중학교 기본 영문법+학교 내신 완벽 대비

LEVEL 3

개정 신판

적중! 중학영문법 3300제

최신 개정 교과서 100% 반영

한눈에 쏙 들어오는 문법 개념 정리

서술형 주관식 대비 실전 문제 강화

책 한 권 분량의 워크북으로 문법 완벽 마스터

꿈을담는틀 Dream Matrix

적중! 중학영문법 3300제 LEVEL 3

교재 개발에 도움을 주신 모든 선생님들께 깊이 감사드립니다.

●● 연구진

이제석 효성양지학원 신경빈 청담어학원 이은미 삼성장학학원
강윤재 천안상록학원 이헌승 스탠다드학원 허성도 목운중학교

●● 검토진

강성규 서울 권도원 서울 권익재 대구 김광수 수원 김규민 인천
김대경 인천 김선미 부산 김성국 평택 김승엽 양산 김연용 수원
김 완 광주 김은경 서울 김자영 수원 김정현 시흥 김진성 인천
김현아 서울 나규성 대전 노준환 안양 류헌규 서울 명가은 서울
문병교 서울 박남숙 전주 박성주 양주 박성환 서울 박영봉 서울
박인환 천안 박재오 김해 박정훈 광주 박종호 대구 박진현 창원
박혜정 고창 반정란 인천 서동준 산본 성하용 인천 여재원 구미
유영목 전주 유주석 성남 유인옥 서울 윤영미 포항 이미정 대구
이상윤 창원 이수현 부산 이연홍 김해 이영주 서울 이장령 창원
이정민 구리 이정아 광주 이종국 청주 이진욱 서울 이충기 화성
이헌승 서울 임희재 구리 장승혁 인천 장용석 경기 정용균 전주
정지훈 서울 정진원 안동 정희숙 하남 주성호 익산 최민석 인천
최수남 강원 최승규 인천

●● 디자인 자문단

권익재 대구 김광수 화성 김민지 의왕 김선유 서울 김정자 부산
김정현 시흥 김희남 서울 나규성 대전 맹기영 경기 명가은 서울
박예지 부산 방성모 대구 오승준 부산 유재국 충남 이광현 해남
이민주 부산 이승용 경기 이재욱 용인 정도영 인천 정해연 전남
주성호 익산 최수남 강원

5판 1쇄 2023년 9월 1일

집필 홍석현, 신영주, 유석, 유대열, 김도선, 김정곤, 이현미, 강명구 **개발책임** 이운영 **편집 기획** 이은정 **영문감수** Sheenae Kim, Esther Kim, Mads Nielsen, Bum Lee **디자인** 이현지, 임성자 **온라인** 강진식 **마케팅** 박진용 **관리** 장희정 **용지** 영지페이퍼 **인쇄 제본** 벽호·GKC **유통** 북앤북

적중! 중학영문법 3300제

LEVEL 3

불규칙 변화 동사표

동사원형	과거	과거분사	의미
awake	awoke	awoken	(잠에서) 깨다
be	was / were	been	~이다, 있다
beat	beat	beaten	때리다, 치다
become	became	become	~해지다, ~이 되다
begin	began	begun	시작하다
bend	bent	bent	구부리다
bind	bound	bound	묶다
bite	bit	bitten	물다
blow	blew	blown	불다
break	broke	broken	깨다
bring	brought	brought	가져오다, 가져다주다
build	built	built	(건물을) 짓다
burn	burned / burnt	burned / burnt	불에 타다
buy	bought	bought	사다, 사 주다
catch	caught	caught	잡다
choose	chose	chosen	고르다, 선택하다
come	came	come	오다
cost	cost	cost	비용이 들다
cut	cut	cut	자르다, 베다
deal	dealt	dealt	다루다
do	did	done	하다
draw	drew	drawn	그리다
drink	drank	drunk	마시다
drive	drove	driven	운전하다
eat	ate	eaten	먹다
fall	fell	fallen	떨어지다
feed	fed	fed	먹이다, 먹이를 주다
feel	felt	felt	(기분이) 들다/느끼다
fight	fought	fought	싸우다
find	found	found	찾다
fly	flew	flown	날다

동사원형	과거	과거분사	의미
forget	forgot	forgotten	잊다, 잊어버리다
forgive	forgave	forgiven	용서하다
freeze	froze	frozen	얼다
get	got	got / gotten	받다, 시키다
give	gave	given	주다
go	went	gone	가다
grow	grew	grown	자라다, 재배하다
have	had	had	가지고 있다, 먹다
hear	heard	heard	듣다
hide	hid	hidden	숨기다
hit	hit	hit	치다, 때리다
hold	held	held	쥐다, 잡다
hurt	hurt	hurt	다치게 하다
keep	kept	kept	유지하다, 계속 있다
know	knew	known	알다, 알고 있다
lay	laid	laid	놓다, 두다
lead	led	led	이끌다
leave	left	left	떠나다
lend	lent	lent	빌려주다
let	let	let	시키다, 허락하다
lie	lay	lain	누워 있다, 눕다
lose	lost	lost	지다, 잃어버리다
make	made	made	만들다
mean	meant	meant	의미하다
meet	met	met	만나다
mistake	mistook	mistaken	실수하다, 오해하다
pay	paid	paid	지불하다
put	put	put	놓다, 두다
quit	quit / quitted	quit / quitted	그만두다
read[ri:d]	read[red]	read[red]	읽다
ride	rode	ridden	타다

동사원형	과거	과거분사	의미
ring	rang	rung	울리다
rise	rose	risen	오르다
run	ran	run	달리다, 운영하다
say	said	said	말하다
see	saw	seen	보다, 알다
seek	sought	sought	찾다, 구하다
sell	sold	sold	팔다
send	sent	sent	보내다
set	set	set	놓다, 세우다
shake	shook	shaken	흔들다
shine	shone	shone	빛나다
shut	shut	shut	닫다
sing	sang	sung	노래하다
sit	sat	sat	앉다
sleep	slept	slept	(잠을) 자다
speak	spoke	spoken	말하다
spend	spent	spent	쓰다, 소비하다
stand	stood	stood	서다, 서 있다, 참다
steal	stole	stolen	훔치다
swim	swam	swum	수영하다
take	took	taken	가지고 가다
teach	taught	taught	가르치다
tell	told	told	말하다, 알려 주다
think	thought	thought	(~라고) 생각하다
throw	threw	thrown	던지다
understand	understood	understood	이해하다
wake	woke	woken	(잠에서) 깨다
wear	wore	worn	입고 있다
win	won	won	이기다
write	wrote	written	(글을) 쓰다

적중! 중학영문법 3300제 주요 특징

1 최신 교육과정 교과서 연계표

중학 영어 교과서의 문법을 분석하여 학교 시험에 완벽하게 대비할 수 있도록 하였습니다.
활용 Tip) 학교 시험 기간에 시험 범위에 해당하는 문법만을 골라 집중적으로 예습 · 복습할 수 있습니다.

2 서술형 대비 강화

학교 시험에 자주 나오는 서술형 문제 유형을 분석하여 출제한 실전 문제를 통해
갈수록 비중이 커져가는 서술형 평가에 완벽하게 대비할 수 있습니다.

3 한눈에 쏙 들어오는 문법 정리

복잡하고 어려운 영문법 내용을 표로 간결하게 정리하였습니다. 또한 출제 빈도가 높은 내용은
좀 더 자세하게 설명하여 문법 내용을 쉽게 이해할 수 있도록 구성하였습니다.

4 나만의 학습 플랜

단원별로 공부한 날짜, 학습 확인 등을 표시할 수 있도록 하였습니다. 자신의 학습 능력과
상황에 따라 스스로 학습 플랜을 완성하고, 문법 학습과 복습에 활용할 수 있습니다.

5 문법 인덱스

책에 수록된 문법 사항을 abc, 가나다 순서로 정리하여
궁금한 문법 사항이 생겼을 때 찾아보기 쉽도록 구성하였습니다.

6 워크북

「적중! 중학영문법 3300제」에 나오는 단어를 테스트할 수 있는 단어 암기장과
내신 대비 추가 문제를 제공합니다.

구성과 특징 Features

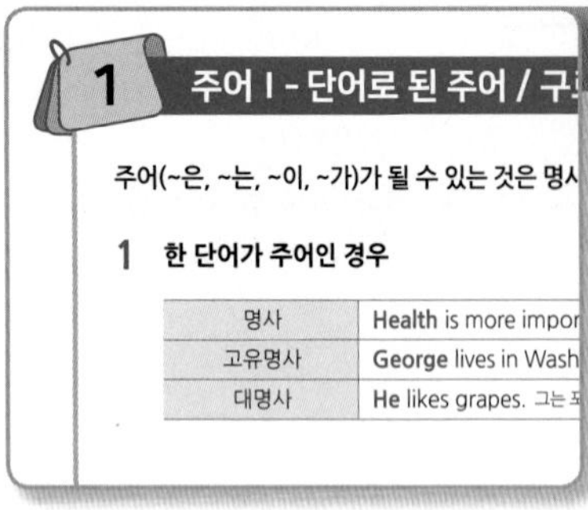
1 주어 I - 단어로 된 주어 / 구

주어(~은, ~는, ~이, ~가)가 될 수 있는 것은 명사

1 한 단어가 주어인 경우

명사	Health is more impor
고유명사	George lives in Wash
대명사	He likes grapes. 그는 포

한눈에 쏙 들어오는 문법 정리

복잡하고 어려운 영문법 내용을 표로 간결하게 정리하였습니다. 또한 출제 빈도가 높은 내용은 좀 더 자세하게 설명하여 문법 내용을 쉽게 이해할 수 있도록 구성하였습니다.

또한 한 단계 심화된 영문법 내용을 !로 제시하여 학교 시험에 출제되는 고난도 문제에도 당황하지 않고 대처할 수 있습니다.

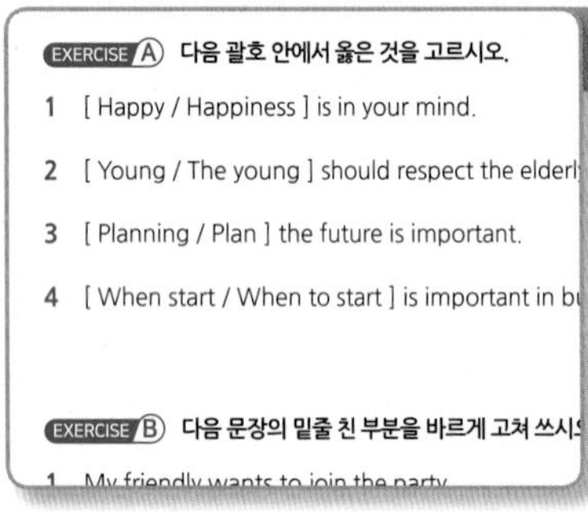
EXERCISE A 다음 괄호 안에서 옳은 것을 고르시오.

1 [Happy / Happiness] is in your mind.

2 [Young / The young] should respect the elderl

3 [Planning / Plan] the future is important.

4 [When start / When to start] is important in bu

EXERCISE B 다음 문장의 밑줄 친 부분을 바르게 고쳐 쓰시오

1 My friendly wants to join the party.

체계적이고 다양한 연습 문제

해당 문법을 익히기에 가장 적합한 유형으로 구성된 연습 문제를 풀면서 문법 개념을 반복적으로 연습하다보면 영문법을 마스터할 수 있습니다.

최근 주관식 문제로 많이 출제되는 영작 문제에 대비할 수 있도록 문장 완성 및 작문 연습 문제를 충분히 실었습니다.

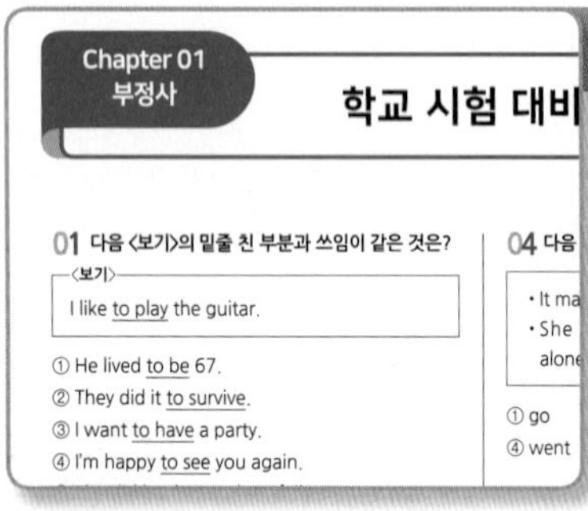
Chapter 01 부정사

학교 시험 대비

01 다음 <보기>의 밑줄 친 부분과 쓰임이 같은 것은?

<보기>
I like to play the guitar.

① He lived to be 67.
② They did it to survive.
③ I want to have a party.
④ I'm happy to see you again.

04 다음

• It ma
• She
alone

① go
④ went

학교 시험 대비 문제

학교 시험에 자주 나오는 문제 유형을 분석하여 출제한 실전 문제를 통해 학교 시험을 완벽하게 대비할 수 있습니다.

특히, 서술형 평가에 대비한 실전 문제를 강화하여 고득점을 받을 수 있는 실력을 키울 수 있습니다.

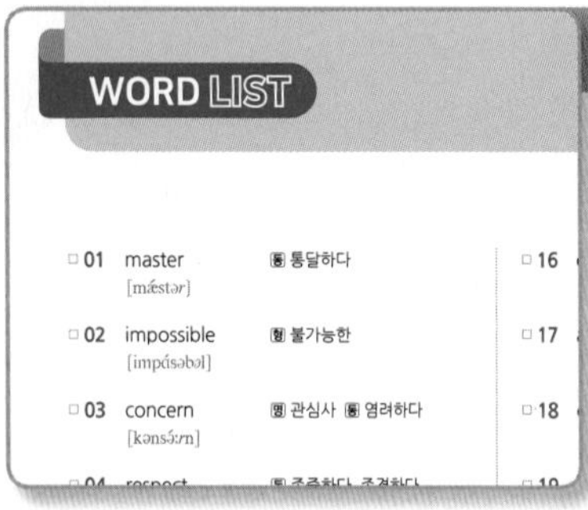
WORD LIST

□ 01 master [mǽstər] 통 통달하다 □ 16
□ 02 impossible [impɑ́səbəl] 형 불가능한 □ 17
□ 03 concern [kənsə́ːrn] 명 관심사 통 염려하다 □ 18

워크북(단어 암기장 + 내신 대비 추가 문제)

본문에 나오는 어휘들을 테스트 할 수 있는 단어 암기장과 서술형으로 자주 나오는 유형을 집중 연습할 수 있는 서술형 대비 문장 연습, 학교 시험 대비 문제가 추가로 제공됩니다.

다음 단원으로 넘어가기 전에 워크북을 활용해 학습한 내용을 확실하게 점검할 수 있습니다.

차례 Contents

문장의 구조

Chapter 01 부정사

Chapter 02 동명사

Chapter 03 분사

Chapter 04 시제

Chapter 05 조동사

학습 플랜 Plan

자신의 학습 능력과 상황에 따라 스스로 학습 플랜을 완성하고, 문법 학습과 복습에 활용해 보세요.

학습 확인 □ 학습률 0% ☑ 1회 학습 ☑☑ 2회 학습 ☑☑☑ 3회 학습 ■ 학습률 100%

단원	공부한 날		학교 시험 대비 문제 점수		학습 확인
	시작한 날짜	마친 날짜			
문장의 구조	월 일	월 일	선택형		□□□
			서술형		
Chapter 01 부정사	월 일	월 일	선택형		□□□
			서술형		
Chapter 02 동명사	월 일	월 일	선택형		□□□
			서술형		
Chapter 03 분사	월 일	월 일	선택형		□□□
			서술형		
Chapter 04 시제	월 일	월 일	선택형		□□□
			서술형		
Chapter 05 조동사	월 일	월 일	선택형		□□□
			서술형		
Chapter 06 수동태	월 일	월 일	선택형		□□□
			서술형		
Chapter 07 대명사	월 일	월 일	선택형		□□□
			서술형		
Chapter 08 형용사와 부사	월 일	월 일	선택형		□□□
			서술형		
Chapter 09 비교	월 일	월 일	선택형		□□□
			서술형		
Chapter 10 전치사	월 일	월 일	선택형		□□□
			서술형		
Chapter 11 관계사	월 일	월 일	선택형		□□□
			서술형		
Chapter 12 접속사	월 일	월 일	선택형		□□□
			서술형		
Chapter 13 가정법	월 일	월 일	선택형		□□□
			서술형		
Chapter 14 일치와 화법	월 일	월 일	선택형		□□□
			서술형		
Chapter 15 특수구문	월 일	월 일	선택형		□□□
			서술형		

문장의 구조

1 주어 I - 단어로 된 주어 / 구로 된 주어
2 주어 II - 절로 된 주어 / 길어진 주어
3 목적어 I - 단어로 된 목적어 / 구로 된 목적어
4 목적어 II - 절로 된 목적어 / 길어진 목적어
5 주격보어 - 명사 / 형용사 · 분사
6 목적격보어 I - 명사 / 형용사 · 분사
7 목적격보어 II - to부정사 / 동사원형 / 분사

1 주어 I - 단어로 된 주어 / 구로 된 주어

주어(~은, ~는, ~이, ~가)가 될 수 있는 것은 명사 및 명사 상당어구이다.

1 한 단어가 주어인 경우

명사	**Health** is more important than money. 건강이 돈보다 더 중요하다.
고유명사	**George** lives in Washington D.C. George는 워싱턴 D.C.에 산다.
대명사	**He** likes grapes. 그는 포도를 좋아한다.

2 구가 주어인 경우 - 명사구

to부정사(구)	**To speak English** is difficult. 영어를 말하는 것은 어렵다. ➡ **It** is difficult **to speak English**.
동명사(구)	**Shopping on the Internet** is convenient. 인터넷에서 쇼핑하는 것은 편리하다. ➡ **It** is convenient **shopping on the Internet**.
the + 형용사	**The rich** grow richer and **the poor** grow poorer. 부자들은 더 부유해지고 가난한 사람들은 더욱 가난해진다.
의문사 + to부정사	**What to do next** is an important question to me. 다음에 무엇을 할지가 내게 중요한 문제이다.

▶▶ 정답과 해설 p.3

EXERCISE A 다음 괄호 안에서 옳은 것을 고르시오.

1 [Happy / Happiness] is in your mind.

2 [Young / The young] should respect the elderly.

3 [Planning / Plan] the future is important.

4 [When start / When to start] is important in business.

EXERCISE B 다음 문장의 밑줄 친 부분을 바르게 고쳐 쓰시오.

1 <u>My friendly</u> wants to join the party.

2 <u>To watching TV</u> is sometimes harmful to kids.

3 <u>True</u> doesn't change forever.

4 <u>To where go</u> hasn't been decided yet.

2 주어 II - 절로 된 주어 / 길어진 주어

1 절이 주어인 경우 - 명사절

that절	**That Peter loves Susan** is true. Peter가 Susan을 사랑하는 것은 사실이다. ➡ **It** is true **that Peter loves Susan**.
whether절	**Whether you are right or not** isn't clear. 네가 옳은지 아닌지는 명확하지 않다.
의문사절	**When we will start** is not important. 우리가 언제 출발할 것인지는 중요하지 않다.
what절	**What we had** was the diamond. 우리가 가졌던 것은 다이아몬드였다.

2 수식을 받아 주어가 길어진 경우

전치사구의 수식을 받은 주어	A trip **to another country** is exciting. 다른 나라로의 여행은 흥미진진하다.
관계대명사절의 수식을 받은 주어	He **who laughs last** laughs best. 마지막으로 웃는 자가 최후의 승자다.

▶▶ 정답과 해설 p.3

EXERCISE A 다음 괄호 안에서 옳은 것을 고르시오.

1 [Whether he will come / That will come] is very important.

2 [Where stay / Where we stay] doesn't matter.

3 [He knows the fact / That he knows the fact] is certain.

4 [The child likes me / Children like me] helped the cats.

5 [The child who likes music / The child what likes music] has great talent.

EXERCISE B 다음 문장의 주어에 밑줄을 그으시오.

1 That he stole the money was not true.

2 What you do is more important than what you say.

3 The girl that just left the shop didn't buy anything.

4 How he came here is mysterious.

5 The problem on the test seems difficult.

3 목적어 I - 단어로 된 목적어 / 구로 된 목적어

목적어(~을, ~를, ~에게)가 될 수 있는 것은 명사 및 명사 상당어구이다.

1 한 단어가 목적어인 경우

명사	We play **baseball** after school. 우리는 방과 후에 야구를 한다.
고유명사	I miss **Eddy** so much. 나는 Eddy가 무척 그립다.
대명사	Everyone likes **her**. 모든 사람들이 그녀를 좋아한다.

2 구가 목적어인 경우 - 명사구

to부정사(구)	I want **to buy a car**. 나는 차 한 대를 구입하고 싶다.
동명사(구)	Jane enjoys **baking bread**. Jane은 빵 굽는 것을 즐긴다.
the + 형용사	Men like **the pretty** more than **the ugly**. 사람들은 못생긴 사람들보다 예쁜 사람들을 더 좋아한다.
의문사 + to부정사	I don't know **when to start**. 나는 언제 시작해야 할지 모르겠다.

▶▶ 정답과 해설 p.3

EXERCISE A **다음 괄호 안에서 옳은 것을 고르시오.**

1 I said [nothing / no] about it.

2 I am interested in [study / studying] English.

3 She forgot [to mail this letter / mail this letter].

4 He taught me [how to make / how to making] a bow.

EXERCISE B **다음 문장의 밑줄 친 부분을 바르게 고쳐 쓰시오.**

1 I want <u>eat</u> some fruit and vegetables.

2 We decided <u>going</u> on a family trip.

3 I don't know <u>where go</u> to study English.

4 Would you mind <u>dance</u> with me?

4 목적어 II - 절로 된 목적어 / 길어진 목적어

1 절이 목적어인 경우 - 명사절

that절 (that 생략 가능)	Columbus believed **(that) the earth is round**. 콜럼버스는 지구가 둥글다고 믿었다.
if(whether)절	I don't know **if he will come**. 나는 그가 올 것인지 모르겠다.
의문사절	Can you tell me **when she left the hotel**? 그녀가 언제 호텔을 떠났는지 내게 말해 줄 수 있니? **＊「의문사 + 주어 + 동사」의 어순**
what절	Tell me more about **what you think**. 네가 생각하는 것에 대해 내게 좀 더 말해줘.

2 수식을 받아 목적어가 길어진 경우

＊선루프 : 실내 환기와 채광을 위해 자동차의 지붕이 열리도록 하는 장치

전치사구의 수식을 받은 목적어	I have **a car with a sunroof**. 나는 ＊선루프가 있는 차를 가지고 있다.
관계대명사절의 수식을 받은 목적어	He likes **women who smile a lot**. 그는 많이 웃는 여성들을 좋아한다.

▶▶ 정답과 해설 p.3

EXERCISE A 다음 괄호 안에서 옳은 것을 고르시오.

1 I think [that / who] he will accept the job.

2 I don't know [what / whether] it will rain tomorrow.

3 I know how [solved he / he solved] the problem.

4 Tell him [what you want / do you want] to do now.

EXERCISE B 다음 문장의 목적어(목적어구, 목적절)에 밑줄을 그으시오.

1 I wonder if he is reliable.

2 He said he would sleep on the sofa.

3 She denied the marriage that he proposed.

4 Are you watching a movie about Kung Fu?

5 I'm not sure why he didn't keep his promise.

6 I thought that she didn't tell a lie.

5 주격보어 - 명사 / 형용사 · 분사

주격보어(주어를 보충 설명)가 될 수 있는 것은 명사 상당어구와 형용사 · 분사이다.

1 명사 상당어구인 경우

명사	The old man is **a professor**. 그 노인은 교수다.
고유명사	The capital of Korea is **Seoul**. 한국의 수도는 서울이다.
대명사	The book is **mine**. 그 책은 나의 것이다.
to부정사(구)	My hobby is **to play soccer**. 나의 취미는 축구하는 것이다.
동명사(구)	Seeing is **believing**. 보는 것이 믿는 것이다. (= 백문이 불여일견이다.)
의문사 + to부정사	My question is **what to choose**. 나의 질문은 무엇을 선택해야 하는가이다.
that절	My opinion is **that we should listen to each other**. 내 의견은 우리가 서로의 말을 들어야 한다는 것이다.
의문사절	The problem is **when he escaped**. 문제는 그가 언제 탈출했는가이다.
what절	We become **what we think**. 우리는 우리가 생각하는 것이 된다.

2 형용사 · 분사인 경우

형용사	He always looks **happy**. 그는 항상 행복해 보인다.
현재분사(능동)	She remained **standing** there for a while. 그녀는 잠시 동안 그곳에 서 있었다.
과거분사(수동)	This hotel remains **closed** during the winter. 이 호텔은 겨울 동안 문을 닫는다.

▶▶ 정답과 해설 p. 3

EXERCISE A **다음 괄호 안에서 옳은 것을 고르시오.**

1 His dream is [visit / to visit] India.

2 They looked [sad / sadly] today.

3 His name became [know / known] all over the world.

EXERCISE B **다음 문장의 밑줄 친 부분을 바르게 고쳐 쓰시오.**

1 The sky in fall looks <u>clearly</u>.

2 Are you <u>interest</u> in 3D movies?

3 The game became more and more <u>excite</u>.

4 My plan is <u>listen</u> to English for 30 minutes every day.

6 목적격보어 I - 명사 / 형용사 · 분사

목적격보어(목적어를 보충 설명)가 될 수 있는 것은 명사, 형용사 · 분사, 준동사이다.

1 명사인 경우

make, choose, elect, name, call, think + 목적어(O) + 명사(OC)

They **made** their son **a doctor**. 그들은 그들의 아들을 의사로 만들었다.

We **elected** him **president**. 우리는 그를 회장으로 선출했다.

They **named** the dog **Boksil**. 그들은 그 개를 복실이라고 이름지었다.

2 형용사 · 분사인 경우

make, keep, leave, find, think + 목적어(O) + 형용사 · 분사(OC)

The song **made** me **happy**. 그 노래는 나를 행복하게 만들었다.

We **left** the door **closed**. 우리는 그 문을 닫아두었다.

I **found** the thief **running** to the car. 나는 그 도둑이 차로 달려가고 있는 것을 발견했다.

▶▶ 정답과 해설 p. 3

EXERCISE A 다음 괄호 안에서 옳은 것을 고르시오.

1 We chose [he / him] chairman of our club.

2 They elected [Edward / for Edward] president.

3 The music made me [sleepily / sleepy].

4 Her mother made her [a teacher / to a teacher].

5 I found you [be happy / happy] with the boy.

EXERCISE B 다음 문장의 밑줄 친 부분을 바르게 고쳐 쓰시오. (틀린 부분이 없으면 ○표)

1 They made <u>she</u> a famous singer.

2 Please keep the drinks <u>coolly</u>.

3 We called Dave <u>a troublemaker</u>.

4 Did you leave the window <u>closing</u>?

7 목적격보어 II - to부정사 / 동사원형 / 분사

1 to부정사인 경우

요청, 명령, 기대 (ask, tell, order, want)	He **asked** me **to turn** off the radio. 그는 나에게 라디오를 꺼달라고 했다.

2 동사원형인 경우

사역동사(have, let, make)	They **made** me **wait** for hours. 그들은 나를 몇 시간 동안 기다리게 했다.
지각동사(see, hear, smell, feel)	I **heard** him **open** the door. 나는 그가 문 여는 소리를 들었다.

※ 지각동사는 동작이 진행 중임을 강조할 때, 목적격보어로 현재분사를 사용한다.

3 분사인 경우

목적어 - 목적격보어 : 능동 관계	I saw **the thief running**. 나는 그 도둑이 달려가고 있는 것을 봤다.
목적어 - 목적격보어 : 수동 관계	I got **my watch repaired**. 나는 내 시계를 수리 받았다.

▶▶ 정답과 해설 p. 3

EXERCISE A 다음 괄호 안에서 옳은 것을 고르시오.

1 I want you [do / to do] the work.

2 This dress makes me [look / to look] fat.

3 My dad asked me [to wash / wash] his car.

4 I smelled something [to burn / burning] in the kitchen.

EXERCISE B 다음 문장의 밑줄 친 부분을 바르게 고쳐 쓰시오.

1 Don't let the students <u>to play</u> in the garden.

2 The doctor told the patients not <u>smoke</u>.

3 My mom asked me <u>doing</u> the dishes.

4 Did you see a dog <u>to run</u> down the street?

FINISH

Chapter 01

부정사

1 주어/보어/목적어 역할을 하는 to부정사
2 진주어/진목적어 역할을 하는 to부정사
3 의문사 + to부정사
4 목적어로 to부정사를 사용하는 동사
5 목적격보어로 to부정사를 사용하는 동사
6 목적격보어로 동사원형을 사용하는 동사
7 명사를 수식하는 to부정사
8 be동사 + to부정사
9 seem〔appear〕 + to부정사
10 목적/결과를 나타내는 to부정사
11 조건을 나타내는 to부정사
12 감정의 원인/판단의 근거를 나타내는 to부정사
13 too ~ to/enough to
14 It takes ~ to부정사
15 대부정사
16 독립부정사
■ 학교 시험 대비 문제

1 주어 / 보어 / 목적어 역할을 하는 to부정사

역할	주어, 보어, 목적어
해석	~하기, ~하는 것
부정	not〔never〕 + to부정사

To master English in a short time **is** impossible. 짧은 시간 안에 영어를 마스터하는 것은 불가능하다. **<주어>**
Her hope is **to make** her father healthy. 그녀의 소망은 그녀의 아버지를 건강하게 만드는 것이다. **<주격보어>**
My hobby is **to listen** to the radio. 나의 취미는 라디오를 듣는 것이다. **<주격보어>**
The doctor advised him **to lose** weight. 의사는 그에게 몸무게를 줄이라고 조언했다. **<목적격보어>**
I hope **to visit** Australia someday. 나는 언젠가 호주에 방문하기를 바란다. **<목적어>**

▶▶ 정답과 해설 p.4

EXERCISE A **다음 문장에서 to부정사를 찾아 밑줄을 긋고, 알맞은 역할을 고르시오.**

1 He wants to get a pair of shoes. [주어 / 보어 / 목적어]

2 Her wish is to travel around the world. [주어 / 보어 / 목적어]

3 To look after the kids here is my job. [주어 / 보어 / 목적어]

4 My one aim at that time was to win the race. [주어 / 보어 / 목적어]

5 To form a good habit is important to everyone. [주어 / 보어 / 목적어]

6 They agreed to be kind to their customers. [주어 / 보어 / 목적어]

7 My wish was to meet him as soon as possible. [주어 / 보어 / 목적어]

8 She wanted to finish the work by ten. [주어 / 보어 / 목적어]

9 Sometimes to make good friends is hard. [주어 / 보어 / 목적어]

10 I decided to take pictures of wild animals. [주어 / 보어 / 목적어]

EXERCISE B **다음 문장에서 어법상 틀린 부분을 찾아 바르게 고쳐 쓰시오.**

1 They wanted invite him to their house.

2 Be near the river is very dangerous.

3 Visit Canada with her family is her only hope.

4 To getting good marks at school is very important to you.

5 Her father's main goal is make a fortune.

EXERCISE C **다음 우리말과 일치하도록 주어진 단어 및 어구를 배열하여 문장을 완성하시오.**

1 나는 그와 함께 파티에 가기를 기대했다. (go, to, expected, to)
➡ I ________________ the party with him.

2 그 배우의 관심사는 다른 사람들에게 신사처럼 보이는 것이다. (to, a gentleman, is, look like)
➡ The actor's concern ________________ to others.

3 어떤 도움도 없이 외국에서 공부하는 것은 불가능했다. (abroad, To, study, without)
➡ ________________ any help was impossible.

4 공원에서 그녀가 한 일은 그녀의 남자 친구인 David에 대해 이야기한 것이 전부였다. (to, about, talk, was)
➡ All she did in the park ________________ her boyfriend, David.

5 다른 사람들에게 친절하게 대하는 것은 자신을 존중하는 것이다. (kind, To, be, to)
➡ ________________ others is to respect oneself.

EXERCISE D **다음 우리말과 일치하도록 주어진 단어를 사용하여 문장을 완성하시오. (필요시 형태 변화)**

1 내 목표는 모든 회원들을 행복하게 만드는 것이다. (make)
➡ My goal ________ ________ ________ every member happy.

2 베푸는 것이 당신을 더 행복하게 만든다. (give, make)
➡ ________ ________ ________ you happier.

3 그는 전쟁이 끝난 후 그들을 만나고 싶어했다. (hope, meet)
➡ He ________ ________ ________ them after the war.

4 그는 나쁜 친구들을 사귀지 않으려고 노력했다. (try, make, not)
➡ He ________ ________ ________ ________ bad friends.

5 영어를 배우는 가장 좋은 방법은 많이 읽는 것이다. (read)
➡ The best way of learning English ________ ________ ________ a lot.

2 진주어 / 진목적어 역할을 하는 to부정사

1 가주어 · 진주어 / 가목적어 · 진목적어

가주어나 가목적어 it을 쓰고 to부정사를 문장 뒤로 보낸다.

It is difficult **to solve** the problem.
그 문제를 푸는 것은 어렵다. **<가주어, 진주어>**

It is difficult **to imagine** life without the Internet.
인터넷 없는 삶을 상상하는 것은 어렵다. **<가주어, 진주어>**

She makes **it** a rule **to wake up** early in the morning.
그녀는 아침에 일찍 일어나는 것을 규칙으로 삼고 있다. **<가목적어, 진목적어>**

2 의미상 주어

to부정사의 의미상 주어가 문장의 주어나 목적어와 일치하지 않는 경우, 의미상 주어는 일반적으로 「for + 목적격」으로 나타낸다.

It is dangerous **for you to swim** in this river. 네가 이 강에서 수영하는 것은 위험하다.
It is natural **for her to be** mad at you. 그녀가 너에게 화내는 것은 당연하다.

+ 사람의 성격이나 태도를 나타내는 형용사 다음에 나오는 to부정사의 의미상 주어는 「of + 목적격」으로 나타낸다.

kind, nice, good, wise, clever, polite, generous, rude, impolite

It was wise **of you to say** so. 네가 그렇게 말한 것은 현명했다.

▶▶ 정답과 해설 p.4

EXERCISE A 다음 괄호 안에서 옳은 것을 고르시오.

1 It is easy [for criminals / of criminals] to get guns these days.

2 It is very cruel [for her / of her] to do such a bad thing.

3 It was impossible [for them / of them] to find out the secret.

4 It will be hard [for him / of him] to come back by six.

5 It was very foolish [for you / of you] to waste your own time on it.

EXERCISE B 다음 문장에서 어법상 틀린 곳을 찾아 바르게 고쳐 쓰시오. (틀린 곳이 없으면 ○표)

1 It is kind for your wife to invite us to the party tonight.

2 It is not so hard of me to answer this question.

3 It was wise of him to choose that.

4 It is important of all the students to eat properly.

5 It is nice for you to show me the way to the park.

6 It was not good for us to buy the tickets there.

EXERCISE C 다음 주어진 문장을 <보기>처럼 바꿔 쓸 때 빈칸에 알맞은 말을 쓰시오.

<보기>
To go to the movies at night is his hobby.
➡ It is his hobby to go to the movies at night.

1 To climb the mountain alone is impossible.
➡ ______________________ to climb the mountain alone.

2 To sing loudly at night is not good.
➡ ______________________ loudly at night.

3 To take a trip to Paris with my mom would be wonderful.
➡ ______________________ a trip to Paris with my mom.

EXERCISE D 다음 우리말과 일치하도록 주어진 단어 및 어구를 사용하여 문장을 완성하시오. (필요시 형태 변화)

1 그는 일반적인 감기 바이러스를 제거하는 것이 쉽다고 생각했다. (think, easy)
➡ He ________ ________ ________ ________ get rid of a common cold virus.

2 그녀는 건강을 위해 간식을 먹지 않는 것을 규칙으로 삼고 있다. (make, a rule, not)
➡ She ________ ________ ____ ____ ________ ________ ________ eat between meals for her health.

3 나는 저녁에 공부하는 것이 더 좋다고 생각한다. (think, better)
➡ I ________ ________ ________ ________ study in the evening.

4 그는 아빠와 노는 것이 재미있다는 것을 알게 되었다. (find, exciting)
➡ He ________ ________ ________ ________ play with his dad.

3 의문사 + to부정사

「의문사 + to부정사」는 주어, 목적어, 보어 역할을 하며, 「의문사 + 주어 + should + 동사원형」으로 전환할 수 있다.

who(m) + to부정사	누가[누구를] ~할지	what + to부정사	무엇을 ~할지
which + (명사) + to부정사	어떤 것을 ~할지	when + to부정사	언제 ~할지
where + to부정사	어디로 ~할지	how + to부정사	어떻게 ~할지, ~하는 방법

How to spend money is very important. 돈을 어떻게 쓸지가 매우 중요하다. **<주어>**
= **How we should spend** money is very important.

I couldn't decide **where to go**. 나는 어디로 갈지 결정할 수 없었다. **<목적어>**
= I couldn't decide **where I should go**.

His concern is **what to do** next. 그의 관심사는 다음에 무엇을 할지이다. **<보어>**
= His concern is **what he should do** next.

! 「why + to부정사」는 쓰지 않는다.

▶▶ 정답과 해설 p.4

EXERCISE A 다음 괄호 안에서 옳은 것을 고르시오.

1 I can't decide [whom / what / which] to marry.

2 She wanted to learn [which / how / why] to drive a car.

3 The host usually tells the guests [what / when / why] to come.

EXERCISE B 다음 우리말과 일치하도록 주어진 단어를 사용하여 문장을 완성하시오.

1 그는 나에게 어떤 것을 선택할지 조언해 주었다. (choose)
➡ He advised me ________ ________ ________ ________.

2 나는 그에게 내게 언제 전화를 걸어야 할지를 말해주지 않았다. (call)
➡ I didn't tell him ________ ________ ________ ________ me.

3 무엇을 사야 할지는 내게 중요한 질문이었다. (buy)
➡ ________ ________ ________ ________ was an important question to me.

4 목적어로 to부정사를 사용하는 동사

want(원하다)	plan(계획하다)	agree(동의하다)	pretend(~인 척하다)
learn(배우다)	need(필요로 하다)	manage(가까스로 ~하다)	promise(약속하다)
tend(~하는 경향이 있다)	mean(의미하다)	expect(기대하다)	choose(선택하다)
hope(희망하다)	wish(바라다)	decide(결정하다)	refuse(거절하다)

I **want to hire** more employees. 나는 더 많은 직원들을 채용하기를 원한다.

I didn't **mean to hurt** them. 나는 그들을 해치려고 의도한 것은 아니었다.

They **agreed to start** after lunch. 그들은 점심 식사 후에 출발하는 데 동의했다.

! 전치사의 목적어 자리에는 to부정사를 사용할 수 없다.

I'm interested in ***to be*** a member of the baseball team. (X)

▶▶ 정답과 해설 p.4

EXERCISE A 다음 괄호 안에서 옳은 것을 고르시오.

1 He decided [buying / to buy / buy] a used car for his sister.

2 The kids in the room pretended [be / to be / being] asleep.

3 Boys tend [skip / to skip / skipping] breakfast more often than girls.

4 She promised [to take / taking / take] you there this time.

EXERCISE B 다음 우리말과 일치하도록 주어진 단어를 사용하여 문장을 완성하시오. (필요시 형태 변화)

1 저는 곧 당신을 만나기를 바랍니다. (hope, see)
➡ I __________ __________ __________ you soon.

2 그들은 방과 후에 수영하는 것을 배울 것이다. (learn, swim)
➡ They will __________ __________ __________ after school.

3 나는 혼자 힘으로 간신히 생계를 꾸려야 했다. (manage, earn)
➡ I had to __________ __________ __________ a living for myself.

4 Jenny는 뉴욕에 있는 그녀의 사촌을 만나기를 기대했다. (expect, see)
➡ Jenny __________ __________ __________ her cousin in New York.

5 목적격보어로 to부정사를 사용하는 동사

ask(요구하다)	invite(초대하다)	want(원하다)	expect(기대하다)
force(강요하다)	drive(몰아가다)	order(명령하다)	require(요구하다)
tell(말하다)	allow(허락하다)	permit(허용하다)	warn(경고하다)
advise(조언하다)	encourage(격려하다)	enable(~할 수 있게 하다)	get(~하게 하다)

She doesn't **allow** me **to meet** him. 그녀는 내가 그를 만나는 것을 허락하지 않는다.

He **advised** his son **to study** in the library. 그는 그의 아들에게 도서관에서 공부하라고 조언했다.

They **told** me **to think** about marriage again. 그들은 나에게 결혼에 대해 다시 생각하라고 말했다.

My daughter **asked** me **not to show** him her report card.
나의 딸이 자신의 성적표를 그에게 보여주지 말라고 내게 부탁했다.

▶▶ 정답과 해설 p. 5

EXERCISE A **다음 괄호 안에서 옳은 것을 고르시오.**

1 The police warned the lady not [walk / to walk / walking] around alone at night.

2 We have to force them [to give / give / giving] up their plans.

3 They expected her [becoming / become / to become] a professor.

4 She allowed him [to go / go / going] abroad to see his aunt.

5 Do you want me [get / to get / getting] you a pretty doll for your birthday?

6 I asked her [call / to call / calling] me after the meeting.

7 He advised her [to not hang / not to hanging / not to hang] out with the girls.

EXERCISE B **다음 문장에서 어법상 틀린 곳을 찾아 바르게 고쳐 쓰시오. (틀린 곳이 없으면 ○표)**

1 Hunger drove them steal some bread.

2 He asked her to wait for him till he came back.

3 We told them to picking up our children at the airport.

4 She advised us to brush our teeth three times a day.

5 The Internet enables us find the information easily.

EXERCISE C 다음 우리말과 일치하도록 주어진 단어를 사용하여 문장을 완성하시오. (필요시 형태 변화)

1 누가 그녀에게 파티에 오라고 했니? (come)
➡ Who asked her ________ ________ to the party?

2 나는 소년들이 학교 운동장에서 활동적으로 놀기를 원한다. (play)
➡ I want boys ________ ________ actively in the playground at school.

3 나의 아버지께서 내가 그의 구두를 닦도록 시키셨다. (get, polish)
➡ My father ________ ________ ________ ________ his shoes.

4 선생님께서 내게 그 동아리에 가입하라고 조언하셨다. (join)
➡ The teacher advised ________ ________ ________ the club.

5 그 상황이 내가 그 학회에 참석하는 것을 허락하지 않았다. (attend)
➡ The situation didn't permit ________ ________ ________ the conference.

6 그녀는 그가 그곳에 같이 가주기를 원했다. (want, go)
➡ She ________ ________ ________ ________ there together.

7 그는 그녀에게 노래에 맞춰 자신과 함께 춤추자고 요청했다. (ask, dance)
➡ He ________ ________ ________ ________ with him to the song.

EXERCISE D 다음 우리말과 일치하도록 주어진 단어를 배열하여 문장을 완성하시오.

1 그녀는 그가 모든 일에 최선을 다하기를 원한다. (to, wants, him, do)
➡ She ______________________________ his best at everything.

2 그는 학생들이 실험실에서 서로 돕도록 격려한다. (students, help, to, encourages)
➡ He ______________________________ one another in the lab.

3 우리는 그들에게 전국 체전에 참가할 것을 요구했다. (to, them, required, take)
➡ We ______________________________ part in the National Sports Festival.

4 의사는 그 환자에게 1회분의 약을 복용하도록 지시했다. (to, patient, take, the, ordered)
➡ The doctor ______________________________ a dose of medicine.

5 나는 그에게 공부할 때 떠들지 말라고 경고했다. (not, warned, him, make, to)
➡ I ______________________________ a noise when studying.

6 목적격보어로 동사원형을 사용하는 동사

1 사역동사 make, have, let, help(준사역동사)

My grandmother doesn't **let** me **go** fishing alone.
나의 할머니께서는 내가 혼자 낚시하러 가도록 허락하지 않으신다.

His suit **made** him **look** handsome. 그의 양복이 그를 잘생겨 보이게 했다.

+ help(준사역동사)는 목적격보어로 to부정사와 동사원형을 모두 사용한다.

Thomas **helped** me **(to) move** my desk. Thomas는 내가 책상을 옮기는 것을 도왔다.

This exercise will **help** you **(to) lose** weight. 이 운동은 네가 살을 빼도록 도와줄 것이다.

+ have / get + 목적어(O) + 목적격보어(OC)

동사(V)	목적어(O)	목적격보어(OC)	O와 OC의 관계
have	사람	동사원형	능동
get		to부정사	
have/get	사물	과거분사	수동

2 지각동사 feel, see, watch, hear, smell, look at

I **heard** my son **turn** on the computer. 나는 내 아들이 컴퓨터를 켜는 소리를 들었다.

He **felt** his feet **hurt** suddenly. 그는 갑자기 발이 아프다고 느꼈다.

+ 지각동사가 진행의 의미를 강조할 때는 목적격보어로 현재분사를 사용하기도 한다.

He **saw** someone **coming** in the room. 그는 누군가가 방 안으로 들어오고 있는 것을 보았다.

▶▶ 정답과 해설 p. 5

EXERCISE A 다음 괄호 안에서 옳은 것을 모두 고르시오.

1 She saw a friend of mine [to sing / sing / singing] a song in the concert.

2 They let her [to know / know / knowing] that she had failed the exam.

3 We heard someone [to knock / knock / knocking] on the door.

4 He made them [to do / do / doing] the dishes.

5 I helped him [to carry / carry / carrying] the heavy boxes.

6 We got our cars [to repair / repairing / repaired] in the town.

EXERCISE B **다음 문장에서 어법상 틀린 곳을 찾아 바르게 고쳐 쓰시오. (틀린 곳이 없으면 ○표)**

1 나는 그가 그 컴퓨터를 고치게 했다.
➡ I made him to fix the computer.

2 그녀는 그가 전화로 이야기하고 있는 것을 들었다.
➡ She heard him talking on the phone.

3 그는 내가 하루 종일 TV를 보도록 허락하지 않는다.
➡ He doesn't let me to watch TV all day long.

4 나는 어제 그들이 함께 테니스 치는 것을 보았다.
➡ I saw them play tennis together yesterday.

5 우리는 아이들에게 거실을 치우도록 시켰다.
➡ We had the kids cleaning the living room.

6 나는 누군가가 내 두 손을 만지는 것을 느꼈다.
➡ I felt someone touch my hands.

7 그들은 방과 후에 우리가 열심히 공부할 수 있도록 도와주었다.
➡ They helped us studied hard after school.

EXERCISE C **다음 우리말과 일치하도록 주어진 단어 및 어구를 사용하여 문장을 완성하시오. (필요시 형태 변화)**

1 우리는 그가 교실 밖으로 뛰어나가는(뛰어나가고 있는) 것을 보았다. (run, see)
➡ We ________ ________ ________ out of the classroom.

2 나는 거미 한 마리가 내 왼쪽 다리 위로 기어 가는(기어 가고 있는) 것을 느꼈다. (a spider, crawl, feel)
➡ I ________ ________ ________ ________ up my left leg.

3 그들은 내가 그 화장실을 사용하도록 허락했다. (let, use)
➡ They ________ ________ ________ the bathroom.

4 너는 누군가가 그 방에서 피아노를 치는(치고 있는) 소리가 들리니? (hear, play, somebody)
➡ Do you ________ ________ ________ the piano in the room?

5 그는 반성문을 쓴 후에 내가 교무실에서 나가도록 허락했다. (get, let)
➡ He ________ ________ ________ out of the teachers' room after writing a letter of apology.

7 명사를 수식하는 to부정사

역할	명사를 뒤에서 수식
해석	~한, ~할
참고	전치사를 수반하는 경우 전치사 생략 불가

The pill is not **the only thing to save** him. 그 약이 그를 구할 유일한 것은 아니다.
We want **something cold to drink**. 우리는 차가운 마실 것을 원한다.

+ 전치사를 수반하는 경우: 전치사가 수식하는 명사에 대한 정확한 의미 관계를 나타낸다.

They had no **house to live in**. 그들은 살 집이 없었다.
He needs **a counselor to talk with**. 그는 함께 대화를 나눌 상담사가 필요하다.

+ -thing, -body, -one으로 끝나는 부정대명사도 to부정사가 뒤에서 수식한다.

▶▶ 정답과 해설 p. 5

EXERCISE A 다음 우리말과 일치하도록 어법상 틀린 부분을 찾아 바르게 고쳐 쓰시오.

1 나는 너와 함께 놀 시간이 없다.
➡ I have no time play with you.

2 그들은 그 문제를 해결할 방법을 알고 있었다.
➡ They knew the way solve the problem.

3 우리는 앉을 몇 개의 큰 의자들이 필요했다.
➡ We needed a few big chairs to sit off.

4 그녀는 그들에게 말할 좋은 소식이 있다.
➡ She has good news tell them.

5 그는 거주할 좋은 장소를 찾았다.
➡ He found a good place to living in.

6 그녀가 Edward에게 쓸 펜 하나를 주었다.
➡ She gave Edward a pen with to write.

7 그들은 기내에서 읽을거리를 찾고 있었다.
➡ They were looking for something read on the plane.

8 그는 요즘 대화를 나눌 친구가 필요하다.
➡ He needs a friend talk with recently.

EXERCISE B **다음 우리말과 일치하도록 주어진 단어 및 어구를 배열하여 문장을 완성하시오.**

1 나는 비밀리에 네게 말할 것이 있다. (tell, something, to, have)
➡ I ______________________ you in secret.

2 엄마는 내게 새 휴대 전화를 사주신다는 약속을 하셨다. (buy, a promise, to, made)
➡ Mom ______________________ me a new cell phone.

3 지금이 필리핀을 방문할 가장 좋은 시기이다. (visit, the best time, to, is)
➡ This ______________________ the Philippines.

4 이 수학 문제를 푸는 가장 좋은 방법은 무엇이었나요? (solve, the best way, to, was)
➡ What ______________________ this math problem?

5 그는 쓸 펜이 하나 필요하다. (write, a pen, to, needs, with)
➡ He ______________________.

6 제게 쓸 종이 한 장만 주세요. (write, paper, to, on)
➡ Give me a piece of ______________________, please.

7 그는 내게 앉을 의자 하나를 가져다주었다. (sit, a chair, to, on)
➡ He brought me ______________________.

8 그가 의지할 누군가가 있다는 것은 다행이었다. (to, someone, on, depend)
➡ It was lucky for him to have ______________________.

EXERCISE C **다음 우리말과 일치하도록 주어진 단어 및 어구를 사용하여 문장을 완성하시오. (필요시 형태 변화)**

1 서울은 방문할 만한 흥미로운 도시다. (an, exciting, visit, city)
➡ Seoul is ________ ________ ________ ________ ________.

2 그녀는 의지할 사람이 아무도 없었다. (no one, on, rely)
➡ She had ________ ________ ________ ________ ________.

3 어떤 사람들은 늘 불평할 무언가를 찾는다. (about, something, complain)
➡ Some people always look for ________ ________ ________ ________.

4 우리는 누울 침대 하나가 필요했다. (a bed, on, lie)
➡ We needed ________ ________ ________ ________ ________.

8 be동사 + to부정사

가능	~할 수 있다 (= can, be able to) *** 수동태로 쓰이는 경우가 많음**	Not a person **was to be seen** in the forest after dark. 어두워진 후에 숲속에서 단 한 사람도 볼 수 없었다.
운명	~할 운명이다 (= be destined to) *** never와 쓰이는 경우가 많음**	She **was never to meet** her husband again. 그녀는 그녀의 남편을 다시는 만나지 못할 운명이었다.
의도	~할 작정이다 (= will, intend to)	If you **are to see** him, apologize to him first. 네가 그를 보고자 한다면, 먼저 그에게 사과해라.
예정	~할 예정이다 (= will, be going to)	They **are to hold** a birthday party tonight. 그들은 오늘 밤에 생일 파티를 열 예정이다.
의무	~해야 한다 (= must, have to)	We **are to complete** the whole course by July 31. 우리는 7월 31일까지 전체 과정을 끝마쳐야 한다.

▶▶ 정답과 해설 p.5

EXERCISE A 다음 밑줄 친 부분의 의미로 알맞은 것을 고르시오.

1 Nothing is to be seen. [예정 / 의무 / 가능]

2 They were to finish the work by noon. [운명 / 의무 / 의도]

3 We are to go to Argentina next month. [가능 / 예정 / 의도]

4 If you are to succeed in business, just do your best. [의도 / 운명 / 가능]

5 They were never to meet again after the meeting. [예정 / 의무 / 운명]

6 Our family is to dine out this evening. [가능 / 예정 / 운명]

7 She was never to see her family again. [운명 / 의무 / 예정]

8 If she is to be a member of our team, she shouldn't do that. [의무 / 의도 / 가능]

9 You are to stop using bad words like that. [예정 / 의도 / 의무]

EXERCISE B 다음 주어진 문장을 <보기>처럼 바꿔 쓸 때 빈칸에 알맞은 말을 쓰시오.

<보기>

She will leave for the big city to make money.
➡ She is to leave for the big city to make money.

1 I am going to meet her in front of the hotel tomorrow.
➡ I ______________________ in front of the hotel tomorrow.

2 She had to come back there by ten o'clock.
➡ She ______________________ there by ten o'clock.

3 If you intend to be a great dancer, you have to take lessons.
➡ If you ______________________, you have to take lessons.

4 Not a cloud can be seen now.
➡ Not a cloud ______________________ now.

5 They were destined never to succeed in business.
➡ They ______________________ in business.

EXERCISE C **다음 우리말과 일치하도록 주어진 단어를 사용하여 문장을 완성하시오. (필요시 형태 변화)**

1 우리는 2주 후에 그 경기에 참가할 예정이다. (participate)
➡ We ________ ________ ________ in the game two weeks later.

2 그들이 그 큰 경기를 이기고자 한다면, 그들은 열심히 훈련해야 한다. (win)
➡ If they ________ ________ ________ the big match, they need to train hard.

3 그녀는 병원에서 그의 곁에 있어야 한다. (be)
➡ She ________ ________ ________ with him in the hospital.

4 그는 죽을 때까지 자신의 딸을 절대 보지 못할 운명이었다. (never, see)
➡ He ________ ________ ________ ________ his daughter until his death.

5 그들은 그 다음 날 휴가를 떠날 예정이었다. (go)
➡ They ________ ________ ________ on a vacation the next day.

6 그는 어떻게든 그녀와 다시 만날 운명이다. (meet)
➡ He ________ her again by any means.

7 작가로서 명성을 얻으려면, 다독이 필수적이다. (gain)
➡ If we ________ ________ ________ fame as writers, we need extensive reading.

8 올해는 강어귀에서 연어 한 마리를 볼 수가 없다. (be seen)
➡ Not a salmon ________ ________ ________ ________ at the mouth of the river this year.

9 seem(appear) + to부정사

1 to부정사 seem(ed)과 to부정사가 동일한 시제일 때

It **seems** (that) he **is** an artist. 그는 예술가인 것 같다.

➡ He **seems to be** an artist. **<seems와 같은 시제>**

It **seemed** (that) he **was** an artist. 그는 예술가인 것 같았다.

➡ He **seemed to be** an artist. **<seemed와 같은 시제>**

2 to have p.p. seem(ed)보다 to부정사가 앞선 시제일 때

It **seems** (that) he **was** an artist. 그는 예술가였던 것 같다.

➡ He **seems to have been** an artist. **<seems보다 앞선 시제>**

It **seemed** (that) he **had been** an artist. 그는 예술가였던 것 같았다.

➡ He **seemed to have been** an artist. **<seemed보다 앞선 시제>**

▶▶ 정답과 해설 p.6

EXERCISE A 다음 주어진 문장을 <보기>처럼 바꿔 쓸 때 빈칸에 알맞은 말을 쓰시오.

<보기>
It appeared that she was a good teacher.
➡ She appeared to be a good teacher.

1 It seemed that he gained weight.
➡ He ______________________ weight.

2 It appears that she is healthy.
➡ She ______________________ healthy.

3 It appeared that they played the violin well.
➡ They ______________________ the violin well.

4 It appeared that she had been an athlete.
➡ She ______________________ an athlete.

5 It seems that she was rich.
➡ She ______________________ rich.

6 It appears that the boy was sorry about his mistake.
➡ The boy ______________________ sorry about his mistake.

EXERCISE B **다음 주어진 문장을 <보기>처럼 바꿔 쓸 때 빈칸에 알맞은 말을 쓰시오.**

〈보기〉
They seemed to fall in love with each other.
➡ It seemed (that) they fell in love with each other.

1 You seem to be diligent.
➡ It ______________________ diligent.

2 He seemed to enjoy the play.
➡ It ______________________ the play.

3 The girl seems to have had a good time.
➡ It ______________________ a good time.

4 You seemed to have known the answer.
➡ It ______________________ the answer.

5 You seem to be very happy nowadays.
➡ It ______________________ very happy nowadays.

EXERCISE C **다음 우리말과 일치하도록 주어진 단어 및 어구를 배열하여 문장을 완성하시오.**

1 당신은 야구 선수인 것 같다. (you, seems, are, It, that)
➡ ______________________ a baseball player.

2 그는 돈 때문에 그녀와 싸웠던 것 같다. (It, that, fought, seems, he)
➡ ______________________ with her for the money.

3 그들이 멍청한 실수를 한 것 같았다. (that, made, seemed, they, It)
➡ ______________________ a foolish mistake.

4 그가 좋은 일자리를 찾았던 것 같았다. (that, seemed, had found, he, It)
➡ ______________________ a good job.

5 그녀는 몰래 그를 도왔던 것 같았다. (she, It, had helped, seemed, him, that)
➡ ______________________ in secret.

10 목적 / 결과를 나타내는 to부정사

1 목적 ~하기 위해 ➡ 「in order to(so as to) + 동사원형」
➡ 「so that + 주어 + can(could) ~」

We **studied** very hard **to pass** the exam. 우리는 시험에 통과하기 위해 매우 열심히 공부했다.
➡ We **studied** very hard **in order to(so as to) pass** the exam.
➡ We **studied** very hard **so that we could pass** the exam.

2 결과 (~해서 결국) …하다

Our grandfather **lived to be** ninety-two. 우리 할아버지께서는 92세까지 사셨다.
He **grew up to become** a movie director. 그는 커서 영화감독이 되었다.

+ 「only(never) + to부정사」는 '결국 ~하다(~하지 못하다)'의 뜻으로 쓰인다.

She tried her best in the contest **only to fail**. 그녀는 시합에서 최선을 다했지만 결국 떨어졌다.

▶▶ 정답과 해설 p.6

EXERCISE A 다음 밑줄 친 부분의 우리말 뜻을 쓰시오.

1 We saved much money to buy a new house.

2 They did everything to find the missing child.

3 He practices hard to become a professional golfer.

4 She paid more attention to his words in order not to disappoint him.

EXERCISE B 다음 우리말과 일치하도록 주어진 단어 및 어구를 배열하여 문장을 완성하시오.

1 그 말은 달아나서 결국 돌아오지 않았다. (never, come back, ran away, to)
➡ The horse ______________________________.

2 나는 밖으로 나가기 위해 신발을 신었다. (to, my shoes, on, go outside, put)
➡ I ______________________________.

3 나는 첫 기차를 놓치지 않으려고 집에서 일찍 출발했다. (early, to, left home, the first train, miss, not)
➡ I ______________________________.

11 조건을 나타내는 to부정사

조건 ~한다면 ➡ 「if + 주어 + 동사 ~」

You **may be** surprised **to see** the animal in the city. 네가 그 도시에서 그 동물을 본다면 놀랄지도 모른다.
➡ You **may be** surprised **if you see** the animal in the city.

I **would be** glad **to join** your ping-pong club. 내가 너희 탁구 동아리에 가입한다면 기쁠 것이다.
➡ I **would be** glad **if I could join** your ping-pong club.

I **would be** happy **to hear** his voice. 그의 목소리를 듣는다면 나는 행복할 것이다.
➡ I **would be** happy **if I could hear** his voice.

▶▶ 정답과 해설 p.6

EXERCISE A 다음 밑줄 친 부분의 우리말 뜻을 쓰시오.

1 She would be upset <u>to see the broken window</u>.

2 I will be happy <u>to see my parents again</u>.

3 <u>To hear her speak Swedish</u>, you would be very surprised.

4 We may be angry <u>to watch our team lose the game</u>.

5 You would be pleased <u>to help the poor</u>.

EXERCISE B 다음 우리말과 일치하도록 주어진 단어를 배열하여 문장을 완성하시오.

1 그는 그 조사 결과를 본다면 놀랄지도 모른다. (the results, see, to, the research, of)
➡ He may be amazed ______________________.

2 그 소식을 듣는다면 그들은 슬퍼할지도 모른다. (the news, hear, to)
➡ They may be sad ______________________.

3 장애인들을 돕는다면 너는 행복함을 느낄지도 모른다. (to, the disabled, help)
➡ You may feel happy ______________________.

4 그 버스를 놓친다면 그는 당황할 것이다. (to, the bus, miss)
➡ He would be embarrassed ______________________.

12 감정의 원인 / 판단의 근거를 나타내는 to부정사

1 **감정의 원인** **~해서 ➡ 「because + 주어 + 동사」**

They were **surprised to see** the working environment. 그들은 그 작업 환경을 보고서 놀랐다.
➡ They were **surprised because they saw** the working environment.

I'm very **happy to meet** you. 나는 너를 만나서 매우 반갑다.
➡ I'm very **happy because I meet** you.

+ 감정을 나타내는 형용사 : delighted, happy, pleased, surprised, sad, grieved, glad

2 **판단의 근거** **~하다니 ➡ 「It ~ of ... + to부정사」**

He can't be **wise to act** like that. 그렇게 행동하다니 그는 현명할 리가 없다.
➡ **It** can't be **wise of him to act** like that.

He must be **brave to save** the little kid. 그 어린 아이를 구하다니 그는 용감한 게 틀림없다.
➡ **It** must be **brave of him to save** the little kid.

▶▶ 정답과 해설 p.6

EXERCISE A **다음 밑줄 친 부분의 우리말 뜻을 쓰시오.**

1 I am very pleased <u>to see you again</u>.

2 She must be silly <u>to do such a stupid thing</u>.

3 We were sad <u>to hear of her failure</u>.

4 He can't be a man of sense <u>to believe it</u>.

5 She is happy <u>to live together with her mom</u>.

EXERCISE B **다음 두 문장의 의미가 같도록 빈칸에 알맞은 말을 쓰시오.**

1 My parents were disappointed to look at my report card.
= My parents were disappointed ______________ my report card.

2 She is foolish to repeat the same mistake again.
= It is foolish ______________ the same mistake again.

3 He is so bold to go against our company policy.
= It is so bold ______________ against our company policy.

13 too ~ to / enough to

1 「too + 형용사(부사) + to부정사」: 너무 ~해서 …할 수 없는

➡ 「so + 형용사(부사) + that + 주어 + can't(couldn't)」

He is **too weak to lift** the table. 그는 너무 허약해서 그 탁자를 들어 올릴 수 없다.

➡ He is **so weak that he can't lift** the table.

+ 사물이 주어인 경우 to부정사의 의미상 주어가 종속절의 주어가 된다.

The box was **too** heavy **for him to lift**. 그 상자는 너무 무거워서 그가 들어 올릴 수 없었다.

➡ **The box** was **so** heavy **that he couldn't lift it**.

2 「형용사(부사) + enough + to부정사」: ~할 만큼 충분히 …한(하게)

➡ 「so + 형용사(부사) + as + to부정사」

➡ 「so + 형용사(부사) + that + 주어 + can(could)」

She was **humorous enough to make** everyone laugh.
그녀는 모든 사람들을 웃게 할 만큼 충분히 재미있었다.

➡ She was **so humorous as to make** everyone laugh.

➡ She was **so humorous that she could make** everyone laugh.

▶▶ 정답과 해설 p. 7

EXERCISE A 다음 주어진 문장을 〈보기〉처럼 바꿔 쓸 때 빈칸에 알맞은 말을 쓰시오.

〈보기〉
We were too full to drink a glass of orange juice.
➡ We were so full that we couldn't drink a glass of orange juice.

1 She is too shy to make a public speech.
➡ She is ______________________ a public speech.

2 This bed is too short for me to sleep on.
➡ This bed is ______________________ on it.

3 The wallet was too big for me to put in my back pocket.
➡ The wallet was ______________________ it in my back pocket.

4 This soup is too hot for me to eat.
➡ This soup is ______________________ it.

EXERCISE B 다음 주어진 문장을 〈보기〉처럼 바꿔 쓸 때 빈칸에 알맞은 말을 쓰시오.

〈보기〉

The man was kind enough to drive us home late at night.
➡ The man was so kind as to drive us home late at night.
➡ The man was so kind that he could drive us home late at night.

1 He is rich enough to buy a new yacht.
➡ He is ______________________ a new yacht.
➡ He is ______________________ a new yacht.

2 She was free enough to read many books.
➡ She was ______________________ many books.
➡ She was ______________________ many books.

3 They are smart enough to pass the exam.
➡ They are ______________________ the exam.
➡ They are ______________________ the exam.

4 He was strong enough to move the desk for himself.
➡ He was ______________________ the desk for himself.
➡ He was ______________________ the desk for himself.

EXERCISE C 다음 우리말과 일치하도록 주어진 단어를 배열하여 문장을 완성하시오.

1 우리는 너무 피곤해서 어제 외출을 할 수 없었다. (go, tired, too, to)
➡ We were ______________________ out yesterday.

2 그녀는 친구들에게 조언을 해줄 만큼 충분히 현명하다. (enough, give, to, wise)
➡ She is ______________________ advice to her friends.

3 너무 어두워서 나는 진입로를 볼 수 없었다. (dark, me, for, too, see, to)
➡ It was ______________________ the driveway.

4 그는 친구들을 유쾌하게 할 만큼 충분히 활기찼다. (to, lively, make, enough)
➡ He was ______________________ his friends cheerful.

14 It takes ~ to부정사

「It takes + 사람 + 시간 + to부정사」: (사람)이 ~하는 데 시간이 … 걸리다

➡「It takes + 시간 + for 사람 + to부정사」

➡「사람 + spend + 시간 + (on) -ing」

It took me about five hours to get there from here by bus.

내가 버스로 여기서 그곳에 가는 데 약 5시간이 걸렸다.

➡ **It took about five hours for me to get** there from here by bus.

➡ **I spent about five hours (on) getting** there from here by bus.

▶▶ 정답과 해설 p.7

EXERCISE A 다음 문장에서 어법상 틀린 곳을 찾아 바르게 고쳐 쓰시오. (틀린 곳이 없으면 ○표)

1 She spent thirty minutes finish her homework.

2 They spent about two hours ending their discussion.

3 It takes three years him to complete the whole course.

4 It took to me one and a half hours to memorize the poem.

5 It took fifteen years for her to see her husband again.

6 It takes me one hour to going to school on foot.

EXERCISE B 다음 세 문장의 의미가 같도록 빈칸에 알맞은 말을 쓰시오.

1 It took her five hours or so to write an article.
= It took five hours or so ________________ an article.
= She spent ________________ an article.

2 It took me forty minutes to give an oral presentation.
= It ________________ to give an oral presentation.
= I spent ________________ an oral presentation.

3 It usually takes him two days to get back from his hometown.
= It usually takes two days ________________ from his hometown.
= He usually spends ________________ back from his hometown.

15 대부정사

대부정사는 문장의 간결성을 위해 앞에서 나온 '동사(구)'를 뒤에서 반복하여 쓰지 않고 생략하여 to만 쓰는 형태를 말한다.

I will **go** with her if she wants **to**. 나는 그녀가 원하면 그녀와 함께 갈 것이다.
= to go

You can **have this doll** if you want **to**. 네가 원하면 이 인형을 가져도 된다.
= to have this doll

A Would you like to **speak English fluently**? 너는 영어를 유창하게 말하고 싶니?
B Yes, I'd like **to**. 응, 그러고 싶어.
= to speak English fluently

▶▶ 정답과 해설 p.7

EXERCISE A **다음 문장에서 어법상 틀린 부분을 찾아 바르게 고쳐 쓰시오.**

1 **A** Do you want to travel to Greece?
B Of course, I'd like.

2 You may go home now if you really want go.

3 He will come here with her if she would like come here.

4 My parents wanted to take pictures, but I didn't to.

EXERCISE B **다음 문장의 밑줄 친 부분 뒤에 생략된 말을 찾아 쓰시오.**

1 **A** Will you watch the movie again?
B Yes, I want to.

2 You may drop by if you want to.

3 **A** Do you want to dance?
B Yes, I'd love to.

4 He drank coffee, but I told him not to.

5 I asked her to play the violin, but she didn't want to.

6 She will do him a favor even if everyone tells her not to.

16 독립부정사

독립부정사는 to부정사가 독립된 의미를 가지면서 문장 전체를 수식한다.

to be sure	확실히	to make a long story short	요약하자면
to be frank(honest)	솔직히	to tell the truth	사실은
to start(begin) with	우선	strange to say	이상하게도
to say the least	적어도	so to speak	말하자면
not to speak of	~은 말할 것도 없이	to make things worse	엎친 데 덮친 격으로

독립부정사는 문장 전체를 수식하며 문장의 앞, 뒤, 중간 어디에도 위치할 수 있다.

He, **to make things worse**, lost her trust as well. 그는 엎친 데 덮친 격으로 그녀의 믿음까지도 잃었다.
She speaks French, **not to speak of** English. 그녀는 영어는 말할 것도 없이 프랑스어도 한다.
He is, **so to speak**, a walking dictionary. 그는 말하자면 걸어 다니는 사전이다.

▶▶ 정답과 해설 p.7

EXERCISE A **다음 문장에서 어법상 틀린 부분을 찾아 바르게 고쳐 쓰시오.**

1 He did a hard job without pay, strangely to say.

2 So speaking, they deceived us by not telling the truth.

3 Make things worse, he can't marry the woman he loves.

4 There were 500 students in the hall, to say the last.

5 To not speak of him, we all were shocked at the news.

6 To tell the true, he wanted to get the chance to meet the mayor.

EXERCISE B **다음 우리말과 일치하도록 빈칸에 알맞은 말을 쓰시오.**

1 엎친 데 덮친 격으로, 우리는 가스를 다 썼다.
➡ ________ ________ ________ ________, we used up the gas.

2 솔직히, 나는 그녀가 생각하는 방식을 좋아하지 않는다.
➡ ________ ________ ________, I don't like the way she thinks.

3 사실은, 나는 너의 이름을 잊어버렸다.
➡ ________ ________ ________ ________, I forgot your name.

학교 시험 대비 문제

맞힌 개수	
선택형	____ / 31
서술형	____ / 24

▶▶ 정답과 해설 p.7

01 다음 〈보기〉의 밑줄 친 부분과 쓰임이 같은 것은?

〈보기〉
I like to play the guitar.

① He lived to be 67.
② They did it to survive.
③ I want to have a party.
④ I'm happy to see you again.
⑤ She did her best only to fail.

02 다음 주어진 문장과 의미가 일치하지 않는 것은?

I studied very hard to get a good score.

① I studied very hard for a good score.
② I studied too hard to get a good score.
③ To get a good score, I studied very hard.
④ I studied very hard in order to get a good score.
⑤ I studied very hard so that I could get a good score.

03 다음 밑줄 친 부분의 쓰임이 나머지 넷과 다른 것은?

① He grew up to be a good pianist.
② I am happy to see him before I leave.
③ I have the power to have control over myself.
④ She was glad to take part in the big game.
⑤ You need to do it to succeed in the company.

04 다음 빈칸에 공통으로 알맞은 것은?

• It made him ________ there by himself.
• She doesn't let me ________ hunting alone.

① go ② go to ③ going
④ went ⑤ to going

고난도

05 다음 중 어법상 틀린 것은?

① He had her bring some toys.
② I heard him turning on the TV.
③ They saw me sing in the festival.
④ She helped him to set up the tent.
⑤ She allowed someone come in the room.

06 다음 중 밑줄 친 부분이 어법상 틀린 것은?

① It is natural for him to do so.
② It is careless of you to trip over a stone.
③ It is stupid of you to make such a mistake.
④ It was impossible of him to win the lottery.
⑤ It was hard for her to admit the truth.

07 다음 빈칸에 들어갈 말로 알맞은 것은?

• It takes me about ten minutes to wash my hair.
= It takes about ten minutes ________ my hair.

① me to wash
② me washing
③ of me to wash
④ for me washing
⑤ for me to wash

08 다음 중 어법상 틀린 것은?

① People want to be famous.
② They decided to buy some food.
③ Lisa agreed starting after breakfast.
④ So to speak, money is everything to him.
⑤ It took too much time for them to play cards.

고난도

09 다음 두 문장의 의미가 서로 일치하지 않는 것은?

① It appears that he is lonely.
= He appears to be lonely.
② It seemed that he had been a robber.
= He seemed to have been a robber.
③ She seemed to have had a hard time.
= It seemed that she had a hard time.
④ It appeared that he played the flute very well.
= He appeared to play the flute very well.
⑤ She seems to have been sorry for her mistake.
= It seems that she was sorry for her mistake.

10 다음 문장을 우리말로 잘못 옮긴 것은?

① He can't be wise to act like that.
➡ 그렇게 행동하다니 그는 현명할 리가 없다.
② I will work here to become a mechanic.
➡ 나는 정비사가 되기 위해 여기서 일할 것이다.
③ We were pleased to ride a horse in the fields.
➡ 우리는 들판에서 말을 탈 수 있었다.
④ He went to London to visit his grandparents.
➡ 그는 조부모님을 방문하기 위해서 런던에 갔다.
⑤ You may be surprised to experience such a strange thing at night.
➡ 여러분이 밤에 그런 이상한 일을 겪는다면 놀랄지도 모른다.

11 다음 밑줄 친 부분이 어법상 틀린 것은?

① He asked us why to go.
② The big problem is what to do next.
③ How we should spend time is important.
④ She couldn't decide where she should go.
⑤ She told him when to finish the project.

12 다음 밑줄 친 부분과 바꿔 쓴 것이 틀린 것은?

① She is to hold a party tomorrow.
➡ is going to hold
② He was to finish the work by six.
➡ had to finish
③ Not a man was to be seen in the jungle.
➡ could be seen
④ We were never to see each other forever.
➡ were destined to see
⑤ If you are to meet him, make an appointment with him first. ➡ intend to meet

13 다음 중 뜻과 어구가 일치하지 않는 것은?

① 확실히 ➡ to be sure
② 우선 ➡ to begin with
③ 말하자면 ➡ so to speak
④ 적어도 ➡ to say the last
⑤ ~은 말할 것도 없이 ➡ not to speak of

14 다음 중 밑줄 친 to부정사의 쓰임이 나머지 넷과 다른 것은?

① His hope is to be at the top.
② She wants to play the game.
③ He hopes not to fail the exam.
④ It is dangerous to swim in the river.
⑤ You must study hard to pass the test.

15 다음 빈칸에 들어갈 말로 알맞지 않은 것은?

Someone ________ me to kneel down.

① told ② made
③ wanted ④ ordered
⑤ expected

16 다음 빈칸에 들어갈 말로 알맞은 것을 모두 고르시오.

We could hear him ________ for help then.

① call ② calls
③ call to ④ calling
⑤ to call

고난도

17 다음 중 어법상 틀린 문장의 수로 알맞은 것은?

- They were to meet at the same place.
- He spoke German, not to speak English.
- It took about an hour us to have lunch there and come back here.
- He would watch too much TV because you didn't tell him not to.

① 1개 ② 2개 ③ 3개
④ 4개 ⑤ 없음

18 다음 중 밑줄 친 부분이 어법상 틀린 것은?

① I saw him get on the bus.
② They got her have the keys.
③ She heard me shut the door.
④ He made his son wash the car.
⑤ We let them play in the ground.

고난도

19 다음 빈칸에 들어갈 말이 바르게 짝지어진 것은?

I need a pen to write ________. And she needs a sheet of paper to write ________.

① on — by ② by — with
③ into — in ④ with — on
⑤ before — on

20 다음 우리말을 영어로 바르게 옮긴 것은?

그는 그들에게 비열한 짓을 하지 말라고 나에게 말했다.

① He told me to play not a dirty trick on them.
② He told me not to play a dirty trick on them.
③ He didn't tell me to play a dirty trick on them.
④ He told not for me to play a dirty trick on them.
⑤ He didn't tell me not to play a dirty trick on them.

21 다음 문장의 의미가 나머지 넷과 다른 것은?

① It was too dark for me to keep going through the woods.
② It was so dark that I could keep going through the woods.
③ It was too dark, so I couldn't keep going through the woods.
④ Because it was too dark, I couldn't keep going through the woods.
⑤ I could have kept going through the woods if it hadn't been too dark.

22 다음 빈칸에 들어갈 말로 알맞은 것은?

• She would be surprised to hear the news. = She would be surprised ________ she heard the news.

① if ② so ③ though
④ while ⑤ so that

23 다음 빈칸에 들어갈 말로 알맞지 않은 것은?

My brother is ________ enough to do that.

① nice ② brave ③ youth
④ strong ⑤ gentle

24 다음 밑줄 친 부분과 쓰임이 같은 것은?

I would be very happy to go there.

① He must be kind to help old people.
② I worked hard only to fail in the exam.
③ She was excited to win the gold medal.
④ Mom will be angry to see the messy desk.
⑤ John got up very early to see the sunrise.

25 다음 중 밑줄 친 부분의 쓰임이 나머지 넷과 다른 것은?

① They both grew up to be lawyers.
② She did everything to save his life.
③ I'm so pleased to get along with you.
④ I left home early to get a seat in the library.
⑤ You're the one to share my feelings with these days.

26 다음 빈칸에 들어갈 말로 가장 알맞은 것은?

> • You are to do your homework before you go out.
> = You ________ your homework before you go out.

① have to do ② intend to do
③ are able to do ④ are going to do
⑤ are destined to do

27 다음 빈칸에 들어갈 말로 알맞지 <u>않은</u> 것은?

> It was ________ of him to do well by the people.

① wise ② nice ③ kind
④ friendly ⑤ natural

고난도

28 다음 중 어법상 <u>틀린</u> 것은?

① Tell me what to do now.
② I have no house to live in.
③ She needed an adviser to talk.
④ He is not the only man to tell a lie.
⑤ They didn't have any water to drink.

고난도

29 다음 두 문장의 의미가 서로 일치하지 <u>않는</u> 것은?

① I'll have her go with you.
   = I'll get her to go with you.
② I don't know which to buy.
   = I don't know which I should buy.
③ I am so sad to have to leave you.
   = I am so sad if I have to leave you.
④ She was so rude that I couldn't stand her.
   = She was too rude for me to stand.
⑤ We tried our best in order not to feel regret for it.
   = We tried our best so that we wouldn't feel regret for it.

30 다음 빈칸에 들어갈 말로 알맞은 것을 <u>모두</u> 고르시오.

> She went to the shopping mall ________ buy a jacket.

① to ② for ③ so that
④ so well ⑤ in order to

31 다음 빈칸에 들어갈 말로 알맞은 것은?

> You don't have to wear jeans if ____________ ________.

① you like
② you don't wanted
③ you don't want to
④ you would want to
⑤ you didn't want to it

서술형

32 다음 우리말과 일치하도록 주어진 단어를 배열하여 문장을 완성하시오.

- 그들은 내가 자신들의 집 앞에 주차하도록 허락하지 않았다. (to, allow, park, me)

➡ They didn't ______________ in front of their house.

33 다음 빈칸에 주어진 단어를 배열하여 대화를 완성하시오.

A Why not ask him to tell you ______________? (classes, to, which, take)

B That's a great idea.

34 다음 우리말과 일치하도록 주어진 단어를 사용하여 문장을 완성하시오. (필요시 형태 변화)

- 그 결과가 그들을 그렇게 생각하도록 만들었다. (make, think)

➡ The result ______________ so.

35 다음 문장의 밑줄 친 부분을 우리말로 해석하시오.

- You don't need to meet them <u>if you don't want to</u>.

➡ ______________

36 다음 두 문장의 뜻이 같도록 빈칸에 알맞은 말을 쓰시오.

- Because I heard the news that you would come back to your homeland, I was so glad.

= I was so glad ________ ________ the news that you would come back to your homeland.

37 다음 우리말과 일치하도록 주어진 단어와 어구를 배열하여 문장을 완성하시오.

- 그는 그녀에게 앉을 의자 하나를 가져다주었다. (to, on, a chair, sit)

➡ He brought her ______________.

[38-39] 다음 우리말과 일치하도록 주어진 단어와 어구를 사용하여 문장을 완성하시오. (필요시 형태 변화)

38

- 나는 매일 아침 잠자리를 정돈하는 것을 규칙으로 삼고 있다. (make, a rule, it)

➡ I make ________ ________ ________ ________ ________ my bed every morning.

39

- 그녀는 자신의 친구들에게 조언을 해줄 만큼 충분히 현명하다. (wise, give)

➡ She is __________ __________ __________ __________ advice to her friends.

[40-41] 다음 두 문장의 뜻이 같도록 주어진 단어를 사용하여 문장을 완성하시오.

40

- He was too afraid to bungee jump.

= He was ____________________ bungee jump. (so, that)

41

- It took me half an hour to find the book.

= It took ____________________ to find the book. (for)

42 다음 우리말과 일치하도록 주어진 단어를 사용하여 문장을 완성하시오.

- 그녀는, 말하자면, 그에게 천사이다. (so)

➡ She, __________ __________ __________, is an angel to him.

43 다음 빈칸에 공통으로 들어갈 말을 쓰시오.

- __________ was wonderful to have dinner with you on Christmas Eve last year.
- I didn't think __________ easy to become an astronaut.

고난도

44 다음 빈칸에 주어진 단어를 배열하여 대화를 완성하시오.

A What's the problem with her?

B She ____________________ her car keys. (to, lost, have, seems)

45 다음 두 문장의 뜻이 같도록 주어진 단어를 사용하여 문장을 완성하시오.

- She seemed to enjoy her first flight. (that)

= It seemed ____________________ her first flight.

[46-47] 다음 두 문장의 뜻이 같도록 빈칸에 알맞은 말을 쓰시오.

46

- She must be brave to train the wild tiger.

= It must be ________ ________ ________ to train the wild tiger.

47

- I forgot what I should buy at the market.

= I forgot ________ ________ ________ at the market.

48 다음 두 문장의 뜻이 같도록 주어진 단어를 배열하여 문장을 완성하시오.

- She turned off the TV so that she wouldn't disturb the sleeping baby.

= She turned off the TV ________________ disturb the sleeping baby.
(to, order, in, not)

49 다음 대화의 내용에 맞도록 주어진 질문에 완전한 문장의 대답을 쓰시오.

A Did you make up your mind?
B Oh, yeah. I think this is not a good time to buy a laptop now.
A OK. Let's not buy a laptop, then.

Q What did they decide?
➡ ________________________________

50 다음 우리말과 일치하도록 주어진 단어를 배열하여 문장을 완성하시오.

- 나의 관심사는 그녀에게 소심해 보이지 않는 것이다. (look, not, is, to)

➡ My concern ________________ timid to her.

51 다음 두 문장의 뜻이 같도록 빈칸에 알맞은 말을 쓰시오.

- If she saw his messy room, she would be very angry with him.

= She would be very angry with him ________ ________ ________ ________ ________.

52 주어진 우리말과 일치하도록 <조건>에 맞게 영작하시오.

<조건>
- 가주어 it을 사용할 것
- 주어진 단어를 모두 사용할 것
- 총 11단어로 문장을 완성할 것

- 우리가 그 과제를 내일까지 끝내는 것은 불가능하다. (finish, the project, by tomorrow)

➡ ______________________

고난도

[53-55] 다음 글을 읽고, to부정사를 사용하여 질문에 답하시오.

Dear Susan,

I had a hard time taking a short trip to the National Museum today. I planned to get up at about 9 in the morning, but I overslept and missed the bus. It was 10:30. So, in a hurry, I headed for my destination. Two hours later, I finally got there. Because it was so crowded, I thought it would be hard to get through every gallery and it would be better to go home early. It was only 2 p.m. when I headed home. To make things worse, I lost my favorite pen there. How did this happen to me? When I got home, it was 3:30 p.m.

Your true friend,
Peter

53 Q What did Peter think when he arrived at the National Museum?
A He thought it was too ______________________
______________________.

54 Q What did Peter decide to do after he thought there were so many people?
A He decided ______________________
______________________.

55 Q How long did it take for him to get home from the National Museum?
A It took ______________________
______________________.

Chapter

02

동명사

1 주어/보어/목적어 역할을 하는 동명사
2 동명사의 의미상 주어
3 목적어로 동명사를 사용하는 동사
4 목적어로 동명사와 to부정사를 모두 사용하는 동사
5 동명사와 현재분사
6 동명사 관용 표현
■ 학교 시험 대비 문제

1 주어 / 보어 / 목적어 역할을 하는 동명사

동명사는 「동사원형+-ing」의 형태로 명사처럼 주어, 보어, 목적어 역할을 한다.

역할	주어, 보어, 목적어
해석	~하기, ~하는 것
부정	not〔never〕 + -ing

Traveling by ship **is** very interesting. 배로 여행하는 것은 아주 흥미롭다. **<주어> * 주어로 쓰일 때는 단수 취급**

Riding a bike **is** good for health. 자전거를 타는 것은 건강에 좋다. **<주어>**

Her hobby is **collecting** coins. 그녀의 취미는 동전을 수집하는 것이다. **<보어>**

He finished **painting** the picture. 그는 그림 그리는 것을 끝마쳤다. **<목적어>**

They are fond of **playing** the flute. 그들은 플루트 연주하는 것을 좋아한다. **<전치사의 목적어>**

+ 주어와 보어로 쓰인 동명사는 to부정사로 바꿔 쓸 수 있다.

Being kind to others is very important.
➡ **To be** kind to others is very important. 다른 사람들에게 친절히 대하는 것은 매우 중요하다.

My job was **teaching** English.
➡ My job was **to teach** English. 나의 직업은 영어를 가르치는 것이었다.

▶▶ 정답과 해설 p. 10

EXERCISE A 다음 문장에서 동명사에 밑줄을 긋고, 사용된 역할을 고르시오.

1 She is poor at speaking German. [주어 / 보어 / 목적어]

2 My dream was going to Europe. [주어 / 보어 / 목적어]

3 Getting up early every morning will be hard. [주어 / 보어 / 목적어]

4 She enjoyed going for a walk after meals. [주어 / 보어 / 목적어]

5 Going out to play is very exciting. [주어 / 보어 / 목적어]

6 He avoided spending some time with me. [주어 / 보어 / 목적어]

7 My plan for this holiday is helping my mom at home. [주어 / 보어 / 목적어]

8 Making friends was too difficult for me. [주어 / 보어 / 목적어]

9 I can't stop playing computer games when I'm alone. [주어 / 보어 / 목적어]

10 Commerce is buying and selling products. [주어 / 보어 / 목적어]

EXERCISE B 다음 문장에서 어법상 틀린 부분을 찾아 바르게 고쳐 쓰시오.

1 I'm looking forward to see you again.

2 Walk in the country road is very pleasant.

3 He didn't stop make fun of me.

4 My favorite thing is play soccer with friends.

5 Talking with some classmates are very interesting.

6 Having a free discussion with members were very useful.

7 They denied going far from here without think of it.

8 The most important thing is put my idea into practice.

EXERCISE C 다음 우리말과 일치하도록 주어진 단어 및 어구를 사용하여 문장을 완성하시오. (필요시 형태 변화)

1 그녀는 동물원에 가는 것에 들떠 있다. (about, go, to)
➡ She is excited ________ ________ ________ the zoo.

2 그때 그녀는 시험 공부를 끝마쳤니? (study, for, the exam)
➡ Did she finish ________ ________ ________ ________ then?

3 그는 그런 끔찍한 일을 목격하고서 놀랐다. (amazed, at, see)
➡ He was ________ ________ ________ such a terrible thing.

4 제가 약속을 지키지 못한 것을 부디 용서하세요. (for, keep)
➡ Please forgive me ________ ________ ________ my word.

5 네 엄마를 실망시키지 않은 것에 대해 고맙다. (for, disappoint)
➡ Thank you ________ ________ ________ your mom.

6 그녀는 자신의 정원에서 아이들과 노는 것을 즐겼다. (enjoy, play, with)
➡ She ________ ________ ________ kids in her yard.

7 그들은 부유하지 않다는 것을 부끄러워한다. (ashamed, of, be)
➡ They are ________ ________ ________ ________ rich.

2 동명사의 의미상 주어

동명사의 의미상 주어는 동명사의 동작을 행하는 주체를 말한다.

1 의미상 주어를 나타내는 경우

동명사의 의미상 주어가 문장의 주어 또는 목적어와 다른 경우, 의미상 주어는 동명사 앞에 소유격 또는 목적격으로 나타낸다.

Some were satisfied with **her being** innocent. 몇몇은 그녀가 무죄라는 것에 만족했다.
She insisted on **her father going** there. 그녀는 그녀의 아버지께서 그곳에 가실 것을 고집했다.
I don't like **him coming** tonight. 나는 오늘 밤에 그가 오는 것이 마음에 들지 않는다.
You must allow for **the bus being** late. 너는 버스가 늦는 것을 고려해야 한다.

2 의미상 주어를 생략하는 경우

동명사의 의미상 주어가 일반인(we, you, they)이거나 문장의 주어 또는 목적어와 같은 경우, 의미상 주어는 생략된다.

Walking fast is good for our health. 빠르게 걷는 것은 건강에 좋다. **<의미상 주어가 일반인>**
(Our)

I like **listening** to her song. 나는 그녀의 노래를 듣는 것을 좋아한다. **<의미상 주어가 문장의 주어와 일치>**
문장의 주어 (my)

Thank you for **giving** me this book. 나에게 이 책을 줘서 고마워. **<의미상 주어가 문장의 목적어와 일치>**
문장의 목적어 (your)

▶▶ 정답과 해설 p. 10

EXERCISE A **다음 문장에서 동명사의 의미상 주어를 찾아 밑줄을 그으시오. (생략된 경우 ×표)**

1 Their being rich enough was their dream of a life in the city.

2 I insisted on my mother coming here quickly.

3 Excuse me for not coming in time.

4 I have a doubt about this being false.

5 He is proud of passing the entrance exam.

6 Thank you for supporting my proposal in Congress.

7 He was so proud of her doing a good job in the business world.

EXERCISE B 다음 문장에서 어법상 틀린 부분을 찾아 바르게 고쳐 쓰시오.

1 Her parents don't like for her using a smart phone.

2 We were proud of she winning the world championship.

3 She was unsatisfied with theirs coming home late.

4 He doesn't like the idea of John come to the party.

5 I won't share the blame for saying not anything about this.

6 He was afraid of to let out a secret.

EXERCISE C 다음 우리말과 일치하도록 주어진 단어 및 어구를 배열하여 문장을 완성하시오.

1 나는 그들이 게으른 것을 이해할 수가 없었다. (idle, their, being)
➡ I couldn't understand ________________.

2 우리는 그가 시험에 떨어진 것에 대해 유감스럽다. (the test, failing, his)
➡ We're sorry about ________________.

3 그녀는 Brian이 이곳에 온다는 생각이 마음에 들었다. (coming, Brian, here)
➡ She liked the idea of ________________.

4 나는 그녀가 우리와 함께 캠핑 가는 것에 찬성하지 않는다. (camping, us, her, going, with)
➡ I don't agree on ________________.

5 그들은 그들의 아들이 시골에서 혼자 사는 것을 싫어했다. (in, living alone, the country, their, son)
➡ They hated ________________.

6 그는 그의 개가 Jane의 아들을 문 것에 대해 그녀에게 사과했다. (dog, son, her, biting, his)
➡ He apologized to Jane for ________________.

7 제가 교실에서 피아노 연습을 해도 될까요? (the classroom, the piano, practicing, my, in)
➡ Do you mind ________________?

8 엄마는 내가 학교에 지각하는 것에 대해 걱정하신다. (school, being, late for, my)
➡ My mom is worried about ________________.

3 목적어로 동명사를 사용하는 동사

enjoy(즐기다)	mind(꺼리다)	avoid(피하다)	quit(그만두다)
delay(미루다)	finish(끝내다)	postpone(연기하다)	stop(멈추다)
suggest(제안하다)	consider(고려하다)	put off(연기하다)	miss(놓치다)
practice(연습하다)	understand(이해하다)	imagine(상상하다)	give up(포기하다)

He **enjoys reading** novels. 그는 소설 읽는 것을 즐긴다.

She didn't **mind taking** the ship. 그녀는 배 타는 것을 상관하지 않았다.

We **finished doing** our work. 우리는 일하는 것을 끝마쳤다.

They're **considering going** with her. 그들은 그녀와 함께 가는 것을 고려하고 있다.

I **put off going** to the dentist. 나는 치과에 가는 것을 연기했다.

+ 목적어로 to부정사를 사용하는 동사

want(원하다)	promise(약속하다)	choose(선택하다)	manage(가까스로 ~하다)
hope(희망하다)	plan(계획하다)	need(필요로 하다)	learn(배우다)
wish(바라다)	decide(결정하다)	agree(동의하다)	afford(~할 여유가 있다)
expect(기대하다)	tend(~하는 경향이 있다)	refuse(거절하다)	pretend(~인 척하다)

▶▶ 정답과 해설 p. 11

EXERCISE A 다음 문장에서 어법상 틀린 부분을 찾아 바르게 고쳐 쓰시오.

1 She delayed to write to him.

2 He practices to play the cello regularly.

3 He wishes have a white Christmas.

4 We don't understand her to coming here.

5 They couldn't imagine to meet him there.

6 My dad promised buying the gift.

7 Do you expect going to Disneyland?

EXERCISE B 다음 우리말과 일치하도록 주어진 단어를 사용하여 문장을 완성하시오. (필요시 형태 변화)

1 그는 건강을 위해 당분간 커피 마시는 것을 그만두었다. (coffee, drink, stop)
➡ He ________ ________ ________ for his health for a while.

2 나는 새벽 두 시 반까지 그 일을 끝마치지 못했다. (finish, do)
➡ I ________ ________ ________ the job until 2:30 a.m.

3 그녀는 남편을 위해 그렇게 말하는 것을 피할 수 없었다. (could, avoid, say)
➡ She ________ ________ ________ so for her husband.

4 그는 가을에 말 타는 것을 즐겼다. (a horse, ride, enjoy)
➡ He ________ ________ ________ ________ in autumn.

5 그들은 끝내 서로 싸우는 것을 포기했다. (fight, up, give)
➡ They finally ________ ________ ________ against each other.

6 그는 내가 옆에서 떠들어도 상관하지 않았다. (mind, make, my)
➡ He ________ ________ ________ ________ noise next to him.

7 나는 그들과 함께 테니스를 칠까 생각하는 중이다. (tennis, play, consider)
➡ I'm ________ ________ ________ together with them.

EXERCISE C **다음 우리말과 일치하도록 주어진 단어를 배열하여 문장을 완성하시오.**

1 나는 매일 그와 대화하는 것을 즐긴다. (having, a, enjoy, conversation)
➡ I ________________________________ with him every day.

2 그들은 해변에서 환상적인 광경을 보는 것을 놓쳤다. (fantastic, sight, the, missed, seeing)
➡ They ________________________________ on the beach.

3 우리는 목적 없이 외국에 가는 것을 이해할 수가 없었다. (abroad, understand, couldn't, going)
➡ We ________________________________ without a purpose.

4 아빠는 갑자기 우리가 소풍 가는 것을 제안하셨다. (going, a, on, suggested, picnic, our)
➡ Dad ________________________________ suddenly.

5 우리는 폭우로 출발을 연기했다. (off, because, put, leaving, of)
➡ We ________________________________ the heavy rain.

6 그는 아침 일찍 일어나는 것을 연습했다. (up, practiced, early, getting)
➡ He ________________________________ in the morning.

7 그녀는 그들과 친하게 지내는 것을 피해야 한다. (company, should, avoid, keeping)
➡ She ________________________________ with them.

4 목적어로 동명사와 to부정사를 모두 사용하는 동사

1 의미 차이가 없는 동사

동명사와 to부정사를 모두 목적어로 쓰며 의미가 달라지지 않는다.

like / love(좋아하다)	hate(싫어하다)	prefer(더 좋아하다)
begin / start(시작하다)	continue(계속하다)	

I **like taking** a bath with hot water. 나는 뜨거운 물로 목욕하는 것을 좋아한다.
= I **like to take** a bath with hot water.

2 의미 차이가 있는 동사

remember, forget, regret, try는 동명사와 to부정사를 모두 목적어로 쓰지만 의미가 달라진다. to부정사는 주로 미래지향적인 뜻을 나타내며 동명사는 주로 과거지향적인 뜻을 나타낸다.

remember	~한 것을 기억하다	I **remember meeting** her. <과거의 일> 나는 그녀를 만난 것을 기억한다.
	~할 것을 기억하다	I **remembered to meet** her. <미래의 일> 나는 그녀를 만나기로 한 것을 기억했다.
forget	~한 것을 잊다	I **forgot meeting** them. <과거의 일> 나는 그들을 만난 것을 잊고 있었다.
	~할 것을 잊다	I **forgot to meet** them. <미래의 일> 나는 그들을 만나기로 한 것을 잊고 있었다.
regret	~한 것을 후회하다	I **regret telling** you the bad news. 나는 너에게 나쁜 소식을 전한 것을 후회한다.
	~하게 되어 유감이다	I **regret to tell** you that I can't accept your offer. 나는 너의 제안을 받아들일 수 없다고 말하게 되어 유감이다.
try	~해 보다	She **tried catching** fish. <시도> 그녀는 (시험 삼아) 물고기를 잡아봤다.
	~하려고 애쓰다	She **tried to catch** fish. <노력> 그녀는 물고기를 잡으려고 애썼다.

! stop은 목적어로 동명사만 쓸 수 있으며, 「stop + to부정사」에서 to부정사는 목적어가 아닌 부사의 역할을 한다.

- stop + v-ing: ~하는 것을 멈추다
- stop + to부정사: ~하기 위해 멈추다

She **stopped chatting** with her friend. 그녀는 그녀의 친구와 이야기하는 것을 멈추었다. **<목적어 역할>**
She **stopped to chat** with her friend. 그녀는 그녀의 친구와 이야기하기 위해 멈추었다. **<부사 역할>**

▶▶ 정답과 해설 p. 11

EXERCISE A 다음 우리말과 일치하도록 괄호 안에서 옳은 것을 고르시오.

1 나는 그 호텔 앞에서 이 차에 탄 것을 기억했다.
➡ I remembered [getting / to get] in this car in front of the hotel.

2 그는 나를 깨우기 위해 오늘 아침 나에게 전화해야 하는 것을 잊고 있었다.
➡ He forgot [calling / to call] me to wake me up this morning.

3 우리는 우리 힘만으로 이 문제들을 풀기 위해 열심히 노력했다.
➡ We tried hard [solving / to solve] these problems all by ourselves.

4 이 나쁜 소식을 당신에게 전하게 되어 유감입니다.
➡ I regret [telling / to tell] you this bad news.

5 그녀는 그의 계획에 대해 너무 무관심한 것을 후회했다.
➡ She regretted [being / to be] so careless about his plan.

EXERCISE B 다음 우리말과 일치하도록 주어진 단어를 사용하여 문장을 완성하시오. (필요시 형태 변화)

1 어젯밤에 비가 내리기 시작했다. (begin, rain)
➡ It ________ ________ last night.

2 나는 내일 도서관에서 그녀를 보기로 한 것을 기억할 것이다. (remember, see)
➡ I will ________ ________ ________ her at the library tomorrow.

3 그녀는 그에게 거짓말한 것을 후회했다. (regret, tell)
➡ She ________ ________ him a lie.

4 그는 계속해서 그 소설을 읽고 있다. (continue, read)
➡ He ________ ________ ________ the novel.

5 나는 네게 그의 메시지를 전해야 하는 것을 잊고 있었다. (forget, give)
➡ I ________ ________ ________ you his message.

6 우리는 그 무거운 바위를 옮기려고 애썼다. (try, move)
➡ We ________ ________ ________ the heavy rock.

7 그는 자신의 첫 컴퓨터에 그렇게 많은 돈을 쓴 것을 결코 잊지 못할 것이다. (never, forget, spend)
➡ He'll ________ ________ ________ so much money on his first computer.

5 동명사와 현재분사

동명사와 현재분사는 둘 다 「동사원형 + -ing」로 형태가 같지만 문장에서의 역할은 서로 다르다.

	동명사	현재분사
형태	동사원형 + -ing	동사원형 + -ing
역할	명사 역할	형용사 역할
해석	~하기 위한, ~하는 것	~하고 있는, ~하는 중인
의미	용도, 목적	동작, 진행
예문	• You'd better not take a **sleeping** pill. 잠들기 위한 약 (= a pill for sleeping) 당신은 수면제를 복용하지 않는 것이 좋을 것이다. • Her job is **helping** sick people. 돕는 것 그녀의 직업은 아픈 사람들을 돕는 것이다.	• Be quiet for the **sleeping** baby. 자고 있는 아기 (= the baby who is sleeping) 자고 있는 아기를 위해 조용히 해라. • She is **helping** sick people. 돕고 있는 그녀는 아픈 사람들을 돕고 있다.

Her hobby is **drawing** pictures. 그녀의 취미는 그림을 그리는 것이다. **<동명사>**

His **smiling** face makes me happy. 그의 웃는 얼굴은 나를 행복하게 만든다. **<현재분사>**

▶▶ 정답과 해설 p. 11

EXERCISE A **다음 밑줄 친 부분의 쓰임을 괄호 안에서 고르시오.**

1 He is a walking dictionary. [동명사 / 현재분사]

2 He was looking for a smoking room in the building. [동명사 / 현재분사]

3 My decision was being with them during the vacation. [동명사 / 현재분사]

4 I enjoyed taking a nap on the grass at school. [동명사 / 현재분사]

5 He was chatting online when they came home. [동명사 / 현재분사]

6 I thought she needed a sleeping pill for some sleep. [동명사 / 현재분사]

7 The crying child in the playground was my sister. [동명사 / 현재분사]

EXERCISE B **다음 밑줄 친 부분을 우리말로 해석하고, 동명사인지 현재분사인지 쓰시오.**

1 He was surfing the Internet in his room. ➡ 검색하고 있었다, 현재분사

2 I enjoy surfing the Internet. ➡ ____________________

3 Someone was watching the waiting room. ➡ ____________________

4 He is waiting for me outside. ➡ ____________________

5 My grandfather needed a walking stick. ➡ ____________________

6 I like the walking boy. ➡ ____________________

7 All living things would die without air. ➡ ____________________

8 They are talking in the living room. ➡ ____________________

9 Look at the sleeping dog on the hill. ➡ ____________________

10 I didn't bring my sleeping bag. ➡ ____________________

EXERCISE C **다음 우리말과 일치하도록 주어진 단어 및 어구를 배열하여 문장을 완성하시오.**
(1. 필요시 형태 변화 2. 동명사 또는 현재분사 사용)

1 당근과 토마토를 먹는 것은 눈에 좋다.
(carrots and tomatoes, good, eat, is, for the eyes)
➡ ____________________

2 Laura는 탈의실에 들어가고 싶지 않았다.
(to go, fit, want, into, didn't, room, the, Laura)
➡ ____________________

3 아마존 강에 살고 있는 분홍색 돌고래들이 있다.
(in, live, the Amazon River, pink dolphins, there, are)
➡ ____________________

4 한 소녀가 풍선을 들고 있다.
(a balloon, hold, is, a girl)
➡ ____________________

5 과속하는 차량들은 매우 위험하다.
(are, dangerous, very, cars, speed)
➡ ____________________

6 동명사 관용 표현

look forward to -ing ~하기를 고대하다	I'm **looking forward to working** with you. 나는 당신과 함께 일하기를 고대하고 있다.
far from -ing 결코 ~이 아닌, ~이기는 커녕	James is **far from being** an honest boy. James는 결코 정직한 소년이 아니다.
prevent(keep, stop) A from -ing A가 ~하는 것을 막다	The heavy rain **prevented me from going** there. 폭우가 나를 그곳에 가지 못하게 했다.
spend + 시간(돈) + -ing ~하는 데 시간(돈)을 소비하다	She **spent ten days setting** up fences. 그녀는 울타리를 치는 데 10일을 보냈다.
be busy -ing ~하느라 바쁘다	She **is busy preparing** dinner. 그녀는 저녁을 준비하느라 바쁘다.
have trouble(difficulty) -ing ~하는 데 어려움을 겪다	Tom **had trouble sleeping** deeply. Tom은 깊이 잠드는 데 어려움을 겪었다.
There is no -ing ~하는 것은 불가능하다	**There is no explaining** the process of making paper. 종이 만드는 과정을 설명하는 것은 불가능하다.
cannot help -ing = cannot but + 동사원형 ~할 수밖에 없다	The player **couldn't help keeping** the rule. = The player **couldn't but keep** the rule. 그 선수는 규칙을 따를 수밖에 없었다.
be worth -ing = be worthwhile -ing(to부정사) ~할 가치가 있다	The museum **is worth visiting**. = The museum is **worth while visiting(to visit)**. 그 박물관은 방문할 만한 가치가 있다.
feel like -ing = want to부정사 ~하고 싶다	I **feel like giving** him a good scolding. 나는 그를 야단치고 싶다.
on -ing = as soon as + 주어 + 동사 ~하자마자	**On seeing** the train coming, he jumped out of the chair. 기차가 오는 것을 보자마자, 그는 의자에서 벌떡 일어났다.
be used(accustomed) to -ing ~에 익숙하다	I'**m used to staying** up till late. 나는 늦게까지 깨어 있는 데 익숙하다.
It is no use(good) -ing ~해봐야 소용없다	**It is no use crying** over spilt milk. 엎질러진 우유를 두고 울어봐야 소용없다.

▶▶ 정답과 해설 p. 11

EXERCISE A 다음 문장에서 어법상 틀린 부분을 찾아 바르게 고쳐 쓰시오.

1 Lisa spent much money fix her camera.

2 This book was worth to reading.

3 She can't help to say yes.

4 I had trouble finish the work in a week.

5 He is looking forward buy a new bag.

6 They are busy to cleaning the living room.

7 Jerry is used to eat spicy Kimchi.

8 The movie is worth to see twice.

9 Peter spends a lot of time play computer games.

EXERCISE B 다음 우리말과 일치하도록 주어진 단어를 사용하여 문장을 완성하시오.
(1. 필요시 형태 변화 2. 동명사 사용)

1 그는 어제 시험을 준비하느라 바빴다. (prepare)
➡ He ________ ________ ________ for the exam yesterday.

2 나는 너에게서 곧 연락 받기를 고대하고 있다. (hear)
➡ I ________ ________ ________ ________ ________ from you soon.

3 나는 저녁으로 맛있는 중국 음식을 먹고 싶다. (eat)
➡ I ________ ________ ________ delicious Chinese food for dinner.

4 그녀는 주말마다 집에서 TV를 보는 데 익숙하다. (watch)
➡ She ________ ________ ________ ________ TV at home every weekend.

5 우리는 우리 아들 때문에 다른 도시로 이사하고 싶었다. (move)
➡ We ________ ________ ________ to another town because of our son.

6 오후에 집에 도착하자마자, 우리는 가방을 풀었다. (get)
➡ ________ ________ home in the afternoon, we unpacked our bags.

7 그는 아이를 습관적으로 나무라는 데 익숙했다. (blame)
➡ He ________ ________ ________ ________ the child out of habit.

8 Daphne를 보자마자, Apollo는 사랑에 빠졌다. (see)
➡ ________ ________ Daphne, Apollo fell in love with her.

9 그는 출근하려고 일어나는 데 종종 어려움을 겪는다. (wake)
➡ He often ________ ________ ________ up for work.

10 그녀에게 말해도 소용없다. (talk)
➡ ________ ________ ________ ________ ________ to her.

Chapter 02
동명사

학교 시험 대비 문제

맞힌 개수	
선택형	____ / 23
서술형	____ / 17

▶▶ 정답과 해설 p. 12

01 다음 문장에서 어법상 틀린 것은?

He ① went ② away ③ without ④ to say ⑤ good-bye.

02 다음 빈칸에 들어갈 말이 바르게 짝지어진 것은?

• She couldn't but ________ no.
• It is no use ________ over spilt milk.

① say — cry
② say — crying
③ saying — cried
④ saying — crying
⑤ said — crying

03 다음 빈칸에 들어갈 말로 알맞지 않은 것은?

We ________ having a conversation with them about it.

① enjoyed ② avoided ③ promised
④ finished ⑤ considered

고난도

04 다음 밑줄 친 부분의 쓰임이 나머지 넷과 다른 것은?

① His job is protecting the people.
② You'd better take a sleeping pill.
③ He liked playing tennis on weekends.
④ He heard someone laughing in the store.
⑤ I'll get a new walking stick for my grandmother.

05 다음 중 어법상 올바른 것은?

① He enjoyed to drink alcohol.
② Please quit to smoke for your health.
③ She avoided keeping company with him.
④ You have to postpone to answer the email.
⑤ Would you mind to close the door, please?

06 다음 빈칸에 들어갈 말로 알맞은 것은?

• 그 책은 끝까지 읽을 가치가 있다.
➡ The book is worth ________ through.

① read ② reading ③ to read
④ will read ⑤ have read

07 다음 밑줄 친 부분의 쓰임이 나머지 넷과 다른 것은?

① His hobby is collecting coins.
② I'm doing business with them.
③ She finished painting the picture.
④ He liked playing the piano.
⑤ Being kind to the elderly is very important.

[08-09] 다음 중 어법상 틀린 것을 고르시오.

고난도

08 ① They like his going there.
② Her being poor is known to all.
③ I'm sure of his arriving on time.
④ We were sorry about her fail the test.
⑤ He doesn't mind my opening the window.

09 ① She was used to stay up late at night.
② I feel like visiting Mr. Brown tomorrow.
③ He spent two weeks writing the report.
④ There is no explaining the process of it.
⑤ They were busy preparing for the exam.

10 다음 빈칸에 공통으로 들어갈 말로 알맞은 것은?

• There is ________ living without any difficulty.
• It is ________ good complaining after buying it carelessly.

① in ② of ③ at
④ no ⑤ to

11 다음 우리말을 영어로 바르게 옮긴 것은?

나는 혼자서 낚시하러 가는 데 익숙하다.

① I used to go fishing alone.
② I'm used to go fishing alone.
③ I'm used of going fishing alone.
④ I'm used in going fishing alone.
⑤ I'm used to going fishing alone.

12 다음 대화의 빈칸에 알맞은 것은?

A How was your trip?
B Great. I'll never forget ________ the scenery in Scotland.

① see ② seen ③ to see
④ seeing ⑤ to be seen

13 다음 두 문장의 의미가 서로 <u>다른</u> 것은?

① I was used to staying at home alone.
= I was accustomed to staying at home alone.

② He cannot help falling in love with her.
= He cannot but fall in love with her.

③ He is looking forward to going to bed.
= He has trouble going to bed.

④ Lots of work kept them from going home.
= Lots of work prevented them from going home.

⑤ She feels like forgetting about everything.
= She wants to forget about everything.

14 다음 밑줄 친 부분의 쓰임이 나머지 넷과 <u>다른</u> 것은?

① She is <u>playing</u> the guitar.

② Look at the <u>sleeping</u> baby.

③ She is a <u>walking</u> dictionary.

④ I'm looking for a <u>smoking</u> room.

⑤ They are walking down the street <u>talking</u> to each other.

고난도

15 다음 중 어법상 <u>틀린</u> 것은?

① Her being rich is known to all.

② My hobby is collecting stamps.

③ We're considering to go with them.

④ I forgot meeting him two years ago.

⑤ Don't bother the sleeping cat on the floor.

16 다음 밑줄 친 부분을 바꿔 쓸 때 의미가 달라지는 것은?

① He hated <u>waiting</u> for her. ➡ to wait

② I regret <u>telling</u> them a lie. ➡ to tell

③ They started <u>to make</u> noise. ➡ making

④ We continued <u>talking</u> to each other. ➡ to talk

⑤ She began <u>complaining</u> about her new boss.
➡ to complain

17 다음 밑줄 친 부분을 우리말로 <u>잘못</u> 옮긴 것은?

① He is looking for <u>a smoking room</u> here.
흡연실

② I was coming home <u>listening</u> to the radio.
들으면서

③ There was <u>a big dancing hall</u> in town.
큰 무도장

④ Over time, <u>all living things</u> would die.
살기 위한 모든 것

⑤ She was <u>a walking dictionary</u> at school.
걸어 다니는 사전

18 다음 빈칸에 알맞은 말이 순서대로 짝지어진 것은?

> • She is tired of ________ care of her dog.
> • ________ in the rain is very dangerous.

① take — Drive
② take — To drive
③ taking — Driving
④ taking — Drive
⑤ to take — Driving

19 다음 빈칸에 buying이 들어갈 수 없는 것은?

① I avoided ________ their product.
② Laura gave up ________ a new car.
③ She enjoyed ________ a brand-new bag.
④ He suggested ________ her a teddy bear.
⑤ She hoped ________ a house with a pool.

20 다음 빈칸에 들어갈 말이 바르게 짝지어진 것은?

> • Don't wake up the ________ dog.
> • He found a snake in his ________ bag.

① sleep — sleeping
② slept — slept
③ slept — sleeping
④ sleeping — slept
⑤ sleeping — sleeping

21 다음 밑줄 친 부분의 쓰임이 〈보기〉와 같은 것은?

> 〈보기〉
> His job is helping poor people.

① Having breakfast is a healthy habit.
② I love studying wild flowers and plants.
③ Are you interested in teaching children?
④ How about going to the movies tonight?
⑤ Her homework is writing about global warming.

22 다음 밑줄 친 부분의 쓰임이 나머지 넷과 다른 것은?

① a dancing girl
② running shoes
③ a walking stick
④ a singing room
⑤ a washing machine

23 다음 중 어법상 틀린 것은?

① Do you mind to leave now?
② We put off starting a new project.
③ They enjoy taking a walk after dinner.
④ I plan to go to the art museum next week.
⑤ The boy avoided answering the math questions.

서술형

24 다음 우리말과 일치하도록 주어진 단어를 배열하시오.

- 나는 부지런하지 않은 것을 부끄러워했다.
(being, of, not)

➡ I was ashamed ______________ diligent.

25 다음 빈칸에 공통으로 들어갈 말을 쓰시오.

- I am accustomed ________ adapting to new surroundings.
- I look forward ________ seeing you on Monday.

26 다음 우리말과 일치하도록 주어진 단어를 사용하여 문장을 완성하시오. (필요시 형태 변화)

- 그는 작년에 그녀에게 거짓말한 것을 후회했다.
(regret, tell)

➡ He ________ ________ her a lie last year.

27 다음 문장에서 어법상 <u>틀린</u> 곳을 찾아 바르게 고쳐 쓰시오.

We missed to see the amazing sight in the sky.

______________ ➡ ______________

28 다음 우리말과 일치하도록 주어진 단어를 사용하여 문장을 완성하시오. (필요시 형태 변화)

- 나는 내일 그를 만나기로 한 것을 기억할 것이다.
(remember, meet)

➡ I will ________ ________ ________ him tomorrow.

29 다음 두 문장의 뜻이 일치하도록 빈칸에 알맞은 말을 쓰시오.

- She didn't like to swim in the river.

= She didn't like ____________ in the river.

고난도

30 다음 주어진 단어를 배열하여 대화를 완성하시오.

A What's wrong with him? He is late again like always. I don't ______________ all the time. (being, his, late, like)

B We have to say something to him this time.

31 다음 문장의 밑줄 친 부분을 우리말로 해석하시오.

• They must allow for <u>the train being a little late</u>.

➡ ______________

32 다음 우리말과 일치하도록 주어진 단어를 사용하여 문장을 완성하시오. (필요시 형태 변화)

• 나는 너를 곧 만나기를 고대하고 있다. (forward, see)

➡ I'm ______ ______ ______ ______ you soon.

33 다음 문장에서 어법상 <u>틀린</u> 부분을 찾아 바르게 고쳐 쓰시오.

I couldn't imagine to meet him there.

______________ ➡ ______________

34 다음 두 문장의 뜻이 일치하도록 빈칸에 알맞은 말을 쓰시오.

• As soon as they heard the sound, they came out of the house to check.

= ______ ______ the sound, they came out of the house to check.

35 다음 우리말과 일치하도록 주어진 단어를 사용하여 문장을 완성하시오. (필요시 형태 변화)

• 폭우는 우리가 축하 행사를 위해 외출하는 것을 방해했다. (stop, go)

➡ Heavy rain ______ ______ ______ ______ out for a celebration.

[36-37] 다음 대화의 내용과 일치하도록, <조건>에 맞게 빈칸에 알맞은 말을 쓰시오.

Waiter	May I take your order, ladies?
Kitty	Not now, but in a few minutes, thank you.
Betty	Look what's happening out there! It was just fine a moment ago.
Kitty	Oh, dear! I forgot to bring my umbrella with me.
Betty	Don't worry. It will stop soon.

<조건>
- 과거시제로 쓸 것
- 각 문장에 to부정사를 사용할 것
- 주어진 단어를 사용할 것 (필요시 형태 변화)

36 It ________________ after Kitty and Betty entered the restaurant. (start, rain)

37 Kitty ________________ her umbrella. (remember, bring)

[38-40] 다음 문장을 <보기>와 같이 바꿔 쓸 때 빈칸에 알맞은 말을 쓰시오.

<보기>
She is kind. And it is known to all the people.
➡ Her being kind is known to all the people.

38 The bus may be late. And you must allow for it.
➡ You must allow for ________________
________________________.

39 They are very noisy. And you can't understand it.
➡ You can't understand ________________
________________________.

40 We didn't give you some information. And we were sorry for it.
➡ We were sorry for ________________
________________________.

Chapter

03

분사

1 명사를 수식하는 분사

분사가 단독으로 쓰일 때는 명사 앞에서, 분사가 구를 이룰 때는 명사 뒤에서 수식한다.

	현재분사	과거분사
형태	-ing	p.p.
의미	~하게 하는, ~하고 있는(능동/진행)	~된, ~한(수동/완료)

It was a **disappointing result**. 그것은 실망스러운 결과였다. **<능동>**

Look at the **broken window**. 그 깨진 창문을 봐. **<수동>**

The boy playing the guitar is my brother. 기타를 치고 있는 그 소년이 나의 남동생이다. **<진행>**

Even **the leaves fallen on the ground** were beautiful. 땅에 떨어진 잎들조차 아름다웠다. **<완료>**

+ 분사는 「주격 관계대명사+be동사」가 생략된 형태로 볼 수 있다.

people **(who are) living** in poverty 가난하게 살아가는 사람들 **<현재분사>**

people **(who are) wounded** in the war 전쟁에서 다친 사람들 **<과거분사>**

▶▶ 정답과 해설 p. 14

EXERCISE A 다음 주어진 단어를 빈칸에 알맞은 형태로 고쳐 쓰시오.

1 The firefighter rushed into the ___________ house. (burn)

2 They found some ___________ treasure. (hide)

3 My lovely sister ___________ Mary is sick. (call)

4 The novel ___________ by a famous writer is very interesting. (write)

5 He saved some money and bought a ___________ car for the tour. (use)

6 I didn't want to make a speech in class in a ___________ voice. (shake)

EXERCISE B 다음 주어진 두 문장을 <보기>와 같이 바꿔 쓸 때 빈칸에 알맞은 말을 쓰시오.

〈보기〉
The woman is my Spanish teacher. She is looking at me.
➡ The woman looking at me is my Spanish teacher.

1 The man is the boss of my company. He is asking me a question.
➡ The man ______________________________ is the boss of my company.

2 The painting is *Waterlilies*. It is filled with flowers.
➡ The painting ________________ is *Waterlilies*.

3 The members are my neighbors. They are attending the meeting.
➡ The members ________________ are my neighbors.

4 What is the language? It is spoken in Mexico.
➡ What is the language ________________?

5 The girls are my classmates. They are cheering their team to victory.
➡ The girls ________________ are my classmates.

6 She was walking on the leaves. They have fallen from the trees.
➡ She was walking on the leaves ________________.

EXERCISE C 다음 우리말과 일치하도록 주어진 단어를 배열하여 문장을 완성하시오.

1 그 나무에서 노래하는 새들은 앵무새다. (the, singing, in, tree)
➡ The birds ________________ are parrots.

2 그녀는 그녀의 친구가 쓴 이야기를 읽고 있었다. (the, written, by, story)
➡ She was reading ________________ her friend.

3 선생님께서 교실에서 잡담하고 있는 여자 아이들을 불렀다. (the, in, chatting, classroom)
➡ The teacher called the girls ________________.

4 그들은 라디오에서 그 충격적인 소식을 들었다. (shocking, the, heard, news)
➡ They ________________ from the radio.

5 그에 의해 페인트 칠해진 그 작은 집은 너무나 아름다웠다. (him, was, by, painted)
➡ The small house ________________ so beautiful.

6 이런 표현들은 이곳에서 구어체로 쓰인다. (language, here, spoken)
➡ These expressions are used in ________________.

7 많은 학생들에 둘러싸인 그 남자는 나의 선생님이다. (lot, students, a, surrounded, of, by)
➡ The man ________________ is my teacher.

2 보어 역할을 하는 분사

	현재분사	과거분사
주격보어	~하면서, ~하게 하는	~된, ~해진
목적격보어	~하는 것을	~되는 것을

She sat **singing** merrily. 그녀는 즐겁게 노래하며 앉아 있었다. **〈주격보어〉**

I felt **relieved** when I finished the hard work. 나는 그 힘든 작업을 끝마쳤을 때 안심이 되었다. **〈주격보어〉**

He saw **her crossing** the road. 그는 그녀가 길을 건너고 있는 것을 보았다. **〈목적격보어〉**

She wants **her computer fixed** by tomorrow. 그녀는 그녀의 컴퓨터가 내일까지 수리되기를 원한다. **〈목적격보어〉**

▶▶ 정답과 해설 p. 14

EXERCISE A 다음 밑줄 친 부분의 쓰임과 같은 것을 〈보기〉에서 골라 기호를 쓰시오.

〈보기〉

ⓐ Wake up the sleeping boy. ⓑ I threw away the broken vase.
ⓒ She sat thinking of him. ⓓ We had your camera fixed already.

1 They came toward him calling his name.

2 The barking dog in the street is a bulldog.

3 I'll keep the door closed for three days.

4 It will be a disappointing result to everybody.

5 He got the machine carried to the factory early in the morning.

6 The woman surrounded by some people was playing the guitar.

EXERCISE B 다음 주어진 두 문장을 〈보기〉와 같이 바꿔 쓸 때 빈칸에 알맞은 말을 쓰시오.

〈보기〉

I saw him at the party. And he was playing the piano.
➡ I saw him playing the piano at the party.

1 I saw some children at night. And they were singing Christmas songs.
➡ I saw some children ______________________ at night.

2 I saw her yesterday. And she was going into your room.

➡ I saw her ______________________ yesterday.

3 I saw a cat. And the cat was hit by a car on the road.

➡ I saw a cat ______________________.

EXERCISE C 다음 우리말과 일치하도록 주어진 단어 및 어구를 배열하여 문장을 완성하시오.

1 그 소녀는 아버지를 찾으며 울고 있었다. (her, looking for, father)

➡ The girl was crying ______________________.

2 그는 그의 시계를 수리받아야 한다. (his, repaired, get, watch)

➡ He must ______________________.

3 나는 사고로 다리가 부러졌다. (leg, had, my, broken)

➡ I ______________________ in the accident.

4 너는 친구들을 오랫동안 기다리게 둬서는 안 된다. (your, waiting, friends, keep)

➡ You shouldn't ______________________ for long.

EXERCISE D 다음 우리말과 일치하도록 주어진 단어를 사용하여 문장을 완성하시오. (필요시 형태 변화)

1 나는 어떤 남자가 밤에 그 집에 침입하고 있는 것을 보았다. (see, break)

➡ I ________ ________ ________ ________ into the house at night.

2 그녀는 그가 경기에서 기뻐 외치는 소리를 들었다. (hear, shout)

➡ She ________ ________ ________ for joy at the game.

3 그들은 그녀가 가족에 의해 홀로 남겨졌다는 것을 알게 되었다. (find, leave)

➡ They ________ ________ ________ alone by her family.

4 나는 기꺼이 그의 가게에서 그녀의 신발을 수선하도록 했다. (have, mend)

➡ I ________ ________ ________ ________ in his shop gladly.

3 감정을 나타내는 분사

종류	현재분사		과거분사	
형태	-ing		p.p.	
개념	주어가 영향을 끼침		주어가 영향을 받음	
해석	~한 감정을 느끼게 하는		~한 감정을 느끼는	
감정 분사	amusing	재미있게 하는	amused	재미있게 느끼는
	exciting		excited	
	interesting		interested	
	boring	지루하게 하는	bored	지루하게 느끼는
	satisfying	만족스럽게 하는	satisfied	만족스럽게 느끼는
	disappointing	실망스럽게 하는	disappointed	실망스럽게 느끼는
	amazing	놀라게 하는	amazed	놀랍게 느끼는
	surprising		surprised	
	confusing	혼란스럽게 하는	confused	혼란스럽게 느끼는
	shocking	충격적으로 만드는	shocked	충격적으로 느끼는

▶▶ 정답과 해설 p. 14

EXERCISE A 다음 괄호 안에서 옳은 것을 고르시오.

1 This is an [amazing / amazed] story.

2 I was [surprising / surprised] at the news from the radio.

3 My report card was [disappointing / disappointed] to me.

4 He was [shocking / shocked] at the strange sight in the sea.

5 She will be [confusing / confused] by the different situation.

EXERCISE B 다음 문장에서 어법상 틀린 곳을 찾아 바르게 고쳐 쓰시오.

1 The audience were satisfying with his lecture.

2 My friends are very interesting in the new game.

3 We were a little boring during his address.

4 I thought going on a trip with her would be satisfied.

5 Riding a horse in the island was amused.

4 분사구문 만드는 법

1 부사절의 주어와 주절의 주어가 일치할 경우

부사절의 접속사와 주어를 생략하고, 부사절의 동사를 -ing 형태로 바꾼다.

~~When he~~ **saw** her, he ran away.
(he = he)

➡ **Seeing** her, he ran away. 그녀를 보자, 그는 도망쳤다.

+ 분사구문으로 전환할 때, 접속사의 의미를 명확하게 하기 위해서 접속사를 남겨두기도 한다.

After she finished her homework, she went to bed early.
➡ **(After) Finishing** her homework, she went to bed early. 숙제를 끝마친 후에, 그녀는 일찍 잤다.

2 부사절의 주어와 주절의 주어가 일치하지 않을 경우

부사절의 접속사를 생략하고 주어는 그대로 둔 채, 부사절의 동사를 -ing 형태로 바꾼다.

~~After~~ **the sun set**, she went out for shopping.
(the sun ≠ she)

➡ **The sun setting**, she went out for shopping. 해가 진 뒤에, 그녀는 쇼핑하러 나갔다.

! 1. 분사구문의 부정형은 분사 앞에 not이나 never를 붙인다.

Not knowing her phone number, I can't call her. 그녀의 전화번호를 몰라서, 나는 그녀에게 전화할 수 없다.

2. 진행형이나 수동형을 분사구문으로 전환할 때 being은 보통 생략한다.

Because I am interested in baseball, I watch almost every game on TV.
= **(Being) Interested** in baseball, I watch almost every game on TV.
야구에 관심이 있어서, 나는 TV로 거의 모든 경기를 본다.

▶▶ 정답과 해설 p. 14

EXERCISE A 다음 두 문장의 뜻이 같도록 분사구문을 사용하여 문장을 완성하시오.

1 While I was staying in Rome, I made some friends.
= While ______________________________, I made some friends.

2 After we finished the work, we went home in a hurry.
= After ______________________________, we went home in a hurry.

3 As spring comes, the birds move northward.
= ______________________________, the birds move northward.

4 As she didn't receive any answer, she called him again.

= ______________________________, she called him again.

EXERCISE B **다음 두 문장의 의미가 같도록 빈칸에 알맞은 말을 쓰시오.**

1 Doing a paper in haste, she got a C in biology.

= As ________ ________ a paper in haste, she got a C in biology.

2 Living in the country, he is very healthy.

= As ________ ________ in the country, he is very healthy.

3 Having many easy words, the book is good for beginners.

= Since ________ ________ many easy words, the book is good for beginners.

4 Leaving the classroom, she turned off the light.

= As ________ ________ the classroom, she turned off the light.

EXERCISE C **다음 우리말과 일치하도록 주어진 단어를 사용하여 〈보기〉와 같이 문장을 완성하시오. (필요시 형태 변화)**

〈보기〉

대도시에 살고 있기 때문에, 나는 많은 사람들을 만날 수 있다. (because, live)

➡ ____Because I live____ in a big city, I can meet many people.

➡ ____Living____ in a big city, I can meet many people.

1 왼쪽으로 돌면, 그 은행을 찾을 것이다. (if, take)

➡ ______________________ a left turn, you will find the bank.

➡ ______________________ a left turn, you will find the bank.

2 돌에 걸려 넘어졌을 때, 그 소년은 울기 시작했다. (when, fall)

➡ ______________________ over a rock, the boy began to cry.

➡ ______________________ over a rock, the boy began to cry.

3 어제 날씨가 화창했기 때문에, 우리는 소풍을 갔다. (because, be)

➡ ______________________ sunny yesterday, we went on a picnic.

➡ ______________________ sunny yesterday, we went on a picnic.

4 도시에서 자랐기 때문에, 그는 시골 생활에 대해 잘 몰랐다. (as, grow up)

➡ ______________________ in the city, he knew little about country life.

➡ ______________________ in the city, he knew little about country life.

5 시간 / 이유 / 부대상황을 나타내는 분사구문

의미	(부사절의) 접속사
시간(~할 때, ~하는 동안, ~하기 전에, ~한 후에)	when, as, while, before, after
이유(~이기 때문에, ~이므로)	because, as, since
부대상황(~하면서, ~하고 나서)	as, while

* 부대상황이란 두 가지 상황이 동시에 일어나거나 연속해서 일어나는 것을 뜻한다.

Before he left home, he said good-bye to his family.

➡ **Leaving** home, he said good-bye to his family. 집을 떠나기 전에, 그는 가족에게 작별 인사를 했다. **<시간>**

Because I got very angry, I didn't want to say anything.

➡ **Getting** very angry, I didn't want to say anything. 너무 화가 나서, 나는 아무 말도 하고 싶지 않았다. **<이유>**

While he smiled brightly, he held out his hand.

➡ **Smiling** brightly, he held out his hand. 밝게 미소를 지으며, 그는 손을 내밀었다. **<부대상황>**

▶▶ 정답과 해설 p. 15

EXERCISE A 다음 문장을 분사구문으로 바꿔 쓰시오.

1 Since he felt sorry for that, he apologized.
➡ ______________________, he apologized.

2 While they sat on the grass, they watched the sunset.
➡ ______________________, they watched the sunset.

3 Because I have no money with me, I can't buy the new shoes.
➡ ______________________, I can't buy the new shoes.

EXERCISE B 다음 두 문장의 뜻이 같도록 주어진 단어를 사용하여 문장을 완성하시오.

1 Being kind to other students, she has lots of friends at school. (Because)
= ______________________, she has lots of friends at school.

2 Watching TV, he has to do his homework first for tomorrow. (Before)
= ______________________, he has to do his homework first for tomorrow.

3 Cleaning my room, I usually listen to the radio. (While)
= ______________________, I usually listen to the radio.

6 조건 / 양보를 나타내는 분사구문

의미	(부사절의) 접속사
조건(~한다면)	if
양보·대조(~이지만, (비록) ~일지라도〔하더라도〕)	though, although, even though, even if

If you turn to the right, you'll find the park.

➡ **Turning** to the right, you'll find the park. 오른쪽으로 돌면, 너는 그 공원을 찾을 것이다. **<조건>**

If you take the medicine, you will get well soon.

➡ **Taking** the medicine, you will get well soon. 그 약을 복용한다면, 너는 곧 좋아질 것이다. **<조건>**

+ although나 though 등이 쓰이는 양보 부사절은 분사구문으로 바꾸더라도 의미를 더 정확하게 전달하기 위해서 일반적으로 접속사를 생략하지 않는다.

Though I live next to his house, I've seldom seen him.

➡ **Though living** next to his house, I've seldom seen him.

그의 옆집에 살지만, 나는 그를 거의 보지 못했다. **<양보 · 대조>**

▶▶ 정답과 해설 p. 15

EXERCISE A 다음 문장을 분사구문으로 바꿔 쓰시오.

1 If you take this train, you'll get there at 10.

➡ ______________________, you'll get there at 10.

2 Although he fell down on the track, he started to run again.

➡ Although ______________________, he started to run again.

3 If it rains tomorrow, we won't go hiking.

➡ ______________________, we won't go hiking.

EXERCISE B 다음 문장의 밑줄 친 부분을 우리말로 해석하시오.

1 <u>Even if hating it</u>, you must do it.

2 <u>Though saving a little money</u>, she was happy with it.

3 <u>Getting some relax after work</u>, you'll get better soon.

4 <u>Buying this new product here</u>, you'll get this free gift.

7 분사구문의 시제와 생략

1 시제

	단순형 시제	완료형 시제
형태	동사원형 + -ing	having p.p.
개념	주절과 같은 시제	주절보다 한 단계 앞선 시제

If you study harder, you'll catch up with him.

➡ **Studying** harder, you'll catch up with him. 더 열심히 공부하면, 너는 그를 따라잡을 것이다.

Because they made no effort, now they get nothing.

➡ **Having made** no effort, now they get nothing.
전혀 노력을 하지 않았기 때문에, 그들은 지금 아무것도 얻지 못한다.

2 생략

	단순형 시제	완료형 시제
형태	(being) + 분사	(having been) + 분사
참고	being과 having been 뒤에 분사가 올 때 being이나 having been을 생략할 수 있다. 일반적으로 형용사나 명사가 올 경우에는 생략하지 않는다.	

As she was tired, she went to bed earlier.

➡ **(Being) Tired**, she went to bed earlier. 피곤해서, 그녀는 평소보다 일찍 잤다.

Although he was scolded for lying, he still tells a lie.

➡ **Although (having been) scolded** for lying, he still tells a lie.
거짓말을 했다가 혼났지만, 그는 아직도 거짓말을 한다.

▶▶ 정답과 해설 p. 15

EXERCISE A 다음 괄호 안에서 옳은 것을 고르시오.

1 Although not [liking / liked] them, I ate all the cookies.

2 [Interesting / Interested] in the game, I get to know a lot about it.

3 Though [invited / inviting] to the show, we couldn't be present at it.

4 [Having / Having had] an accident, she knows well how much pain the patients feel.

5 [Studying / Having studied] hard, Sarah is confident about the English test.

6 [Looking / Having looked] at the blue sky, they sat on the bench in the garden.

7 Although [finishing / having finished] his homework, he didn't bring it to school.

EXERCISE B 다음 우리말과 일치하도록 주어진 단어를 사용하여 <보기>와 같이 문장을 완성하시오. (필요시 형태 변화)

<보기>
이번에 좋은 성적을 받는다면, 나는 약간의 보상을 받을 것이다. (if, get)
➡ ___If I get___ good grades this time, I will be given some reward.
➡ ___Getting___ good grades this time, I will be given some reward.

1 그 소식에 매우 놀랐었지만, 지금 그녀는 괜찮다. (though, surprise)
➡ ______________ at the news, now she is okay with that.
➡ ______________ at the news, now she is okay with that.

2 아침을 먹지 않았기 때문에, 우리는 배가 많이 고팠다. (since, have)
➡ ______________ breakfast in the morning, we were so hungry.
➡ ______________ breakfast in the morning, we were so hungry.

3 나의 손목시계를 어제 고쳤기 때문에, 나는 기분이 좋다. (because, have)
➡ ______________ my watch repaired yesterday, I am feeling good.
➡ ______________ my watch repaired yesterday, I am feeling good.

4 또렷한 글씨체로 쓰여 있어서, 이 리포트는 읽기가 쉽다. (as, write)
➡ ______________ in a clear hand, this report is easy to read.
➡ ______________ in a clear hand, this report is easy to read.

5 무엇인가에 긴장하면, 나는 식사를 거의 하지 못한다. (if, nervous)
➡ ______________ about something, I can hardly have a meal.
➡ ______________ about something, I can hardly have a meal.

EXERCISE C 다음 우리말과 일치하도록 주어진 단어 및 어구를 사용하여 문장을 완성하시오. (필요시 형태 변화)

1 그녀의 행동에 몹시 실망해서, 나는 그녀와 말하고 싶지 않다. (disappoint)
➡ ______________ badly at her behavior, I don't want to talk with her.

2 나의 돈을 전부 잃어버렸기 때문에, 지금 나는 나의 계획을 포기해야 한다. (lose)
➡ ______________ all my money, now I have to give up my plan.

3 나의 진정한 친구라면, 내게 조언을 좀 해줘. (be, my true friend)
➡ ______________, please give me some advice.

8 with + (대)명사 + 분사

「with + (대)명사 + 분사」는 '~을 …한 채로'의 뜻으로, 분사가 (대)명사의 상태나 동작을 나타내며 주된 상황에 부수적으로 일어나는 상황을 설명한다. (대)명사와 분사의 관계가 능동이면 현재분사, 수동이면 과거분사를 쓴다.

He entered the gate **with his students following** him.
그는 그의 학생들이 그를 뒤따르게 한 채 출입문으로 들어섰다. **〈능동〉**

She was watching me **with her arms folded**. 그녀는 팔짱을 낀 채로 나를 쳐다보고 있었다. **〈수동〉**

I was listening to music **with my eyes closed**. 나는 눈을 감은 채로 음악을 듣고 있었다. **〈수동〉**

▶▶ 정답과 해설 p. 15

EXERCISE A **다음 밑줄 친 부분에서 틀린 부분을 찾아 바르게 고쳐 쓰시오.**

1 She sat with her legs crossing.

2 I studied math with my cat sat next to me.

3 They usually fall asleep with the light turning on.

4 She ran around the park with her pet kept pace with her.

5 Although it rained, the gentleman walked with his umbrella folding.

EXERCISE B **다음 우리말과 일치하도록 주어진 단어를 배열하여 문장을 완성하시오.**

1 그는 문을 닫은 채로 시험공부를 했다. (the, closed, with, door)
➡ He studied for an exam ______________________.

2 그녀는 국이 끓어 넘치게 둔 채 그만 잠이 들었다. (the, with, boiling, soup)
➡ She just fell asleep ______________________ over.

3 우리는 선풍기를 틀어 놓은 채로 책을 읽었다. (set, electric, with, an, fan)
➡ We read a book ______________________ in motion.

4 그들은 아이들이 그 경기를 보게 한 채 체스를 두었다. (kids, watching, with, their)
➡ They played chess ______________________ the game.

5 그녀는 아기를 거실에서 놀게 한 채 요리를 하고 있었다. (her, with, playing, baby)
➡ She was cooking ______________________ in the living room.

9 관용적 분사구문

Frankly speaking	솔직히 말하면	Compared with	~와 비교해서
Speaking of	~에 관해 말하면	Assuming (that)	~이라 하면
Considering	~을 고려하면	Seeing (that)	~으로 보건대
Judging from	~으로 판단하건대	Generally speaking	일반적으로 말하면
Admitting (that)	~은 인정하지만	Strictly speaking	엄밀히 말하면

Frankly speaking, she is not reliable. 솔직히 말하면, 그녀는 신뢰할 수가 없다.

Generally speaking, Koreans are kind. 일반적으로 말하면, 한국인들은 친절하다.

Judging from his accent, he is from England. 그의 억양으로 판단하건대, 그는 영국 출신이다.

Assuming (that) it snows tomorrow, what should we do? 내일 눈이 내린다면, 우리는 무엇을 해야 할까?

▶▶ 정답과 해설 p. 15

EXERCISE A 다음 문장의 밑줄 친 부분을 우리말로 해석하시오.

1 Generally speaking, women live longer than men.

2 Frankly speaking, he is too young to go there.

3 Strictly speaking, this is not correct.

4 Speaking of movies, I don't like horror movies.

5 Judging from her way of doing things, she is not an American.

EXERCISE B 다음 빈칸에 가장 알맞은 표현을 <보기>에서 골라 문장을 완성하시오.

<보기>

Admitting Speaking of Strictly speaking Considering Assuming

1 ______________ her age, she looks young.

2 ______________ the history exam, isn't it too difficult?

3 ______________, it is not a novel but a short story.

4 ______________ that you are rich enough, you shouldn't waste your money.

5 ______________ that she is still alive, how old would she be now?

학교 시험 대비 문제

맞힌 개수	
선택형	____ / 26
서술형	____ / 21

▶▶ 정답과 해설 p. 16

01 다음 우리말을 영어로 잘못 옮긴 것은?

① 깨진 유리창 ➡ a broken window
② 타고 있는 양초 ➡ a burning candle
③ 중고차 ➡ a using car
④ 삶은 달걀 두 개 ➡ two boiled eggs
⑤ 떠오르는 태양 ➡ the rising sun

고난도

02 다음 밑줄 친 부분이 어법상 옳은 것은?

① We know a guy calling Brian at school.
② They sat surrounding by some students.
③ She saw the breaking truck on the street.
④ I heard her boring speech for over an hour.
⑤ He got lots of letters writing in Japanese from his fans.

03 다음 빈칸에 들어갈 말로 알맞은 것은?

> ________ that it really happens, we can't accept it as a fact easily.

① Seeing ② Considering
③ Judging ④ Admitting
⑤ Compared

04 다음 밑줄 친 부분에서 문맥상 생략된 말로 어색한 것은?

① Left alone, he began to be lonely.
➡ When
② Used carefully, it will give long service.
➡ Though
③ There being no bus, she had to walk home.
➡ As
④ Living in the country, I can't meet many people. ➡ Because
⑤ Leaving his office, he turned off the computer.
➡ Before

05 다음 밑줄 친 부분의 쓰임이 나머지 넷과 다른 것은?

① He got out of the burning house.
② The man living next door is my uncle.
③ The boy was chasing the barking dog.
④ His parents felt relieved after he got home.
⑤ The leaves fallen from the tree are beautiful.

06 다음 중 어법상 옳은 것은?

① Don't leave the baby cried.
② They got the problems solved.
③ You may be amazing at the news.
④ He rushed home screamed aloud.
⑤ She saw me picked up one-dollar bill on the floor.

07 다음 빈칸에 들어갈 말로 알맞은 것은?

- After the sun set, we went out for shopping.

➡ ____________________, we went out for shopping.

① Set ② Setting
③ Having set ④ Not setting
⑤ The sun setting

08 다음 빈칸에 들어갈 말로 알맞은 것은?

- The final match excited all the people there.

= All the people there ____________ about the final match.

① was exciting ② were excited
③ was excited ④ were exciting
⑤ was being excited

09 다음 중 어법상 어색한 것은?

① He went for a walk with his pet following him.
② She was staring at me with her legs crossing.
③ I often listen to music with my dog sitting next to me.
④ We sometimes talk to each other with the light turned off.
⑤ They read the book with their child taking a nap on the grass.

10 다음 중 밑줄 친 부분이 어법상 틀린 것은?

① Admitted that ② you are ③ young, you ④ should be ⑤ responsible for your acts.

11 다음 밑줄 친 부분에 생략된 말로 알맞은 것은?

- Because she was confused with the problems, she couldn't do anything by herself.

➡ __________ confused with the problems, she couldn't do anything by herself.

① Having ② Being
③ Having been ④ Not being
⑤ Not having been

12 다음 중 밑줄 친 부분이 어법상 틀린 것은?

① I thought it was a disappointed result.
② The boy looked at the broken window.
③ The girl playing the piano is my daughter.
④ He swept the leaves fallen on the balcony.
⑤ She was watching the burning tree on the farm.

13 다음 우리말을 바르게 영작한 것은?

날씨가 추웠기 때문에, 우리는 하루 종일 집에 있었다.

① Being cold, we stayed at home all day long.
② It being cold, we stayed at home all day long.
③ Not it being cold, we stayed at home all day long.
④ Though it was cold, we stayed at home all day long.
⑤ Before it had been cold, we stayed at home all day long.

고난도

14 다음 밑줄 친 부분을 분사구문으로 바꿔 쓴 것이 어법상 틀린 것은?

① When she saw him, she ran away.
➡ Seeing him
② After I had read the novel, I lent it to him.
➡ Reading the novel
③ As he was tired from overworking, he fell asleep soon.
➡ Tired from overworking
④ While she stayed in Paris, she made many new friends.
➡ While staying in Paris
⑤ Since we didn't know what we should do, we reported to the police.
➡ Not knowing what we should do

15 다음 밑줄 친 부분을 바르게 고친 것으로 짝지어진 것은?

The boy wear blue jeans was chat with Cathy.

① worn — chat
② wears — chatted
③ wears — chatting
④ wearing — chatted
⑤ wearing — chatting

16 다음 대화의 빈칸에 알맞은 것은?

A	What did you do right after the accident?
B	____________, we called 119.

① Known what to do
② Knowing what to do
③ Not known what to do
④ We knowing what to do
⑤ Not knowing what to do

17 다음 빈칸에 들어갈 말로 알맞은 것은?

• 솔직히 말하면, 나는 느끼한 음식을 좋아하지 않는다. ➡ ____________, I don't like greasy food.

① Frankly spoken ② Frankly speaking
③ Speaking frank ④ We speak frankly
⑤ We speaking frank

18 다음 빈칸에 공통으로 들어갈 말로 알맞은 것은?

- They are dancing ________ the radio turned on.
- She watched a music video ________ the door closed.

① on ② off ③ in
④ out ⑤ with

19 다음 빈칸에 들어갈 말이 바르게 짝지어진 것은?

- ________ down the street, we saw the man ________ down.
- Not ________ any answer, he sent her an email today.

① Walking — fallen — received
② Walked — fallen — receiving
③ Walking — falling — received
④ Walked — falling — receiving
⑤ Walking — falling — receiving

[20-21] 다음 두 문장의 뜻이 같도록 빈칸에 들어갈 알맞은 말을 고르시오.

20

- As he visited the theater before, he knows where we can buy tickets.

= ____________ the theater before, he knows where we can buy tickets.

① Visit ② Being visiting
③ Having ④ Being visited
⑤ Having visited

21

- Since she didn't know what to say, she kept silent for a long time.

= ____________ what to say, she kept silent for a long time.

① Knowing not ② Having not
③ Not knowing ④ Not having
⑤ Knowing that

고난도

22 다음 빈칸에 알맞은 것을 모두 고르시오.

____________, I closed my eyes and took a deep breath.

① Tiring ② Being tired
③ As I was tired ④ When I tired
⑤ Although I was tired

[23-24] 다음 두 문장을 한 문장으로 바꿔 쓸 때 빈칸에 알맞은 것을 고르시오.

23

- I saw the vase. It was filled with flowers.

➡ I saw the vase ________ with flowers.

① fill ② filled ③ filling
④ being fill ⑤ having filled

24

- The man is my German teacher.
  He is looking at me.
  ➡ The man ________ at me is my German teacher.

① look ② looked ③ looking
④ is looking ⑤ having looked

25 다음 빈칸에 들어갈 말로 알맞은 것은?

- 계속해서 싸우는 것 때문에 혼났지만, 그들은 아직도 무언가를 두고 싸우고 있다.
  ➡ Though ________ for continuously fighting, they are still fighting over something.

① they not ② scolded
③ scolded not ④ having scolded
⑤ scolding

26 다음 밑줄 친 부분이 어법상 올바른 것은?

① When he was young, he learned English.
➡ Being young, he learned English.
② As she was tired, she couldn't focus on it.
➡ Been tired, she couldn't focus on it.
③ If you turn to the left, you'll find the bank.
➡ Turned to the left, you'll find the bank.
④ Though they live in the city, they don't live a modern life.
➡ Not living in the city, they don't live a modern life.
⑤ She put on her coat, and she left her apartment.
➡ Put on her coat, she left her apartment.

서술형

고난도

27 다음 문장을 분사구문으로 바꿔 쓸 때 빈칸에 알맞은 말을 쓰시오.

- As I lost my cell phone, I can't call anybody now.
  ➡ ________ my cell phone, I can't call anybody now.

고난도

28 다음 우리말과 일치하도록 주어진 단어를 사용하여 분사구문을 완성하시오. (필요시 형태 변화)

- 며칠 전에 그 파티에 초대받았지만, 지금 우리는 파티에 갈 수가 없다. (invite)
  ➡ ________ to the party a few days ago, now we can't go to the party.

29 다음 빈칸에 들어갈 말로 알맞은 말을 쓰시오.

- While she smiled happily, she hugged her son tightly.
  = ________ ________, she hugged her son tightly.

30 다음 우리말과 일치하도록 주어진 단어를 사용하여 문장을 완성하시오. (필요시 형태 변화)

- 그를 전에 보았기 때문에, 나는 그가 어떻게 생겼는지 안다. (see)

➡ __________ __________ him before, I know what he looks like.

31 다음 우리말과 일치하도록 주어진 단어를 배열하여 문장을 완성하시오.

- 그는 교통사고로 왼쪽 다리가 부러졌다. (his, broken, leg, had, left)

➡ He ____________________ in a car accident.

32 다음 문장을 분사구문으로 바꿔 쓸 때 빈칸에 알맞은 말을 쓰시오.

- If you are not able to swim, you'd better put on a life jacket.

➡ ____________________, you'd better put on a life jacket.

[33-34] 다음 두 문장의 뜻이 같도록 빈칸에 알맞은 말을 쓰시오.

33

- She found herself in a strange room. And she was left alone.

= She found herself __________ __________ in a strange room.

고난도

34

- Having spent all the money, he couldn't buy a new jacket.

= Since __________ __________ __________ all the money, he couldn't buy a new jacket.

35 다음 밑줄 친 부분을 우리말로 해석하시오.

- The players injured in the game were sent to the hospital.

➡ ____________________ 병원으로 보내졌다.

36 다음 문장에서 어법상 틀린 부분을 찾아 바르게 고쳐 쓰시오.

They heard their names calling.

_______________ ➡ _______________

37 다음 우리말과 일치하도록 주어진 단어를 배열하여 문장을 완성하시오.

• Benjamin과 Sharon은 운전사를 기다리게 한 채 작별 인사를 했다.
(waiting, with, driver, the)
➡ Benjamin and Sharon said goodbye _______________.

38 다음 밑줄 진 부분을 분사구문으로 만들 때, 빈칸에 알맞은 말을 쓰시오.

• If I find her address, I'll send her an invitation.
➡ _______________, I'll send her an invitation.

39 다음 우리말과 일치하도록 주어진 단어를 사용하여 문장을 완성하시오. (필요시 형태 변화)

• 그녀는 소년들이 노래를 따라 부르게 둔 채 피아노를 연주했다. (boy, sing)
➡ She played the piano _______ _______ _______ _______ along.

40 다음 괄호 안의 단어를 빈칸에 알맞은 형태로 바꿔 쓰시오.

The quality of the goods was _______. However, I wasn't _______ with the service of the store at all. (satisfy)

41 다음 두 문장을 한 문장으로 바꿔 쓸 때 빈칸에 알맞은 말을 쓰시오.

• Look at the girls. They are cheering their team to victory.
= Look at the girls _______ _______ _______ to victory.

[42-45] 다음 문장에서 어법상 틀린 부분을 찾아 바르게 고쳐 쓰시오. (단, 분사구문으로 쓸 것)

42 I saw a girl crossed the road at a red light.

➡ ______________________

43 The police officer saw the thief is running away with the jewels.

➡ ______________________

44 She had the broken car repair for use.

➡ ______________________

45 He had some mistakes correcting in the document.

➡ ______________________

고난도

[46-47] 다음 글을 읽고, <조건>에 맞도록 문장을 완성하시오.

> The class started as usual. The teacher called the students' names. But when he called Sarah's name, there was no reply. The teacher thought for a moment, and then just opened the textbook. I really wondered what happened to Sarah. But because I didn't get along with her, I couldn't call her that day.

<조건>

- 분사구문으로 쓸 것
- 주어진 단어와 어구만 사용할 것 (필요시 형태 변화)

46 ______________________, Sarah was not in class. (call, the teacher, when, by)

47 ______________________, I couldn't call Sarah. (her, get along, not, with)

Chapter 04

시제

1 미래를 나타내는 표현
2 과거와 현재완료
3 현재완료 I - 계속/경험 용법
4 현재완료 II - 완료/결과 용법
5 현재완료진행
6 과거완료
7 과거완료진행
■ 학교 시험 대비 문제

1 미래를 나타내는 표현

1 현재시제나 현재진행시제는 확실히 정해진 가까운 미래를 나타낼 수 있다.

My train **arrives** at 6:00 **tomorrow morning**. 내가 탈 기차는 내일 아침 6시에 도착할 것이다.

Joel **is flying** to New York **next week**. Joel은 다음 주에 (비행기를 타고) 뉴욕에 갈 것이다.

2 시간이나 조건의 부사절에서는 현재시제로 미래를 나타낸다.

I will wait here **until** you **finish** your work.
네가 일을 끝마칠 때까지 나는 여기에서 기다릴 것이다. **<시간 부사절>**

If it **is** fine tomorrow, I will play basketball outside.
내일 날씨가 맑다면, 나는 밖에서 농구를 할 것이다. **<조건 부사절>**

+ 상태를 나타내는 동사는 진행형으로 쓸 수 없다.

소유	have, own, belong to
감각	see, hear, feel, smell, taste
감정	like, love, hate, want, wish, need, prefer
인식	know, think, believe, forget, remember, understand

I ***am liking*** him. (×) He ***is knowing*** the girl. (×) I'***m having*** a pet. (×)

! have가 '먹다'의 의미로 쓰일 때는 진행형으로 쓸 수 있다.

I'**m having** dinner. (○) 나는 저녁을 먹고 있다.

▶▶ 정답과 해설 p. 18

EXERCISE A 다음 괄호 안에서 옳은 것을 고르시오.

1 We will play with the soccer team if we [win / won] on Friday.

2 I'll come when I [finish / finished] my homework.

3 If the weather [is / will be] snowy tomorrow, I will go skiing.

4 Mark [leaved / is leaving] for Sydney next week.

5 I will go out when my sister [arrives / arrived] at home.

6 If it [won't rain / doesn't rain] tomorrow, let's go to the park.

7 He [came / comes] here next week.

2 과거와 현재완료

과거	현재완료
과거에 시작되어 과거에 끝난 일 또는 상태를 나타내며 현재와의 연관성은 없다. • I **lived** in Germany two years ago. 나는 2년 전에 독일에 살았다. (지금은 어디에 사는지 알 수 없음)	과거에 일어난 일이 현재까지 영향을 미친다. • I lived in Germany two years ago. + I still live in Germany. 나는 2년 전에 독일에 살았다. 나는 아직도 독일에 산다. → I **have lived** in Germany for two years. 나는 2년째 독일에 살고 있다. (2년 전에 독일에 살았고 지금도 독일에 살고 있음)
명백한 과거를 나타내는 부사(구)인 의문사 when, yesterday, last, ago, just now(방금 전), 「in + 연도」 등과 함께 쓴다. • **When did** you **go** to the museum? 너는 그 미술관에 언제 갔니? • She **painted** this picture **last week**. 그녀는 이 그림을 지난주에 그렸다.	과거를 나타내는 부사(구)와 함께 쓰지 않는다. • **Have** you ever **been** to the museum? 너는 그 미술관에 가본 적이 있니? • She **has painted** this picture **since last week**. 그녀는 이 그림을 지난주부터 그렸다. • She has painted this picture ***last week***. (×)

현재완료 평서문	have(has) + p.p.	She **has passed** the driving test. 그녀는 운전면허 시험에 합격했다.
현재완료 부정문	have(has) + not + p.p.	She **hasn't passed** the driving test. 그녀는 운전면허 시험에 합격하지 못했다.
현재완료 의문문	Have(Has) + 주어 + p.p. ~? — Yes, 주어 + have(has). — No, 주어 + haven't(hasn't).	A **Has** she **passed** the driving test? 그녀는 운전면허 시험에 합격했니? B Yes, she **has**. / No, she **hasn't**. 응, 그랬어. / 아니, 그렇지 않았어.

▶▶ 정답과 해설 p. 18

EXERCISE A 다음 괄호 안에서 옳은 것을 고르시오.

1 I [lived / have lived] in Beijing. I don't live there now.

2 Yesterday it [rained / has rained] all morning.

3 World War II [broke out / has broken out] in 1939.

4 Has he [finish / finished] the work?

5 Sam [has arrived / arrived] here yesterday.

6 I [moved / have moved] here four years ago. And I still live here.

7 I met Ann two years ago. I still know her now. I [know / have known] Ann for two years.

3 현재완료 I - 계속 / 경험 용법

1 계속 용법

의미	~해오고 있다, ~해왔다
함께 쓰이는 어구	for, since, How long ~?

It **has rained since** yesterday. 어제부터 비가 내리고 있다.

I **have lived** here **for** three years. 나는 여기서 3년째 살고 있다.

+ 「for + 기간」(~동안) vs. 「since + 과거시점」(~이후로)

I **have had** the yellow bicycle **for** 7 years. 나는 7년째 노란 자전거를 가지고 있다.

I **have had** the yellow bicycle **since** 2015. 나는 2015년부터 노란 자전거를 가지고 있다.

+ since 뒤에 절이 올 수도 있는데, 이 경우 since 절에는 주로 과거시제를 사용한다.

I **have played** the violin **since I went** to elementary school.
나는 초등학교에 다닌 이후로 바이올린을 연주하고 있다.

2 경험 용법

의미	~해본 적이 있다
함께 쓰이는 어구	ever, never, before, once, twice, ~ times

Have you **ever ridden** a horse **before**? 너는 전에 말을 타본 적이 있니?

She **has fallen** down the stairs **several times**. 그녀는 여러 번 그 계단에서 넘어진 적이 있다.

▶▶ 정답과 해설 p. 18

EXERCISE A 다음 밑줄 친 부분의 쓰임으로 옳은 것을 고르시오.

1 Have you ever trained a dog? [경험 / 계속]

2 I have known Diana for ten years. [경험 / 계속]

3 Mike has eaten at the nice restaurant twice. [경험 / 계속]

4 She has had the shoes since 2016. [경험 / 계속]

5 I've never seen that kind of bread. [경험 / 계속]

6 Daniel has lived in Canada for five years. [경험 / 계속]

7 How long have you known him? [경험 / 계속]

EXERCISE B 다음 괄호 안에서 옳은 것을 고르시오.

1 The president has been in China [for / since] yesterday.

2 The weather has been sunny [for / since] three days.

3 She has been interested in planets [for / since] she was a child.

4 I have worn glasses [for / since] last month.

5 Jane has studied Chinese [for / since] three years.

6 The oil spill in the Gulf hasn't stopped [for / since] about a month.

7 Mr. Brown hasn't been in the office [for / since] 3 o'clock.

8 Sarah has worked at the university [for / since] 2004.

EXERCISE C 다음 우리말과 일치하도록 주어진 단어를 사용하여 문장을 완성하시오. (필요시 형태 변화)

1 나는 일주일째 기침을 하고 있다. (have)
➡ _________ _________ a cough _________ a week.

2 Jenny는 낚시를 가본 적이 없다. (never, go)
➡ Jenny _________ _________ _________ fishing.

3 너는 해변에서 일몰을 본 적이 있니? (ever, see)
➡ _________ you _________ _________ the sunset at the beach?

4 Harry는 Sally가 태어났을 때부터 그녀를 돌보고 있다. (take)
➡ Harry _________ _________ care of Sally _________ she was born.

5 우리는 2007년부터 많은 변화를 만들어 왔다. (make)
➡ We _________ _________ a lot of changes _________ 2007.

6 진수는 게임을 좋아한다. 하지만 그는 체스를 해본 적이 없다. (never, play)
➡ Jinsu likes games. But he _________ _________ _________ chess.

7 박 선생님은 나의 과학 선생님이다. 그녀는 8년째 과학을 가르치고 있다. (teach)
➡ Ms. Park is my science teacher. She _________ _________ science _________ eight years.

4 현재완료 II - 완료 / 결과 용법

1 완료 용법

의미	이미 ~했다, 막 ~했다
함께 쓰이는 어구	just, already, yet * yet은 부정문과 의문문에서만 쓰이며 부정문에서는 '아직', 의문문에서는 '이제'의 의미를 갖는다. 의문문에서는 굳이 해석하지 않기도 한다. already나 just는 주로 have와 p.p. 사이에 위치하지만, yet은 주로 문장의 가장 끝에 위치한다.

I **have just eaten** lunch. 나는 방금 점심을 먹었다.

I **haven't read** today's newspaper **yet**. 나는 아직 오늘 신문을 읽지 못했다.

Has it **stopped** raining **yet**? 이제 비가 그쳤니?

2 결과 용법

의미	~해 버렸다, ~해 버려서 지금 …하다
자주 쓰이는 표현	go, lose, come, leave, buy

I **have lost** my teddy bear. 나는 내 테디 베어(곰 인형)를 잃어버렸다.

My friend, Tony, **has gone** to London. 내 친구 Tony는 런던으로 가 버렸다.

+ have been to(경험) vs. have gone to(결과)

have been to (경험)	~에 다녀왔다, ~에 가본 적이 있다	I **have been to** Paris. 나는 파리에 가본 적이 있다.
have gone to (결과)	~에 갔다, 가 버렸다 (그래서 지금 여기에 없다)	He **has gone to** Paris. 그는 파리로 가 버렸다. (그래서 지금 여기에 없다.)

▶▶ 정답과 해설 p. 18

EXERCISE A 다음 밑줄 친 부분의 쓰임으로 옳은 것을 고르시오.

1 The train has just left. [완료 / 결과]

2 I have already finished my work. [완료 / 결과]

3 They have gone to Rome. [완료 / 결과]

4 She hasn't eaten breakfast yet. [완료 / 결과]

5 He has lost his bicycle. [완료 / 결과]

EXERCISE B 다음 괄호 안에서 옳은 것을 고르시오.

1 He [has been to / has gone to] Jeju Island on business. Now he is in Seoul.

2 Liz [has been to / has gone to] Dubai. She still stays there.

3 Linda is back home now. She [has been to / has gone to] Singapore.

4 They [have been to / have gone to] Greece. They are enjoying their holidays there.

5 A Did you have lunch?

B Yes, I did. I [have been to / have gone to] the Chinese restaurant.

EXERCISE C 다음 우리말과 일치하도록 주어진 단어를 사용하여 문장을 완성하시오. (필요시 형태 변화)

1 내가 가장 좋아하는 계절인 봄이 벌써 왔다. (already, come)
➡ Spring, my favorite season, _______ _______ _______.

2 너는 이제 숙제를 했니? (do)
➡ _______ _______ _______ your homework yet?

3 누군가가 방금 교실에 있는 거울을 깨뜨렸다. (just, break)
➡ Somebody _______ _______ _______ the mirror in the classroom.

4 Amy는 아직 그녀의 어머니로부터 소포를 받지 못했다. (get, yet)
➡ Amy _______ _______ the parcel from her mother yet.

5 그는 남아메리카에 있는 칠레로 가 버렸다. (go)
➡ He _______ _______ _______ Chile in South America.

6 나는 이미 오늘 일을 끝마쳤다. (already, finish)
➡ I _______ _______ _______ today's work.

7 그 교수는 방금 회의실에 도착했다. (just, arrive)
➡ The professor _______ _______ _______ at the conference room.

8 나는 네 휴대 전화를 잃어버렸다. (lose)
➡ I _______ _______ my cell phone.

9 Paul은 이메일 쓰는 것을 이미 끝냈다. (already, finish)
➡ Paul _______ _______ _______ writing the email.

10 Jane은 그 서점에서 책을 한 권 샀다. (buy)
➡ Jane _______ _______ a book at the bookstore.

5 현재완료진행

「have(has) been + -ing」: (계속) ~해오고 있다

현재완료진행은 과거의 어느 시점부터 현재까지 진행되어 온 동작이나 사건을 나타낸다.

He was playing the piano. He is still playing it now.
그는 피아노를 연주하고 있었다. 그는 지금도 계속 그것을 연주하고 있다.

➡ He **has been playing** the piano. 그는 피아노를 계속 연주하고 있다.

He **has been jogging** since 8 o'clock. 그는 8시부터 조깅을 하고 있다.

She **has been studying** Chinese for 6 months. 그녀는 6개월째 중국어를 공부하고 있다.

+ 현재진행 vs. 과거진행 vs. 현재완료진행

현재진행	현재의 한 시점에 진행되고 있는 동작 He **is watching** TV now. 그는 지금 TV를 시청하고 있다.
과거진행	과거의 한 시점에 진행되고 있던 동작 He **was watching** TV when his mother called him. 그의 어머니가 그를 불렀을 때 그는 TV를 시청하고 있었다.
현재완료진행	과거에 시작되어 현재까지 진행되어 온 동작 He **has been watching** TV for two hours. 그는 두 시간째 TV를 시청하고 있다.

▶▶ 정답과 해설 p. 18

EXERCISE A 다음 주어진 단어를 사용하여 현재완료진행 문장을 완성하시오. (필요시 형태 변화)

1 I ______________________ this website since 2006. (run)

2 He ______________________ for his girlfriend since 6 o'clock. (wait)

3 Peter and Paul ______________________ their bikes all day. (ride)

4 Susan ______________________ on the computer for too long. (work)

5 You ______________________ to music since 12:30. (listen)

6 The family ______________________ dinner for 30 minutes. (have)

7 I ______________________ in this city since this summer. (live)

8 She ______________________ to him for three hours. (talk)

EXERCISE B 다음 두 문장을 <보기>와 같이 한 문장으로 바꿔 쓸 때 빈칸에 알맞은 말을 쓰시오.

<보기>
They started to wait for a bus two hours ago. They are still waiting for it.
➡ They have been waiting for a bus for two hours.

1 It started to rain yesterday. It is still raining even today.
➡ It ______________________ since yesterday.

2 They started lying in the sun three hours ago. They are still lying in the sun now.
➡ They ______________________ for three hours.

3 My parents started to wait for Brian three hours ago. They are still waiting for Brian now.
➡ My parents ______________________ for three hours.

4 Maria started studying German in January. She is still studying German now.
➡ Maria ______________________ since January.

5 They began to swim two hours ago. They are still swimming.
➡ They ______________________ for two hours.

6 He began to play computer games an hour ago. He is still playing computer games.
➡ He ______________________ for an hour.

EXERCISE C 다음 우리말과 일치하도록 주어진 단어를 사용하여 문장을 완성하시오. (필요시 형태 변화)

1 나는 집을 한 채 사려고 5년째 돈을 모으고 있다. (save)
➡ I ________ ________ ________ money for five years to buy a house.

2 우리는 태어났을 때부터 음악을 듣고 있다. (listen)
➡ We ________ ________ ________ to music since we were born.

3 그 귀여운 강아지가 3시간째 자고 있다. (sleep)
➡ The cute puppy ________ ________ ________ for three hours.

4 내가 집에 온 후로 비가 내리고 있다. (rain)
➡ It ________ ________ ________ since I came home.

5 너는 이 귀걸이를 얼마나 오래 착용해오고 있니? (wear)
➡ How long ________ ________ ________ ________ these earrings?

6 과거완료

「had + p.p.」: (특정 과거 시점보다 더 이전에) ~했었다

과거완료는 과거보다 더 이전에 시작된 일이 과거 어느 시점까지 영향을 미치는 것을 나타낸다.

He **had been** ill **for** three days when I visited him. 내가 그를 방문했을 때 그는 사흘 동안 아팠었다. **<계속>**
I **had never eaten** tacos before I came here. 나는 여기 오기 전에 타코를 먹어 본 적이 없었다. **<경험>**
She **had already cooked** lunch when I arrived. 내가 도착했을 때 그녀는 이미 점심 요리를 끝마쳤었다. **<완료>**
When we arrived there, they **had gone** to the train station.
우리가 거기에 도착했을 때, 그들은 (이미) 기차역으로 떠나 버렸다. **<결과>**

+ 대과거는 과거에 순차적으로 일어난 두 가지 사건 중 먼저 일어난 사건을 가리키며, 과거완료와 같은 형태인 「had + p.p.」를 써서 나타낸다.

We talked about the movie that we **had seen**. 우리는 우리가 본 영화에 대해 이야기했다.
(We talked about the movie: 나중에 일어난 사건 / that we had seen: 먼저 일어난 사건)

+ before나 after 등의 접속사를 사용하여 확실한 시간의 전후 관계를 알 수 있는 경우, 과거완료 대신 단순 과거형을 써서 나타낼 수 있다.

▶▶ 정답과 해설 p. 19

EXERCISE A 다음 괄호 안에서 옳은 것을 고르시오.

1 I didn't want to watch the movie because I [have seen / had seen] it.

2 The plane [has just taken off / had just taken off] when I got to the airport.

3 He lost the shoes that he [has bought / had bought] the day before yesterday.

4 Jim pretended that something [has happened / had happened] to him.

5 She [have lived / had lived] in Seoul before she came here.

6 I knew that she [had broken / has been broken] the window.

EXERCISE B 다음 문장에서 어법상 틀린 곳을 찾아 바르게 고쳐 쓰시오.

1 Peter has already left when Julia got to the park.

2 Because my bike has broken on my way here, I couldn't arrive in time.

3 They have been married for twenty years before they moved here.

EXERCISE C **다음 두 문장을 <보기>와 같이 한 문장으로 연결할 때 빈칸에 알맞은 말을 쓰시오.**

〈보기〉
The soccer team cried for joy. They won the match.
➡ The soccer team cried for joy because they had won the match.

1 They didn't know how to go. They missed the last train.
➡ They didn't know how to go because ______________________.

2 I decided to help the victims. I saw the earthquake in Haiti.
➡ I decided to help the victims after ______________________.

3 The grass looked greener than yesterday. It rained at night.
➡ The grass looked greener than yesterday after ______________________.

4 Jack couldn't buy the notebooks. He spent all his money.
➡ Jack couldn't buy the notebooks because ______________________.

EXERCISE D **다음 우리말과 일치하도록 주어진 단어 또는 어구를 사용하여 문장을 완성하시오. (필요시 형태 변화)**

1 어느 날 우리는 어떤 배가 태평양에서 사라졌다는 소식을 들었다. (disappear)
➡ One day we heard a ship ________ ________ in the Pacific.

2 나는 Allen이 교통사고를 당했다는 소식을 들어서 매우 슬펐다. (have)
➡ I was so sad to hear that Allen ________ ________ a car accident.

3 내가 학교에 도착했을 때 수업은 이미 시작해 있었다. (already, begin)
➡ The class ________ ________ ________ when I arrived at school.

4 나는 2008년에 태어났고, 나의 형은 1년 먼저 태어났다. (be born)
➡ I was born in 2008, and my brother ________ ________ ________ a year before.

5 Dorothy는 이탈리아로 이사 오기 전까지 올리브 나무를 본 적이 전혀 없었다. (never, see)
➡ Dorothy ________ ________ ________ an olive tree before she moved to Italy.

6 나는 지난 토요일에 농구 경기를 보러 갔다. 하지만 표는 이미 매진되어 있었다. (be sold)
➡ I went to see a basketball game last Saturday. But the tickets ________ ________ ________ out already.

7 그녀가 거기에 도착했을 때 그 가게는 막 문을 닫았다. (just, close)
➡ The store ________ ________ ________ when she arrived there.

7 과거완료진행

「had been + -ing」: ~하고 있었다

과거완료진행은 과거의 어느 시점 이전부터 그 시점까지 진행되어 온 동작이나 사건을 나타낸다.

Many people **had been looking** at Monet's *Waterlilies* when I arrived at the gallery.
내가 미술관에 도착했을 때 많은 사람들이 모네의 <수련>을 보고 있었다.

I **had been sleeping** for 12 hours when the doorbell rang.
초인종이 울렸을 때 나는 12시간 동안 자고 있었다.

▶▶ 정답과 해설 p. 19

EXERCISE A 다음 괄호 안에서 옳은 것을 고르시오.

1 I was sad when I sold my car. I [have been driving / had been driving] the car since May 2012.

2 The UN is discussing the agenda. They [have been discussing / had been discussing] it for two hours.

3 Dona is listening to music. She likes Beethoven. She [has been listening / had been listening] to the music since 2 o'clock.

4 I [have been talking / had been talking] with my friend for a half hour before the bus came.

EXERCISE B 다음 우리말과 일치하도록 주어진 단어를 사용하여 문장을 완성하시오. (필요시 형태 변화)

1 내가 역에 도착했을 때, 내 친구들은 나를 한 시간째 기다리고 있었다. (wait)
➡ When I arrived at the station, my friends ________ ________ ________ for me for an hour.

2 경기가 시작될 때까지, 사람들은 30분 동안 줄을 서 있었다. (stand)
➡ By the time the game began, people ________ ________ ________ in line for 30 minutes.

3 그는 영국으로 건너가기 전에 5년 동안 영어를 공부하고 있었다. (study)
➡ He ________ ________ ________ English for five years before he went over to the UK.

학교 시험 대비 문제

맞힌 개수	
선택형	____ / 36
서술형	____ / 11

▶▶ 정답과 해설 p. 19

01 다음 두 문장을 한 문장으로 바꿔 쓸 때 빈칸에 알맞은 것은?

> • He lost his passport. Now he doesn't have it.
> ➡ He ________ his passport.

① lose ② is losing
③ was losing ④ has lost
⑤ have lost

02 다음 우리말을 영어로 바르게 옮긴 것은?

> 그는 오늘 밤에 나를 보러 올 것이다.

① He came to see me tonight.
② He is coming to see me tonight.
③ He has come to see me tonight.
④ He had come to see me tonight.
⑤ He was coming to see me tonight.

03 다음 대화의 밑줄 친 단어를 바르게 고쳐 쓴 것은?

> **A** What's this?
> **B** It's a book about wild animals. I <u>read</u> it since last week.

① will read ② am reading
③ was reading ④ have read
⑤ had been reading

04 다음 빈칸에 들어갈 말이 바르게 짝지어진 것은?

> • I have already ________ pizza for dinner.
> • He had never ________ a camel before he visited the zoo.

① eat — seeing ② ate — seen
③ eaten — see ④ ate — see
⑤ eaten — seen

05 다음 밑줄 친 부분과 쓰임이 같은 것은?

> <u>Have</u> you ever <u>seen</u> the horse there?

① I <u>have</u> just <u>eaten</u> breakfast.
② I <u>have been</u> to France three times.
③ It <u>has been raining</u> since yesterday.
④ <u>Have</u> you <u>studied</u> math for two hours?
⑤ He <u>has had</u> the cell phone for one year.

고난도
06 다음 중 어법상 올바른 것은?

① They have married next week.
② He was ill in bed since last month.
③ I have climbed Mt. Seorak last Sunday.
④ I will wait here until the train will arrive.
⑤ I lost the umbrella that I had bought for my mom.

07 다음 밑줄 친 부분의 쓰임이 나머지 넷과 다른 것은?

① Snow is still falling heavily.
② Tom is coming to see me next week.
③ I'm taking five courses next semester.
④ Jenny is having a birthday party tomorrow.
⑤ He is leaving for New York the day after tomorrow.

08 다음 대답이 나올 수 있는 질문으로 알맞은 것은?

No, I've never been there.

① Where has he gone?
② Did you like Cape Town?
③ Cape Town is beautiful, isn't it?
④ Does Cape Town have much rain?
⑤ Have you ever been to Cape Town?

09 다음 빈칸에 들어갈 말이 바르게 짝지어진 것은?

• He has been interested in drawing ________ he was young.
• She has been sick ________ four days.

① for — for ② for — since
③ since — for ④ since — while
⑤ since — since

10 다음 두 문장을 한 문장으로 바꿔 쓸 때 빈칸에 알맞은 것은?

• Steve went to China. So he is not here.
➡ Steve has ________ to China.

① go ② going ③ been
④ gone ⑤ went

11 다음 중 짝지어진 대화가 어색한 것은?

① **A** How long have you been there?
B I've been here for a week.
② **A** Have you ever met a movie star?
B No, I didn't.
③ **A** What were you doing at nine last night?
B I was listening to music.
④ **A** Has your son lost his schoolbag?
B Yes, he has.
⑤ **A** Did you watch the soccer game last Sunday?
B No, I didn't watch it.

고난도

12 다음 밑줄 친 부분이 어법상 틀린 것은?

① She is going to buy some fruits.
② She usually goes to work by subway.
③ She left here the day before yesterday.
④ She has returned from America last Sunday.
⑤ She was doing homework when I entered the room.

13 다음 빈칸에 들어갈 말로 알맞은 것은?

When I got to the bus station, the bus ______________.

① already leave ② already left
③ has already left ④ had already left
⑤ will have already left

14 다음 우리말과 일치하도록 빈칸에 들어갈 말로 알맞은 것은?

• 그녀는 30년째 영어를 가르치고 있다.
➡ She ________ English for thirty years.

① teaches ② is teaching
③ has taught ④ had taught
⑤ taught

고난도
15 다음 중 어법상 틀린 것은?

① It's been raining for two days.
② When I got there, he had already gone.
③ I have been to Jeju Island several times.
④ Why have you been looking for the teacher?
⑤ He is playing computer games since two o'clock.

16 다음 빈칸에 들어갈 말로 알맞은 것은?

My brother ______________ on the computer when I entered the room.

① draws ② is drawing
③ has drawn ④ has been drawing
⑤ had been drawing

17 다음 빈칸에 들어갈 말로 알맞은 것은?

• 아이들은 30분째 쓰레기를 줍고 있다.
➡ The children have been ________ up the trash for thirty minutes.

① pick ② picked
③ picking ④ to pick
⑤ to picking

18 다음 대화의 빈칸에 알맞은 것은?

A Have you cleaned your room?
B No, I ________.
A Can you tell me why?
B I have a lot of homework.

① am not ② don't
③ didn't ④ haven't
⑤ hasn't

19 다음 중 어법상 올바른 것은?

① I have been a doctor in 1990.
② The train has left thirty minutes ago.
③ He has finished the work yesterday.
④ When did you buy your smartphone?
⑤ Have you written the essay last night?

20 다음 밑줄 친 단어를 바르게 고쳐 쓴 것은?

> Yesterday I lost the cap that my brother buy for me.

① buys ② have bought
③ is buying ④ has bought
⑤ had bought

21 다음 밑줄 친 부분과 쓰임이 같은 것은?

> Tom has just finished his speech.

① He has used the product before.
② I have always wanted to climb Mt. Jiri.
③ We have not decided what to order yet.
④ She has lost her backpack on the subway.
⑤ Eddy has worked in a bank for three years.

22 다음 밑줄 친 단어의 형태가 바르게 짝지어진 것은?

> The baseball team shout for joy yesterday because it win the World Series.

① shout — won
② shouted — have won
③ shouted — had won
④ had shouted — have won
⑤ had shouted — had won

고난도

23 다음 문장에서 어법상 틀린 것은?

> Kevin is(①) a 16-year-old(②) boy who lives(③) in Boston with his parents and(④) his two brothers. He lives(⑤) there for 10 years.

24 다음 밑줄 친 단어의 형태가 바르게 짝지어진 것은?

> My parents have visit Hongdo three times. But I have never be to the island. They promised to take me there.

① visit — am ② visit — was
③ visited — be ④ visited — was
⑤ visited — been

25 다음 중 어법상 틀린 것은?

① He's been ill for about ten months.
② I've had a cold for nearly a month.
③ We've been married since four years.
④ Michael hasn't been in class since this afternoon.
⑤ She hasn't eaten anything since the day before yesterday.

26 다음 빈칸에 들어갈 말로 알맞지 않은 것은?

I have ________ seen such a house.

① never ② often ③ not
④ already ⑤ since

27 다음 빈칸에 들어갈 말로 알맞은 것은?

I'll come as soon as I ________ my project.

① finish ② finished
③ was finish ④ had finished
⑤ will have finished

28 다음 중 어법상 올바른 것은?

① She has slept since 20 hours.
② Have you ever been to Canada?
③ He has lived in Vietnam for 2014.
④ I know Jimmy since he was young.
⑤ Wendy has been to Japan. She is still there.

29 다음 밑줄 친 단어를 바르게 고쳐 쓴 것은?

When I saw him at the airport, he was not wearing the ring. I thought that he lose it.

① has lost ② loses
③ had lost ④ was losing
⑤ is losing

30 다음 밑줄 친 부분과 쓰임이 같은 것은?

She has been away from home for two years.

① He has lost his key.
② They have gone to Prague.
③ I have seen the musical once.
④ I have lived here since I was born.
⑤ I have already finished making invitation cards.

31 다음 밑줄 친 부분의 쓰임이 나머지 넷과 다른 것은?

① I have never had any pets.
② He has once seen a shark.
③ Have you ever tried sushi?
④ I have been to Canada before.
⑤ Two years have passed since she died.

32 다음 중 밑줄 친 부분이 어법상 틀린 것은?

① She has never been to China before.
② We have been studying for three hours.
③ John has already left when his sister got there.
④ My parents had gone to bed when I got home.
⑤ I borrowed some money because I had lost my purse.

33 다음 중 어법상 틀린 것은?

① I have lost my pencil.
② They have gone to India.
③ He has bought a new camera.
④ Have you ever been to China?
⑤ We have known each other since we are ten years old.

34 다음 두 문장의 밑줄 친 부분의 쓰임이 서로 다른 것은?

① Minji has just cleaned the kitchen.
Has she read the essay yet?
② My sister has lost her wallet.
John has gone to the Netherlands.
③ We have been in Spain for 3 years.
How long have you been in Spain?
④ I have seen her twice.
Have you eaten Turkish food before?
⑤ I have written the book since last month.
She has visited Paris three times.

고난도
35 다음 밑줄 친 부분이 어법상 틀린 것은?

① She has had dinner yet.
② The film has just finished.
③ He has just received a letter.
④ Tom and Jane have already arrived.
⑤ Jenny hasn't told me about the accident yet.

36 다음 빈칸에 들어갈 말로 알맞지 않은 것은?

John has lived here ________.

① since 2009
② last month
③ since last week
④ for a long time
⑤ for three months

서술형

고난도

37 다음 글에서 틀린 부분을 찾아 바르게 고쳐 쓰시오.

There are many kinds of flowers at the fair. They are beautiful. Especially white roses are smelling sweet.

__________ ➡ __________

38 다음 주어진 단어를 사용하여 빈칸에 알맞은 말을 쓰시오.

She has written many novels since she __________ eighteen. (be)

[39-40] 다음 우리말과 일치하도록 주어진 단어를 사용하여 문장을 완성하시오. (필요시 형태 변화)

39

- 그는 나에게 두바이를 여러 번 방문했었다고 말했다. (visit)

➡ He told me that he __________ __________ Dubai several times.

40

- 그가 도착하기 전에 나는 그를 오랫동안 기다리고 있었다. (wait)

➡ I __________ __________ __________ for him for a long time before he arrived.

[41-42] 다음 두 문장을 한 문장으로 바꿔 쓸 때 빈칸에 알맞은 말을 쓰시오.

41

- It started to rain yesterday. It is still raining.

➡ It __________ __________ __________ since yesterday.

42

- I bought the coat seven years ago. Now I still wear it.

➡ I __________ __________ the coat for seven years.

고난도

43 **다음 문장에서 어법상 틀린 부분을 찾아 바르게 고쳐 쓰시오.**

> When we were in elementary school, we learned that Admiral Yi Sunsin had defeated the Japanese navy in 1597.

__________ ➡ __________

[44-45] 다음 〈보기〉를 참고하여 주어진 상황을 한 문장으로 쓰시오.

〈보기〉

Matt lost his watch. He still can't find it.

thirty minutes ago — now

➡ Matt has lost his watch.

44 Brian went to China. He is not here.

in 2018 — now

➡ __________

45 It started to rain. It is still raining.

yesterday — now

➡ __________

고난도

[46-47] 다음 글을 읽고, 주어진 어구를 사용하여 글을 완성하시오. (필요시 형태 변화)

46

> Kate went to the "Green" restaurant last Saturday. Henry went to the restaurant, too. But they didn't see each other. Henry left the restaurant at 6:00 p.m. Kate arrived there at 7:00 p.m. So, when Kate arrived at the restaurant, Henry __________ (go home) already.

47

> Our family came back from our vacation. When we arrived at home, we were very surprised. The things in the living room were scattered all over the place. We thought that __________ (thief, break into) the house. So, we called the police.

Chapter
05

조동사

1 can / could

능력, 가능	~할 수 있다 (= be able to)	I **can** drive a car without any help. 나는 어떤 도움 없이도 차를 운전할 수 있다. = I **am able to** drive a car without any help. Jake **could** solve the problem thanks to his teacher. Jake는 그의 선생님 덕분에 그 문제를 풀 수 있었다.
허가	~해도 된다 ~해도 될까요?	You **can** use my laptop if you need. 필요하다면 너는 내 노트북 컴퓨터를 사용해도 된다. **Can** I ask you a question? 제가 질문 하나 해도 될까요?
요청	~해주시겠어요?	**Can(Could)** you close the door? 문을 닫아주시겠어요?
추측	~일까? ~일 리가 없다	**Can** it be true? 그게 사실일까? He **can't** be here. 그가 여기 있을 리가 없다.
부정형	can ↔ can't(cannot) / could ↔ couldn't(could not)	

+ 중요 표현

cannot help -ing(= cannot but + 동사원형) : ~하지 않을 수 없다
cannot ~ without -ing : ~할 때마다 …하게 된다
cannot ~ too ... : 아무리 ~해도 지나치지 않다

! 조동사는 2개를 나란히 사용할 수 없기 때문에, can이 다른 조동사와 같이 쓰이는 경우에는 반드시 be able to를 사용해야 한다.

You **will be able to** catch up with him. 너는 그를 따라 잡을 수 있을 것이다.

▶▶ 정답과 해설 p. 22

EXERCISE A **다음 괄호 안에서 옳은 것을 고르시오.**

1 [Can / Will] I have some tea or something?

2 It [cannot / can] be true. He is telling a lie.

3 I couldn't help [weep / weeping] at the sad news.

4 We [can / is able to] see a great view from the bedroom window.

EXERCISE B **다음 문장의 밑줄 친 부분과 쓰임이 같은 것을 <보기>에서 골라 기호를 쓰시오.**

<보기>
ⓐ Mammals <u>can't</u> breathe in the water except whales.
ⓑ My best friend <u>can't</u> be a liar.

1 We can't live without air.

2 She can't be so young; she must be over thirty.

3 He can't find the answer to that question.

4 I saw her at the library five minutes ago. She can't be at home.

5 Even Hercules can't beat everyone.

EXERCISE C 다음 주어진 문장을 <보기>와 같이 바꿔 쓰시오.

<보기>
I can earn more money for my family.
➡ I am able to earn more money for my family.

1 Jenny can ride a bike now.
➡ Jenny ______________ ride a bike now.

2 We couldn't tell him about his father's death.
➡ We ______________ tell him about his father's death.

3 Can you classify all these papers?
➡ ______________ classify all these papers?

4 He can say his name, but he can't write it.
➡ He __________ say his name, but he __________ write it.

EXERCISE D 다음 우리말과 일치하도록 주어진 단어를 사용하여 문장을 완성하시오. (필요시 형태 변화)

1 나는 내일까지 이 보고서를 끝낼 수 없을 것이다. (will, able)
➡ I ______ ______ ______ ______ finish this report by tomorrow.

2 나는 그녀를 기억할 때마다 울게 된다. (can, remember)
➡ I ______ ______ her without crying.

3 나는 그의 조언을 따를 수밖에 없었다. (help, follow)
➡ I ______ ______ ______ his advice.

4 차를 운전할 때는 아무리 주의해도 지나치지 않다. (can, careful)
➡ You ______ ______ ______ ______ when driving a car.

2 may / might

허가	~해도 된다 ~해도 될까요?	You **may** enter the room. 너는 그 방에 들어가도 된다. **May** I open the box? 제가 그 상자를 열어봐도 될까요? — Yes, you **may**. 응, 그래. / No, you **may not**. 아니, 그럴 수 없어.
추측	~일지도 모른다	I **may(might)** be going to England to study. 나는 공부하러 영국에 가게 될지도 모른다. He **may not** be a good husband to her. 그는 그녀에게 좋은 남편이 아닐지도 모른다.
부정형	may ↔ may not / might ↔ might not	

+ 추측을 의미하는 may와 might는 서로 구분 없이 사용하며, 시제 일치가 필요한 경우에는 항상 might를 사용한다.

Jane **thought** the man **might** steal the ring. Jane은 그 남자가 그 반지를 훔쳤을지도 모른다고 생각했다.

+ 중요 표현

「may(might) well + 동사원형」: ~하는 것이 당연하다

「may(might) as well + 동사원형」: ~하는 편이 낫다

▶▶ 정답과 해설 p.22

EXERCISE A 다음 문장의 밑줄 친 부분과 쓰임이 같은 것을 <보기>에서 골라 기호를 쓰시오.

<보기>

ⓐ He may be very busy these days.　　ⓑ You may use the printer for free.

1 This article may not be true.

2 May I have your phone number?

3 You may watch TV from now on.

4 She may not be an actress.

5 You may borrow my cell phone.

6 He may leave Seoul soon.

EXERCISE B 다음 우리말과 일치하도록 주어진 단어를 사용하여 문장을 완성하시오. (필요시 형태 변화)

1 그가 그의 아들을 자랑스러워하는 것은 당연하다. (well, be)
➡ He ______________________ proud of his son.

2 그는 10시간째 운전하고 있다. 그가 졸린 것은 당연하다. (well, sleepy)
➡ He has driven for 10 hours. He ______________________.

3 비가 많이 오고 있다. 우리는 집에 머무는 편이 낫다. (well, stay)
➡ It is raining hard. We ______________________ at home.

3 must / have to

의무 · 필요	~해야 한다 (= have(has) to)	You **must** keep it in mind. 너는 그것을 명심해야 한다. You **have to** listen to his words. 너는 그의 말을 들어야 한다. We **have to** drive slowly in the school zone. 우리는 어린이 보호구역에서는 천천히 운전해야 한다.
강한 추측	~임에 틀림없다	You **must** be tired. 너는 피곤한 게 틀림없다. She **must** be sick in bed. 그녀는 아파서 누워있는 게 틀림없다.
부정형	must ↔ must not / have to ↔ don't(doesn't) have to	

+ must의 과거형은 had to로 나타낸다.

He **had to** sell his house last year. 그는 작년에 그의 집을 팔아야 했다.

! must not과 don't have to의 뜻이 전혀 다르므로 주의해야 한다.

You **must not** wear glasses. 너는 안경을 써서는 안 된다. **<금지> (= should not)**

You **don't have to** wear glasses. 너는 안경을 쓸 필요가 없다. **<불필요> (= need not)**

▶▶ 정답과 해설 p. 22

EXERCISE A 다음 괄호 안에서 옳은 것을 고르시오.

1 She [must / have / has] to eat more fresh fruit.

2 She [will / have / has] to take care of her brother.

3 We can't use the public transportation. So we [have to / need not / must not] rent a car.

4 He [must / have / had] to help his sister do the dishes.

5 He [must / must not / cannot] be innocent. Nobody witnessed him at the murder scene.

6 You [may / have to / cannot] study hard, or you would fail the exam.

7 You don't have a driver's license. You [must / have to / has to] not drive a car.

EXERCISE B 다음 문장의 밑줄 친 부분과 쓰임이 같은 것을 <보기>에서 골라 기호를 쓰시오.

<보기>

ⓐ A driver must stop when he sees a red light.

ⓑ He must be a fool to do such a thing.

1 She must be happy to have such a good husband.

2 You must keep the safety rules here.

3 He's very funny. He must be a comedian.

4 Patients must follow the doctor's order.

5 You must get on the boat by 10:30.

6 The Prime Minister must control both parties to avoid the worst case.

EXERCISE C **다음 주어진 문장을 <보기>와 같이 바꿔 쓰시오.**

<보기>

You need not prepare the meal.

➡ You don't have to prepare the meal.

1 The customers need not pay for the broken product.

➡ The customers __________________ pay for the broken product.

2 Now the Korean soccer team need not fear European teams.

➡ Now the Korean soccer team __________________ fear European teams.

3 She need not worry about that. I can handle it myself.

➡ She __________________ worry about that. I can handle it myself.

EXERCISE D **다음 우리말과 일치하도록 주어진 단어를 배열하여 문장을 완성하시오.**

1 너는 재미로 벌레를 죽여서는 안 된다. 그건 나쁜 것이다. (kill, bugs, not, must)

➡ You __________________________ for fun. It's a bad thing.

2 그녀는 평화를 되찾기 위해 무언가를 해야만 할 것이다. (do, to, have, will)

➡ She __________________________ something to regain peace.

3 너는 그들에게 영어 단어들을 발음하는 방법을 가르칠 필요가 없다. (to, don't, teach, have)

➡ You __________________________ them how to pronounce English words.

4 Karl은 열쇠를 잃어버려서 창문을 통해서 들어가야 했다. (through, go, had, the window, to)

➡ Karl lost his keys, so he __________________________.

4 should / ought to

(도덕적) 의무	~해야 한다	The rich **should** donate more for the poor. 부자들은 가난한 사람들을 위해 더 많이 기부해야 한다. We **ought to** keep the law and order to maintain peace. 우리는 평화를 유지하기 위해 법과 질서를 지켜야 한다.
부정형	should ↔ should not(shouldn't) / ought to ↔ ought not to(oughtn't to)	

You **should** wear a seat belt while driving. 너는 운전할 때 안전벨트를 매야 한다.

We **ought to** try to do our best at all times. 우리는 항상 최선을 다하려고 노력해야 한다.

+ 요구 · 주장 · 제안을 나타내는 동사 또는 감정 · 판단을 나타내는 말 다음의 that절에서 should를 쓰며, 이때 should는 생략할 수 있다.

요구 · 주장 · 제안을 나타내는 동사	suggest, demand, order, advise, recommend, insist
감정 · 판단을 나타내는 말	necessary, essential, natural, strange, surprising, a pity

My wife **suggested that** we **(should)** have dinner at a fine restaurant.
나의 아내는 고급 레스토랑에서 저녁을 먹자고 제안했다.

It is **essential that** you **(should)** be here soon. 네가 이곳에 빨리 와야 하는 것은 기본적인 것이다.

▶▶ 정답과 해설 p.22

EXERCISE A 다음 괄호 안에서 옳은 것을 고르시오.

1 Do you think I [should / ought] to look for another job?

2 We don't know what we [ought / should] do.

3 The doctor suggested that I [would / should] take a walk every morning.

4 He insisted that I [accept / accepted] it, but I rejected.

5 Any man who killed someone [ought to not / ought not to] be released.

EXERCISE B 다음 우리말과 일치하도록 주어진 단어를 사용하여 문장을 완성하시오. (필요시 형태 변화)

1 그것은 Hena의 잘못이다. 그녀는 그에게 사과해야 한다. (apologize)
➡ It's Hena's fault. She __________ __________ to him.

2 아이들은 그 약을 먹어서는 안 된다. (take)
➡ Children __________ __________ __________ the pill.

5 will / would / used to

will	미래(= be going to)	I **will** be seventeen next year. 나는 내년에 17살이 된다.
	의지(~할 것이다)	I **will** punish you for it. 내가 그것에 대해 너에게 벌을 줄 것이다.
will, would	요청(~해주시겠어요?)	**Will** you check my schedule? 제 일정을 확인해주시겠어요? **Would** you marry me? 저와 결혼해주시겠어요?
would, used to	과거의 습관(~하곤 했다)	I **would** play with Mary in the garden when I was young. = I **used to** play with Mary in the garden when I was young. 나는 어렸을 때 정원에서 Mary와 함께 놀곤 했다.
used to	과거의 상태(~이었다)	The library **used to** be a school. 그 도서관은 (예전에는) 학교였다.
부정형	will ↔ won't(will not) / would ↔ would not(wouldn't) / used to ↔ used not to	

+ used to vs. be used to부정사 vs. be used to -ing

used to	~하곤 했다, ~이었다
be used to부정사	~하기 위해 사용되다 *** to부정사의 부사적 용법**
be used to -ing	~하는 데 익숙하다

The museum **used to** be a fortress. 그 박물관은 (예전에) 요새였다.
The gate **was used to protect** the palace. 그 성문은 궁을 보호하기 위해 사용되었다.
The girls **are used to standing** on the stage. 그 소녀들은 무대에 서는 데 익숙하다.

▶▶ 정답과 해설 p.23

EXERCISE A 다음 괄호 안에서 옳은 것을 고르시오.

1 I [will / would] send the parcel to my uncle next Tuesday.

2 I [will / used] not break my promise before I die.

3 Bill [will / would] sleep with a loud snore when he was young.

4 Our shop [is going to / was going to] be closed tomorrow.

EXERCISE B 다음 문장의 빈칸에 would와 used to 중에서 알맞은 말을 골라 쓰시오. (답 2개 가능)

1 This is where the temple ____________ be.

2 My father ____________ go fishing on weekends.

3 ______ you pass me the salt, please?

4 I think the summer days are hotter than they ______ be.

5 Her hair ______ be blonde, but it turned gray.

6 I never thought that I ______ be a doctor when I grew up.

7 My father ______ give me a ride on his bicycle when I was young.

EXERCISE C **다음 문장의 밑줄 친 부분과 쓰임이 같은 것을 <보기>에서 골라 기호를 쓰시오.**

<보기>
ⓐ She used to go to the theater with her mother.
ⓑ The funds will be used to help the poor.
ⓒ We are used to working with the musicians.

1 My sister used to go swimming every Sunday.

2 I am not used to being treated like a big star.

3 Today's younger generation is used to searching information on the Internet.

4 I used to feel lonely when I was in New York.

5 Air conditioners are used to keep us cool in hot summer.

6 Gary used to work in a toy factory, but he quit the job last week.

EXERCISE D **다음 우리말과 일치하도록 주어진 단어를 사용하여 문장을 완성하시오. (필요시 형태 변화)**

1 그는 예전의 그가 아니다. (be)
➡ He is not what he ______ ______ ______.

2 그녀는 방과 후에 친구들과 테니스를 치곤 했다. (play tennis)
➡ She ______ ______ ______ with her friends after school.

3 할머니 댁에는 강아지가 한 마리 있었다. (be)
➡ There ______ ______ ______ a puppy in my grandmother's house.

6 had better / would rather

had better	강한 충고 (~하는 게 좋겠다)	You **had better** take an umbrella because it might rain. 비가 올지도 모르기 너는 때문에 우산을 가져가는 게 좋겠다. You **had better** stop bullying him. 너는 그를 괴롭히는 것을 그만두는 게 좋겠다.
would rather	선택 (~하겠다, ~하고 싶다)	I **would rather** stay at home. 나는 집에 있겠다. I **would rather** live in the country. 나는 시골에서 살겠다.
부정형	had better ↔ had better not / would rather ↔ would rather not	

+ would rather A than B (B하느니 차라리 A 하겠다)

I **would rather** stay at home **than** go out. 나는 외출하느니 차라리 집에 있겠다.

▶▶ 정답과 해설 p.23

EXERCISE A 다음 문장에서 어법상 틀린 부분을 찾아 바르게 고쳐 쓰시오.

1 You had better to go to the hospital.

2 You had not better stay here anymore.

3 I would rather go on a bicycle as take a crowded bus.

4 I would rather walk than taking the subway.

EXERCISE B 다음 우리말과 일치하도록 주어진 단어를 사용하여 문장을 완성하시오. (필요시 형태 변화)

1 너는 이번에 그것을 포기하는 게 좋겠다. (give)
➡ You _________ _________ _________ it up this time.

2 나는 너에게 사실을 말하느니 차라리 떠나겠다. (leave)
➡ I _________ _________ _________ than tell you the truth.

3 너는 밖에 나가지 않는 게 좋겠다. (go)
➡ You _________ _________ _________ _________ outside.

4 나는 그런 타블로이드 신문을 읽느니 차라리 TV를 보겠다. (would)
➡ I _________ _________ watch TV _________ read such a tabloid.

7 do

일반동사	'~을 하다'의 의미로 쓰임	I **did** everything I could do. 나는 내가 할 수 있는 것은 다 했다.
대동사	앞의 동사를 가리킴	Women **have** a longer life span than men **do**. 여자들은 남자들보다 수명이 더 길다.
조동사	의문문, 부정문에서 쓰임	**Do** you play any musical instruments? 너는 악기를 연주하니? We **didn't** receive your fax. 우리는 네가 보낸 팩스를 받지 못했다.
강조의 조동사	일반동사를 강조함	I **do love** you. 나는 너를 정말 사랑한다. This pearl **does look** real, but it's not. 이 진주는 정말 진짜처럼 보이지만 진짜가 아니다.

▶▶ 정답과 해설 p.23

EXERCISE A 다음 문장의 밑줄 친 부분과 쓰임이 같은 것을 〈보기〉에서 골라 기호를 쓰시오.

〈보기〉
ⓐ I will do the right thing. ⓑ Why do you read the book?
ⓒ He does like blue jeans. ⓓ Sarah loves ice cream and so does Susan.

1 You really did a good job.

2 I'm sorry that we didn't have more time to talk.

3 What did you do on Christmas Eve?

4 I am working harder nowadays than I did.

5 I did believe in you, but you deceived me.

EXERCISE B 다음 우리말과 일치하도록 주어진 단어와 do를 사용하여 문장을 완성하시오. (필요시 형태 변화)

1 그는 다시는 담배를 피우지 않겠다고 정말로 맹세했다. (swear)
➡ He ________ ________ not to smoke again.

2 자동차 사고로 죽는 것보다 더 많은 수의 사람들이 암으로 죽는다. (than)
➡ People die more from cancer ________ ________ ________ from car accidents.

3 저의 무례한 태도에 대해 진심으로 사과드립니다. (apologize)
➡ I ________ ________ for my impolite attitude.

4 나는 대부분의 남자아이들이 그런 것처럼 그 미식축구팀에 들어가고 싶다. (most boys)
➡ I want to join the football team as ________ ________ ________.

8 조동사 + have p.p.

should have p.p.	후회 · 유감 (~했어야 했다)	He might even die. We **should have called** 119 earlier. 그는 심지어 죽을지도 모른다. 우리는 119에 더 일찍 전화를 했어야 했다.
may(might) have p.p.	약한 추측 (~했을지도 모른다)	You **might have convinced** my wife but not me. 너는 내 아내를 설득했을지 모르지만 나는 그렇지 않다.
must have p.p.	강한 추측 (~했음에 틀림없다)	The house was empty. The whole family **must have left** last night. 그 집은 비어 있었다. 온 가족이 어젯밤에 떠난 것이 틀림없다.
cannot have p.p.	강한 부정의 추측 (~했을 리가 없다)	She **cannot have told** a lie. She is such an honest girl. 그녀가 거짓말을 했을 리가 없다. 그녀는 정말 정직한 소녀이다.
부정형	should have p.p. ↔ should not have p.p. may(might) have p.p. ↔ may(might) not have p.p. must have p.p. ↔ must not have p.p.	

▶▶ 정답과 해설 p.23

EXERCISE A 다음 괄호 안에서 옳은 것을 고르시오.

1 I [should / cannot] not have said so. Everybody took me for a liar.

2 The kids were very polite. They [should / must] have been educated well.

3 He [should / must] have passed the ball to me. If so, we could have won the game.

4 He [should / cannot] have done such a thing. He is always kind to everyone.

5 You were stupid to try to climb up there. You [might / cannot] have killed yourself.

6 If you had come earlier, you [might / must] have met the salesman. Unfortunately, he's gone.

7 He [cannot / must] have paid a lot of money for the meal. The restaurant was very big and luxurious.

EXERCISE B 다음 우리말과 일치하도록 밑줄 친 부분을 바르게 고쳐 쓰시오.

1 지난 겨울 어디에선가 대지진이 있었던 게 틀림없다.
➡ There must be a big earthquake somewhere last winter.

2 Jenny가 늦는다. 그녀는 그 회의에 대해 잊었을지도 모른다.
➡ Jenny is late. She may forgot about the meeting.

3 나는 Ann에게 오늘 아침 전화했어야 했는데 잊어버렸다.

➡ I should phone Ann this morning, but I forgot.

4 나는 열쇠를 찾을 수 없다. 나는 열쇠를 집에 놓고 온 것이 틀림없다.

➡ I can't find my keys. I must leave them at home.

5 그 개가 네가 한 말을 이해했을 리가 없다.

➡ The dog can't understand what you said.

EXERCISE C 다음 주어진 단어를 사용하여 <보기>와 같이 문장을 완성하시오. (필요시 형태 변화)

〈보기〉

You spilled the water. You should have been more careful. (should, be)

1 My wallet is not in my pocket. I ______________________ it in the toilet. (must, leave)

2 People are angry with their president. He ______________________ the public interest. (should, promote)

3 James passed Cathy without even saying hello. He ______________________ her. (cannot, see)

EXERCISE D 다음 우리말과 일치하도록 주어진 단어 및 어구를 사용하여 문장을 완성하시오. (필요시 형태 변화)

1 길이 젖어 있다. 밤 사이에 비가 왔던 게 틀림없다. (it, rain)

➡ The road is wet. ________ ________ ________ ________ during the night.

2 그는 그녀를 만났을 리가 없다. 그녀는 그때 해외에서 공부하고 있었다. (meet, her)

➡ He ________ ________ ________ ________. She was studying abroad at that time.

3 나는 너를 어디에서도 보지 못했다. 너는 도서관에서 하루 종일 시간을 보냈던 게 틀림없다. (spend)

➡ I couldn't see you anywhere. You ________ ________ ________ all day in the library.

4 우리의 결혼은 결국 깨졌다. 우리는 서로의 말을 들어줬어야 했다. (listen to)

➡ Our marriage finally broke up. We ________ ________ ________ ________ each other.

Chapter 05
조동사

학교 시험 대비 문제

맞힌 개수	
선택형	____ / 29
서술형	____ / 16

▶▶ 정답과 해설 p.23

01 다음 중 밑줄 친 부분과 바꿔 쓸 수 있는 것은?

They aren't able to walk anymore because it's too hot.

① may not ② cannot ③ must not
④ will not ⑤ should not

02 다음 빈칸에 들어갈 말로 알맞은 것은?

• 너는 피곤한 게 틀림없다.
➡ You ________ be tired.

① must ② would ③ have to
④ ought to ⑤ cannot

03 다음 빈칸에 들어갈 말로 알맞은 것은?

I ________ sleep on the floor when I was a child.

① used ② used to
③ am used to ④ was used to
⑤ get used to

고난도

04 다음 문장에서 어법상 틀린 것은?

She(①) suggested(②) that(③) he breaks(④) the bad habit(⑤).

고난도

05 다음 중 어법상 옳은 것은?

① He have to pay me back.
② You must come home by 7.
③ You will must clean the bathroom.
④ The police musted catch the criminal.
⑤ She doesn't has to be nervous about it.

06 다음 빈칸에 공통으로 들어갈 말로 알맞은 것은?

• His father ________ be late tonight.
• ________ I open this box which you gave me?

① do (Do) ② may (May)
③ used to (Used to) ④ should (Should)
⑤ would (Would)

07 다음 중 어법상 올바른 것은?

① He is used to get lots of phone calls every day.
② This computer will not work well.
③ There would be a pond in the forest.
④ I am used to have a bad cold in winter.
⑤ I would live in Vancouver when I was eleven.

08 다음 빈칸에 들어갈 말로 알맞은 것은?

> I thought that the man wandering around ________ be a thief.

① may ② might ③ can
④ will ⑤ did

09 다음 밑줄 친 did와 쓰임이 같은 것은?

> I did hear a lot about you.

① He doesn't play chess.
② I like her more than you do.
③ I did follow my teacher's advice.
④ I don't understand what they did.
⑤ My sister does homework after dinner.

10 다음 중 문장의 의미가 나머지 넷과 다른 것은?

① You must return the book to the library.
② You might return the book to the library.
③ You have to return the book to the library.
④ You ought to return the book to the library.
⑤ You should return the book to the library.

11 다음 빈칸에 들어갈 말로 가장 알맞은 것은?

> • I think you shouldn't talk back to your father.
> = You'd ________ ________ talk back to your father.

① rather than ② better not
③ should not ④ not better
⑤ must not

12 다음 대화의 빈칸에 가장 알맞은 것은?

> **A** Susan didn't pass the audition for the main role.
> **B** Oh, that's too bad. She ____________ more.

① may have practiced
② must have practiced
③ might have practiced
④ would have practiced
⑤ should have practiced

13 다음 빈칸에 공통으로 들어갈 말로 알맞은 것은?

> • You ________ carry out your duty.
> • We ________ protect the environment.

① may ② shall ③ should
④ could ⑤ might

14 다음 중 빈칸에 would(Would)가 들어가기에 어색한 것은?

① ________ you fill out this card?

② You ________ better go back home.

③ I ________ like to talk to you for a while.

④ Dean ________ take a walk before breakfast.

⑤ He thought that the plants ________ grow well.

고난도

15 다음 중 어법상 틀린 것은?

① You will can fight the enemy.

② He won't be able to run anymore.

③ It cannot have been easy for him.

④ We were not able to turn the tables.

⑤ I was able to keep up with the pace.

16 다음 빈칸에 들어갈 말로 알맞은 것은?

He looked pale. He ________ sick.

① must have been

② should have been

③ cannot have been

④ doesn't have to be

⑤ wouldn't have been

17 다음 빈칸에 들어갈 말이 바르게 짝지어진 것은?

• The game was already over. We ________ earlier. • There were no people in the stadium. The game ________ over.

① must have come — must have been

② should have come — must have been

③ must have come — should have been

④ should have come — should have been

⑤ cannot have come — mustn't have been

18 다음 밑줄 친 did의 쓰임이 나머지 넷과 다른 것은?

① We did appreciate it.

② I did think you were right.

③ She did marry twice before.

④ He did not make a reservation.

⑤ He did feel sorry for the orphan.

19 다음 빈칸에 들어갈 말로 알맞은 것은?

• 나는 교외에 살았었지만, 지금 나는 도시에 산다. ➡ I ________ live in the suburbs, but I live in the city now.

① is ② would ③ should

④ has to ⑤ used to

20 다음 빈칸에 들어갈 말로 알맞은 것은?

> You give me inspiration as you ________ ten years ago.

① are ② have ③ do
④ did ⑤ should

고난도
21 다음 주어진 문장과 의미가 같은 것은?

> I'm sorry that I didn't watch the game.

① I had better watch the game.
② I was going to watch the game.
③ I must have watched the game.
④ I should have watched the game.
⑤ I was not supposed to watch the game.

22 다음 중 어법상 틀린 것은?

① He hasn't to help her work.
② You must not enter the office.
③ You will have to pay the debt.
④ You need not buy a new cell phone.
⑤ We don't have to do foul play to win the game.

23 다음 빈칸에 들어갈 말로 알맞은 것은?

> • 너는 너의 개를 당장 수의사에게 데려가는 게 좋겠다.
> ➡ You ________ take your dog to the vet right away.

① used to ② cannot ③ had better
④ might ⑤ would rather

24 다음 밑줄 친 부분의 의미가 나머지 넷과 다른 것은?

① My father can't drive a car.
② I can't go to her birthday party.
③ Can I borrow your umbrella?
④ He can't solve the problem easily.
⑤ What if you can't go to the concert?

25 다음 중 어법상 틀린 것은?

① He did do a good job. It was perfect.
② The concert is going to start at midnight.
③ You failed the exam. You should have studied more.
④ I recommended that he exercises on a regular basis.
⑤ I used to have pimples on my face, but I don't have any now.

26 다음 중 밑줄 친 might의 의미가 나머지 넷과 다른 것은?

① He might have a cold.
② Do you think it might rain?
③ That wall is so weak that it might fall.
④ It might be broken because it's too weak.
⑤ Mother allowed that Mike might go out with his girlfriend.

27 다음 밑줄 친 부분과 바꿔 쓸 수 없는 것은?

① Can I get some water?
➡ May
② You should not open the door.
➡ must not
③ I cannot swim in the deep river.
➡ am not able to
④ This place used to be a large castle.
➡ would
⑤ She must go to her room to fix her makeup.
➡ should

고난도

28 다음 두 문장의 뜻이 서로 다른 것은?

① It is certain that Bill had a cold.
= Bill must have had a cold.
② It is possible that she was upset.
= She may have been upset.
③ I'm sure that he didn't study hard.
= He cannot have studied hard.
④ I'm sorry that you didn't do your best.
= You should have done your best.
⑤ I regret that I ate so much ice cream last night.
= I should have eaten so much ice cream last night.

고난도

29 다음 중 <보기>의 밑줄 친 부분과 의미가 같은 것을 모두 고른 것은?

<보기>
You made a big mistake. He must be very upset.

ⓐ The report must be false.
ⓑ You must hand in the paper by tomorrow.
ⓒ We must take care of the weak in our society.
ⓓ My teacher knows about everything. He must know my secret.

① a, b ② a, d ③ a, c, d
④ b, c, d ⑤ a, b, c, d

서술형

30 다음 주어진 단어를 사용하여 대화의 빈칸에 알맞은 말을 쓰시오. (필요시 형태 변화)

A What does she need to do?
B She ________ ________ ________ enough sleep. (have, get)

[31-32] 다음 우리말과 일치하도록 주어진 단어를 배열하여 문장을 완성하시오.

31

• 나는 네게 거짓말을 하느니 차라리 침묵하겠다.
(than, would, I, a lie, keep, silent, you, tell, rather)

➡ ____________________
____

32

• 너는 그 이야기에 대해 내게 말하지 않는 게 좋겠다.
(not, better, tell, had)

➡ You ____________ me about the story.

고난도

33 다음 두 문장을 한 문장으로 바꿔 쓸 때 빈칸에 알맞은 말을 쓰시오.

• My sister was very thin as a child. But now she is not.

➡ My sister ________ ________ ________ very thin as a child.

34 다음 문장에서 어법상 틀린 부분을 찾아 바르게 고쳐 쓰시오.

He suggested that we went shopping after school.

____________ ➡ ____________

35 다음 주어진 단어를 사용하여 우리말을 영작하시오. (필요시 형태 변화)

A Why are you crying?
B I'm so disappointed. I failed my driver's test.
A That's OK. You can do better next time.
B Thank you for saying so. 나는 좀 더 연습을 했어야 했어. (practice, more)

➡ ____________________

36 다음 문장을 미래시제로 바꿔 쓸 때 빈칸에 알맞은 말을 쓰시오.

• I can download all of the files at once.

➡ ____________ all of the files at once.

[37-39] 다음 주어진 우리말과 일치하도록 <조건>에 맞게 문장을 완성하시오.

〈조건〉

• 모든 문장에 used를 사용할 것

37 이 우유는 초콜릿을 만드는 데 사용된다.

➡ ________________ make chocolate.

38 그는 밤늦게 까지 일하곤 했다.

➡ ________________ until late at night.

39 나는 밤에 공부하는 것에 익숙하다.

➡ ________________ at night.

[40-42] 다음 문장을 주어진 조동사를 사용하여 반대되는 내용의 문장으로 바꿔 쓰시오.

40 Minho cannot have stayed at home.
(must)

➡ Minho ________________________.

41 Brian believes the news must be true.
(cannot)

➡ Brian believes the news ____________
________________________.

42 James must have stolen the money.
(cannot)

➡ James ________________________.

[43-45] 다음 그림을 보고, 주어진 단어를 사용하여 문장을 완성하시오.

43

He ________________________.
(can, guitar)

44

Clerk You ________________________.
(may, chair)

45

Old man The sign says you ____________
________________________.
(must, here)

FINISH

Chapter 06

수동태

1 수동태 만드는 법

He opened the window. 그는 창문을 열었다.
주어 동사 목적어

➡ The window **was opened by him**. 그 창문은 그에 의해 열렸다.
be동사 + p.p. by + 행위자

① 주어와 목적어의 위치를 바꾼다.
② 동사는 「be동사 + p.p.」의 형태로 바꾼다. 이 때 주어의 수와 시제 일치에 주의한다.
③ 자리가 바뀐 주어(He)를 목적격(him)으로 바꾸고 그 앞에는 전치사 by를 붙인다.
④ 행위자가 일반인이거나 불특정인일 경우에는 「by + 행위자」를 생략한다.

Joe did not write the report. Joe는 그 보고서를 쓰지 않았다. **<부정문>**

➡ The report **was not written by Joe**. 그 보고서는 Joe에 의해 쓰여지지 않았다.

Does your father cook your meals on Sundays?
너의 아버지는 일요일마다 너의 식사를 요리하시니? **<의문사가 없는 의문문>**

➡ **Are** your meals **cooked by your father** on Sundays?
너의 식사는 일요일마다 너의 아버지에 의해 요리되니?

When did he paint this picture? 그는 언제 이 그림을 그렸니? **<의문사가 있는 의문문>**

➡ When **was** this picture **painted by him**? 이 그림은 언제 그에 의해 그려졌니?

Who designs the building? 누가 그 건물을 설계하니? **<who가 주어인 의문문>**

➡ **By whom is** the building **designed**? 누구에 의해 그 빌딩이 설계되니?

! 상태를 나타내는 타동사는 수동태로 쓸 수 없다.

have, cost, resemble, lack, fit, hold, meet, become, suit

I **have** a nice car. (○) ➡ A nice car ***is had by me***. (×)
나는 좋은 차가 한 대 있다.

▶▶ 정답과 해설 p.25

EXERCISE A 다음 문장을 수동태로 바꿔 쓸 때 빈칸에 알맞은 말을 쓰시오.

1 Saint-Exupéry wrote *The Little Prince*.
➡ *The Little Prince* __________ __________ by Saint-Exupéry.

2 Tom and Mary ate five hamburgers.
➡ Five hamburgers __________ __________ by Tom and Mary.

3 She makes special food on Sundays.
➡ Special food is made __________ __________ on Sundays.

4 Mother Teresa helped the poor.
➡ The poor __________ __________ __________ Mother Teresa.

5 The farmer doesn't grow the lemon tree.
➡ The lemon tree __________ __________ by the farmer.

EXERCISE B 다음 우리말과 일치하도록 주어진 단어를 사용하여 문장을 완성하시오. (필요시 형태 변화)

1 그 도둑은 경찰에 의해 일본에서 잡혔다. (catch)
➡ The thief __________ __________ by the police in Japan.

2 리포트가 학생들에 의해 제출되었다. (hand)
➡ The reports __________ __________ in by the students.

3 그 음악은 매년 여름에 공원에서 그 오케스트라에 의해 연주된다. (play)
➡ The music __________ __________ at the park by the orchestra every summer.

4 그 다리들은 오늘날의 증가하는 교통 문제를 해결하기 위해 지어졌다. (build)
➡ The bridges __________ __________ to solve today's increasing traffic problems.

EXERCISE C 다음 문장을 수동태로 바꿔 쓰시오.

1 Russia held the 2018 World Cup.
➡ ____

2 UNICEF helps the poor children in the world.
➡ ____

3 The Naro Space Center in Korea launched a satellite.
➡ ____

4 Kim Hongdo painted the cultural landscapes of the Joseon Dynasty.
➡ ____

2 조동사의 수동태

1 긍정문 「조동사 + be + p.p.」

He **can open** the window. 그는 창문을 열 수 있다.

➡ The window **can be opened (by him)**. 그 창문은 (그에 의해) 열려질 수 있다.

We **should follow** the new policy. 우리는 새로운 정책을 따라야 한다.

➡ The new policy **should be followed (by us)**. 새로운 정책은 (우리에 의해) 따라져야 한다.

2 부정문 「조동사 + not + be + p.p.」

They **cannot watch** the video on this website. 그들은 이 웹사이트에서 그 비디오를 볼 수 없다.

➡ The video on this website **cannot be watched (by them)**.
이 웹사이트에서 그 비디오는 (그들에 의해) 보여질 수 없다.

▶▶ 정답과 해설 p.25

EXERCISE A 다음 문장의 밑줄 친 부분을 바르게 고쳐 쓰시오.

1 The sweater can't <u>buy</u> by you. It's sold out.

2 Their love story will <u>write</u> by an author.

3 The building ought to <u>design</u> by Bob.

4 Carpets should <u>be not used</u> in this place.

5 He will <u>not be accepted</u> the reports written in pen.

6 The document is going to <u>sign</u> by Mark.

EXERCISE B 다음 문장을 수동태로 바꿔 쓸 때 빈칸에 알맞은 말을 쓰시오.

1 We can prepare something for the festival.
➡ Something ________ ________ ________ for the festival.

2 He may surprise you.
➡ You ________ ________ ________ by him.

3 She will make a decision next Monday.
➡ A decision ________ ________ ________ by her next Monday.

3 진행형 수동태

「be동사 + being + p.p.」

He **is opening** the window. 그는 창문을 열고 있다.

➡ The window **is being opened** by him. 그 창문은 그에 의해 열려지고 있다.

She **is baking** a cake. 그녀는 케이크를 굽고 있다.

➡ A cake **is being baked** by her. 케이크는 그녀에 의해 구워지고 있다.

▶▶ 정답과 해설 p.26

EXERCISE A **다음 문장을 수동태로 바꿔 쓸 때 빈칸에 알맞은 말을 쓰시오.**

1 They are preparing the exams.
➡ The exams ________ ________ ________ by them.

2 The pollution is destroying the river.
➡ The river ________ ________ ________ by the pollution.

3 My father was using the computer.
➡ The computer ________ ________ ________ by my father.

4 The children were making the paper boats.
➡ The paper boats ________ ________ ________ by the children.

5 We are not considering his career for this project.
➡ His career ________ ________ ________ ________ by us for this project.

EXERCISE B **다음 문장을 수동태로 바꿔 쓰시오.**

1 My twin sisters are cleaning the room.
➡ ____

2 The math teacher is collecting the test sheets.
➡ ____

3 He isn't making coffee at the moment.
➡ ____

4 Many volunteers were helping the African countries.
➡ ____

4 완료형 수동태

「have(has, had) + been + p.p.」

He **has opened** the window. 그는 창문을 열었다. **<현재완료>**
➡ The window **has been opened** by him. 그 창문은 그에 의해 열려졌다.

I **have used** this camera since last month. 나는 지난달부터 이 카메라를 사용해왔다. **<현재완료>**
➡ This camera **has been used** since last month by me. 이 카메라는 지난달부터 나에 의해 사용되어졌다.

The company **had sold** the item worldwide. 그 회사는 그 물건을 전 세계에 팔았었다. **<과거완료>**
➡ The item **had been sold** worldwide by the company. 그 물건은 그 회사에 의해 전 세계로 팔렸었다.

▶▶ 정답과 해설 p.26

EXERCISE A 다음 문장을 수동태로 바꿔 쓰시오.

1 Joel has suggested a new project.
➡ ______________________________

2 They haven't finished the decoration of the shop yet.
➡ ______________________________

3 The Smiths had invited me to their wedding party.
➡ ______________________________

4 The family have painted the wall.
➡ ______________________________

5 Tom and Jerry had broken the vase.
➡ ______________________________

EXERCISE B 다음 우리말과 일치하도록 주어진 단어를 사용하여 문장을 완성하시오. (필요시 형태 변화)

1 많은 고래들이 1970년대부터 일본에 의해 포획되어졌다. (catch)
➡ Many whales ________ ________ ________ by Japan since the 1970s.

2 그 면바지는 방금 나의 어머니에 의해 다림질되어졌다. (iron)
➡ The cotton pants ________ just ________ ________ by my mother.

3 피겨스케이팅의 채점제가 최근에 바뀌었다. (change)
➡ The scoring system in figure skating ________ ________ ________ recently.

5 4형식 문장의 수동태

1 4형식 문장의 수동태

4형식 문장은 간접목적어와 직접목적어를 각각 주어로 하는 두 가지 수동태가 가능하다.

He gave me a present. 그는 나에게 선물 하나를 주었다.

➡ **I was given** a present by him. 나는 그에 의해 선물 하나를 받았다. **<간접목적어가 주어>**

➡ **A present was given to** me by him. 선물 하나가 그에 의해 나에게 주어졌다. **<직접목적어가 주어>**

2 직접목적어를 수동태의 주어로 쓸 때

직접목적어를 수동태의 주어로 쓸 때 간접목적어 앞에는 to, for, of와 같은 전치사가 온다.
이때 전치사는 동사에 따라 달라진다.

to	give, hand, pass, read, sell, send, teach, write
for	make, buy, cook, get, find
of	ask

Jane bought me a chocolate cake. Jane은 나에게 초콜릿 케이크 하나를 사주었다.

➡ **A chocolate cake was bought for** me by Jane. 초콜릿 케이크 하나가 나를 위해서 Jane에 의해 구매되었다.

! 수여동사 make, buy, cook, get, read, sell, write 등은 직접목적어만을 수동태의 주어로 쓸 수 있다.

She bought him **a new watch**. 그녀는 그에게 새 손목시계를 사주었다.

➡ **A new watch** was bought **for** him by her. (○) 새 손목시계가 그를 위해서 그녀에 의해 구매되었다.

➡ ***He*** was bought **a new watch** by her. (×)

▶▶ 정답과 해설 p.26

EXERCISE A 다음 문장을 수동태로 바꿔 쓸 때 빈칸에 알맞은 말을 쓰시오.

1 Morris gave Mitch the greatest lesson.

➡ ________ was given the greatest lesson by Morris.

➡ The greatest lesson was given ________ Mitch by Morris.

2 I make my grandmother some food on Sundays.

➡ ________ ________ is made ________ my grandmother by me on Sundays.

3 Sarah bought her parents the tickets for the musical *Cats*.

➡ The tickets for the musical *Cats* ________ ________ ________ her parents by Sarah.

4 Her dad gave Ann some storybooks.

➡ Ann ________ ________ some storybooks by her dad.

➡ Some storybooks ________ ________ ________ Ann by her dad.

5 She made her daughter a pretty doll.

➡ A pretty doll ________ ________ ________ her daughter by her.

EXERCISE B 다음 문장을 수동태로 바꿔 쓸 때 빈칸에 알맞은 말을 쓰시오.

1 My mom made me the blue sweater.

➡ The blue sweater ______________________________ by my mom.

2 The referee gave Ronald the penalty.

➡ Ronald ______________________________ by the referee.

3 I passed her the salt and sugar.

➡ The salt and sugar ______________________________ by me.

4 My father will buy my brother some books.

➡ Some books ______________________________ by my father.

5 The man sold the boy the bicycle for the price of one pound.

➡ The bicycle ______________________________ for the price of one pound by the man.

EXERCISE C 다음 우리말과 일치하도록 주어진 단어를 사용하여 문장을 완성하시오. (필요시 형태 변화)

1 흰 장미 한 다발이 그에 의해 그녀에게 주어졌다. (give)

➡ A bunch of white roses ________ ________ ________ her by him.

2 많은 연애 편지가 로미오에 의해 줄리엣에게 쓰여졌다. (write)

➡ A lot of love letters ________ ________ ________ Juliet by Romeo.

3 그는 판사에 의해 2년형을 선고받았다. (give)

➡ He ________ ________ a two-year prison sentence ________ the judge.

4 특별한 선물이 Cindy의 제일 친한 친구를 위해 그녀에 의해 구입되었다. (buy)

➡ A special gift ________ ________ ________ Cindy's best friend by her.

6 5형식 문장의 수동태

5형식 문장의 목적격보어 명사, 형용사, to부정사는 수동태로 전환할 때 「be동사+p.p.」 뒤에 그대로 쓴다. 5형식 문장의 목적어만 수동태의 주어가 될 수 있고, 목적격보어는 주어가 될 수 없다.

They called him Chris. 그들은 그를 Chris라고 불렀다.
주어 동사 목적어 목적격보어

➡ He was called Chris by them. 그는 그들에 의해 Chris라고 불렸다.
be동사 + p.p. by + 행위자

① 목적어를 주어로 한다.
② 동사를 「be동사 + p.p.」의 형태로 바꾼다.
③ 5형식 문장의 목적격보어를 그대로 써준다.

We called **him** **"the Little Prince."** 우리는 그를 '어린 왕자'라고 불렀다. **<목적격보어 - 명사>**
➡ **He** was called **"the Little Prince"** by us. (○) 그는 우리에 의해 '어린 왕자'라고 불렸다.
➡ ***"The Little Prince"*** was called **him** by us. (×)

The smile makes **her relieved**. 그 미소가 그녀를 안심시킨다. **<목적격보어 - 형용사>**
➡ **She** is made **relieved** by the smile. 그녀는 그 미소에 의해 안심이 된다.

I told **him to come back** here. 나는 그에게 여기로 돌아오라고 말했다. **<목적격보어 - to부정사>**
➡ **He** was told **to come back** here by me. 그는 나에 의해 여기로 돌아오라고 들었다.

▶▶ 정답과 해설 p.26

EXERCISE A 다음 두 문장의 뜻이 같도록 빈칸에 알맞은 말을 쓰시오.

1 We named our cat "Duri."
= Our cat ________ ________ "Duri."

2 They elected Ban Ki-moon UN Secretary General in 2006.
= Ban Ki-moon ________ ________ UN Secretary General in 2006.

3 The roof was painted white by Tom.
= Tom ________ the roof ________.

4 The concert was considered successful by the audience.
= The audience ________ the concert ________.

5 I was allowed to play the computer game for 30 minutes by my mom.
= My mom ________ me ________ ________ the computer game for 30 minutes.

EXERCISE B 다음 문장을 수동태로 바꿔 쓰시오.

1 They called the girl "Little Queen."
➡ ____________________

2 People considered her a genius.
➡ ____________________

3 The company forced her to resign.
➡ ____________________

4 The fact makes the case more difficult.
➡ ____________________

5 They have chosen him the leader of the group.
➡ ____________________

6 We advised the colleagues in our office to stop smoking.
➡ ____________________

EXERCISE C 다음 우리말과 일치하도록 주어진 단어를 사용하여 문장을 완성하시오. (필요시 형태 변화)

1 그는 강원도 도지사로 당선되었다. (elect)
➡ He ________ ________ governor of Gangwondo.

2 이율곡은 신사임당에 의해 훌륭한 학자로 만들어졌다. (make)
➡ Yi Yulgok ________ ________ a great scholar ________ Sin Saimdang.

3 그 들판은 그 농부들에 의해 평평하게 만들어졌다. (make, farmers)
➡ The field ________ ________ flat ________ ________ ________.

4 그는 판사에 의해 그 음모를 계획한 것에 대해 유죄라고 판결받았다. (find, guilty)
➡ He ________ ________ ________ of planning the plot by the judge.

5 자원봉사자들은 도시 청소를 도와줄 것을 부탁받았다. (ask, help)
➡ Volunteers ________ ________ ________ ________ clean up the city.

7 지각 · 사역동사의 수동태

1 지각동사의 목적격보어가 동사원형인 경우, 수동태에서는 to부정사로 바뀐다.

She **heard** birds **sing**. 그녀는 새들이 지저귀는 것을 들었다.

➡ Birds **were heard to sing** by her. 새들이 지저귀는 것이 그녀에게 들렸다.

+ 지각동사의 목적격보어가 현재분사인 경우, 수동태 문장에 그대로 쓴다.

Tom **saw** her **playing** soccer. Tom은 그녀가 축구를 하고 있는 것을 보았다.

➡ She **was seen playing** soccer by Tom. 그녀가 축구를 하고 있는 것이 Tom에게 보였다.

2 사역동사 make의 목적격보어가 동사원형인 경우, 수동태에서는 to부정사로 바뀐다.

Mom **made** me **clean** the room. 엄마는 내가 방을 청소하게 하셨다.

➡ I **was made to clean** the room by Mom. 나는 엄마에 의해 방을 청소하게 되었다.

※ 사역동사 중에서 make만 수동태로 쓸 수 있다.

▶▶ 정답과 해설 p.26

EXERCISE A 다음 문장을 수동태로 바꿔 쓸 때 빈칸에 알맞은 말을 쓰시오.

1 We saw Peter put his hands on his face.
➡ Peter ______________________ his hands on his face.

2 They saw him explore the tropical forests on TV.
➡ He ______________________ the tropical forests by them on TV.

3 I heard the supporters shout at the players.
➡ The supporters ______________________ at the players by me.

4 She makes Ashley look like a movie star.
➡ Ashley ______________________ like a movie star by her.

5 We noticed the group have a strong voice.
➡ The group ______________________ a strong voice.

6 She made the builder fix her kitchen last month.
➡ The builder ______________________ her kitchen last month by her.

7 They saw the whales jump in the water.
➡ The whales ______________________ in the water.

EXERCISE B **다음 문장을 수동태로 바꿔 쓰시오.**

1 I saw Jack go to the coffee shop.

➡ ______________________________

2 They heard Mr. Kim ask about the accident.

➡ ______________________________

3 These issues make them think about the project.

➡ ______________________________

4 I saw my brother and sister play basketball together.

➡ ______________________________

5 The Prime Minister makes him improve safety.

➡ ______________________________

6 The CEO made you get in touch with the world.

➡ ______________________________

7 I heard the baby cry all night.

➡ ______________________________

EXERCISE C **다음 우리말과 일치하도록 빈칸에 알맞은 말을 쓰시오. (필요시 형태 변화)**

1 쥐 한 마리가 나무에 올라가고 있는 것이 그들에게 보였다. (see, climb)

➡ A mouse ________ ________ ________ a tree by them.

2 그 아이들은 그들의 부모에 의해 그들의 손을 너무 자주 씻게 된다. (make, wash)

➡ The children ________ ________ ________ ________ their hands too frequently by their parents.

3 UFO 3대가 들판에 착륙하고 있는 것이 Sam에게 목격되었다. (observe, land)

➡ Three UFOs ________ ________ ________ in the field by Sam.

4 Steve Jobs가 iPod 4에 대해 발표하는 것이 들렸다. (hear, do)

➡ Steve Jobs ________ ________ ________ a presentation about iPod 4.

5 그 문어가 우승자를 예언하고 있는 것이 들렸다. (hear, predict)

➡ The octopus ________ ________ ________ the final winner.

9 by 이외의 전치사를 쓰는 수동태

「be동사 + p.p. + with(at, in, of 등) 행위자」

보통 「by + 목적격」으로 수동태의 행위자를 나타내지만, by 이외에 다른 전치사가 쓰이는 경우도 많다.

A lot of tourists **filled** Paris. 많은 관광객들이 파리를 채웠다.

➡ Paris **was filled with** a lot of tourists. 파리는 많은 관광객들로 가득 찼다.

be covered with	~으로 덮여 있다	be satisfied with	~에 만족하다
be pleased with	~에 기뻐하다	be disappointed with	~에 실망하다
be filled with	~으로 가득 차다	be surprised at	~에 놀라다
be interested in	~에 관심이 있다	be worried about	~에 대해 걱정하다
be made of	~으로 만들어지다 (물리적 변화)	be made from	~으로 만들어지다 (화학적 변화)
be tired of	~에 싫증나다	be tired from(with)	~으로 피곤하다
be known as	~로(서) 알려지다 (자격)	be known for	~으로 알려지다 (이유)
be known to	~에게 알려지다 (대상)	be made up of	~으로 구성되다

* be made of는 '나무로 만든 책상'처럼 재료의 형태가 남아있는 물리적 변화를 나타낼 때 쓰며, be made from은 '우유로 만든 치즈'처럼 재료의 성질이 변해 형태가 남아있지 않은 화학적 변화를 나타낼 때 쓴다.

▶▶ 정답과 해설 p.27

EXERCISE A 다음 빈칸에 알맞은 말을 <보기>에서 골라 문장을 완성하시오.

<보기>
at in about with of for

1 I was surprised _________ his powerful speech.

2 We are interested _________ the green campaign.

3 People are pleased _________ the street performance in Swiss.

4 They are not worried _________ air pollution.

5 This table is made _________ wood.

6 The roof is covered _________ snow.

7 She is satisfied _________ his new way of working.

8 They are known _________ their kindness.

EXERCISE B **다음 문장을 수동태로 바꿔 쓰시오.**

1 The history of South Africa interested me.

➡ ______________________________

2 Starfish covered the beach.

➡ ______________________________

3 The news pleased all the classmates.

➡ ______________________________

4 The storm and thunder worry me.

➡ ______________________________

5 The new book will satisfy the readers.

➡ ______________________________

6 The video on YouTube might interest you.

➡ ______________________________

EXERCISE C **다음 우리말과 일치하도록 주어진 단어를 사용하여 빈칸에 알맞은 말을 쓰시오. (필요시 형태 변화)**

1 그는 그 결과에 놀랐다. (surprise)

➡ He ________ ________ ________ the result.

2 고객들은 훌륭한 서비스에 만족한다. (satisfy)

➡ Customers ________ ________ ________ the great service.

3 나는 살찌는 것에 대해 몹시 걱정한다. (worry)

➡ I'm deeply ________ ________ gaining weight.

4 우리 팀은 심판의 판정에 실망했다. (disappoint)

➡ Our team ________ ________ ________ the referee's decision.

5 그들은 멸종 동물들에 관심이 있다. (interest)

➡ They ________ ________ ________ extinct animals.

6 지구의 71%가 물로 덮여 있다. (cover)

➡ 71% of the earth ________ ________ ________ water.

7 그 CD는 많은 유명한 곡으로 가득 차 있다. (fill)

➡ The CD ________ ________ ________ lots of well-known songs.

10 목적어가 절인 경우의 수동태

다음 동사들의 목적어가 that절인 경우 두 가지 수동태로 바꿔 쓸 수 있다.

believe	report	think	consider	say

① 가주어 It을 문두에 놓고 that절을 뒤로 보내서 It is ... that ~ 형태의 수동태를 만들 수 있다.

② that절의 주어를 전체 문장의 주어로 하여 수동태를 만들 수 있다. 이때 that절의 동사는 to부정사로 바뀐다.

They say that the family comes from Poland. 그들은 그 가족이 폴란드 출신이라고 말한다.

➡ **It is said that** the family comes from Poland. 그 가족은 폴란드 출신이라고 한다.

➡ The family **is said to come** from Poland.

▶▶ 정답과 해설 p. 27

EXERCISE A 다음 두 문장의 뜻이 같도록 빈칸에 알맞은 말을 쓰시오.

1 They say that he enjoys dancing and tennis.
= It ________ ________ that he enjoys dancing and tennis.

2 They said that the car was in a good condition.
= It ________ ________ that the car was in a good condition.

3 They believed that the story was written by the king.
= It ________ ________ that the story was written by the king.

4 They believed that the wolf escaped from a zoo.
= ________ ________ was believed ________ ________ from a zoo.

5 It was said that the woman was wearing sunglasses.
= ________ ________ was said ________ ________ wearing sunglasses.

EXERCISE B 다음 문장을 주어진 단어로 시작하는 수동태로 바꿔 쓰시오.

1 They say that Susan is a passionate soccer fan.
➡ It ______________________________ a passionate soccer fan.
➡ Susan ______________________________ a passionate soccer fan.

2 They said that Bill Gates donated much money.

➡ It ________________________________ much money.

➡ Bill Gates ________________________________ much money.

3 They thought that only 10 soldiers survived the battle.

➡ It ________________________________ the battle.

➡ Only 10 soldiers ________________________________ the battle.

4 They believe that the robbers have fled from the city.

➡ It ________________________________ from the city.

➡ The robbers ________________________________ from the city.

5 They think that the album has sold more than 10 million units worldwide.

➡ It ________________________________ more than 10 million units worldwide.

➡ The album ________________________________ more than 10 million units worldwide.

EXERCISE C **다음 우리말과 일치하도록 주어진 단어를 사용하여 빈칸에 알맞은 말을 쓰시오. (필요시 형태 변화)**

1 한국인들은 그들의 근면성으로 유명하다고 한다. (It, say)

➡ ________ ________ ________ ________ Koreans are famous for their diligence.

2 DHA는 두뇌 발달에 중요한 것으로 여겨진다. (It, think)

➡ ________ ________ ________ ________ DHA is important for brain development.

3 대부분의 은하계는 매우 거대한 블랙홀을 가지고 있다고 여겨진다. (think, contain)

➡ Most galaxies ________ ________ ________ ________ extremely large black holes.

4 올해 태어난 사람들이 창의력이 있고 관대하다고 한다. (It, say)

➡ ________ ________ ________ ________ people born in this year are creative and generous.

5 옷과 보석을 만드는 것과 같은 취미들이 정말 인기가 있다고 한다. (say, be)

➡ Hobbies like making clothes and jewelry ________ ________ ________ ________ really popular.

6 Amanda는 일을 구하기 위해 런던으로 향하고 있다고 믿어졌다. (believe, be)

➡ Amanda ________ ________ ________ ________ heading to London to find work.

Chapter 06
수동태

학교 시험 대비 문제

맞힌 개수	
선택형	_____ / 34
서술형	_____ / 11

▶▶ 정답과 해설 p.28

01 다음 문장을 수동태로 바꿔 쓸 때 빈칸에 알맞은 것은?

• He did not write the essay.
➡ The essay ____________ by him.

① is not written
② has not written
③ was not written
④ was not writing
⑤ did not written

02 다음 빈칸에 들어갈 말이 바르게 짝지어진 것은?

• Today people ________ their cars too often.
• Ginger ________ in making tea.

① use — is using
② use — is used
③ are using — uses
④ are used — uses
⑤ are used — is used

03 다음 밑줄 친 부분 중 생략할 수 <u>없는</u> 것은?

① He is respected <u>by everyone</u>.
② English is spoken in Canada <u>by people</u>.
③ His bag was taken <u>by someone</u> in the library.
④ The window was broken in the morning <u>by somebody</u>.
⑤ The bridge was built 100 years ago <u>by a British company</u>.

04 다음 빈칸에 들어갈 말로 알맞은 것은?

The birds ____________ into the sky this morning by him.

① saw to fly
② were saw fly
③ was seen fly
④ is seen to fly
⑤ were seen to fly

[05-06] 다음 문장을 수동태로 바르게 바꿔 쓴 것을 고르시오.

05

Jane returned the pen in the afternoon.

① Jane has returned the pen in the afternoon.
② The pen is returned by Jane in the afternoon.
③ Jane was returned by the pen in the afternoon.
④ The pen was returned by Jane in the afternoon.
⑤ The pen was returning by Jane in the afternoon.

06

Lincoln gave him the chance.

① He is given the chance by Lincoln.
② He was given the chance by Lincoln.
③ The chance was given for him by Lincoln.
④ The chance is given to him by Lincoln.
⑤ He was given to the chance by Lincoln.

고난도

07 다음 중 밑줄 친 부분이 어법상 틀린 것은?

① The shop is run by my mom.
② Eggs are used to make bread.
③ A lot of fish are raised in the pond.
④ The farmer was bought a goat by her.
⑤ The photo was taken in the 19th century.

고난도

08 다음 중 수동태로 바꿔 쓸 수 없는 것을 모두 고른 것은?

ⓐ I have a nice bike.
ⓑ The boy bought a yellow bicycle.
ⓒ The earthquake destroyed the city.
ⓓ The weather changes every day.

① ⓐ, ⓑ
② ⓐ, ⓓ
③ ⓐ, ⓑ, ⓒ
④ ⓑ, ⓒ, ⓓ
⑤ ⓐ, ⓑ, ⓒ, ⓓ

고난도

09 다음 문장을 수동태로 바르게 바꿔 쓴 것은?

People say that love always wins.

① Love is said always winning.
② Love is saying to always win.
③ It says that love always wins.
④ It is said that love always wins.
⑤ People are said that love always wins.

10 다음 빈칸에 들어갈 말로 알맞지 않은 것은?

The village is known for ________.

① the oldest castle
② the tomato festival
③ its beautiful scenery
④ everyone in Europe
⑤ their kindness to tourists

11 다음 중 밑줄 친 부분을 주어로 수동태를 만들 수 없는 것은?

① Tony told Jane his address.
② Mr. Jackson teaches us music.
③ Ellen gave her friend some candy.
④ I will ask my teacher the question.
⑤ Jane makes her brother a model plane.

12 다음 문장을 수동태로 바꿔 쓸 때 빈칸에 알맞은 것은?

• The judge found him guilty.
➡ He __________ guilty by the judge.

① is found ② was found
③ were found ④ has been found
⑤ has been founding

13 다음 문장을 수동태로 바르게 바꿔 쓴 것은?

He looked at the Egyptian statue.

① The Egyptian statue is looked at him.
② The Egyptian statue was looked at him.
③ The Egyptian statue was looked by him.
④ The Egyptian statue is looked at by him.
⑤ The Egyptian statue was looked at by him.

14 다음 빈칸에 들어갈 말이 바르게 짝지어진 것은?

• We are worried __________ the future.
• The table is made __________ the oak tree.

① about — of ② with — from
③ from — from ④ about — as
⑤ as — for

15 다음 빈칸에 들어갈 말이 〈보기〉와 같은 것은?

〈보기〉
The tower __________ built in 1500.

① The river __________ been polluted lately.
② The rules must __________ obeyed by students.
③ Used paper and bottles can __________ recycled.
④ Mike __________ being punished by his father then.
⑤ The cars __________ now being repaired by David.

16 다음 중 어법상 올바른 것은?

① The problem has just been solving.
② The timetable has just been changed.
③ The town has destroyed by the hurricane.
④ He has been taken this medicine for a month.
⑤ This house has used as Mr. Kim's office since last year.

17 다음 문장을 수동태로 바르게 바꿔 쓴 것은?

We should protect elephants from hunters.

① Elephants should protect us by hunters.
② Elephants should protect hunters by us.
③ Hunters are being protected by elephants.
④ Elephants should be protected from hunters.
⑤ Elephants should have protected from hunters.

고난도

18 다음 빈칸에 들어갈 말이 바르게 짝지어진 것은?

> • He is looked up ________ by his family.
> • Poor people must not be looked down ________ by rich people.

① to — over ② at — in
③ with — on ④ after — of
⑤ to — on

[19-20] 다음 빈칸에 들어갈 말로 알맞은 것을 고르시오.

19

> • 금메달은 신지애에 의해 획득되었다.
> ➡ The gold medal ________ by Sin Jiae.

① wins ② won
③ has won ④ is winning
⑤ was won

20

> • 그녀는 규칙적으로 식사를 하라고 의사에 의해 충고받았다.
> ➡ She ________ meals regularly by the doctor.

① advised to have
② was advised have
③ advised to be had
④ was advised having
⑤ was advised to have

[21-22] 다음 문장을 수동태로 바꿔 쓸 때 빈칸에 들어갈 말로 알맞은 것을 고르시오.

고난도

21

> • They thought that everyone had the ability.
> ➡ ________ that everyone had the ability.

① It is thought
② It was thought
③ They are thought
④ They were thought
⑤ Everyone was thought

22

> • My uncle has helped the poor since 2010.
> ➡ The poor ________ by my uncle since 2010.

① have helped ② were helped
③ have been helped ④ were been helped
⑤ have been helping

23 다음 빈칸에 들어갈 말이 나머지 넷과 <u>다른</u> 것은?

① He is interested ________ religion.
② The roof is covered ________ snow.
③ We are pleased ________ his comeback.
④ The garden is filled ________ white roses.
⑤ The player was satisfied ________ the score.

24 다음 밑줄 친 부분을 묻는 의문문으로 알맞은 것은?

The table was carried <u>by Thomas and his father</u>.

① Whom did the table carry?
② Who has carried the table?
③ Who was the table carried?
④ By whom was the table carried?
⑤ By whom was carried the table?

25 다음 빈칸에 들어갈 말로 알맞은 것은?

• 고래가 바다에서 잡히고 있다. ➡ Whales ______________ in the ocean.

① was caught ② have caught
③ are catching ④ had been caught
⑤ are being caught

26 다음 문장을 수동태로 바르게 바꿔 쓴 것은?

We elected Mr. Gates our chairman.

① Mr. Gates was elected by our chairman.
② Mr. Gates was elected our chairman by us.
③ Our chairman was elected us by Mr. Gates.
④ Our chairman was elected Mr. Gates by us.
⑤ We were elected our chairman by Mr. Gates.

27 다음 우리말을 영어로 바르게 옮긴 것은?

초인종이 울리는 것이 내게 들렸다.

① The door bell is heard ring by me.
② The door bell heard to ring by me.
③ The door bell was heard ring by me.
④ The door bell is heard to ring by me.
⑤ The door bell was heard ringing by me.

28 다음 빈칸에 들어갈 말로 알맞은 것은?

• 몇 명의 천재들은 과거에 비웃음을 받았다. ➡ A few geniuses ______________ in the past.

① was laugh ② was looked
③ were looked at ④ were laughed at
⑤ were looked after

29 다음 밑줄 친 부분의 쓰임이 <u>어색한</u> 것은?

① The sweater <u>is made of</u> wool.
② The city <u>is known for</u> its hot springs.
③ Robert <u>is pleased with</u> her email.
④ Jack's class <u>is made up of</u> 20 students.
⑤ The island <u>is filled of</u> wonderful things.

고난도

30 다음 중 어법상 틀린 것은?

① The book was published in 2010.
② *Snow White* is read in a lot of languages.
③ The school bus was driven by Mr. Redford.
④ Baseball is played almost all over the world.
⑤ The company was developed the new smart phone.

31 다음 중 수동태로 바르게 바꿔 쓴 것은?

① People call the woman Ms. White.
➡ Ms. White is called the woman.
② They chose Jack chairman.
➡ Chairman was chosen by Jack.
③ The news made her unhappy.
➡ She was made unhappy by the news.
④ The manager made him a famous actor.
➡ He made the manager a famous actor.
⑤ The magazine asks readers to email their questions.
➡ Readers are asked email their questions by the magazine.

32 다음 문장을 수동태로 바르게 바꿔 쓴 것은?

The boy was reading a comic book.

① A comic book was been read by the boy.
② A comic book was being read by the boy.
③ A comic book had been read by the boy.
④ A comic book was been reading by the boy.
⑤ A comic book has being reading by the boy.

33 다음 빈칸에 들어갈 말로 알맞은 것은?

• We should keep milk and meat in the refrigerator. = Milk and meat ______________ in the refrigerator.

① are keep
② should keep
③ are should keep
④ should be kept
⑤ should keep been

34 다음 빈칸에 들어갈 말이 바르게 짝지어진 것은?

• My father's shirts have ________ ironed by my mother. • The decision will ________ made by children. • My favorite song was ________ played in the street.

① being — be — be
② being — been — been
③ being — be — been
④ been — been — being
⑤ been — be — being

서술형

고난도

35 다음 우리말과 일치하도록 어법상 틀린 부분을 찾아 바르게 바꿔 쓰시오.

• 그 아기는 방과 후에 Jenny에 의해 돌보아진다.
➡ The baby is taken care by Jenny after school.

__________ ➡ __________

36 다음 밑줄 친 부분을 어법상 바르게 고쳐 쓰시오.

• It was said that the temperature of the Earth rose.
➡ The temperature of the Earth was said rising.

37 다음 문장을 수동태로 바꿔 쓸 때 빈칸에 알맞은 말을 쓰시오.

• I saw the boy going to the cinema.
➡ The boy was seen __________ to the cinema by me.

38 다음 우리말과 일치하도록 주어진 어구를 사용하여 문장을 완성하시오. (필요시 형태 변화)

• James는 캘리포니아에서 고모에 의해 키워졌다. (bring up)
➡ James __________ __________ __________ by his aunt in California.

39 다음 문장을 수동태로 바꿔 쓸 때 빈칸에 알맞은 말을 쓰시오.

• I will write my parents a letter of thanks.
➡ A letter of thanks __________ __________ __________ __________ my parents by me.

40 다음 우리말과 일치하도록 빈칸에 알맞은 말을 쓰시오.

• 한국 사람들은 매우 성실하다고 한다.
➡ __________ __________ __________ __________ Korean people are very diligent.

[41-43] 다음 표를 보고, 두 항목을 연결하여 <보기>와 같이 문장을 쓰시오.

Helen Keller (make / a great person)	Anne Sullivan
41 *Romeo and Juliet* (write)	Shakespeare
42 the *Sunflowers* (draw)	Van Gogh
43 the ozone layer (destroy)	carbon dioxide

<보기>

Helen Keller was made a great person by Anne Sullivan.

41 ______________________

42 ______________________

43 ______________________

[44-45] 다음 그림을 보고, 괄호 안에 주어진 단어를 사용하여 <보기>와 같이 문장을 완성하시오.

<보기>

(win)

Name : Kim Yuna

The gold medal *was won by Kim Yuna* at the Winter Olympics.

44

(call)

Name: Jack

Jack ______________________ when he was a middle school student.

45

(teach)

Name : Ms. Alice

English ______________________ every Monday.

Chapter

07

대명사

1 재귀대명사
2 부정대명사 one ~ the other ... 등
3 부정대명사 all / none / each / every 등
4 부정대명사 somebody / anything 등
■ 학교 시험 대비 문제

1 재귀대명사

1 재귀 용법

문장의 주어가 가리키는 대상이 동사나 전치사의 목적어와 동일할 때 재귀대명사를 사용하며, 생략이 불가능하다.

I saw **myself** in the mirror. 나는 거울 속에서 내 자신을 봤다.
She laughed at **herself**. 그녀는 자신을 비웃었다.

2 강조 용법

주어 또는 목적어와 동격으로 쓰여 의미를 강조하며, 생략이 가능하다. 이때 재귀대명사는 강조하는 대상 바로 뒤에 오거나 문장 끝에 올 수 있다.

Jessica **(herself)** came back. (바로) Jessica가 돌아왔다.
He had painted the picture **(himself)**. 그는 그 그림을 (직접) 그렸었다.

3 관용 표현

by oneself	혼자, 홀로 (= alone) * **by itself 저절로, 자동으로 (= automatically)**
for oneself	혼자 힘으로, 스스로 (= independently, without other's help)
in itself	그 자체가, 본질적으로 (= naturally, by nature)
of itself	자연히, 자발적으로 (= spontaneously)
help oneself to	~을 마음껏 먹다
enjoy oneself	즐겁게 보내다 (= have a good time)
talk to oneself	혼잣말을 하다
between ourselves	우리끼리 얘기지만 (= in confidence)

▶▶ 정답과 해설 p.30

EXERCISE A 다음 문장의 빈칸에 알맞은 재귀대명사를 쓰시오.

1 I ______________ wouldn't do such a stupid thing.

2 She was very careful not to hurt ______________.

3 The first thing for you to do is to know ______________.

4 The boy tried to solve the problem for ______________.

5 Help ______________ to the dishes.

6 The old man lives in that remote house by ___________.

7 He looks at ___________ in the mirror every morning.

8 She wrote the novel ___________.

9 Let me introduce ___________ to you.

10 Did you enjoy ___________ at the party?

11 The door opened by ___________.

12 I will use all of my efforts to develop ___________.

EXERCISE B 다음 우리말과 일치하도록 주어진 단어 및 어구를 배열하여 문장을 완성하시오.

1 우리는 파티에서 과일을 마음껏 먹었다. (fruit, ourselves, helped, to)
➡ We ______________________________ at the party.

2 Alice와 Doris는 직접 그 스티커들을 모았다. (themselves, collected, the stickers)
➡ Alice and Doris ______________________________.

3 Emma, 너는 그 사진을 스스로 찍었니? (for, the photo, take, yourself, did, you)
➡ Emma, ______________________________?

4 그는 학생들이 스스로 생각하게 했다. (themselves, think, for)
➡ He made students ______________________________.

5 재활용 과정 그 자체가 환경에 도움이 됩니까? (itself, in, helpful)
➡ Is the recycling process ______________________________ to the environment?

6 우리 어머니는 종종 혼잣말을 하신다. (to, often, herself, talks)
➡ My mother ______________________________.

7 우리끼리 얘기지만, 그는 그녀와 정말로 결혼하고 싶어 한다. (ourselves, Between)
➡ ______________________________, he really wants to marry her.

8 Dave는 혼자 힘으로 그 연을 만들었다. (himself, for, the kite)
➡ Dave made ______________________________.

2 부정대명사 one ~ the other ... 등

one : (불특정한) 하나 / another : 또 다른 하나 / the other : 나머지 하나 / some : 전체 중 일부
the others : 나머지 모두 / others : 다른 일부 / other + 복수명사 : 다른 ~것들

one ~ the other ... (둘 중) 하나는 ~, 나머지 하나는 …

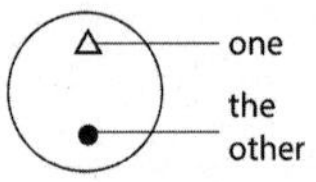

He has two books in his bag. **One** is on economics and **the other** is on literature. 그는 가방에 책이 두 권 있다. 한 권은 경제학에 관한 것이고, 다른 한 권은 문학에 관한 것이다.

one ~ another ... the other - (셋 중) 하나는 ~, 또 다른 하나는 …, 나머지 하나는 -

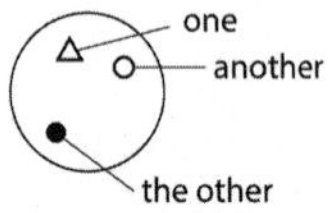

They have three sons. **One** is a middle school student, **another** is a university student, and **the other** is a soldier. 그들은 아들이 세 명 있다. 한 명은 중학생이고, 다른 한 명은 대학생이고, 나머지 한 명은 군인이다.

one ~ another ... (셋 이상에서) 하나는 ~, 다른 하나는 …

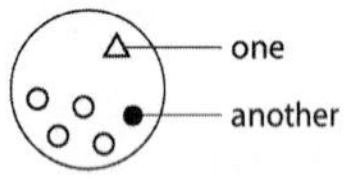

A How about this shirt? 이 셔츠 어때요?
B I don't like this **one**. Show me **another**.
이것은 마음에 들지 않아요. 다른 것을 보여주세요.

one ~ the others ... (정해진 범위 안에서) 하나는 ~, 나머지는 모두 …

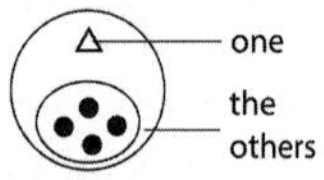

I went shopping with five of my friends. **One** bought a book for a present, but **the others** didn't decide what to buy. 나는 친구 다섯 명과 함께 쇼핑을 갔다. 한 명은 선물로 책 한 권을 샀지만, 나머지 친구들은 모두 무엇을 살지 결정하지 못했다.

some ~ the others ... (정해진 범위 안에서) 몇몇은 ~, 나머지는 모두 …

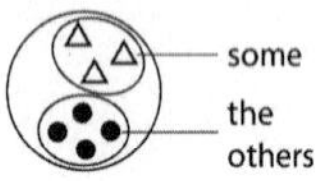

There are 30 students in my class. **Some** of them would like to go to the mountains for a picnic and **the others** want to stay at home. 우리 반에는 30명의 학생이 있다. 그들 중 몇몇은 소풍으로 산에 가고 싶어 하고 나머지는 모두 집에 있기를 원한다.

some ~ others ... (정해지지 않은 다수 중에서) 몇몇은 ~, 다른 일부는 …

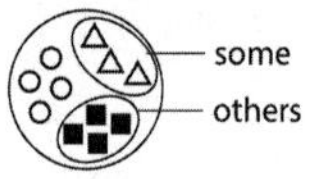

You can see a lot of different shapes on the page. **Some** are triangles and **others** are squares. 너는 그 페이지에서 다양한 모양들을 많이 볼 수 있다. 몇 개는 삼각형이고 몇 개는 사각형이다.

▶▶ 정답과 해설 p.30

EXERCISE A 다음 빈칸에 알맞은 것을 <보기>에서 골라 문장을 완성하시오. (대·소문자 변화 가능)

〈보기〉

one   another   others   the other   the others

1 Here are four suitcases, but I can carry only two. Please bring ____________.

2 The twins are alike, so it is difficult to tell one from ______________.

3 ______________ of them is a girl and the others are all boys.

4 Some writers are greater than ______________.

5 I can't go skiing. For one thing I'm busy; for ______________ I have no money.

6 They have two little daughters: ______________ is a baby and the other is a girl of nine.

7 Children should be taught how to get along with ______________.

EXERCISE B 다음 문장에서 어법상 틀린 부분을 찾아 바르게 고쳐 쓰시오.

1 Try to be kind to other.

2 I don't like this scarf. Show me the other.

3 I have two cats: one is black and another is white.

4 Some people like apples and other like oranges.

5 He has four sons. One is a teacher, another is a doctor, and others are drivers.

6 Between these two, it is difficult to tell one from another.

7 I have ten apples. One is blue and the other are red.

EXERCISE C 다음 우리말과 일치하도록 주어진 단어를 배열하여 문장을 완성하시오.

1 그에게는 개 두 마리가 있다. 한 마리는 흰색이고 다른 한 마리는 검은색이다.
(the, black, One, is, white, and, is, other)
➡ He has two dogs. ____

2 연필 세 자루가 있다. 한 자루는 내 것이고 나머지는 모두 내 동생 것이다.
(others, my, One, is, are, mine, brother's, and, the)
➡ There are three pencils. ______________________________________

3 어떤 소년들은 축구를 좋아하지만 어떤 소년들은 그것을 좋아하지 않는다.
(Some, boys, but, don't, it, like, soccer, others, like)
➡ ____

3 부정대명사 all / none / each / every 등

all (of) 모두 (all (of) + 단수명사 → 단수 취급) (all (of) + 복수명사 → 복수 취급)	**All of her salary goes** to clothes. 그녀의 월급은 모두 옷에 쓰인다. **All the members were** against his idea. 모든 회원들이 그의 생각에 반대했다.
none (of) 하나도(누구도) ~없다(않다) (none (of) + 단수명사 → 단수 취급) (none (of) + 복수명사 → 단수/복수 취급)	**None of the information is** useful to me. 그 정보는 내게 하나도 쓸모가 없다. **None of my friends is(are)** here yet. 내 친구들은 아직 아무도 여기에 오지 않았다.
each 각자 (each + 단수명사 → 단수 취급)	**Each answer is** worth 20 points. 각각의 정답은 20점이다.
each of 각자 (each of + 복수명사 → 단수 취급)	**Each of the students has** to pay for the entrance ticket. 그 학생들 각자 입장권을 사야 한다.
every 모든 (every + 단수명사 → 단수 취급)	**Every boy has** his own desk. 모든 소년이 각자 자신의 책상을 가지고 있다. **＊「every + 기수사 + 복수명사」: ~마다 ex) every two weeks 2주마다**
both 둘 다 (복수 취급)	**Both** (of the) books **are** full of funny stories. (그) 책 두 권 모두 재미있는 이야기로 가득 차 있다.
either 둘 중 어느 쪽 하나 (단수 취급)	**Either** of the books **is** mine. 그 책들 중 한 권은 내 것이다.
neither 둘 중 어느 쪽도 아닌 (단수 취급)	**Neither** of the books **is** interesting. 그 책들 중 어느 것도 재미있지 않다.

▶▶ 정답과 해설 p.31

EXERCISE A 다음 괄호 안에서 옳은 것을 고르시오.

1 Every student [like / likes] to be challenged.

2 All of the material in this book [is / are] interesting.

3 Either of the two sisters [is / are] willing to pay for the gift.

4 Each country [has / have] its own history and tradition.

5 All of my brothers [is / are] tall.

6 Neither of the two teams [deserve / deserves] to play in the finals.

7 Both of the boys [was / were] nice to me.

8 Either of the pencils [is / are] mine.

9 Each of the monkeys in the cage [play / plays] to the audience.

10 Neither of the workers in the office [are / is] busy.

11 All of these shops [was / were] opened on weekends.

EXERCISE B 다음 문장에서 어법상 틀린 부분을 찾아 바르게 고쳐 쓰시오.

1 Both of them knows me very well.

2 Not all water are good enough to drink.

3 Every girl are working hard.

4 All of my family leave home at seven.

5 I don't like neither of these shoes.

6 All of the rocks in the bag is worthless.

7 All of the people was disgusted with the media.

8 None of the money were spent to buy books.

EXERCISE C 다음 우리말과 일치하도록 주어진 단어 및 어구를 배열하여 문장을 완성하시오.

1 모든 규칙에는 예외가 있다. (has, rule, its, Every)
➡ ______________________ exceptions.

2 그는 차를 두 대 가지고 있는데 어느 것도 작동되지 않는다. (of, works, them, neither)
➡ He has two cars, but ______________________.

3 그 재킷들은 하나도 나한테 맞지 않아서 구입하지 않았다. (of, None, fitted, the, jackets)
➡ ______________________ me, so I didn't buy one.

4 모든 어린이들은 한국에서 법에 의해 학교에 가야 한다. (children, to school, go, All, must)
➡ ______________________ in Korea by law.

5 내 친구와 나 둘 다 너를 그곳에서 봐서 놀랐다. (my friend, I, Both, were, and, surprised)
➡ ______________________ to see you there.

4 부정대명사 somebody / anything 등

-body, -one	• 사람을 대신함. 형용사(구)가 수식할 때는 뒤에서 수식함. **Everybody** has the right to talk about his own thought. 모두가 자신의 생각을 말할 권리가 있다.
-thing	• 사물을 대신함. 형용사(구)가 수식할 때는 뒤에서 수식함. Have I said **something** wrong? 내가 뭔가 잘못 말했니? I have **nothing** to do with the terrible accident. 나는 그 끔찍한 사건과 아무 관련이 없다. * **have nothing to do with ~와 아무 관련이 없다**
some-	• 긍정문, 긍정의 답을 기대하거나 권유를 나타내는 의문문에 사용 (something, somebody, someone, somewhere) Any doctor would try to say **something** to please his patients. 어떤 의사라도 환자를 기쁘게 할 무언가를 말하려고 할 것이다. **〈긍정문〉** Would you like **something** to drink? 마실 것을 좀 드릴까요? **〈권유문〉**
any-	• 부정문, 의문문, 조건문에 사용 (anything, anybody, anyone, anywhere) I don't know **anything** about it. 나는 그것에 대해 아무것도 모른다. **〈부정문〉** Do you have **anything** to ask? 질문할 것이 있니? **〈의문문〉** If **anybody** comes earlier than expected, tell him I'll be here soon. 누군가 예상보다 일찍 온다면, 그에게 내가 곧 여기에 올 거라고 말해줘. **〈조건문〉**

▶▶ 정답과 해설 p. 31

EXERCISE A 다음 빈칸에 알맞은 것을 〈보기〉에서 골라 문장을 완성하시오. (대 · 소문자 변화 가능)

〈보기〉
something somewhere somebody anything anywhere

1 ______________ phoned me today, but he didn't tell me his name.

2 She didn't say ______________ about her job when I spoke to her.

3 I'm sure you'll find it ______________ if you keep looking for it.

4 Can I speak to you for a moment? I want to discuss ______________ with you.

5 **A** Have you seen my handbag ______________?
B Yes, I think it's somewhere in the living room.

6 ______________ took my children to the amusement park.

7 Laura was hiding ______________ in her backpack.

8 I saw your brother, who didn't say ______________ to me.

Chapter 07
대명사

학교 시험 대비 문제

맞힌 개수	
선택형	_____ / 23
서술형	_____ / 11

▶▶ 정답과 해설 p.31

01 다음 빈칸에 들어갈 말로 알맞은 것은?

> Bob lost his job. It's going to be difficult for him to find ________ job.

① other's ② other ③ another
④ the other ⑤ the another

02 다음 문장에서 wrong이 들어갈 알맞은 곳은?

> I (①) realized (②) that I (③) was doing (④) something (⑤).

[03-05] 다음 빈칸에 들어갈 말로 알맞은 것을 고르시오.

고난도
03

> Each of the ________________ own cage.

① lion in the zoo has its
② lions in the zoo has its
③ lion in the zoo have their
④ lions in the zoo has their
⑤ lions in the zoo have their

04

> All of the athletes who took part in the international games should be very proud of ____________.

① them ② himself
③ oneself ④ themselves
⑤ yourselves

05

> There are two ways of mass communication.
> The newspaper is one.
> Television is ____________.

① other ② the other
③ another ④ the others
⑤ second

06 다음 중 어법상 틀린 것은?

① Each of the girls is beautiful.
② Both of the boys is believed to study hard.
③ I don't like this one. Can you show me another?
④ Every student studies hard to prepare for the midterm.
⑤ All of the students are quite busy doing their homework.

07 다음 빈칸에 들어갈 말이 바르게 짝지어진 것은?

> There are many people in this restaurant. ________ are waiting in line, and ________ are having their meals.

① Ones — others
② Some — others
③ Some — the other
④ One — the other
⑤ Some — another

고난도

08 다음 중 어법상 올바른 것은?

① Both books is full of sad stories.
② You need to answer each questions.
③ Some people tries to climb high mountains.
④ Every man wants to have a break from work.
⑤ Each one have his or her own right to express their opinion.

09 다음 중 밑줄 친 부분의 쓰임이 나머지 넷과 <u>다른</u> 것은?

① He made this chair <u>himself</u>.
② She fell down and hurt <u>herself</u>.
③ Luckily they could seat <u>themselves</u>.
④ We started to introduce <u>ourselves</u> to the crowd.
⑤ Sarah looks at <u>herself</u> in the mirror every morning.

10 다음 빈칸에 들어갈 말이 바르게 짝지어진 것은?

> There are six foreign students in our class. ________ of them are Japanese and ________ are British.

① One — the other
② One — another
③ One — the others
④ Some — the other
⑤ Some — the others

11 다음 중 밑줄 친 부분이 어법상 <u>틀린</u> 것은?

① I don't like this skirt. Show me <u>another</u>.
② Here are four books. One is mine and <u>others</u> are Mary's.
③ She has many friends. Some are kind and <u>others</u> are unkind.
④ There are two pens. One is mine and <u>the other</u> is my sister's.
⑤ She bought three notebooks. One is red, <u>another</u> is black, and the other is blue.

12 다음 빈칸에 들어갈 말로 알맞은 것은?

> The national soccer team has done well this year. All of members ________ very hard.

① is
② does
③ has tried
④ have tried
⑤ has been tried

13 다음 빈칸에 들어갈 말이 바르게 짝지어진 것은?

• I'm proud of ________.
• Don't worry about the dogs. We can take care of them ________.

① me — us
② myself — us
③ me — ourselves
④ myself — ourselves
⑤ ourselves — ourselves

14 다음 중 밑줄 친 부분을 생략할 수 있는 것은?

① Can he find the way out by himself?
② Does she sometimes talk to herself?
③ Sue herself doesn't think she'll be rich.
④ We'll keep this rumor between ourselves.
⑤ Some people are so selfish that they only think of themselves.

고난도
15 다음 중 어법상 틀린 것은?

① There were four boys. One of the boys stayed inside and the others went out.
② The white one is bigger and the black one is smaller.
③ Some students want to play basketball, and the other wants to play baseball.
④ She has two daughters. One has brown hair, and the other has black hair.
⑤ He has three pets. One is a dog, another is a cat, and the other is a rabbit.

16 다음 밑줄 친 부분이 어법상 틀린 것은?

She ① has been to three countries. ② One is England, ③ other is France, ④ and ⑤ the other is Turkey.

[17-18] 다음 중 밑줄 친 부분의 쓰임이 나머지 넷과 다른 것을 고르시오.

17

① Take care of yourselves during the vacation.
② Fortunately he didn't hurt himself badly falling down.
③ The movie itself isn't very impressive but I like the music.
④ Be careful because the pan is very hot. You may hurt yourself.
⑤ She got out of the bathtub and dried herself with a towel.

18

① She baked the cake herself.
② I looked at myself in the mirror.
③ Did you enjoy yourself at the party?
④ Can you imagine yourself in ten years?
⑤ He dropped a boiling teapot and hurt himself.

19 다음 빈칸에 들어갈 말이 바르게 짝지어진 것은?

I got two presents. ________ was from my mom, ________ was from my friend.

① One — another ② Some — two
③ Some — others ④ One — the other
⑤ One — the others

고난도

20 다음 괄호 안에 주어진 동사의 형태가 알맞은 것끼리 짝지어진 것은?

• Each of the children (have) their own dream. • All of these tomatoes (look) fresh.

① have — look ② has — look
③ have — looks ④ has — looks
⑤ have — are looking

21 다음 빈칸에 들어갈 말이 바르게 짝지어진 것은?

• She couldn't see ________ in the dark. • Before you say ________, you have to think it over.

① anything — anything
② everything — nothing
③ something — anything
④ anything — something
⑤ something — something

22 다음 우리말을 영어로 바르게 옮긴 것은?

John은 그곳에 혼자 가려고 했다.

① John tried to go there in himself.
② John tried to go there of himself.
③ John tried to go there by himself.
④ John tried to go there with himself.
⑤ John tried to go there from himself.

23 다음 빈칸에 들어갈 말로 알맞지 않은 것은?

________________ is going to take part in the marathon.

① Each student
② Both of the students
③ Each of the students
④ Neither of the students
⑤ Every student in this class

서술형

24 다음 중 어법상 틀린 부분을 찾아 바르게 고쳐 쓰시오.

When we go on holiday, we always enjoy themselves.

________________ ➡ ________________

[25-27] 다음 빈칸에 들어갈 말로 알맞은 것을 <보기>에서 골라 쓰시오. (대·소문자 변화 가능)

<보기>

each　　all　　none

25

• 도시의 모든 건물들은 지진이 일어났을 때 붕괴되었다.

➡ ________ the buildings in town collapsed during the earthquake.

26

• 요즘에는 학생 각자 자신의 컴퓨터를 집에 가지고 있다.

➡ These days ________ student has his or her own computer at home.

27

• 정말 길고 지루한 날이었다. 우리가 방문한 곳들은 하나도 흥미롭지 않았다.

➡ It was a very long and boring day. ________ of the places that we visited was interesting.

28 다음 밑줄 친 them을 바르게 고쳐 쓰시오.

Children need to be careful because they can hurt <u>them</u> during the winter.

29 다음 글에서 어법상 틀린 부분을 찾아 바르게 고쳐 쓰시오.

I have two books. One is about cooking, and the others is about science.

________________ ➡ ________________

30 다음 빈칸에 공통으로 들어갈 말을 쓰시오.

• I don't like this cap. Can you show me ________?

• She has three brothers. One lives in Beijing, ________ lives in Chicago, and the other lives in New York.

[31-32] 다음 문장에서 어법상 <u>틀린</u> 부분을 찾아 바르게 고쳐 쓰시오.

31

Some people like to rest in their free time. The others like to travel.

_______________ ➡ _______________

32

I have seen three monsters. One of them was a witch. Other was a vampire. The other was my mom without makeup!

_______________ ➡ _______________

[33-34] 다음 그림을 보고 <조건>에 맞게 빈칸에 알맞은 말을 쓰시오.

<조건>

• 다음 중 하나를 선택하여 쓸 것 (중복사용 불가)

one some another the other the others

33 I don't like this shirt. Show me __________.

34 There are five shirts. __________ is very expensive, but __________ aren't.

Chapter

08

형용사와 부사

1 형용사의 쓰임

1 한정적 용법 명사를 꾸며줌

We enjoyed a **wonderful scene**. 우리는 멋진 풍경을 즐겼다.

I heard a **wonderful song**. 나는 멋진 노래를 들었다.

2 서술적 용법 주어나 목적어의 상태를 설명함

She is **happy**. 그녀는 행복하다. **<주격보어 → 주어 설명>**

Singing always makes **her happy**. 노래하는 것은 항상 그녀를 행복하게 만든다. **<목적격보어 → 목적어 설명>**

+ 한정적 / 서술적 용법으로만 쓰이는 형용사

한정적 용법으로만 쓰이는 형용사	only, main, elder, former, mere
서술적 용법으로만 쓰이는 형용사	afraid, alike, alive, alone, ashamed, asleep, awake, sorry, pleased

▶▶ 정답과 해설 p. 33

EXERCISE A **다음 문장의 밑줄 친 부분을 바르게 고쳐 쓰시오.**

1 I have never heard of such an impression story.

2 We were satisfied with the reason price of the restaurant.

3 I happened to meet a very intelligence person the other day.

4 We will find another effect way to improve the current water pollution.

5 It is not easy to have a truth friend.

EXERCISE B **다음 우리말과 일치하도록 주어진 단어를 배열하시오.**

1 이 책은 대단히 어려운 것 같다. (book, very, difficult, This, seems)

➡ ______________________________

2 나의 형은 의사가 되었다. (became, My, doctor, a, brother, elder)

➡ ______________________________

3 그 왕자는 그녀를 행복하게 해주었다. (her, prince, happy, The, made)

➡ ______________________________

2 주의해야 할 형용사의 어순

1 「부정대명사 + 형용사」

-one, -body, -thing, -where로 끝나는 대명사는 형용사가 뒤에서 수식한다.

Would you get me **anything cold** to drink? 제게 차가운 마실 것을 가져다 주시겠어요?
Was there **anything interesting** at the party? 파티에 흥미로운 무언가가 있었니?

2 「such + a(an) + 형용사 + 명사」

형용사가 such와 함께 쓰일 때 형용사의 어순에 유의한다.

It is **such a lovely day** today. 오늘은 정말 멋진 날이다.
He was **such a kind teacher**. 그는 정말 친절한 선생님이었다.

▶▶ 정답과 해설 p. 33

EXERCISE A **다음 문장의 밑줄 친 부분을 바르게 고쳐 쓰시오.**

1 There must be <u>attractive something</u> about her.

2 I have never seen <u>a such beautiful</u> woman before.

3 I wish <u>happy something</u> could take place every day.

4 She is <u>such nice a</u> teacher that every student likes her.

5 You shouldn't make <u>a such foolish</u> mistake anymore.

6 Let's go <u>nice somewhere</u> for dinner this evening.

EXERCISE B **다음 주어진 단어를 배열하여 문장을 완성하시오.**

1 Would you like to have ________ ________ to drink? (cold, something)

2 Are you looking for ________ ________ to live? (quiet, somewhere)

3 Was there ________ ________ about the result of the survey? (wrong, anything)

4 They haven't met ________ ________ ________ ________ in person. (famous, a, such, director)

5 Stella is ________ ________ ________ ________ that people smile whenever they meet her. (a, girl, cute, such)

3 the + 형용사

「the + 형용사」: ~한 사람들

「the + 형용사」가 주어로 쓰일 때 복수 취급을 한다.

The rich send their kids to private schools. 부자들은 그들의 아이들을 사립학교에 보낸다. <= Rich people>

He worked at the local hospital for **the disabled** on a voluntary basis.
그는 자원봉사로 장애인들을 위해 지역 병원에서 일했다. <= disabled people>

He has announced a new project to help **the homeless**.
그는 노숙자들을 돕기 위한 새 계획을 발표했다. <= homeless people>

▶▶ 정답과 해설 p.33

EXERCISE A 다음 영영풀이가 뜻하는 단어를 「the + 형용사」의 형태로 쓰시오.

1 people who are young ➡ ______________

2 people who own lots of money ➡ ______________

3 people who don't have enough money ➡ ______________

4 people who have nowhere to live ➡ ______________

5 people who are unable to see ➡ ______________

6 people who are unable to hear ➡ ______________

7 people who suffer from physical disabilities ➡ ______________

EXERCISE B 다음 괄호 안에서 옳은 것을 고르시오.

1 Do you think the rich [is / are] always happy?

2 She decided to devote all her life to helping [a / the] blind.

3 You are not allowed to park here. This is for [a / the] disabled.

4 After the accident, the injured [was / were] taken to hospital.

5 [A / ×] homeless man on the street begged me to give him some change.

6 The increasing number of [a / the] jobless has become a social problem.

7 He must be [a / the] deaf man. He seems to hear nothing.

4 some / any

some	주로 긍정문, 권유문, 긍정의 대답 예상	약간의, 몇몇의, 조금	+ 셀 수 있는 복수명사 셀 수 없는 명사
any	주로 의문문, 조건문	약간의, 몇몇의, 조금	
	부정문	조금도, 하나도, 전혀	

I have **some books**. 나는 책을 몇 권 가지고 있다. **<긍정문>**

Would you like **some coffee**? 커피 좀 드시겠어요? **<권유문>**

Was there **any furniture** in the room? 그 방에 가구가 좀 있었니? **<의문문>**

He doesn't have **any money** with him. 그는 가지고 있는 돈이 전혀 없다. **<부정문>**

She didn't buy **any souvenirs** for you. 그녀는 너를 위한 기념품을 전혀 사지 않았다. **<부정문>**

She needs to prepare **some milk**. 그녀는 우유를 좀 준비해야 한다. **<긍정문>**

▶▶ 정답과 해설 p. 33

EXERCISE A **다음 괄호 안에서 옳은 것을 고르시오.**

1 I am going to buy [any / some] new clothes.

2 Do you have [any / some] children?

3 Look! There are [any / some] birds flying above the trees.

4 Have you ever met [any / some] famous movie stars?

5 They bought [any / some] bread, but they didn't buy [any / some] butter.

6 We can't go skiing. There isn't [any / some] snow.

EXERCISE B **다음 우리말과 일치하도록 주어진 단어를 사용하여 문장을 완성하시오. (필요시 형태 변화)**

1 나는 신선한 공기를 좀 쐬려고 창문을 열었다. (air, fresh)
➡ I opened the window to get ________ ________ ________.

2 이 근처에는 좋은 호텔들이 하나도 없다. (hotel, good)
➡ There are not ________ ________ ________ around here.

3 질문이 좀 더 있다면, 언제든지 내게 질문해도 좋습니다. (question, further)
➡ If you have ________ ________ ________, you can ask me at any time.

5 many / much / a lot of

many	+ 셀 수 있는 복수명사	Do you have **many books**? 너는 많은 책을 갖고 있니?
much	+ 셀 수 없는 명사	I don't have **much interest** in physics. 나는 물리학에 많은 관심이 없다.
a lot of, lots of, plenty of	+ 셀 수 있는 복수명사 + 셀 수 없는 명사	I have **a lot of books**. 나는 많은 책을 갖고 있다. **Lots of people** saw the UFO. 많은 사람들이 그 UFO를 보았다.

▶▶ 정답과 해설 p. 33

EXERCISE A **다음 괄호 안에서 옳은 것을 모두 고르시오.**

1 We usually have [many / a lot of] snow in winter here.

2 Were there [many / much] people at the party?

3 Is there [many / much] milk in the jar?

4 I used to read [a lot of / much / many] books when I was in college.

5 I think she doesn't have [many / much / lots of] interest in football.

6 I didn't feel like eating. So I didn't eat [many / much / a lot of] food.

EXERCISE B **다음 우리말과 일치하도록 주어진 단어를 사용하여 문장을 완성하시오. (필요시 형태 변화)**

1 커피에 설탕을 얼마나 많이 넣을까요? (sugar)
➡ How _________ _________ do you want in your coffee?

2 사람들은 이 강에 물고기가 많다고 말한다. (fish)
➡ People say there are _________ _________ _________ in this river.

3 어제 도로에 차들이 많았니? (car)
➡ Were there _________ _________ on the road yesterday?

4 나는 작년에 많은 돈을 저축하지 못했다. (money)
➡ I didn't save _________ _________ last year.

5 그 도서관에는 많은 책들이 있다. (book)
➡ There are _________ _________ _________ in the library.

6 few / a few / little / a little

1 「few(거의 없는) / a few(조금, 약간의) + 셀 수 있는 복수명사」

He has **a few books** to read. 그는 읽을 책이 몇 권 있다.

He has **few books** to read. 그는 읽을 책이 거의 없다.

2 「little(거의 없는) / a little(조금, 약간의) + 셀 수 없는 명사」

She has **a little water** to drink. 그녀는 마실 물이 조금 있다.

She has **little water** to drink. 그녀는 마실 물이 거의 없다.

+ 「quite a few 상당수의 / only a few 극소수의 + 셀 수 있는 복수명사」

Quite a few tourists are allowed to visit the island. 상당수의 관광객들이 그 섬에 방문하도록 허락되었다.

Only a few tourists are allowed to visit the island. 극소수의 관광객들만이 그 섬에 방문하도록 허락되었다.

▶▶ 정답과 해설 p.34

EXERCISE A 다음 괄호 안에서 옳은 것을 고르시오.

1 I borrowed [a few / little / a little] books yesterday.

2 She can speak [few / a few / a little] Spanish.

3 We need to go shopping. We have [few / little / a little] eggs.

4 There will be [a few / little / a little] interesting movies on TV tonight.

5 The refrigerator is almost empty. There is [a little / little / a few] food in it.

EXERCISE B 다음 빈칸에 few, a few, little, a little 중 알맞은 것을 넣어 문장을 완성하시오.

1 He is nearly broke. He has ________ money.

2 He is lonely and sad because he has ________ friends.

3 There was ________ snow last week, so we couldn't go skiing.

4 I happened to meet Sarah on the street ________ ________ days ago.

5 She put on ________ ________ perfume before going out.

6 ________ ________ students like old pop songs.

7 부사의 형태와 쓰임

부사의 형태	예
형용사 + -ly	active**ly**, beautiful**ly**, certain**ly**, definite**ly** *cf.* 명사 + -ly → 형용사 : love - love**ly**, friend - friend**ly**
자음 + y → ily	eas**ily**, happ**ily**, heav**ily**, luck**ily**, prett**ily**
형용사와 부사의 형태와 의미가 같은 경우	early, enough, fast, high, last, long
형용사와 부사의 형태는 같지만 의미가 다른 경우	pretty 형 예쁜 부 꽤, 매우 well 형 건강한 부 잘
-ly를 붙이면 다른 뜻이 되는 부사	hard 형 단단한, 어려운, 힘든 부 열심히, 심하게 / hardly 부 거의 ~하지 않다 (= seldom, rarely, scarcely) late 형 늦은 부 늦게 / lately 부 최근에 (= recently, nowadays) high 형 높은 부 높게 / highly 부 매우 near 형 가까운 부 가까이 / nearly 부 거의 most 형 대부분의, 가장 많은 부 가장 많이 / mostly 부 주로

The girl is **pretty**. 그 소녀는 예쁘다. **<형 예쁜>**

The work was **pretty** difficult. 그 일은 매우 어려웠다. **<부 꽤, 매우>**

He was **late** for school this morning. 그는 오늘 아침에 학교에 늦었다. **<형 늦은>**

The train arrived **late**. 그 기차는 늦게 도착했다. **<부 늦게>**

They moved to this town **lately**. 그들은 최근에 이 마을로 이사 왔다. **<부 최근에>**

It is **hard** work. 그것은 힘든 일이다. **<형 힘든>**

He worked very **hard**. 그는 매우 열심히 일했다. **<부 열심히>**

She **hardly** has breakfast. 그녀는 아침을 거의 먹지 않는다. **<부 거의 ~하지 않다>**

부사의 쓰임	예문
동사를 수식	She **dances** **beautifully**. 그녀는 아름답게 춤춘다.
형용사를 수식	You are a **very** **good** cook. 당신은 아주 훌륭한 요리사다.
다른 부사를 수식	He speaks English **very** **fluently**. 그는 영어를 아주 유창하게 한다.
문장 전체를 수식	**It was very windy** **yesterday**. 어제는 바람이 많이 불었다.

+ 전치사구(전치사 + 명사)는 문장에서 부사 또는 형용사와 동일한 역할을 한다.

She drove on the snowy road **with care**. (= carefully)

그녀는 눈 덮인 도로에서 조심스럽게 운전했다. **<전치사구: 부사 역할>**

The books **on the desk** are mine. 책상 위에 있는 그 책들은 내 것이다. **<전치사구: 형용사 역할>**

▶▶ 정답과 해설 p.34

EXERCISE A 다음 밑줄 친 부사가 수식하는 단어 또는 문장을 쓰시오.

1 He used to run fast when young.

2 The meal was absolutely fantastic.

3 The boy did very well on the difficult math exam.

4 I happened to see her at the cafeteria this morning.

EXERCISE B 다음 괄호 안에서 옳은 것을 고르시오.

1 You should drive [careful / carefully] on the icy road.

2 Has your whole family moved to this town [late / lately]?

3 Penguins use their wings [most / mostly] for swimming.

4 It was surprising that [near / nearly] one third of the students failed the exam.

EXERCISE C 다음 두 문장의 뜻이 같도록 빈칸에 알맞은 부사를 넣어 문장을 완성하시오.

1 You had better handle the vase with care.
= You had better handle the vase ________.

2 She sat down and read the letter in silence.
= She sat down and read the letter ________.

3 Have you ever talked to a famous singer in person?
= Have you ever talked to a famous singer ________?

EXERCISE D 다음 우리말과 일치하도록 주어진 단어를 사용하여 문장을 완성하시오. (필요시 형태 변화)

1 이 건물은 새로 지어진 오페라 극장이다. (built, new)
➡ This building is a ________ ________ opera theater.

2 그는 그녀의 훈훈한 이야기에 깊이 감동받았다. (moved, deep)
➡ He was ________ ________ by her heartwarming story.

3 당신은 너무 시끄럽게 음악을 연주해서는 안 된다. (loud, too)
➡ You shouldn't play the music ________ ________.

8 빈도부사

빈도부사는 어떤 일이 일어나는 빈번한 정도를 나타내는 부사이다.

0% — 50% — 100%

never (결코 ~않는)	hardly seldom rarely scarcely (거의 ~않는)	sometimes at times now and then from time to time (가끔)	often (자주)	usually (보통)	always (항상)

빈도부사의 위치	예문
일반동사 앞	I **sometimes go** for a swim. 나는 가끔 수영하러 간다.
be동사 뒤	She **is always** kind to others. 그녀는 항상 다른 사람들에게 친절하다.
조동사 뒤	I **will always** remember you. 나는 너를 항상 기억할 것이다.
have와 p.p. 사이	I **have never been** to Spain. 나는 스페인에 가본 적이 없다. **<완료시제>**
be동사와 p.p. 사이	The room **is always cleaned**. 그 방은 항상 청소되어 있다. **<수동태>**

▶▶ 정답과 해설 p. 34

EXERCISE A **다음 괄호 안에 주어진 단어가 들어갈 자리에 ∨ 표시를 하시오.**

1 Do you have breakfast? (usually)

2 I have lost my wallet. (sometimes)

3 I could recognize her at the party. (hardly)

4 The garden is watered automatically. (always)

EXERCISE B **다음 우리말과 일치하도록 주어진 단어를 배열하여 문장을 완성하시오.**

1 그녀는 항상 남들에게 예의바르다. (always, to, polite, is)
➡ She ______________________________ others.

2 그들은 주말마다 가끔 테니스를 친다. (play, on, sometimes, tennis)
➡ They ______________________________ weekends.

3 그는 중국에 가본 적이 전혀 없다. (never, to, has, been)
➡ He ______________________________ China.

4 그는 내가 말하고 있는 것을 거의 이해하지 못한다. (can, understand, what, hardly)
➡ He ______________________________ I'm saying.

9 일반동사 + 부사 vs. 연결동사 + 형용사

1 일반동사 + 부사 : 부사가 동사를 수식함

She **sings beautifully**. 그녀는 아름답게 노래한다. **<sings를 수식>**

Owls **fly silently**. 부엉이는 조용히 난다. **<fly를 수식>**

He **stood silently** at the funeral. 그는 장례식장에서 조용히 서 있었다. **<stood를 수식>**

2 연결동사 + 형용사 : 형용사가 주어를 설명함

She **looks beautiful**. 그녀는 아름다워 보인다. **<She = beautiful>**

He **became famous**. 그는 유명해졌다. **<He = famous>**

Please **keep silent** in the library. 도서관에서 조용히 해주세요. **<생략된 주어 You = silent>**

+ 연결동사(2형식 동사)의 종류

연결동사(2형식 동사)는 주어의 상태를 나타내는 동사로서 주격보어를 필요로 한다.

상태를 나타내는 동사	be, seem, appear, become
감각을 나타내는 동사	look, sound, smell, taste, feel
변화 또는 불변화를 나타내는 동사	go, grow, get, turn / stay, remain, keep

▶▶ 정답과 해설 p.34

EXERCISE A 다음 괄호 안에서 옳은 것을 고르시오.

1 The flowers on the table smell [good / well].

2 She sat down and kept reading the book [silent / silently].

3 She looked very [graceful / gracefully] at the party last week.

4 The newly swept beach became really [peaceful / peacefully].

EXERCISE B 다음 문장에서 어법상 틀린 부분을 찾아 바르게 고쳐 쓰시오.

1 The shoes you are wearing look comfortably.

2 He became famously after publishing his first book.

3 I expected they would dance beautiful in the scene.

4 The price of the metal watch doesn't seem reasonably to me.

10 타동사 + 부사

1 「타동사 + 대명사 + 부사」

타동사와 부사가 함께 쓰여 동사구를 이룰 때 목적어가 대명사인 경우 항상 동사와 부사 사이에 온다.

You need to **put** it **on**. (○)　　You need to ***put on*** it. (×)
너는 그것을 입어야 한다.

2 「타동사 + 부사 + 명사」, 「타동사 + 명사 + 부사」

목적어가 명사인 경우 목적어는 동사와 부사 사이에 위치하거나 부사 뒤에 올 수 있다.

You need to **put on your coat**. (○)　　You need to **put your coat on**. (○)
너는 네 코트를 입어야 한다.

bring up ~을 키우다, 기르다	look up (사전에서) ~을 찾아보다	take off ~을 벗다
call off ~을 취소하다	pick up ~을 태우러 가다, 집다	throw away ~을 버리다
check out ~을 확인하다	put off ~을 미루다	try on ~을 입어보다
figure out ~을 이해하다	put on ~을 입다	turn down ~을 거절하다
fill in ~을 작성하다	put out (촛불 등을) 끄다	turn in ~을 제출하다
give up ~을 포기하다	see off ~을 배웅하다	turn on / off ~을 켜다 / 끄다
hand in ~을 제출하다	set up ~을 세우다	turn up (소리 등을) 높이다
look after ~을 돌보다	switch on / off ~을 켜다 / 끄다	write down ~을 받아 적다

▶▶ 정답과 해설 p.34

EXERCISE A 다음 괄호 안에서 올바른 것을 고르시오.

1 Those shoes look really nice. Can I [try on them / try them on]?

2 I am going to [pick up her / pick her up] at the airport this afternoon.

3 I can't hear the TV. Could you [turn up it / turn it up] a little bit?

EXERCISE B 다음 우리말과 일치하도록 빈칸에 알맞은 말을 쓰시오.

1 안이 어둡네. 불을 켜 줄래?
➡ It's dark inside. Can you ________ ________ the light, please?

2 그 연필은 정말 오래됐다. 너는 그걸 버려도 된다.
➡ The pencil is really old. You can ________ ________ ________.

3 소방관들은 Church Street에 발생한 불을 끌 수 있었다.
➡ The firefighters were able to ________ ________ the fire on Church Street.

Chapter 08
형용사와 부사

학교 시험 대비 문제

맞힌 개수	
선택형	____ / 40
서술형	____ / 9

▶▶ 정답과 해설 p.34

01 다음 중 단어의 성격이 나머지 넷과 다른 것은?

① carefully ② kindly ③ lovely
④ safely ⑤ bravely

02 다음 빈칸에 들어갈 말이 순서대로 짝지어진 것은?

- Would you like ________ cookies?
- I haven't seen ________ science fiction films at all.

① any — any ② any — some
③ some — some ④ some — any
⑤ one — any

03 다음 중 어법상 틀린 것은?

① I was afraid to talk to a foreigner.
② They say Betty and I are much alike.
③ He is the only teacher that I like in my school.
④ We can see alive animals at a zoo.
⑤ The loud noise made them stay awake all night long.

고난도

04 다음 중 밑줄 친 부분의 해석이 틀린 것은?

① It's warm inside. Take off your coat.
➡ ~을 벗다

② I put on the cardigan that he gave me.
➡ ~을 입다

③ Don't forget to turn off the light when you go out.
➡ ~을 끄다

④ We need to call off the meeting tomorrow.
➡ ~을 통보하다

⑤ When you're out, she will look after Jimmy and Karen.
➡ ~을 돌보다

05 다음 빈칸에 들어갈 말로 알맞은 것은?

- 나는 인터넷으로 역사에 관한 책 몇 권을 주문했다.
➡ I ordered ________ books about history online.

① few ② a few ③ little
④ a little ⑤ a lot of

06 다음 밑줄 친 부분과 바꿔 쓸 수 있는 것은?

She devoted all her life to helping the poor.

① a poor ② any poor
③ poverty ④ poor people
⑤ some poor people

07 다음 두 단어의 관계가 나머지 넷과 다른 것은?

① nice — nicely ② friend — friendly
③ silent — silently ④ happy — happily
⑤ wonderful — wonderfully

[08-09] 다음 중 어법상 틀린 것을 모두 고르시오.

08

① They have always treated me well.
② She would often go to the movies alone.
③ I can hardly understand what you are saying.
④ I never have seen such an interesting person.
⑤ I visit sometimes New York to see my grandma.

고난도

09

① I think she is not a friendly person.
② The students are talking very loudly.
③ We have successful finished the work.
④ The pretty girl kindly showed me the way.
⑤ You can easy find the place along the street.

고난도

10 다음 빈칸에 알맞은 말을 모두 고르시오.

It ________ hotter and hotter.

① became ② were ③ made
④ got ⑤ seem

11 다음 밑줄 친 부분의 쓰임이 같은 것은?

① Do you feel well this morning?
I didn't do very well on the test.
② She looks so pretty today.
He tried to talk pretty loudly.
③ Raise your glasses high.
The diamond was sold at a high price.
④ He studied very hard to pass it.
It is hard for me to pass the exam.
⑤ We stayed up late yesterday.
I woke up late, so I missed the first train.

12 다음 밑줄 친 부분 중 어법상 올바른 것은?

① I have many work to do today.
② There are many bread on the plate.
③ They didn't have many information.
④ There were lots of furnitures in the hall.
⑤ How many hours did you spend waiting in line?

13 다음 빈칸에 들어갈 말로 알맞은 것은?

The sun is shining ________ over her head.

① silently ② usually ③ brightly
④ beautiful ⑤ famously

14 다음 중 어법상 틀린 것은?

① He never tells a lie.
② She sometimes gets sad.
③ Jane has never tried Turkish food.
④ I would often go out for a walk after dinner.
⑤ They seldom have played football after school.

15 다음 빈칸에 들어갈 말로 알맞은 것을 모두 고르시오.

> • 이것은 시각 장애인들을 위한 잡지다.
> ➡ This is a magazine for ________.

① blind ② a blind ③ the blind
④ blinds ⑤ blind people

16 다음 중 어법상 틀린 것은?

① Don't give up the chance.
② Would you turn it on?
③ I'm going to turn off it right away.
④ Let me throw away the used paper.
⑤ Would you see him off instead of me?

17 다음 빈칸에 들어갈 말로 알맞은 것은?

> Do you have ________ money with you?

① a lot ② any ③ few
④ a few ⑤ many

18 다음 짝지어진 두 문장의 의미가 서로 다른 것은?

① Have you seen her recently?
➡ Have you seen her lately?
② She has studied very hard lately.
➡ She seems to have hardly studied recently.
③ She took a lot of interesting pictures on her trip.
➡ She took a number of interesting pictures on her trip.
④ They will provide us with lots of good programs.
➡ They will provide us with plenty of good programs.
⑤ The government started a project for the homeless.
➡ The government started a project for people who have no place to live in.

19 다음 빈칸에 공통으로 들어갈 말로 알맞은 것은?

> • Don't put it ________ until Monday, will you?
> • Take it ________ and try this shirt on.

① to ② for ③ off
④ at ⑤ on

20 다음 빈칸에 들어갈 말로 알맞지 않은 것은?

I have ________ books to read.

① a lot of ② a few ③ a little
④ plenty of ⑤ lots of

21 다음 밑줄 친 much의 쓰임이 나머지 넷과 다른 것은?

① Don't put much sugar in your tea.
② Let's save much money this year.
③ She drank much water after class.
④ Thank you very much for the flowers.
⑤ I found much information on the Internet.

고난도

22 다음 중 어법상 틀린 것을 모두 고르시오.

① It sounds greatly.
② The bread smelled good.
③ You don't look well today.
④ They looked very friendly.
⑤ His answer made her angrily.

23 다음 빈칸에 들어갈 말이 바르게 짝지어진 것은?

• Kathy is shy, but she has ________ friends. • I had ________ time to have a meal, so I skipped it.

① few — a little ② a lot of — few
③ a little — a few ④ a few — little
⑤ a little — a little

24 다음 빈칸에 공통으로 들어갈 말로 알맞은 것은?

• It is raining ________ outside. • Her face seems as ________ as a rock. • He is trying ________ to write an English diary.

① heavily ② strong ③ hard
④ mostly ⑤ highly

[25-26] 다음 밑줄 친 부분이 어법상 틀린 것을 고르시오.

25

① Look at that sleeping puppy.
② Some of the strawberries look fresh.
③ Could I have cold something to drink?
④ He tried to read as many books as he could.
⑤ The homeless are people who have no place to live in.

26

① He owns a pretty big house in the country.
② Did you meet famous anybody at the party?
③ Why don't we go somewhere nice for dinner?
④ I have never met such a great teacher like him.
⑤ There were lots of terrible things that occurred today.

27 다음 밑줄 친 부분과 뜻이 일치하지 않는 것은?

① You must switch on the light.
➡ turn on

② The mayor canceled the meeting.
➡ call off

③ Switch off the lights as you go out.
➡ Turn off

④ You should turn in your paper tomorrow.
➡ hand in

⑤ He offered me help, but I denied his offer.
➡ turn in

28 다음 빈칸에 들어갈 말로 알맞은 것은?

> • 상당수의 여행객들이 매년 그 성당을 방문한다.
> ➡ Quite ________ tourists visit the cathedral every year.

① little ② a little ③ few
④ a few ⑤ much

[29-32] 다음 중 어법상 틀린 것을 고르시오.

29

① I have little money with me.
② Does she have many friends?
③ I have to memorize a lot of word.
④ She drinks a lot of milk every day.
⑤ There were a few students in the library.

30

① She would often come to see us.
② You have always done it this way.
③ They don't usually have their dinner early.
④ My homework always is checked on Thursdays.
⑤ He hardly understood what the foreigner said.

31

① Why don't you try this on?
② Take your shoes off, please.
③ I won't forget to turn off the TV.
④ Could I turn it off a few minutes later?
⑤ I'm going to pick up her in front of the station.

32

> ① The young ② was serving ③ food ④ to the elderly ⑤ at the party.

33 다음 빈칸에 들어갈 말로 알맞은 것은?

> As it suddenly ________ cold, I put on my overcoat.

① had ② made ③ became
④ let ⑤ took

[34-35] 다음 중 밑줄 친 부분이 어법상 틀린 것을 고르시오.

34

① The idea will never work in practice.
② He usually studies with the music on.
③ My father sometimes works overtime.
④ My family seldom visits an amusement park.
⑤ This is the place which I always have wanted to visit.

35

① Could you give me some tips?
② I don't have any friends in this school.
③ Linda didn't want to buy any clothes at all.
④ If you have some questions, please ask me at any time.
⑤ I picked up some apples and put them in the shopping cart.

36 다음 괄호 안에 주어진 단어가 들어갈 곳으로 알맞은 것은?

> When I don't know (①) how to express (②) myself in English, I (③) refer (④) to the dictionary (⑤). (often)

고난도

37 다음 중 어법상 올바른 것은?

① The rich is not always happy.
② We haven't had some food yet.
③ This parking place is for a disabled.
④ Your suggestion sounds wonderfully.
⑤ What part of the movie did you like most?

[38-39] 다음 중 어법상 틀린 것을 고르시오.

38

① They give free food to the poor.
② The unemployed are increasing.
③ The young likes this kind of music.
④ There is a special class for the handicapped.
⑤ There are seats for the weak and the elderly on the subway.

고난도

39

① The scarf looked very lovely.
② You must keep silently in church.
③ They closed the shop quickly and left.
④ She tells her story very interestingly.
⑤ Rivers and lakes turn green in hot weather.

40 다음 중 밑줄 친 부분이 어법상 틀린 것은?

① I met my old friend a few days ago.
② In the street, there were a few children.
③ He was angry because there was few food.
④ There are only a few characters in the novel.
⑤ She speaks little Korean, so she can't understand me.

서술형

41 다음 우리말과 일치하도록 빈칸에 알맞은 말을 쓰시오.

- 나는 그의 강의에서 흥미로운 것을 찾지 못했다.

➡ I found ________ ________ in his lecture.

42 다음 글에서 어법상 틀린 곳을 찾아 바르게 고쳐 쓰시오.

Try to learn before you visit a foreign country. It's helpful to know something about the custom of the country to make people feel happily with you.

________ ➡ ________

43 다음 우리말과 일치하도록 주어진 단어를 사용하여 문장을 완성하시오. (필요시 형태 변화)

- 그녀가 한 말이 나를 기쁘게 했다. (make, happy)

➡ What she said ________ ________ ________.

44 다음 빈칸에 공통으로 들어갈 단어를 쓰시오.

- I'm really full. I had ________ food.
- She was smart ________ to answer the difficult question.
- I don't have ________ money to buy the expensive jacket.

45 다음 대화의 빈칸에 알맞은 말을 쓰시오.

A Can I talk to you for a minute?
B Sorry, I don't have ________ time right now. I'll call you after school.

고난도

[46-47] 다음 Andy의 가족 소개글을 읽고, <보기>와 같이 문장을 완성하시오.

Let me introduce my family to you. My dad is an English teacher at a middle school. He treats the students kindly. He plays tennis very well. My mom is good at cooking. She drives very carefully. My sister, Jenny, plays the piano wonderfully. When she describes something, she writes about it creatively.

<보기>

Andy's father is a kind English teacher at a middle school. He is a good tennis player.

46 Andy's mother is ______________________.
She is ______________________.

47 Andy's sister, Jenny, is ______________________
______________________.
She is ______________________.

[48-49] 다음 우리말과 일치하도록 <조건>에 맞게 문장을 쓰시오.

<조건>

- 주어진 단어를 모두 사용할 것
- <보기>에서 하나만 선택하여 문장을 완성할 것

<보기>

little a little few a few

48 그들의 집은 작았고, 가구가 거의 없었다.
(home, and, small, was, their, furniture, had)
➡ ______________________

49 운동이 건강에 좋다는 것을 부인하는 의사는 거의 없다.
(good, doctors, health, deny, for, is, exercise, that)
➡ ______________________

Chapter

09

비교

1 as + 원급 + as

1 「as + 원급 + as」: ~만큼 …한(하게)

My girlfriend is 16 years old. I am 16 years old, too.

➡ My girlfriend is **as old as** I am. 내 여자 친구는 나와 동갑이다.

※ as 뒤의 「주어 + 동사」는 목적격으로 바꿔 쓸 수 있다.

2 「not as(so) + 원급 + as」: ~만큼 …하지 않은

A car is **not as(so) fast as** a plane. 자동차는 비행기만큼 빠르지 않다.

His camera is **not as(so) good as** mine. 그의 카메라는 내 것만큼 좋지 않다.

3 「배수사 + as + 원급 + as」: ~배로 …한(하게)

My father's shirt is **twice as big as** mine. 나의 아버지의 셔츠는 내 것보다 두 배 크다.

Kate's pencil is **three times as long as** mine. Kate의 연필은 내 것보다 세 배 길다.

▶▶ 정답과 해설 p.37

EXERCISE A **다음 우리말과 일치하도록 주어진 단어를 사용하여 문장을 완성하시오.**

1 너의 방은 내 것만큼 크다. (big)

➡ Your room is ______________________ mine.

2 오페라는 영화만큼 재미있다. (interesting)

➡ The opera is ______________________ the movie.

3 비행기는 기차보다 두 배 빠르다. (fast)

➡ The plane is ______________________ the train.

4 나는 너보다 두 배 많은 책을 읽어야 한다. (many, books)

➡ I have to read ______________________ you.

5 내 카메라는 네 것만큼 비싸지 않다. (expensive)

➡ My camera ______________________ yours.

6 Jenny는 나만큼 열심히 일하지 않는다. (work, hard)

➡ Jenny ______________________ I do.

7 너는 내가 가진 책의 절반을 가지고 있다. (books, many, half)

➡ You have ______________________ I do.

2 as + 원급 + as possible

「as + 원급 + as possible」: 가능한 한 ~한(하게)
= 「as + 원급 + as + 주어 + can(could)」

He tries to read **as many** books **as possible**.
➡ He tries to read **as many** books **as he can**. 그는 가능한 한 많은 책을 읽으려고 노력한다.

She promised to send me an email **as soon as possible**.
➡ She promised to send me an email **as soon as she could**.
그녀는 가능한 한 빨리 나에게 이메일을 보낼 것을 약속했다.

▶▶ 정답과 해설 p.37

EXERCISE A 다음 두 문장의 뜻이 같도록 빈칸에 알맞은 말을 쓰시오.

1 I am going to read as many English books as possible.
= I am going to read as many English books as ________ ________.

2 She decided to save as much money as she could.
= She decided to save as much money as ________.

3 He drew the beautiful picture as quickly as possible.
= He drew the beautiful picture as quickly as ________ ________.

4 Can you send me your new photo as soon as possible?
= Can you send me your new photo as soon as ________ ________?

EXERCISE B 다음 우리말과 일치하도록 주어진 단어를 사용하여 문장을 완성하시오.

1 가능한 한 빨리 나에게 다시 전화주세요. (soon)
➡ Please call me back ________ ________ ________ ________.

2 당신은 영어 말하기를 가능한 한 많이 연습할 필요가 있습니다. (much)
➡ You need to practice speaking English ________ ________ ________ ________.

3 우리는 가능한 한 많은 장소들을 방문할 계획이었다. (many, places)
➡ We planned to visit ________ ________ ________ ________ ________.

4 그 남자는 가능한 한 빨리 달리려고 애썼다. (fast)
➡ The man tried to run ________ ________ ________ ________ ________.

3 비교급 + than

1 「비교급 + than」: ~보다 더 …한(하게)

A soccer ball is **bigger than** a baseball.
축구공이 야구공보다 더 크다.

A cheetah runs **faster than** a zebra.
치타는 얼룩말보다 더 빨리 달린다.

2 비교하는 대상의 종류가 같을 때 ➡ 소유대명사로 바꿔 쓸 수 있음

My bag is heavier than **your bag**. 나의 가방은 너의 가방보다 더 무겁다.

➡ My bag is heavier than **yours**. (○) **<소유대명사>**

➡ My bag is heavier than ***you***. (×)

cf. **The prices** in Paris are higher than **the prices** in London. 파리의 물가는 런던의 물가보다 더 높다.

➡ **The prices** in Paris are higher than **those** in London. **<대명사>**

3 than 다음에 나오는 「주어 + 동사」 ➡ 목적격으로 바꿔 쓸 수 있음

He plays tennis well. I don't play tennis well.

➡ He plays tennis better than **I do**. 그는 나보다 테니스를 더 잘 친다.

➡ He plays tennis better than **me**.

+ junior(연하의), senior(연상의), superior(뛰어난), inferior(열등한), prefer(~을 더 좋아하다) 등 라틴어에서 유래한 단어의 비교급 문장에서는 than 대신에 to를 쓴다.

I **prefer** a brand new car **to** a used one. 나는 중고차보다 신형차를 더 선호한다.

▶▶ 정답과 해설 p.37

EXERCISE A **다음 문장의 밑줄 친 부분을 소유대명사로 바꿔 쓰시오.**

1 My laptop is heavier than your laptop.

2 Your umbrella is bigger than my umbrella.

3 His watch is more expensive than her watch.

4 Her answer to the question was better than our answer.

5 Jiho's story is more interesting than Yujin's story.

EXERCISE B 다음 <보기>를 참고하여 비교급 문장을 완성하시오.

<보기>
His brother isn't very tall. He is taller than his brother.

1 His plan isn't very good. Your plan is ____________________.

2 That bread doesn't smell fresh. This bread smells ____________________.

3 These jeans aren't very cheap. Those jeans are ____________________.

4 Her idea didn't seem reasonable. Your idea seemed ____________________.

EXERCISE C 다음 두 문장을 <보기>와 같이 한 문장으로 바꿔 쓰시오.

<보기>
He can run very fast. I can't run fast.
➡ He can run faster than me.

1 She is 17 years old. I am 15 years old.
➡ ____________________

2 You are 174 cm tall. He is 171 cm tall.
➡ ____________________

3 These oranges taste good. Those oranges taste terrible.
➡ ____________________

4 The math exam was very difficult. The English exam wasn't difficult.
➡ ____________________

EXERCISE D 다음 두 문장의 뜻이 같도록 <보기>에서 알맞은 단어를 골라 문장을 완성하시오.

<보기>
prefer junior senior

1 She is two years older than me. = She is two years __________ to me.

2 He is three years younger than you. = He is three years __________ to you.

3 I like apples more than oranges. = I __________ apples to oranges.

4 less + 원급 + than

「*A* less + 원급 + than *B*」: A는 B보다 덜 ~하다
➡ 「*A* not as(so) + 원급 + as *B*」: A는 B만큼 ~하지 않다
➡ 「*B* 비교급 + than *A*」: B는 A보다 더 ~하다

Her younger sister is **less beautiful than** her. 그녀의 여동생은 그녀보다 덜 아름답다.
➡ Her younger sister **isn't as beautiful as** her. 그녀의 여동생은 그녀만큼 아름답지 않다.
➡ She is **more beautiful than** her younger sister. 그녀는 그녀의 여동생보다 더 아름답다.

▶▶ 정답과 해설 p.37

EXERCISE A 다음 문장을 <보기>와 같이 바꿔 쓸 때 빈칸에 알맞은 말을 쓰시오.

<보기>
Her younger sister dances less beautifully than her.
➡ Her younger sister doesn't dance as beautifully as her.
➡ She dances more beautifully than her younger sister.

1 My English is less good than your English.
➡ My English ______________________ your English.
➡ Your English ______________________ my English.

2 This city isn't as big as Seoul.
➡ This city ______________________ Seoul.
➡ Seoul ______________________ this city.

3 Football is more popular than baseball here.
➡ Baseball ______________________ football here.
➡ Baseball ______________________ than football here.

4 My answer was less short than your answer.
➡ My answer ______________________ your answer.
➡ Your answer ______________________ my answer.

5 She can play the piano better than me.
➡ I can't play the piano ______________________ her.
➡ I can play the piano ______________________ her.

5 비교급 강조

「much(a lot, even, still, far) + 비교급」: 훨씬 더 ~한

She is **much smarter than** you think. 그녀는 네가 생각하는 것보다 훨씬 더 똑똑하다.

Tom runs **a lot faster than** Mark. Tom은 Mark보다 훨씬 더 빨리 달린다.

! very는 '매우'라는 뜻으로 원급을 강조하는 표현이다.

She is **very** smart. (○) 그녀는 매우 똑똑하다.

She is ***very*** smarter than you think. (×)

▶▶ 정답과 해설 p. 37

EXERCISE A **다음 괄호 안에서 옳은 것을 고르시오.**

1 Canada is a [very / much] big country.

2 China is [very / much] bigger than my country.

3 I found him [very / much] more intelligent than I had expected.

4 The movie we watched last night was [very / a lot] boring.

5 Last week, she had to do [very / even] more work than usual.

EXERCISE B **다음 우리말과 일치하도록 주어진 단어 또는 어구를 사용하여 문장을 완성하시오. (필요시 형태 변화)**

1 그는 나보다 훨씬 더 영어를 잘한다. (much, well)
➡ He can speak English ________ ________ ________ I can.

2 학생들은 그 시험이 이전보다 훨씬 더 어렵다는 것을 알게 되었다. (a lot, difficult)
➡ The students found the test ________ ________ ________ ________ ________ ever before.

3 수영장의 물이 평소보다 훨씬 더 차가웠다. (a lot, cold)
➡ The water of the pool was ________ ________ ________ ________ usual.

4 그녀는 그녀의 언니보다 훨씬 더 예쁘다. (much, beautiful)
➡ She is ________ ________ ________ ________ her sister.

6 the + 비교급, the + 비교급

「The 비교급 + 주어 + 동사, the 비교급 + 주어 + 동사」: ~하면 할수록, 더 …한
= 「As + 주어 + 동사 + 비교급, 주어 + 동사 + 비교급」

The longer she stayed abroad, **the more** she missed her family.
그녀가 외국에 더 오래 있을수록, 그녀는 가족을 더 많이 그리워했다.
= As she stayed abroad **longer**, she missed her family **more**.

▶▶ 정답과 해설 p.37

EXERCISE A 다음 두 문장의 뜻이 같도록 빈칸에 알맞은 말을 쓰시오.

1 As you read more, you become wiser.
= ________ ________ you read, ________ ________ you become.

2 As she saved more, she became richer.
= ________ ________ she saved, ________ ________ she became.

3 As you exercise more, you will be stronger.
= ________ ________ you exercise, ________ ________ you will be.

4 If you practice speaking English harder, you can speak it more fluently.
= ________ ________ you practice speaking English, ________ ________ ________ you can speak it.

EXERCISE B 다음 우리말과 일치하도록 주어진 단어를 사용하여 문장을 완성하시오. (필요시 형태 변화)

1 더 높이 올라갈수록, 더 추워진다. (high, cold)
➡ ________ ________ you go up, ________ ________ it becomes.

2 날씨가 더 좋을수록, 나는 더 행복함을 느낀다. (good, happy)
➡ ________ ________ the weather is, ________ ________ I feel.

3 네가 여기에 오래 머무를수록, 너는 이 도시를 더 많이 좋아할 것이다. (long, much)
➡ ________ ________ you stay here, ________ ________ you would like this city.

4 그들이 공급을 줄일수록, 가격은 더 높이 올라간다. (little, high)
➡ ________ ________ they supply, ________ ________ the price goes up.

7 비교급 + and + 비교급

「비교급 + and + 비교급」: 점점 더 ~한

It is getting **colder and colder** these days. (○) 요즘 날씨가 점점 더 추워지고 있다.

It is getting ***more and more cold*** these days. (×)

He began to run **faster and faster** after the middle of the race.

그는 경주 중반 이후에 점점 더 빨리 뛰기 시작했다.

+ 비교급이 「more + 원급」 형태일 때는 「more and more + 원급」 형태로 표현한다.

The question made her **more and more confused**. (○) 그 질문은 그녀를 점점 더 혼란스럽게 만들었다.

The question made her ***more confused and more confused***. (×)

▶▶ 정답과 해설 p. 37

EXERCISE A 다음 우리말과 일치하도록 주어진 단어를 사용하여 문장을 완성하시오. (필요시 형태 변화)

1 최근에 날씨가 점점 더 더워지고 있다. (hot)
➡ It is getting ______________________ lately.

2 수술 후에, 그의 건강은 점점 더 좋아졌다. (good)
➡ After the operation, his health has become ______________________.

3 그녀는 차를 점점 더 천천히 운전했다. (slowly)
➡ She drove her car ______________________.

4 그 신제품은 시장에서 점점 더 인기를 얻고 있다. (popular)
➡ The new product has grown ______________________ in the market.

5 버스를 기다리면서, 그녀는 점점 더 초조해졌다. (nervous)
➡ While waiting for the bus, she felt ______________________.

6 그가 계속 너무 많이 먹는다면 그는 아마 점점 더 뚱뚱해질 것이다. (fat)
➡ He will probably get ______________________ if he keeps eating too much.

7 그가 운동을 규칙적으로 함에 따라, 그는 점점 더 건강해졌다. (healthy)
➡ As he kept exercising regularly, he became ______________________.

8 그 경기장의 관중들은 점점 더 흥분했다. (excited)
➡ The crowd at the stadium became ______________________.

8 the + 최상급

「the + 최상급」: 가장 ~한(하게)

Andy is **older than** Billy.
Andy는 Billy보다 나이가 더 많다.

Chris is **younger than** Billy.
Chris는 Billy보다 나이가 더 어리다.

Andy is **the oldest** of the three boys.
Andy는 세 소년들 중 나이가 가장 많다.

Chris is **the youngest** of the three boys.
Chris는 세 소년들 중 나이가 가장 어리다.

Andy, 17 Billy, 15 Chris, 14

She is **the most famous** person in town. 그녀는 마을에서 가장 유명한 사람이다.
What is **the longest** river in the world? 세계에서 가장 긴 강은 무엇이니?

+ 최상급 구문에서는 '~중에서'의 의미인 「in + 단수명사(장소·단체)」 또는 「of + 복수명사」를 써서 범위를 나타내기도 한다.

Tom is the tallest boy **in my class**. Tom은 우리 반에서 키가 가장 큰 소년이다.
He is the smartest student **of the three boys**. 그는 세 명의 소년 중에서 가장 똑똑한 학생이다.

+ 부사의 최상급 앞에서는 the를 생략할 수 있으며, 최상급 앞에 소유격이 있는 경우는 the를 쓰지 않는다.

He runs **(the) fastest** of us all. 그는 우리 모두 중에서 가장 빨리 달린다. **<부사의 최상급 앞>**
She is **my best** friend. 그녀는 나의 가장 친한 친구이다. **<최상급 앞에 소유격이 올 때>**

▶▶ 정답과 해설 p.38

EXERCISE A **다음 그림을 보고, 주어진 단어를 사용하여 문장을 완성하시오.**

1 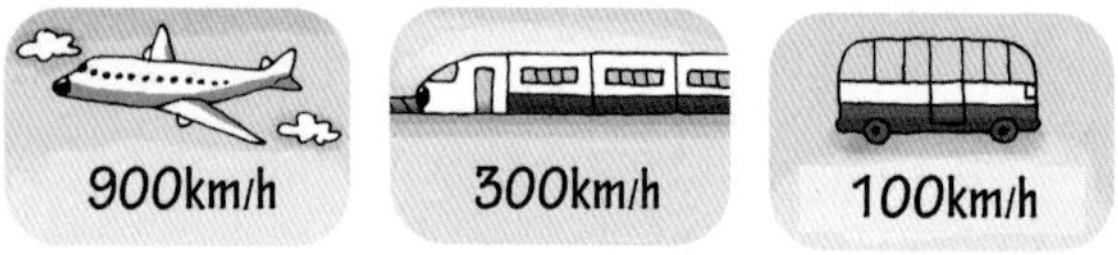

(fast, slow)

An airplane is ________ than a train.

A bus is ________ than a train.

The airplane is ________ ________ public transportation of the three.

The bus is ________ ________ public transportation of the three.

2

Mt. Everest

Mt. Kilimanjaro

Mt. Fuji

(high, low)

Mt. Everest is __________ than Mt. Kilimanjaro.

Mt. Fuji is __________ than Mt. Kilimanjaro.

Mt. Everest is __________ __________ mountain of the three.

Mt. Fuji is __________ __________ mountain of the three.

EXERCISE B **다음 주어진 단어를 사용하여 〈보기〉와 같이 최상급 문장을 완성하시오. (필요시 형태 변화)**

〈보기〉
The cheetah is __the fastest animal__ in the world. (fast, animal)

1 Jupiter is ______________________________ in the solar system. (big, planet)

2 Yesterday was ______________________________ of the year. (hot, day)

3 The Burj Khalifa is ______________________________ in the world. (tall, building)

4 Chile is ______________________________ in the world. (long, country)

5 Soccer is ______________________________ in my country. (popular, sport)

6 My family is ______________________________ in my life. (important, thing)

EXERCISE C **다음 우리말과 일치하도록 주어진 단어를 사용하여 문장을 완성하시오. (필요시 형태 변화)**

1 오늘은 내 인생에서 가장 행복한 날이다. (happy)
➡ Today is __________ __________ day of my life.

2 서울은 우리나라에서 가장 큰 도시이다. (big)
➡ Seoul is __________ __________ city in my country.

3 이것은 내 앨범에서 가장 아름다운 사진이다. (beautiful)
➡ This is __________ __________ __________ picture in my album.

9 one of the + 최상급 + 복수명사

「one of the + 최상급 + 복수명사」: 가장 ~한 것들 중 하나 * 단수 취급

She is **one of the smartest students** in my class. 그녀는 우리 반에서 가장 똑똑한 학생들 중 한 명이다.

He was **one of the wisest kings** in the world. 그는 세상에서 가장 현명한 왕들 중 한 명이었다.

A crocodile is **one of the most dangerous animals** in the world.
악어는 세상에서 가장 위험한 동물들 중 하나이다.

+ 「the + 최상급 + 명사 + (that) + 주어 + have (ever) p.p.」: ~한 것 중에서 가장 …한

The movie was great. It was **the best movie I had ever watched**.
그 영화는 훌륭했다. 그것은 내가 봤던 것 중에서 최고의 영화였다.

▶▶ 정답과 해설 p.38

EXERCISE A 다음 우리말과 일치하도록 주어진 단어를 사용하여 문장을 완성하시오. (필요시 형태 변화)

1 그는 우리 반에서 가장 똑똑한 학생들 중 한 명이다. (bright, student)
➡ He is ________ ________ ________ ________ ________ in my class.

2 그녀는 그리스에서 가장 인기 있는 가수들 중 한 명이었다. (popular, singer)
➡ She was ________ ________ ________ ________ ________ ________ in Greece.

3 야구는 내 인생에서 가장 중요한 것들 중 하나이다. (important, thing)
➡ Baseball is ________ ________ ________ ________ ________ ________ in my life.

4 이 스파게티는 우리가 요리한 것 중에서 가장 형편없는 요리다. (bad, dish, cook)
➡ This spaghetti is ________ ________ ________ we ________ ________ ________.

5 그것은 그가 봤던 것 중에서 가장 지루한 영화였다. (boring, film, watch)
➡ That was ________ ________ ________ ________ he ________ ________ ________.

6 그 마을은 그녀가 방문했던 곳 중에서 가장 아름다운 곳이었다. (beautiful, place, visit)
➡ The village was ________ ________ ________ ________ she ________ ________ ________.

7 그녀는 팀에서 가장 훌륭한 선수들 중 한 명이다. (good, player)
➡ She is ________ ________ ________ ________ ________ in the team.

8 이 케이크는 내가 먹어본 것 중에서 가장 맛있는 케이크이다. (delicious, cake, eat)
➡ This is ________ ________ ________ ________ I ________ ________ ________.

10 원급과 비교급을 이용한 최상급 표현

「the + 최상급」: 가장 ~하다
➡ 「비교급 + than any other + 단수명사」: 다른 어떤 것보다 더 ~하다
➡ 「비교급 + than all the other + 복수명사」: 다른 모든 것들보다 더 ~하다
➡ 「부정주어 ... 비교급 + than ~」: 어떤 것도 ~보다 더 …하지 않다
➡ 「부정주어 ... as(so) + 원급 + as ~」: 어떤 것도 ~만큼 …하지 않다

Eric is **the tallest boy** in school. Eric은 학교에서 가장 키가 큰 소년이다.
➡ Eric is **taller than any other boy** in school. Eric은 학교에서 다른 어떤 소년보다 키가 더 크다.
➡ Eric is **taller than all the other boys** in school. Eric은 학교에서 다른 모든 소년들보다 키가 더 크다.
➡ **No (other) boy** in school is **taller than** Eric. 학교에서 (다른) 어떤 소년도 Eric보다 키가 더 크지 않다.
➡ **No (other) boy** in school is **as(so) tall as** Eric. 학교에서 (다른) 어떤 소년도 Eric만큼 키가 크지 않다.

▶▶ 정답과 해설 p.38

EXERCISE A 다음 우리말과 일치하도록 빈칸에 알맞은 말을 쓰시오.

1 런던은 영국에서 가장 큰 도시이다.
➡ London is ________ ________ ________ in England.
➡ London is bigger than ________ ________ ________ in England.
➡ No other city in England is bigger ________ London.

2 David는 학교에서 테니스를 가장 잘 친다.
➡ David plays tennis ________ ________ in school.
➡ ________ ________ in school plays tennis better ________ David.
➡ No one in school plays tennis ________ ________ as David.

3 Jennie는 우리 반에서 가장 예의바른 학생이다.
➡ Jennie is ________ ________ ________ in our class.
➡ Jennie is politer than ________ ________ ________ ________ in our class.
➡ No other student in our class is ________ than Jennie.

4 우리 엄마는 가족들 중에서 가장 조심스럽게 운전하신다.
➡ My mom drives ________ ________ ________ in my family.
➡ No one in my family drives ________ ________ as my mom.
➡ ________ ________ in my family drives more carefully ________ my mom.

EXERCISE B 다음 문장을 <보기>와 같이 바꿔 쓰시오.

<보기>

The church is the oldest building in town.
➡ The church is older than any other building in town.
➡ The church is older than all the other buildings in town.
➡ No other building in town is older than the church.
➡ No other building in town is as old as the church.

1 Jolly sings the best in class.
➡ Jolly sings ______________________________.
➡ Jolly sings ______________________________.
➡ No other student in class sings ______________________________.
➡ No other student in class sings ______________________________.

2 Professor Charles is the most famous scholar in the university.
➡ Professor Charles is ______________________________.
➡ Professor Charles is ______________________________.
➡ No other scholar in the university is ______________________________.
➡ No other scholar in the university is ______________________________.

3 The red roses look the most beautiful in the garden.
➡ The red roses look ______________________________.
➡ The red roses look ______________________________.
➡ No other flower in the garden looks ______________________________.
➡ No other flower in the garden looks ______________________________.

4 My teacher explains things the most clearly in school.
➡ My teacher explains things ______________________________.
➡ My teacher explains things ______________________________.
➡ No other teacher in school explains things ______________________________.
➡ No other teacher in school explains things ______________________________.

5 Chile is the longest country in the world.
➡ Chile is ______________________________.
➡ Chile is ______________________________.
➡ No other country in the world is ______________________________.
➡ No other country in the world is ______________________________.

Chapter 09
비교

학교 시험 대비 문제

맞힌 개수	
선택형	____ / 23
서술형	____ / 30

▶▶ 정답과 해설 p.38

01 다음 빈칸에 들어갈 말로 알맞은 것은?

> I would like you to stay here as ________ as you want.

① many ② quicker ③ long
④ sooner ⑤ more

02 다음 빈칸에 들어갈 말로 알맞은 것은?

> • I like soccer more than baseball.
> = I prefer soccer ________ baseball.

① by ② than ③ to
④ with ⑤ for

고난도
03 다음 중 어법상 올바른 것을 모두 고르시오.

① He didn't run as fast as I was.
② In fact, I am senior to him.
③ She dances as beautiful as her sister.
④ The football match last night was much boring.
⑤ These oranges look a lot fresher than those in the box.

고난도
04 다음 중 어법상 올바른 것은?

① She is as beautifully as her sister.
② He can run faster than any other boys in class.
③ He is a most intelligent person I have ever met.
④ The harder you practice, the better you will play the guitar.
⑤ In a couple of weeks, it will be more and more cold.

05 다음 중 짝지어진 두 문장의 의미가 서로 다른 것은?

① He is less tall than his brother.
➡ He is not as tall as his brother.
② I like English more than math.
➡ I prefer English to math.
③ She is younger than me.
➡ She is senior to me.
④ As people grow older, they become wiser.
➡ The older people grow, the wiser they become.
⑤ Nothing is as important as health.
➡ Health is the most important thing of all.

고난도

06 다음 중 어법상 올바른 것을 모두 고르시오.

① No one can sing as beautifully as you.
② My laptop is very heavier than yours.
③ Seoul is bigger than any other cities in Korea.
④ He was much more intelligent than I had expected.
⑤ I preferred tea than coffee when staying in England.

07 다음 빈칸에 들어갈 말로 알맞은 것은?

I tried to solve the problem as ________ as I could.

① quick ② quicker
③ quickly ④ more quick
⑤ more quickly

08 다음 중 어법상 틀린 것은?

① Eddie is the tallest boy in school.
② No other boy in school is as tall as Eddie.
③ No other boy in school is taller than Eddie.
④ Eddie is taller than any other boy in school.
⑤ Eddie is taller than all the other boy in school.

09 다음 중 어법상 올바른 것을 모두 고르시오.

① He runs very faster than I do.
② One of the best activity is going swimming.
③ The prices in London are much higher than Seoul.
④ I need to read twice as many books as I used to.
⑤ She felt more and more nervous before the interview.

[10-11] 다음 빈칸에 들어갈 말로 알맞지 않은 것을 고르시오.

10

The water of the lake was ________ colder than I had thought.

① very ② much ③ a lot
④ even ⑤ still

11

She isn't as ________ as you think.

① smart ② clever ③ friendly
④ kindly ⑤ intelligent

12 다음 중 짝지어진 두 문장의 의미가 서로 다른 것은?

① Your car isn't as old as mine.
➡ My car is older than your car.
② My watch is cheaper than yours.
➡ My watch is not as expensive as yours.
③ She likes coffee more than tea.
➡ She prefers coffee to tea.
④ He is the fastest student in school.
➡ No other student in school is as fast as him.
⑤ She can dance better than all the other girls in class.
➡ No other girl in class can't dance as well as she.

13 다음 빈칸에 들어갈 말이 바르게 짝지어진 것은?

• You look ________ beautiful today.
• She looks ________ younger than her age.

① very — very ② very — much
③ little — a lot ④ a lot — even
⑤ even — very

14 다음 중 어법상 틀린 것은?

① Jennie can run the fastest in class.
② No other girl in class can run as fast as Jennie.
③ No other girl in class can run faster than Jennie.
④ Jennie can run faster than any other girls in class.
⑤ Jennie can run faster than all the other girls in class.

15 다음 빈칸에 들어갈 말로 알맞은 것은?

• His work is less important than mine.
= His work is ________ important as mine.

① as ② so ③ not as
④ more ⑤ not less

고난도

16 다음 중 어법상 올바른 것은?

① This is a longest bridge in Korea.
② He doesn't cook as good as I do.
③ She plays the piano better than I am.
④ Their house was twice as big as ours.
⑤ Seoul is one of the biggest city in Korea.

17 다음 중 어법상 틀린 것은?

① Susan is the busiest in my office.
② Who is the cutest baby among them?
③ I think this red shirt is the better in this shop.
④ What is the highest mountain in the world?
⑤ I think math is the most difficult subject of all.

18 다음은 100미터 달리기 결과를 나타낸 표이다. 표의 내용과 일치하는 것은?

Tom	Mike	David
13.5 sec	14.5 sec	15 sec

① Tom is slower than David.
② David is faster than Mike.
③ David is much faster than Tom.
④ Mike is the fastest runner of the three.
⑤ David is the slowest runner of the three.

19 다음 빈칸에 들어갈 말로 알맞은 것은?

• That computer isn't as expensive as this one.
= That computer is ________ expensive than this one.

① little ② least
③ more ④ less
⑤ most

20 다음 빈칸에 들어갈 말로 알맞지 않은 것은?

His new music is ________ more creative than his previous music.

① far ② even
③ very ④ much
⑤ a lot

고난도

21 다음 중 어법상 올바른 것은?

① She tried to run as fast as she can.
② It has been more and more warm lately.
③ Actually she is junior than me.
④ The work was much more difficult as I had expected.
⑤ He is one of the most influential scientists in the world.

22 다음 문장에서 어법상 틀린 것은?

Thomas Edison is ① known as ② one of ③ the greatest ④ inventor ⑤ in the world.

23 다음 중 문장의 의미가 나머지 넷과 다른 것은?

① The box is lighter than my bag.
② My bag is heavier than the box.
③ My bag isn't so heavy as the box.
④ The box isn't so heavy as my bag.
⑤ The box is less heavy than my bag.

서술형

24 다음 우리말과 일치하도록 주어진 단어를 사용하여 문장을 완성하시오.

• 네가 운동을 많이 할수록, 너는 더 건강하게 될 것이다. (much, healthy)

➡ ________ ________ you exercise, ________ ________ you will become.

[25-27] 다음 두 문장의 뜻이 같도록 빈칸에 알맞은 말을 쓰시오.

25

• He tried to read as many books as possible.
= He tried to read as many books as ________ ________.

26

• Nothing is as important as the environmental movement.
= The environmental movement is ________ ________ ________ thing.

27

• As we climbed up higher, it became colder.
= ________ ________ we climbed up, ________ ________ it became.

28 다음 밑줄 친 부분을 어법에 맞게 고쳐 쓰시오.

He is <u>one of great scientist</u> in the world.

➡ ____________________

29 다음 우리말과 일치하도록 빈칸에 알맞은 말을 쓰시오.

• 나는 가능한 한 빨리 너에게 이메일을 보낼 것이다.

➡ I am going to send you an email ________ ________ ________ ________.

30 **다음 우리말과 일치하도록 주어진 단어를 사용하여 문장을 완성하시오. (필요시 형태 변화)**

- 샌프란시스코의 기후는 시애틀의 기후보다 더 온화하다. (mild, Seattle)

➡ The climate of San Francisco is ________ ________ ________ ________ ________.

31 **다음 밑줄 친 부분을 어법에 맞게 고쳐 쓰시오.**

She is <u>very more pretty</u> than you thought.

➡ ________________________

[32-35] 다음 두 문장의 뜻이 같도록 빈칸에 알맞은 말을 쓰시오.

32

- If you start it sooner, you can finish it faster.

= ________ ________ you start it, ________ ________ you can finish it.

33

- He is older than his co-worker.

= He is ________ to his co-worker.

34

- The Eiffel Tower is the most famous place in Paris.

= No other place in Paris is more ________ ________ the Eiffel Tower.

35

- This theater is the oldest building in town.

= No other building in town is as ________ ________ ________ ________.

[36-38] 다음 우리말과 일치하도록 주어진 단어를 사용하여 문장을 완성하시오.

36

- 야구는 한국에서 가장 인기 있는 스포츠 중 하나이다. (popular, sport)

➡ Baseball is ________ ________ ________ ________ ________ ________ in Korea.

37

- 점점 더 적은 수의 학생들이 그 시험을 통과했다. (few)

➡ ________ ________ ________ students have passed the exam.

38

- 이 강의 오염이 점점 더 심각해졌다. (serious)

➡ The pollution of this river has become ________ ________ ________ ________.

39 다음 표를 보고, 빈칸에 알맞은 말을 쓰시오.

Ann	Sarah	Susan
15 years old	14 years old	17 years old

- Ann is ________ than Susan.
- Sarah is ________ ________ of the three girls.
- Susan is ________ ________ of the three girls.

40 다음 우리말과 일치하도록 빈칸에 알맞은 말을 쓰시오.

- 그는 나보다 두 배 더 많은 책을 가지고 있다.

➡ He has ________ ________ many books ________ I do.

41 다음 우리말과 일치하도록 주어진 단어를 사용하여 문장을 완성하시오. (필요시 형태 변화)

- 그가 그 마을에 더 오래 머물수록, 그는 그곳을 더 많이 좋아했다. (long, much)

➡ ________ ________ he stayed in the village, ________ ________ he liked the place.

[42-47] 다음 표를 보고, 빈칸에 알맞은 말을 쓰시오.

Sarah	Lisa	Julie
163 cm	167 cm	163 cm
gets up at 7:00	gets up at 6:30	gets up at 6:30

42 Lisa is ________ than Sarah.

43 Julie is ________ ________ ________ Sarah.

44 Lisa is ________ ________ of the three girls.

45 Julie gets up ________ than Sarah.

46 Sarah gets up ________ than Lisa.

47 Julie gets up ________ ________ ________ Lisa.

[48-53] 다음 신제품 목록을 보고, 주어진 단어 중에서 알맞은 것을 선택하여 빈칸에 알맞은 말을 쓰시오.

모델명	Grand Star	Duocraft	Thunder
종류	sedan	compact car	sports car
가격	$ 30,000	$ 10,000	$ 20,000
시속	250 km/h	200 km/h	300 km/h

48 (fast / slow)
Duocraft is ________ than Grand Star.

49 (fast / slow)
Thunder is ________ than Duocraft.

50 (fast / slow)
Thunder is ________ ________ car of the three brand-new vehicles.

51 (expensive / cheap)
Grand Star is ________ ________ ________ ________ as Duocraft.

52 (expensive / cheap)
Thunder is ________ ________ ________ as Duocraft.

53 (expensive / cheap)
Duocraft is ________ ________ car of the three brand-new vehicles.

[15-16] 다음 빈칸에 들어갈 말이 바르게 짝지어진 것을 고르시오.

15

- The girl is watering the garden ________ a bucket.
- Traveling ________ ship was a wonderful experience.

① in — by　② in — through
③ with — by　④ by — with
⑤ with — through

16

- Henry first met her at the concert ________ 2010.
- Can you make it at the bookstore ________ 4 o'clock?

① in — on　② at — in　③ in — at
④ on — to　⑤ on — in

17 다음 빈칸에 들어갈 말로 알맞은 것은?

I have lived in this house ________ 1975.

① in　② on　③ till
④ from　⑤ since

18 다음 밑줄 친 부분이 어법상 틀린 것은?

① My ball rolled down the hill.
② I took a candy bar out of my pocket.
③ We have to drive through the tunnel.
④ He went into the room to get his bag.
⑤ Ted swam among the Han River last week.

서술형

19 다음 주어진 단어를 사용하여 우리말을 영작하시오.

- 그 남자는 그 문 쪽으로 걸어갔다.
(walked, the door)

➡ ________________________________

20 다음 우리말과 일치하도록 빈칸에 알맞은 말을 쓰시오.

- 놀랍게도, 그는 다시 성공했다.

➡ __________ my __________, he has succeeded again.

21 다음 중 어법상 틀린 곳을 찾아 바르게 고쳐 쓰시오.

- I found a seat among the two ladies.

__________ ➡ __________

[22-23] 다음 우리말과 일치하도록 <조건>에 맞게 문장을 쓰시오.

<조건>
- 7-9 단어로 쓸 것
- 주어진 어구를 사용할 것 (필요시 형태 변화)

22 그는 두 달 동안 유럽을 여행했다.
(travel around Europe)
➡ ______________________________

23 나는 여름 방학 동안 자원봉사를 할 것이다.
(do volunteer work)
➡ ______________________________

[24-29] 다음 Jane의 일기를 읽고, at, on, in 중에서 알맞은 전치사를 넣어 문장을 완성하시오.

Sunday, August 18th

I got up **24** ________ 6:30 early **25** ________ the morning, because I had a lot of things to do. I usually stay in bed late **26** ________ Sundays, but my mom woke me up. I had breakfast with my family **27** ________ 7 o'clock and left home for the place where I was supposed to meet my friends. Today was my best friend's birthday, so we had a party at his place. He was born **28** ________ 2006, and just turned 15. Celebrating his birthday, we had lunch together and decided to go to the cinema **29** ________ the evening.

[30-31] 다음 그림을 보고, 주어진 단어를 사용하여 문장을 완성하시오. (단, 현재진행시제로 쓸 것)

30

(soccer, the park)
Two boys ______________________________
______________________________.

31

(run, the school)
Two boys ______________________________
______________________________.

Chapter
11

관계사

1 주격 관계대명사 - who / which / that
2 목적격 관계대명사 - whom / which / that
3 소유격 관계대명사 - whose / of which
4 관계대명사 that
5 관계대명사 what
6 전치사 + 관계대명사
7 관계대명사의 생략
8 관계부사 I - where / when
9 관계부사 II - why / how
10 관계사의 계속적 용법
11 복합관계대명사
12 복합관계부사
■ 학교 시험 대비 문제

1 주격 관계대명사 - who / which / that

관계대명사는 접속사와 대명사의 역할을 하며, 선행사를 수식하는 형용사절을 이끈다.

선행사	주격 관계대명사
사람	who
동물, 사물	which
사람, 동물, 사물, 「사람 + 동물」, 「사람 + 사물」, 최상급, 서수, all, every, the only, the same 등이 포함된 경우	that

1 주격 관계대명사를 사용하여 문장 연결하기

Some students came to our school. + **They** looked like high school students.
어떤 학생들이 우리 학교에 왔다. + 그들은 고등학생처럼 보였다.

➡ **Some students who** looked like high school students came to our school.
고등학생처럼 보이는 어떤 학생들이 우리 학교에 왔다.

2 주격 관계대명사가 포함된 문장 구조
「선행사 + 주격 관계대명사 + (관계사절의) 동사」

The girl who is standing there is Tiffany. 저기 서 있는 그 소녀는 Tiffany이다. **<선행사 : 사람>**

I'm looking for **a herb which will cure** any disease for the eyes.
나는 눈병을 치료할 약초를 찾고 있다. **<선행사 : 사물>**

▶▶ 정답과 해설 p.43

EXERCISE A 다음 괄호 안에서 옳은 것을 고르시오.

1 The woman [who / which] visited me yesterday is my girlfriend.

2 The necklaces [which / who] lay on the table are hers.

3 People who [take / takes] care of their health are wise.

4 The street [which / who] was covered with snow looked dangerous.

5 There are many people who [eat / eats] with their hands in India.

6 She lives in the house [who / which] is clean and well decorated.

EXERCISE B 다음 문장에서 어법상 틀린 부분을 찾아 바르게 고쳐 쓰시오.

1 We will stay at the hostel who is cheap and nice.

2 Bring me the toothbrush what is on the shelf.

3 This is the novel who will be helpful to you.

4 My neighbor has a dog which look like a wolf.

5 The city which once were the richest in the world is now being destroyed.

6 Michael works for a company that make computers.

7 They look after patients which might die soon in nursing homes.

8 The new concert hall that can hold tens of thousands of people are going to open next year.

EXERCISE C 다음 주어진 두 문장을 <보기>와 같이 바꿔 쓸 때 빈칸에 알맞은 말을 쓰시오.

〈보기〉

The machine is now repaired. It broke down.
➡ The machine which broke down is now repaired.

1 I like the sitcom. It makes me very happy.
➡ I like ________________ me very happy.

2 Where is the meat? It was in the refrigerator.
➡ Where is ________________ in the refrigerator?

3 The man told me you were busy. He answered the phone.
➡ ________________ told me you were busy.

4 The building has been rebuilt. It was destroyed in the events.
➡ ________________ in the events has been rebuilt.

5 Do you know the woman? She is talking to Tom.
➡ Do you know ________________ Tom?

6 The professor was an African-American. He had influenced my theory.
➡ ________________ my theory was an African-American.

7 I like the man. The man is diligent.
➡ I like ________________ diligent.

2 목적격 관계대명사 - whom / which / that

선행사	목적격 관계대명사
사람	whom〔who〕
동물, 사물	which
사람, 동물, 사물, 「사람 + 동물」, 「사람 + 사물」, 최상급, 서수, all, every, the only, the same 등이 포함된 경우	that

* 목적격 관계대명사의 선행사가 사람인 경우, whom 대신 who를 쓰기도 한다.

1 목적격 관계대명사를 사용하여 문장 연결하기

The dress is not expensive. + Ann bought **it**. 그 드레스는 비싸지 않다. + Ann은 그것을 샀다.

➡ **The dress which〔that〕** Ann bought is not expensive. Ann이 산 그 드레스는 비싸지 않다.

2 목적격 관계대명사가 포함된 문장 구조 「선행사 + 목적격 관계대명사 + 주어 + 동사(목적어 없음)」

The house which we moved into was beautiful.
우리가 이사 간 그 집은 아름다웠다. **<선행사 : 사물>**

I saw **the man whom〔who〕 the police are searching for**.
나는 경찰이 찾고 있는 그 사람을 봤다. **<선행사 : 사람>**

▶▶ 정답과 해설 p.43

EXERCISE A 다음 괄호 안에서 옳은 것을 고르시오.

1 He spoke of the rainbow [whom / which] he had seen.

2 I forget most of the films [which / where] I watched.

3 All of them know the man [whom / whose] he mentioned.

4 There are a lot of safety rules [which / of which] you have to know before diving.

5 The office [who / which] Gregory worked for was full of books.

6 The task [which / who] he took on had a bad effect on his health.

EXERCISE B 다음 문장에서 어법상 틀린 부분을 찾아 바르게 고쳐 쓰시오.

1 I didn't understand the language what they were speaking.

2 The girl whom you met her at the party was an actress.

3 The bus which I took it got to the library twenty minutes later.

4 Where is the book whom I was reading?

5 You may know the film where James Cameron made in 1990s.

6 Do you remember the name of the institute whose Jimmy Carter founded?

EXERCISE C 다음 주어진 두 문장을 <보기>와 같이 바꿔 쓸 때 빈칸에 알맞은 말을 쓰시오.

<보기>
Is this the magazine? You ordered it from Amazon yesterday.
➡ Is this the magazine which you ordered from Amazon yesterday?

1 I refused the check. The company offered it to me.
➡ I refused ______________________ to me.

2 The eye doctor is famous. I saw her at the hospital.
➡ ______________________ at the hospital is famous.

3 Did you receive the postcards? I had sent them last month.
➡ Did you receive ______________________ last month?

4 Jennifer told me about the car. She was eager to buy it.
➡ Jennifer told me about ______________________ to buy.

5 Susan was working harder than anyone else. I paid her for the job.
➡ ______________________ harder than anyone else.

6 What are you going to do with the money? I gave you that money.
➡ What are you going to do with ______________________?

7 The woman often takes a walk in Central Park. I took a picture of her.
➡ ______________________ often takes a walk in Central Park.

8 Those houses are now gaining popularity. American Indians built them hundreds of years ago.
➡ ______________________ hundreds of years ago are now gaining popularity.

3 소유격 관계대명사 - whose / of which

선행사	소유격 관계대명사
사람	whose
동물, 사물	whose, of which

* of which는 주로 문어체에서 사용되는 표현으로, 실제 회화에서는 거의 사용되지 않는다.

1 소유격 관계대명사를 사용하여 문장 연결하기

I saw **a girl**. + **Her** hair came down to her waist.
나는 한 소녀를 보았다. + 그녀의 머리카락은 허리까지 내려왔다.

➡ I saw **a girl whose** hair came down to her waist. 나는 머리카락이 허리까지 내려오는 한 소녀를 보았다.

2 소유격 관계대명사가 포함된 문장 구조
「선행사 + 소유격 관계대명사 + 명사 + 동사」

The girl whose father is my boss works for the restaurant.
아버지가 내 상사인 그 소녀는 식당에서 일한다. **<선행사 : 사람>**

He has to repair **the chair whose legs are broken**.
그는 다리가 부러진 그 의자를 고쳐야 한다. **<선행사 : 사물>**

+ 소유격 관계대명사 vs. 목적격 관계대명사

소유격 관계대명사	「소유격 관계대명사 + 명사」를 포함한 완전한 문장 I have a friend **whose sister likes me**. 나는 여동생이 나를 좋아하는 친구가 한 명 있다.
목적격 관계대명사	「목적격 관계대명사 + 명사(대명사)」를 포함한 불완전한 문장 I have a friend **whom they like**. 나는 그들이 좋아하는 친구가 한 명 있다.

* 소유격 관계대명사는 관계대명사 that으로 바꿔 쓸 수 없다.

▶▶ 정답과 해설 p.43

EXERCISE A 다음 괄호 안에서 옳은 것을 고르시오.

1 Here comes the bus [of which / which] the roof is green.

2 I remember the soldier [whom / whose] accent is unique.

3 I've found the car keys [which / of which] you were looking for.

4 I drove the truck [whose / whom] engine seemed worn.

5 There's a TV show tonight [which / whose] you like.

6 The employer [whose / who] father was the mayor is a difficult person to work with.

7 My sister [which / whose] major is psychology works now at a hospital.

EXERCISE B 다음 문장에서 어법상 틀린 부분을 찾아 바르게 고쳐 쓰시오.

1 The book who cover was worn is mine.

2 Do you know the name of the hotel which view is great?

3 Do you remember the people whose we met in Italy?

4 The woman that name was familiar to me must be one of my friends.

5 He has a bicycle which wheels are very old.

6 I met a girl which father is a famous singer.

7 A boy who name was Paul came into the shop.

EXERCISE C 다음 주어진 두 문장을 <보기>와 같이 바꿔 쓸 때 빈칸에 알맞은 말을 쓰시오.

<보기>
She likes a man. His sister is a doctor. ➡ She likes a man whose sister is a doctor.

1 The car looked dangerous. Its door was broken.
➡ ________________ was broken looked dangerous.

2 I work for a company. The president of the company is in his early thirties.
➡ I work for ________________ is in his early thirties.

3 He doesn't trust his friends. Their concerns are only about money.
➡ He doesn't trust ________________ are only about money.

4 I have never been to Egypt. Its capital is Cairo.
➡ I have never been to ________________ is Cairo.

5 The young usually don't make efforts to succeed. Their parents are rich.
➡ ________________ are rich usually don't make efforts to succeed.

4 관계대명사 that

1 관계대명사 that을 주로 쓰는 경우

선행사 : 「사람 + 동물(사물)」	Look at **the girl and the dog that** are walking on the street. 길을 걷고 있는 저 소녀와 개를 봐.
선행사 : something, anything	There is **nothing that** I can give you. 내가 너에게 줄 수 있는 것이 없다.
선행사 : 형용사의 최상급	She is **the bravest** woman **that** I know. 그녀는 내가 아는 가장 용감한 여자다.
선행사 : 서수, all, every, the only, the same	**All that** I know is that she is a liar. 내가 아는 전부는 그녀가 거짓말쟁이라는 것이다.

2 관계대명사 that을 쓸 수 없는 경우

소유격	I know a girl ***that*** mother is a famous actress. (×) I know a girl **whose** mother is a famous actress. (○) 나는 어머니가 유명한 배우인 한 소녀를 안다.
전치사 뒤	The classmates ***with that*** I study are very kind. (×) The classmates **with whom** I study are very kind. (○) 내가 함께 공부하는 반 친구들은 매우 친절하다.
쉼표 뒤 (계속적 용법)	Julia told me about her new job, ***that*** she's enjoying very much. (×) Julia told me about her new job, **which** she's enjoying very much. (○) Julia는 나에게 그녀의 새 직업에 대해 얘기했는데, 그녀는 그것을 매우 즐기고 있다.

▶▶ 정답과 해설 p.43

EXERCISE A 다음 괄호 안에서 옳은 것을 고르시오.

1 Man is the only animal [which / that] laughs and weeps.

2 The girl for [whom / that] I was waiting didn't show up.

3 The first thing [that / what] you should do is exercise.

4 There are three men in the office, [that / who] are all millionaires.

EXERCISE B 다음 문장에서 어법상 틀린 부분을 찾아 바르게 고쳐 쓰시오.

1 The soup contains mushrooms, that he does not like.

2 He is the strongest man whose I have ever seen.

3 I had a dream in that I picked up a golden ring.

5 관계대명사 what

1 관계대명사 what

① 관계대명사 what은 '~하는 것'이라는 의미이며 the thing(s) which〔that〕로 바꿔 쓸 수 있다.
② 명사절을 이끌며 문장에서 주어, 목적어, 보어 역할을 한다.

I always believe **what** my mom says. 나는 나의 엄마가 말하는 것을 항상 믿는다.
➡ I always believe **the thing which〔that〕** my mom says.

What you have to do is (to) study hard. 네가 해야 하는 것은 열심히 공부하는 것이다. **<주어>**
This is **what happened yesterday**. 이것은 어제 일어난 일이다. **<보어>**
You should follow **what your parents say**. 너는 너희 부모님이 말씀하시는 것을 따라야 한다. **<목적어>**

2 관계대명사 what vs. 접속사 that

관계대명사 what	「관계대명사 what + 불완전한 문장」 I believe **what she told us** at the meeting. 나는 그녀가 그 회의에서 우리에게 말한 것을 믿는다.
접속사 that	「접속사 that + 완전한 문장」 I believe **that she told the truth** at the meeting. 나는 그녀가 그 회의에서 진실을 말했다고 믿는다.

3 관계대명사 what vs. 의문사 what

관계대명사 what (~하는 것)	일반적인 타동사와 함께 쓰임 I **bought what** he was selling. 나는 그가 팔고 있는 것을 샀다.
의문사 what (무엇)	의문, 불확실을 나타내는 동사와 함께 쓰임 (ask, wonder, don't know) I **asked what** he was selling. 나는 그가 무엇을 팔고 있는지 물어보았다.

▶▶ 정답과 해설 p.44

EXERCISE A 다음 괄호 안에서 옳은 것을 고르시오.

1 She told me [what / that] she knew.

2 People tend to avoid doing [what / that] is difficult.

3 We know [what / that] the next day will be difficult.

4 [What / Which] is done cannot be undone.

5 [What / That] the weather forecaster said about today proved to be wrong.

6 I don't believe [that / what] he is saying.

7 I know [what / that] she will win first prize.

8 When I heard [that / what] you said, I was surprised.

9 The police doubted [what / that] the boy was telling the truth.

10 [That / What] is learned in the cradle is carried to the grave.

EXERCISE B 다음 밑줄 친 단어가 관계대명사이면 '관', 의문사이면 '의'로 쓰시오.

1 Show me what is in your pocket.

2 I wonder what is in your pocket.

3 What do you want to be when you grow up?

4 What I want to get is that cute cat.

5 I want to know what this sentence really means.

6 Never put off till tomorrow what you can do today.

7 I don't believe what you have just said.

EXERCISE C 다음 우리말과 일치하도록 주어진 단어 또는 어구를 사용하여 문장을 완성하시오. (필요시 형태 변화)

1 너는 네가 뿌린 것을 거둬야 한다. (you, sow)
➡ You must reap ________ ________ ________.

2 나의 아버지가 남긴 것을 누가 받을까? (father, leave)
➡ Who will receive ________ ________ ________ ________?

3 민수는 그의 선생님이 말한 것을 기억할 수 없었다. (teacher, say)
➡ Minsu couldn't remember ________ ________ ________ ________.

4 나는 그녀가 하고 있는 일을 신경 쓰지 않는다. (be doing)
➡ I don't care ________ ________ ________ ________.

5 그들은 내가 전에 했던 것을 되풀이했다. (do, before)
➡ They repeated ________ ________ ________ ________ ________.

6 전치사 + 관계대명사

1 전치사가 포함된 관계대명사의 문장 구조
「선행사 + 전치사 + 관계대명사 + 완전한 문장」

They taught me **the methods through which I could get an A** in English.
그들은 나에게 영어에서 A를 받을 수 있는 방법들을 가르쳐 주었다.

2 전치사의 위치 변환

관계대명사가 전치사의 목적어인 경우, 전치사는 관계대명사 앞 또는 관계대명사절 끝에 올 수 있다.

This is the restaurant. He had dinner at the restaurant.
이곳이 그 레스토랑이다. 그는 그 레스토랑에서 저녁을 먹었다.

➡ This is the restaurant **at which** he had dinner. 이곳이 그가 저녁을 먹은 레스토랑이다. **<관계대명사 앞>**

*** 전치사가 관계대명사 앞에 올 경우 : 관계대명사 생략 불가, 관계대명사를 that으로 바꿔 쓸 수 없음**

➡ This is the restaurant **which** he had dinner **at**. **<관계대명사절 끝>**

*** 전치사가 관계대명사절 끝에 올 경우 : 관계대명사 생략 가능, 관계대명사를 that으로 바꿔 쓸 수 있음**

! 관계대명사 that 앞에는 전치사를 쓸 수 없다.

The subject ***in that*** I'm interested is English. (×)
The subject **in which** I'm interested is English. (○) 내가 관심 있는 과목은 영어다.

▶▶ 정답과 해설 p.44

EXERCISE A 다음 괄호 안에서 옳은 것을 고르시오.

1 I want to see the fog [which / for which] London is famous.

2 *The Cats* is the name of the musical [which / in which] ran for over ten years.

3 The person [whom / from whom] you got the information from is my sister.

4 The man [whom / by whom] you are standing is Mr. Kim.

5 The age [which / at which] people can begin driving depends on the law.

6 He is the nephew [to whom / for whom] I bought this toy.

7 She had a big cushion [in which / on which] she could sit.

8 I have many friends [with whom / whom] I can play.

9 Do you have a pen [on which / with which] you can write?

EXERCISE B **다음 주어진 두 문장을 <보기>와 같이 바꿔 쓸 때 빈칸에 알맞은 말을 쓰시오.**

〈보기〉

The man is my roommate. I'm staying with him.
➡ The man with whom I'm staying is my roommate.
➡ The man whom(that) I'm staying with is my roommate.

1 She met her old friend. She used to play the piano with him.
➡ She met ______________________________.
➡ She met ______________________________.

2 Have you read the article? I told you about it.
➡ Have you read ______________________?
➡ Have you read ______________________?

3 I remembered the name of the guy. I spoke to him on the phone.
➡ I remembered ______________________ on the phone.
➡ I remembered ______________________ on the phone.

4 The boy will be moved to another club. Everybody would like to play with him.
➡ The boy ______________________ will be moved to another club.
➡ The boy ______________________ will be moved to another club.

EXERCISE C **다음 우리말과 일치하도록 주어진 단어를 배열하여 문장을 완성하시오.**

1 이곳이 우리가 살고 있는 집이다. (been, which, in, have, we)
➡ This is the house ______________________ living.

2 네가 찾고 있던 지갑은 서랍 안에 있다. (you, for, looking, were)
➡ The wallet which ______________________ is in the drawer.

3 여기에 내가 가장 간단한 설명을 찾을 수 있는 그 책이 있다. (which, I, find, can, in)
➡ Here is the book ______________________ the simplest explanation.

4 내가 기내에서 싸웠던 그 승객은 매우 수다스러웠다. (with, a fight, I, had)
➡ The passenger whom ______________________ on the plane was very talkative.

7 관계대명사의 생략

1 목적격 관계대명사는 생략이 가능하다.

Have you ever heard the song **(that)** she wrote? 너는 그녀가 쓴 노래를 들어 본 적이 있니?

2 「주격 관계대명사 + be동사」는 생략이 가능하다.

There is a great sculpture **(which is)** made of marble in the Louvre.
루브르 박물관에는 대리석으로 만들어진 위대한 조각품이 있다.

! 계속적 용법의 관계사와 전치사 뒤에 오는 목적격 관계대명사는 생략할 수 없다.

I went to China, **where** I met her. 나는 중국에 갔는데, 거기서 그녀를 만났다. **<계속적 용법>**
The man **with whom** I was talking was Tom. 나와 이야기하고 있던 그 남자는 Tom이었다. **<전치사+관계대명사>**

▶▶ 정답과 해설 p.44

EXERCISE A 다음 문장에서 생략 가능한 부분에 밑줄을 그으시오.

1 The letter that you had sent was not delivered yet.

2 The girl who was sitting by me was chatting with her friend.

3 The soldier who was injured in the battle is being carried to the hospital.

4 I can't go to the film festival that you recommended.

5 The girl that I gave a party for is singing a song.

EXERCISE B 다음 문장에서 관계대명사가 생략된 곳에 V 표시를 한 후, 생략된 말을 쓰시오.

1 The party we went to last night was amazing.

2 The concert planned to begin at 3 o'clock was cancelled.

3 Ramen was made in 1950s by a man called Ando.

4 Exercise helps control our weight by using extra calories we ate.

5 Who's the girl dancing with your brother?

8 관계부사 I - where / when

관계부사는 형용사절을 이끌며, 절 안에서 부사 역할을 한다.

선행사	관계부사	전치사+관계대명사
the place, the house (장소)	where	in〔on, at〕 which
the time, the day (시간)	when	at〔on, in〕 which

1 관계부사를 사용하여 문장 연결하기

This is **the hotel**. + The accident happened **in this hotel**.
이곳이 그 호텔이다. + 그 사건은 이 호텔에서 일어났다.
➡ This is **the hotel where** the accident happened. 이곳이 그 사건이 일어난 호텔이다.
➡ This is **the hotel in which** the accident happened.

The day will come. + The world ends **on that day**. 그날이 올 것이다. + 세상은 그때 끝난다.
➡ **The day when** the world ends will come. 세상이 끝나는 날이 올 것이다.
➡ **The day on which** the world ends will come.

2 관계부사 vs. 관계대명사

관계부사	•「선행사+관계부사+완전한 문장」 This is the parking lot **where** everybody may pull the car. (the parking lot: 선행사 / where: 관계부사 / everybody: 주어 / may pull: 동사 / the car: 목적어) 이곳은 누구나 차를 세워도 되는 주차장이다.
관계대명사	•「선행사+관계대명사+불완전한 문장」 This is the parking lot **which** everybody can use. (the parking lot: 선행사 / which: 관계대명사 / everybody: 주어 / can use: 동사 (목적어가 빠져 있음)) 이곳은 누구나 이용할 수 있는 주차장이다.

▶▶ 정답과 해설 p.44

EXERCISE A 다음 괄호 안에서 옳은 것을 고르시오.

1 The house [which / where] I live will be torn down soon.

2 Can you recognize the house [which / where] we visited?

3 England is one of the few countries [which / where] people drive on the left.

4 Tomorrow is the day [which / when] I've been waiting for.

5 There was a time [where / when] people could live without a car.

6 The post office is the place [which / where] people can send a package.

7 Is this the place [where / which] you talked about last time?

8 There is a wallet on the floor [where / which] the guest dropped.

EXERCISE B **다음 주어진 두 문장을 <보기>와 같이 바꿔 쓸 때, 빈칸에 알맞은 말을 쓰시오.**

> <보기>
> Please show me the way to the hotel. I am staying there now.
> ➡ Please show me the way to the hotel where〔at which〕 I am staying now.

1 The city is near the lake. I used to live in that city.
➡ The city ______________________ is near the lake.

2 May is a beautiful month. At that time, all living things come to life.
➡ May is a beautiful month ______________________.

3 The time will soon come. We can see the reunification of Korea at that time.
➡ The time ______________________ will soon come.

4 Rocky was born in the city. There was a gang fight every day in that city.
➡ Rocky was born in the city ______________________.

5 The day was her wedding anniversary. My aunt's store opened that day.
➡ The day ______________________ was her wedding anniversary.

EXERCISE C **다음 우리말과 일치하도록 주어진 단어를 배열하여 문장을 완성하시오.**

1 나는 우리가 만난 그날을 기억한다. (we, met, when)
➡ I remember the day ______________________.

2 Roswell은 그녀가 태어난 도시이다. (she, born, where, was)
➡ Roswell is the town ______________________.

3 누군가가 내가 기다리고 있던 방으로 들어왔다. (I, where, waiting, was)
➡ Someone entered the room ______________________.

4 그때는 내가 해외로 나갔던 해였다. (abroad, when, went, I)
➡ That was the year ______________________.

9 관계부사 II - why / how

선행사	관계부사	전치사 + 관계대명사
the reason (이유)	why	for which
the way (방법)	how	in which

1 관계부사를 사용하여 문장 연결하기

That is **the reason**. + She has never laughed before **for that reason**.
그것이 그 이유다. + 그녀는 그 이유로 전에 한 번도 웃어본 적이 없다.

➡ That is **the reason why** she has never laughed before.

➡ That is **the reason for which** she has never laughed before.
그것이 그녀가 전에 한 번도 웃어본 적이 없는 이유다.

2 관계부사의 생략

관계부사 앞에 선행사가 있는 경우 관계부사를 생략할 수 있다.

Today is **the day (when)** I can relax. 오늘은 내가 쉴 수 있는 날이다.

3 선행사의 생략

관계부사의 선행사가 the place, the time, the reason과 같이 일반적인 경우나 문맥상 알 수 있는 경우에는 생략할 수 있다.

Today is **(the day) when** I can relax. 오늘은 내가 쉴 수 있는 날이다.

cf. 특정한 때나 장소를 나타내는 선행사는 생략할 수 없다.

This is the only day **when** I can relax. 이 날은 내가 쉴 수 있는 유일한 날이다. **<선행사 the only day 생략 불가>**

! 선행사 the way와 관계부사 how는 함께 쓸 수 없으며 둘 중 하나를 생략해야 한다.

That's **the way** it works. (○) 그게 그것이 작동하는 방식이다.

➡ That's **how** it works. (○)　　That's ***the way how*** it works. (×)

▶▶ 정답과 해설 p.45

EXERCISE A 다음 괄호 안에서 옳은 것을 고르시오.

1 There is no reason [why / how] I should be responsible for our failure.

2 I came to know [the way / the way how] you love me.

3 The reason [which / why] the team lost the game was the injuries of the key players.

▶▶ 정답과 해설 p.45

EXERCISE A 다음 주어진 문장을 <보기>와 같이 바꿔 쓸 때, 빈칸에 알맞은 말을 쓰시오.

〈보기〉
We climbed to the top of the mountain, which was a great experience.
➡ We climbed to the top of the mountain, and it was a great experience.

1 We had been waiting for the princess, who didn't show up.
➡ We had been waiting for the princess, ______________________.

2 Sam offered to let me stay in his cottage, which was very nice of him.
➡ Sam offered to let me stay in his cottage, ______________________.

EXERCISE B 다음 주어진 두 문장을 <보기>와 같이 바꿔 쓸 때, 빈칸에 알맞은 말을 쓰시오.

〈보기〉
Our flight was delayed. This means we had to stay at the airport all night.
➡ Our flight was delayed, which means we had to stay at the airport all night.

1 The neighbor was found dead. It was a shock to that village.
➡ ______________________ a shock to that village.

2 Brian passed the exam. It was good news to his family.
➡ ______________________ good news to his family.

3 Eric didn't answer the phone. This made his mother worried.
➡ ______________________ his mother worried.

EXERCISE C 다음 주어진 두 문장을 <보기>와 같이 바꿔 쓸 때, 빈칸에 알맞은 말을 쓰시오.

〈보기〉
I visited Paris. I met an old friend of mine there.
➡ I visited Paris, where I met an old friend of mine.

1 He found a good restaurant. He had a meal there.
➡ He found a good restaurant, ______________________.

2 I arrived there on Monday. I saw the rainbow that day.
➡ I arrived there on Monday, ______________________.

3 We met him in the harbor yesterday. We were just leaving for the island then.
➡ We met him in the harbor yesterday, ______________________.

11 복합관계대명사

복합관계대명사는 선행사를 포함하기 때문에 복합관계대명사 앞에는 선행사가 없다.

복합관계대명사	명사절	부사절
whoever	~하는 사람은 누구든지 = anyone who	누가 ~하더라도 = no matter who
whomever	~하는 사람은 누구든지 = anyone whom	누구를 ~하더라도 = no matter whom
whichever	~하는 것은 어느 것이든지 = anything that	어느 것이(을) ~하더라도 = no matter which
whatever	~하는 것은 무엇이든지 = anything that	무엇이(을) ~하더라도 = no matter what

Whoever breaks the rule will be punished. **<명사절>**
규칙을 위반하는 사람은 누구든지 처벌 받을 것이다. **<= Anyone who>**

Whoever may tell you about me, you don't have to believe it. **<부사절>**
누가 너에게 나에 관한 말을 하더라도, 너는 그것을 믿을 필요가 없다. **<= No matter who>**

+ 복합관계대명사 whatever vs. 관계대명사 what

My father gave me **whatever** I need.
나의 아버지는 내가 필요로 하는 것이 무엇이든지 내게 주셨다. **<anything that : '무제한'의 의미>**

My father gave me **what** I need.
나의 아버지는 내가 필요로 하는 것을 내게 주셨다. **<the thing that : '제한'의 의미>**

▶▶ 정답과 해설 p.45

EXERCISE A 다음 괄호 안에서 옳은 것을 고르시오.

1 [Who / Whoever] wants to eat this cake may take it.

2 No matter [what / when] you say, he will not change his mind.

3 [Whoever / whom] wants to meet him can enter the room.

4 [Whatever / However] you say, I won't believe you.

5 [Which / Whichever] you may choose, they'll reject it.

6 Write down [whatever / however] comes to your mind.

7 He will give this invitation to [whichever / whomever] he likes.

8 You should remember there is always risk [whatever / whoever] you do.

EXERCISE B 다음 주어진 문장을 <보기>와 같이 바꿔 쓸 때, 빈칸에 알맞은 말을 쓰시오.

〈보기〉

Do whatever you need to do. ➡ Do anything that you need to do.
Whatever she does, I understand. ➡ No matter what she does, I understand.

1 I will give her whatever she needs.
➡ I will give her ____________________.

2 Whatever happens to your company, it's none of my business.
➡ ____________________, it's none of my business.

3 Whomever you ask, you'll not get an answer.
➡ ____________________, you'll not get an answer.

4 Whatever they choose, they can't have it.
➡ ____________________, they can't have it.

5 Whoever wins, it isn't important for me.
➡ ____________________, it isn't important for me.

EXERCISE C 다음 우리말과 일치하도록 주어진 단어를 사용하여 문장을 완성하시오. (필요시 형태 변화)

1 네가 하고 싶은 것은 무엇이든지 해라. (like, you)
➡ Do ______ ______ ______ to do.

2 우리에게 무슨 일이 일어나더라도, 우리는 우리나라를 지켜낼 것이다. (happen, may)
➡ ______ ______ ______ to us, we will defend our country.

3 우리는 우리가 좋아하는 누구에게든지 선물을 줄 것이다. (like, we)
➡ We will give a present to ______ ______ ______.

4 네가 어떤 동아리에 가입하더라도, 회원들은 너를 환영해줄 것이다. (club, may, join, you)
➡ ______ ______ ______ ______ ______, the members will welcome you.

5 너의 계획이 무엇이더라도, 나는 너와 함께 갈 것이다. (plan, is)
➡ ______ ______ ______ ______, I'll go with you.

12 복합관계부사

복합관계부사는 선행사를 포함하기 때문에 복합관계부사 앞에는 선행사가 없다.

복합관계부사	장소·시간의 부사절 〈긍정〉	양보의 부사절 〈대립〉
wherever	~(하는 곳은) 어디든지 = in(at) any place where	어디에서 ~하더라도 = no matter where
whenever	~(할 때는) 언제든지, ~할 때마다 = at any time when	언제 ~하더라도 = no matter when
however	—	아무리 ~하더라도 = no matter how

Wherever you go, people will welcome you. **〈장소의 부사절〉**
네가 가는 곳 어디든지, 사람들은 너를 환영할 것이다. **〈= In any place where〉**

Wherever you may go, I will be waiting for you here. **〈양보의 부사절〉**
네가 어디에 가더라도, 나는 이곳에서 너를 기다릴 것이다. **〈= No matter where〉**

! however가 쓰인 문장은 어순에 주의해야 한다.
「however+형용사(부사)+주어+동사」 → 「no matter how+형용사(부사)+주어+동사」

However hard it may be, you must solve the problem. 그것이 아무리 어렵더라도, 너는 그 문제를 풀어야 한다.
➡ **No matter how hard** it may be, you must solve the problem.

▶▶ 정답과 해설 p.45

EXERCISE A 다음 괄호 안에서 옳은 것을 고르시오.

1 [Wherever / However] much I may try, things are getting worse.

2 Please be seated [wherever / however] you like.

3 [Whichever / Wherever] he appeared, his fans followed him.

EXERCISE B 다음 우리말과 일치하도록 주어진 단어를 사용하여 문장을 완성하시오. (필요시 형태 변화)

1 네가 어디에 가더라도, 너는 그것을 발견하지 못할 것이다. (go, you)
➡ _________ _________ _________, you will not find it.

2 나는 뭔가를 사고 싶을 때마다 쇼핑을 하러 갈 것이다. (want, I)
➡ I'm going shopping _________ _________ _________ to buy something.

3 그 여자가 아무리 예쁘더라도, 나는 내 마음을 바꾸지 않겠다. (is, the woman, pretty)
➡ _________ _________ _________ _________ _________, I won't change my mind.

Chapter 11
관계사

학교 시험 대비 문제

맞힌 개수	
선택형	____ / 39
서술형	____ / 9

▶▶ 정답과 해설 p.45

01 다음 빈칸에 들어갈 말로 알맞은 것은?

> My daughter ________ just returned from abroad will go to high school.

① who ② whose ③ whom
④ what ⑤ which

고난도

02 다음 빈칸에 공통으로 들어갈 말로 알맞은 것은?

> • ________ you say, I will not go to his party.
> • ________ has a beginning also has an end.

① Whoever ② Whatever
③ Whenever ④ Wherever
⑤ Whichever

03 다음 빈칸에 들어갈 말로 알맞은 것은?

> • This is the thing which you should do before you go to high school.
> = This is ________ you should do before you go to high school.

① which ② that ③ what
④ where ⑤ when

고난도

04 다음 중 어법상 올바른 것은?

① I know the way how you did it.
② He didn't understand that you said.
③ She was offered a good job, that she declined.
④ He teaches a boy whose talent is very unique.
⑤ Japan is the country where is famous for hot springs.

05 다음 대화의 빈칸에 알맞은 것은?

> A Who's that girl ________ hair is black?
> B She's one of my classmates.
> A Where is she from?
> B I heard she's from Korea.

① who ② whom ③ whose
④ which ⑤ in which

[06-08] 다음 빈칸에 들어갈 말로 알맞은 것을 고르시오.

06

> Is this the house ________ ghosts appear?

① which ② that ③ what
④ where ⑤ who

07

> This is the village in ________ I lived until I entered the high school.

① which ② that ③ where
④ at which ⑤ what

08

> Don't tell others ________ you are going to do.

① who ② whom ③ that
④ which ⑤ what

고난도

09 다음 중 어법상 틀린 것은?

① The people whom I work with are all kind.
② He has some money which he can buy a car.
③ The forms which we had to fill in were not simple.
④ She had a holiday during which she saw her family.
⑤ This is the reason for which we have to defend ourselves.

10 다음 빈칸에 들어갈 말로 알맞은 것은?

> The cottage ________ we stayed last winter was too expensive.

① which ② where ③ when
④ there ⑤ here

11 다음 밑줄 친 부분 대신 사용할 수 있는 것은?

> England was an empire on which the sun never set.

① who ② whom ③ where
④ when ⑤ how

고난도

12 다음 빈칸에 들어갈 말로 알맞은 것은?

> • She found her lost children, and they were all alive.
> = She found her lost children, ________ were all alive.

① who ② whom ③ whose
④ that ⑤ what

13 다음 문장의 빈칸에 생략된 말로 가장 알맞은 것은?

The products ________ delivered were different from those of last year.

① that is ② that was ③ that are
④ that were ⑤ what are

14 다음 빈칸에 들어갈 말로 알맞은 것은?

I like the book ________ cover is well designed.

① which ② that ③ in which
④ what ⑤ whose

15 다음 중 빈칸에 들어갈 말이 나머지 넷과 다른 것은?

① The house ________ we live needs fixing.
② This is the apartment ________ I was looking for.
③ I know this area ________ the war broke out first.
④ The lake ________ we were swimming was very deep.
⑤ I will go to the city ________ I can meet many people.

16 다음 두 문장을 한 문장으로 연결할 때 빈칸에 알맞은 것은?

• There are a few students.
• Their memories are better than others.
➡ There are a few students ________ memories are better than others.

① whom ② that ③ when
④ whose ⑤ where

17 다음 빈칸에 들어갈 말로 알맞은 것은?

My mom wanted to finish the party earlier, ________ was impossible.

① who ② which ③ that
④ what ⑤ where

18 다음 빈칸에 들어갈 말로 알맞은 것은?

• No matter what happens, I'll be on your side.
= ________ happens, I'll be on your side.

① Whichever ② Whoever
③ Whatever ④ However
⑤ Whenever

고난도

19 다음 문장의 밑줄 친 부분과 쓰임이 같은 것은?

What is important right now is how to carry that heavy box.

① I wonder what brought her here.
② I want to know what her name is.
③ What kind of food do you like best?
④ What I planned yesterday was useless.
⑤ What are you going to do when you grow up?

20 다음 빈칸에 공통으로 들어갈 말로 알맞은 것은?

• Do you know ________ broke the vase?
• I have a friend ________ can teach you how to dance.

① as ② if ③ who
④ how ⑤ where

고난도

21 다음 중 어법상 틀린 것은?

① Ann is hiding what she is afraid of.
② Ann is hiding something she is afraid of.
③ Ann is hiding something that she is afraid of.
④ Ann is hiding something of that she is afraid.
⑤ Ann is hiding something of which she is afraid.

22 다음 두 문장을 한 문장으로 바꿔 쓸 때 빈칸에 들어갈 말로 알맞은 것은?

• The house will be rebuilt.
• We have lived in the house.
➡ The house ________ we have lived in will be rebuilt.

① which ② where ③ in which
④ what ⑤ wherever

23 다음 중 어법상 틀린 것은?

① This is the town my son was born in.
② This is the town which my son was born.
③ This is the town where my son was born.
④ This is the town which my son was born in.
⑤ This is the town in which my son was born.

24 다음 빈칸에 들어갈 말로 알맞은 것은?

You are the only person ________ witnessed the accident.

① whose ② whom ③ which
④ what ⑤ that

25 다음 중 빈칸에 들어갈 말이 나머지 넷과 다른 것은?

① This is _________ I am late for school.
② That's exactly _________ I'm talking about.
③ She's not satisfied with _________ she has now.
④ Read these sentences and find _________ is wrong.
⑤ _________ I am trying to tell you may hurt you.

26 다음 두 문장을 한 문장으로 연결할 때 빈칸에 들어갈 말로 알맞은 것은?

> • The hotel was once on fire.
> • That made it lose its fame.
> ➡ The hotel was once on fire, _________ made it lose its fame.

① that ② which ③ what
④ where ⑤ and

27 다음 중 어법상 어색한 것은?

① Charlie had a cat which everybody liked.
② The car which Jane is driving is her father's.
③ The girl whom Mike likes lives near my house.
④ The movie whom we saw yesterday was very good.
⑤ The comic book which I read last night was funny.

28 다음 중 밑줄 친 부분을 생략할 수 없는 것은?

① This is the house of which I spoke.
② Can I borrow the book that you bought?
③ Is this the bag which you are looking for?
④ The girl whom you asked out is my girlfriend.
⑤ You can see many girls who are hanging around.

고난도

29 다음 빈칸에 들어갈 말로 알맞은 것은?

> We reached the point _________ the government should decide whether or not to send the troops.

① who ② when ③ how
④ why ⑤ what

30 다음 빈칸에 들어갈 말로 알맞은 것은?

> • I met the woman, who invited me to dinner.
> = I met the woman, _________ she invited me to dinner.

① whom ② whoever ③ and
④ but ⑤ that

31 다음 우리말과 일치하도록 빈칸에 알맞은 말을 모두 고르시오.

> • 너는 그들이 갑자기 떠난 이유를 알고 있니?
> ➡ Do you know ________ they left suddenly?

① how ② why ③ however
④ the way ⑤ the reason

32 다음 빈칸에 들어갈 말이 나머지 넷과 다른 것은?

① This is ________ I am always thinking.
② She always wears ________ is in fashion.
③ I didn't understand ________ my teacher explained.
④ Let me tell you the story ________ I heard from Dad.
⑤ ________ he is trying to say is the top secret of his company.

고난도

33 다음 문장의 빈칸에 알맞은 것은?

> My dog, ________ I looked for ten years, died last month.

① who ② which ③ whose
④ of which ⑤ after which

34 다음 중 밑줄 친 부분을 생략할 수 없는 것은?

① The kid whom I met looked pretty.
② She is the student that all teachers like.
③ We live in an age in which technology is incredibly important.
④ Chess is the game which I am interested in.
⑤ The sculpture which was made by Rodin moved us.

35 다음 밑줄 친 부분이 어법상 틀린 것은?

① Seoul is the city in which I grew up.
② Please give me a chair on which I can sit.
③ The man is the writer whose book sells well.
④ I know a girl who mother runs a big company.
⑤ The place where you were born is in reconstruction.

36 다음 중 어법상 올바른 것은?

① This is how MERS spreads.
② This is the place which we spent many years.
③ Is there any reason how you avoided me?
④ I don't know what she got angry with me.
⑤ This is the restroom in where you may wash yourself.

37 다음 빈칸에 들어갈 말이 바르게 짝지어진 것은?

- I like the season ________ the flowers are in full bloom.
- Let me tell you ________ I got there.

① which — when ② which — why
③ when — which ④ when — how
⑤ what — what

38 다음 빈칸에 들어갈 말로 알맞은 것은?

- 우리가 아무리 일찍 출발하더라도, 우리는 비행기를 탈 수가 없다.

➡ No matter ________ early we start, we can't catch the flight.

① when ② where ③ how
④ why ⑤ what

39 다음 문장에서 생략할 수 있는 것은?

Do ① you ② know ③ the man ④ who is ⑤ standing on the beach?

서술형

40 다음 두 문장을 한 문장으로 바꿔 쓰시오.

- The city was full of many tourists.
- We visited that city during summer vacation.

➡ ____
____

41 다음 두 문장을 한 문장으로 연결할 때 빈칸에 알맞은 말을 쓰시오.

- There are many reasons.
- I have changed my mind for the reasons.

➡ There are many reasons ________ I have changed my mind.

42 다음 문장에서 어법상 틀린 곳을 찾아 바르게 고쳐 쓰시오.

I have to sell the house where my grandfather built.

________________ ➡ ________________

[43-45] 다음 James의 메모를 읽고, <조건>에 맞게 <보기>와 같이 문장을 완성하시오.

Tiffany	She has been on a variety of TV shows.
Jessica	She graduated from an international school.
Yoona	My friend likes her best.
Yuri	Her nickname is Black Pearl.

<조건>

- 선행사 the girl에 알맞은 관계대명사를 사용할 것
- 괄호 안에 적힌 단어 수에 맞게 쓸 것

<보기>

Tiffany is the girl who has been on a variety of TV shows.

43 (6단어) Jessica is the girl ______________________________.

44 (5단어) Yoona is the girl ______________________________.

45 (5단어) Yuri is the girl ______________________________.

[46-48] 다음 여름 방학 때 했던 일을 읽고, 알맞은 관계부사를 사용하여 문장을 완성하시오.

46

I stayed at the hotel for a week.
Susan

Susan talked about the hotel ______________________________.

47

I enjoyed swimming on the beach.
Brian

Brian talked about the beach ______________________________.

48

I went on a camping trip to Mt. Jiri.
Paul

Paul talked about Mt. Jiri ______________________________.

Chapter

12

접속사

1 등위접속사 and / but / or / so
2 상관접속사
3 명사절을 이끄는 접속사 I - that
4 명사절을 이끄는 접속사 II - if / whether
5 간접의문문
6 so / so that ~ / so ~ that ...
7 부사절을 이끄는 접속사 I - 원인 / 양보
8 부사절을 이끄는 접속사 II - 시간
9 부사절을 이끄는 접속사 III - 조건
10 주의해야 할 접속사 - as / while
11 접속부사
■ 학교 시험 대비 문제

1 등위접속사 and / but / or / so

등위접속사는 문법상 대등한 단어와 단어, 구와 구, 절과 절을 연결시켜주는 역할을 한다.

and	~와, 그리고	Harry **and** Sally were good friends. Harry와 Sally는 좋은 친구였다. Out of the frying pan **and** into the fire. 튀김팬에서 불속으로(엎친 데 덮친 격) Harry is handsome **and** Sally is cute. Harry는 잘생기고 Sally는 귀엽다.
but	그러나, 하지만	Harry loves Sally, **but** she doesn't love him. Harry는 Sally를 사랑하지만, 그녀는 그를 사랑하지 않는다.
or	또는, 즉	He **or** she had to leave this town. 그 또는 그녀가 이 마을을 떠나야만 했다. H1N1, **or** the new flu virus, continues to spread all over the world. H1N1, 즉 신종 독감 바이러스가 전 세계로 계속 퍼져 나간다.
so	그래서	Kate was tired, **so** she went to bed early. Kate는 피곤해서 일찍 잤다.

▶▶ 정답과 해설 p.48

EXERCISE A **다음 괄호 안에서 옳은 것을 고르시오.**

1 The show was good [and / but / so] boring.

2 Which one do you prefer, pears [and / but / or] grapes?

3 The host will prepare special food [and / but / so] decorate his house.

4 I entered my password [and / or / but] checked my emails.

5 She invited everyone, [so / but / or] only two of them came.

6 Which do you want to wear, sneakers [or / and / but] high heels?

7 He hid behind a tree, [and / but / or] his mother soon found him out.

8 She studied very hard, [but / or / so] she got a good grade.

9 Do you work at a hospital [and / but / or] a kindergarten?

10 I'm not sure whether I'll stay here [so / and / or] go abroad.

2 상관접속사

both *A* and *B*	A, B 둘 다 (복수 취급)	**Both** mother **and** child are fine. 어머니와 아이 둘 다 괜찮다.
not *A* but *B*	A 가 아니라 B (B에 수 일치)	He is **not** a lawyer **but** an accountant. 그는 변호사가 아니라 회계사다.
either *A* or *B*	A, B 둘 중 하나 (B에 수 일치)	**Either** the mother **or** the child is ill. 어머니와 아이 둘 중 하나는 아프다.
neither *A* nor *B*	A, B 둘 다 아닌 (B에 수 일치)	**Neither** she **nor** I plan to attend the meeting. 그녀도 나도 그 회의에 참석할 계획이 없다.
not only *A* but also *B* = *B* as well as *A*	A뿐만 아니라 B도 (B에 수 일치)	**Not only** I **but also** she is going to join the party. 나뿐만 아니라 그녀도 파티에 참석할 것이다. ➡ She **as well as** I is going to join the party.

▶▶ 정답과 해설 p.49

EXERCISE A 다음 괄호 안에서 옳은 것을 고르시오.

1 You must answer with either yes [and / or] no.

2 I have neither time [or / nor] money to travel abroad.

3 It's not a shame for both men [and / or] women to cry in front of others.

4 I'd like to learn not only English [but / or] also Chinese to become a diplomat.

5 [Both / Either] my mother [and / or] father were very strict when I was young.

6 The car accident did not happen on Monday, [and / but] on Friday.

EXERCISE B 다음 문장에서 어법상 틀린 곳을 찾아 바르게 고쳐 쓰시오.

1 Either you or I is going to the concert.

2 Not only you but also he are responsible for the case.

3 I think that either he or you is wrong.

4 Both Christie and Sarah has studied science.

5 She as well as I don't play the violin.

EXERCISE C 다음 두 문장을 <보기>와 같이 바꿔 쓸 때 빈칸에 알맞은 말을 쓰시오.

〈보기〉

I am interested in hip hop. I am also interested in computer games.
➡ I am interested not only in hip hop but also in computer games.
➡ I am interested in computer games as well as in hip hop.

1 Mary is beautiful. Mary is also smart.
➡ Mary is ____________________.
➡ Mary is ____________________.

2 Coffee makes me relieved. Coffee also makes me comfortable.
➡ Coffee makes me ____________________.
➡ Coffee makes me ____________________.

3 Smoking is bad for myself. Smoking is also bad for others.
➡ Smoking is bad ____________________.
➡ Smoking is bad ____________________.

4 The World Cup brought a dream to South Africa. The World Cup also brought hope to South Africa.
➡ The World Cup brought ____________________ to South Africa.
➡ The World Cup brought ____________________ to South Africa.

EXERCISE D 다음 우리말과 일치하도록 빈칸에 알맞은 말을 쓰시오.

1 헬렌 켈러는 들을 수도 볼 수도 없었다.
➡ Helen Keller could ________ hear ________ see.

2 Jane은 피아노와 바이올린 둘 다 연주할 수 있다.
➡ Jane can play ________ the piano ________ the violin.

3 민호와 나 둘 중 하나는 반장으로 선출될 것이다.
➡ ________ Minho ________ I will be selected class president.

4 Mata Hari는 아름다운 댄서였을뿐만 아니라 냉철한 스파이였다.
➡ Mata Hari was a cold-hearted spy ________ ________ ________ a beautiful dancer.

5 너와 그 둘 다 그 모임에 참석해야 한다.
➡ ________ you ________ he have to attend the meeting.

3 명사절을 이끄는 접속사 I - that

that절은 주어, 목적어, 보어 역할을 한다. 목적어절을 이끄는 접속사 that은 생략할 수 있다.

That he lied is not certain. **<주어 역할 : ~라는 것은>**

➡ **It** is not certain **that** he lied. 그가 거짓말을 했다는 것은 확실하지 않다.

I think **that** Michael is innocent. **<목적어 역할 : ~라는 것을> that 생략 가능**

➡ I think Michael is innocent. 나는 Michael이 무죄라고 생각한다.

The only problem is **that** this car is too expensive. **<보어 역할 : ~라는 것>**

유일한 문제는 이 차가 너무 비싸다는 것이다.

+ 접속사 that vs. 관계사 that

접속사 that	선행사 없음 (that + 완전한 문장)	I believe **that** love doesn't change. 나는 사랑이 변하지 않는다고 믿는다.
관계사 that	선행사 + that + 불완전한 문장	I believe in **love that** doesn't change. 나는 변하지 않는 사랑을 믿는다.

▶▶ 정답과 해설 p.49

EXERCISE A 다음 문장을 <보기>와 같이 가주어를 사용하여 바꿔 쓸 때 빈칸에 알맞은 말을 쓰시오.

<보기>
That he was dead is true. ➡ It is true that he was dead.

1 That students do their homework is important.
➡ ________________ students do their homework.

2 That he exercises in the morning is false.
➡ ________________ he exercises in the morning.

EXERCISE B 다음 문장에서 that이 생략된 부분을 찾아 V 표시를 하시오.

1 I think we have to deal with the pollution problem first.

2 I want you to know I can't wait any longer.

3 Everyone in town knows you are such a good guy.

4 I've heard you were a high school teacher.

4 명사절을 이끄는 접속사 II - if / whether

If / whether절은 '~인지 아닌지'라는 뜻으로, whether절은 주어, 목적어, 보어 역할을 하는 반면 if절은 주어로 쓰이지 않으며 보어로도 거의 쓰이지 않는다.

Whether he believes me or not is of no importance. **<주어 역할 : ~인지 아닌지는> if절 불가**
그가 나를 믿는지 아닌지는 중요하지 않다.

I want to know **if** it is true. **<목적어 역할 : ~인지 아닌지를>**
나는 그것이 사실인지 아닌지 알고 싶다.

My concern is **whether** my family is alive **or not**. **<보어 역할 : ~인지 아닌지>**
내 관심사는 나의 가족이 살아있는지 아닌지다.

+ 명사절 if vs. 부사절(조건절) if

명사절 if	~인지 아닌지	• 의문유발동사와 함께 쓰이며 명사절로 목적어 역할을 함 • 미래시제와 함께 쓰일 수 있음 I wonder **if he will come**. 나는 그가 올지 안 올지 궁금하다. *** 의문유발동사: ask, wonder, doubt, be not sure 등 의문이나 불확실을 나타내는 동사**
부사절 if (조건절)	~라면	• 완전한 문장의 앞뒤에 쓰임 • 미래시제와 함께 쓰일 수 없음 I will leave here **if he comes**. 나는 그가 온다면 이곳을 떠날 것이다.

▶▶ 정답과 해설 p. 49

EXERCISE A 다음 괄호 안에 알맞은 접속사를 고르시오.

1 I wonder [that / if] Yuri will make it.

2 [If / Whether] she will come or not doesn't matter.

3 I'm wondering [that / if] this dress fits her.

4 I think [that / whether] she will be in touch with him.

5 I don't know [that / whether] he will arrive tonight or not.

6 Did you think [that / if] Maria hated Linda?

EXERCISE B 다음 문장의 밑줄 친 if(If)와 쓰임이 같은 것을 <보기>에서 골라 기호를 쓰시오.

<보기>
ⓐ I don't know <u>if</u> he will leave tonight.
ⓑ I will be very sad <u>if</u> he leaves tonight.

1 If you buy this new product, you won't regret it.

2 May I ask if you are married?

3 You can call me any time if you need me.

4 I was wondering if your company could help us at this time.

5 What will happen if I don't agree with that opinion?

6 Call me up any time if there is any way I can help you.

EXERCISE C **다음 문장에서 어법상 틀린 곳을 찾아 바르게 고쳐 쓰시오.**

1 I want to know that she loves me or not.

2 If the team will lose or not makes no difference.

3 I am not sure that my patient will recover or not.

4 You will pass the exam if you will do your best.

5 If you will leave without a word, all of them will panic.

6 That my wife is pregnant or not is still uncertain.

EXERCISE D **다음 우리말과 일치하도록 주어진 단어와 어구를 배열하여 문장을 완성하시오.**

1 나는 그가 내 친구인지 아닌지 모르겠다. (my friend, is, or not, he, whether)
➡ I'm not sure ______________________.

2 그가 올지 안 올지가 쟁점이다. (or not, will, Whether, come, he)
➡ ______________________ is the issue.

3 나는 그것이 가능한지 아닌지를 모르겠다. (it, possible, whether, or not, is)
➡ I don't know ______________________.

4 나는 우리 팀이 경기를 이길지 아닐지 모르겠다. (the game, win, if, our team, will)
➡ I am not sure ______________________.

5 그녀는 그에게 그가 계산을 했는지 안 했는지를 물어보았다. (he, or not, the bill, whether, paid)
➡ She asked him ______________________.

5 간접의문문

간접의문문은 문장 안에서 의문사 또는 의문사 역할을 하는 접속사(if / whether)로 연결된 절을 말하며, 문장에서 주어, 목적어, 보어 역할을 한다.

1 의문사가 없는 의문문 「접속사 if(whether) + 주어 + 동사」

I wonder. + Is he my new English teacher?

➡ I wonder **if he is** my new English teacher. 나는 그가 나의 새로운 영어 선생님인지 궁금하다.

2 의문사가 있는 의문문 「의문사 + 주어 + 동사」

Do you know? + When does the store close?

➡ Do you know **when the store closes**? 너는 그 가게가 언제 문을 닫는지 아니?

+ 주절의 동사가 think, believe, suppose, imagine, guess와 같이 불확실이나 추측을 나타낼 때는 간접의문문의 의문사가 문장 맨 앞에 온다.

Do you **think**? + **Why** did she cry?

➡ **Why** do you **think** she cried? 너는 그녀가 왜 울었다고 생각하니?

▶▶ 정답과 해설 p. 49

EXERCISE A **다음 괄호 안에서 옳은 것을 고르시오.**

1 I'd like to know [that / whether] she bought a smart phone.

2 Did you know [where / whether] she came from?

3 Can you tell me [where / if] he is now?

4 Do you know [if / how] much I should pay?

5 [Where do you think / Do you think where] she lives?

6 I wonder [if / that] she looks beautiful.

7 [Do you think what / What do you think] I have in my hand?

8 I want to know [what / whether] her name is.

9 I'm not sure [when / if] I can finish this by this Friday.

EXERCISE B 다음 주어진 두 문장을 연결하여 한 문장으로 바꿔 쓰시오.

1 No one knows. Are they alive or not?
➡ No one knows ______________________.

2 I don't know. How should I repair this broken chair?
➡ I don't know ______________________.

3 I wonder. When did the accident happen?
➡ I wonder ______________________.

4 Let me see. Did you leave something in the theater?
➡ Let me see ______________________.

5 Do you suppose? How long does it take?
➡ ______________________

6 Do you think? Who is the most reliable player?
➡ ______________________

EXERCISE C 다음 우리말과 일치하도록 주어진 단어들을 배열하여 문장을 완성하시오.

1 너는 비용이 얼마나 들지 알고 있니? (will, how, cost, it, much)
➡ Do you have any idea ______________________?

2 너는 이 블로그가 왜 인기 있는지 아니? (this blog, popular, why, is)
➡ Do you know ______________________?

3 너는 독감이 얼마나 오래 지속될 거라고 생각하니? (you, How, do, long, think)
➡ ______________________ the flu will last?

4 너는 그녀 혼자서 등교할 수 있는지 알고 있니? (she, school, if, go, can, to)
➡ Do you know ______________________ by herself?

5 너는 그 대통령의 가장 위대한 업적이 무엇이라고 생각하니? (do, think, What, is, you)
➡ ______________________ the president's greatest achievement?

6 so / so that ~ / so ~ that ...

so	그래서, ~해서	• I felt very tired, **so** I went to bed early. 나는 너무 피곤해서 일찍 잤다. ➡ **Because** I felt very tired, I went to bed early.
so that ~	~하기 위해서, ~할 수 있도록	• Make plans **so that** you **may control** yourself. 네 자신을 통제할 수 있도록 계획을 세워라. ➡ Make plans **in order that** you **may control** yourself. ➡ Make plans **(in order) to control** yourself. ➡ Make plans **so as to control** yourself.
so ~ that ...	매우 ~ 해서 …한	• The box is **so big that I can put** all of my clothes in **it**. 그 상자는 매우 커서 그 안에 내 모든 옷을 넣을 수 있다. ➡ The box is **big enough for me to put** all of my clothes in. • I was **so exhausted that I couldn't walk**. 나는 너무 지쳐서 걸을 수 없었다. ➡ I was **too exhausted to walk**.

▶▶ 정답과 해설 p.50

EXERCISE A 다음 괄호 안에서 옳은 것을 고르시오.

1 He talked louder [so that / in order] I could hear him.

2 She closed the door, [so / to] the guests couldn't see her.

3 [So / Because] he pulled out the sword, I had to fight him.

4 The light comes from behind him, [so / because] we can't see his face exactly.

5 Check the bus schedule [in order / so] not to be late for school.

6 She is so smart [that / enough] she can solve the math problem.

7 The shoes were [so / too] expensive for me to buy.

8 I caught a cold, [so / because] I'm going to see a doctor.

EXERCISE B 다음 문장을 주어진 단어를 사용하여 <보기>와 같이 바꿔 쓸 때 빈칸에 알맞은 말을 쓰시오.

<보기>

Try harder in order to succeed. (can)
➡ Try harder so that you can succeed.

1 Change your mind in order to survive. (may)
➡ Change your mind ______________________.

2 They climbed higher in order to get a better view. (might)
➡ They climbed higher ______________________.

3 We installed the heating devices in order to prevent catching colds. (could)
➡ We installed the heating devices ______________________.

EXERCISE C 다음 문장을 <보기>와 같이 바꿔 쓸 때 빈칸에 알맞은 말을 쓰시오.

<보기>
- He is so wise that he can handle the work.
  ➡ He is wise enough to handle the work.
- He is so young that he can't go to the gym.
  ➡ He is too young to go to the gym.

1 I was so tired that I couldn't work overtime.
➡ I was ______________________.

2 Gary's grandfather is so healthy that he can drive his car.
➡ Gary's grandfather is ______________________.

3 This book was so difficult that we couldn't understand it.
➡ This book was ______________________.

4 My English was so good that I could get an interpreter's job.
➡ My English was ______________________ an interpreter's job.

EXERCISE D 다음 우리말과 일치하도록 주어진 단어와 어구를 배열하여 문장을 완성하시오.

1 나의 아버지는 내가 잡을 수 있도록 공을 약하게 던졌다. (catch, that, so, I, it, could)
➡ My father threw the ball softly ______________________.

2 그녀는 너무 바빠서 내게 전화할 수 없었다. (she, couldn't, so, call, busy, that, me)
➡ She was ______________________.

3 그 거리는 너무 좁아서 차들이 통과할 수 없다. (too, the cars, narrow, to pass, for, through)
➡ The streets are ______________________.

7 부사절을 이끄는 접속사 I - 원인 / 양보

원인	because, as ~ 때문에	**As** I want to lose weight, I have to keep jogging. 나는 살을 빼기를 원하기 때문에, 계속 조깅을 해야 한다. Susan dumped him **because** he was always late when they had a date. Susan은 그가 데이트를 할 때 항상 늦었기 때문에 그를 차버렸다.
양보·대조	though, although, even though (비록) ~이지만 <사실>	**Though** I am retired, I'd like to keep working. 나는 은퇴했지만, 계속 일을 하고 싶다. ➡ **Although** I am retired, I'd like to keep working. ➡ **Even though** I am retired, I'd like to keep working.
	even if ~하더라도 <가정>	It's all right **even if** you can't do it. 네가 그것을 할 수 없더라도 괜찮다.

+ 전치사와 비교

접속사	전치사
because + 주어 + 동사	because of + 명사〔대명사 / 동명사〕
though〔although, even though〕+ 주어 + 동사	despite〔in spite of〕+ 명사〔대명사 / 동명사〕

▶▶ 정답과 해설 p. 50

EXERCISE A 다음 괄호 안에서 옳은 것을 고르시오.

1 [Because / Although] she is not famous, she must be a talented writer.

2 Ted couldn't drive a car [because / although] he drank too much.

3 Linda lives with her grandparents [because / although] her parents are in hospital.

4 [Because / Though] my foot was injured, I played soccer yesterday.

5 He knows the way to the place [because / even though] he has never visited there.

6 I can't get to sleep [though / because] it is very noisy.

7 [Even if / Because] she comes to see me, I won't meet her.

EXERCISE B 다음 문장에서 어법상 틀린 곳을 찾아 바르게 고쳐 쓰시오. (틀린 곳이 없으면 ○표)

1 Because a hurricane, they went to the basement.

2 Although injuries, they rushed into the finish line.

3 He was criticized by all the villagers because of he was rude.

4 Her voice was shaking despite all her efforts to control it.

5 Although he was a good musician, his performance was really terrible.

6 I want to protect pandas because there are only 1800 left on Earth.

EXERCISE C 다음 문장을 <보기>와 같이 바꿔 쓸 때 빈칸에 알맞은 말을 쓰시오.

<보기>
I like Julia so much, but she always turns her eyes away from me.
➡ Although I like Julia so much, she always turns her eyes away from me.

1 The man is in trouble, but he is cheerful all the time.
➡ ________________, he is cheerful all the time.

2 She had a criminal record, but the owner hired her.
➡ ________________, the owner hired her.

3 He studies hard in his class, but his grades aren't good.
➡ ________________, his grades aren't good.

4 I had all the necessary qualifications, but I didn't get the job.
➡ ________________, I didn't get the job.

EXERCISE D 다음 문장을 <보기>와 같이 바꿔 쓸 때 빈칸에 알맞은 말을 쓰시오.

<보기>
Because he lied, nobody believed his words.
➡ Because of his lie, nobody believed his words.

1 Because she is shy, she never talks to others at a party.
➡ ________________, she never talks to others at a party.

2 She said bad things about other girls because she was jealous.
➡ She said bad things about other girls ________________.

3 Although she was poor, she was able to go to college.
➡ ________________, she was able to go to college.

8 부사절을 이끄는 접속사 II - 시간

when	~할 때	I was doing my homework **when** Tom called me. Tom이 내게 전화했을 때 나는 숙제를 하고 있었다.
as	~할 때, ~하면서 * when으로 바꿔 쓸 수 있음	**As** I entered the bathroom, the lights went out suddenly. 내가 욕실에 들어갔을 때, 불이 갑자기 나갔다.
before	~ 전에	Don't count your chickens **before** they are hatched. 부화되기도 전에 병아리를 세지 마라.(김칫국부터 마시지 마라.)
after	~ 후에	**After** the war was over, they punished the general. 전쟁이 끝난 후에, 그들은 그 장군을 처벌했다.
while	~하는 동안	The telephone rang **while** I was asleep. 내가 자고 있는 동안 전화벨이 울렸다.
until, till	~할 때까지	Why don't we wait **until** it stops raining? 비가 그칠 때까지 기다리는 게 어때?
since	~이후로 * 주로 현재완료에서 쓰임	Two years have passed **since** I came here. 내가 여기에 온 후로 2년이 지났다.
as soon as	~하자마자 * on -ing로 바꿔 쓸 수 있음	**As soon as** I picked up the phone, the call ended. 내가 수화기를 들자마자, 전화가 끊어졌다. ➡ **On** my **picking** up the phone, the call ended. 부사절과 주절의 주어가 다른 경우 동명사의 의미상 주어를 소유격으로 나타냄

+ 부사절을 이끄는 when vs. 명사절을 이끄는 when

My family will have a party **when** my father **comes** home.
나의 가족은 아버지가 집에 오시면 파티를 할 것이다. **〈부사절: ~할 때〉 미래시제 불가**

Nobody knows **when** my father **will come** home.
아무도 나의 아버지가 언제 집에 오실지 모른다. **〈명사절: 언제〉 미래시제 가능**

▶▶ 정답과 해설 p.50

EXERCISE A 다음 괄호 안에서 옳은 것을 고르시오.

1 Please call me back [although / as soon as] you get this message.

2 What were you doing there [while / even if] she was on the phone?

3 We never recognize the value of health [after / before] we lose it.

4 He dropped the plate [while / until] he was taking it out of the cupboard.

5 You may take a rest [after / while] you finish the work.

6 Let's wait [as / until] it stops raining.

7 He packed his suitcase [before / after] he went to the airport.

EXERCISE B 다음 문장의 빈칸에 알맞은 것을 <보기>에서 골라 문장을 완성하시오.

<보기>

while since after

1 Ten years have passed ________ my uncle died.

2 Stay put ________ I take a picture of you.

3 ________ he graduated from college, he became a lawyer.

EXERCISE C 다음 문장에서 어법상 틀린 곳을 찾아 바르게 고쳐 쓰시오. (틀린 곳이 없으면 ○표)

1 Please write me back when you will have time.

2 I want to know when you will bring it back.

3 He always complains when he will eat out.

4 I don't know when the game will be over.

5 What do you do when you have free time?

EXERCISE D 다음 문장을 <보기>와 같이 바꿔 쓸 때 빈칸에 알맞은 말을 쓰시오.

<보기>

As soon as the robbers saw the cop, they ran away.
➡ On seeing the cop, the robbers ran away.

1 As soon as she ate the rotten tomato, she spat it out.
➡ ______________________, she spat it out.

2 As soon as the repairman fixed the vending machine, he left.
➡ ______________________, the repairman left.

3 As soon as they left, it began to rain.
➡ ______________________, it began to rain.

4 As soon as she finished the work, she rushed to her house.
➡ ______________________, she rushed to her house.

9 부사절을 이끄는 접속사 III - 조건

if	~라면	• 부사절에서 미래시제 대신 현재시제 사용 We will stay at home **if** it **rains** tomorrow. (○) 내일 비가 오면 우리는 집에 머물 것이다. We will stay at home **if** it ***will rain*** tomorrow. (×) • 명령문, and ~ ➡ if절 **Go** straight ahead, **and** you will find the building. 곧장 가라, 그러면 너는 그 건물을 찾을 것이다. ➡ **If** you go straight ahead, you will find the building. 곧장 가면, 너는 그 건물을 찾을 것이다.
unless	~가 아니라면	• unless는 if ~ not과 바꿔 쓸 수 있음 **Unless** you keep the promise, he will be mad at you. ➡ **If** you **don't** keep the promise, he will be mad at you. 네가 그 약속을 지키지 않으면, 그가 네게 화를 낼 것이다. • 명령문, or ~ ➡ unless절 **Make** haste, **or** you will be late. 서둘러라, 그렇지 않으면 너는 늦을 것이다. ➡ **Unless** you make haste, you will be late. 서두르지 않으면, 너는 늦을 것이다.

▶▶ 정답과 해설 p. 51

EXERCISE A 다음 문장을 <보기>와 같이 바꿔 쓸 때 빈칸에 알맞은 말을 쓰시오.

<보기>
Unless you study hard, you'll fail.
➡ If you don't study hard, you'll fail.

1 Unless you have any further questions, I will finish the meeting.
➡ ______________________, I will finish the meeting.

2 Unless you wear a jacket, you will catch a cold.
➡ ______________________, you will catch a cold.

3 Unless you apologize to him, he won't forgive you.
➡ ______________________, he won't forgive you.

4 Unless you have a passport, you're not allowed to board.
➡ ______________________, you're not allowed to board.

5 Unless you read between the lines, you can't understand the sentence.
➡ ______________________, you can't understand the sentence.

EXERCISE B 다음 문장을 <보기>와 같이 바꿔 쓸 때 빈칸에 알맞은 말을 쓰시오.

<보기>
Do your best, and you will win another medal.
➡ If you do your best, you will win another medal.

1 Visit Paris, and you can see the Eiffel Tower.
➡ ______________________, you can see the Eiffel Tower.

2 Try to be patient, and happiness will be yours.
➡ ______________________, happiness will be yours.

3 Be kind to others, and they will be more kind to you.
➡ ______________________, they will be more kind to you.

4 Sing for me, and I'll be happy.
➡ ______________________, I'll be happy.

5 Turn to your right, and you'll find the subway station.
➡ ______________________, you'll find the subway station.

EXERCISE C 다음 문장을 <보기>와 같이 바꿔 쓸 때 빈칸에 알맞은 말을 쓰시오.

<보기>
Unless you do your best, you won't get a chance.
➡ Do your best, or you won't get a chance.

1 Unless you are around me, I can't do anything.
➡ ______________________ I can't do anything.

2 Unless you find a way to make a living, you will get into trouble.
➡ ______________________ you will get into trouble.

3 Unless you listen to my warning, you will be in danger.
➡ ______________________ you will be in danger.

4 Unless you do your homework, you can't watch TV.
➡ ______________________ you can't watch TV.

5 Unless you run away right now, you will be caught by the bear.
➡ ______________________ you will be caught by the bear.

10 주의해야 할 접속사 - as / while

1 as

이유	~ 때문에	The game was cancelled **as** it rained a lot. 비가 많이 왔기 때문에 그 경기는 취소되었다.
시간	~할 때	I saw him **as** he got off the bus. 나는 그가 버스에서 내릴 때 그를 보았다.
비례	~함에 따라, ~할수록	**As** she grew older, she became more patient. 나이가 들수록, 그녀는 참을성이 많아졌다.
양태	~하듯이, ~ 대로	**As** food nourishes our body, books nourish our minds. 음식이 우리의 몸에 영양을 주듯이, 책은 우리의 정신에 영양을 준다.

* 양태란 어떤 행동이나 사람, 사물을 표현할 때 다른 사람이나 사물과 연관 지어 표현하는 것을 뜻한다.

2 while

시간	~ 하는 동안	**While** they were away, a thief broke into their house. 그들이 나가 있는 동안, 도둑이 그들의 집에 침입했다.
양보 · 대조	~이지만, ~인 반면에	Teens agreed to the agenda, **while** adults didn't. 십 대들은 그 안건에 동의한 반면에, 성인들은 그러지 않았다.

▶▶ 정답과 해설 p. 51

EXERCISE A **다음 밑줄 친 As(as)와 같은 의미로 쓰인 것을 <보기>에서 골라 기호를 쓰시오.**

<보기>

ⓐ As time went by, people changed.
ⓑ He missed his parents all the time as he was born an orphan.
ⓒ I saw an old friend as I was leaving the airport.
ⓓ They didn't do as they were told.

1 The phone rang as I was asleep on the couch.

2 As he grew older, he became wiser.

3 Mary often listens to the radio as she works in the kitchen.

4 You can do as you wish.

5 As it was an election day last Thursday, we didn't go to school.

6 Behave as I told you.

7 As the door was open, her cat ran away from home.

EXERCISE B 다음 문장의 밑줄 친 부분을 우리말로 해석하시오.

1 Jason cut in suddenly as she was talking.

2 Do in Rome as the Romans do.

3 As it grew darker, it became colder.

4 I drank a soft drink while I was reading a newspaper.

5 I started to think about my family while I was praying in church.

6 While some spoke English, most of the people spoke Spanish.

7 As I don't like meat, I usually have vegetables.

EXERCISE C 다음 두 문장을 접속사 as(As)를 사용하여 한 문장으로 만드시오.

1 He grew older. He got thinner.
➡ ______________________________

2 She is on a diet. She skips dinner.
➡ ______________________________

3 Sarah saw her father. She visited the company.
➡ ______________________________

EXERCISE D 다음 우리말과 일치하도록 주어진 단어를 사용하여 문장을 완성하시오. (필요시 형태 변화)

1 그는 나이가 들수록, 그의 건강에 대해 더 많이 걱정하게 되었다. (as, grow, old)
➡ ______________________, he became more worried about his health.

2 내가 저녁을 요리하는 동안 너는 그 아이들을 돌봐줄 수 있니? (while, dinner, cook)
➡ Can you look after the children ______________________?

3 나는 빨간 양말을 고른 반면에, 그녀는 노란 것을 골랐다. (choose, socks, while)
➡ ______________________, she chose yellow ones.

4 그들이 떠나려고 할 때, 그는 그들에게 집까지 태워다 주겠다고 제안했다. (leave, as)
➡ ______________________, he offered them a ride home.

11 접속부사

however	그러나	People think that giraffes are slow. **However**, they are actually very fast. 사람들은 기린이 느리다고 생각한다. 그러나, 사실 기린은 매우 빠르다.
therefore	그러므로, 그래서	I think. **Therefore**, I exist. 나는 생각한다. 그러므로, 나는 존재한다.
as a result	그 결과, 결과적으로	The company offers its employees many benefits. **As a result**, they stay there for a long time. 그 회사는 직원들에게 많은 혜택을 제공한다. 그 결과, 그들은 오랫동안 그곳에 남아 있는다.
for example, for instance	예를 들면	In India, you can see many unusual things. **For example**, some coins have square sides there. 인도에서, 너는 많은 특이한 것들을 볼 수 있다. 예를 들면, 그곳의 어떤 동전은 사각형이다.
in addition, besides	게다가, 더욱이	The food in this restaurant is excellent. **In addition**, the servers are very kind. 이 레스토랑의 음식은 훌륭하다. 게다가, 직원들도 매우 친절하다.
in other words	즉, 다시 말해서	Ben is good at breaking the ice. **In other words**, he always starts a good conversation. Ben은 서먹한 분위기 깨는 것을 잘한다. 다시 말해서, 그는 항상 즐거운 대화를 시작한다.
on the other hand, in contrast, on the contrary	반면에, 대조적으로	The Japanese economy is close to recession. **On the other hand**, the Korean economy is on the rise. 일본 경제는 경기 침체에 다가섰다. 반면에, 한국 경제는 상승 중이다.

▶▶ 정답과 해설 p. 51

EXERCISE A **다음 괄호 안에서 옳은 것을 고르시오.**

1 She failed to make a flight reservation. [Therefore / However], she couldn't join the trip.

2 The hunter has been watching over the woods for a long time. [Therefore / However], nothing appeared from there.

3 The tsunami swept the town. [As a result / In contrast], so many people lost their houses.

4 People from different cultures think about the space differently. [Therefore / For example], South Americans stand closer than Asians when they talk.

5 I have not finished my homework yet. [However / For example], my sister has already finished her homework.

6 Non-count nouns don't have a plural form. [On the other hand / For example], "milk" is a non-count noun.

Chapter 12
접속사

학교 시험 대비 문제

맞힌 개수	
선택형	____ / 35
서술형	____ / 13

▶▶ 정답과 해설 p.51

01 다음 빈칸에 들어갈 말로 알맞은 것은?

• Although he ran very fast, he didn't win the race.
= He ran very fast, ________ he didn't win the race.

① or ② and ③ but
④ since ⑤ because

02 다음 빈칸에 공통으로 들어갈 말로 알맞은 것은?

• ________ no one was watching the store, they stole the money in the safe.
• In my office, Steven is lazy ________ Paul is diligent.

① when(When) ② as(As)
③ while(While) ④ that(That)
⑤ although(Although)

03 다음 빈칸에 들어갈 말로 알맞은 것은?

My new roommate is not only rude ________ also lazy.

① and ② so ③ or
④ but ⑤ if

04 다음 빈칸에 들어갈 말로 알맞은 것은?

• The musician had to go abroad because his country gave him up.
= His country gave him up, ________ the musician had to go abroad.

① that ② why ③ so
④ or ⑤ but

05 다음 빈칸에 들어갈 말로 어색한 것은?

________________, we will go on a picnic.

① If it is fine tomorrow
② If it doesn't rain tomorrow
③ If we are not busy tomorrow
④ Unless it is not fine tomorrow
⑤ Unless we are busy tomorrow

고난도
06 다음 중 빈칸에 while이 들어갈 수 있는 것은?

① I began to cook ________ I was hungry.
② Be seated ________ wait until I call your name.
③ I'm telling you the secret ________ you are my friend.
④ Some people sleep ________ others study all night.
⑤ You should call the police ________ you see the suspect.

[07-08] 다음 빈칸에 들어갈 말로 알맞은 것을 고르시오.

07

If it ________ tomorrow, I will stay at home.

① rains ② rained ③ rain
④ will rain ⑤ is going to rain

08

Speak slowly, ____________ nobody will understand you.

① and ② then ③ so
④ or ⑤ but

고난도

09 다음 밑줄 친 if의 쓰임이 나머지 넷과 다른 것은?

① I doubt if he will come in time.
② I asked him if he could help me.
③ I wonder if you are free this weekend.
④ I'm not sure if she will come to see me.
⑤ I will be thankful to you if you give me a hand.

10 다음 두 문장을 한 문장으로 연결할 때 빈칸에 알맞은 것은?

- They are exporting coals.
- And they are also exporting natural gas.

➡ They are exporting not only coals ________ also natural gas.

① and ② but ③ or
④ as ⑤ to

고난도

11 다음 밑줄 친 that의 쓰임이 나머지 넷과 다른 것은?

① He thinks that she is a liar.
② The truth is that he is guilty.
③ I believe that the rumor is not true.
④ My problem is that I feel hungry all the time.
⑤ The concert that I was interested in was cancelled.

고난도

12 다음 중 어법상 틀린 것은?

① It is certain if the war will happen.
② Tell me if you can go on an errand.
③ The waiter asked me if I was ready.
④ I doubt if she will listen to his advice.
⑤ I am not sure if the man is a foreigner.

13 다음 중 밑줄 친 부분과 바꿔 쓸 수 있는 것은?

He scored the winning goal even though he missed his chance twice.

① if ② as ③ although
④ whether ⑤ because

14 다음 우리말과 일치하도록 빈칸에 들어갈 말로 알맞은 것은?

- 축구는 아르헨티나뿐만 아니라 한국에서도 매우 인기 있다.

➡ Soccer is very popular in Korea __________ in Argentina.

① as far as ② as well as
③ as soon as ④ as long as
⑤ as many as

15 다음 빈칸에 들어갈 말이 바르게 짝지어진 것은?

- The rainforests in the world are disappearing. __________, we must take actions.
- The play was so fantastic. __________, I didn't enjoy it much.

① So — Although
② So — Because
③ Therefore — Though
④ Therefore — However
⑤ However — Therefore

[16-17] 다음 빈칸에 공통으로 알맞은 것을 고르시오.

16

- Clean your room __________ I make dinner.
- __________ we were playing soccer, someone stole our clothes.

① but〔But〕 ② or〔Or〕
③ while〔While〕 ④ because〔Because〕
⑤ so〔So〕

17

- I'm not sure __________ I trust myself.
- __________ you say it's true, I'll believe it.

① if〔If〕 ② that〔That〕
③ whether〔Whether〕 ④ although〔Although〕
⑤ even if〔Even if〕

18 다음 중 빈칸에 that이 들어갈 수 있는 것은?

① Do you think __________ I am a liar?
② I am not sure __________ Korea will win or not.
③ Everybody likes her __________ she is very kind.
④ Neighbors are noisy, __________ I can't sleep at night.
⑤ Ann likes to study English, __________ Jake likes to study math.

19 다음 문장의 밑줄 친 부분과 바꿔 쓸 수 있는 것은?

I watched her <u>while</u> she took a walk.

① as ② if ③ or
④ but ⑤ during

고난도

20 다음 문장의 밑줄 친 부분을 바르게 바꿔 쓴 것은?

> The thief went out through the back door so that we could not see him.

① in order to see him
② not in order to see him
③ in order for us not to see him
④ not in order for us to see him
⑤ in order not that we could see him

21 다음 두 문장을 한 문장으로 바르게 바꿔 쓴 것은?

> • I wonder.
> • Can she recognize me?

① I wonder if can she recognize me.
② I wonder if she can recognize me.
③ I wonder that she can recognize me.
④ I wonder how can she recognize me.
⑤ I wonder what she can recognize me.

22 다음 중 어법상 틀린 것은?

① I doubt if you can make it.
② Ask me if you have any problem.
③ I don't know if he will visit her.
④ If she likes the present is not clear to me.
⑤ Whether you can go or not makes no difference to me.

고난도

23 다음 밑줄 친 as(As)의 뜻이 나머지 넷과 다른 것은?

① Leave the matter as it is.
② As I was pulling out the car, I hit the car behind me.
③ Someone went out as I was making a speech.
④ The train slowed down as it approached the station.
⑤ A deer suddenly ran out as we were driving along the road.

24 다음 빈칸에 공통으로 들어갈 말로 알맞은 것은?

> • If you won't go with me, I won't go, ________.
> • You must be ________ naive or stupid.

① too ② either ③ neither
④ also ⑤ both

고난도

25 다음 두 문장의 뜻이 서로 다른 것은?

① Be patient, or you will fail.
➡ If you are not patient, you will fail.
② After it was dark, they went home.
➡ They didn't go home until it was dark.
③ Although my dad is old, he is strong.
➡ My dad is old, but he is strong.
④ If you don't lose your temper, I will see you again.
➡ Unless you lose your temper, I will see you again.
⑤ I bought a present for her because tomorrow is her birthday.
➡ Tomorrow is her birthday so that I bought a present for her.

26 다음 우리말과 일치하도록 빈칸에 들어갈 말로 알맞은 것은?

> • 신사 숙녀 여러분, 다치지 않도록 안전벨트를 매주세요.
> ➡ Ladies and gentlemen, please fasten your seat belt ______________.

① unless you get hurt
② so you will get hurt
③ if you don't get hurt
④ and you will get hurt
⑤ so that you may not get hurt

27 다음 빈칸에 들어갈 말이 바르게 짝지어진 것은?

> • I think that either he or you ______ guilty.
> • Both he and his friend ______ innocent.

① is — is ② are — is ③ is — are
④ are — are ⑤ am — is

28 다음 빈칸에 들어갈 말로 알맞은 것은?

> • If you don't change your mind, I will leave you right now.
> ➡ ________ you change your mind, I will leave you right now.

① In case ② While ③ As if
④ Unless ⑤ Whatever

고난도

29 다음 중 밑줄 친 부분의 뜻이 서로 같은 것은?

① As we grow older, our bodies become weaker.
You can go as you please.
② Can you look after her while I am away?
She likes vegetables, while I like meat.
③ If you remember the lesson, you will be successful.
Nobody asked if you were right.
④ I loved history when I was in school.
When the movie was over, she was crying.
⑤ I did my best so that I could win the prize.
He was so fearful that he couldn't drive a car.

30 다음 빈칸에 들어갈 말로 알맞은 것은?

> **A** What's up? You look serious.
> **B** Oh, I lost my hairpin. Maybe I dropped it on my way home.
> **A** I'm not sure ________ we can find it, but let's try.

① so ② as ③ if
④ what ⑤ while

31 다음 빈칸에 공통으로 들어갈 말로 알맞은 것은?

> • ________ of my illness, I couldn't go to school.
> • I didn't meet him ________ he was a man from an unknown company.

① if(If) ② but(But)
③ instead(Instead) ④ because(Because)
⑤ in spite of(In spite of)

32 다음 글의 빈칸에 가장 알맞은 것은?

If we went back billions of years, we would find that everything was blue and only the sea plants under the water were green. ____________, there were only two colors: blue and green.

① Besides ② However
③ For example ④ In addition
⑤ In other words

33 다음 빈칸에 들어갈 말이 바르게 짝지어진 것은?

• Many students got a flu, ________ our school was closed. • He should stop smoking ________ take a rest for the time being.

① so — but ② so — and
③ but — and ④ but — or
⑤ or — but

34 다음 빈칸에 공통으로 들어갈 말로 알맞은 것은?

• Her problem is ________ she can't ride a bike. • The address ________ he wrote down is wrong.

① what ② that ③ whom
④ which ⑤ whether

35 다음 밑줄 친 while(While)의 뜻이 나머지 넷과 다른 것은?

① I fell asleep while I was watching TV.
② The robber ran away while the officer listened to music.
③ While I was going down the stairs, I broke my glasses.
④ While my wife goes shopping, I take care of the children.
⑤ Westerners shake hands when greeting each other, while Asians bow.

서술형

36 다음 두 문장을 한 문장으로 연결할 때 빈칸에 알맞은 말을 쓰시오.

• Please tell me. • Have you been to New York? ➡ Please tell me ________ you have been to New York.

[37-39] 다음 두 문장의 뜻이 같도록 빈칸에 알맞은 말을 쓰시오.

37

• I did my best, but I lost the game. = ________ I did my best, I lost the game.

38

- Unless you hurry up, you will miss the plane.

= If you _________ _________ _________, you will miss the plane.

39

This watch is so cheap that I can buy it.
= This watch is cheap _________ for me to buy.

40 다음 두 문장을 한 문장으로 바꿔 쓰시오.

- I don't know.
- Did she get the message?

➡ ________________________________
____

[41-43] 다음 두 문장의 뜻이 같도록 빈칸에 알맞은 말을 쓰시오.

41

- You are smart and your friend is smart, too.

= _________ you _________ your friend are smart.

42

- Does he want to change his job?

= I am wondering _________ he _________ to change his job.

43

- Although the rain was heavy, the concert ended successfully.

= The concert ended successfully _________ the heavy rain.

44 다음 두 문장을 한 문장으로 바꿔 쓰시오.

- She didn't keep her promise.
- I was so upset.

➡ I ________________________________
________________________________.

[45-46] 다음 주어진 대화를 읽고, <보기>와 같이 문장을 완성하시오.

James	Nice to meet you, Mary. Where do you live?
Mary	I live on 4th Avenue.

<보기>

James is asking Mary where she lives.

45

Mike	Do you have any questions?
Lisa	Please tell me. How old is your girlfriend?

Lisa is asking Mike ______________________.

46

Betty	Hi. Have you seen Nancy these days?
Brian	No, I haven't.

Betty wants to know ______________________

______________________.

[47-48] 다음 그림을 보고, 주어진 접속사를 사용하여 한 문장으로 바꿔 쓰시오.

47

She is kind.
She shows a stranger the way.

(so)

____

48

I'm strong.
I can do the hard work.

(because)

____

Chapter

13

가정법

1 가정법 과거

「If + 주어 + 동사의 과거형 ~, 주어 + 조동사의 과거형 + 동사원형 …」: 만약 ~한다면, …할 텐데

① 가정법 과거는 현재 사실과 반대되는 가정이나 가능성이 없는 상상을 나타낸다.
② 가정법 과거에서 if절의 동사가 be동사일 경우, 주어의 인칭과 수에 상관없이 were를 쓴다.
(구어체에서는 was를 쓰기도 한다.)
③ 가정법과 직설법 동사의 긍정·부정은 서로 정반대가 된다.
④ 가정법의 과거시제는 직설법에서 현재시제가 된다.

If I **knew** her email address, I **would send** an email to her. **<가정법 과거>**
만약 내가 그녀의 이메일 주소를 안다면, 그녀에게 이메일을 보낼 텐데.
➡ **As** I don't know her email address, I can't send an email to her. **<직설법 현재>**
➡ I don't know her email address, **so** I can't send an email to her. **<직설법 현재>**

+ 단순 조건절을 이끄는 if는 어느 정도 일어날 가능성이 있는 일에 대한 조건을 나타낸다.

If you behave badly again, you will be punished. 네가 다시 예의 없이 행동하면, 혼날 것이다.
※ 조건을 나타내는 부사절에서는 현재시제로 미래를 나타낸다.
If it **rains** tomorrow, I'll stay at home. 내일 비가 오면, 나는 집에 있을 것이다.

! 가정법에서 if를 생략하면 주어와 동사가 도치된다.

If I were rich, I would spend all my time traveling. 만약 내가 부자라면, 내 모든 시간을 여행하는 데 쓸 텐데.
➡ **Were I rich**, I would spend all my time traveling.

▶▶ 정답과 해설 p.54

EXERCISE A 다음 괄호 안에서 옳은 것을 고르시오.

1 If he [is / were] here, he would listen to me.

2 If you [give / gave] him a big hand, he will be happy with that.

3 If Tom [has / had] enough time, he could go camping with his family.

4 If they [can / could] swim in the pond, they will go swimming with us.

5 If we [can / could] help them right now, it would be nice for us, too.

6 If she [does / did] such a good thing, she would be loved by everyone here.

7 If I [were / are] you, I would not buy too much fatty food.

EXERCISE B 다음 문장을 <보기>와 같이 바꿔 쓸 때 빈칸에 알맞은 말을 쓰시오.

〈보기〉
If he knew it well, he could tell me about it.
➡ As he doesn't know it well, he can't tell me about it.
➡ He doesn't know it well, so he can't tell me about it.

1 If he lived here, I could see him every day.
➡ As ______________________________.

2 If she were here, she could help us.
➡ ______________________, so ______________________.

3 She is not a wise woman, so she makes such a mistake.
➡ If ______________________________.

4 As I don't have enough money, I can't buy a beautiful house.
➡ If ______________________________.

5 You are not a bird, so you can't fly to me.
➡ If ______________________________.

EXERCISE C 다음 우리말과 일치하도록 주어진 단어를 사용하여 문장을 완성하시오. (필요시 형태 변화)

1 만약 그가 그녀의 이름을 알고 있다면, 그가 네게 말해 줄 텐데. (if, know, will tell)
➡ ______ ______ ______ her name, ______ ______ ______ you.

2 만약 그가 선생님의 말씀을 주의 깊게 듣는다면, 그는 답을 알 수 있을 텐데. (if, listen, can know)
➡ ______ ______ ______ to his teacher carefully, ______ ______ ______ the answer.

3 만약 내가 그녀의 입장이라면, 나는 그의 제안을 받아들일 텐데. (if, be, will accept)
➡ ______ ______ ______ in her position, ______ ______ ______ his proposal.

4 만약 그녀가 시간이 충분히 있다면, 그녀는 그 책을 끝까지 읽을 텐데. (if, have, will read)
➡ ______ ______ ______ enough time, ______ ______ ______ through the book.

2 가정법 과거완료

「If + 주어 + had p.p. ~, 주어 + 조동사의 과거형 + have p.p. …」: 만약 ~했다면, …했을 텐데

① 가정법 과거완료는 과거 사실과 반대되는 가정이나 가능성이 없는 상상을 나타낸다.
② 가정법과 직설법 동사의 긍정·부정은 서로 정반대가 된다.
③ 가정법의 과거완료 시제는 직설법에서 과거시제가 된다.

If she **had been** more careful, she **would not have gotten** hurt. **<가정법 과거완료>**
만약 그녀가 더 조심했다면, 다치지 않았을 텐데.
➡ **As** she was not more careful, she got hurt. **<직설법 과거>**
➡ She was not more careful, **so** she got hurt. **<직설법 과거>**

▶▶ 정답과 해설 p.54

EXERCISE A 다음 괄호 안에서 옳은 것을 고르시오.

1 If we [had / had had] our car then, we could have saved time.

2 He would have gotten there if he [started / had started] early in the morning.

3 If they [asked / had asked] for advice, they wouldn't have had any trouble.

4 She could have made a happy life if she [were / had been] alive.

5 If we [worked / had worked] hard, we would have made a lot of money.

EXERCISE B 다음 문장을 <보기>와 같이 바꿔 쓸 때 빈칸에 알맞은 말을 쓰시오.

<보기>
If I had known her, I could have asked her for help.
➡ As I didn't know her, I couldn't ask her for help.
➡ I didn't know her, so I couldn't ask her for help.

1 If you had told me the fact, it would have been much better.
➡ As ______________________________.

2 If they hadn't been so tired, they would have gone out.
➡ As ______________________________.

3 If he hadn't laughed at me, I would have been close to him.
➡ ____________________, so ____________________.

4 As he was not my father, he didn't understand me.

➡ If ______________________________.

5 They didn't have enough money, so they couldn't help her.

➡ If ______________________________.

6 As he didn't know my phone number, he didn't call me.

➡ If ______________________________.

EXERCISE C 다음 우리말과 일치하도록 어법상 틀린 부분을 찾아 바르게 고쳐 쓰시오.

1 만약 그들이 부자였다면, 그들은 아파트를 살 수 있었을 텐데.

➡ If they had been rich, they could buy an apartment.

2 만약 그가 조심해서 운전을 했더라면, 그는 다치지 않았을 텐데.

➡ He wouldn't have been injured if he drove carefully.

3 만약 내가 돈이 있었다면, 나는 그에게 좀 빌려주었을 텐데.

➡ I would not have lent him some money if I had had any.

4 만약 그녀가 나를 도와주지 않았다면, 나는 곤경에 처했을 텐데.

➡ I would been in trouble if she hadn't helped me.

5 만약 우리가 더 이른 버스를 탔더라면, 우리는 제 시간에 거기 도착할 수 있었을 텐데.

➡ If we caught the earlier bus, we could have gotten there on time.

EXERCISE D 다음 우리말과 일치하도록 주어진 단어와 어구를 사용하여 문장을 완성하시오. (필요시 형태 변화)

1 만약 그가 좀 더 일찍 내게 경고했더라면, 나는 그렇게 하지 않았을 텐데. (if, warn, will do)

➡ ______ ______ ______ ______ me earlier, ______ ______ ______ ______ so.

2 만약 우리가 바쁘지 않았다면, 우리는 축구를 할 수 있었을 텐데. (if, be, may play)

➡ ______ ______ ______ ______ busy, we ______ ______ ______ soccer.

3 만약 내가 좀 더 젊었더라면, 나는 좀 더 많은 일들을 할 수 있었을 텐데. (can do, if, be)

➡ ______ ______ ______ ______ more things ______ ______ ______ ______ a little younger.

3 I wish + 가정법

1 I wish+가정법 과거 현재와 반대되는 소망

「I wish + 주어 + 동사의 과거형」: ~라면 좋을 텐데
➡ 「I am sorry (that) + 주어 + 동사의 현재형」

I wish I **had** my own computer. 나만의 컴퓨터가 있으면 좋을 텐데. **<가정법 과거>**
➡ I'm sorry I **don't have** my own computer. 나만의 컴퓨터가 없어 유감이다. **<직설법 현재>**

I wish I **could** be a hero. 내가 영웅이 될 수 있다면 좋을 텐데.
➡ I'm sorry I **can't be** a hero. 내가 영웅이 될 수 없어 유감이다.

2 I wish+가정법 과거완료 과거와 반대되는 소망

「I wish + 주어 + had p.p.」: ~했더라면 좋았을 텐데
➡ 「I am sorry (that) + 주어 + 동사의 과거형」

I wish I **had worked** harder. 내가 더 열심히 일했더라면 좋았을 텐데. **<가정법 과거완료>**
➡ I'm sorry I **didn't work** harder. 내가 더 열심히 일하지 않았던 것이 유감이다. **<직설법 과거>**

▶▶ 정답과 해설 p. 54

EXERCISE A 다음 괄호 안에서 옳은 것을 고르시오.

1 I wish he [takes / took] care of his baby.

2 I wish I [have / had] learned how to skate.

3 I wish I [can / could] lend you my notebook.

4 I wish my father [could / had] bought me a toy train.

5 I wish the woman [would / have] come to the party.

EXERCISE B 다음 주어진 문장을 <보기>와 같이 바꿔 쓸 때 빈칸에 알맞은 말을 쓰시오.

<보기>
I wish I could speak English well.
➡ I'm sorry I can't speak English well.

1 I wish I were his partner at the party.
➡ ______________________ his partner at the party.

2 I wish I were not poor at singing.

➡ ______________________ at singing.

3 I'm sorry you are not there with them.

➡ ______________________ there with them.

4 I wish I had listened to her advice.

➡ ______________________ to her advice.

5 I'm sorry she didn't go fishing with us.

➡ ______________________ fishing with us.

6 I'm sorry I didn't stop smoking for my health.

➡ ______________________ smoking for my health.

EXERCISE C **다음 우리말과 일치하도록 주어진 단어 또는 어구를 사용하여 문장을 완성하시오. (필요시 형태 변화)**

1 그가 용감한 남자라면 좋을 텐데. (wish, be)

➡ ______ ______ ______ ______ a brave man.

2 내가 저 무지개 너머 어딘가로 갈 수 있다면 좋을 텐데. (wish, can go)

➡ ______ ______ ______ ______ ______ somewhere over the rainbow.

3 나는 매일 대화를 나눌 친구 한 명이 있다면 좋을 텐데. (wish, have)

➡ ______ ______ ______ ______ a friend to talk with every day.

4 내가 영국에서 호주까지 여행을 갔더라면 좋았을 텐데. (wish, take)

➡ ______ ______ ______ ______ ______ a trip from England to Australia.

5 내 숙모가 나와 함께 쇼핑몰에 갔더라면 좋았을 텐데. (wish, my aunt, go)

➡ ______ ______ ______ ______ ______ ______ with me to the mall.

6 내가 그 경기에 참가할 또 다른 기회가 있었더라면 좋았을 텐데. (wish, have)

➡ ______ ______ ______ ______ ______ another chance to take part in the match.

7 다음 주 금요일까지 당신이 나와 함께 이곳에 머문다면 좋을 텐데. (wish, will stay)

➡ ______ ______ ______ ______ ______ here with me until next Friday.

4 as if + 가정법

1 as if+가정법 과거 주절의 시제와 일치하는 시점의 일에 반대되는 상황을 가정

「as if + 주어 + 동사의 과거형」: 마치 ~인 것처럼(현재 사실과 반대되는 가정)

He **looks** **as if** he **were** happy. 그는 마치 행복한 것처럼 보인다.
(looks: 현재 / were: 과거(현재의 일에 반대되는 상황))

➡ In fact, he **is not** happy. 사실 그는 행복하지 않다.
(is not: 현재)

He **looked** **as if** he **were** happy. 그는 마치 행복한 것처럼 보였다.
(looked: 과거 / were: 과거(과거의 일에 반대되는 상황))

➡ In fact, he **wasn't** happy. 사실 그는 행복하지 않았다.
(wasn't: 과거)

2 as if+가정법 과거완료 주절의 시제 그 이전의 일에 반대되는 상황을 가정

「as if + 주어 + had p.p.」: 마치 ~였던 것처럼(과거 사실과 반대되는 가정)

She **talks** **as if** she **had not known** the story. 그녀는 마치 그 이야기를 몰랐던 것처럼 이야기한다.
(talks: 현재 / had not known: 과거완료(현재 이전-과거-의 일에 반대되는 상황))

➡ In fact, she **knew** the story. 사실 그녀는 그 이야기를 알았다.
(knew: 과거)

She **talked** **as if** she **had not known** the story. 그녀는 마치 그 이야기를 몰랐던 것처럼 이야기했다.
(talked: 과거 / had not known: 과거완료(과거 이전의 일에 반대되는 상황))

➡ In fact, she **had known** the story. 사실 그녀는 그 이야기를 알았었다.
(had known: 과거완료)

▶▶ 정답과 해설 p. 55

EXERCISE A 다음 괄호 안에서 어법상 옳은 것을 고르시오.

1 He talks as if he [can / could] answer all the questions. But he can't.

2 He thinks as if they [are / were] his parents. But they aren't his parents.

3 They talk as if they [could / can] hide their secrets forever. In fact, they can't.

4 He seems as if he [liked / had liked] my sister. But he didn't like her.

5 He talked as if he [had gotten / got] angry about it. In fact, he hadn't gotten angry about it at all.

6 She looks as if she [has / had] a lot of friends. In fact, she doesn't have a lot of friends.

EXERCISE B 다음 주어진 문장을 <보기>와 같이 바꿔 쓸 때 빈칸에 알맞은 말을 쓰시오.

〈보기〉
She talks as if she were an actress.
➡ In fact, she is not an actress.

1 She looks as if she had been thirsty.
➡ In fact, ______________________.

2 She says as if she could climb up the tall tree.
➡ In fact, ______________________.

3 In fact, we are not surprised at this.
➡ We talk ______________________.

4 In fact, they didn't win the game.
➡ They talk ______________________.

5 In fact, they had a fight with each other.
➡ They look ______________________.

EXERCISE C 다음 우리말과 일치하도록 주어진 단어와 어구를 사용하여 문장을 완성하시오. (필요시 형태 변화)

1 그들은 마치 공포 영화를 좋아하는 것처럼 이야기한다. (as if, like)
➡ They talk ______ ______ ______ ______ horror movies.

2 그녀는 마치 자신의 약속을 지키고 싶었던 것처럼 말한다. (as if, want)
➡ She speaks ______ ______ ______ ______ ______ to keep her promise.

3 너는 마치 고등학생인 것처럼 보인다. (as if, be)
➡ You look ______ ______ ______ ______ a high school student.

4 그들은 마치 그녀가 오랫동안 그들을 싫어했던 것처럼 느꼈다. (as if, hate)
➡ They felt ______ ______ ______ ______ ______ them for a long time.

5 너는 마치 깊은 바닷속에서 보물을 찾을 수 있는 것처럼 이야기한다. (as if, can find)
➡ You talk ______ ______ ______ ______ ______ the treasure in the deep sea.

5 Without (But for) 가정법

1 가정법 과거

Without (But for) + 명사(구) ➡ If it were not for + 명사(구) ➡ Were it not for + 명사(구)	, 주어 + 조동사의 과거형 + 동사원형	~가 없다면

Without (But for) her advice, I **would fail**. 그녀의 조언이 없다면, 나는 실패할 것이다.
➡ **If it were not for** her advice, I **would fail**.
➡ **Were it not for** her advice, I **would fail**. <if 생략 도치>

2 가정법 과거완료

Without (But for) + 명사(구) ➡ If it had not been for + 명사(구) ➡ Had it not been for + 명사(구)	, 주어 + 조동사의 과거형 + have p.p.	~가 없었다면

Without (But for) his help, I **couldn't have succeeded.** 그의 도움이 없었다면, 나는 성공하지 못했을 것이다.
➡ **If it hadn't been for** his help, I **couldn't have succeeded.**
➡ **Had it not been for** his help, I **couldn't have succeeded.** <if 생략 도치>

▶▶ 정답과 해설 p.55

EXERCISE A 다음 주어진 문장을 <보기>와 같이 바꿔 쓸 때 빈칸에 알맞은 말을 쓰시오.

<보기>
If it were not for water, nothing could live.
➡ Were it not for water, nothing could live.
➡ Without (But for) water, nothing could live.

1 If it were not for hope, life would be harder.
➡ ______________________, life would be harder.
➡ ______________________, life would be harder.

2 If it hadn't been for the accident, we could have arrived in the city.
➡ ______________________, we could have arrived in the city.
➡ ______________________, we could have arrived in the city.

3 If it hadn't been for him, I couldn't have done it.
➡ ______________________, I couldn't have done it.
➡ ______________________, I couldn't have done it.

4 If it were not for the keys, she couldn't get back in her office.

➡ ______________________________, she couldn't get back in her office.

➡ ______________________________, she couldn't get back in her office.

5 If it were not for the scholarship, he couldn't be at college.

➡ ______________________________, he couldn't be at college.

➡ ______________________________, he couldn't be at college.

EXERCISE B 다음 주어진 문장을 <보기>와 같이 바꿔 쓸 때 빈칸에 알맞은 말을 쓰시오.

〈보기〉

Without〔But for〕 their attack, we would win the war.

➡ Were it not for their attack, we would win the war.

1 Without〔But for〕 the guide, they would be lost in the jungle.

➡ ______________________________, they would be lost in the jungle.

2 Without〔But for〕 the trouble, we would have taken a good rest.

➡ ______________________________, we would have taken a good rest.

3 Without〔But for〕 the warning sign, he would have caused a traffic accident.

➡ ______________________________, he would have caused a traffic accident.

4 Without〔But for〕 the weapons, they couldn't fight against their enemy.

➡ ______________________________, they couldn't fight against their enemy.

EXERCISE C 다음 우리말과 일치하도록 주어진 단어와 어구를 배열하여 문장을 완성하시오.

1 내 신용카드가 없다면, 나는 지금 결제할 수 없을 것이다. (for, it, not, Were, my, credit card)

➡ ______________________________, I couldn't pay for it now.

2 그 잡지가 없었다면, 나는 매우 지루했을 것이다. (it, been, the magazine, for, If, hadn't)

➡ ______________________________, I would have been so bored.

3 그 우산이 없었다면, 그는 비를 맞으며 집에 걸어왔을 것이다. (not, the umbrella, for, been, it, Had)

➡ ______________________________, he would have walked home in the rain.

6 혼합가정법

「If + 주어 + had p.p. ~, 주어 + 조동사의 과거형 + 동사원형 ~」: 만약 ~했다면 …할 텐데

혼합가정법은 과거 사실과 반대되는 가정을 나타내며 과거의 일이 현재까지 영향을 미치는 경우에 쓴다.
혼합가정법은 주절과 종속절의 시제가 다르다.

If he **hadn't helped** me then, I **shouldn't be** well off now. * **well off: 부유한, 잘 사는, 형편이 좋은**

만약 그가 그때 나를 도와주지 않았다면, 나는 지금 잘 살고 있지 못할 텐데.

➡ **As** he helped (과거) me then, I am (현재) well off now. 그가 그때 나를 도와줘서, 나는 지금 잘 살고 있다.

➡ He helped (과거) me then, **so** I am (현재) well off now.

※ 보통 주절에 현재를 나타내는 부사가 존재한다. ex) now, today

▶▶ 정답과 해설 p. 55

EXERCISE A 다음 두 문장의 뜻이 같도록 빈칸에 알맞은 말을 쓰시오.

1 As he didn't take her advice then, he isn't happy now.
= If ______________ her advice then, he might be happy now.

2 She didn't leave, so her family can be with her.
= Her family couldn't be with her if ______________.

3 As he didn't fail, he works for this company.
= If ______________, he couldn't work for this company.

EXERCISE B 다음 우리말과 일치하도록 주어진 단어 또는 어구를 사용하여 문장을 완성하시오. (필요시 형태 변화)

1 만약 그녀가 내 스마트폰을 고장 내지 않았다면, 나는 그것을 사용할 수 있을 텐데. (if, break)
➡ ______ ______ ______ ______ my smart phone, I could use it.

2 만약 그가 그의 지갑을 잃어버렸다면, 내게 돈을 전혀 빌려줄 수 없을 텐데. (can lend)
➡ ______ ______ ______ me any money if he had lost his wallet.

3 만약 내가 오늘 아침에 식사를 했더라면, 지금 배고프지 않을 텐데. (if, eat)
➡ ______ ______ ______ ______ breakfast this morning, I would not be hungry now.

Chapter 13
가정법

학교 시험 대비 문제

맞힌 개수	
선택형	_____ / 25
서술형	_____ / 18

▶▶ 정답과 해설 p. 55

01 다음 중 가정법 문장이 아닌 것은?

① If I were a bird, I could fly to you.
② I'll go with you if you are ready for it.
③ If she knew it, she would tell me about it.
④ If I had enough money, I could buy the house.
⑤ If he were a wise man, he wouldn't make such a mistake.

고난도

02 다음 두 문장의 뜻이 같도록 할 때 어법상 틀린 것을 모두 고르시오.

① Without the long hard training, they ② couldn't have made the Olympic team.
= ③ Have it not been ④ to the long hard training, they couldn't ⑤ have made the Olympic team.

03 다음 빈칸에 들어갈 말로 알맞은 것은?

If he ________ careful, he wouldn't have been injured.

① were ② will be
③ had been ④ have been
⑤ hasn't been

04 다음 빈칸에 알맞은 말이 순서대로 짝지어진 것은?

• I wish I ________ sing well now.
➡ I'm sorry that I can't sing well now.
• I wish I ________ in a big house.
➡ I'm sorry that I didn't live in a big house.

① can — lived ② could — lived
③ will — had lived ④ can — had lived
⑤ could — had lived

05 다음 빈칸에 들어갈 말로 알맞은 것은?

If you came to the party, you ____________ yourself.

① enjoy ② would enjoy
③ will enjoy ④ would be enjoyed
⑤ would have enjoyed

06 다음 빈칸에 들어갈 말로 알맞은 것은?

If I ________ rich enough, I would buy new things at that store.

① am ② were ③ be
④ have been ⑤ had been

07 다음 두 문장의 뜻이 서로 다른 것은?

① If they were here with us, they could help us.
= They are not here with us, so they can't help us.

② As she doesn't live here, I can't see her every day.
= I couldn't see her every day if she lived here.

③ I didn't know him well, so I couldn't ask him for help.
= If I had known him well, I could have asked him for help.

④ As you were not my mother, you didn't understand my mistake.
= If you had been my mother, you would have understood my mistake.

⑤ If he had had enough money, he could have helped them.
= He didn't have enough money, so he couldn't help them.

08 다음 빈칸에 들어갈 말로 알맞은 것은?

If she had known his phone number, she ________ him.

① could be called ② couldn't call
③ might had called ④ wouldn't call
⑤ would have called

09 다음 빈칸에 들어갈 말이 바르게 짝지어진 것은?

• If I ________ in his shoes, I could accept her proposal.
➡ As I ________ in his shoes, I can't accept her proposal.
➡ I am not in his shoes, ________ I can't accept her proposal.

① was — am — or
② am — was — so
③ were — am not — so
④ was — were not — or
⑤ were — was not — so

10 다음 우리말과 일치하지 않는 것은?

① 만약 비가 내리고 있지 않다면, 나는 축구를 할 텐데.
➡ I would play soccer if it were not raining.

② 만약 그가 충분한 시간이 있다면, 그는 그 책을 끝까지 읽을 텐데.
➡ He would read through the book if he had enough time.

③ 만약 그가 조심해서 운전을 했었다면, 그는 다치지 않았을 텐데.
➡ If he had driven carefully, he wouldn't have been injured.

④ 만약 우리가 부자였다면, 우리는 그 스포츠카를 살 수 있었을 텐데.
➡ If we have been rich, we could have bought the sports car.

⑤ 만약 네가 이 일로부터 자유롭다면, 너는 어디든지 갈 수 있을 텐데.
➡ You could go anywhere if you were free from this work.

11 다음 빈칸에 들어갈 말이 바르게 짝지어진 것은?

> • We were busy, so we didn't play tennis with them.
> = If we ______ busy, we ______ ______ tennis with them.

① were — will play
② had been — might play
③ have been — wouldn't play
④ has been — could been played
⑤ hadn't been — might have played

12 다음 빈칸에 들어갈 말이 바르게 짝지어진 것은?

> • He acts as if he ______ her. In fact, he didn't meet her.
> • She is dancing as if she ______ a dancer. In fact, she isn't a dancer.

① met — were
② met — weren't
③ had met — were
④ had met — weren't
⑤ had met — had been

13 다음 빈칸에 들어갈 말로 알맞은 것은?

> If she ______ it up, she could have completed the project.

① gave ② gives
③ hadn't given ④ were given
⑤ had been given

14 다음 우리말을 영어로 옮길 때 어법상 틀린 것은?

> • 그녀가 만약 그의 이름을 알았다면, 너에게 말해 주었을 텐데.
> ➡ She would ① tell you if she ② had known ③ his name.
> ➡ She ④ didn't know his name, so ⑤ he didn't tell you.

15 다음 우리말과 일치하도록 빈칸에 들어갈 말이 바르게 짝지어진 것은?

> • 만약 네가 더 열심히 공부한다면, 너는 그 시험에 합격할 수 있을 텐데.
> ➡ ______ you worked harder, you could pass the exam.
> ➡ ______ you don't work harder, you can't pass the exam.
> ➡ You don't work harder, ______ you can't pass the exam.

① As — So — if ② So — If — as
③ If — As — so ④ As — If — so
⑤ So — As — if

16 다음 대화의 밑줄 친 부분과 뜻이 일치하는 것은?

> A Why were you absent from the meeting yesterday? You promised!
> B I wanted to attend the meeting. But I had a bad cough. So I had to see a doctor.

① If I had a bad cough, I would attend the meeting.
② If I would have a bad cough, I could attend the meeting.
③ If I had had a bad cough, I will have attended the meeting.
④ If I didn't have a bad cough, I could have attend the meeting.
⑤ If I hadn't had a bad cough, I would have attended the meeting.

17 다음 우리말과 일치하지 않는 것은?

① 그 지도가 없다면, 우리는 그곳에 도착하지 못할 것이다.
➡ Were it not for the map, we couldn't get there.
② 그녀가 없었다면, 나는 그것을 할 수 없었을 것이다.
➡ If it hadn't been for her, I couldn't have done it.
③ 공기가 없다면, 우리는 숨조차 쉴 수 없을 것이다.
➡ Without air, we couldn't even breathe.
④ 물이 없다면, 아무것도 지구상에서 생존할 수 없다.
➡ But for water, nothing could survive on the earth.
⑤ 그 사고가 없었다면, 그들은 제시간에 이곳에 도착할 수 있었을 것이다.
➡ Hadn't it not been for the accident, they could have arrived here in time.

18 다음 우리말을 영어로 바르게 옮긴 것은?

> 그녀는 마치 나를 찾고 있었던 것처럼 거짓말을 한다.

① She tells a lie as if she had looked for me.
② I'm sorry she looked for me.
③ In fact, she really looked for me.
④ She tells a lie as if she hadn't looked for me.
⑤ She told a lie as if she would have looked for me.

고난도

19 다음 두 문장의 뜻이 서로 다른 것은?

① In fact, she is not happy.
= She looks as if she were happy.
② I'm sorry I don't have my computer.
= I wish I had my computer.
③ If I were tall and smart, I would be so happy.
= As I'm not tall and smart, I'm not so happy.
④ He talks as if he hadn't known the news.
= In fact, he knew the news.
⑤ I wish I had learned more from you.
= I'm sorry I can't learn more from you.

20 다음 빈칸에 들어갈 말로 알맞은 것은?

> If he ________ her address, he would send a postcard to her.

① knew ② had know
③ knows ④ haven't known
⑤ hadn't known

21 다음 우리말을 영어로 바르게 옮긴 것은?

만약 내가 내 카메라를 고쳤다면, 나는 지금 사진을 찍을 수 있을 텐데.

① I would take photos now if you had the camera repaired.
② If I have my camera repaired, I could have taken photos.
③ If you had the camera repaired, I would take photos now.
④ If I had had my camera repaired, I could take photos now.
⑤ I could have photos now if you have had the camera repaired.

22 다음 빈칸에 들어갈 말로 알맞은 것은?

He talked as if he hadn't ________ the fact.

① knew ② known ③ know
④ knows ⑤ been knew

23 다음 빈칸에 들어갈 수 없는 것을 모두 고르시오.

________, I could finish the thing sooner.

① If you helped me
② If you could help me
③ If you can help me
④ If you would help me
⑤ If you will help me

24 다음 문장의 우리말 뜻이 틀린 것은?

① If I had money, I could buy the car.
➡ 만약 내가 돈이 있다면, 나는 그 차를 살 수 있을 텐데.
② If you had followed her advice, you wouldn't have failed.
➡ 만약 네가 그녀의 조언을 따랐다면, 너는 실패하지 않았을 텐데.
③ If she had been careful, she wouldn't have gotten hurt.
➡ 만약 그녀가 조심했더라면, 그녀는 다치지 않았을 텐데.
④ If she worked hard, she could do better.
➡ 만약 그녀가 열심히 일한다면, 그녀는 더 잘 할 수 있을 텐데.
⑤ If he had had some money, he could have lived in a large apartment.
➡ 만약 그가 돈이 없었다면, 그는 넓은 아파트에서 살 수 없었을 텐데.

25 다음 주어진 문장의 의미로 알맞은 것은?

He acts as if he were honest.

① In fact, he is honest.
② In fact, he isn't honest.
③ In fact, he was honest.
④ In fact, he wasn't honest.
⑤ In fact, he had been honest.

서술형

[26-31] 다음 두 문장의 뜻이 같도록 빈칸에 알맞은 말을 쓰시오.

26 (한 단어)

• Had it not been for her help, he couldn't have achieved his goal.
= ________ her help, he couldn't have achieved his goal.

27

• I wish I had my own room.
= ________ ________ I don't have my own room.

28

• If it were not for fresh water, nothing could live.
= ________ ________ fresh water, nothing could live.

29

• If she had the book, she could lend it to us.
= As she ________ ________ the book, she ________ ________ it to us.

30

• I'm sorry I can't speak English well.
= I wish I ________ ________ English well.

31

• She acted as if she ________ ________ a princess.
= In fact, she hadn't been a princess.

고난도

32 **다음 우리말과 일치하도록 틀린 부분을 찾아 바르게 고쳐 쓰시오. (답 2개)**

- 만약 그들이 그렇게 피곤하지 않았다면, 그들은 함께 외출했을 텐데.

➡ If they ① hadn't been so tired, they ② would not have gone out together.

➡ ③ So they ④ were so tired, they ⑤ didn't go out together.

__________ ➡ __________

__________ ➡ __________

33 **다음 세 문장의 뜻이 같도록 빈칸에 알맞은 말을 쓰시오.**

- He didn't tell me the problem, so I couldn't help him.

= If ______ ______ ______ me the problem, I could have helped him.

= As ______ ______ ______ me the problem, I couldn't help him.

34 **다음 우리말과 일치하도록 주어진 단어를 사용하여 문장을 완성하시오. (필요시 형태 변화)**

- 만약 우리가 그것을 알고 있었다면, 우리는 네게 말해주었을 텐데. (if, know)

➡ ______ ______ ______ ______ it, we would have told you.

35 **다음 우리말과 일치하도록 빈칸에 알맞은 말을 쓰시오. (한 단어)**

- 나의 부모님의 사랑이 없었다면, 나는 이렇게 잘 자라지 못했을 것이다.

➡ Had it ______ been for my parents' love, I couldn't have grown up well like this.

[36-37] 다음 두 문장의 뜻이 같도록 빈칸에 알맞은 말을 쓰시오.

36

- She looks as if she were in a gloomy mood.

= In fact, ______ ______ ______ in a gloomy mood.

37

- He broke his cell phone a few days ago, so he can't call anyone now.

= If he ______ ______ his cell phone, he ______ ______ anyone now.

[38-40] 다음 우리말을 주어진 지시사항에 따라 영작하시오.

만약 그녀가 정오부터 혼자 일을 하지 않았다면, 그녀는 제시간에 그 일을 끝낼 수 있었을 텐데.

38 ______________________________,
she could have finished the work in time.
(if를 사용한 가정법 문장)

39 ______________________________,
she couldn't finish the work in time.
(as를 사용한 직설법 문장)

40 ______________________________
____
(so를 사용한 직설법 문장)

[41-43] 다음 우리말을 주어진 지시사항에 따라 영작하시오.

그의 조언이 없었다면, 나는 슬픔을 극복할 수 없었을 것이다.

41 ______________________________,
I couldn't have overcome my grief.
(without을 사용한 문장)

42 ______________________________,
I couldn't have overcome my grief.
(if를 사용한 문장)

43 ______________________________,
I couldn't have overcome my grief.
(if를 생략한 문장)

Chapter 14

일치와 화법

1 수 일치 I - 단수주어 + 단수동사

구/절	• To believe (믿는 것), Believing (믿는 것), What you believe (네가 믿는 것) **Keeping friends is** more important than making friends. 친구를 유지하는 것이 친구를 사귀는 것보다 더 중요하다. **What you know is** not true. 네가 알고 있는 것은 사실이 아니다.
one of +복수명사	• one of my books (내 책들 중 하나), one of my daughters (내 딸들 중 한 명) **One of your apples was** rotten. 네 사과들 중 하나가 썩었다.
the number of +복수명사	• the number of people (사람들의 수), the number of books (책의 수) **The number of people** in the airplane **is** three hundred. 비행기 안에 있는 사람들의 수는 300명이다.
every, each	• every person (모든 사람), every class (모든 수업), each desk (각각의 책상), each candy (각각의 사탕) **Every student has** a cellphone. 모든 학생들이 휴대 전화를 가지고 있다. **Each person has** his or her own point of view. 각자 자신의 관점을 가지고 있다.
학과명(-ics)	• mathematics (수학), economics (경제학), politics (정치학), physics (물리학) **Politics is** very complicated. 정치학은 매우 복잡하다.
길이, 시간, 거리 단위	• 10 centimeters (10센티미터), twenty years (20년) **Seven miles is** a long way to walk. 7마일은 걷기에 먼 길이다.
복수형 고유명사	• the United States of America (미국), the United Nations (유엔) **The United Nations is** located in New York. UN은 뉴욕에 있다.
부정주어	• no one (아무도), nobody (누구도), nothing (아무것도) **No one dances** on the stage. 아무도 무대에서 춤을 추지 않는다.
관용어	• news (뉴스), customs (관세), species (종), series (시리즈) **The news is** very shocking. 그 뉴스는 매우 충격적이다.

▶▶ 정답과 해설 p.58

EXERCISE A **다음 괄호 안에서 옳은 것을 고르시오.**

1 Every student [has / have] an email address.

2 Reading many books [is / are] good for your mind.

3 The number of his students [is / are] small.

4 Mathematics [was / were] my favorite subject.

5 No news [is / are] good news.

6 Each [singers / singer] has a headphone.

7 The United States of America [is / are] a big country.

8 One of her students [speaks / speak] French well.

9 Every singer [plays / play] his or her part in the opera.

EXERCISE B 다음 문장의 밑줄 친 부분을 바르게 고쳐 쓰시오. (틀린 곳이 없으면 ○표)

1 Making new friends are not easy.

2 Every girl in this room looks happy.

3 Economics are very important to my business.

4 No one helps him with his homework.

5 Each traveler in this island need his or her own swimsuit.

6 The number of cars in Seoul are increasing rapidly.

EXERCISE C 다음 우리말과 일치하도록 주어진 단어를 사용하여 문장을 완성하시오. (필요시 형태 변화)

1 보는 것이 믿는 것이다. (to, be)
➡ ________ ________ ________ to believe.

2 모든 쓰레기통이 가득 차 있었다. (every, be)
➡ ________ garbage can ________ full.

3 사람들의 수는 60명이었다. (number, be)
➡ ________ ________ ________ people ________ 60.

4 5년은 긴 시간이다. (year, be)
➡ ________ ________ ________ a long time.

5 나이 들어 나쁜 습관들을 바꾸는 것은 힘들다. (habits, be)
➡ Changing ________ ________ ________ difficult in old age.

6 내 학생들 중에 한 명은 배우다. (be)
➡ ________ ________ my students ________ an actor.

2 수 일치 II - 복수주어 + 복수동사

짝을 이루는 명사	• glasses (안경), pants (바지), scissors (가위), socks (양말), shoes (신발) **Your glasses were** broken. 너의 안경은 깨졌다. **The shoes** in the store **are** very expensive. 그 가게에 있는 신발은 매우 비싸다.
a number of + 복수명사	• a number of cars (많은 차들), a number of students (많은 학생들) **A number of girls were** using the lipstick. 많은 소녀들이 그 립스틱을 사용하고 있었다. **〈a number of = many〉**
the + 형용사	• the poor (가난한 사람들), the rich (부자들), the young (청년들), the handicapped (장애인들) **The rich don't** regard one dollar as a small amount of money. 부자들은 1달러를 적은 돈으로 여기지 않는다. **〈the + 형용사 = 형용사 + people〉**
both *A* and *B*	• both the man and the woman 그 남자와 그 여자 둘 다 **Both** the singer **and** the actor **were** absent. 그 가수와 그 배우 둘 다 불참했다.

▶▶ 정답과 해설 p. 58

EXERCISE A 다음 괄호 안에서 옳은 것을 고르시오.

1 Her pants [is / are] too tight.

2 Both you and I [am / are] wrong.

3 Gloves [is / are] needed for safety reasons.

4 A number of students [was / were] absent yesterday.

5 The young [has / have] to look on the bright side of life.

6 Both Jane and David [is / are] going to join the forum.

EXERCISE B 다음 문장의 밑줄 친 부분을 바르게 고쳐 쓰시오. (틀린 곳이 없으면 ○표)

1 My shoes <u>were</u> worn out.

2 The poor <u>is</u> not always unhappy.

3 <u>Weren't</u> her glasses cheap?

4 <u>Does</u> a number of kids have a smartphone?

5 I don't like the rich who <u>doesn't</u> have a beautiful mind.

3 주의해야 할 수 일치

A and *B*	The A and B ➡ 단수 취급 (A=B)	**The** novelist **and** teacher **is** my homeroom teacher. 소설가이자 교사인 그분이 나의 담임 선생님이다.
	The A and the B ➡ 복수 취급 (A≠B)	**The** novelist **and the** teacher **are** my uncles. 그 소설가와 그 교사가 나의 삼촌들이다.
all	사물(모든 것) ➡ 단수 취급	**All is** over. 모든 것이 끝났다.
	사람(모든 사람들) ➡ 복수 취급	**All are** ready for enjoying the party. 모두가 그 파티를 즐길 준비가 되어 있다.
most〔half, part, 분수〕 of	+ 단수명사 ➡ 단수 취급	**Half of** the orange **is** red. 그 오렌지의 절반이 빨갛다.
	+ 복수명사 ➡ 복수 취급	**Half of** the tomatoes **are** red. 그 토마토들의 절반이 빨갛다.
some〔any〕 of	+ 불가산명사 ➡ 단수 취급	**Any of** his advice **doesn't** seem helpful. 그의 어떠한 조언도 도움이 될 것 같지 않다.
	+ 가산명사 ➡ 복수 취급	If **any of** your friends **are** interested in it, just let me know. 네 친구들 중 누구라도 그것에 관심이 있으면, 내게 알려줘.
집합명사	집합체 ➡ 단수 취급	My **family is** a small one. 나의 가족은 소가족이다.
	구성원 ➡ 복수 취급	My **family are** all early risers. 나의 가족들은 모두 일찍 일어난다.

+ 책이나 영화 제목 등의 작품명은 단수 취급한다.

***Romeo and Juliet* was** written by Shakespeare.

〈로미오와 줄리엣〉은 셰익스피어에 의해 쓰였다.

▶▶ 정답과 해설 p.58

EXERCISE A 다음 괄호 안에서 옳은 것을 고르시오.

1 Half of the houses in the village [was / were] burnt down.

2 Most of the students [does / do] not know his name.

3 The singer and the writer [is / are] coming into the room.

EXERCISE B 다음 문장의 밑줄 친 부분을 바르게 고쳐 쓰시오. (틀린 곳이 없으면 ○표)

1 The famous doctor and writer <u>has</u> two sons.

2 Three fourths of the earth's surface <u>are</u> water.

3 My team <u>encourages</u> one another everyday.

4 시제 일치의 원칙

주절	종속절	예문
현재 현재완료 미래	모든 시제 가능	• He **believes** that you **are** his friend. 현재 현재 그는 네가 그의 친구라고 믿는다. • He **has believed** that you **will be** his friend. 현재완료 미래 그는 네가 그의 친구가 될 거라고 믿어왔다. • He **will believe** that you **were** his friend. 미래 과거 그는 네가 그의 친구였다고 믿을 것이다.
과거	과거 또는 과거완료만 가능	• She **said** that she **read** a book everyday. 과거 과거 그녀는 책을 매일 읽는다고 말했다. • She **said** that she **had read** a book everyday. 과거 과거완료 그녀는 책을 매일 읽었다고 말했다. • She **said** that she **would read** a book everyday. 과거 과거시제의 종속절에서 미래의 일을 나타낼 때는 would 사용 그녀는 책을 매일 읽을 거라고 말했다.

▶▶ 정답과 해설 p.58

EXERCISE A 다음 괄호 안에서 옳은 것을 고르시오.

1 I thought that he [was / is] too late for the meeting.

2 He said that he [will return / would return] it within a week.

3 She told me that she [can't come / couldn't come] to the party.

4 He thought that I [was / am] sick then.

EXERCISE B 다음 문장의 밑줄 친 부분을 바르게 고쳐 쓰시오. (틀린 곳이 없으면 ○표)

1 I will tell him that I cleaned the car.

2 The stone was so heavy that he can't lift it.

3 She said that she has been in Korea for three years.

4 My teacher thinks that I will win the first prize.

5 Did you notice that the answer of the last question is wrong?

5 시제 일치의 예외

1 불변의 진리, 현재의 습관, 속담, 시간표 : 항상 현재시제

We **learned** that the Earth **moves** around the Sun.
우리는 지구가 태양 주위를 돈다는 것을 배웠다. **<불변의 진리>**

He **said** that he **drinks** tea after dinner every day.
그는 매일 저녁 식사 후에 차를 마신다고 말했다. **<현재의 습관>**

*** 습관을 나타내는 부사 : on weekends 주말마다, every morning 매일 아침, every day 매일**

My grandma **said** that the early bird **catches** the worm.
나의 할머니는 일찍 일어나는 새가 벌레를 잡는다고 말씀하셨다. **<속담>**

He **said** that the train **leaves** every ten minutes.
그는 기차가 10분마다 출발한다고 말했다. **<시간표>**

2 역사적 사실 : 항상 과거시제

Our teacher **said** World War II **broke** out in 1939.
우리 선생님은 2차 세계대전이 1939년에 발발했다고 말씀하셨다.

▶▶ 정답과 해설 p.58

EXERCISE A 다음 괄호 안에서 옳은 것을 고르시오.

1 I told her that I always [went / go] fishing on weekends.

2 My father said that light [traveled / travels] faster than sound.

3 I learned that the Second World War [have ended / ended] in 1945.

4 I learned that knowledge [was / is] power.

5 Jim said that he [will run / runs] every morning.

6 She said that Hangeul [is / was] invented by King Sejong in 1443.

7 I know that three times two [is / was] six.

8 We knew that New York [is / was] bigger than London.

EXERCISE B 다음 괄호 안에 주어진 단어를 사용하여 문장을 완성하시오. (필요시 형태 변화)

1 She said that she __________ up at five every morning. (get)

2 The teacher said that the earth ________ round. (be)

3 He did not know that the moon ________ in the east. (rise)

4 My friend told me that time ________ gold. (be)

5 My teacher said that America ________ its independence from England in 1776. (declare)

6 The guide said that the earliest plane ________ for London at 6 a.m. every day. (leave)

EXERCISE C **다음 문장에서 어법상 틀린 부분을 찾아 바르게 고쳐 쓰시오. (틀린 곳이 없으면 ○표)**

1 The professor is saying that the Civil War has broken out in 1861.

2 I remembered that a rolling stone gathered no moss.

3 The timetable says the next train arrives exactly at 9 a.m.

4 It reminded the scholar that spring comes after winter.

5 My mother always told us that age is just a number.

6 He will say that the Korean War had broken out in 1950.

7 The stewardess told me that the last plane for Japan always leaves at 9 p.m.

8 My friend said that walls had ears.

EXERCISE D **다음 우리말과 일치하도록 주어진 단어 또는 어구를 배열하여 문장을 완성하시오.**

1 나의 삼촌은 고기를 먹지 않는다고 말했다. (meat, doesn't, eat, he, that)
➡ My uncle said ________________________.

2 그 경찰관은 정직이 최선의 방책이라고 말했다. (is, honesty, the best, that, policy)
➡ The police officer said ________________________.

3 그는 그의 아버지가 항상 5시에 일어나신다고 말했다. (gets, that, up, his father, always)
➡ He said ________________________ at 5.

4 나의 독일어 선생님은 독일이 1990년에 통일되었다고 말씀하셨다. (unified, Germany, that, was)
➡ My German teacher said ________________________ in 1990.

6 화법 전환 I - 평서문

평서문의 화법 전환(직접화법 → 간접화법)		
① 전달동사	say → say, say to → tell	
② 접속사	콤마(,)와 인용부호(" ") → that(생략 가능)	
③ 인칭	that절의 인칭대명사를 전달자의 입장에 맞게 변경	
④ 시제	주절의 시제가 과거일 경우 종속절의 시제를 바꿈	
⑤ 부사(구) 및 지시어 변경	부사(구)	ago → before　here → there　last → the previous today → that day　next → the following now → then, at that time　next week → the next week last night → the night before, the previous night yesterday → the day before, the previous day tomorrow → the day after, the next day
	지시어	this → that　these → those

1 주절이 현재일 경우 : 시제 변화 없이 그대로 사용

He **says to** me, " I **am(was)** very busy." **<직접화법>** 그는 나에게 "나는 너무 바빠(바빴어)."라고 말한다.

전달동사↓　접속사↓　↓인칭　↓시제

He **tells** me that he **is(was)** very busy. **<간접화법>** 그는 나에게 굉장히 바쁘다고(바빴다고) 말한다.

2 주절이 과거일 경우 : 종속절을 한 단계 이전의 시제로 바꿈

He **said to** me, " I **am(was)** very busy." **<직접화법>** 그는 나에게 "나는 너무 바빠(바빴어)."라고 말했다.

전달동사↓　접속사↓　↓인칭　↓시제

He **told** me that he **was(had been)** very busy. **<간접화법>** 그는 나에게 굉장히 바쁘다고(바빴다고) 말했다.

▶▶ 정답과 해설 p.58

EXERCISE A 다음 문장을 간접화법으로 바꿔 쓸 때 괄호 안에서 옳은 것을 고르시오.

1 She says, "I am busy."
➡ She [says / tells] that [I am / she is] busy.

2 She said to him, "I will go on a picnic."
➡ She told him that [she will / she would] go on a picnic.

3 He said to me, "I met Tony yesterday."
➡ He told me that he [met / had met] Tony [the day before / that day].

4 He said to me, "I saw your bike in the park."
➡ He told me that [I / he] [saw / had seen] [my bike / his bike] in the park.

EXERCISE B 다음 문장을 간접화법으로 바꿔 쓸 때 빈칸에 알맞은 말을 쓰시오.

1 She says, "I will keep the promise."
➡ She says ______________________.

2 He said to me, "You are kind to my brother."
➡ He told me ______________________.

3 Judy says, "My parents are cooking in the kitchen."
➡ Judy says ______________________.

4 Mary said to me, "I will go there tomorrow."
➡ Mary told me ______________________.

5 He said, "I met her three days ago."
➡ He said ______________________.

6 She said to me, "I saw your father last night."
➡ She told me ______________________.

EXERCISE C 다음 문장을 직접화법으로 바꿔 쓸 때 빈칸에 알맞은 말을 쓰시오.

1 She said that she was very happy.
➡ She said, ______________________

2 I said that he was crying then.
➡ I said, ______________________

3 She told me that she could help me.
➡ She said to me, ______________________

4 He said that he had bought that camera.
➡ He said, ______________________

5 He told me that they would come back soon.
➡ He said to me, ______________________

6 She said that she had made pizza for me.
➡ She said, ______________________

7 화법 전환 II - 의문문

의문문의 화법 전환(직접화법 → 간접화법)	
① 전달동사	say / say to → ask
② 접속사	콤마(,)와 인용부호(" ") 삭제 ➡ 의문사 + 주어 + 동사(의문사가 있는 간접의문문) ➡ if〔whether〕+ 주어 + 동사(의문사가 없는 간접의문문)
③ 인칭	간접의문문의 인칭대명사 및 지시대명사 변경
④ 시제	주절의 시제에 맞춰 종속절의 시제를 바꿈

1 의문사가 있는 경우 : 의문사 + 주어 + 동사

She **said to** me, " Where do you live? " **〈직접화법〉** 그녀는 나에게 "너는 어디에 사니?"라고 말했다.

전달동사 ↓ 생략 ↓ 의문사가 있는 의문문

She **asked** me **where** I lived. **〈간접화법〉** 그녀는 나에게 어디 사는지 물었다.

2 의문사가 없는 경우 : if〔whether〕+ 주어 + 동사

She **said to** me, " Do you love me? " **〈직접화법〉** 그녀는 나에게 "너는 나를 사랑하니?"라고 말했다.

전달동사 ↓ 생략 ↓ 의문사가 없는 의문문

She **asked** me **if〔whether〕** I loved her. **〈간접화법〉** 그녀는 나에게 그녀를 사랑하는지 물었다.

▶▶ 정답과 해설 p. 59

EXERCISE A **다음 문장을 간접화법으로 바꿔 쓸 때 괄호 안에서 옳은 것을 고르시오.**

1 She said to the boy, "Can you speak English?"
➡ She asked the boy [if / that] [he / she] could speak English.

2 He said to me, "Why are you crying?"
➡ He [said / asked] me why [was I crying / I was crying].

3 I said to Peter, "How old are you?"
➡ I [asked / asked to] Peter how old [you were / he was].

4 I said to him, "Who wrote the letter?"
➡ I [told / asked] him who [wrote / had written] the letter.

5 He said to me, "Will you open the door?"
➡ He asked me [if / that] I [will / would] open the door.

6 Julie said to him, "Is this your book?"
➡ Julie asked him [whether / that] [was that / that was] his book.

EXERCISE B 다음 문장을 간접화법으로 바꿔 쓸 때 빈칸에 알맞은 말을 쓰시오.

1 Mom said to me, "What are you doing?"
➡ Mom asked me ______________________.

2 I said to Bill, "Are you sleepy?"
➡ I asked Bill ______________________.

3 Mike said to me, "Which book did you read?"
➡ Mike asked me ______________________.

4 Ted said to her, "How do you go to school?"
➡ Ted asked her ______________________.

EXERCISE C 다음 문장을 직접화법으로 바꿔 쓸 때 빈칸에 알맞은 말을 쓰시오.

1 I asked him what he was thinking about.
➡ I said to him, ______________________

2 My friend asked me whether I was busy then.
➡ My friend said to me, ______________________

3 The doctor asked him if he had smoked a lot.
➡ The doctor said to him, ______________________

4 Jim asked me who had closed the door.
➡ Jim said to me, ______________________

EXERCISE D 다음 우리말과 일치하도록 주어진 단어 또는 어구를 배열하여 문장을 완성하시오.

1 James는 저것이 누구의 차인지 물었다. (car, was, whose, that)
➡ James asked ______________________.

2 나는 그녀가 어디에서 영어를 공부하고 있는지 물었다. (she, where, was, English, studying)
➡ I asked ______________________.

3 그녀는 내가 농구를 좋아하는지 물었다. (I, basketball, liked, if)
➡ She asked ______________________.

4 그는 내게 내가 독서를 좋아하는지 물었다. (was, if, I, fond of, reading)
➡ He asked me ______________________.

8 화법 전환 III - 명령문

명령문의 화법 전환(직접화법 → 간접화법)	
① 전달동사	say / say to → tell, advise(충고), order(명령), ask(부탁)
② 접속사	콤마(,)와 인용부호(" ") 삭제
③ 명령문	(긍정명령문) 동사원형 ➡ to부정사 (부정명령문) 동사원형 ➡ 「not + to부정사」

1 긍정명령문 : to부정사로 나타냄

The officer **said to** the soldiers, "**Fire**!" **<직접화법>** 그 장교는 군사들에게 "발사하라!"라고 말했다.

전달동사 ↓ 생략 ↓ to부정사

The officer **ordered** the soldiers **to fire**. **<간접화법>** 그 장교는 군사들에게 발사하라고 명령했다.

2 부정명령문 : 「not + to부정사」로 나타냄

The teacher **said to** the students, "**Don't make** noise." **<직접화법>** 선생님은 학생들에게 "떠들지 마라." 라고 말씀하셨다.

전달동사 ↓ 생략 ↓ not+to부정사

The teacher **told** the students **not to make** noise. **<간접화법>** 선생님은 학생들에게 떠들지 말라고 말씀하셨다.

▶▶ 정답과 해설 p. 59

EXERCISE A 다음 문장을 간접화법으로 바꿔 쓸 때 괄호 안에서 옳은 것을 고르시오.

1 She says to him, "Be careful."
➡ She tells him [to be / that be] careful.

2 Mom said to me, "Don't go near the fire."
➡ Mom told me [to go not / not to go] near the fire.

3 He said to me, "Please lend me your pen."
➡ He asked me [to lend / if lend] him [his / my] pen.

4 My dad said to me, "Please come home early."
➡ My dad [said / asked] me [to come / I come] home early.

5 The doctor said to me, "Don't drink coffee too much."
➡ The doctor [said / advised] me [to / not to] drink coffee too much.

6 The plumber said to me, "Change the faucet."
➡ The plumber [said / advised] me [to change / not to change] the faucet.

EXERCISE B 다음 간접화법 또는 직접화법으로 바꿔 쓴 문장에서 어법상 틀린 부분을 찾아 바르게 고쳐 쓰시오.

1 He said to me, "Don't be late."
➡ He told me to do not be late.

2 She told Bob to pass her the ball.
➡ She said to Bob, "Pass you the ball."

3 The boy said to me, "Follow me this way, please."
➡ The boy asked me follow him this way.

EXERCISE C 다음 문장을 직접화법으로 바꿔 쓸 때 빈칸에 알맞은 말을 쓰시오.

1 He ordered me not to move.
➡ He said to me, ______________________________

2 My father told me to move those boxes to the garage.
➡ My father said to me, ______________________________

3 He asked his friend to wait there till he returned.
➡ He said to his friend, ______________________________

4 Sue told him not to worry about her.
➡ Sue said to him, ______________________________

EXERCISE D 다음 괄호 안에 주어진 단어를 사용하여 간접화법으로 바꿔 쓰시오. (필요시 형태 변화)

1 Bob said to her, "Look at me." (tell)
➡ Bob ________ her ______________________________.

2 She said to me, "Please help me." (ask)
➡ She ________ me ______________________________.

3 The officer said to his soldiers, "Start immediately." (order)
➡ The officer ________ his soldiers ______________________________.

4 The doctor said to me, "Don't smoke too much." (advise)
➡ The doctor ________ me ______________________________.

Chapter 14
일치와 화법

학교 시험 대비 문제

맞힌 개수	
선택형	____ / 25
서술형	____ / 12

▶▶ 정답과 해설 p. 59

[01-02] 다음 빈칸에 들어갈 말로 알맞은 것을 고르시오.

01

The Olympic Games ________ held in Seoul in 1988.

① has ② had ③ was
④ are ⑤ were

02

Every country ________ a national flag.

① has ② have ③ is
④ are ⑤ having

03 다음 문장을 직접화법으로 바르게 고쳐 쓴 것은?

She said that her son was the biggest joy of her life.

① She told, "Her son is the biggest joy of my life."
② She said, "Her son is the biggest joy of his life."
③ She said, "My son is the biggest joy of my life."
④ She said, "My son was the biggest joy of my life."
⑤ She told me, "My son was the biggest joy of my life."

고난도

04 다음 빈칸에 들어갈 말이 바르게 짝지어진 것은?

Every plate, fork, and glass in the house ________ dirty. All the children's clothes ________ dirty, too. Each of the children ________ a problem. I want to help them.

① is — is — has ② is — are — have
③ is — are — has ④ are — are — has
⑤ are — is — have

05 다음 간접화법으로 바꿔 쓴 문장에서 틀린 것은?

• Kate said to Tom, "I'm sorry you don't understand me."
➡ Kate told(①) Tom that(②) she is(③) sorry he didn't(④) understand her(⑤).

고난도

06 다음 중 어법상 올바른 것은?

① Curry and rice are popular in Korea.
② *Gulliver's Travels* were written by Swift.
③ Two thirds of the building has been completed.
④ Some of our money were spent in buying tickets.
⑤ Half of the students was wearing Korean dresses.

07 다음 중 문장 전환이 바르지 않은 것은?

① John said to me, "Will you marry me?"
➡ John asked me if I would marry him.

② She said to me, "What do you want to be?"
➡ She asked me what I wanted to be.

③ I said, "Is he coming to the party?"
➡ I asked that he was coming to the party.

④ Tom said to me, "I will call you tomorrow."
➡ Tom told me that he would call me the next day.

⑤ My mother said to me, "I'm proud of you."
➡ My mother told me that she was proud of me.

08 다음 간접화법으로 바꿔 쓴 문장에서 틀린 것은?

> • He said to me, "I was happy to see you."
> ➡ He told(①) me that he(②) was(③) happy(④) to see me(⑤).

고난도

09 다음 중 어법상 틀린 것은?

① Who was absent?

② Is your family all early risers?

③ Is bread and butter your favorite dish?

④ The famous poet and novelist was born in 1872.

⑤ The people over 19 years old have the right to vote.

10 다음 빈칸에 들어갈 말로 알맞은 것은?

> The young ______________.

① behave as if he knew everything

② behaves as if he knew everything

③ behave as if he knows everything

④ behave as if they knew everything

⑤ behaves as if they knew everything

11 다음 빈칸에 들어갈 말로 알맞은 것은?

> • He said to me, "I will help you tomorrow."
> = He told me that he ______________.

① will help you tomorrow

② helped you the next day

③ was helping me tomorrow

④ would help me the next day

⑤ would help you the next day

12 다음 간접화법으로 바꿔 쓴 문장에서 틀린 것은?

> • He said to me, "I came here to see you."
> ➡ He told(①) me that he(②) came(③) there(④) to see me(⑤).

고난도

13 다음 밑줄 친 부분이 어법상 틀린 것은?

① It seemed that they would win.
② It is clear that he majored in math.
③ I think he is good at playing soccer.
④ They say she is the smartest student in my class.
⑤ They thought that she has been interested in psychology.

14 다음 빈칸에 들어갈 말로 알맞은 것은?

Physics ________ not taught in this school.

① have ② had ③ is
④ are ⑤ were

15 다음 문장을 간접화법으로 바꿔 쓸 때 빈칸에 알맞은 것은?

• The teacher said, "John, don't sing so loud." ➡ The teacher told John ________ sing so loud.

① not to ② to ③ not do
④ never ⑤ don't

16 다음 빈칸에 들어갈 말이 바르게 짝지어진 것은?

• Alcott's *Little Women* ________ very popular then. • The characters in *Little Women* ________ to be adults.

① is — want ② are — wants
③ were — want ④ was — want
⑤ was — wants

17 다음 빈칸에 들어갈 말로 알맞은 것은?

• The goalkeeper said to Brian, "Don't kick the ball here." = The goalkeeper told Brian ________ kick the ball ________.

① to not — here ② not to — here
③ don't — there ④ to — there
⑤ not to — there

18 다음 빈칸에 들어갈 말로 알맞은 것은?

He said that he ________ along the river every morning.

① run ② runs ③ will run
④ had run ⑤ was running

19 다음 문장을 간접화법으로 바르게 바꿔 쓴 것은?

He said to me, "I received this letter."

① He said me that I had received that letter.
② He told me that I have received that letter.
③ He told me that he has received that letter.
④ He told me that he had received that letter.
⑤ He told me that he has received this letter.

고난도

20 다음 빈칸에 들어갈 말이 바르게 짝지어진 것은?

• Most of the students ______________ disappointed with the result. • Two thirds of the planet ______________ covered with water.

① was — is ② were — are
③ was — are ④ were — is
⑤ were — have

21 다음 문장을 간접화법으로 바르게 바꿔 쓴 것은?

He said to me, "Do you know her email address?"

① He asked me if I knew her email address.
② He asked me that I knew her email address.
③ He asked me if you knew her email address.
④ He told me that you knew her email address.
⑤ He asked me that you knew her email address.

고난도

22 다음 중 어법상 틀린 것은?

① They thought it would rain.
② She thought that he was very brave.
③ She says that the movie was shocking.
④ She says that she bought a new smart phone.
⑤ He didn't know if she has ever watched the movie.

23 다음 문장을 직접화법으로 바르게 바꿔 쓴 것은?

He asked her if she was hurt.

① He asked her, "Is she hurt?"
② He told to her, "Do you hurt?"
③ He asked her, "Was she hurt?"
④ He said to her, "Are you hurt?"
⑤ He said to her, "If she was hurt?"

24 다음 빈칸에 들어갈 말로 알맞은 것은?

The rich __________ looking for the chance to invest their money.

① is ② has ③ keeps on
④ are ⑤ is going to

25 다음 중 어법상 틀린 것은?

① It is true that he is honest.
② She thinks that the food is delicious.
③ She remembered that he was very kind.
④ He said that he will go to bed at 10 every day.
⑤ He thinks that the exam was very difficult.

서술형

26 다음 문장의 밑줄 친 부분을 바르게 고쳐 쓰시오.

He thought that the exam is difficult.

__________ ➡ __________

27 다음 대화의 밑줄 친 부분을 바르게 고쳐 쓰시오.

A Did you see her at the party?
B Yes, I remember I see her at the party.

__________ ➡ __________

28 다음 우리말과 일치하도록 주어진 단어와 어구를 배열하시오. (필요시 형태 변화)

• 자동차의 수가 증가하고 있다. (cars, have, increasing, the number of, been)
➡ __________

29 다음 대화의 내용과 일치하도록 빈칸에 알맞은 단어를 쓰시오.

Teacher	Do you know what causes objects to fall?
Students	Of course. Gravity.

➡ Students knew that gravity __________ objects to fall.

30 다음 문장에서 어법상 틀린 부분을 찾아 바르게 고쳐 쓰시오.

Looking up new words are very important in learning languages.

__________ ➡ __________

고난도

31 다음 문장을 직접화법으로 바꿔 쓸 때 빈칸에 알맞은 말을 쓰시오.

• I asked Sam how he could play chess so well.
➡ I said to Sam, "How __________ __________ play chess so well?"

32 다음 주어진 단어를 배열하여 문장을 완성하시오.

The doctor advised me __________.
(to, get, sleep, enough)

33 **다음 우리말과 일치하도록 〈조건〉에 맞게 문장을 쓰시오.**

〈조건〉
- 각 문장에 반드시 단어 number를 포함할 것
- 필요시 주어진 단어의 형태를 변형할 것
- (1)은 총 9단어, (2)는 총 8단어로 쓸 것

(1) 많은 사람들이 버스를 기다리고 있다. (wait for)

➡ ________________________________

(2) 학생들의 수가 매년 감소하고 있다. (decrease)

➡ ________________________________

[34-35] 다음 대화를 읽고, 대화의 내용에 대한 요약문을 완성하시오.

Julie	How was your weekend, James?
James	Great! I went to the French village in Seoul.
Julie	I didn't know there was a French village in Seoul. Can you tell me more about it?

34 Julie asked James, firstly, ________________

________________________________.

35 Julie asked James, secondly, ________________

____

the French village in Seoul.

[36-37] 다음 그림을 보고, 주어진 말풍선의 대사를 참고하여 〈보기〉와 같이 문장을 완성하시오.

〈보기〉

Study in the library.

My teacher told me to study in the library.

36

Take your umbrella.

My sister told me ________________

________________________________.

37

Don't talk about it anymore.

Paul told me ________________

________________________________.

Chapter

15

특수구문

1 강조 I - 동사를 강조하는 do

「do(does, did) + 일반동사(동사원형)」: 정말 ~하다

평서문에 do를 사용해서 일반동사를 강조할 수 있다.

A Do you love your wife? 당신은 아내를 사랑합니까?

B Yes, I **do love** her. 네, 저는 그녀를 정말 사랑합니다.

▶▶ 정답과 해설 p.62

EXERCISE A 다음 빈칸에 강조하는 말을 넣어 문장을 완성하시오.

1 **A** Do you like ice cream?
B Yes, I ________ like ice cream.

2 **A** Do they want to see me?
B Yes, they ________ want to see you.

3 **A** Is Linda a good tennis player?
B Yes, she ________ play tennis well.

4 **A** Did you know what happened yesterday?
B Of course, I ________ know what happened.

5 **A** How was your travel to Istanbul? Did you enjoy it?
B Absolutely, I ________ enjoy my traveling there.

EXERCISE B 다음 밑줄 친 부분을 바르게 바꿔 쓰시오.

1 **A** He has a car, doesn't he?
B Certainly, he <u>do has</u> a car.

2 **A** Who painted this wonderful picture?
B Actually, I <u>did painted</u> it.

3 **A** Do you like watching football games?
B Yes, I <u>do watching</u> football games a lot.

4 **A** She plays the guitar well, doesn't she?
B Yes, she <u>does plays</u> the guitar well.

2 강조 II - It ~ that 강조 구문

「It is(was) ~ that ...」: …인 것은 바로 ~이다

It과 that 사이에 주어, 목적어, 부사구(절) 중 강조하고자 하는 말을 넣어 강조구문을 만들 수 있다. It ~ that 강조 구문에서 동사와 형용사는 강조할 수 없으며, 강조하는 대상에 따라 that 대신 who, which, where, when 등을 사용할 수 있다.

John bought a bag at the store yesterday. John은 어제 그 가게에서 가방을 샀다.

➡ **It was John that(who)** bought a bag at the store yesterday. **〈주어 강조〉**
어제 그 가게에서 가방을 산 사람은 바로 John이었다.

➡ **It was a bag that(which)** John bought at the store yesterday. **〈목적어 강조〉**
John이 어제 그 가게에서 산 것은 바로 가방이었다.

➡ **It was at the store that(where)** John bought a bag yesterday. **〈장소 강조〉**
John이 어제 가방을 산 곳은 바로 그 가게였다.

➡ **It was yesterday that(when)** John bought a bag at the store. **〈시간 강조〉**
John이 그 가게에서 가방을 산 때는 바로 어제였다.

+ It ~ that 강조 구문 vs. It ~ that 가주어·진주어 구문

It was at the library **that** I first met her. **〈It ~ that 강조 구문〉**
내가 그녀를 처음 만난 곳은 바로 도서관이었다.

It is difficult **that** you speak English fluently. **〈It ~ that 가주어·진주어 구문〉**
네가 영어를 유창하게 말하는 것은 어렵다.

▶▶ 정답과 해설 p. 62

EXERCISE A 다음 문장의 밑줄 친 부분을 〈보기〉와 같이 바꿔 쓰시오.

〈보기〉
Brian showed me how to solve the math problem.
➡ It was Brian that showed me how to solve the math problem.

1 Ernest Hemingway wrote *the Old Man and the Sea*.
➡ It was ____________ that ____________.

2 Chris Columbus directed the film *Harry Potter*.
➡ It was ____________ that ____________.

3 I happened to see Sarah on the street last week.
➡ It was ____________ that ____________.

4 You helped me get over difficulties.
➡ It was ____________ that ____________.

3 도치 I - 장소 부사구

「장소 부사구+동사+주어」

장소나 방향을 나타내는 부사구가 강조되어 문장 앞에 오게 되면 주어와 동사의 어순이 도치된다. 이때 동사의 형태는 바뀌지 않는다.

A man with a big hat came **along the road**.
➡ **Along the road** came a man with a big hat. 길을 따라서 커다란 모자를 쓴 한 남자가 왔다.

An old castle stood **on the top of the hill**.
➡ **On the top of the hill** stood an old castle. 그 언덕 꼭대기에 오래된 성 하나가 서 있었다.

! 주어가 대명사인 경우에는 도치가 일어나지 않는다.

Here she comes. (○) 여기 그녀가 온다.
Here ***comes*** she. (×)

▶▶ 정답과 해설 p. 62

EXERCISE A 다음 문장의 밑줄 친 부분을 강조하여 도치한 문장으로 바꿔 쓰시오.

1 A new computer was <u>in the room</u>.
➡ ______________________________

2 A red car appeared <u>from around the corner</u>.
➡ ______________________________

3 A few tall trees stand <u>next to the museum</u>.
➡ ______________________________

4 The bank I work for is <u>next to the bakery</u>.
➡ ______________________________

5 The sea horse lives <u>in warm seas</u>.
➡ ______________________________

6 An old woman came <u>out of the car</u>.
➡ ______________________________

7 A computer lab which students can use is <u>in the library</u>.
➡ ______________________________

4 도치 II - so〔neither〕+ 동사 + 주어

so + 동사 + 주어	~도 역시 그렇다 (긍정문에 동의하는 표현)	A I am interested in music. 나는 음악에 흥미가 있어. B **So am I.** (= I am interested in music, too.) 나도 그래(나도 또한 음악에 흥미가 있어).
neither + 동사 + 주어	~도 역시 그렇지 않다 (부정문에 동의하는 표현)	A I don't like physics. 나는 물리학을 좋아하지 않아. B **Neither do I.** (= I don't like physics, either.) 나도 그래(나도 또한 물리학을 좋아하지 않아). * Neither don't I. (×)

※ '또한'이라는 의미를 나타내기 위해 긍정문에는 too를, 부정문에는 either를 붙인다.

▶▶ 정답과 해설 p. 62

EXERCISE A 다음 괄호 안에서 옳은 것을 고르시오.

1 A I am happy to see you. B I am happy, [too / either].

2 A I don't like dancing. B Neither [do / does] we.

3 A I am so hungry. B So [am / do] I.

4 A I am not tired. B I am not tired, [either / neither].

5 A He likes soccer. B So [is / does] she.

6 A She has already watched the film. B So [does / has] he.

7 A She can play the violin. B So [do / can] I.

8 A I haven't finished my homework yet. B Neither [did / have] we.

EXERCISE B 다음 대화의 응답과 같은 뜻이 되도록 빈칸에 알맞은 말을 쓰시오.

1 A I am not good at English.
B I am not good at it, either. ➡ ________ ________ ________.

2 A I have been to China once.
B We have been there, too. ➡ ________ ________ ________.

3 A I can't play the guitar well.
B He can't play it, either. ➡ ________ ________ ________.

5 도치 III - 부정어

부정어 not, no, never, hardly, seldom 등이 강조되어 문장 앞에 오는 경우 어순이 도치된다.

1 「부정어 + do〔does, did〕+ 주어 + 동사원형」: 동사의 시제가 현재나 과거일 때

I hardly ride my bike to school.

➡ **Hardly do I ride** my bike to school. 나는 학교에 자전거를 타고 가는 일이 거의 없다.

2 「부정어 + have〔조동사〕+ 주어 + 동사」: 동사의 시제가 완료시제이거나 조동사가 있을 때

He has never met such a beautiful woman before.

➡ **Never has he met** such a beautiful woman before.

그는 전에 그렇게 아름다운 여인을 만난 적이 전혀 없었다.

*** 완료시제에서는 주어 뒤에 p.p.형태의 동사가 오고 조동사가 쓰였을 때는 동사원형이 온다.**

▶▶ 정답과 해설 p.62

EXERCISE A 다음 문장을 〈보기〉와 같이 부정어를 강조하는 문장으로 바꿔 쓰시오.

〈보기〉
He seldom goes to the movies.
➡ Seldom does he go to the movies.

1 She has never been to Brazil before.
➡ ______________________ to Brazil before.

2 I rarely read the morning paper nowadays.
➡ ______________________ the morning paper nowadays.

3 She seldom has a cup of tea before going to bed.
➡ ______________________ a cup of tea before going to bed.

4 I could hardly understand what she was trying to tell me.
➡ ______________________ what she was trying to tell me.

5 They had never heard of such a stupid idea.
➡ ______________________ of such a stupid idea.

6 He has not mentioned a single word about the happening.
➡ Not a single word ______________________ about the happening.

6 생략

1 반복되는 동일 어구의 생략

She stayed at home and **(she)** watched TV all evening. 그녀는 집에 머무르며 저녁 내내 TV를 보았다.

A Would you like to go to the party with me tonight? 오늘 밤 저와 함께 그 파티에 가시겠습니까?

B I'd love to **(go)**, but I can't. 저는 가고 싶지만, 그럴 수 없어요. **<to부정사에서 동사원형 생략>**

2 목적격 관계대명사의 생략

This is the watch **(which)** I bought yesterday. 이것은 내가 어제 산 손목시계다.

***「전치사+목적격 관계대명사」에서 목적격 관계대명사는 생략할 수 없다.**

3 「주격 관계대명사+be동사」의 생략

I was given a letter **(which was)** written in English. 나는 영어로 쓰인 한 통의 편지를 받았다.

▶▶ 정답과 해설 p.62

EXERCISE A **다음 문장에서 생략할 수 있는 부분에 밑줄을 그으시오.**

1 I opened the window and I looked out at the street.

2 This is the book that I want to read.

3 He talked to his friend who was sitting at the table.

4 I will go with her if she wants to go.

EXERCISE B **다음 문장에서 특정 어구가 생략된 부분에 V 표시를 한 후, 생략된 어구를 쓰시오.**

1 My mother doesn't always buy me everything I want.

2 She received my phone call but didn't talk to me.

3 The girl waiting at the door is my cousin, Jenny.

4 I asked her to play the violin, but she did not want to.

5 She brought me a book written by one of her favorite writers.

6 The handsome man she spoke to is her English teacher.

학교 시험 대비 문제

맞힌 개수	
선택형	____/ 20
서술형	____/ 11

▶▶ 정답과 해설 p.63

01 다음 중 밑줄 친 do의 쓰임이 나머지 넷과 다른 것은?

① She does enjoy dancing.
② I do like singing very much.
③ I do yoga every morning.
④ They did like traveling in Europe.
⑤ He did find a way to solve the problem.

02 다음 밑줄 친 that의 쓰임이 <보기>와 같은 것은?

<보기>
It is my smartphone that I left on the bus.

① I think that she is a kind person.
② Who is that girl coming toward us?
③ It is English that I am really interested in.
④ The English test wasn't that difficult.
⑤ It must be difficult that you finish the work in time.

03 다음 문장에서 어법상 틀린 것은?

① Around them ② was ③ lots of ④ wooden ⑤ baskets and tables.

04 다음 우리말을 영어로 바르게 옮긴 것을 모두 고르시오.

그는 오후에 테니스를 거의 치지 않는다.

① He hardly plays tennis in the afternoon.
② He plays hardly tennis in the afternoon.
③ Hardly he do plays tennis in the afternoon.
④ Hardly do he plays tennis in the afternoon.
⑤ Hardly does he play tennis in the afternoon.

고난도

05 다음 중 밑줄 친 that의 쓰임이 나머지 넷과 다른 것은?

① It was yesterday that I lost my watch.
② It was my brother that broke the window.
③ It was my father that helped me finish the work.
④ It was at the bus stop that I met her for the first time.
⑤ It is hard that you master English within a short period of time.

06 다음 빈칸에 공통으로 들어갈 말로 알맞은 것은?

• She ________ her homework before dinner.
• I ________ see an active volcano in Japan.

① was ② did ③ had
④ took ⑤ made

고난도

07 다음 중 어법상 틀린 것은?

① A I'm sorry to hear that.
 B So am I.

② A I like playing football very much.
 B So does she.

③ A I wasn't good at English.
 B Neither was I.

④ A She had a good meal this morning.
 B So had I.

⑤ A I haven't watched the film yet.
 B Neither have I.

08 다음 빈칸에 들어갈 말로 알맞은 것은?

> Behind the art museum ________ the boys and the girls.

① stands ② stand ③ standing
④ to stand ⑤ be stood

09 다음 중 어법상 올바른 것을 모두 고르시오.

① A I'm happy to see you again.
 B I'm happy, either.

② A I wasn't disappointed with the result.
 B I wasn't disappointed, neither.

③ A I enjoyed watching the film.
 B So was I.

④ A I had a good time at the party.
 B So did I.

⑤ A I haven't heard from her recently.
 B Neither have I.

10 다음 밑줄 친 that의 쓰임이 〈보기〉와 같은 것은?

> 〈보기〉
> It was at the library that I found her ID card.

① Is that bag over there yours?
② I believed that he would keep his promise.
③ That he made such a foolish mistake is strange.
④ It was last week that he finally passed the exam.
⑤ It is important that you should learn how to drive.

11 다음 중 문장 전환이 어법상 틀린 것은?

① It was yesterday that she arrived here.
 ➡ She arrived here yesterday.

② She has never been to New York.
 ➡ Never she has been to New York.

③ Do you know the girl who is waiting by the door?
 ➡ Do you know the girl waiting by the door?

④ To speak Japanese fluently is hard for you.
 ➡ It is hard for you to speak Japanese fluently.

⑤ They stayed at home and watched a football match.
 ➡ They stayed at home and they watched a football match.

고난도

12 **다음 중 어법상 올바른 것을 모두 고르시오.**

① This is the house she used to live in.
② In a castle lived a beautiful princess.
③ Hardly he does read a morning paper.
④ I was not surprised to hear the news, neither.
⑤ The machine using to make coffee needs repairing.

13 **다음 중 밑줄 친 부분을 생략할 수 없는 것은?**

① I like a man who is filled with self-confidence.
② I went to the window and I opened it.
③ There is a boy who speaks English well.
④ Do you know the girls who are standing over there?
⑤ You may go home now if you really want to go.

고난도

14 **다음 우리말을 영어로 바르게 옮긴 것을 모두 고르시오.**

그녀는 전에 런던에 가본 적이 전혀 없다.

① Never she has been to London before.
② She has never been to London before.
③ Never have she been to London before.
④ Never has she been to London before.
⑤ She never has been to London before.

[15-16] 다음 중 밑줄 친 부분의 쓰임이 나머지 넷과 다른 것을 고르시오.

고난도

15 ① Her mom did stay at home all day.
② I have to do the dishes after dinner.
③ He did teach me how to grow roses.
④ It does cost lots of money to stay at the hotel.
⑤ She does act as if she were the devil.

고난도

16 ① It was a pity that she broke her arm.
② It was last night that I heard the news.
③ It is my father that is reading a newspaper.
④ It was at the park that I met him.
⑤ It was my parents that sent me a card on my birthday.

17 **다음 밑줄 친 부분을 생략할 수 없는 것은?**

① The dinner itself was really delicious.
② English is the subject which Sam likes most.
③ You can have this doll if you want to have this doll.
④ The house in which I lived has a beautiful scenery.
⑤ He drank coffee, but I told him not to drink coffee.

18 다음 중 어법상 틀린 것은?

① On the bench sat the man.
② Over our school flew an airplane.
③ Right over our heads an eagle flew.
④ Next to the bakery is the bank I work for.
⑤ Under the ground run pipes for gas and water.

19 다음 대화의 빈칸에 들어갈 말로 알맞은 것은?

A I'm not good at science.
B ________ I didn't pass the exam.

① So am I. ② So did I.
③ Neither do I. ④ Neither am I.
⑤ I was good at it.

20 다음 중 어법상 틀린 것은?

① A I wasn't busy then.
B Neither was I.
② A I have been to India.
B So am I.
③ A Tom plays the piano very well.
B So does Mary. Mary is a pianist!
④ A My father takes a walk every day.
B So do I.
⑤ A I don't know why he had to leave so early.
B Neither do I.

서술형

[21-22] 다음 B의 응답과 같은 뜻이 되도록 빈칸에 알맞은 말을 쓰시오.

21

A Never have I met such a boring person.
B I haven't, either.
= ________ ________ ________.

22

A It was a good dinner. I enjoyed the food.
B I enjoyed it, too.
= ________ ________ ________.

[23-25] 다음 문장을 〈보기〉와 같이 바꿔 쓰시오.

〈보기〉
• He seldom goes out for lunch.
➡ Seldom does he go out for lunch.

23 I hardly skip my breakfast.
➡ ________________________

24 She has seldom missed her music class.
➡ ________________________

25 They have never tried Turkish food before.
➡ ________________________

[26-28] 다음 우리말과 일치하도록 <보기>와 같이 문장을 완성하시오.

<보기>

A She is not good at English.
B Neither is he. (그도 그래.)

26 A I enjoy reading a lot.
B ______________________ (나도 그래.)

27 A He can't swim very well.
B ______________________ (그녀도 그래.)

28 A He has finished his homework.
B ______________________ (Jane도 그래.)

[29-31] 다음 문장을 <조건>에 맞게 바꿔 쓰시오.

• He helped me find my pen at the library yesterday.

<조건>

• 'It ~ that …' 강조구문을 이용할 것
• 괄호 안에 적힌 내용을 강조하는 형태로 쓸 것

29 (he)

____

____

30 (at the library)

____

____

31 (yesterday)

____

____

우리 학교 교과서 연계표

※ 다락원(강용순) 연계표 : 홈페이지 제공

금성(최인철)		적중! 중학영문법 3300제 Level 3		
1과	사역동사	Ch.01 부정사	6 목적격보어로 동사원형을 사용하는 동사	p.24
	동명사 관용 표현	Ch.02 동명사	6 동명사 관용 표현	p.60
2과	the + 비교급 ~, the + 비교급 ~	Ch.09 비교	6 the + 비교급, the + 비교급	p.198
	to부정사(의미상 주어)	Ch.01 부정사	2 진주어 / 진목적어 역할을 하는 to부정사	p.18
3과	not only A but also B	Ch.12 접속사	2 상관접속사	p.259
	I wish 가정법 과거	Ch.13 가정법	3 I wish + 가정법	p.290
4과	과거완료	Ch.04 시제	6 과거완료	p.100
	원급비교	Ch.09 비교	1 as + 원급 + as	p.192
5과	so ~ that	Ch.12 접속사	6 so / so that ~ / so ~ that ...	p.266
	지각동사	Ch.01 부정사	6 목적격보어로 동사원형을 사용하는 동사	p.24
6과	It ~ that 강조 구문	Ch.15 특수구문	2 강조 II – It ~ that 강조 구문	p.327
	분사구문	Ch.03 분사	5 시간 / 이유 / 부대상황을 나타내는 분사구문	p.77
7과	to부정사(부사적 용법)	Ch.01 부정사	10 목적 / 결과를 나타내는 to부정사	p.327
	도치	Ch.15 특수구문	4 도치 II – so(neither) + 동사 + 주어	p.329
8과	접속사 whether	Ch.12 접속사	4 명사절을 이끄는 접속사 II – if / whether	p.262

능률(김성곤)		적중! 중학영문법 3300제 Level 3		
1과	현재완료진행	Ch.04 시제	5 현재완료진행	p.98
	관계대명사 what	Ch.11 관계사	5 관계대명사 what	p.235
2과	관계대명사 계속적 용법	Ch.11 관계사	10 관계사의 계속적 용법	p.244
	분사	Ch.03 분사	1 명사를 수식하는 분사	p.70
3과	과거완료	Ch.04 시제	6 과거완료	p.100
	접속사 since	Ch.12 접속사	8 부사절을 이끄는 접속사 II – 시간	p.270
4과	접속사 if	Ch.12 접속사	9 부사절을 이끄는 접속사 III – 조건	p.272
	조동사 수동태	Ch.06 수동태	2 조동사의 수동태	p.134
5과	to부정사(의미상 주어)	Ch.01 부정사	2 진주어 / 진목적어 역할을 하는 to부정사	p.18
	관계부사	Ch.11 관계사	8 관계부사 I – where / when 9 관계부사 II – why / how	p.240 p.242
6과	the + 비교급 ~, the + 비교급 ~	Ch.09 비교	6 the + 비교급, the + 비교급	p.198
	분사구문	Ch.03 분사	1 명사를 수식하는 분사	p.70
7과	가정법 과거	Ch.13 가정법	1 가정법 과거	p.286
	so that	Ch.12 접속사	6 so / so that ~ / so ~ that ...	p.266

능률(양현권)		적중! 중학영문법 3300제 Level 3		
1과	to부정사(의미상 주어)	Ch.01 부정사	2 진주어 / 진목적어 역할을 하는 to부정사	p.18
	관계대명사 계속적 용법	Ch.11 관계사	10 관계사의 계속적 용법	p.244
2과	It ~ that 강조 구문	Ch.15 특수구문	2 강조 II – It ~ that 강조 구문	p.327
	think + 목적어 + 목적격보어	문장의 구조	6 목적격보어 I – 명사 / 형용사·분사	p.13
3과	간접의문문	Ch.12 접속사	5 간접의문문	p.264
	사역동사	Ch.01 부정사	6 목적격보어로 동사원형을 사용하는 동사	p.24
4과	과거완료	Ch.04 시제	6 과거완료	p.100
	분사구문	Ch.03 분사	5 시간 / 이유 / 부대상황을 나타내는 분사구문	p.77
5과	의문사 + to부정사	Ch.01 부정사	3 의문사 + to부정사	p.20
	the + 비교급 ~, the + 비교급 ~	Ch.09 비교	6 the + 비교급, the + 비교급	p.198
6과	간접화법	Ch.14 일치와 화법	7 화법 전환 II – 의문문	p.315
	지각동사	Ch.01 부정사	6 목적격보어로 동사원형을 사용하는 동사	p.24
7과	가정법 과거	Ch.13 가정법	1 가정법 과거	p.286
	so ~ that	Ch.12 접속사	6 so / so that ~ / so ~ that ...	p.266

동아(윤정미)		적중! 중학영문법 3300제 Level 3		
1과	간접의문문	Ch.12 접속사	5 간접의문문	p.264
	to부정사(형용사적 용법)	Ch.01 부정사	7 명사를 수식하는 to부정사	p.26
2과	make + 목적어 + 형용사	문장의 구조	6 목적격보어 I – 명사 / 형용사 · 분사	p.13
	so that	Ch.12 접속사	6 so / so that ~ / so ~ that ...	p.266
3과	관계대명사 계속적 용법	Ch.11 관계사	10 관계사의 계속적 용법	p.244
	It ~ that 강조 구문	Ch.15 특수구문	2 강조 II – It ~ that 강조 구문	p.327
4과	현재완료진행	Ch.04 시제	5 현재완료진행	p.98
	의문사 + to부정사	Ch.01 부정사	3 의문사 + to부정사	p.20
5과	분사	Ch.03 분사	1 명사를 수식하는 분사	p.70
	원급 비교	Ch.09 비교	1 as + 원급 + as	p.192
6과	과거완료	Ch.04 시제	6 과거완료	p.100
	관계대명사 what	Ch.11 관계사	5 관계대명사 what	p.235
7과	분사구문	Ch.03 분사	1 명사를 수식하는 분사	p.70
	접속사 as	Ch.12 접속사	10 주의해야 할 접속사 – as / while	p.274
8과	to부정사(의미상 주어)	Ch.01 부정사	2 진주어 / 진목적어 역할을 하는 to부정사	p.18
	가정법 과거	Ch.13 가정법	1 가정법 과거	p.286

동아(이병민)		적중! 중학영문법 3300제 Level 3		
1과	to부정사(의미상 주어)	Ch.01 부정사	2 진주어 / 진목적어 역할을 하는 to부정사	p.18
	관계대명사 what	Ch.11 관계사	5 관계대명사 what	p.235
2과	수 일치	Ch.14 일치와 화법	1 수 일치 I – 단수주어 + 단수동사	p.306
	조동사 수동태	Ch.06 수동태	2 조동사의 수동태	p.134
3과	사역동사	Ch.01 부정사	6 목적격보어로 동사원형을 사용하는 동사	p.24
	It ~ that 강조 구문	Ch.15 특수구문	2 강조 II – It ~ that 강조 구문	p.327
4과	the + 비교급 ~, the + 비교급 ~	Ch.09 비교	6 the + 비교급, the + 비교급	p.198
	접속사 since	Ch.12 접속사	7 부사절을 이끄는 접속사 I – 원인 / 양보	p.268
5과	가정법 과거	Ch.13 가정법	1 가정법 과거	p.286
	의문사 + to부정사	Ch.01 부정사	3 의문사 + to부정사	p.20
6과	so that	Ch.12 접속사	6 so / so that ~ / so ~ that ...	p.266
	enough to	Ch.01 부정사	13 too ~ to / enough to	p.35
7과	소유격 관계대명사	Ch.11 관계사	3 소유격 관계대명사 – whose / of which	p.232
	접속사 while	Ch.12 접속사	10 주의해야 할 접속사 – as / while	p.274
8과	분사구문	Ch.03 분사	5 시간 / 이유 / 부대상황을 나타내는 분사구문	p.77
	과거완료	Ch.04 시제	6 과거완료	p.100

미래엔(최연희)		적중! 중학영문법 3300제 Level 3		
1과	관계대명사 what	Ch.11 관계사	5 관계대명사 what	p.235
	접속사 although	Ch.12 접속사	7 부사절을 이끄는 접속사 I – 원인 / 양보	p.268
2과	It ~ that 강조 구문	Ch.15 특수구문	2 강조 II – It ~ that 강조 구문	p.327
	관계대명사 계속적 용법	Ch.11 관계사	10 관계사의 계속적 용법	p.244
3과	분사	Ch.03 분사	1 명사를 수식하는 분사	p.70
	강조의 do	Ch.15 특수구문	1 강조 I – 동사를 강조하는 do	p.326
4과	간접의문문	Ch.12 접속사	5 간접의문문	p.264
	과거완료	Ch.04 시제	6 과거완료	p.100
5과	분사구문	Ch.03 분사	5 시간 / 이유 / 부대상황을 나타내는 분사구문	p.77
	not only A but also B	Ch.12 접속사	2 상관접속사	p.259
6과	관계부사	Ch.11 관계사	8 관계부사 I – where / when 9 관계부사 II – why / how	p.240 p.242
	접속부사	Ch.12 접속사	11 접속부사	p.276
7과	소유격 관계대명사	Ch.11 관계사	3 소유격 관계대명사 – whose / of which	p.232
	가정법 과거	Ch.13 가정법	1 가정법 과거	p.286

비상(김진완)		적중! 중학영문법 3300제 Level 3		
1과	관계대명사 what	Ch.11 관계사	5 관계대명사 what	p.235
	관계부사	Ch.11 관계사	8 관계부사 I – where / when 9 관계부사 II – why / how	p.240 p.242
2과	to부정사(의미상 주어)	Ch.01 부정사	2 진주어 / 진목적어 역할을 하는 to부정사	p.18
	현재완료진행	Ch.04 시제	5 현재완료진행	p.98
3과	접속사 if	Ch.12 접속사	4 명사절을 이끄는 접속사 II – if / whether	p.262
	과거완료	Ch.04 시제	6 과거완료	p.100
4과	분사	Ch.03 분사	1 명사를 수식하는 분사	p.70
	to부정사(가목적어 it)	Ch.01 부정사	2 진주어 / 진목적어 역할을 하는 to부정사	p.18
5과	분사구문	Ch.03 분사	5 시간 / 이유 / 부대상황을 나타내는 분사구문	p.77
	so that	Ch.12 접속사	6 so / so that ~ / so ~ that ...	p.266
6과	강조구문	Ch.15 특수구문	2 강조 II – It ~ that 강조 구문	p.327
	사역동사	Ch.01 부정사	6 목적격보어로 동사원형을 사용하는 동사	p.24
7과	접속사 as	Ch.12 접속사	10 주의해야 할 접속사 – as / while	p.274
	수 일치	Ch.14 일치와 화법	3 주의해야 할 수 일치	p.309
8과	가정법 과거	Ch.13 가정법	1 가정법 과거	p.286
	with + 목적어 + 분사	Ch.03 분사	8 with + (대)명사 + 분사	p.81

YBM(박준언)		적중! 중학영문법 3300제 Level 3		
1과	강조의 do	Ch.15 특수구문	1 강조 I – 동사를 강조하는 do	p.326
	관계대명사 what	Ch.11 관계사	5 관계대명사 what	p.235
2과	현재완료진행	Ch.04 시제	5 현재완료진행	p.98
	분사	Ch.03 분사	1 명사를 수식하는 분사	p.70
3과	It ~ that 강조 구문	Ch.15 특수구문	2 강조 II – It ~ that 강조 구문	p.327
	사역동사	Ch.01 부정사	6 목적격보어로 동사원형을 사용하는 동사	p.24
4과	to부정사(의미상 주어)	Ch.01 부정사	2 진주어 / 진목적어 역할을 하는 to부정사	p.18
	가정법 과거	Ch.13 가정법	1 가정법 과거	p.286
5과	과거완료	Ch.04 시제	6 과거완료	p.100
	so that	Ch.12 접속사	6 so / so that ~ / so ~ that ...	p.266
6과	관계대명사 계속적 용법	Ch.11 관계사	10 관계사의 계속적 용법	p.244
	to부정사(부사적 용법)	Ch.01 부정사	10 목적 / 결과를 나타내는 to부정사	p.32
7과	관계부사 how	Ch.11 관계사	9 관계부사 II – why / how	p.242
	the + 비교급 ~, the + 비교급 ~	Ch.09 비교	6 the + 비교급, the + 비교급	p.198
8과	분사구문	Ch.03 분사	5 시간 / 이유 / 부대상황을 나타내는 분사구문	p.77
	be worth ~ing	Ch.02 동명사	6 동명사 관용 표현	p.60
9과	I wish 가정법 과거	Ch.13 가정법	3 I wish + 가정법	p.290
	간접의문문	Ch.12 접속사	5 간접의문문	p.264

YBM(송미정)		적중! 중학영문법 3300제 Level 3		
1과	too ~ to	Ch.01 부정사	13 too ~ to / enough to	p.35
	to부정사의 부정	Ch.01 부정사	1 주어 / 보어 / 목적어 역할을 하는 to부정사	p.16
2과	분사구문	Ch.03 분사	5 시간 / 이유 / 부대상황을 나타내는 분사구문	p.77
	접속사 if	Ch.12 접속사	4 명사절을 이끄는 접속사 II – if / whether	p.262
3과	the + 비교급 ~, the + 비교급 ~	Ch.09 비교	6 the + 비교급, the + 비교급	p.198
	It ~ that 강조 구문	Ch.15 특수구문	2 강조 II – It ~ that 강조 구문	p.327
4과	접속사 although	Ch.12 접속사	7 부사절을 이끄는 접속사 I – 원인 / 양보	p.268
	seem to부정사	Ch.01 부정사	9 seem(appear) + to부정사	p.30
5과	관계대명사 what	Ch.11 관계사	5 관계대명사 what	p.235
	현재완료진행	Ch.04 시제	5 현재완료진행	p.98
6과	원급비교	Ch.09 비교	1 as + 원급 + as	p.192
	과거완료	Ch.04 시제	6 과거완료	p.100
7과	가정법 과거	Ch.13 가정법	1 가정법 과거	p.286
	so that	Ch.12 접속사	6 so / so that ~ / so ~ that ...	p.266
8과	not only A but also B	Ch.12 접속사	2 상관접속사	p.259
	접속사 while	Ch.12 접속사	10 주의해야 할 접속사 – as / while	p.274

지학사(민찬규)		적중! 중학영문법 3300제 Level 3		
1과	관계대명사 what	Ch.11 관계사	5 관계대명사 what	p.235
	지각동사	Ch.01 부정사	6 목적격보어로 동사원형을 사용하는 동사	p.24
2과	to부정사(의미상 주어)	Ch.01 부정사	2 진주어 / 진목적어 역할을 하는 to부정사	p.18
	분사	Ch.03 분사	1 명사를 수식하는 분사	p.70
3과	not only A but also B	Ch.12 접속사	2 상관접속사	p.259
	간접의문문	Ch.12 접속사	5 간접의문문	p.264
4과	과거완료	Ch.04 시제	6 과거완료	p.100
	to부정사(부사적 용법)	Ch.01 부정사	10 목적 / 결과를 나타내는 to부정사	p.32
5과	부정대명사	Ch.07 대명사	2 부정대명사 one ~ the other ... 등	p.160
	분사구문	Ch.03 분사	4 분사구문 만드는 법	p.75
6과	It ~ that 강조 구문	Ch.15 특수구문	2 강조 II – It ~ that 강조 구문	p.327
	접속부사 however	Ch.12 접속사	11 접속부사	p.276
7과	가정법 과거	Ch.13 가정법	1 가정법 과거	p.286
	keep + 목적어 + 형용사	문장의 구조	6 목적격보어 I – 명사 / 형용사 · 분사	p.13
8과	too ~ to	Ch.01 부정사	13 too ~ to / enough to	p.35
	no one	Ch.14 일치와 화법	1 수 일치 I – 단수주어 + 단수동사	p.306

천재(이재영)		적중! 중학영문법 3300제 Level 3		
1과	관계대명사 what	Ch.11 관계사	5 관계대명사 what	p.235
	지각동사	Ch.01 부정사	6 목적격보어로 동사원형을 사용하는 동사	p.24
2과	분사	Ch.03 분사	1 명사를 수식하는 분사	p.70
	접속사 since, though	Ch.12 접속사	7 부사절을 이끄는 접속사 I – 원인 / 양보 8 부사절을 이끄는 접속사 II – 시간	p.268 p.270
3과	현재완료진행	Ch.04 시제	5 현재완료진행	p.98
	so ~ that	Ch.12 접속사	6 so / so that ~ / so ~ that ...	p.266
4과	관계부사	Ch.11 관계사	8 관계부사 I – where / when 9 관계부사 II – why / how	p.240 p.242
	접속사 if, whether	Ch.12 접속사	4 명사절을 이끄는 접속사 II – if / whether	p.262
5과	과거완료	Ch.04 시제	6 과거완료	p.100
	It ~ that 강조 구문	Ch.15 특수구문	2 강조 II – It ~ that 강조 구문	p.327
6과	to부정사(의미상 주어)	Ch.01 부정사	2 진주어 / 진목적어 역할을 하는 to부정사	p.18
	가정법 과거	Ch.13 가정법	1 가정법 과거	p.286
7과	분사구문	Ch.03 분사	5 시간 / 이유 / 부대상황을 나타내는 분사구문	p.77
	조동사 수동태	Ch.06 수동태	2 조동사의 수동태	p.134
8과	조동사 have p.p.	Ch.05 조동사	8 조동사 + have p.p.	p.122
	관계대명사 계속적 용법	Ch.11 관계사	10 관계사의 계속적 용법	p.244

천재(정사열)		적중! 중학영문법 3300제 Level 3		
1과	접속사 if / whether	Ch.12 접속사	4 명사절을 이끄는 접속사 II – if / whether	p.234
	관계대명사 계속적 용법	Ch.11 관계사	10 관계사의 계속적 용법	p.246
2과	과거완료	Ch.04 시제	6 과거완료	p.100
	비교급 강조	Ch.09 비교	5 비교급 강조	p.197
3과	enough to	Ch.01 부정사	13 too ~ to / enough to	p.35
	not only A but also B	Ch.12 접속사	2 상관접속사	p.259
4과	분사구문	Ch.03 분사	5 시간 / 이유 / 부대상황을 나타내는 분사구문	p.77
	관계대명사 what	Ch.11 관계사	5 관계대명사 what	p.235
5과	가정법 과거	Ch.13 가정법	1 가정법 과거	p.286
	소유격 관계대명사	Ch.11 관계사	3 소유격 관계대명사 – whose / of which	p.232
6과	the + 비교급 ~, the + 비교급 ~	Ch.09 비교	6 the + 비교급, the + 비교급	p.198
	It ~ that 강조 구문	Ch.15 특수구문	2 강조 II – It ~ that 강조 구문	p.327
7과	화법전환	Ch.14 일치와 화법	6 화법 전환 I – 평서문	p.313
	접속사 if	Ch.12 접속사	4 명사절을 이끄는 접속사 II – if / whether	p.262
8과	부정대명사	Ch.07 대명사	2 부정대명사 one ~ the other ... 등	p.160
	5형식	문장의 구조	7 목적격보어 II – to부정사 / 동사원형 / 분사	p.14

INDEX 찾아보기

영문

A

B

C

D

E

F

H

I

한글

ㄱ

ㄷ

ㅁ

ㅂ

ㅅ

ㅇ

ㅈ

ㅌ

ㅍ

ㅎ

*

적중! 중학영문법 3300제

LEVEL 3

정답+워크북

적중! 중학영문법 3300제

LEVEL 3

정답과 해설

문장의 구조

1 주어 I - 단어로 된 주어 / 구로 된 주어 ▸▸ p.8

A

1 Happiness
2 The young
3 Planning
4 When to start

B

1 My friend
2 To watch TV 또는 Watching TV
3 Truth
4 Where to go

2 주어 II - 절로 된 주어 / 길어진 주어 ▸▸ p.9

A

1 Whether he will come
2 Where we stay
3 That he knows the fact
4 Children like me
5 The child who likes music

B

1 That he stole the money was not true.
2 What you do is more important than what you say.
3 The girl that just left the shop didn't buy anything.
4 How he came here is mysterious.
5 The problem on the test seems difficult.

3 목적어 I - 단어로 된 목적어 / 구로 된 목적어 ▸▸ p.10

A

1 nothing
2 studying
3 to mail this letter
4 how to make

B

1 to eat
2 to go
3 where to go
4 dancing

4 목적어 II - 절로 된 목적어 / 길어진 목적어 ▸▸ p.11

A

1 that
2 whether
3 he solved
4 what you want

B

1 I wonder if he is reliable.
2 He said he would sleep on the sofa.
3 She denied the marriage that he proposed.
4 Are you watching a movie about Kung Fu?
5 I'm not sure why he didn't keep his promise.
6 I thought that she didn't tell a lie.

5 주격보어 - 명사 / 형용사 · 분사 ▸▸ p.12

A

1 to visit
2 sad
3 known

B

1 clear
2 interested
3 exciting
4 to listen 또는 listening

6 목적격보어 I - 명사 / 형용사 · 분사 ▸▸ p.13

A

1 him
2 Edward
3 sleepy
4 a teacher
5 happy

B

1 her
2 cool
3 ○
4 closed

7 목적격보어 II - to부정사 / 동사원형 / 분사 ▸▸ p.14

A

1 to do
2 look
3 to wash
4 burning

B

1 play
2 to smoke
3 to do
4 run 또는 running

Chapter 01 부정사

1 주어 / 보어 / 목적어 역할을 하는 to부정사

▸▸ p. 16~17

A

1 to get, 목적어
2 to travel, 보어
3 To look, 주어
4 to win, 보어
5 To form, 주어
6 to be, 목적어
7 to meet, 보어
8 to finish, 목적어
9 to make, 주어
10 to take, 목적어

B

1 invite → to invite
2 Be → To be(Being)
3 Visit → To visit(Visiting)
4 To getting → To get(Getting)
5 make → to make(making)

C

1 expected to go to
2 is to look like a gentleman
3 To study abroad without
4 was to talk about
5 To be kind to

D

1 is to make
2 To give makes
3 hoped to meet
4 tried not to make
5 is to read

2 진주어 / 진목적어 역할을 하는 to부정사

▸▸ p. 18~19

A

1 for criminals
2 of her
3 for them
4 for him
5 of you

B

1 for → of
2 of → for
3 ○
4 of → for
5 for → of
6 ○

C

1 It is impossible
2 It is not good to sing
3 It would be wonderful to take

D

1 thought it easy to
2 makes it a rule not to
3 think it better to
4 found it exciting to

3 의문사 + to부정사

▸▸ p. 20

A

1 whom
2 how
3 when

B

1 which I should choose
2 when he should call
3 What I should buy

4 목적어로 to부정사를 사용하는 동사

▸▸ p. 21

A

1 to buy
2 to be
3 to skip
4 to take

B

1 hope to see
2 learn to swim
3 manage to earn
4 expected to see

5 목적격보어로 to부정사를 사용하는 동사

▶▶ p.22~23

A

1 to walk
2 to give
3 to become
4 to go
5 to get
6 to call
7 not to hang

B

1 steal → to steal
2 ○
3 picking → pick
4 ○
5 find → to find

C

1 to come
2 to play
3 got me to polish
4 me to join
5 me to attend
6 wanted him to go
7 asked her to dance

D

1 wants him to do
2 encourages students to help
3 required them to take
4 ordered the patient to take
5 warned him not to make

6 목적격보어로 동사원형을 사용하는 동사

▶▶ p.24~25

A

1 sing, singing
2 know
3 knock, knocking
4 do
5 to carry, carry
6 repaired

B

1 to 삭제
2 ○
3 to 삭제
4 ○
5 cleaning → clean
6 ○
7 studied → study 또는 to study

C

1 saw him run(running)
2 felt a spider crawl(crawling)
3 let me use
4 hear somebody play(playing)
5 let me get

7 명사를 수식하는 to부정사

▶▶ p.26~27

A

1 play → to play
2 solve → to solve
3 off → on
4 tell → to tell
5 living → live
6 with to write → to write with
7 read → to read
8 talk → to talk

B

1 have something to tell
2 made a promise to buy
3 is the best time to visit
4 was the best way to solve
5 needs a pen to write with
6 paper to write on
7 a chair to sit on
8 someone to depend on

C

1 an exciting city to visit
2 no one to rely on
3 something to complain about
4 a bed to lie on

8 be동사 + to부정사

▶▶ p.28~29

A

1 가능
2 의무
3 예정
4 의도
5 운명
6 예정
7 운명
8 의도
9 의무

B

1 am to meet her

2 was to come back

3 are to be a great dancer

4 is to be seen

5 were never to succeed

C

1	are to participate	2	are to win
3	is to be	4	was never to see
5	were to go	6	is to meet
7	are to gain	8	is to be seen

9 seem(appear) + to부정사

▶▶ p. 30~31

A

1 seemed to gain

2 appears to be

3 appeared to play

4 appeared to have been

5 seems to have been

6 appears to have been

B

1 seems (that) you are

2 seemed (that) he enjoyed

3 seems (that) the girl had

4 seemed (that) you had known

5 seems (that) you are

C

1 It seems that you are

2 It seems that he fought

3 It seemed that they made

4 It seemed that he had found

5 It seemed that she had helped him

10 목적 / 결과를 나타내는 to부정사

▶▶ p. 32

A

1 새 집 한 채를 사기 위해

2 그 실종된 아이를 찾기 위해

3 프로 골프 선수가 되기 위해

4 그를 실망시키지 않기 위해

B

1 ran away never to come back

2 put my shoes on(put on my shoes) to go outside

3 left home early not to miss the first train

11 조건을 나타내는 to부정사

▶▶ p. 33

A

1 그 깨진 유리창을 본다면

2 나의 부모님을 다시 만난다면

3 그녀가 스웨덴어를 하는 것을 듣는다면

4 우리 팀이 경기에서 지는 것을 본다면

5 가난한 사람들을 돕는다면

B

1 to see the results of the research

2 to hear the news

3 to help the disabled

4 to miss the bus

12 감정의 원인 / 판단의 근거를 나타내는 to부정사

▶▶ p. 34

A

1 너를 다시 만나서

2 그런 어리석은 일을 하다니

3 그녀의 실패에 대해 들어서

4 그것을 믿다니

5 그녀의 엄마와 함께 살아서

B

1 because they looked at

2 of her to repeat   3 of him to go

13 too ~ to / enough to

▸▸ p.35~36

A

1 so shy that she can't make
2 so short that I can't sleep
3 so big that I couldn't put
4 so hot that I can't eat

B

1 so rich as to buy, so rich that he can buy
2 so free as to read, so free that she could read
3 so smart as to pass, so smart that they can pass
4 so strong as to move, so strong that he could move

C

1 too tired to go
2 wise enough to give
3 too dark for me to see
4 lively enough to make

14 It takes ~ to부정사

▸▸ p.37

A

1 finish → (on) finishing
2 ○
3 him → for him
4 to → 삭제
5 ○
6 going → go

B

1 for her to write, five hours or so (on) writing
2 took forty minutes for me, forty minutes (on) giving
3 for him to get back, two days (on) getting

15 대부정사

▸▸ p.38

A

1 like → like to (travel to Greece)
2 go → to (go home now)
3 come here → to (come here)
4 to → want to (take pictures)

B

1 watch the movie again
2 drop by
3 dance
4 drink coffee(it)
5 play the violin
6 do him a favor

16 독립부정사

▸▸ p.39

A

1 strangely → strange
2 speaking → to speak
3 Make → To make
4 last → least
5 To not → Not to
6 true → truth

B

1 To make things worse
2 To be frank(honest)
3 To tell the truth

Chapter 01 학교 시험 대비 문제

▸▸ p.40~48

01 ③ **02** ② **03** ③ **04** ① **05** ⑤ **06** ④ **07** ⑤ **08** ③ **09** ③ **10** ③ **11** ① **12** ④ **13** ④ **14** ⑤ **15** ② **16** ①, ④ **17** ② **18** ② **19** ④ **20** ② **21** ② **22** ① **23** ③ **24** ④ **25** ⑤ **26** ① **27** ⑤ **28** ③ **29** ③ **30** ①, ⑤ **31** ③

서술형 **32** allow me to park **33** which classes to take **34** made them think **35** 네가 그러고 싶지 않다면(네가 그들을 만나고 싶지 않다면) **36** to hear **37** a chair to sit on **38** it a rule to make **39** wise enough to give **40** so afraid that he couldn't **41** half an hour for me **42** so to speak **43** It(it) **44** seems to have lost **45** that she enjoyed **46** brave of her **47** what to buy **48** in order not to **49** They decided not to buy a laptop. **50** is not to look **51** to see his messy room **52** It is impossible for us to finish the project by tomorrow. **53** crowded (for him) to get through every gallery **54** to go home early **55** one and a half hours for him to get home 또는 him one and a half hours to get home

01 **해설** 보기와 ③은 명사적 용법으로 쓰여서 목적어 역할을 한다. 나머지는 부사적 용법으로 ①⑤ 결과, ② 목적, ④ 감정의 원인을 나타낸다.

해석 나는 기타 연주하는 것을 좋아한다.

02 **해설** ② too ~ to부정사는 '너무 ~해서 …할 수 없다'는 뜻으로 부정적 결과를 나타내므로 나머지 넷과 의미가 다르다.

해석 나는 좋은 점수를 받기 위해 매우 열심히 공부했다.

03 **해설** ③은 명사(the power)를 수식하는 형용사적 용법으로 쓰였다. 나머지는 모두 부사적 용법으로 ① 결과, ②④ 감정의 원인, ⑤ 목적을 나타낸다.

04 **해설** 사역동사는 목적격보어로 동사원형을 사용한다.

해석 • 그것은 그가 혼자서 그곳에 가도록 만들었다.
• 그녀는 내가 혼자서 사냥하러 가도록 허락하지 않는다.

05 **해설** ⑤ allow는 목적격보어로 to부정사를 사용하므로 come → to come

06 **해설** ④ impossible은 사람의 성격을 나타내는 형용사가 아니므로 to부정사의 의미상 주어를 「for + 목적격」으로 나타내야 한다.

07 **해설** 「It takes + 사람 + 시간 + to부정사」 → 「It takes + 시간 + for 사람 + to부정사」

해석 나는 머리를 감는 데 10분 정도 걸린다.

08 **해설** ③ agree는 목적어로 to부정사를 사용하는 동사이므로 starting → to start

09 **해설** ③ 「주어 + seemed + to have p.p.」 = 「It seemed that + 주어 + had p.p.」이므로 had → had had

10 **해설** ③ 우리는 들판에서 말을 타게 되어서 기뻤다.

11 **해설** ① 「why + to부정사」는 사용할 수 없다.

12 **해설** ④ 부정어 never가 있으므로 were destined to see → were destined never to see

13 **해설** to say the least : 적어도

14 **해설** ⑤는 부사적 용법으로 '목적'을 나타낸다. 나머지는 명사적 용법으로 ① 보어, ②③ 목적어, ④ 진주어 역할을 한다.

15 **해설** 목적격보어(to kneel down)가 to부정사이므로 동사원형을 목적격보어로 취하는 made(사역동사)는 알맞지 않다.
kneel down : 무릎을 꿇다

16 **해설** 지각동사(hear)는 목적격보어로 동사원형이나 현재분사를 사용한다.

해석 우리는 그때 그가 도와달라고 부르는(부르고 있는) 소리를 들을 수 있었다.

17 **해설** not to speak → not to speak of(~은 말할 것도 없이), 「It takes + 시간 + for 사람 + to부정사」

해석 • 그들은 같은 장소에서 만날 예정이었다.
• 그는 영어뿐만 아니라 독일어도 할 줄 알았다.
• 우리가 그곳에서 점심을 먹고 이곳으로 돌아오는 데 약 한 시간이 걸렸다.
• 그는 네가 그에게 그러지 말라고 말하지 않았기 때문에 텔레비전을 아주 많이 봤을 것이다.

18 **해설** ② get은 목적격보어로 to부정사를 사용하므로 have → to have

19 **해설** 가지고 쓸 필기도구이므로 with / 표면 위에 무엇인가를 쓸 종이이므로 on

해석 나는 쓸 펜 한 자루가 필요하다. 그리고 그녀는 쓸 종이 한 장이 필요하다.

20 **해설** ② tell은 목적격보어로 to부정사를 사용하고 to부정사의 부정형은 to부정사 앞에 not을 써서 나타낸다.
play a dirty trick on : ~에게 비열한 짓을 하다

21 **해설** 「too + 형용사(부사) + to부정사」는 「so + 형용사(부사) + that + 주어 + can't(couldn't)」로 바꿔 쓸 수 있다.

22 **해설** to부정사구 to hear the news가 조건의 의미를 나타내므로 접속사 if가 알맞다.

해석 그녀가 그 소식을 듣는다면 놀랄 것이다.

23 **해설** 「형용사(부사) + enough + to부정사」 구문이므로 명사(youth)는 빈칸에 알맞지 않다.

24 **해설** 주어진 문장과 ④는 조건을 나타내고 나머지는 각각 ① 판단의 근거, ② 결과, ③ 감정의 원인, ⑤ 목적을 나타낸다.

해석 나는 그곳에 가면 매우 행복할 것이다.

25 **해설** ⑤ 명사 the one을 수식하는 형용사적 용법으로 쓰였다. 나머지는 부사적 용법으로 ① 결과, ②④ 목적, ③ 감정의 원인을 나타낸다.

26 **해설** ① 의무를 나타내는 be to 용법이므로 have to do로 바꿔 쓸 수 있다.

해석 너는 외출하기 전에 숙제를 해야 한다.

27 **해설** ⑤ natural은 사람의 성격을 나타내는 말이 아니므로 의미상 주어를 of him으로 쓸 수 없다.
do well by : ~에게 잘하다

28 **해설** ③ 의미상 함께 의논할 사람을 필요로 하고 있기 때문에 to부정사 뒤에 전치사 with가 필요하다.

29 **해설** ③ 의미상 '떠나야 하기 때문에 슬픈 것'이므로, if가 아닌 원인을 나타내는 because로 써야 한다.

30 해설 목적을 나타내는 to부정사는 in order to[so as to]로 바꿔 쓸 수 있다.

31 해설 앞에서 나온 to부정사구가 반복될 때 to만 쓰고 동사원형은 생략할 수 있다.

해석 네가 원하지 않으면 청바지를 입을 필요가 없다.

서술형

32 해설 allow는 목적격보어로 to부정사를 사용한다.

33 해설 「which + (명사) + to부정사」: 어떤 것을 ~할지

해석 A 네가 어떤 수업을 들어야 할지 알려 달라고 그에게 부탁하는 게 어때?

B 그거 좋은 생각이야.

34 해설 사역동사 made는 목적격보어로 동사원형을 사용한다.

35 해설 밑줄 친 부분의 대부정사(to)는 앞에 나온 to meet them을 대신한다.

36 해설 because가 이끄는 절을 감정의 원인을 나타내는 to부정사로 표현할 수 있다.

해석 나는 네가 고국으로 돌아온다는 소식을 듣고서 무척 기뻤다.

37 해설 의자 위에 앉는 것이므로 접촉을 나타내는 전치사 on과 함께 사용한다.

38 해설 가목적어 it을 사용한다. a rule은 목적격보어이며 to make는 진목적어이다.

39 해설 「형용사 + enough + to부정사」: ~할 만큼 충분히 …한

40 해설 「too + 형용사[부사] + to부정사」는 「so + 형용사[부사] + that + 주어 + can't[couldn't]」로 바꿔 쓸 수 있는데, 주절의 동사가 과거형이므로 couldn't를 쓴다.

해석 그는 너무 두려워서 번지 점프를 할 수 없었다.

41 해설 「It takes + 사람 + 시간 + to부정사」는 「It takes + 시간 + for 사람 + to부정사」로 바꿔 쓸 수 있다.

해석 나는 그 책을 찾는 데 30분이 걸렸다.

42 해설 so to speak : 말하자면

43 해설 가주어 / 가목적어 It[it]

해석 • 작년 크리스마스 이브에 너와 함께 저녁을 먹은 것은 멋졌다.

• 나는 우주비행사가 되는 것이 쉽다고 생각하지 않았다.

44 해설 '~인 것 같은 것'은 현재, '자동차 열쇠를 잃어버린 것'은 그 이전의 과거를 나타내므로 「seem + to have p.p.」로 나타낸다.

해석 A 그녀에게 무슨 문제가 있니?

B 그녀는 자동차 키를 잃어버렸던 것 같아.

45 해설 to부정사(to enjoy)의 형태이므로 seemed와 시제가 같은 「It seemed that + 주어 + 동사(과거)」로 쓸 수 있다.

해석 그녀는 첫 비행을 즐긴 것 같았다.

46 해설 판단의 근거를 나타내는 to부정사는 「It ~ of ... to부정사」 형태의 가주어·진주어 구문으로 바꿔 쓸 수 있다.

해석 그녀가 그 야생 호랑이를 훈련시키다니 용감한 게 틀림없다.

47 해설 「의문사 + 주어 + should + 동사원형」은 「의문사 + to부정사」로 바꿔 쓸 수 있다.

해석 나는 시장에서 무엇을 사야 할지 잊어버렸다.

48 해설 목적을 나타내는 to부정사는 in order to부정사로 바꿔 쓸 수 있고, 부정형은 in order not to로 나타낸다.

해석 그녀는 잠자고 있는 아기를 방해하지 않으려고 텔레비전을 껐다.

49 해설 decide는 목적어로 to부정사를 사용하는 동사인데 의미상 부정형으로 나타내야 하므로 to 앞에 not을 붙인다.

해석 A 너는 결정했니?

B 응, 그래. 지금은 노트북 컴퓨터를 사기에 좋은 때는 아니라고 생각해.

A 그래. 그럼 노트북 컴퓨터를 사지 말자.

Q 그들은 무엇을 결정했는가?

→ 그들은 노트북 컴퓨터를 사지 않기로 결정했다.

50 해설 to부정사의 부정형은 to부정사 앞에 not[never]을 붙여서 나타낸다.

51 해설 If가 이끄는 조건절을 조건을 나타내는 to부정사로 바꿔 쓸 수 있다.

해석 만약 그녀가 그의 지저분한 방을 본다면, 그녀는 그에게 무척 화를 낼 것이다.

52 해석 진주어 역할을 하는 to부정사를 뒤로 보내고 가주어 It을 문장 앞에 쓴다. to부정사의 의미상 주어가 문장의 주어와 다른 경우, 「for + 목적격」의 형태로 나타낸다.

[53-55]

해석 Susan에게,

나는 오늘 국립 박물관으로 가는 짧은 여행을 하면서 힘든 시간을 보냈어. 나는 아침 9시쯤 일어날 계획이었지만 늦잠을 자버려서 버스를 놓쳤어. 10시 30분이었지. 그래서 나는 서둘러서 목적지로 향했어. 2시간 후에, 나는 드디어 그곳에 도착했어. 사람들로 너무 붐벼서 나는 모든 전시관을 돌아보기가 힘들테니 집에 일찍 가는 게 좋겠다고 생각했어. 내가 집으로 향했을 때는 딱 2시였어. 엎친 데 덮친 격으로, 나는 내가 가장 좋아하는 펜을 그곳에서 잃어버렸어. 어떻게 나에게 이런 일이 일어났지? 내가 집으로 돌아왔을 때는 오후 3시 30분이었어.

너의 진정한 벗,
Peter가

53 해설 too ~ to부정사는 '너무 ~해서 …할 수 없다'는 뜻으로 부정적 결과를 나타낸다.
해석 **Q** Peter가 국립 박물관에 도착했을 때 무슨 생각을 했는가?
A 그는 사람들로 너무 붐벼서 모든 전시관을 돌아볼 수 없다고 생각했다.

54 해설 decide는 목적어로 to부정사를 사용하는 동사다.
해석 **Q** 그곳에 사람들이 너무 많다고 생각한 후에 Peter는 어떻게 하기로 결정했는가?
A 그는 집에 일찍 가기로 결정했다.

55 해설 「It takes + 시간 + for 사람 + to부정사」 = 「It takes + 사람 + 시간 + to부정사」
해석 **Q** 그가 국립 박물관에서 집에 가기까지 얼마나 걸렸는가?
A 그가 집에 오는 데 1시간 30분이 걸렸다.

Chapter 02 동명사

1 주어 / 보어 / 목적어 역할을 하는 동명사

▸▸ p.50~51

A

1 speaking, 목적어
2 going, 보어
3 Getting, 주어
4 going, 목적어
5 Going, 주어
6 spending, 목적어
7 helping, 보어
8 Making, 주어
9 playing, 목적어
10 buying, selling, 보어

B

1 see → seeing
2 Walk → Walking 또는 To walk
3 make → making
4 play → playing 또는 to play
5 are → is
6 were → was
7 think → thinking
8 put → putting 또는 to put

C

1 about going to
2 studying for the exam
3 amazed at seeing
4 for not keeping
5 for not disappointing
6 enjoyed playing with
7 ashamed of not being

2 동명사의 의미상 주어

▸▸ p.52~53

A

1 Their
2 my mother
3 ×
4 this
5 ×
6 ×
7 her

B

1 for her → her
2 she → her 또는 삭제
3 theirs → their
4 come → coming
5 saying not → not saying
6 to let → letting

C

1 their being idle
2 his failing the test
3 Brian coming here
4 her going camping with us
5 their son living alone in the country
6 his dog biting her son
7 my practicing the piano in the classroom
8 my being late for school

3 목적어로 동명사를 사용하는 동사

▶▶ p.54~55

A

1 to write → writing
2 to play → playing
3 have → to have
4 to → 삭제
5 to meet → meeting
6 buying → to buy
7 going → to go

B

1 stopped drinking coffee
2 didn't finish doing
3 couldn't avoid saying
4 enjoyed riding a horse
5 gave up fighting
6 didn't mind my making
7 considering playing tennis

C

1 enjoy having a conversation
2 missed seeing the fantastic sight
3 couldn't understand going abroad
4 suggested our going on a picnic
5 put off leaving because of
6 practiced getting up early
7 should avoid keeping company

4 목적어로 동명사와 to부정사를 모두 사용하는 동사

▶▶ p.56~57

A

1 getting
2 to call
3 to solve
4 to tell
5 being

B

1 began raining
2 remember to see
3 regretted telling
4 continues to read
5 forgot to give
6 tried to move
7 never forget spending

5 동명사와 현재분사

▶▶ p.58~59

A

1 현재분사
2 동명사
3 동명사
4 동명사
5 현재분사
6 동명사
7 현재분사

B

2 인터넷 검색하는 것, 동명사
3 대기실, 동명사
4 기다리고 있다, 현재분사
5 지팡이, 동명사
6 걷고 있는 소년, 현재분사
7 살아 있는 것들, 현재분사
8 거실, 동명사
9 잠자고 있는 개, 현재분사
10 침낭, 동명사

C

1 Eating carrots and tomatoes is good for the eyes.
2 Laura didn't want to go into the fitting room.
3 There are pink dolphins living in the Amazon River.
4 A girl is holding a balloon.
5 Speeding cars are very dangerous.

6 동명사 관용 표현

▶▶ p.60~61

A

1 fix → fixing
2 to → 삭제
3 to say → saying
4 finish → finishing
5 buy → to buying
6 to → 삭제
7 eat → eating
8 to see → seeing
9 play → playing

B

1 was busy preparing
2 am looking forward to hearing
3 feel like eating
4 is used(accustomed) to watching
5 felt like moving
6 On getting
7 was used(accustomed) to blaming
8 On seeing
9 has trouble(difficulty) waking
10 It is no use(good) talking

Chapter 02 학교 시험 대비 문제

▶▶ p.62~68

01 ④ 02 ② 03 ③ 04 ④ 05 ③ 06 ② 07 ② 08 ④ 09 ① 10 ④ 11 ⑤ 12 ④ 13 ③ 14 ④ 15 ③ 16 ② 17 ④ 18 ③ 19 ⑤ 20 ⑤ 21 ⑤ 22 ① 23 ①

서술형 24 of not being 25 to 26 regretted telling 27 to see → seeing 28 remember to meet 29 swimming 30 like his being late 31 기차가 조금 늦는 것 32 looking forward to seeing 33 to meet → meeting 34 On hearing 35 stopped us from going 36 started to rain 37 didn't remember to bring 38 the bus being late 39 their(them) being very noisy 40 not giving you some information

01 해설 ④ 전치사 without의 목적어로 동명사가 와야 하므로 to say를 saying으로 써야 한다.
해석 그는 작별 인사도 없이 떠났다.

02 해설 cannot but + 동사원형 : ~할 수밖에 없다
It is no use -ing : ~해봐야 소용없다
해석 • 그녀는 '아니'라고 대답할 수밖에 없었다.
• 엎질러진 우유를 두고 울어봐야 소용없다.

03 해설 promise는 목적어로 to부정사를 사용하는 동사이다.

04 해설 ④의 laughing은 현재분사로, 나머지는 모두 동명사로 쓰였다. ④ laughing 웃고 있는 ① protecting 보호하는 것 ② sleeping 잠들기 위한 ③ playing (테니스를) 치는 것 ⑤ walking 걷기 위한

05 해설 enjoy, quit, avoid, postpone, mind는 동명사를 목적어로 사용하는 대표적인 동사들이다.
① to drink → drinking ② to smoke → smoking ④ to answer → answering ⑤ to close → closing

06 해설 be worth -ing : ~할 가치가 있다

07 해설 ②의 doing은 현재진행형에 사용된 현재분사로, 나머지는 동명사로 쓰였다. ① collecting 모으는 것 ② doing 하고 있는 ③ painting 그리는 것 ④ playing 연주하는 것 ⑤ Being (친절하게) 대하는 것

08 해설 의미상 주어 her 뒤에 전치사의 목적어 역할을 하는 동명사가 와야 알맞다. fail → failing

09 해설 ① be used to -ing : ~에 익숙하다 stay → staying ② feel like -ing : ~하고 싶다 ③ 「spend + 시간(돈) + -ing」 : ~하는 데 시간(돈)을 소비하다 ④ There is no -ing : ~하는 것은 불가능하다 ⑤ be busy -ing : ~하느라 바쁘다

10 해설 There is no -ing : ~하는 것은 불가능하다
It is no use(good) -ing : ~해봐야 소용없다
해석 • 아무런 어려움 없이 사는 것은 불가능하다.
• 그것을 경솔하게 사고 난 후에 불평해도 소용없다.

11 해설 ⑤ be used to -ing : ~하는 데 익숙하다
① 「used to + 동사원형」 : ~하곤 했다
② 「be used to + 동사원형」 : ~에 쓰이다, 사용되다

12 해설 과거에 대한 일이므로 forget의 목적어로 동명사를 사용하는 것이 알맞다.
해석 A 여행은 어땠니?
B 멋졌어. 난 스코틀랜드의 풍경을 본 것을 절대 잊지 못할 거야.

13 해설 ① be used(accustomed) to -ing : ~하는 데 익숙하다 ② cannot help -ing (= cannot but + 동사원형) : ~할 수밖에 없다 ③ look forward to -ing : ~하기를 고대하다 / have trouble -ing : ~하는 데 어려움을 겪다 ④ keep(prevent) A from -ing : A를 ~하지 못하게 하다 ⑤ feel like -ing (= want to부정사) : ~하고 싶다

14 해설 ④의 smoking은 용도나 목적(a room for smoking)을 나타내므로 동명사로, 나머지는 현재분사로 쓰였다.
① playing 연주하고 있는 ② sleeping 자고 있는 ③ walking 걸어 다니는 ④ smoking 담배를 피우기 위한 ⑤ talking 이야기하면서

15 해설 consider는 목적어로 동명사를 사용한다. to go → going
① 주어로 쓰인 동명사 being ② 보어로 쓰인 동명사 collecting ④ forget의 목적어로 쓰인 동명사 meeting ⑤ 현재분사 sleeping

16 해설 ② regret은 과거에 일어난 일을 후회할 때는 목적어로 동명사를 사용하고(나는 그들에게 거짓말한 것을 후회한다.), 미래에 일어날 일에 대한 유감을 나타낼 때는 to부정사를 사용한다.(나는 그들에게 거짓말을 해야 하는 것이 유감이다.)
① hate, ③ start, ④ continue, ⑤ begin은 목적어로 동명사와 to부정사를 모두 사용하며 의미가 달라지지 않는다.

17 해설 ④의 living은 '살아 있는'의 의미로 동작이나 상태를 나타내는 현재분사로 쓰였다. ① 동명사 ② 현재분사 ③ 동명사 ⑤ 현재분사

18 해설 첫 번째 빈칸은 전치사의 목적어 자리이므로 동명사가 알맞고, 두 번째 빈칸은 주어 자리이므로 동명사 또는 to부정사가 알맞다.

해석 • 그녀는 그녀의 개를 돌보는 데 싫증이 났다.
• 빗속에서 운전하는 것은 매우 위험하다.

19 해설 ⑤ hope는 to부정사를 목적어로 취하는 동사이므로 to buy가 알맞다.

20 해설 첫 번째 빈칸에는 '잠을 자고 있는'이라는 진행, 동작의 의미로 빈칸 뒤의 명사 dog를 수식하는 현재분사 sleeping이 알맞다. 두 번째 빈칸에는 '잠을 자기 위한'이라는 용도를 나타내는 동명사 sleeping이 알맞다.

해석 • 잠자고 있는 개를 깨우지 마라.
• 그는 침낭에서 뱀을 발견했다.

21 해설 보기와 ⑤는 보어 역할을 한다.

해석 그의 직업은 가난한 사람들을 돕는 것이다.

22 해설 ①은 현재분사, 나머지는 동명사로 쓰였다.
① 춤추고 있는 소녀 ② 운동화 ③ 지팡이 ④ 노래방 ⑤ 세탁기

23 해설 ① mind는 동명사를 목적어로 취하는 동사이므로 to leave를 leaving으로 써야 한다.

서술형

24 해설 전치사 of 뒤에 동사가 올 경우 동명사 형태가 알맞다. 동명사의 부정형은 동명사 바로 앞에 not을 쓴다.

25 해설 be accustomed to -ing : ~에 익숙하다 / look forward to -ing : ~을 고대하다

해석 • 나는 새로운 환경에 적응하는 것에 익숙하다.
• 나는 월요일에 너를 만나는 것을 고대한다.

26 해설 이미 지난 일(과거)을 후회하고 있으므로 regret의 목적어로 동명사를 사용한다.

27 해설 miss는 목적어로 동명사를 사용한다.

해석 우리는 하늘에서 놀라운 광경을 보는 것을 놓쳤다.

28 해설 앞으로 있을 일(미래)이므로 remember의 목적어로 to부정사를 사용해야 한다.

29 해설 like는 동명사와 to부정사를 모두 목적어로 사용하는 동사이다.

해석 그녀는 강에서 수영하는 것을 좋아하지 않았다.

30 해설 일반동사 like는 동명사와 to부정사를 모두 목적어로 취한다. 동명사의 의미상 주어는 소유격(his)으로 나타내며 동명사 바로 앞에 위치한다.

해석 **A** 그에게 무슨 일이 있니? 그가 언제나처럼 또 늦네. 나는 그가 항상 늦는 것이 마음에 들지 않아.
B 우리는 이번에 그에게 뭔가 말해야 해.

31 해설 동명사의 의미상 주어 the train이 동명사의 행위 주체이므로 먼저 해석한다.
allow for : ~을 고려하다

해석 그들은 기차가 조금 늦는 것을 고려해야 한다.

32 해설 look forward to -ing : ~하기를 고대하다

33 해설 imagine은 목적어로 동명사를 사용한다.

해석 나는 그곳에서 그를 만나는 것을 상상할 수 없었다.

34 해설 on -ing = 「as soon as + 주어 + 동사」 : ~ 하자마자

해석 그들은 그 소리를 듣자마자, 확인하기 위해 집 밖으로 나왔다.

35 해설 stop A from -ing : A가 ~하는 것을 막다

[36-37]

해석 **Waiter** 주문하시겠습니까, 숙녀분들?
Kitty 지금 말고 몇 분 후에요, 고맙습니다.
Betty 밖에 무슨 일이 일어나는지 봐! 방금 전까지 날씨가 좋았는데.
Kitty 오 이런, 나는 우산을 가지고 오는 걸 잊었어.
Betty 걱정 마. 곧 그칠 거야.

36 해설 start는 목적어로 to부정사와 동명사를 모두 사용할 수 있다.

해석 Kitty와 Betty가 레스토랑에 들어온 후에 비가 오기 시작했다.

37 해설 과거의 시점에서 미래에 해야 할 일에 대해 설명하고 있으므로 to bring을 사용한다.

해석 Kitty는 우산을 가져오는 것을 기억하지 못했다.

[38-40]

해석 <보기> 그녀가 친절하다는 것은 모든 사람들에게 알려져 있다.

38 해설 동명사의 의미상 주어가 문장의 주어나 목적어와 일치하지 않으므로 동명사 앞에 의미상 주어 the bus를 쓴다.

해석 너는 버스가 늦는 것을 고려해야 한다.

39 해설 동명사의 의미상 주어가 문장의 주어와 일치하지 않으므로 동명사 앞에 의미상 주어 their(them)를 쓴다.

해석 너는 그들이 매우 시끄러운 것을 이해하지 못한다.

40 해설 동명사의 의미상 주어가 문장의 주어와 일치하므로 의미상 주어를 생략한다. 부정어 not은 동명사 앞에 위치한다.

해석 우리는 너에게 정보를 주지 못한 것에 대해 유감스러웠다.

Chapter 03 분사

1 명사를 수식하는 분사

▸▸ p. 70~71

A

1 burning 2 hidden 3 called
4 written 5 used 6 shaking

B

1 asking me a question
2 filled with flowers
3 attending the meeting
4 spoken in Mexico
5 cheering their team to victory
6 fallen from the trees

C

1 singing in the tree
2 the story written by
3 chatting in the classroom
4 heard the shocking news
5 painted by him was
6 spoken language here
7 surrounded by a lot of students

2 보어 역할을 하는 분사

▸▸ p. 72~73

A

1 ⓒ 2 ⓐ 3 ⓓ
4 ⓐ 5 ⓓ 6 ⓑ

B

1 singing Christmas songs
2 going into your room
3 hit by a car on the road

C

1 looking for her father
2 get his watch repaired
3 had my leg broken
4 keep your friends waiting

D

1 saw a man breaking(break)
2 heard him shouting(shout)
3 found her left
4 had her shoes mended

3 감정을 나타내는 분사

▸▸ p. 74

A

1 amazing 2 surprised
3 disappointing 4 shocked
5 confused

B

1 satisfying → satisfied
2 interesting → interested
3 boring → bored
4 satisfied → satisfying
5 amused → amusing

4 분사구문 만드는 법

▸▸ p. 75~76

A

1 (being) staying in Rome
2 finishing the work
3 Spring coming
4 Not receiving any answer

B

1 she did 2 he lives
3 it (the book) has 4 she left

C

1 If you take, Taking
2 When he fell, Falling
3 Because it was, It being
4 As he grew up, Growing up

5 시간 / 이유 / 부대상황을 나타내는 분사구문

▸▸ p. 77

A

1 Feeling sorry for that

2 Sitting on the grass

3 Having no money with me

B

1 Because she is kind to other students

2 Before he watches TV

3 While I clean my room

6 조건 / 양보를 나타내는 분사구문

▸▸ p. 78

A

1 Taking this train

2 falling down on the track

3 It raining tomorrow

B

1 그것을 싫어하더라도

2 적은 돈을 저축했지만

3 퇴근해서 좀 쉬면

4 여기서 이 신상품을 구매하면

7 분사구문의 시제와 생략

▸▸ p. 79~80

A

1 liking

2 Interested

3 invited

4 Having had

5 Having studied

6 Looking

7 having finished

B

1 Though she was surprised, Though (having been) surprised

2 Since we didn't have, Not having

3 Because I had, Having had

4 As it is written, (Being) Written

5 If I am nervous, Being nervous

C

1 (Having been) Disappointed

2 Having lost

3 Being my true friend

8 with + (대)명사 + 분사

▸▸ p. 81

A

1 crossing → crossed

2 sat → sitting

3 turning → turned

4 kept → keeping

5 folding → folded

B

1 with the door closed

2 with the soup boiling

3 with an electric fan set

4 with their kids watching

5 with her baby playing

9 관용적 분사구문

▸▸ p. 82

A

1 일반적으로 말하면

2 솔직히 말하면

3 엄밀히 말하면

4 영화에 관해 말하면

5 그녀의 행동 방식으로 판단하건대

B

1 Considering

2 Speaking of

3 Strictly speaking

4 Admitting

5 Assuming

Chapter 03 학교 시험 대비 문제

▶▶ p.83~90

01 ③ 02 ④ 03 ④ 04 ② 05 ④ 06 ② 07 ⑤ 08 ② 09 ② 10 ① 11 ② 12 ① 13 ② 14 ② 15 ⑤ 16 ⑤ 17 ② 18 ⑤ 19 ⑤ 20 ⑤ 21 ③ 22 ②, ③ 23 ② 24 ③ 25 ② 26 ①

서술형 **27** Having lost **28** (Having been) Invited **29** Smiling happily **30** Having seen **31** had his left leg broken **32** Not being able to swim **33** left alone **34** he had spent **35** 경기에서 다친 선수들이 **36** calling → called **37** with the driver waiting **38** Finding her address **39** with the boys singing **40** satisfying, satisfied **41** cheering their team **42** I saw a girl crossing the road at a red light. **43** The police officer saw the thief running away with the jewels. **44** She had the broken car repaired for use. **45** He had some mistakes corrected in the document. **46** when called by the teacher **47** Not getting along with her

01 해설 ③ 중고차는 의미상 '사용되어진' 차를 뜻하므로 수동을 의미하는 used로 써야 한다.

02 해설 ④ '지루한'의 의미이므로 현재분사가 쓰인 것이 알맞다. 나머지는 수동인 ① called, ② surrounded, ③ broken, ⑤ written 형태가 알맞다.

03 해설 ④ 문맥상 '~은 인정하지만'의 의미가 알맞다.
해석 그것이 실제로 일어나는 것은 인정하지만, 우리는 그것을 쉽게 사실로 받아들일 수 없다.

04 해설 ② 문맥상 조건을 나타내는 If가 오는 것이 자연스럽다.

05 해설 ④는 주격보어의 역할을 하고, 나머지는 명사의 앞뒤에서 명사를 수식하는 역할을 한다.

06 해설 ② '문제'는 누군가에 의해 풀려야 하는 대상이므로 수동의 의미가 알맞다. 나머지는 각각 ① crying, ③ amazed, ④ screaming, ⑤ picking (pick)으로 써야 한다.

07 해설 주절의 주어와 부사절의 주어가 서로 다를 때 분사구문에 부사절의 주어를 남겨 둔다.
해석 해가 진 뒤에, 우리는 쇼핑하러 나갔다.

08 해설 ② 사람들이 감정을 느끼는 것이므로 과거분사 형태가 알맞고, 주어가 복수이므로 were excited를 써야 한다.
해석 모든 사람들이 결승전에 흥분했었다.

09 해설 ② 목적어인 her legs는 행위를 당하는 대상이므로 수동의 의미인 crossed로 써야 한다.

10 해설 Although we admit that you are young을 분사구문으로 바꾼 것으로 Admitting으로 써야 한다. Admitting (that): ~은 인정하지만
해석 네가 어린 것은 인정하지만, 너는 네 행동에 책임을 져야 한다.

11 해설 ② 부사절의 시제가 주절과 같고 수동태인 것으로 보아 Being이 생략되었음을 알 수 있다.
해석 그 문제들로 혼란스러웠기 때문에, 그녀는 혼자서 아무것도 할 수 없었다.

12 해설 ① result(결과)가 감정을 느끼는 것(실망한)이 아니라 감정을 전달하는 의미(실망스러운)이므로 disappointing으로 써야 한다.

13 해설 ② 부사절의 주어와 주절의 주어가 다르므로 날씨를 나타내는 비인칭 주어 it을 분사구문에서 생략하지 않고 남겨 둔다.

14 해설 ② 부사절의 시제가 주절의 시제보다 앞선 시제이므로 Having read로 써야 한다.

15 해설 The boy를 수식하는 wear는 소년이 바지를 '입고 있는' 것이므로 wearing이 알맞다. 주어 The boy가 '이야기를 하고 있는' 상황이므로 chat은 진행시제를 나타내는 chatting으로 써야 한다.
해석 청바지를 입은 그 소년은 Cathy와 이야기를 나누고 있었다.

16 해설 부사절 As we didn't know what to do를 분사구문 형태로 바꾼 것이다.
해석 **A** 너는 사고 직후에 무엇을 했니?
B 무엇을 해야 할지 몰라서, 우리는 119에 전화했어.

17 해설 Frankly speaking : 솔직히 말하면

18 해설 「with + (대)명사 + 분사」의 형태로 동시상황의 의미를 나타낸다.
해석 • 그들은 라디오를 켜둔 채로 춤을 추고 있다.
• 그녀는 문을 닫아둔 채로 뮤직 비디오를 보았다.

19 해설 동시상황을 나타내는 분사구문 Walking / 목적어 the man의 능동적 행위를 나타내는 현재분사 falling / 이유를 나타내는 분사구문 receiving
해석 • 거리를 걸어가다가, 우리는 그 남자가 넘어지는 것을 봤다.
• 아무 응답을 받지 못해서, 그는 오늘 그녀에게 이메일을 보냈다.

20 해설 부사절의 시제가 주절의 시제보다 앞서므로 「Having p.p.」 형태의 완료형 분사구문이 알맞다.
해석 전에 그 극장에 와본 적이 있어서, 그는 우리가 어디에서 티켓을 살 수 있는지 안다.

21 해설 접속사와 주어 she를 생략하고 부정어를 문두에

위치시키는 것에 유의하여 분사구문을 만든다.

해석 무슨 말을 해야 할지 몰라서, 그녀는 오랫동안 침묵을 지켰다.

22 해설 이유를 나타내는 접속사 As가 쓰인 부사절 ③과 접속사와 주어가 생략된 분사구문 ②가 빈칸에 알맞다.

해석 피곤해서, 나는 눈을 감고 심호흡을 했다.

23 해설 지각동사 saw의 목적어 the vase는 꽃으로 채워지는 대상이므로 수동의 의미를 나타내는 과거분사 filled가 알맞다.

해석 나는 그 꽃병이 꽃들로 채워져 있는 것을 보았다.

24 해설 능동, 진행의 의미를 나타내는 현재분사구가 The man을 뒤에서 수식하는 형태이다.

해석 나를 바라보고 있는 그 남자는 나의 독일어 선생님이시다.

25 해설 부사절의 시제가 주절보다 앞서므로 완료형 시제로 쓴 (having been) scolded가 알맞다.

26 해설 ② Been tired → (Being) Tired ③ Turned → Turning ④ Not living → (Though) Living ⑤ Put → Putting

서 술 형

27 해설 부사절의 시제는 과거이고 주절의 시제는 현재이므로 「Having p.p.」의 형태가 알맞다.

해석 내 휴대 전화를 잃어버렸기 때문에, 나는 지금 아무에게도 전화할 수 없다.

28 해설 부사절의 시제가 주절의 시제보다 앞서고 수동의 의미가 되어야 하므로 「Having been + p.p.」의 형태가 알맞다. 이때 Having been은 생략이 가능하다.

29 해설 접속사 While과 주어 she를 생략하고 Smiling happily 형태의 분사구문으로 쓴다.

해석 행복하게 미소지으며, 그녀는 그녀의 아들을 힘껏 껴안았다.

30 해설 분사구문의 시제(과거)가 주절의 시제(현재)보다 앞서므로 「Having + p.p.」의 형태를 사용한다.

31 해설 목적어인 his left leg는 사고를 당해서 '부러진' 것이므로 수동의 의미를 나타내는 과거분사(broken)를 써야 한다.

32 해설 분사구문에서 부정어 not은 분사 앞에 온다.

해석 수영을 할 수 없다면, 너는 구명조끼를 입는 게 좋겠다.

33 해설 found의 목적어 herself가 낯선 방에 홀로 남겨진 상황이므로 수동의 의미를 나타내는 과거분사 left가 알맞다.

해석 그녀는 자신이 낯선 방에 홀로 남겨졌다는 것을 알게 되었다.

34 해설 완료형 분사구문(Having spent ~)이 쓰인 것으로 보아 부사절의 시제가 주절의 시제(과거)보다 앞선 시제임을 알 수 있으므로 과거완료 시제로 나타낸다.

해석 돈을 다 썼기 때문에, 그는 새 재킷을 살 수 없었다.

35 해설 과거분사구(injured in the game)가 명사(The players)를 뒤에서 수식하는 형태이다.

36 해설 지각동사 heard의 목적어(their names)와 목적격보어의 관계가 수동이므로 calling을 called로 써야 한다.

해석 그들은 그들의 이름이 불리는 것을 들었다.

37 해설 「with + (대)명사 + 분사」의 형태로 동시상황의 의미를 나타낼 수 있다.

38 해설 접속사(If)와 주어(I)를 생략하고 Finding her address 형태의 분사구문으로 쓸 수 있다.

해석 그녀의 주소를 알게 되면, 나는 그녀에게 초대장을 보낼 것이다.

39 해설 「with + (대)명사 + 분사」 형태의 분사구문으로, the boys가 노래하는 것이므로 능동의 의미를 나타내는 현재분사 singing을 쓰는 것이 알맞다.

40 해설 상품의 질이 만족스러움을 주는 것이므로 첫 번째 빈칸에는 현재분사가 알맞고, 두 번째 빈칸에는 내가 만족하지 못하는 것이므로 과거분사가 알맞다.

해석 그 상품의 품질은 만족스러웠다. 하지만, 나는 그 가게의 서비스에 전혀 만족하지 않았다.

41 해설 the girls가 자신들의 팀을 응원하고 있는 상황이므로 능동의 의미를 나타내는 현재분사를 쓴다.

해석 자신들의 팀이 승리하라고 응원하고 있는 그 소녀들을 봐라.

42 해설 지각동사 saw의 목적격보어가 능동의 의미로 쓰였으므로 현재분사 crossing을 쓴다.

해석 나는 빨간 불에 길을 건너고 있는 소녀를 보았다.

43 해설 지각동사 saw의 목적격보어가 능동의 의미로 쓰였으므로 현재분사 running 또는 동사원형 cross를 쓴다.

해석 그 경찰은 도둑이 보석을 가지고 달아나고 있는 것을 보았다.

44 해설 have는 목적어와 목적격보어의 관계가 수동일 때 「have + 목적어(사물) + 목적격보어(p.p.)」의 형태로 쓴다.

해석 그녀는 그 고장 난 차를 쓸 수 있게 수리 받았다.

45 **해설** have는 목적어와 목적격보어의 관계가 수동일 때 「have + 목적어(사물) + 목적격보어(p.p.)」의 형태로 쓴다.

해석 그는 그 문서에서 몇 가지 실수를 바로잡았다.

[46-47]

해석 수업이 평소처럼 시작되었다. 선생님께서 학생들의 이름을 불렀다. 하지만 선생님께서 Sarah를 불렀을 때, 아무런 대답이 없었다. 선생님께서는 잠시 생각하시더니 그냥 교과서를 펼치셨다. 나는 Sarah에게 무슨 일이 있는지 정말 궁금했다. 그러나 나는 그녀와 잘 지내지 못했기 때문에 그날 그녀에게 전화를 할 수 없었다.

46 **해설** 시간의 부사절 when Sarah was called by the teacher를 분사구문 being called by the teacher로 만들고 접속사의 의미를 명확하게 하기 위해 when을 남겨둔 뒤, being을 생략한 형태이다.

해석 선생님에 의해 (이름이) 불렸을 때, Sarah는 수업에 없었다.

47 **해설** 이유의 부사절 because I didn't get along with her를 분사구문으로 만든 형태이다. 분사구문의 부정은 「not[never] + -ing」의 형태로 나타낸다.

해석 그녀와 잘 지내지 못해서, 나는 Sarah에게 전화를 할 수 없었다.

Chapter 04 시제

1 미래를 나타내는 표현

▸▸ p.92

A

1	win	**2**	finish
3	is	**4**	is leaving
5	arrives	**6**	doesn't rain
7	comes		

2 과거와 현재완료

▸▸ p.93

A

1	lived	**2**	rained
3	broke out	**4**	finished
5	arrived	**6**	moved
7	have known		

3 현재완료 I - 계속 / 경험 용법

▸▸ p.94~95

A

1	경험	**2**	계속	**3**	경험
4	계속	**5**	경험	**6**	계속
7	계속				

B

1	since	**2**	for	**3**	since
4	since	**5**	for	**6**	for
7	since	**8**	since		

C

1	I've had, for	**2**	has never gone
3	Have, ever seen	**4**	has taken, since
5	have made, since	**6**	has never played
7	has taught, for		

4 현재완료 II - 완료 / 결과 용법

▸▸ p.96~97

A

1	완료	**2**	완료	**3**	결과
4	완료	**5**	결과		

B

1	has been to	**2**	has gone to
3	has been to	**4**	have gone to
5	have been to		

C

1	has already come	**2**	Have you done
3	has just broken	**4**	hasn't gotten[got]
5	has gone to	**6**	have already finished
7	has just arrived	**8**	have lost
9	has already finished	**10**	has bought

5 현재완료진행

▸▸ p.98~99

A

1	have been running	**2**	has been waiting
3	have been riding	**4**	has been working
5	have been listening	**6**	have been having
7	have been living	**8**	has been talking

B

1 has been raining
2 have been lying in the sun
3 have been waiting for Brian
4 has been studying German
5 have been swimming
6 has been playing computer games

C

1 have been saving 2 have been listening
3 has been sleeping 4 has been raining
5 have you been wearing

6 과거완료

▶▶ p. 100~101

A

1 had seen
2 had just taken off
3 had bought
4 had happened
5 had lived
6 had broken

B

1 has already left → had already left
2 has broken → had broken
3 have been → had been

C

1 they had missed the last train
2 I had seen(I saw) the earthquake in Haiti
3 it had rained(it rained) at night
4 he had spent all his money

D

1 had disappeared
2 had had
3 had already begun
4 had been born
5 had never seen
6 had been sold
7 had just closed

7 과거완료진행

▶▶ p. 102

A

1 had been driving
2 have been discussing
3 has been listening
4 had been talking

B

1 had been waiting
2 had been standing
3 had been studying

Chapter 04 학교 시험 대비 문제

▶▶ p. 103~110

01 ④ 02 ② 03 ④ 04 ⑤ 05 ② 06 ⑤ 07 ① 08 ⑤ 09 ③ 10 ④ 11 ② 12 ④ 13 ④ 14 ③ 15 ⑤ 16 ⑤ 17 ③ 18 ④ 19 ④ 20 ⑤ 21 ③ 22 ③ 23 ⑤ 24 ⑤ 25 ③ 26 ⑤ 27 ① 28 ② 29 ③ 30 ④ 31 ⑤ 32 ③ 33 ⑤ 34 ⑤ 35 ① 36 ②

서술형 **37** are smelling → smell **38** was **39** had visited **40** had been waiting **41** has been raining **42** have worn **43** had defeated → defeated **44** Brian has gone to China. **45** It has been raining since yesterday. **46** had gone home **47** a thief had broken into

01 해설 과거에 여권을 잃어버려서 현재 가지고 있지 않다는 의미이므로 과거의 일이 현재까지 영향을 미치고 있음을 알 수 있다. 따라서 빈칸에는 현재완료 시제가 알맞다.

해석 그는 그의 여권을 잃어버렸다. 지금 그는 그것을 가지고 있지 않다.
→ 그는 그의 여권을 잃어버렸다.

02 해설 go, come, leave, arrive 등과 같은 동사는 현재진행형을 써서 가까운 미래를 나타낼 수 있다.

03 해설 since last week는 '지난주부터 지금까지 쭉'이라는 뜻이므로 현재완료의 계속 용법과 함께 쓰인다. (현재완료진행형도 가능함)

해석 **A** 이건 뭐니?
B 그것은 야생 동물에 관한 책이야. 나는 지난주부터 그것을 읽고 있어.

04 **해설** 첫 번째 문장은 현재완료의 완료 용법, 두 번째 문장은 과거완료의 경험 용법이므로 빈칸에는 과거분사가 들어가야 한다.

해석 • 나는 이미 저녁으로 피자를 먹었다.
• 그는 그 동물원을 방문하기 전에 낙타를 본 적이 없었다.

05 **해설** 주어진 문장과 ②는 현재완료의 경험 용법으로 쓰였다. ① 완료 ③ 현재완료진행 ④⑤ 계속

해석 너는 거기서 그 말을 본 적이 있니?

06 **해설** ① have married → will marry ② was ill → has been ill(현재완료의 계속 용법) ③ have climbed → climbed ④ will arrive → arrives(시간 부사절)

07 **해설** ① 현재진행시제, ②③④⑤ 미래시제를 나타내는 현재진행형

08 **해설** have never been이라는 표현으로 보아 현재완료를 사용하여 경험을 묻는 의문문이 알맞다.

해석 아니, 나는 거기에 가본 적이 없어.

09 **해설** he was young은 과거시점을 나타내므로 since를, four days는 기간을 나타내므로 for를 쓴다.

해석 • 그는 어렸을 때부터 그림 그리는 데 관심이 있었다.
• 그녀는 4일째 아팠다.

10 **해설** have gone to : ~로 가 버렸다(결과) / have been to : ~에 가본 적이 있다(경험)

해석 Steve는 중국에 갔다. 그래서 그는 여기에 없다.
→ Steve는 중국에 가 버렸다.

11 **해설** Have you p.p. ~?로 묻는 현재완료 의문문에서, 긍정이면 Yes, I have.로, 부정이면 No, I haven't.로 대답한다.

12 **해설** ④의 last Sunday는 과거를 나타내는 부사구이므로 과거시제와 함께 쓰인다. has returned → returned

13 **해설** 버스가 떠난 시점은 내가 버스 정류장에 도착했던 시점(과거)보다 먼저 일어난 일이므로 과거완료 형태가 알맞다.

해석 내가 버스 정류장에 도착했을 때 버스는 이미 떠나 버렸다.

14 **해설** '30년 전에 영어를 가르치기 시작해서 지금까지 계속 가르치고 있다'는 의미이므로 빈칸에는 현재완료(계속 용법)가 알맞다.

15 **해설** ⑤의 since로 보아 그 앞에는 현재완료나 현재완료진행시제가 쓰여야 하므로 has played나 has been playing으로 써야 한다.

16 **해설** 남동생이 컴퓨터로 그림을 그리고 있던 것은 내가 방에 들어간 시점보다 이전의 일이므로 과거완료 또는 과거완료진행시제가 알맞다.

해석 내가 방에 들어갔을 때 내 남동생은 컴퓨터로 그림을 그리고 있었다.

17 **해설** 현재완료진행형은 「have(has) been + -ing」의 형태로 나타낸다.

18 **해설** 현재완료 의문문 Have you p.p. ~?에 대해 긍정으로 대답할 때는 Yes, I have.로, 부정으로 대답할 때는 No, I haven't.로 한다.

해석 **A** 네 방을 청소했니?
B 아니요, 안 했어요.
A 이유를 말해줄 수 있니?
B 숙제가 많아요.

19 **해설** ① have been → was
② has left → left
③ has finished → finished
⑤ Have you written → Did you write

20 **해설** 형이 나에게 모자를 사준 것은 내가 모자를 잃어버린 것보다 먼저 일어난 일이므로 과거완료 형태를 써야 한다.

해석 어제 나는 형이 나에게 사 준 모자를 잃어버렸다.

21 **해설** 주어진 문장과 ③은 현재완료의 완료 용법으로 쓰였다. ① 경험 ②⑤ 계속 ④ 결과

해석 Tom은 방금 연설을 끝마쳤다.

22 **해설** 명백한 과거를 나타내는 부사인 yesterday로 보아 과거시제인 shouted가 알맞다. 월드 시리즈에서 우승한 것은 기뻐서 소리지른 것보다 먼저 일어난 사건이므로 과거완료 형태인 had won이 알맞다.

해석 그 야구팀은 월드 시리즈에서 우승했기 때문에 어제 기뻐서 소리 질렀다.

23 **해설** ⑤ lives → has lived 또는 has been living
과거의 어느 시점부터 지금까지 10년 동안 계속 살고 있으므로 현재완료나 현재완료진행시제로 써야 한다.

해석 Kevin은 부모님과 두 형제와 함께 보스턴에 사는 16살 소년이다. 그는 그곳에서 10년째 살고 있다.

24 **해설** visit의 경우 문맥상 '세 번 방문한 적이 있다'는 의미이고, be의 경우 문맥상 '한 번도 가본 적이 없다'는 의미이므로 경험을 나타내는 현재완료 형태로 써야 한다. 따라서 각각 visited와 been이 알맞다.

해석 나의 부모님은 홍도에 세 번 다녀오셨다. 하지만 나는 그 섬에 한 번도 가본 적이 없다. 그들은 나를 그곳에 데려가기로 약속하셨다.

25 **해설** 「since + 과거시점」, 「for + 기간」이 오므로 ③은 for four years로 써야 한다.

26 **해설** since는 과거시점을 나타내는 말 앞에 쓰이므로 빈칸에 알맞지 않다.

27 **해설** 시간이나 조건을 나타내는 부사절에서는 현재시제로 미래를 나타내므로 빈칸에는 현재시제가 알맞다.

해석 나는 프로젝트를 끝내자마자 올 것이다.

28 **해설** ① since → for

③ for → since

④ know → have known

⑤ has been to → has gone to

29 **해설** 그가 반지를 잃어버린 시점은 내가 생각했던 시점보다 이전이므로 lose는 과거완료 형태가 알맞다.

해석 내가 그를 공항에서 보았을 때, 그는 반지를 끼고 있지 않았다. 나는 그가 그것을 잃어버렸다고 생각했다.

30 **해설** 주어진 문장과 ④는 현재완료의 계속 용법으로 쓰였다.

①② 결과 ③ 경험 ⑤ 완료

해석 그녀는 2년째 집을 떠나 지내고 있다.

31 **해설** ⑤ 현재완료의 계속 ①②③④ 경험

32 **해설** ③ John이 떠난 것은 그의 여동생이 도착한 시점(과거)보다 더 이전이므로 과거완료로 나타내야 한다. (→ had already left)

33 **해설** ⑤의 since 다음에는 과거시점이 오는 것이 알맞다. are → were

34 **해설** ⑤의 첫 번째 문장은 현재완료의 계속, 두 번째 문장은 경험을 나타낸다.

① 완료 ② 결과 ③ 계속 ④ 경험

35 **해설** 현재완료의 완료 용법에서 yet은 부정문과 의문문에 사용되며, 부정문에서는 '아직', 의문문에서는 '이제'의 의미로 쓰인다.

36 **해설** ②의 last month는 과거를 나타내는 부사구이므로 과거시제와 함께 쓰인다.

서술형

37 **해설** 감각동사 smell은 진행형으로 쓰이지 않는다.

해석 그 박람회에는 많은 종류의 꽃들이 있다. 그것들은 아름답다. 특히 흰장미는 향기로운 냄새가 난다.

38 **해설** since가 접속사로 쓰일 경우 일반적으로 since 앞에는 현재완료가, since 뒤에는 과거시제가 온다. (현재완료의 계속 용법)

해석 그녀는 18살이었을 때부터 많은 소설을 써왔다.

39 **해설** 그가 두바이를 여러 번 방문한 것은 그가 나에게 말한 것보다 먼저 일어난 일이므로 과거완료 형태인 had visited로 쓴다.

40 **해설** 내가 오랫동안 그를 기다리고 있었던 것은 그가 도착했던 것보다 먼저 일어난 일이므로 과거완료나 과거완료진행시제를 쓰는 것이 알맞다. 빈칸이 세 개 주어졌으므로 과거완료진행시제인 had been waiting을 써서 문장을 완성한다.

41 **해설** '어제부터 내리기 시작한 비가 지금도 내리고 있다'는 의미이므로 빈칸에는 현재완료진행형을 쓴다.

해석 어제 비가 내리기 시작했다. 비는 아직도 내리고 있다.

→ 비가 어제부터 계속 내리고 있다.

42 **해설** '7년 전에 산 코트를 지금도 입고 있다'는 의미이므로 빈칸에는 현재완료시제를 사용한다. (wear - wore - worn)

해석 나는 그 코트를 7년 전에 샀다. 지금도 여전히 나는 그것을 입는다.

→ 나는 7년째 그 코트를 입고 있다.

43 **해설** 'in 1597'과 같이 명백한 과거를 나타내는 말이 올 때는 과거시제를 쓴다. (역사적인 사실)

해석 우리가 초등학교를 다닐 때, 우리는 이순신 장군이 1597년에 일본 해군을 물리쳤다는 것을 배웠다.

[44-45]

해석 <보기> Matt는 시계를 잃어버렸다. 그는 그것을 아직 찾지 못하고 있다. → Matt는 시계를 잃어버렸다.

44 **해설** 중국에 가서 지금 여기에 없으므로 현재완료의 결과 용법을 사용하여 표현한다.

해석 Brian은 중국에 갔다. 그는 여기에 없다.

→ Brian은 중국으로 가버렸다.

45 **해설** 어제 시작된 일(비가 내리기 시작함)이 현재까지 진행 중이므로 현재완료진행시제를 사용한다.

해석 비가 오기 시작했다. 비가 아직도 내리고 있다.

→ 비가 어제부터 내리고 있다.

46 해설 Henry가 집에 간 것은 Kate가 식당에 도착한 것보다 먼저 일어난 일이므로 과거완료 형태를 써야 한다.

해석 Kate는 지난주 토요일에 'Green' 레스토랑에 갔다. Henry도 그 레스토랑에 갔다. 하지만 그들은 서로 만나지 못했다. Henry는 오후 6시에 레스토랑을 떠났다. Kate는 그곳에 오후 7시에 도착했다. 그래서 Kate가 레스토랑에 도착했을 때, Henry는 이미 집에 가고 없었다.

47 해설 누군가가(도둑이) 집에 침입한 것은 우리가 그것을 알게 된 것보다 먼저 일어난 일이므로 과거완료 형태를 사용한다.

해석 우리 가족은 휴가에서 돌아왔다. 우리가 집에 도착했을 때 우리는 굉장히 놀랐다. 거실에 있는 물건들이 사방에 흩어져 있었다. 우리는 집에 도둑이 침입했다고 생각했다. 그래서 우리는 경찰을 불렀다.

Chapter 05 조동사

1 can / could

▸▸ p. 112~113

A
1 Can　2 cannot　3 weeping
4 can

B
1 ⓐ　2 ⓑ　3 ⓐ
4 ⓑ　5 ⓐ

C
1 is able to　2 weren't able to
3 Are you able to　4 is able to, isn't able to

D
1 won't be able to　2 cannot remember
3 couldn't help following
4 cannot be too careful

2 may / might

▸▸ p. 114

A
1 ⓐ　2 ⓑ　3 ⓑ
4 ⓐ　5 ⓑ　6 ⓐ

B
1 may(might) well be
2 may(might) well be sleepy
3 may(might) as well stay

3 must / have to

▸▸ p. 115~116

A
1 has　2 has　3 have to
4 had　5 must　6 have to
7 must

B
1 ⓑ　2 ⓐ　3 ⓑ
4 ⓐ　5 ⓐ　6 ⓐ

C
1 don't have to
2 doesn't have to
3 doesn't have to

D
1 must not kill bugs
2 will have to do
3 don't have to teach
4 had to go through the window

4 should / ought to

▸▸ p. 117

A
1 ought　2 should　3 should
4 accept　5 ought not to

B
1 should apologize
2 should not take 또는 oughtn't to take

5 will / would / used to
▶▶ p. 118~119

A

1	will	**2**	will
3	would	**4**	is going to

B

1	used to	**2**	would 또는 used to
3	Would	**4**	used to
5	used to	**6**	would
7	would 또는 used to		

C

1	ⓐ	**2**	ⓒ	**3**	ⓒ
4	ⓐ	**5**	ⓑ	**6**	ⓐ

D

1	used to be	**2**	would play tennis
3	used to be		

6 had better / would rather
▶▶ p. 120

A

1 to go → go
2 had not better → had better not
3 as → than
4 taking → take

B

1	had better give	**2**	would rather leave
3	had better not go	**4**	would rather, than

7 do
▶▶ p. 121

A

1	ⓐ	**2**	ⓑ	**3**	ⓐ
4	ⓓ	**5**	ⓒ		

B

1	did swear	**2**	than they do
3	do apologize	**4**	most boys do

8 조동사 + have p.p.
▶▶ p. 122~123

A

1	should	**2**	must	**3**	should
4	cannot	**5**	might	**6**	might
7	must				

B

1 must have been
2 may(might) have forgotten
3 should have phoned
4 must have left
5 can't(cannot) have understood

C

1	must have left	**2**	should have promoted
3	cannot have seen		

D

1	It must have rained	**2**	cannot have met her
3	must have spent	**4**	should have listened to

Chapter 05 학교 시험 대비 문제
▶▶ p. 124~130

01 ② **2** ① **03** ② **04** ④ **05** ② **06** ② **07** ② **08** ② **09** ③ **10** ② **11** ② **12** ⑤ **13** ③ **14** ② **15** ① **16** ① **17** ② **18** ④ **19** ⑤ **20** ④ **21** ④ **22** ① **23** ③ **24** ③ **25** ④ **26** ⑤ **27** ④ **28** ⑤ **29** ②

서술형 **30** has to get **31** I would rather keep silent than tell you a lie. **32** had better not tell **33** used to be **34** went → (should) go **35** I should have practiced more. **36** I will be able to download **37** This milk is used to **38** He used to work **39** I am used to studying **40** must have stayed at home **41** cannot be true **42** cannot have stolen the money **43** can play the guitar **44** may sit on this chair **45** must not smoke here

01 **해설** be not able to = cannot(~할 수 없다)
해석 날씨가 너무 더워서 그들은 더 이상 걸을 수 없다.
02 **해설** must : ~임에 틀림없다(강한 추측)
03 **해설** used to : ~하곤 했다(과거의 습관)
해석 나는 어렸을 때 바닥에서 자곤 했다.

04 해설 ④ 제안을 나타내는 동사 suggest(ed)가 쓰인 문장이다. that절 안에 should가 생략되었으므로 동사원형 break로 써야 한다.

해석 그녀는 그가 나쁜 버릇을 고쳐야 한다고 제안했다.

05 해설 ① have → has ③ must → have to
④ musted → had to ⑤ has → have

06 해설 ② 추측과 허가의 의미로 모두 쓰일 수 있는 조동사는 may[May]이다.

해석 • 그의 아버지는 오늘 밤에 늦을지도 모른다.
• 네가 나에게 준 이 상자를 열어봐도 되니?

07 해설 ① get → getting ③ would → used to
④ am used to → used to
⑤ would → used to

08 해설 주절의 시제가 과거형이므로 약한 추측을 의미하는 may와 might 중에서 시제가 일치되는 might가 알맞다.

해석 나는 어슬렁거리는 그 남자가 도둑일지도 모른다고 생각했다.

09 해설 주어진 문장과 ③ 강조, ① 부정문에 쓰이는 조동사, ② like를 대신하는 대동사, ④ ⑤ '하다'라는 의미의 일반동사

해석 나는 너에 대해 정말 많이 들었다.

10 해설 ②의 might는 '~일지도 모른다'는 뜻이며, ①의 must, ③의 have to, ④의 ought to, ⑤의 should는 '~해야 한다'는 뜻으로 쓰였다.

11 해설 had better는 '강한 권유'의 의미로 should, must와 비슷한 의미를 나타내며 부정형은 had better not으로 쓴다. You had better not은 You'd better not으로 줄여 쓸 수 있다.

해석 나는 네가 아버지에게 말대꾸하지 말아야 한다고 생각한다.
= 너는 아버지에게 말대꾸하지 않는 게 좋겠다.

12 해설 오디션에서 떨어진 상황이므로 과거에 연습을 열심히 하지 않은 것에 대한 유감을 나타내는 의미로 「should have p.p.」가 알맞다.

해석 **A** Susan은 주인공을 뽑는 오디션에 합격하지 못했어.
B 오, 안됐구나. 그녀는 연습을 더 했어야 했어.

13 해설 '~해야 한다'는 의미의 조동사가 필요하므로 should가 알맞다.

해석 • 너는 너의 임무를 수행해야 한다.
• 우리는 환경을 보호해야 한다.

14 해설 ② 문맥상 '~하는 게 좋겠다'의 의미를 나타내는 had better가 알맞다.

15 해설 조동사는 2개를 나란히 사용할 수 없으므로 will 다음에 can이 올 때는 be able to로 써야 한다.

16 해설 must have p.p. : ~했음에 틀림없다

해석 그는 창백해 보였다. 그는 아팠던 게 틀림없다.

17 해설 should have p.p. : ~했어야 했는데(과거에 대한 후회나 유감)
must have p.p. : ~했음에 틀림없다(과거에 대한 강한 추측)

해석 • 경기가 이미 끝났다. 우리는 더 일찍 왔어야 했다.
• 경기장에 사람이 아무도 없었다. 경기가 끝난 것이 틀림없다.

18 해설 ④ 부정문에 쓰인 조동사, ①②③⑤ 강조

19 해설 used to : ~이었다(과거의 상태)

20 해설 주절의 동사 give를 받는 대동사가 나와야 한다. 과거를 나타내는 ten years ago가 있으므로 과거형 did가 알맞다.

해석 너는 10년 전에 그랬던 것처럼 내게 영감을 준다.

21 해설 ④ 과거에 대한 후회나 유감의 표시는 「should have p.p.」로 나타낼 수 있다.

해석 그 경기를 못 봐서 나는 유감이다.

22 해설 3인칭 단수주어일 때 has to의 부정형은 doesn't have to이다.

23 해설 had better + 동사원형 : ~하는 게 좋겠다

24 해설 ③ 허가(~해도 될까요?), ①②④⑤ 능력[가능](~할 수 없다)

25 해설 ④ 제안을 나타내는 동사 recommend(ed)가 쓰였으므로 that절 안에서 should가 생략된 것을 알 수 있다. 따라서 exercise로 써야 한다.

26 해설 ① ② ③ ④ '~일지도 모른다'는 추측의 의미, ⑤ '~해도 된다'는 허가의 의미

27 해설 ④ used to가 '과거의 상태'를 나타낼 경우 would로 바꿔 쓸 수 없다.

28 해설 ⑤ 어젯밤에 아이스크림을 너무 많이 먹은 것에 대해 후회하는 내용이므로 「should have p.p.」의 부정형 「should not have p.p.」가 알맞다.

29 해설 보기와 ⓐ ⓓ 강한 추측(~임에 틀림없다), ⓑ ⓒ 의무(~해야 한다)

해석 ⓐ 그 보도는 가짜인 게 틀림없다.
ⓑ 너는 과제물을 내일까지 제출해야 한다.
ⓒ 우리는 우리 사회의 약자들을 돌봐야 한다.
ⓓ 나의 선생님은 모든 것을 알고 계신다. 그는 내 비밀을 알고 있는 게 틀림없다.

서술형

30 **해설** need to는 have to로 바꿔 쓸 수 있는데 주어가 3인칭 단수이므로 has to 형태가 알맞다.
해석 **A** 그녀는 무엇을 해야 하니?
B 그녀는 충분한 수면을 취해야 해.

31 **해설** would rather A than B : B하느니 차라리 A하겠다

32 **해설** had better(~하는 게 좋겠다)의 부정형은 had better not이다.

33 **해설** '아주 말랐었다'는 과거의 상태를 말하고 있으므로 used to를 써서 나타낸다.
해석 내 여동생은 어렸을 때 무척 말랐었다.

34 **해설** 제안을 나타내는 동사 suggest(ed)가 쓰였으므로 (should) go로 써야 한다.
해석 그는 우리가 방과 후에 쇼핑을 하러 가야 한다고 주장했다.

35 **해설** 후회의 의미를 나타내는 '~했어야 했는데'는 「should have p.p.」를 사용하여 표현한다.
해석 **A** 너 왜 울고 있니?
B 나는 정말 실망했어. 나 운전면허 시험에서 떨어졌어.
A 괜찮아. 너는 다음 번엔 더 잘할 수 있을 거야.
B 그렇게 말해줘서 고마워. 나는 좀 더 연습을 했어야 했어.

36 **해설** 조동사 will과 can을 함께 쓸 수 없으므로 can을 be able to로 바꿔 쓴다.
해석 나는 모든 파일들을 한 번에 내려받을 수 있다.
→ 나는 모든 파일들을 한 번에 내려받을 수 있을 것이다.

37 **해설** '~하는 데 사용되다'라는 의미의 「be used to부정사」를 사용한다.

38 **해설** '~하곤 했다(습관), ~이었다(상태)'라는 의미의 「used to부정사」를 사용한다.

39 **해설** '~하는 데 익숙하다'라는 의미의 「be used to -ing」를 사용한다.

40 **해설** '~했을 리가 없다'의 「cannot have p.p.」를 '~했음에 틀림없다'의 「must have p.p.」를 사용해 바꿔 쓴다.
해석 민호는 집에 있었을 리가 없다.
→ 민호는 집에 있었던 게 틀림없다.

41 **해설** '~임에 틀림없다'의 must를 '~일 리가 없다'의 cannot을 사용해 바꿔 쓴다.
해석 Brian은 그 뉴스가 사실임에 틀림없다고 믿는다.
→ Brian은 그 뉴스가 사실일 리가 없다고 믿는다.

42 **해설** '~했음에 틀림없다'의 「must have p.p.」를 '~했을 리가 없다'의 「cannot have p.p.」를 사용해 바꿔 쓴다.
해석 James가 그 돈을 훔쳤던 게 틀림없다.
→ James가 그 돈을 훔쳤을 리가 없다.

43 **해설** 능력을 나타내는 can을 사용하여 문장을 완성한다.
해석 그는 기타를 칠 수 있다.

44 **해설** 허가를 나타내는 may를 사용하여 문장을 완성한다.
해석 당신은 이 의자에 앉아도 됩니다.

45 **해설** 금지를 나타내는 must not을 사용하여 문장을 완성한다.
해석 표지판에 이곳에서 담배를 피워서는 안 된다고 쓰여 있군.

Chapter 06 수동태

1 수동태 만드는 법

▶▶ p. 132~133

A

1 was written
2 were eaten
3 by her
4 were helped by
5 isn't grown

B

1 was caught
2 were handed
3 is played
4 were built

C

1 The 2018 World Cup was held by Russia.
2 The poor children in the world are helped by UNICEF.
3 A satellite was launched by the Naro Space Center in Korea.
4 The cultural landscapes of the Joseon Dynasty were painted by Kim Hongdo.

2 조동사의 수동태

▶▶ p. 134

A

1 be bought
2 be written
3 be designed
4 not be used
5 not accept
6 be signed

B

1 can be prepared 2 may be surprised
3 will be made

3 진행형 수동태
▶▶ p. 135

A

1 are being prepared 2 is being destroyed
3 was being used 4 were being made
5 is not being considered

B

1 The room is being cleaned by my twin sisters.
2 The test sheets are being collected by the math teacher.
3 Coffee isn't being made by him at the moment.
4 The African countries were being helped by many volunteers.

4 완료형 수동태
▶▶ p. 136

A

1 A new project has been suggested by Joel.
2 The decoration of the shop has not(hasn't) been finished yet (by them).
3 I had been invited to their wedding party by the Smiths.
4 The wall has been painted by the family.
5 The vase had been broken by Tom and Jerry.

B

1 have been caught 2 have, been ironed
3 has been changed

5 4형식 문장의 수동태
▶▶ p. 137~138

A

1 Mitch, to 2 Some food, for
3 were bought for
4 was given, were given to
5 was made for

B

1 was made for me
2 was given the penalty
3 were passed to her
4 will be bought for my brother
5 was sold to the boy

C

1 was given to 2 were written to
3 was given, by 4 was bought for

6 5형식 문장의 수동태
▶▶ p. 139~140

A

1 was named 2 was elected
3 painted, white 4 considered, successful
5 allowed, to play

B

1 The girl was called "Little Queen" (by them).
2 She was considered a genius (by people).
3 She was forced to resign by the company.
4 The case is made more difficult by the fact.
5 He has been chosen the leader of the group (by them).
6 The colleagues in our office were advised to stop smoking (by us).

C

1 was elected
2 was made, by
3 was made, by the farmers
4 was found guilty
5 were asked to help

7 지각 · 사역동사의 수동태
▶▶ p. 141~142

A

1 was seen to put 2 was seen to explore
3 were heard to shout 4 is made to look
5 was noticed to have 6 was made to fix
7 were seen to jump

B

1 Jack was seen to go to the coffee shop by me.
2 Mr. Kim was heard to ask about the accident (by them).
3 They are made to think about the project by these issues.
4 My brother and sister were seen to play basketball together by me.
5 He is made to improve safety by the Prime Minister.
6 You were made to get in touch with the world by the CEO.
7 The baby was heard to cry all night by me.

C

1 was seen climbing
2 are made to wash
3 were observed landing
4 was heard doing
5 was heard predicting

8 동사구의 수동태

▸▸ p. 143~144

A

1 is being looked at
2 is looked after
3 mustn't be laughed at
4 is looked up to

B

1 An old man was run over by a car.
2 Starving African children should be taken care of by us.
3 Websites about the environment were looked at by them.
4 In *the Jungle Book*, the orphan Mowgli is brought up by animals in the jungle.
5 His plan was laughed at by his boss.

C

1 My computer was turned off by my cat.
2 His mistake was laughed at by his friends.
3 The newborn dogs were looked after by her.
4 An eight-year-old boy was run over by a school bus.
5 The professor is looked up to by the students.
6 Mike was always made fun of by his classmates.
7 The girl watering the flowers is being looked at by me.

9 by 이외의 전치사를 쓰는 수동태

▸▸ p. 145~146

A

1 at
2 in
3 with
4 about
5 of
6 with
7 with
8 for

B

1 I was interested in the history of South Africa.
2 The beach was covered with starfish.
3 All the classmates were pleased with the news.
4 I am worried about the storm and thunder.
5 The readers will be satisfied with the new book.
6 You might be interested in the video on YouTube.

C

1 was surprised at
2 are satisfied with
3 worried about
4 was disappointed with
5 are interested in
6 is covered with
7 is filled with

10 목적어가 절인 경우의 수동태

▸▸ p. 147~148

A

1 is said
2 was said
3 was believed
4 The wolf, to escape
5 The woman, to be

B

1 is said that Susan is, is said to be
2 was said that Bill Gates donated, was said to donate
3 was thought that only 10 soldiers survived, were thought to survive
4 is believed that the robbers have fled, are believed to have fled
5 is thought that the album has sold, is thought to have sold

C

1 It is said that
2 It is thought that
3 are thought to contain
4 It is said that
5 are said to be
6 was believed to be

Chapter 06 학교 시험 대비 문제

▶▶ p. 149~156

01 ③ 02 ② 03 ⑤ 04 ⑤ 05 ④ 06 ② 07 ④ 08 ② 09 ④ 10 ④ 11 ⑤ 12 ② 13 ⑤ 14 ① 15 ④ 16 ② 17 ④ 18 ⑤ 19 ⑤ 20 ⑤ 21 ② 22 ③ 23 ① 24 ④ 25 ⑤ 26 ② 27 ⑤ 28 ④ 29 ⑤ 30 ⑤ 31 ③ 32 ② 33 ④ 34 ⑤

서술형 **35** taken care → taken care of **36** was said to rise **37** going **38** was brought up **39** will be written to **40** It is said that **41** *Romeo and Juliet* was written by Shakespeare. **42** *The Sunflowers* was drawn by Van Gogh. **43** The ozone layer is destroyed [being destroyed] by carbon dioxide. **44** was called "Dancing King" **45** is taught to (the students) by Ms. Alice

01 해설 수동태의 부정은 「be동사 + not + p.p.」의 형태이다. 주어가 단수이고, 시제가 과거이므로 be동사는 was를 쓴다.
해석 그는 그 에세이를 쓰지 않았다.
→ 그 에세이는 그에 의해 쓰여지지 않았다.

02 해설 첫 번째 문장은 자가용을 사용하는 주체인 사람들(people)이 주어이므로 능동태 문장이다. 두 번째 문장은 차를 만드는 데 사용되는 재료인 생강(Ginger)이 주어이므로 수동태 문장이다.
해석 • 오늘날 사람들은 자가용을 너무 자주 사용한다.
• 생강은 차를 만드는 데 사용된다.

03 해설 「by + 행위자」는 일반인이거나 불특정인일 경우에 생략할 수 있다. ⑤는 행위자가 a British company로 구체적으로 명시되어 있으므로 생략할 수 없다.

04 해설 this morning으로 보아 시제가 과거임을 알 수 있다. 주어는 복수이므로 동사는 were를 쓴다. 지각동사가 사용된 능동태에서 목적격보어인 동사원형은 수동태에서 to부정사로 바뀐다.
해석 새들이 하늘로 날아가는 것이 오늘 아침에 그에게 보였다.

05 해설 목적어인 the pen은 주어 자리로 이동하고, 동사 returned는 「be동사 + p.p.」로 바뀐다. 과거시제이므로 be동사는 was를 쓴다.
해석 Jane은 오후에 그 펜을 돌려주었다.

06 해설 give는 간접목적어와 직접목적어 둘 다를 주어로 하여 수동태 전환이 가능하다. 직접목적어가 주어로 쓰일 경우 간접목적어 앞에는 전치사 to를 써야 한다.
해석 Lincoln은 그에게 기회를 주었다.

07 해설 buy는 간접목적어(사람)를 주어로 하는 수동태를 만들 수 없는 동사다.
④ She bought the farmer a goat.
→ The farmer was bought a goat by her. (×)
→ A goat was bought for the farmer by her. (○)

08 해설 ⓐ의 have는 상태를 나타내는 동사이고, ⓓ의 change는 목적어가 없는 자동사이므로 수동태로 쓰일 수 없다.
해석 ⓐ 나는 좋은 자전거가 있다.
ⓑ 그 소년은 노란 자전거를 샀다.
ⓒ 지진이 도시를 파괴했다.
ⓓ 날씨는 매일 변한다.

09 해설 People say that love always wins.
→ It is said that love always wins.
→ Love is always said to win.
해석 사람들은 사랑이 항상 이긴다고 말한다. / 사랑이 항상 이긴다고 한다.

10 해설 be known for : ~으로 알려져 있다, 유명하다(이유)
be known to : ~에게 알려져 있다(대상)

11 해설 make는 간접목적어를 수동태의 주어로 쓸 수 없는 동사이다.

12 해설 능동태의 동사가 found로 과거시제이므로 수동태에서 was found가 되어야 한다.
find ~ guilty 유죄 판결을 내리다
해석 판사는 그에게 유죄 판결을 내렸다.
→ 그는 판사에 의해 유죄 판결을 받았다.

13 해설 look at은 하나의 동사로 취급하여 수동태를 만든다.
해석 그는 이집트 조각상을 바라보았다.

14 해설 be worried about : ~에 대해 걱정하다
be made of : ~으로 만들어지다 (물리적 변화)
해석 • 우리는 미래에 대해 걱정한다.
• 그 탁자는 참나무로 만들어진다.

15 **해설** 보기와 ④ was, ① has, ② be, ③ be, ⑤ are
해석 그 탑은 1500년에 지어졌다.

16 **해설** ① has just been solving → has just been solved
③ has destroyed → has been destroyed
④ has been taken → has taken
⑤ has used → has been used

17 **해설** 조동사의 수동태 : 「조동사 + be p.p.」
④에서 by us는 일반인을 나타내므로 생략되었다.
해석 우리는 사냥꾼으로부터 코끼리를 보호해야 한다.

18 **해설** look up to : ~을 존경하다 / look down on : ~을 멸시하다
수동태로 전환될 때 동사구는 하나의 동사처럼 간주되므로 전치사(부사)를 반드시 함께 써야 한다.
해석 • 그는 그의 가족에 의해 존경받는다.
• 가난한 사람들이 부유한 사람들에 의해 멸시받아서는 안 된다.

19 **해설** 주어가 The gold medal이고, 「by + 행위자」가 있으므로 수동태 형태가 알맞다.

20 **해설** The doctor advised her to have meals regularly.
→ She was advised to have meals regularly by the doctor.

21 **해설** They thought that everyone had the ability.
→ It was thought that everyone had the ability.
→ Everyone was thought to have the ability.
해석 그들은 모든 사람들이 능력을 가졌다고 생각했다.
→ 모든 사람들은 능력을 가졌다고 여겨졌다.

22 **해설** 현재완료의 수동태는 「have(has) been p.p.」로 나타낸다.
해석 나의 삼촌은 2010년부터 가난한 사람들을 돕고 있다.
→ 가난한 사람들은 2010년부터 나의 삼촌에게 도움을 받고 있다.

23 **해설** ①의 빈칸에는 in, ②~⑤의 빈칸에는 모두 with가 알맞다.

24 **해설** by Thomas and his father는 행위자이므로 행위자를 묻는 질문을 해야 한다. 따라서 「By whom + be동사 + 주어 + p.p. ~?」의 형태로 질문한 ④가 알맞다.
해석 그 탁자는 Thomas와 그의 아버지에 의해 운반되었다.

25 **해설** 고래가 누군가에 의해 잡히고 있는 것이므로 수동태를 써야 한다. 잡히고 있는 현재의 동작을 나타내고 있으므로 현재진행형 수동태를 사용한다.

26 **해설** 5형식 문장의 목적격보어는 수동태의 주어로 쓰일 수 없다.
해석 우리는 Gates 씨를 우리의 의장으로 선출했다.

27 **해설** 지각동사의 목적격보어는 수동태에서 to부정사 또는 현재분사(-ing)의 형태로 쓰인다. '들렸다'고 했으므로 be동사는 과거시제 was를 써야 한다.

28 **해설** '~을 비웃다'라는 뜻의 동사구는 laugh at이다. 수동태로 바꿔 쓸 때 전치사 at도 함께 쓰는 것에 유의한다.

29 **해설** '~을 채우다'라는 뜻의 동사 fill은 수동태로 전환될 때 전치사 with를 쓴다.
be filled with : ~으로 가득 차다

30 **해설** ⑤ 행위를 한 주체가 주어이므로 능동태가 알맞다.
was developed → developed

31 **해설** ① → The woman is called Ms. White.
② → Jack was chosen chairman.(choose - chose - chosen)
④ → He was made a famous actor by the manager.
⑤ → Readers are asked to email their questions by the magazine.

32 **해설** 과거진행형의 수동태는 「was(were) being p.p.」의 형태로 나타낸다.
해석 그 소년은 만화책을 읽고 있었다.

33 **해설** 능동태 문장의 목적어가 주어로 쓰이고 있으므로 수동태가 되어야 한다.
조동사가 있는 수동태는 「조동사 + be p.p.」의 형태로 쓴다.
해석 우리는 우유와 고기를 냉장고에 보관해야 한다.
= 우유와 고기는 냉장고에 보관되어야 한다.

34 **해설** 완료형 수동태 : 「have(has) + been + p.p.」
조동사의 수동태 : 「조동사 + be + p.p.」
진행형 수동태 : 「be동사 + being + p.p.」
해석 • 나의 아버지의 셔츠들은 나의 어머니에 의해 다림질 되었다.
• 그 결정은 어린이들에 의해 내려질 것이다.
• 내가 가장 좋아하는 노래가 길에서 연주되고 있었다.

서술형

35 해설 take care of(~을 돌보다)는 수동태로 바꿔 쓸 때 하나의 동사처럼 간주되므로 전치사 of를 빠뜨리지 않도록 주의한다.

36 해설 that절의 주어가 수동태 문장의 주어로 전환될 경우, that절의 동사는 to부정사로 바뀐다.

해석 지구의 온도가 상승했다고 했다.

37 해설 지각동사의 목적격보어가 현재분사인 경우, 수동태 문장에 그대로 쓴다.

해석 나는 그 소년이 영화관에 가고 있는 것을 보았다.
→ 그 소년이 영화관에 가고 있는 것이 나에게 보였다.

38 해설 bring up은 '양육하다'라는 뜻으로 수동태로 전환될 때 하나의 동사로 취급한다.

39 해설 write가 쓰인 문장을 수동태로 바꿔 쓸 때 직접목적어가 주어로 쓰일 경우 간접목적어 앞에 전치사 to를 써야 한다.

해석 나는 나의 부모님께 감사 편지를 쓸 것이다.
→ 감사 편지는 나에 의해 나의 부모님께 쓰여질 것이다.

40 해설 People say that Korean people are very diligent.
→ It is said that Korean people are very diligent (by people).

[41-43]

해설 「be동사 + p.p. + by 행위자」의 수동태 형태가 알맞다.

해석 41 <로미오와 줄리엣>은 셰익스피어에 의해 쓰여졌다.

42 <해바라기>는 반 고흐에 의해 그려졌다.

43 오존층은 이산화탄소에 의해 파괴된다(파괴되고 있다).

[44-45]

해석 <보기> 금메달은 동계올림픽에서 김연아에 의해 획득되었다.

44 해설 Jack이 '댄싱킹'으로 불렸으므로 5형식 문장의 수동태 형태로 그림을 묘사한다.

해석 Jack은 중학생 때 '댄싱킹'이라고 불렸다.

45 해설 Alice 선생님이 학생들에게 영어를 가르치고 있는 모습이므로 4형식 문장의 수동태 형태로 그림을 묘사한다.

해석 영어는 월요일마다 Alice 선생님에 의해 (학생들에게) 가르쳐진다.

Chapter 07 대명사

1 재귀대명사

▸▸ p. 158~159

A

1 myself
2 herself
3 yourself (yourselves)
4 himself
5 yourself (yourselves)
6 himself
7 himself
8 herself
9 myself
10 yourself(yourselves)
11 itself
12 myself

B

1 helped ourselves to fruit
2 collected the stickers themselves
또는 themselves collected the stickers
3 did you take the photo for yourself
4 think for themselves
5 in itself helpful
6 often talks to herself
7 Between ourselves
8 the kite for himself

2 부정대명사 one ~ the other ... 등

▸▸ p. 160~161

A

1 the others
2 the other
3 One
4 others
5 another
6 one
7 others

B

1 other → others
2 the other → another
3 another → the other
4 other → others
5 others → the others
6 another → the other
7 the other → the others

C

1 One is white and the other is black.
2 One is mine and the others are my brother's.
3 Some boys like soccer but others don't like it.

3 부정대명사 all / none / each / every 등 ▸▸ p. 162~163

A

1 likes **2** is **3** is
4 has **5** are **6** deserves
7 were **8** is **9** plays
10 is **11** were

B

1 knows → know **2** are → is
3 are → is **4** leave → leaves
5 neither → either **6** is → are
7 was → were **8** were → was

C

1 Every rule has its
2 neither of them works
3 None of the jackets fitted
4 All children must go to school
5 Both my friend and I were surprised

4 부정대명사 somebody / anything 등 ▸▸ p. 164

A

1 Somebody **2** anything
3 somewhere **4** something
5 anywhere **6** Somebody
7 something **8** anything

Chapter 07 학교 시험 대비 문제

▸▸ p. 165~170

01 ③ **02** ⑤ **03** ② **04** ④ **05** ② **06** ② **07** ② **08** ④ **09** ① **10** ⑤ **11** ② **12** ④ **13** ④ **14** ③ **15** ③ **16** ③ **17** ③ **18** ① **19** ④ **20** ② **21** ④ **22** ③ **23** ②

서술형 **24** themselves → ourselves **25** All **26** each **27** None **28** themselves **29** the others → the other **30** another **31** The others → Others **32** Other → Another **33** another **34** One, the others

01 **해설** '또 다른 하나'를 의미하는 것은 another이다.
해석 Bob은 일자리를 잃었다. 그가 다른 일을 찾는 것은 어려울 것이다.

02 **해설** -thing으로 끝나는 대명사는 형용사가 뒤에서 수식하므로 wrong은 something 다음인 ⑤에 들어가야 한다.
해석 나는 내가 무언가를 잘못하고 있다는 것을 깨달았다.

03 **해설** 「each of + 복수명사」 → 단수 취급
해석 동물원에 있는 사자들은 각각 자신의 우리가 있다.

04 **해설** All of the athletes를 지칭하는 재귀대명사 themselves가 알맞다.
해석 국제 경기에 참가했던 모든 선수들은 자신을 매우 자랑스러워해야 한다.

05 **해설** 둘 중 하나는 one, 다른 하나는 the other로 나타낸다.
해석 대중 매체에는 두 가지 수단이 있다. 신문이 하나다. 텔레비전이 나머지 하나다.

06 **해설** ② both는 복수 취급하므로 be동사는 are가 알맞다. is → are

07 **해설** 정해지지 않은 다수 중 일부는 some, 다른 일부는 others로 나타낸다.
해석 이 레스토랑에는 많은 사람들이 있다. 몇몇은 줄을 서서 기다리고 있고, 몇몇은 식사를 하고 있다.

08 **해설** ④ 「every + 단수명사」는 단수 취급한다.
① both는 복수 취급한다. is → are
② 「each + 단수명사」이므로 each questions → each question
③ 주어가 복수이므로 tries → try
⑤ 「each + 단수명사」는 단수 취급한다. have → has

09 **해설** ①의 himself는 생략이 가능한 강조 용법으로, 나머지는 생략이 불가능한 재귀 용법으로 쓰였다.
③ seat oneself 앉다, 자리를 잡다

10 **해설** 6명 중 몇몇은 some, 나머지 모두는 the others로 표현한다.
「some ~ others ...」: (정해지지 않은 다수 중) 몇몇은 ~, 다른 일부는 …
「some ~ the others ...」: (정해진 범위 안에서) 몇몇은 ~, 나머지는 모두 …
해석 우리 반에는 6명의 외국인 학생들이 있다. 그들 중 몇 명은 일본인이고 나머지는 모두 영국인이다.

11 **해설** ②는 의미상 나머지 세 개 모두를 뜻하므로 the others가 알맞다.
「one ~ the others ...」: (셋 이상에서) 하나는 ~ 나머지는 모두 …
① another : 또 다른 하나
③「some ~ others ...」: (정해지지 않은 다수 중) 몇몇은 ~, 다른 일부는 …
④「one ~ the other ...」: (둘 중) 하나는 ~, 나머지 하나는 …
⑤「one ~ another ... the other -」: (셋 중) 하나는 ~, 또 다른 하나는 …, 나머지 하나는 -

12 **해설** 의미상 완료시제이고 주어가 복수이므로 have tried가 알맞다.
「All (of) + 복수 명사」→ 복수 취급
해석 축구 국가 대표팀은 올해 잘했다. 모든 선수들이 매우 열심히 노력했다.

13 **해설** 첫 번째 빈칸에는 I를 가리키는 재귀대명사 myself가 알맞고(재귀 용법), 두 번째 빈칸에는 We를 가리키는 ourselves가 알맞다(강조 용법).
해석 • 나는 내 자신이 자랑스럽다.
• 그 개들에 대해 걱정하지 마. 우리가 직접 그것들을 돌볼 수 있어.

14 **해설** ③의 herself는 강조 용법으로 쓰인 재귀대명사이므로 생략이 가능하다.

15 **해설** 정해지지 않은 다수 중 일부는 some, 다른 일부는 others로 나타낸다.

16 **해설** 「one ~ another ... the other -」: (셋 중) 하나는 ~, 또 다른 하나는 …, 나머지 하나는 - ③ other → another
해석 그녀는 세 나라에 가봤다. 한 곳은 영국, 또 한 곳은 프랑스, 나머지 한 곳은 터키이다.

17 **해설** ③의 itself는 강조 용법으로 쓰인 재귀대명사로 생략해도 의미 차이가 없다. 나머지는 재귀 용법으로 쓰였다.

18 **해설** ①은 강조 용법으로 쓰인 재귀대명사이고, 나머지는 재귀 용법으로 쓰였다.

19 **해설** 둘 중에서 하나와 나머지 하나를 표현할 때는 「one ~ the other ...」를 사용한다.
해석 나는 선물을 두 개 받았다. 하나는 엄마한테, 나머지 하나는 친구한테 받았다.

20 **해설** 「each of + 복수명사」는 단수 취급하므로 has가 알맞다. 「all of + 복수명사」는 복수 취급하므로 look이 알맞다.
해석 • 아이들은 각자 자신만의 꿈이 있다.
• 이 토마토들 모두 신선해 보인다.

21 **해설** 부정문에는 anything을, 긍정문에는 something을 쓴다.
해석 • 그녀는 어둠 속에서 아무것도 볼 수 없었다.
• 너는 무언가를 말하기 전에 그것에 대해 충분히 생각해야 한다.

22 **해설** by oneself : 혼자서, 홀로(= alone)

23 **해설** 이어지는 동사 is가 단수형이므로 복수 취급하는 Both는 빈칸에 들어갈 수 없다.

서술형

24 **해설** we를 지칭하는 재귀대명사 ourselves가 알맞다.
enjoy oneself : 즐거운 시간을 보내다
해석 우리는 휴가를 가면, 항상 즐겁게 보낸다.

25 **해설** '모든' 건물이 붕괴되었다고 했으므로 All이 알맞다.

26 **해설** '각자' 컴퓨터를 가지고 있다고 했으므로 each가 알맞다.

27 **해설** 방문한 곳들이 '하나도 흥미롭지 않았다'고 했으므로 None이 알맞다.

28 **해설** Children을 가리키는 재귀대명사 themselves가 알맞다.
해석 어린아이들은 겨울 동안 다칠 수도 있기 때문에 조심해야 한다.

29 **해설** 둘 중 나머지 하나를 뜻하므로 the other가 알맞다.
해석 나는 책 두 권이 있다. 하나는 요리에 관한 것이고, 나머지 하나는 과학에 관한 것이다.

30 **해설** another는 '또 다른 하나'의 의미로 쓰인다. 셋 중 두 번째를 말할 때는 another를 사용한다. 「one ~ another ... the other -」: (셋 중) 하나는 ~, 또 다른 하나는 …, 나머지 하나는 -
해석 • 나는 이 모자가 마음에 안 들어요. 다른 것을 보여주실 수 있나요?
• 그녀는 세 명의 오빠가 있다. 한 명은 베이징에 살고, 또 한 명은 시카고에 살고, 나머지 한 명은 뉴욕에 산다.

31 **해설** (정해지지 않은 다수 중에서) 몇몇은 ~, 다른 일부는 … : some ~ others ...
해석 어떤 사람들은 여가 시간에 쉬는 것을 좋아한다. 다른 사람들은 여행하는 것을 좋아한다.

32 **해설** (셋 중) 하나는 ~, 또 다른 하나는 …, 나머지 하나는 - : one ~ another ... the other -

해석 나는 세 괴물을 만났다. 그것들 중 하나는 마녀였다. 다른 하나는 뱀파이어였다. 나머지 하나는 화장하지 않은 우리 엄마였다!

33 **해설** 셋 이상에서 '또 다른 하나'를 가리킬 때는 another를 사용한다.

해석 저는 이 셔츠가 마음에 들지 않아요. 다른 것을 보여주세요.

34 **해설** 정해진 범위 안에서 '하나'를 가리킬 때는 one을 '나머지 모두'를 가리킬 때는 the others를 사용한다.

해석 다섯 벌의 셔츠가 있어요. 하나는 매우 비싸고, 나머지 모두(전부)는 그렇지 않아요.

Chapter 08 형용사와 부사

1 형용사의 쓰임

▶▶ p. 172

A

1 impressive 2 reasonable
3 intelligent 4 effective
5 true

B

1 This book seems very difficult.
2 My elder brother became a doctor.
3 The prince made her happy.

2 주의해야 할 형용사의 어순

▶▶ p. 173

A

1 something attractive
2 such a beautiful
3 something happy 4 such a nice
5 such a foolish 6 somewhere nice

B

1 something cold 2 somewhere quiet
3 anything wrong 4 such a famous director
5 such a cute girl

3 the + 형용사

▶▶ p. 174

A

1 the young 2 the rich
3 the poor 4 the homeless
5 the blind 6 the deaf
7 the disabled

B

1 are 2 the 3 the
4 were 5 A 6 the
7 a

4 some / any

▶▶ p. 175

A

1 some 2 any
3 some 4 any
5 some, any 6 any

B

1 some fresh air 2 any good hotels
3 any further questions

5 many / much / a lot of

▶▶ p. 176

A

1 a lot of 2 many
3 much 4 a lot of, many
5 much, lots of 6 much, a lot of

B

1 much sugar 2 lots(plenty) of fish
3 many cars 4 much money
5 lots(plenty) of books

6 few / a few / little / a little

▸▸ p. 177

A

1 a few 2 a little 3 few
4 a few 5 little

B

1 little 2 few 3 little
4 a few 5 a little 6 A few

7 부사의 형태와 쓰임

▸▸ p. 178~179

A

1 run 2 fantastic 3 well
4 I happened to see her at the cafeteria

B

1 carefully 2 lately
3 mostly 4 nearly

C

1 carefully 2 silently
3 personally

D

1 newly built 2 deeply moved
3 too loudly

8 빈도부사

▸▸ p. 180

A

1 Do you usually have breakfast?
2 I have sometimes lost my wallet.
3 I could hardly recognize her at the party.
4 The garden is always watered automatically.

B

1 is always polite to
2 sometimes play tennis on
3 has never been to
4 can hardly understand what

9 일반동사 + 부사 vs. 연결동사 + 형용사

▸▸ p. 181

A

1 good 2 silently
3 graceful 4 peaceful

B

1 comfortably → comfortable
2 famously → famous
3 beautiful → beautifully
4 reasonably → reasonable

10 타동사 + 부사

▸▸ p. 182

A

1 try them on 2 pick her up
3 turn it up

B

1 switch(turn) on 2 throw it away
3 put out

Chapter 08 학교 시험 대비 문제

▸▸ p. 183~190

01 ③ 02 ④ 03 ④ 04 ④ 05 ② 06 ④ 07 ② 08 ④, ⑤ 09 ③, ⑤ 10 ①, ④ 11 ⑤ 12 ⑤ 13 ③ 14 ⑤ 15 ③, ⑤ 16 ③ 17 ② 18 ② 19 ③ 20 ③ 21 ④ 22 ①, ⑤ 23 ④ 24 ③ 25 ③ 26 ② 27 ⑤ 28 ④ 29 ③ 30 ④ 31 ⑤ 32 ② 33 ③ 34 ⑤ 35 ④ 36 ③ 37 ⑤ 38 ③ 39 ② 40 ③

서술형 41 nothing interesting 42 happily → happy 43 made me happy 44 enough 45 any 46 a good cook, a careful driver 47 a wonderful pianist(piano player), a creative writer 48 Their home was small, and had little furniture. 49 Few doctors deny that exercise is good for health.

01 **해설** ③ 「명사 + -ly」 → 형용사, ①②④⑤ 「형용사 + -ly」 → 부사

02 **해설** 첫 번째 문장은 권유문이므로 빈칸에는 some이 알맞고, 두 번째 문장은 부정문이므로 빈칸에는 any가 알맞다.

해석 • 쿠키 좀 드시겠어요?
• 나는 공상 과학 영화를 전혀 본 적이 없다.

03 **해설** ④ alive는 서술적 용법으로만 쓰이는 형용사이므로 live로 써야 한다.

04 **해설** ④ call off : ~을 취소하다

05 **해설** '몇몇의'라는 의미로 셀 수 있는 복수명사 앞에 쓸 수 있는 것은 a few이다.

06 **해설** the poor : 가난한 사람들(= poor people)

해석 그녀는 가난한 사람들을 돕는 데 그녀의 평생을 바쳤다.

07 **해설** ② 명사 — 형용사, ①③④⑤ 형용사 — 부사

08 **해설** 빈도부사는 일반동사 앞, be동사·조동사 뒤, have와 p.p. 사이에 위치한다.
④ never have seen → have never seen
⑤ visit sometimes → sometimes visit

09 **해설** 동사를 수식하는 부사가 와야 하므로 ③ successful → successfully ⑤ easy → easily

10 **해설** ①, ④ 빈칸 뒤에 형용사 보어가 있으므로 상태나 변화를 나타내는 연결동사가 와야 한다. ②, ⑤는 주어가 단수(It)이므로 알맞지 않다.

11 **해설** ⑤의 두 문장 모두 late가 '늦게'(부사)라는 의미로 쓰였다.
① 건강한(형용사) — 잘(부사)
② 예쁜(형용사) — 아주, 꽤(부사)
③ 높이(부사) — 높은(형용사)
④ 열심히(부사) — 어려운(형용사)

12 **해설** ① work는 셀 수 없는 명사이므로 many → much ② bread는 셀 수 없는 명사이므로 are → is, many → much ③ information은 셀 수 없는 명사이므로 many → much ④ furniture는 셀 수 없는 명사이므로 were → was, furnitures → furniture

13 **해설** 동사를 수식하는 부사가 들어가야 하고, 의미상 brightly가 알맞다.

해석 태양이 그녀의 머리 위로 밝게 빛나고 있다.

14 **해설** ⑤ 빈도부사는 have와 p.p. 사이에 와야 하므로 seldom have played → have seldom played

15 **해설** '시각 장애인들'이라는 복수 보통명사의 의미는 the blind 또는 blind people로 나타낼 수 있다.

16 **해설** ③ 목적어가 대명사일 때 반드시 타동사와 부사 사이에 와야 하므로 turn off it → turn it off

17 **해설** money는 셀 수 없는 명사이므로 any가 알맞다. 셀 수 있는 복수명사 앞에 오는 ③, ④, ⑤는 알맞지 않다. ① a lot은 '많이'의 뜻을 가진 부사이다.

해석 너는 돈을 좀 가지고 있니?

18 **해설** ② 첫 번째 문장의 hard는 '열심히'를 뜻하는 부사이고, 두 번째 문장의 hardly는 '거의 ~하지 않다'를 뜻하는 빈도부사이므로 두 문장의 의미가 같지 않다.

19 **해설** put off : ~을 미루다 / take off : ~을 벗다

해석 • 그것을 월요일까지 미루지 마라, 알겠니?
• 그것을 벗고 이 셔츠를 입어라.

20 **해설** little, a little은 셀 수 없는 명사 앞에 온다.

21 **해설** ④ '매우, 훨씬'의 뜻으로 비교급을 강조하는 말, ①②③⑤ '많은'을 뜻하는 수량 형용사

22 **해설** ① 감각동사 sound 다음에 보어로 형용사가 와야 하므로 greatly → great
⑤ 5형식 문장에서 목적격보어로 형용사가 와야 하므로 angrily → angry

23 **해설** 복수명사(friends) 앞이고 의미상 '약간 있는'이 적절하므로 a few, 셀 수 없는 명사(time) 앞이고 의미상 '거의 없는'이 적절하므로 little

해석 • Kathy는 수줍음이 많지만, 친구가 몇 명 있다.
• 나는 밥 먹을 시간이 거의 없어서, 식사를 건너뛰었다.

24 **해설** ③ hard가 각각 '많이(부사), 딱딱한(형용사), 열심히(부사)'의 의미로 쓰였다.

해석 • 밖에 비가 많이 오고 있다.
• 그녀의 얼굴이 돌처럼 딱딱하게 굳은 것 같다.
• 그는 영어 일기를 쓰기 위해 열심히 노력하는 중이다.

25 **해설** -thing으로 끝나는 대명사는 형용사가 뒤에서 수식하므로 cold something → something cold

26 **해설** ② -body로 끝나는 대명사는 형용사가 뒤에서 수식하므로 famous anybody → anybody famous

27 **해설** ⑤ deny : ~을 거절하다(= turn down)

28 **해설** 셀 수 있는 복수명사 앞에 올 수 있고 의미상 '상당수'를 뜻하는 Quite a few가 알맞다.

29 해설 ③ '많은'을 뜻하는 a lot of 뒤에 온 word는 셀 수 있는 명사이므로 words로 써야 알맞다.

30 해설 빈도부사는 be동사와 p.p. 사이에 오므로 always is checked → is always checked

31 해설 ⑤ 타동사와 부사 사이에 대명사가 와야 하므로 pick up her → pick her up

32 해설 The young은 Young people의 의미이다. 복수 취급을 하므로 was를 were로 써야 한다.

해석 젊은 사람들이 파티에서 어르신들에게 음식을 대접하고 있었다.

33 해설 ③ 빈칸 뒤에 형용사 cold가 보어로 쓰였으므로 상태나 변화를 나타내는 연결동사가 들어가야 하고, 의미상 became이 알맞다.

해석 날씨가 갑자기 추워져서 나는 외투를 입었다.

34 해설 빈도부사는 have와 p.p. 사이에 와야 하므로 always have wanted → have always wanted

35 해설 조건문에서는 any를 쓰므로 some → any

36 해설 ③ often은 빈도부사이므로 일반동사인 refer 앞에 오는 것이 알맞다.

해석 나는 영어로 자신을 표현하는 방법을 모를 때, 종종 그 사전을 참조한다.

37 해설 ⑤ most는 '가장 많이'의 뜻을 나타내는 부사이다.
① The rich는 복수 취급하므로 is → are
② 부정문에는 any를 사용하므로 some → any
③ '몸이 불편한 사람들'을 뜻하므로 a disabled → the disabled
④ 감각동사 sound 뒤에는 형용사가 오므로 wonderfully → wonderful

38 해설 ③「the + 형용사」는 복수 취급하므로 likes → like

39 해설 ② keep은 상태를 나타내는 연결동사로 형용사와 함께 쓰므로 silently → silent

40 해설 ③ food는 셀 수 없는 명사이므로 few → little

서술형

41 해설 -one, -body, -thing, -where로 끝나는 부정대명사는 형용사가 뒤에서 수식한다.

42 해설 감각동사 feel 뒤에는 형용사가 온다.

해석 외국에 방문하기 전에 공부를 하려고 노력해라. 사람들이 너와 함께 있는 것을 즐거워하게 하기 위해서 그 나라의 관습에 대한 것을 아는 것이 도움이 된다.

43 해설 「make + 목적어 + 목적격보어」의 5형식 문장이며, 목적격보어 자리에 형용사가 와서 목적어의 상태를 설명한다.

44 해설 enough 형 충분한 부 충분히

해석
• 나는 정말 배부르다. 나는 충분한 음식을 먹었다.
• 그녀는 그 어려운 질문에 대답할 수 있을 만큼 충분히 똑똑했다.
• 나는 그 비싼 재킷을 살 수 있을 만큼 충분한 돈이 없다.

45 해설 부정문에서 '조금도, 하나도, 전혀'를 의미하는 any가 알맞다.

해석 **A** 잠깐 얘기 좀 할 수 있을까?
B 미안한데, 나는 지금 시간이 전혀 없어. 방과 후에 내가 네게 전화할게.

[46-47]

해석 나의 가족을 너에게 소개할게. 나의 아빠는 중학교 영어 선생님이다. 그는 학생들을 친절하게 대한다. 그는 테니스를 정말 잘 친다. 나의 엄마는 요리를 매우 잘 한다. 그녀는 운전을 굉장히 조심스럽게 한다. 내 여동생 Jenny는 피아노를 정말 잘 친다. 그녀가 무언가를 묘사할 때 그녀는 그것을 창의적으로 쓴다.

<보기> Andy의 아버지는 친절한 중학교 영어 선생님이다. 그는 훌륭한 테니스 선수이다.

46 해설 is good at cooking → a good cook
drives very carefully → a careful driver

해석 Andy의 어머니는 훌륭한 요리사다. 그녀는 조심스러운 운전자다.

47 해설 plays the piano wonderfully → a wonderful pianist(piano player)
writes ~ creatively → a creative writer

해석 Andy의 여동생인 Jenny는 뛰어난 피아노 연주자다. 그녀는 창의적인 작가다.

48 해설 furniture는 셀 수 없는 명사이므로 '(양이) 거의 없는'이라는 뜻의 little로 수식한다.

49 해설 doctors는 복수 명사이므로 '(수가) 거의 없는'이라는 뜻의 few로 수식한다.

Chapter 09 비교

1 as + 원급 + as

▸▸ p. 192

A

1 as big as　　2 as interesting as

3 twice as fast as

4 twice as many books as

5 isn't as(so) expensive as

6 doesn't work as(so) hard as

7 half as many books as

2 as + 원급 + as possible

▸▸ p. 193

A

1 I can　2 possible　3 he could　4 you can

B

1 as soon as possible

2 as much as possible

3 as many places as possible

4 as fast as he could

3 비교급 + than

▸▸ p. 194~195

A

1 yours　2 mine　3 hers　4 ours　5 Yujin's

B

1 better than his (plan)

2 fresher than that (bread)

3 cheaper than these (jeans)

4 more reasonable than hers(her idea)

C

1 She is older than me.

2 You are taller than him.

3 These oranges taste better than those (oranges).

4 The math exam was more difficult than the English exam.

D

1 senior　2 junior　3 prefer

4 less + 원급 + than

▸▸ p. 196

A

1 isn't as(so) good as, is better than

2 is less big than, is bigger than

3 isn't as(so) popular as, is less popular

4 wasn't as(so) short as, was shorter than

5 as well as, less well than

5 비교급 강조

▸▸ p. 197

A

1 very　2 much　3 much

4 very　5 even

B

1 much better than　2 a lot more difficult than

3 a lot colder than　4 much more beautiful than

6 the + 비교급, the + 비교급

▸▸ p. 198

A

1 The more, the wiser　2 The more, the richer

3 The more, the stronger

4 The harder, the more fluently

B

1 The higher, the colder　2 The better, the happier

3 The longer, the more　4 The less, the higher

7 비교급 + and + 비교급

▸▸ p. 199

A

1 hotter and hotter　2 better and better

3 more and more slowly

4 more and more popular

5 more and more nervous

6 fatter and fatter　7 healthier and healthier

8 more and more excited

8 the + 최상급

▶▶ p.200~201

A

1 faster, slower, the fastest, the slowest

2 higher, lower, the highest, the lowest

B

1 the biggest planet　2 the hottest day

3 the tallest building　4 the longest country

5 the most popular sport

6 the most important thing

C

1 the happiest　2 the biggest

3 the most beautiful

9 one of the + 최상급 + 복수명사

▶▶ p.202

A

1 one of the brightest students

2 one of the most popular singers

3 one of the most important things

4 the worst dish, have ever cooked

5 the most boring film, had ever watched

6 the most beautiful place, had ever visited

7 one of the best players

8 the most delicious cake, have ever eaten

10 원급과 비교급을 이용한 최상급 표현

▶▶ p.203~204

A

1 the biggest city, any other city, than

2 the best, No one, than, as(so) well

3 the politest student, all the other students, politer

4 the most carefully, as(so) carefully, No one, than

B

1 better than any other student in class,
better than all the other students in class,
better than Jolly,
as(so) well as Jolly

2 more famous than any other scholar in the university,
more famous than all the other scholars in the university,
more famous than Professor Charles,
as(so) famous as Professor Charles

3 more beautiful than any other flower in the garden,
more beautiful than all the other flowers in the garden,
more beautiful than the red roses,
as(so) beautiful as the red roses

4 more clearly than any other teacher in school,
more clearly than all the other teachers in school,
more clearly than my teacher,
as(so) clearly as my teacher

5 longer than any other country in the world,
longer than all the other countries in the world,
longer than Chile,
as(so) long as Chile

Chapter 09 학교 시험 대비 문제

▶▶ p.205~212

01 ③ **02** ③ **03** ②, ⑤ **04** ④ **05** ③ **06** ①, ④ **07** ③ **08** ⑤ **09** ④, ⑤ **10** ① **11** ④ **12** ⑤ **13** ② **14** ④ **15** ③ **16** ④ **17** ③ **18** ⑤ **19** ④ **20** ③ **21** ⑤ **22** ④ **23** ③

서술형 **24** The more, the healthier **25** he could **26** the most important **27** The higher, the colder **28** one of the greatest scientists **29** as soon(quickly) as possible **30** milder than that of Seattle **31** much(a lot, even, still, far) prettier **32** The sooner, the faster **33** senior **34** famous than **35** old as this theater **36** one of the most popular sports **37** Fewer and fewer **38** more and more serious **39** younger, the youngest, the oldest **40** twice as, as **41** The longer, the more **42** taller **43** as tall as **44** the tallest **45** earlier **46** later **47** as early as **48** slower **49** faster **50** the fastest **51** three times as expensive **52** twice as expensive **53** the cheapest

01 해설 as long as : ~만큼 오래
해석 나는 네가 원하는 만큼 오래 이곳에 머물면 좋겠다.

02 해설 prefer A to B : B보다 A를 더 좋아하다
해석 나는 야구보다 축구를 더 좋아한다.

03 해설 ① I was → I did
② 라틴어에서 유래한 단어의 비교급 문장에서는 than 대신 to를 쓴다.
③ 동사 dances를 수식하는 부사 beautifully가 알맞다.
④ 원급을 강조하므로 much → very
⑤ much, a lot, even, still, far는 비교급을 강조하는 표현이다.

04 해설 ① 주격보어로 형용사의 원급이 와야 하므로 beautifully → beautiful
② 「비교급 + than any other + 단수명사」, boys → boy
③ 최상급이나 서수 앞에는 the를 쓴다. a most → the most
⑤ more and more cold → colder and colder

05 해설 younger than = junior to, older than = senior to

06 해설 ① 「부정주어 ... as(so) + 원급 + as ~」, 동사를 꾸며주는 부사의 원급 beautifully가 알맞다.
② very는 원급을 강조하는 표현이며 비교급을 강조할 때는 much, a lot, even, still, far를 쓴다.
③ 「비교급 + than any other + 단수명사」, cities → city
④ much, a lot, even, still, far는 비교급을 강조하는 표현이다.
⑤ prefer A to B : B보다 A를 더 좋아하다, than → to

07 해설 동사를 꾸며주는 부사의 원급이 알맞다.
해석 나는 가능한 한 빨리 그 문제를 해결하려고 노력했다.

08 해설 ⑤ 「비교급 + than all the other + 복수명사」, boy → boys

09 해설 ① very → much(a lot, even, still, far)
② 「one of the + 최상급 + 복수명사」, activity → activities
③ 비교의 대상이 Seoul이 아니라 Seoul의 prices(물가)이므로 Seoul → those in Seoul

10 해설 very는 형용사나 부사의 원급을 강조할 때 사용하고, 비교급을 강조할 때는 much, a lot, still, even, far 등을 사용한다.

11 해설 「be동사 + 주격보어」의 형태가 되어야 하므로 as와 as 사이에는 형용사의 원급이 와야 하는데 ④의 kindly는 부사이다.

12 해설 부정주어 No other 뒤에 can이 와야 부정의 뜻이 된다. can't → can

13 해설 very는 형용사나 부사의 원급을 강조할 때 사용하고, 비교급을 강조할 때는 much, a lot, still, even, far 등을 사용한다.
해석 • 너는 오늘 정말 아름다워 보인다.
• 그녀는 그녀의 나이보다 훨씬 더 어려 보인다.

14 해설 「비교급 + than any other + 단수명사」, girls → girl

15 해설 「less + 원급 + than」 → 「not as(so) + 원급 + as」
해석 그의 일은 나의 일보다 덜 중요하다. → 그의 일은 나의 일만큼 중요하지 않다.

16 해설 ① 최상급 앞에는 the를 쓴다. a longest → the longest
② 동사 cook을 수식하는 부사의 원급이 알맞다. good → well
③ I am → I do
⑤ 「one of the + 최상급 + 복수명사」, city → cities

17 해설 ③ better 앞에 정관사 the가 있고, 범위를 나타내는 전치사구 in this shop이 있으므로 최상급 best로 써야 알맞다.

18 해설 셋 중에서 Tom이 가장 빠르고, David가 가장 느리므로 ⑤가 표의 내용과 일치한다.

19 해설 「not as(so) + 원급 + as」 → 「less + 원급 + than」
해석 저 컴퓨터는 이것만큼 비싸지 않다.
= 저 컴퓨터는 이것보다 덜 비싸다.

20 해설 빈칸 다음에 비교 표현인 more creative than이 오므로 빈칸에는 비교급을 강조하는 말이 들어가야 한다. very는 원급을 강조하는 말이다.
해석 그의 새 음악은 그의 이전 음악보다 훨씬 더 창조적이다.

21 해설 ① can → could
② more and more warm → warmer and warmer
③ than → to
④ as → than

22 해설 ④ inventor → inventors
「one of the + 최상급 + 복수명사」 : 가장 ~한 것들 중 하나

해석 토마스 에디슨은 세계에서 가장 위대한 발명가들 중 한 사람으로 알려져 있다.

23 해설 ③은 내 가방이 상자보다 가볍다는 의미이고, 나머지는 내 가방이 상자보다 무겁다는 의미이다.

서술형

24 해설 「the + 비교급 ~, the + 비교급 …」: ~하면 할수록, 더 …한

25 해설 「as + 원급 + as possible」= 「as + 원급 + as + 주어 + can(could)」: 가능한 한 ~한(하게)

해석 그는 가능한 한 많은 책을 읽으려고 노력했다.

26 해설 「부정주어 ... as(so) + 원급 + as ~」= 「the + 최상급」

해석 어떤 것도 환경 운동만큼 중요하지 않다.
= 환경 운동이 가장 중요한 것이다.

27 해설 「the + 비교급 ~, the + 비교급 …」: ~하면 할수록, 더 …한

해석 우리가 높이 올라갈수록, 점점 더 추워졌다.

28 해설 「one of the + 최상급 + 복수명사」: 가장 ~한 것들 중 하나

해석 그는 세계에서 가장 훌륭한 과학자들 중 한 명이다.

29 해설 as soon(quickly) as possible : 가능한 한 빨리

30 해설 비교의 대상이 Seattle이 아니라 Seattle의 climate(기후)이므로 대명사 that을 써야 한다.

31 해설 비교급을 강조할 때는 much, a lot, still, even, far 등을 사용한다. pretty의 비교급은 prettier이다.

해석 그녀는 네가 생각했던 것보다 훨씬 더 예쁘다.

32 해설 「the + 비교급 ~, the + 비교급 …」: ~하면 할수록, 더 …한

해석 네가 그것을 빨리 시작할수록, 너는 그것을 더 빨리 끝낼 수 있다.

33 해설 older than = senior to, younger than = junior to

해석 그는 그의 동료보다 나이가 더 많다.

34 해설 「the + 최상급」→「부정주어 ... 비교급 + than ~」

해석 에펠 탑은 파리에서 가장 유명한 곳이다.
= 파리에서 다른 어떤 곳도 에펠 탑보다 더 유명하지 않다.

35 해설 「the + 최상급」→「부정주어 ... as (so) + 원급 + as ~」

해석 이 극장은 마을에서 가장 오래된 건물이다.
= 마을에서 다른 어떤 건물도 이 극장만큼 오래되지 않았다.

36 해설 「one of the + 최상급 + 복수명사」: 가장 ~한 것들 중 하나

37 해설 「비교급 + and + 비교급」: 점점 더 ~한

38 해설 「비교급 + and + 비교급」: 점점 더 ~한
비교급이 「more + 원급」 형태일 때는 「more and more + 원급」으로 표현한다.

39 해설 비교급과 최상급을 사용하여 문장을 완성한다.

해석
- Ann은 Susan보다 어리다.
- Sarah는 세 소녀들 중 가장 어리다.
- Susan은 세 소녀들 중 가장 나이가 많다.

40 해설 「twice(three times, half 등의 배수사) + as + 원급 + as」: ~배로 …한

41 해설 「the + 비교급 ~, the + 비교급 …」: ~하면 할수록, 더 …한

[42-47]

해설 동등 비교 「as + 원급 + as」, 비교급, 최상급을 사용하여 문장을 완성한다.

해석
42 Lisa는 Sarah보다 키가 더 크다.
43 Julie는 Sarah만큼 키가 크다.
44 Lisa는 세 여자 아이들 중에서 가장 키가 크다.
45 Julie는 Sarah보다 더 일찍 일어난다.
46 Sarah는 Lisa보다 더 늦게 일어난다.
47 Julie는 Lisa만큼 일찍 일어난다.

[48-53]

해설 「비교급 + than」: ~보다 …한(하게), 「the + 최상급」: 가장 ~한(하게), 「배수사 + as + 원급 + as」: ~배로 …한(하게)을 사용하여 문장을 완성한다.

해석
48 Duocraft는 Grand Star보다 더 느리다.
49 Thunder는 Duocraft보다 더 빠르다.
50 Thunder는 세 가지 신형 자동차들 중에서 가장 빠르다.
51 Grand Star는 Duocraft보다 세 배 비싸다.
52 Thunder는 Duocraft보다 두 배 비싸다.
53 Duocraft는 세 가지 신형 자동차들 중에서 가장 싸다.

Chapter 10 전치사

1 시간 전치사 I - at / on / in

▶▶ p.214

A

1 in 2 on 3 at 4 in 5 on

B

1 in July 2 on Monday
3 at the end of this month

2 시간 전치사 II - before / after 등

▶▶ p.215

A

1 in 2 within 3 in
4 After 5 before

B

1 be announced in two weeks
2 the country the day after tomorrow
3 fail to graduate within four years
4 often goes to bed after
5 before getting out of the room

3 시간 전치사 III - for / during 등

▶▶ p.216

A

1 for 2 by 3 by
4 during 5 until(till) 6 from
7 since 8 for 9 from

4 장소·위치 전치사 I - at / in 등

▶▶ p.217

A

1 over 2 under 3 on
4 in 5 above 6 in

5 장소·위치 전치사 II - in front of / behind 등

▶▶ p.218

A

1 behind 2 in front of
3 around 4 between
5 among 6 by(beside, next to)

6 방향 전치사

▶▶ p.219~220

A

1 along 2 across 3 down
4 up 5 out of 6 into
7 over 8 through 9 toward(s)

B

1 through, into 2 down, into
3 out of

C

1 dived into the deep water
2 get out of his office
3 went into the kitchen

7 수단·도구 / 재료·원료 전치사

▶▶ p.221

A

1 in 2 by 3 from
4 of 5 into 6 in
7 of 8 with 9 through

8 원인·이유 / 목적·결과 전치사

▶▶ p.222

A

1 of 2 for 3 on
4 To 5 into 6 at
7 for

Chapter 10 학교 시험 대비 문제

▶▶ p.223~226

01 ③ 02 ③ 03 ④ 04 ① 05 ③ 06 ② 07 ① 08 ③ 09 ④ 10 ① 11 ③ 12 ② 13 ④ 14 ④ 15 ③ 16 ③ 17 ⑤ 18 ⑤

서술형 19 The man walked to(toward(s)) the door. 20 To, surprise 21 among → between 22 He traveled around Europe for two months. 23 I will do volunteer work during the summer vacation. 24 at 25 in 26 on 27 at 28 in 29 in 30 are playing soccer in the park 31 are running to(toward(s)) the school

01 **해설** 전치사 at은 '~에'의 의미로 감정의 원인을 나타낸다. be angry at : ~에 화가 나다

해석 나는 그의 실수에 화가 났다.

02 **해설** under : ~의 바로 아래에(떨어져서)

03 **해설** '커튼 뒤에 숨었다'의 의미가 되어야 하므로 behind가 알맞다.

해석 그들은 커튼 뒤에 숨었다.

04 **해설** to는 감정의 명사와 함께 쓰여 '~하게도'의 의미를 나타내므로 For → To

해석 굉장히 슬프게도, 그의 아버지가 그의 생일날 아침에 돌아가셨다.

05 **해설** in + 국가명 / at + 한 지점

해석 • 7월은 한국에서 가장 더운 달이다.
• 공항에 굉장히 많은 사람들이 있다.

06 **해설** in : ~이 지나면

07 **해설** '~이 지나면'의 의미로 시간의 경과를 나타내는 전치사 in / '~으로'의 뜻으로 사망의 직접적인 원인을 나타내는 전치사 of

해석 • 그녀는 며칠 지나면 나아질 것이다.
• 그녀의 아버지는 암으로 돌아가셨다.

08 **해설** ③ 소년들이 선생님 '주변에' 모였다는 의미가 되어야 하므로 among → around

09 **해설** '~을 위하여, ~하러'를 뜻하는 전치사 for가 알맞다. go (out) for a walk : 산책하러 나가다

10 **해설** '~까지'의 의미로 동작이나 상태의 계속을 나타내는 till〔until〕이 알맞다.

해석 나는 그들을 오늘 저녁 6시까지 기다릴 것이다.

11 **해설** on weekdays : 주중에, on weekends : 주말에

해석 그 제과점은 주중에 오전 9시부터 오후 8시까지 연다.

12 **해설** '원료(화학적 변화)'를 나타낼 때는 전치사 from을 사용한다.

13 **해설** 일정한 기간을 나타내는 '~동안'이라는 뜻의 전치사 for는 현재완료 시제와 주로 함께 쓰인다.

14 **해설** ① on → over ② over → on ③ on → over ⑤ over → on

15 **해설** with : ~을 가지고(도구) / by : ~을 타고(교통수단)

해석 • 그 소녀는 양동이로 정원에 물을 주고 있다.
• 배를 타고 여행하는 것은 멋진 경험이었다.

16 **해설** in + 연도 / at + 구체적인 시각
make it : 약속 시간에 맞춰 오다

해석 • Henry는 2010년에 콘서트에서 그녀를 처음 만났다.
• 너는 4시에 서점에 올 수 있니?

17 **해설** since는 '~부터'의 뜻으로 현재완료시제와 함께 쓰인다.

해석 나는 1975년부터 이 집에서 살고 있다.

18 **해설** 한강을 수영해서 건넜다는 의미가 되어야 하므로 among → across 또는 한강에서 수영을 했다는 의미로 in도 가능하다.

서술형

19 **해설** 방향의 전치사 to〔toward(s)〕: ~ 쪽으로

20 **해설** 「to one's + 감정의 명사」: ~하게도

21 **해설** '(둘) ~ 사이에'의 의미이므로 among → between (among은 셋 이상일 때 씀)

해석 나는 두 여성 사이에서 자리를 하나 찾았다.

22 **해설** for + 주로 숫자와 함께 쓰여 일정한 기간을 나타내는 표현

23 **해설** during + 특정한 때를 나타내는 표현

[24-29]

해설 at + 구체적인 시각·시점 / on + 날짜, 요일, 특정한 날 / in + 아침, 오후, 저녁, 연도, 월, 계절

해석 8월 18일 일요일
나는 아침 일찍 6시 30분에 일어났다. 왜냐하면 할 일이 많았기 때문이다. 나는 보통 일요일마다 늦게까지 침대에 누워있지만 엄마가 나를 깨우셨다. 나는 7시에 가족들과 함께 아침을 먹고 집에서 나와 친구들을 만나기로 한 장소로 향했다. 오늘은 내 가장 친한 친구의 생일이어서 그의 집에서 파티가 있었다. 그는 2006년에 태어났고 막 15살이 되었다. 그의 생일을 축하하며 우리는 점심을 함께 먹었고 저녁에 영화를 보러 가기로 결정했다.

30 **해설** in : ~에서(비교적 넓은 장소)

해석 두 소년이 공원에서 축구를 하고 있다.

31 **해설** to〔toward(s)〕: ~ 쪽으로

해석 두 소년이 학교 쪽으로 달려가고 있다.

Chapter 11 관계사

1 주격 관계대명사 - who / which / that

▸▸ p.228~229

A

1	who	2	which
3	take	4	which
5	eat	6	which

B

1 who → which 또는 that
2 what → which 또는 that
3 who → which 또는 that
4 look → looks
5 were → was
6 make → makes
7 which → who 또는 that
8 are → is

C

1 the sitcom which(that) makes
2 the meat which(that) was
3 The man who(that) answered the phone
4 The building which(that) was destroyed
5 the woman who(that) is talking to
6 The professor who(that) had influenced
7 the man who(that) is

2 목적격 관계대명사 - whom / which / that

▸▸ p.230~231

A

1	which	2	which
3	whom	4	which
5	which	6	which

B

1 what → which 또는 that
2 her → 삭제
3 it → 삭제
4 whom → which 또는 that
5 where → which 또는 that
6 whose → which 또는 that

C

1 the check which(that) the company offered
2 The eye doctor who(m)(that) I saw
3 the postcards which(that) I had sent
4 the car which(that) she was eager
5 Susan who(m)(that) I paid for the job was working
6 the money which(that) I gave you
7 The woman who(m)(that) I took a picture of
8 Those houses which(that) American Indians built

3 소유격 관계대명사 - whose / of which

▸▸ p.232~233

A

1	of which	2	whose
3	which	4	whose
5	which	6	whose
7	whose		

B

1 who → whose
2 which → whose
3 whose → who(m) 또는 that
4 that → whose
5 which → whose
6 which → whose
7 who → whose

C

1 The car whose door
2 a company whose president
3 his friends whose concerns
4 Egypt whose capital
5 The young whose parents

4 관계대명사 that

▸▸ p.234

A

1	that	2	whom
3	that	4	who

B

1	that → which	2	whose → that
3	that → which		

5 관계대명사 what

▸▸ p.235~236

A

1 what　2 what　3 that
4 What　5 What　6 what
7 that　8 what　9 that
10 What

B

1 관　2 의　3 의
4 관　5 의　6 관
7 관

C

1 what you sow
2 what my father left
3 what his teacher said
4 what she is doing
5 what I had done before

6 전치사 + 관계대명사

▸▸ p.237~238

A

1 for which　2 which
3 whom　4 by whom
5 at which　6 for whom
7 on which　8 with whom
9 with which

B

1 her old friend with whom she used to play the piano,
her old friend whom(that) she used to play the piano with
2 the article about which I told you,
the article which(that) I told you about
3 the name of the guy to whom I spoke,
the name of the guy whom(that) I spoke to
4 with whom everybody would like to play,
whom(that) everybody would like to play with

C

1 in which we have been
2 you were looking for
3 in which I can find
4 I had a fight with

7 관계대명사의 생략

▸▸ p.239

A

1 that　2 who was
3 who was　4 that
5 that

B

1 The party that(which) we went to last night was amazing.
2 The concert which(that) was planned to begin at 3 o'clock was cancelled.
3 Ramen was made in 1950s by a man who(that) was called Ando.
4 Exercise helps control our weight by using extra calories that(which) we ate.
5 Who's the girl who(that) is dancing with your brother?

8 관계부사 I – where / when

▸▸ p.240~241

A

1 where　2 which
3 where　4 which
5 when　6 where
7 which　8 which

B

1 where(in which) I used to live
2 when(at which) all living things come to life
3 when(at which) we can see the reunification of Korea
4 where(in which) there was a gang fight every day
5 when(on which) my aunt's store opened

C

1 when we met
2 where she was born
3 where I was waiting
4 when I went abroad

9 관계부사 II - why / how

▸▸ p.242~243

A

1	why	**2**	the way
3	why	**4**	how
5	why	**6**	the way

B

1 how[the way] my boss dealt with the job
2 How[The way] the police treated
3 Why[The reason] he was arrested
4 why[the reason] she cancelled the date
5 Why[The reason] they live a long life

C

1 the way those cats wash
2 The reason I'm here
3 the way he speaks to me
4 why he got angry

10 관계사의 계속적 용법

▸▸ p.244~245

A

1 but she didn't show up
2 and it was very nice of him

B

1 The neighbor was found dead, which was
2 Brian passed the exam, which was
3 Eric didn't answer the phone, which made

C

1 where he had a meal
2 when I saw the rainbow
3 when we were just leaving for the island

11 복합관계대명사

▸▸ p.246~247

A

1	Whoever	**2**	what
3	Whoever	**4**	Whatever
5	Whichever	**6**	whatever
7	whomever	**8**	whatever

B

1 anything that she needs
2 No matter what happens to your company
3 No matter whom you ask
4 No matter what they choose
5 No matter who wins

C

1 whatever you like
2 Whatever may happen
3 whomever we like
4 Whichever club you may join
5 Whatever your plan is

12 복합관계부사

▸▸ p.248

A

1	However	**2**	wherever
3	Wherever		

B

1 Wherever you go
2 whenever I want
3 However pretty the woman is

Chapter 11 학교 시험 대비 문제

▸▸ p.249~256

01 ① **02** ② **03** ③ **04** ④ **05** ③ **06** ④ **07** ① **08** ⑤ **09** ② **10** ② **11** ③ **12** ① **13** ④ **14** ⑤ **15** ② **16** ④ **17** ② **18** ③ **19** ④ **20** ③ **21** ④ **22** ① **23** ② **24** ⑤ **25** ① **26** ② **27** ④ **28** ① **29** ② **30** ③ **31** ②, ⑤ **32** ④ **33** ⑤ **34** ③ **35** ④ **36** ① **37** ④ **38** ③ **39** ④

서술형 **40** The city which[that] we visited during summer vacation was full of many tourists. **41** why **42** where → which 또는 that **43** who graduated from an international school **44** whom[who] James' friend likes best **45** whose nickname is Black Pearl **46** where she stayed for a week **47** where he enjoyed swimming **48** where he went on a camping trip

01 **해설** 선행사 My daughter와 관계사절을 연결하는 주격 관계대명사 who가 알맞다.
해석 해외에서 방금 돌아온 나의 딸은 고등학교에 갈 것이다.

02 **해설** 첫 번째 빈칸에는 동사 say의 목적어 역할을 하면서 부사절을 이끄는 복합관계대명사 whatever(= No matter what)가 알맞다. 두 번째 빈칸에는 has의 주어 역할을 하면서, 두 번째 has의 주어절을 이끄는 복합관계대명사 whatever(= Anything that)가 알맞다.
① say 뒤에 사람 목적어가 올 수 없으므로 whoever는 답이 될 수 없다.
⑤ 의미상 선택의 의미가 아니기 때문에 whichever는 어색하다.
해석 • 네가 무슨 말을 하더라도, 나는 그의 파티에 가지 않을 것이다.
• 시작이 있는 것은 무엇이든지 또한 끝도 있다.

03 **해설** the thing which에서 선행사 the thing을 포함할 수 있는 관계대명사는 what이다.
해석 이것은 네가 고등학교에 가기 전에 해야 하는 것이다.

04 **해설** ① the way how → the way〔how〕
② 선행사가 없고 뒤에 불완전한 문장이 온다. that → what
③ that은 콤마 다음에 쓸 수 없다.(계속적 용법 불가능) that → which
⑤ 관계부사 다음에는 완전한 문장이 온다. where→ which〔that〕

05 **해설** 사람을 나타내는 선행사 that girl 뒤에 명사 hair가 나오므로 소유격 관계대명사 whose가 알맞다.
해석 **A** 머리카락이 검은색인 저 소녀는 누구니?
B 그녀는 우리 반 친구들 중 한 명이야.
A 그녀는 어디에서 왔니?
B 나는 그녀가 한국에서 왔다고 들었어.

06 **해설** 장소를 나타내는 선행사(the house)가 있고 뒤에 완전한 문장이 나오므로 관계부사 where가 들어가야 한다.
해석 이곳이 귀신이 나타나는 집이니?

07 **해설** 「선행사 + 전치사 + 관계대명사」의 구조로, 선행사가 the village이고 빈칸 앞에 전치사 in이 있으므로 목적격 관계대명사 which가 알맞다.
해석 이곳은 내가 고등학교에 들어갈 때까지 살았던 마을이다.

08 **해설** 선행사가 없고 뒤에 불완전한 문장이 나오므로 관계대명사 what이 알맞다. others가 의미상 선행사가 될 수 없다는 점에 주의한다.
해석 네가 하려고 하는 것을 다른 사람들에게 말하지 마라.

09 **해설** ② 돈으로(with money) 차를 살 수 있다는 내용이므로 전치사 with가 필요하다.

10 **해설** 선행사가 The cottage(별장)로 장소를 나타내며, 다음에 완전한 문장이 나오므로 관계부사 where가 알맞다.
해석 우리가 지난 겨울에 묵었던 별장은 너무 비쌌다.

11 **해설** 장소를 나타내는 선행사가 올 때 「전치사 + 관계대명사」는 관계부사 where로 바꿔 쓸 수 있다.
해석 영국은 절대로 해가 지지 않는 제국이었다.

12 **해설** 「접속사 + 대명사」는 관계대명사로 바꿔 쓸 수 있다. 선행사가 lost children이고, 접속사가 and이므로 계속적 용법의 주격 관계대명사 who가 알맞다.
해석 그녀는 잃어버린 아이들을 찾았고, 그들은 모두 살아있었다.

13 **해설** delivered가 과거분사이므로 빈칸에 생략된 말은 「주격 관계대명사 + be동사」이다. 선행사 The products가 복수이고 시제 일치가 필요하므로 be동사는 were를 쓴다.
해석 배달된 물건들은 작년의 것들과 달랐다.

14 **해설** 선행사가 the book이고 뒤에 명사가 왔으므로 소유격 관계대명사 whose가 알맞다.
해석 나는 표지 디자인이 잘 된 그 책이 마음에 든다.

15 **해설** ①, ③, ④, ⑤는 장소를 나타내는 선행사가 있고, 빈칸 뒤에 완전한 문장이 이어지므로 관계부사 where가 알맞지만, ②는 관계사 뒤에 불완전한 문장이 나오므로 관계대명사 which〔that〕를 써야 한다.

16 **해설** 선행사가 students(사람)이고 빈칸 뒤에 명사가 오므로 빈칸에 알맞은 것은 소유격 관계대명사 whose이다.
해석 • 몇몇 학생들이 있다.
• 그들의 기억력은 다른 학생들보다 더 좋다.
→ 기억력이 다른 학생들보다 더 좋은 몇몇 학생들이 있다.

17 **해설** 빈칸 앞에 콤마(,)가 있고, 의미상 앞 문장 전체가 선행사에 해당하므로 관계대명사 which가 알맞다. 콤마(,) 뒤에는 관계대명사 that을 쓸 수 없다는 점에 주의한다.
해석 엄마는 파티를 더 일찍 끝내길 원했지만 그것은 불가능했다.

18 **해설** No matter what은 복합관계대명사 Whatever로 바꿔 쓸 수 있다.
해석 무슨 일이 일어나더라도, 나는 네 편이 될 것이다.

19 **해설** 주어진 문장과 ④의 What은 선행사를 포함하는 주격 관계대명사로 쓰였다.
①, ②는 간접의문문을 이끄는 의문사, ③은 의문형용사, ⑤는 의문대명사로 쓰였다.
해석 지금 당장 중요한 것은 저 무거운 상자를 어떻게 옮길지이다.

20 **해설** 첫 번째 빈칸에는 간접의문문에서 사람을 묻는 의문사 who가 들어가고, 두 번째 빈칸에는 선행서 a friend를 수식하는 주격 관계대명사 who나 that이 들어간다. 따라서 공통으로 들어갈 말로 알맞은 것은 who이다.
해석 • 너는 누가 꽃병을 깼는지 아니?
• 나는 너에게 춤추는 법을 가르쳐줄 수 있는 친구가 있다.

21 **해설** 전치사 뒤에는 관계대명사 that을 쓸 수 없다.

22 **해설** 선행사가 있고 관계사절이 전치사로 끝나는 불완전한 문장이므로 목적격 관계대명사 which를 써야 한다.
해석 • 그 집은 재건축될 것이다.
• 우리는 그 집에서 살고 있다.
→ 우리가 살고 있는 그 집은 재건축될 것이다.

23 **해설** 관계대명사 뒤에는 불완전한 문장이 오며, 「전치사+관계대명사」 또는 관계부사 뒤에는 완전한 문장이 온다. ② 관계대명사 which 뒤에 완전한 문장이 나왔으므로 which를 where로 써야 한다.
① 전치사가 관계대명사절 끝에 올 경우 관계대명사를 생략할 수 있다.

24 **해설** 선행사를 제한하는 the only 등의 형용사가 오는 경우 관계대명사 that을 써야 한다.
해석 너는 그 사고를 목격한 유일한 사람이다.

25 **해설** ②, ③, ④, ⑤는 선행사가 없고 뒤에 불완전한 문장이 나오므로 관계대명사 what(What)이 알맞다. ①은 선행사는 없으나 뒤에 완전한 문장이 나오므로 의미상 관계부사 why 또는 선행사 the reason이 오는 것이 알맞다.

26 **해설** 콤마(,)가 있으므로 관계사의 계속적 용법이고, 뒤에 동사가 왔으므로 앞 문장 전체를 선행사로 하는 주격 관계대명사 which가 알맞다.
해석 • 그 호텔은 한때 불이 났었다.
• 그것이 호텔의 명성을 잃게 만들었다.
→ 그 호텔은 한때 불이 났었고, 그것이 호텔의 명성을 잃게 만들었다.

27 **해설** ④ 선행사 The movie가 사물이므로 whom을 which 또는 that으로 써야 한다.

28 **해설** ① 전치사 of 뒤에 관계대명사가 위치하고 있으므로 생략할 수 없다. ②, ③, ④ 목적격 관계대명사는 생략이 가능하다. ⑤ 「주격 관계대명사+be동사」는 생략이 가능하다.

29 **해설** 선행사 the point(시점, 때)는 시간을 나타내는 표현이고, 뒤에 완전한 문장이 나오므로 관계부사 when을 써야 한다.
해석 우리는 정부가 군대를 보낼지 말지를 결정해야만 하는 시점에 도달했다.

30 **해설** 계속적 용법의 관계대명사는 「접속사+대명사」로 바꿔 쓸 수 있다. 주절과 관계사절이 대립적인 의미가 아니므로 접속사 and가 알맞다.
해석 나는 그 여자를 만났고, 그녀는 나를 저녁 식사에 초대했다.

31 **해설** 이유를 나타내는 관계부사 why 또는 선행사 the reason이 의미상 알맞다.

32 **해설** ①, ②, ③, ⑤는 선행사가 없으므로 관계대명사 what(What)이 알맞다.
④는 선행사가 the story이므로 목적격 관계대명사 which나 that이 알맞다.

33 **해설** My dog died last month.와 I looked after him for ten years.의 두 문장이 「전치사+관계대명사」에 의해 연결된 형태이다. 관계사절에 전치사 after가 빠져 있으므로 after which가 알맞다.
해석 내가 십 년간 돌본 나의 개가 지난달에 죽었다.

34 **해설** ③ 전치사 뒤에 쓰인 관계대명사는 생략할 수 없다.
①, ② 목적격 관계대명사는 생략할 수 있다. ④ 전치사가 관계사절 끝에 올 경우 관계대명사를 생략할 수 있다. ⑤ 「주격 관계대명사+be동사」는 생략할 수 있다.

35 **해설** ④는 선행사가 a girl이고 뒤에 명사가 나오므로 소유격 관계대명사 whose가 알맞다.

36 **해설** ② 선행사가 the place이므로 관계부사 where를 써야 한다. ③ 선행사가 any reason이므로 how 대신 why를 써야 한다. ④ what을 관계부사로 바꿔야 하는데 의미상 why가 자연스럽다. ⑤ 선행사가 the restroom이므로 「전치사+관계대명사」인 in which 또는 관계부사인 where로 써야 한다.

37 **해설** 첫 번째 문장의 선행사는 때를 나타내는 the season이며, 뒤에 완전한 문장이 나오므로 관계

부사 when이 알맞다. 두 번째 문장은 선행사가 없고 뒤에 완전한 문장이 나오므로 관계부사 how가 알맞다.

해석 • 나는 꽃들이 활짝 피는 그 계절을 좋아한다. (in full bloom : 활짝 핀)
• 내가 그곳에 어떻게 갔는지 네게 말해 줄게.

38 **해설** 「no matter how + 형용사〔부사〕+ 주어 + 동사」 : 아무리 ~하더라도

39 **해설** 「주격 관계대명사 + be동사」는 생략할 수 있다.
해석 너는 해변에 서 있는 그 남자를 아니?

서술형

40 **해설** 두 번째 문장의 that city는 첫 번째 문장의 The city를 가리키므로 목적격 관계대명사 which〔that〕를 사용한다.
해석 • 그 도시는 많은 관광객들로 가득 차 있었다.
• 우리는 여름 방학 동안에 그 도시를 방문했다.
→ 우리가 여름 방학 동안에 방문한 그 도시는 많은 관광객들로 가득 차 있었다.

41 **해설** 선행사가 reasons이고, 뒤에 완전한 문장이 나오므로 관계부사 why가 알맞다.
해석 • 많은 이유들이 있다.
• 나는 그 이유들로 마음을 바꾸었다.
→ 내가 마음을 바꾼 많은 이유들이 있다.

42 **해설** 장소를 나타내는 선행사 the house가 있지만 관계사 뒤가 불완전(목적어가 빠진 형태)하므로 관계부사 대신 목적격 관계대명사를 써야 한다.
해석 나는 내 할아버지가 지은 그 집을 팔아야 한다.

[43-45]
해석 **Tiffany** 그녀는 다양한 TV 쇼에 출연했다.
Jessica 그녀는 국제 학교를 졸업했다.
Yoona 내 친구는 그녀를 가장 좋아한다.
Yuri 그녀의 별명은 '흑진주'이다.
<보기> Tiffany는 다양한 TV 쇼에 출연한 소녀이다.

43 **해설** 선행사 the girl이 사람이고 주어 역할을 하므로 주격 관계대명사 who를 사용한다.
해석 Jessica는 국제 학교를 졸업한 소녀이다.

44 **해설** 선행사 the girl이 사람이고 목적어 역할을 하므로 목적격 관계대명사 whom〔who〕을 사용한다.
해석 윤아는 James의 친구가 가장 좋아하는 소녀이다.

45 **해설** 선행사 the girl이 사람이고 명사 nickname을 수식하고 있으므로 소유격 관계대명사 whose를 사용한다.
해석 유리는 별명이 '흑진주'인 소녀이다.

[46-48]
해석 **Susan** 나는 일주일 동안 그 호텔에서 지냈다.
Brian 나는 해변에서 수영을 즐겼다.
Paul 나는 지리산으로 캠핑을 갔다.

46 **해설** 선행사가 장소(the hotel)이므로 관계부사 where를 사용한다.
해석 Susan은 일주일 동안 지낸 그 호텔에 대해 이야기했다.

47 **해설** 선행사가 장소(the beach)이므로 관계부사 where를 사용한다.
해석 Brian은 수영을 즐긴 해변에 대해 이야기했다.

48 **해설** 선행사가 장소(Mt. Jiri)이므로 관계부사 where를 사용한다. 관계부사 where는 to which로 바꿔 쓸 수 있다. 장소나 시간을 나타내는 전치사는 주로 at, in, on이 오지만, 선행사에 따라서 at, in, on 이외의 다른 전치사가 올 수도 있다.
해석 Paul은 캠핑을 간 지리산에 대해 이야기했다.

Chapter 12 접속사

1 등위접속사 and / but / or / so

▸▸ p.258

A

1	but	2	or
3	and	4	and
5	but	6	or
7	but	8	so
9	or	10	or

2 상관접속사

▸▸ p.259~260

A

1 or　2 nor
3 and　4 but
5 Both, and　6 but

B

1 is → am　2 are → is
3 is → are　4 has → have
5 don't → doesn't

C

1 not only beautiful but also smart
smart as well as beautiful
2 not only relieved but also comfortable
comfortable as well as relieved
3 not only for myself but also for others
for others as well as for myself
4 not only a dream but also hope
hope as well as a dream

D

1 neither, nor　2 both, and
3 Either, or　4 as well as
5 Both, and

3 명사절을 이끄는 접속사 I - that

▸▸ p.261

A

1 It is important that
2 It is false that

B

1 I think (that) we have to deal with the pollution problem first.
2 I want you to know (that) I can't wait any longer.
3 Everyone in town knows (that) you are such a good guy.
4 I've heard (that) you were a high school teacher.

4 명사절을 이끄는 접속사 II - if / whether

▸▸ p.262~263

A

1 if　2 Whether
3 if　4 that
5 Whether　6 that

B

1 ⓑ　2 ⓐ
3 ⓑ　4 ⓐ
5 ⓑ　6 ⓑ

C

1 that → whether(if)
2 If → Whether
3 that → whether(if)
4 will do → will 삭제
5 will leave → will 삭제
6 That → Whether

D

1 whether he is my friend or not
2 Whether he will come or not
3 whether it is possible or not
4 if our team will win the game
5 whether he paid the bill or not

5 간접의문문

▸▸ p.264~265

A

1 whether　2 where
3 where　4 how
5 Where do you think　6 if
7 What do you think　8 what
9 if

B

1 whether they are alive or not
2 how I should repair this broken chair
3 when the accident happened
4 if(whether) you left something in the theater
5 How long do you suppose it takes?
6 Who do you think is the most reliable player?

C

1 how much it will cost
2 why this blog is popular
3 How long do you think
4 if she can go to school
5 What do you think is

6 so / so that ~ / so ~ that ...

▸▸ p.266~267

A

1 so that
2 so
3 Because
4 so
5 in order
6 that
7 too
8 so

B

1 so that you may survive
2 so that they might get a better view
3 so that we could prevent catching colds

C

1 too tired to work overtime
2 healthy enough to drive his car
3 too difficult for us to understand
4 good enough for me to get

D

1 so that I could catch it
2 so busy that she couldn't call me
3 too narrow for the cars to pass through

7 부사절을 이끄는 접속사 I - 원인 / 양보

▸▸ p.268~269

A

1 Although
2 because
3 because
4 Though
5 even though
6 because
7 Even if

B

1 Because → Because of
2 Although → Despite(In spite of)
3 because of → because
4 ○
5 ○
6 ○

C

1 Although the man is in trouble
2 Although she had a criminal record
3 Although he studies hard in his class
4 Although I had all the necessary qualifications

D

1 Because of her shyness
2 because of her jealousy
3 Despite(In spite of) her poverty

8 부사절을 이끄는 접속사 II - 시간

▸▸ p.270~271

A

1 as soon as
2 while
3 before
4 while
5 after
6 until
7 before

B

1 since
2 while
3 After

C

1 will have → have
2 ○
3 will eat out → eats out
4 ○
5 ○

D

1 On eating the rotten tomato
2 On fixing the vending machine
3 On their leaving
4 On finishing the work

9 부사절을 이끄는 접속사 III - 조건

▸▸ p.272~273

A

1 If you don't have any further questions
2 If you don't wear a jacket
3 If you don't apologize to him
4 If you don't have a passport
5 If you don't read between the lines

B

1 If you visit Paris
2 If you try to be patient
3 If you are kind to others
4 If you sing for me
5 If you turn to your right

C

1 Be around me, or
2 Find a way to make a living, or
3 Listen to my warning, or
4 Do your homework, or
5 Run away right now, or

10 주의해야 할 접속사 - as / while

▸▸ p.274~275

A

1	ⓒ	2	ⓐ	3	ⓒ
4	ⓓ	5	ⓑ	6	ⓓ
7	ⓑ				

B

1 그녀가 말하고 있을 때
2 로마인들이 하는 대로
3 어두워질수록
4 (내가) 신문을 읽는 동안
5 (내가) 교회에서 기도하는 동안
6 몇몇은 영어를 말하는 반면에
7 나는 고기를 좋아하지 않기 때문에

C

1 As he grew older, he got thinner.
2 As she is on a diet, she skips dinner.
3 Sarah saw her father as she visited the company.

D

1 As he grew older
2 while I cook dinner
3 While I chose red socks
4 As they were leaving

11 접속부사

▸▸ p.276

A

1	Therefore	2	However
3	As a result	4	For example
5	However	6	For example

Chapter 12 학교 시험 대비 문제

▸▸ p.277~284

01 ③ 02 ③ 03 ④ 04 ③ 05 ④ 06 ④ 07 ① 08 ④ 09 ⑤ 10 ② 11 ⑤ 12 ① 13 ③ 14 ② 15 ④ 16 ③ 17 ① 18 ① 19 ① 20 ③ 21 ② 22 ④ 23 ① 24 ② 25 ⑤ 26 ⑤ 27 ④ 28 ④ 29 ④ 30 ③ 31 ④ 32 ⑤ 33 ② 34 ② 35 ⑤

서술형 36 if(whether) 37 Though(Although, Even though) 38 don't hurry up 39 enough 40 I don't know if(whether) she got the message. 41 Both, and 42 if(whether), wants 43 despite(in spite of) 44 was so upset because(as) she didn't keep her promise 45 how old his girlfriend is 46 if(whether) he(Brian) has seen Nancy these days 47 She is kind, so she shows a stranger the way. 48 I can do the hard work because I'm strong. 또는 Because I'm strong, I can do the hard work.

01 **해설** Although는 '~이지만'의 뜻을 가진다. 문맥상 '그러나'의 의미로 역접을 나타내는 접속사 but이 빈칸에 알맞다.
해석 그는 매우 빨리 달렸지만, 경주에서 이기지 못했다.

02 **해설** 첫 번째 빈칸에는 '~동안'을 의미하는 while / 두 번째 빈칸에는 '~인 반면에'를 의미하는 while
해석 • 아무도 그 가게를 보지 않는 동안, 그들은 금고 안의 돈을 훔쳤다.
• 나의 사무실에서, Steven은 게으른 반면에 Paul은 부지런하다.

03 **해설** not only A but also B : A뿐만 아니라 B도
해석 내 새 룸메이트는 무례할 뿐만 아니라 게으르다.

04 해설 문맥상 '그래서'의 의미로 결과의 내용을 나타내는 so가 알맞다.

해석 그 음악가는 그의 나라가 그를 포기해서 외국으로 가야 했다.

= 그의 나라가 그를 포기해서, 그 음악가는 외국으로 가야 했다.

05 해설 unless는 if ~ not의 의미로 이미 부정의 의미를 갖고 있으므로 부정어와 함께 사용하지 않는다.

06 해설 ④ '~인 반면에'를 의미하는 while, ① ③ because 또는 as, ② and, ⑤ if 또는 when

07 해설 If가 '~라면'의 의미로 부사절을 이끌 때는 미래시제 대신에 현재시제를 사용한다.

해석 내일 비가 온다면, 나는 집에 머물 것이다.

08 해설 「명령문, or ~」: '~해라, 그렇지 않으면 …할 것이다'

해석 천천히 말해라, 그렇지 않으면 아무도 네 말을 이해하지 못할 것이다.

09 해설 ⑤의 if는 '~라면'의 뜻으로 부사절을 이끈다. 나머지 if는 '~인지 아닌지'의 뜻으로 명사절을 이끈다.

10 해설 not only A but also B : A뿐만 아니라 B도

해석 그들은 석탄뿐만 아니라 천연가스도 수출하고 있다.

11 해설 ⑤ 관계대명사, ①②③④ 명사절을 이끄는 접속사

12 해설 It is not certain의 경우에는 '확실하지 않다'는 의문의 뜻을 품고 있기 때문에 '~인지 아닌지'의 if나 whether가 이끄는 절이 오지만 It is certain의 경우에는 강한 확신을 나타내므로 '~하다는 것'의 that이 이끄는 절이 와야 한다.

13 해설 even though, though, although는 모두 '~이지만'의 의미이다.

해석 그는 (비록) 두 번의 기회를 놓쳤지만 결승골을 넣었다.

score the winning goal : 결승골을 넣다

14 해설 '~뿐만 아니라'의 뜻이므로 as well as가 알맞다.

15 해설 첫 번째 빈칸에는 앞뒤 문장이 인과관계이므로 Therefore가 알맞고, 두 번째 빈칸에는 앞뒤 문장이 역접의 관계이므로 However가 알맞다.

해석 • 세계의 열대우림들이 사라지고 있다. 그러므로, 우리는 행동을 취해야 한다.

• 그 연극은 정말 환상적이었다. 그러나, 나는 그것을 많이 즐기지 못했다.

16 해설 문맥상 '~하는 동안'을 의미하는 while(While)이 알맞다.

해석 • 내가 저녁을 만드는 동안 네 방을 청소해라.

• 우리가 축구를 하는 동안 누군가가 우리의 옷을 훔쳤다.

17 해설 '~인지 아닌지'의 뜻으로 명사절을 이끄는 if / '~라면'의 뜻으로 부사절을 이끄는 if

해석 • 나는 내가 자신을 믿는지 아닌지 모르겠다.

• 네가 그것이 사실이라고 말하면, 나는 그것을 믿을 것이다.

18 해설 ① 동사 think의 목적절을 연결하는 접속사가 필요하므로 that이 알맞다.

문맥상 ②는 whether, ③은 because 또는 as, ④는 so, ⑤는 while이 알맞다.

19 해설 while이 '~하는 동안'의 뜻으로 쓰였으므로 '~할 때'를 의미하는 as로 바꿔 쓸 수 있다.

해석 나는 그녀가 산책하는 동안 그녀를 지켜보았다.

20 해설 so that ~ 구문은 in order to 구문으로 바꿔 쓸 수 있다. that절의 주어(we)가 주절의 주어(The thief)와 다르므로 의미상 주어를 for us로 나타내고, 부정어 not은 to부정사 앞에 오는 것에 유의한다.

해석 그 도둑은 우리가 그를 보지 못하도록 뒷문을 통해 나갔다.

21 해설 의문사가 없는 의문문을 간접의문문으로 연결할 때는 「if(whether) + 주어 + 동사」의 어순으로 쓴다.

22 해설 If절은 주어로 쓰지 않으므로 Whether로 써야 한다.

23 해설 ① '~대로', ②③④⑤ '~할 때'

24 해설 either는 부정문에서 '~도 또한 (않다)'의 뜻으로 사용된다. either A or B는 'A 또는 B 둘 중 하나'의 의미로 쓰인다.

해석 • 네가 나와 함께 가지 않는다면, 나도 가지 않을 것이다.

• 너는 순진하거나 어리석은 게 틀림없다.

25 해설 because는 '~ 때문에'의 뜻이므로 '그래서'를 의미하는 so로 써야 한다.

26 해설 '당신이 다치지 않도록'의 의미가 되어야 하므로 so that ~ 구문이 알맞다.

27 해설 ④ either A or B는 B에 수를 일치시키고, both A and B의 경우 복수 취급을 하므로 두 개의 빈칸 모두 are가 알맞다.

해석 • 나는 그와 당신 중 한 명이 유죄라고 생각한다.

• 그와 그의 친구 둘 다 결백하다.

28 해설 If ~ not은 Unless로 바꿔 쓸 수 있다.

해석 네가 마음을 바꾸지 않는다면, 나는 지금 당장 너를 떠날 것이다.

29 해설 ④ 둘 다 '~할 때'의 의미로 시간을 나타내는 부사

절이다.

① ~함에 따라, ~대로 ② ~하는 동안, ~인 반면에 ③ ~라면, ~인지 아닌지 ⑤ ~하기 위해(~하도록), 매우 ~해서 …한

30 해설 I'm not sure 뒤에 오는 접속사이므로 문맥상 '~인지 아닌지'를 의미하는 if가 알맞다.

해석 A 무슨 일이니? 심각해 보인다.

B 오, 내 머리핀을 잃어버렸어. 아마 집에 오는 길에 떨어뜨린 것 같아.

A 우리가 그것을 찾을 수 있을지는 모르겠지만, 한번 찾아보자.

31 해설 because of + 명사〔대명사 / 동명사〕 / because + 주어 + 동사

해석 • 내 병 때문에, 나는 학교에 갈 수 없었다.

• 그는 모르는 회사에서 온 사람이기 때문에 나는 그를 만나지 않았다.

32 해설 빈칸 뒤의 내용이 앞의 내용에 대한 요약이므로 '즉, 다시 말해서'에 해당하는 In other words가 알맞다.

해석 수십억 년을 거슬러 올라가보면 우리는 모든 것이 파랬고 오직 물 아래의 바다 식물들만이 초록색이었음을 발견할 것이다. 다시 말해서, 그곳엔 파란색, 초록색 오직 두 가지 색만이 있었다.

33 해설 첫 번째 빈칸에는 '그래서'를 의미하는 so가 알맞고, 두 번째 빈칸에는 '그리고'를 의미하는 and가 알맞다.

해석 • 많은 학생들이 독감에 걸려서 우리 학교는 휴교했다.

• 그는 담배 피우는 것을 그만두고 당분간 쉬어야 한다.

34 해설 be동사의 보어절을 이끄는 접속사 that / 선행사 The address를 수식하는 관계사절을 이끄는 that

해석 • 그녀의 문제는 그녀가 자전거를 탈 수 없다는 것이다.

• 그가 적어둔 주소는 틀리다.

35 해설 ⑤ '~인 반면에', ①②③④ '~하는 동안'

서술형

36 해설 의문사가 없는 의문문을 간접의문문으로 쓸 때는 접속사 if 또는 whether를 사용한다.

해석 당신이 뉴욕에 가본 적이 있는지 제게 말씀해 주세요.

37 해설 문맥상 '~이지만'을 의미하는 Though〔Although, Even though〕가 알맞다.

해석 나는 최선을 다했지만, 경기에 졌다.

38 해설 unless는 if ~ not과 같은 의미로 사용된다. hurry up은 일반동사이므로 부정형으로 don't를 사용한다.

해석 서두르지 않으면, 너는 비행기를 놓칠 것이다.

39 해설 「so + 형용사〔부사〕+ that + 주어 + can」은 「형용사〔부사〕+ enough to + 동사원형」으로 바꿔 쓸 수 있다.

해석 이 손목시계는 매우 싸서 내가 그것을 살 수 있다.

40 해설 의문사가 없는 의문문을 간접의문문으로 연결할 때는 「if〔whether〕+ 주어 + 동사」의 어순으로 쓴다.

해석 나는 그녀가 그 메시지를 받았는지 모르겠다.

41 해설 both A and B : A, B 둘 다

해석 너와 네 친구 둘 다 똑똑하다.

42 해설 의문사가 없는 의문문을 간접의문문 형태로 바꾼 것이므로 「if〔whether〕+ 주어 + 동사」의 형태로 써야 한다.

해석 나는 그가 그의 직업을 바꾸기를 원하는지 궁금하다.

43 해설 「though〔although, even though〕+ 주어 + 동사」는 「despite〔in spite of〕+ 명사〔대명사 / 동명사〕」로 바꿔 쓸 수 있다.

해석 비가 많이 내렸지만, 콘서트는 성공적으로 끝났다.

44 해설 주어가 I로 시작하며 문맥상 화가 난 이유가 뒤에 이어지는 것이 적절하므로 '~ 때문에'의 의미를 가진 접속사를 써야 한다.

해석 나는 그녀가 약속을 지키지 않았기 때문에 무척 화가 났다.

[45-46]

해석 **James** 만나서 반가워, Mary. 너는 어디에 사니?

Mary 나는 4번 가에 살아.

<보기> James가 Mary에게 어디에 사는지 물어보고 있다.

45 해설 의문사가 있는 간접의문문은 「의문사 + 주어 + 동사」의 어순으로 쓴다.

해석 **Mike** 질문 있니?
Lisa 내게 말해줘. 네 여자 친구는 몇 살이니?
Lisa는 Mike에게 그의 여자 친구가 몇 살인지 물어보고 있다.

46 **해설** 의문사가 없는 간접의문문은 「if(whether)+주어+동사」의 어순으로 쓴다.
해석 **Betty** 안녕. 너 요즘에 Nancy를 본 적 있니?
Brian 아니, 없어.
Betty는 그가(Brian이) 요즘에 Nancy를 본 적이 있는지 알고 싶어 한다.

[47-48]

47 **해설** so는 '그래서'를 의미하므로 「원인, so+결과」의 형태로 쓴다.
해석 그녀는 친절해서, 모르는 사람에게 길을 알려준다.

48 **해설** because는 '~때문에, 왜냐하면'을 의미하므로 「결과+because+원인」의 형태로 쓴다.
해석 나는 힘이 세기 때문에, 힘든 일을 할 수 있다.

Chapter 13 가정법

1 가정법 과거

▶▶ p.286~287

A
1 were 2 give
3 had 4 can
5 could 6 did
7 were

B
1 he doesn't live here, I can't see him every day
2 She is not here, she can't help us
3 she were a wise woman, she would not make such a mistake
4 I had enough money, I could buy a beautiful house
5 you were a bird, you could fly to me

C
1 If he knew, he would tell
2 If he listened, he could know
3 If I were, I would accept
4 If she had, she would read

2 가정법 과거완료

▶▶ p.288~289

A
1 had had 2 had started
3 had asked 4 had been
5 had worked

B
1 you didn't tell me the fact, it was not(wasn't) much better
2 they were so tired, they didn't go out
3 He laughed at me, I was not(wasn't) close to him
4 he had been my father, he would(could) have understood me
5 they had had enough money, they could have helped her
6 he had known my phone number, he would(could) have called me

C
1 buy → have bought
2 drove → had driven
3 would not → would
4 been → have been
5 caught → had caught

D
1 If he had warned, I wouldn't have done
2 If we hadn't been, might have played
3 I could have done, if I had been

3 I wish + 가정법

▶▶ p.290~291

A
1 took 2 had 3 could
4 had 5 would

B
1 I'm sorry I'm not 2 I'm sorry I'm poor
3 I wish you were 4 I'm sorry I didn't listen
5 I wish she had gone 6 I wish I had stopped

C

1 I wish he were
2 I wish I could go
3 I wish I had
4 I wish I had taken
5 I wish my aunt had gone
6 I wish I had had
7 I wish you would stay

4 as if + 가정법

▸▸ p.292~293

A

1 could
2 were
3 could
4 had liked
5 had gotten
6 had

B

1 she was not thirsty
2 she cannot(can't) climb up the tall tree
3 as if we were surprised at this
4 as if they had won the game
5 as if they hadn't had a fight with each other

C

1 as if they liked
2 as if she had wanted
3 as if you were
4 as if she had hated
5 as if you could find

5 Without(But for) 가정법

▸▸ p.294~295

A

1 Were it not for hope,
Without(But for) hope
2 Had it not been for the accident,
Without(But for) the accident
3 Had it not been for him,
Without(But for) him
4 Were it not for the keys,
Without(But for) the keys
5 Were it not for the scholarship,
Without(But for) the scholarship

B

1 Were it not for the guide
2 Had it not been for the trouble
3 Had it not been for the warning sign
4 Were it not for the weapons

C

1 Were it not for my credit card
2 If it hadn't been for the magazine
3 Had it not been for the umbrella

6 혼합가정법

▸▸ p.296

A

1 he had taken
2 she had left
3 he had failed

B

1 If she hadn't broken
2 He couldn't lend
3 If I had eaten

Chapter 13 학교 시험 대비 문제

▸▸ p.297~304

01 ② 02 ③, ④ 03 ③ 04 ⑤ 05 ② 06 ② 07 ② 08 ⑤ 09 ③ 10 ④ 11 ⑤ 12 ③ 13 ③ 14 ① 15 ③ 16 ⑤ 17 ⑤ 18 ① 19 ⑤ 20 ① 21 ④ 22 ② 23 ③, ⑤ 24 ⑤ 25 ②

서술형 26 Without 27 I'm sorry 28 But for 29 doesn't have, can't lend 30 could speak 31 had been 32 ② would not → would ③ So → As 33 he had told, he didn't tell 34 If we had known 35 not 36 she is not 37 hadn't broken, could call 38 If she hadn't worked alone from noon 39 As she worked alone from noon 40 She worked alone from noon, so she couldn't finish the work in time. 41 Without his advice 42 If it had not(hadn't) been for his advice 43 Had it not been for his advice

01 해설 ②는 단순 조건절이고, 나머지는 가정법 문장이다.

02 해설 주절이 「주어 + 조동사의 과거형 + have p.p.」인 것으로 보아 가정법 과거완료 문장이다. 이때 If it hadn't been for는 Had it not been for로 바꿔 쓸 수 있으므로 Have를 Had로, to를 for로 써야 한다.

해석 그 길고 힘든 훈련이 없었다면, 그들은 올림픽 팀을 만들지 못했을 것이다.

03 해설 가정법 과거완료 문장이므로 if절은 「If + 주어 + had p.p.」의 형태가 알맞다.

해석 만약 그가 조심했다면, 그는 다치지 않았을 텐데.

04 해설 첫 번째 빈칸에는 현재 사실에 대한 소망을 나타내므로 「I wish + 가정법 과거」가 알맞다. 두 번째 빈칸에는 과거 사실에 대한 소망을 나타내므로 「I wish + 가정법 과거완료」가 알맞다.

해석 • 내가 지금 노래를 잘 부를 수 있으면 좋을 텐데.
→ 내가 지금 노래를 잘 부를 수 없어서 유감이다.
• 내가 큰 집에서 살았더라면 좋을 텐데.
→ 내가 큰 집에서 살지 못했던 것이 유감이다.

05 해설 가정법 과거는 「If + 주어 + 동사의 과거형 ~, 주어 + 조동사의 과거형 + 동사원형 …」의 형태이다.

해석 만약 네가 파티에 온다면, 너는 재미있게 즐길 텐데.

06 해설 가정법 과거 문장이므로 If절의 be동사는 were를 사용한다.

해석 만약 내가 충분히 부자라면, 저 가게에서 신상품들을 살 텐데.

07 해설 ②는 의미상 couldn't를 could로 써야 한다. 가정법과 직설법은 의미상 긍정과 부정의 관계가 정반대이다.

08 해설 가정법 과거완료 문장이므로 주절은 「주어 + 조동사의 과거형 + have p.p.」의 형태가 알맞다.

해석 만약 그녀가 그의 전화번호를 알았다면, 그녀는 그에게 전화했을 텐데.

09 해설 첫 번째 빈칸은 주절의 의미와 형태로 보아 가정법 과거 문장이므로 were가 알맞다. 두 번째 빈칸은 종속접속사 as를 사용한 직설법 현재 문장이므로 am not이 알맞다. 세 번째 빈칸은 결과를 나타내는 등위접속사 so가 알맞다.

해석 만약 내가 그의 입장이라면, 나는 그녀의 제안을 받아들일 수 있을 텐데.
→ 나는 그의 입장이 아니기 때문에, 그녀의 제안을 받아들일 수 없다.
→ 나는 그의 입장이 아니어서 그녀의 제안을 받아들일 수 없다.

10 해설 가정법 과거완료는 「If + 주어 + had p.p. ~, 주어 + 조동사의 과거형 + have p.p.」의 형태이다. If절의 have를 had로 써야 한다.

11 해설 가정법 과거완료 문장이므로 if절은 「If + 주어 + had p.p.」의 형태이고, 주절은 「주어 + 조동사의 과거형 + have p.p.」의 형태가 알맞다. 직설법을 가정법으로 바꿀 때 긍정·부정은 정반대가 된다.

해석 우리는 바빠서 그들과 함께 테니스를 치지 않았다.
→ 만약 우리가 바쁘지 않았다면, 우리는 그들과 함께 테니스를 쳤을지도 모를 텐데.

12 해설 첫 번째 문장은 과거 사실과 반대되는 가정이다. 주절의 시제가 현재이므로 「as if + 가정법 과거완료」의 형태가 알맞다. 두 번째 문장은 현재 사실과 반대되는 가정이다. 주절의 시제가 현재이므로 「as if + 가정법 과거」의 형태가 알맞다.

해석 • 그는 마치 그녀를 만났던 것처럼 행동한다. 사실 그는 그녀를 만나지 않았다.
• 그녀는 마치 무용수인 것처럼 춤을 추고 있다. 사실 그녀는 무용수가 아니다.

13 해설 가정법 과거완료 문장이고 의미상 '포기하지 않았다면'이 되어야 하므로 hadn't given이 알맞다.

해석 만약 그녀가 그것을 포기하지 않았다면, 그녀는 그 프로젝트를 완성할 수 있었을 텐데.

14 해설 과거 사실과 반대되는 가정이므로 가정법 과거완료 문장이다. if절은 「if + 주어 + had p.p.」의 형태가 되어야 하므로 have told가 알맞다.

15 해설 첫 번째 빈칸은 가정법 과거이므로 If, 두 번째 빈칸은 종속접속사가 이끄는 직설법 현재이므로 As, 세 번째 빈칸은 원인과 결과를 이어주는 등위접속사 so가 알맞다.

16 해설 기침이 심해서 어제 모임에 참석하지 못했다는 내용이므로 가정법 과거완료 형태로 쓰는 것이 알맞다.

해석 **A** 너는 왜 어제 모임에 참석하지 않았니? 너는 약속했잖아!
B 나는 그 모임에 참석하고 싶었어. 하지만 나는 심한 기침이 났어. 그래서 진찰을 받으러 가야 했어.

17 해설 Hadn't it not에서 부정 표현이 중복되므로 Had로 써야 한다.

18 해설 '거짓말을 하는' 것은 현재, '찾고 있었던 것처럼'은 과거이다. 따라서 주절은 현재시제이고 과거 사실에 반대되는 가정을 하고 있으므로, '마치 ~였던 것처럼'의 의미를 가진 「as if + 가정법 과거완료 (주어 + had p.p.)」의 형태로 나타낼 수 있다.

19 해설 ⑤는 「I wish + 가정법 과거완료」 형태의 문장이므로 직설법 과거로 표현할 때 I'm sorry I didn't 〔couldn't〕 learn more from you.로 써야 한다.

20 **해설** 가정법 과거 문장이므로 If절에 쓰인 일반동사는 과거형이 알맞다.
해석 만약 그가 그녀의 주소를 안다면, 그는 그녀에게 엽서를 보낼 텐데.

21 **해설** 혼합가정법 문장이므로 If절은 가정법 과거완료를 쓰고 주절은 가정법 과거를 쓴다.

22 **해설** 「as if+가정법 과거완료」 형태의 문장이므로 「as if+주어+had p.p.」의 형태가 알맞다.
해석 그는 마치 그 사실을 몰랐던 것처럼 이야기했다.

23 **해설** 가정법 과거에서 If절의 동사는 기본적으로 과거형을 사용한다.

24 **해설** ⑤는 '만약 그가 돈이 있었다면, 그는 넓은 아파트에서 살 수 있었을 텐데.'의 뜻이다.

25 **해설** 「as if+가정법 과거」이고 주절이 현재시제이므로 현재 사실과 반대되는 상황에 대한 가정을 나타낸다.
해석 그는 마치 정직한 것처럼 행동한다.

서술형

26 **해설** Had it not been for 또는 If it hadn't been for는 Without 또는 But for로 바꿔 쓸 수 있다.
해석 그녀의 도움이 없었다면, 그는 그의 목표를 달성하지 못했을 것이다.

27 **해설** 「I wish+가정법 과거」→「I'm sorry+직설법 현재」
해석 나만의 방이 있으면 좋을 텐데.
= 나만의 방이 없어 유감이다.

28 **해설** 「If it were not for+명사(구)」=「Were it not for+명사(구)」
=「But for+명사(구)」=「Without+명사(구)」
해석 맑은 물(담수)이 없다면, 아무것도 살 수 없을 것이다.

29 **해설** 가정법 과거 문장을 직설법 현재로 바꿀 때 긍정·부정은 정반대가 된다.
해석 만약 그녀가 그 책을 가지고 있다면, 우리에게 그것을 빌려줄 수 있을 텐데.
= 그녀는 그 책을 가지고 있지 않기 때문에, 우리에게 그것을 빌려줄 수 없다.

30 **해설** 「I wish+가정법 과거」→「I'm sorry+직설법 현재」 가정법과 직설법 동사의 긍정·부정은 서로 정반대가 된다.
해석 내가 영어를 잘할 수 없어 유감이다.
= 내가 영어를 잘할 수 있으면 좋을 텐데.

31 **해설** 주절의 시제가 과거이고, 직설법 문장에서 동사가 과거완료이므로 「as if+가정법 과거완료」의 형태가 알맞다. 가정법과 직설법 동사의 긍정·부정은 서로 정반대가 된다.
해석 그녀는 마치 공주였던 것처럼 연기했다.
= 사실 그녀는 공주가 아니었다.

32 **해설** ② 의미상 '외출했을 텐데'의 뜻이므로 would가 알맞다. ③ 직설법에서 쓰이는 종속접속사는 as이다.

33 **해설** so를 사용한 직설법 과거 문장을 가정법 과거완료와 as가 이끄는 직설법 과거 문장으로 바꿔 쓴 형태이다.
해석 그가 나에게 그 문제를 말해주지 않아서 나는 그를 도울 수 없었다.
= 만약 그가 나에게 그 문제를 말해주었다면, 나는 그를 도울 수 있었을 텐데.

34 **해설** 가정법 과거완료 문장이므로 if절은 「If+주어+had p.p.」의 형태가 알맞다.

35 **해설** If it hadn't been for my parents' love에서 If가 생략되어 도치된 형태이다.

36 **해설** 「as if+가정법 과거」를 직설법으로 바꾸면 시제는 주절과 같은 현재시제가 되고 긍정·부정은 정반대가 된다.
해석 그녀는 마치 우울한 기분인 것처럼 보인다.
= 사실 그녀는 우울한 기분이 아니다.

37 **해설** 혼합가정법 문장이므로 if절은 「If+주어+had p.p.」의 형태로, 주절은 「주어+조동사의 과거형+동사원형」의 형태를 사용한다.
해석 그는 며칠 전에 휴대 전화를 고장 내서 지금 아무에게도 전화를 할 수 없다.
= 만약 그가 휴대 전화를 고장 내지 않았다면, 그는 지금 누구에게든지 전화를 할 수 있을 텐데.

38 **해설** 가정법 과거완료 문장이므로 if절은 「If+주어+had p.p.」의 형태로 쓴다.

39 **해설** 가정법 과거완료 문장을 as를 사용한 직설법 과거 문장으로 쓴다. 이때 가정법과 직설법 동사의 긍정·부정은 서로 정반대가 된다.

40 **해설** 가정법 과거완료 문장을 원인과 결과를 이어주는 등위접속사 so를 사용한 직설법 과거 문장으로 쓴다.

41 **해설** 「Without+명사(구), 주어+조동사의 과거형+have p.p.」: ~이 없었다면

42 **해설** 「Without+명사(구)」→「If it hadn't been for+명사(구)」

43 **해설** 가정법 문장에서 if가 생략될 경우 주어와 동사가 도치된다. →「Had it not been for+명사(구)」

Chapter 14 일치와 화법

1 수 일치 I - 단수주어 + 단수동사

▶▶ p. 306~307

A

1 has
2 is
3 is
4 was
5 is
6 singer
7 is
8 speaks
9 plays

B

1 is
2 ○
3 is
4 ○
5 needs
6 is

C

1 To see is
2 Every, was
3 The number of, was
4 Five years is
5 bad habits is
6 One of, is

2 수 일치 II - 복수주어 + 복수동사

▶▶ p. 308

A

1 are
2 are
3 are
4 were
5 have
6 are

B

1 ○
2 are
3 ○
4 Do
5 don't

3 주의해야 할 수 일치

▶▶ p. 309

A

1 were
2 do
3 are

B

1 ○
2 are → is
3 encourages → encourage

4 시제 일치의 원칙

▶▶ p. 310

A

1 was
2 would return
3 couldn't come
4 was

B

1 ○
2 couldn't
3 had been
4 ○
5 was

5 시제 일치의 예외

▶▶ p. 311~312

A

1 go
2 travels
3 ended
4 is
5 runs
6 was
7 is
8 is

B

1 gets
2 is
3 rises
4 is
5 declared
6 leaves

C

1 has broken → broke
2 gathered → gathers
3 ○
4 ○
5 ○
6 had broken → broke
7 ○
8 had → have

D

1 that he doesn't eat meat
2 that honesty is the best policy
3 that his father always gets up
4 that Germany was unified

6 화법 전환 I - 평서문

▶▶ p. 313~314

A

1 says, she is
2 she would
3 had met, the day before
4 he, had seen, my bike

B

1 (that) she will keep the promise
2 (that) I was kind to his brother
3 (that) her parents are cooking in the kitchen
4 (that) she would go there the next day(the day after)
5 (that) he had met her three days before
6 (that) she had seen my father the previous night (the night before)

C

1 "I am very happy."
2 "He is crying now."
3 "I can help you."
4 "I bought this camera."
5 "They will come back soon."
6 "I made pizza for you."

7 화법 전환 II - 의문문

▶▶ p.315~316

A

1 if, he	2 asked, I was crying
3 asked, he was	4 asked, had written
5 if, would	6 whether, that was

B

1 what I was doing
2 if(whether) he was sleepy
3 which book I had read
4 how she went to school

C

1 "What are you thinking about?"
2 "Are you busy now?"
3 "Did you smoke a lot?"
4 "Who closed the door?"

D

1 whose car that was
2 where she was studying English
3 if I liked basketball
4 if I was fond of reading

8 화법 전환 III - 명령문

▶▶ p.317~318

A

1 to be	2 not to go
3 to lend, my	4 asked, to come
5 advised, not to	6 advised, to change

B

1 to do not be → not to be
2 you → me
3 follow → to follow, this → that

C

1 "Don't move."
2 "Move these boxes to the garage."
3 "Wait here till I return."
4 "Don't worry about me."

D

1 told, to look at him
2 asked, to help her
3 ordered, to start immediately
4 advised, not to smoke too much

Chapter 14 학교 시험 대비 문제

▶▶ p.319~324

01 ③ **02** ① **03** ③ **04** ③ **05** ③ **06** ③ **07** ③ **08** ③ **09** ② **10** ④ **11** ④ **12** ③ **13** ⑤ **14** ③ **15** ① **16** ④ **17** ⑤ **18** ② **19** ④ **20** ④ **21** ① **22** ⑤ **23** ④ **24** ④ **25** ④

서술형 **26** is → was 또는 had been **27** see → saw **28** The number of cars has been increasing. **29** causes **30** are → is **31** can you **32** to get enough sleep **33** (1) A number of people are waiting for the bus. (2) The number of students is decreasing every year. **34** how his weekend had been **35** if he could tell her more about **36** to take my umbrella **37** not to talk about it anymore

01 **해설** ③ 복수형 고유명사는 단수 취급하고, 역사적인 사실은 과거시제로 나타내며 의미상 수동의 형태가 알맞다.

해석 올림픽이 1988년에 서울에서 개최되었다.

02 해설 의미상 have 동사가 알맞고 every는 단수 취급하므로 단수동사(has)가 와야 한다.

03 해설 ③ 전달동사는 said를 그대로 쓰고, her는 직접화법에서 my가 되며, be동사 was는 현재시제 is로 써야 한다.

해석 그녀는 그녀의 아들이 삶의 가장 큰 기쁨이라고 말했다.

04 해설 「every + 단수명사」 → 단수 취급 / 「all + 복수명사」 → 복수 취급 / 「each of + 복수명사」 → 단수 취급

해석 그 집의 모든 접시, 포크, 그리고 유리컵들은 더럽다. 모든 아이들의 옷도 역시 더럽다. 그 아이들 각자 문제를 가지고 있다. 나는 그들을 도와주고 싶다.

05 해설 주절이 과거시제(told)이므로 종속절의 is를 과거시제인 was로 써야 한다.

해석 Kate는 Tom에게 "네가 나를 이해하지 못해 유감이야."라고 말했다.

→ Kate는 Tom에게 그가 그녀를 이해하지 못해 유감이라고 말했다.

06 해설 「분수 + of + 단수명사」는 단수 취급하므로 ③이 어법상 올바르다.

① A and B(하나의 개념) → 단수 취급

② 작품명 → 단수 취급

④ some of + 불가산명사 → 단수 취급

⑤ half of + 복수명사 → 복수 취급

07 해설 의문사가 없는 의문문은 접속사 if〔whether〕를 사용하여 간접화법을 만든다.

that → if〔whether〕

08 해설 ③ 주절이 과거시제(told)이므로 종속절은 한 시제 앞선 과거완료로 나타내야 한다. 따라서 had been으로 써야 한다.

해석 그는 나에게 "나는 너를 만나서 반가워."라고 말했다.

→ 그는 나에게 나를 만나서 반가웠다고 말했다.

09 해설 ② 의미상 family가 가족 구성원을 의미하므로 복수 취급하여 Is를 Are로 써야 한다. ③ bread and butter는 '버터 바른 빵'이라는 뜻으로 단수 취급한다.

10 해설 The young은 Young people을 의미하는 복수명사이므로 동사는 behave가 알맞으며, 대명사는 they를 사용한다.

해석 젊은이들은 마치 그들이 모든 것을 아는 것처럼 행동한다.

11 해설 전달동사의 시제가 과거(told)이므로 종속절의 시제도 would help가 되고, 목적어 you는 me가 된다. tomorrow는 the next day로 바뀐다.

해석 그는 나에게 "내가 내일 너를 도와줄게."라고 말했다.

= 그는 나에게 다음 날 나를 도와주겠다고 말했다.

12 해설 전달동사(told)가 과거시제이므로, 종속절의 시제는 과거보다 앞선 시제인 과거완료 had come으로 써야 한다.

해석 그는 나에게 "나는 너를 만나러 이곳에 왔어."라고 말했다.

→ 그는 나에게 나를 만나러 그곳에 왔다고 말했다.

13 해설 ⑤ 주절이 과거이면 종속절의 시제는 과거 또는 과거완료여야 하므로 was interested 또는 had been interested가 알맞다.

14 해설 학과명은 단수 취급하고 의미상 수동의 형태가 알맞으므로 is가 알맞다.

해석 물리학은 이 학교에서 가르치지 않는다.

15 해설 직접화법을 간접화법으로 바꿀 때 부정명령문은 「not + to부정사」로 나타낸다.

해석 선생님이 "John, 너무 크게 노래를 부르지 마라."라고 말씀하셨다.

→ 선생님이 John에게 너무 크게 노래를 부르지 말라고 말씀하셨다.

16 해설 첫 번째 빈칸에는 Little Women이 책 이름이므로 단수 취급하며, then은 과거를 나타내는 부사이므로 was를 쓰고, 두 번째 빈칸은 주어 The characters가 복수명사이므로 want를 써야 한다.

해석 • Alcott의 〈작은 아씨들〉은 그때 매우 인기 있었다.

• 〈작은 아씨들〉의 등장인물들은 어른이 되고 싶어 한다.

17 해설 부정명령문이므로 「not + to부정사」를 써서 연결하고, 부사 here는 there로 바꾼다.

해석 그 골키퍼는 Brian에게 "공을 여기서 차지 마."라고 말했다.

= 그 골키퍼는 Brian에게 거기서 공을 차지 말라고 말했다.

18 해설 every morning으로 미루어 볼 때 현재의 습관임을 알 수 있으므로 현재시제가 알맞다. he는 3인칭 단수이므로 ①은 정답이 될 수 없다.

해석 그는 매일 아침에 강을 따라 달린다고 말했다.

19 해설 ④ 주어 I는 he로, 지시어 this는 that으로, 과거는 한 단계 앞선 시제인 과거완료로 바꿔야 한다.

해석 그는 나에게 "내가 이 편지를 받았어."라고 말했다.

20 **해설** 첫 번째 빈칸은 Most of 뒤에 복수명사가 왔으므로 복수동사가 알맞다. 두 번째 빈칸은 분수 표현 뒤에 단수명사가 왔으므로 단수동사가 알맞다.

해석 • 대부분의 학생들은 그 결과에 실망했다.
• 그 행성의 3분의 2는 물로 덮여 있다.

21 **해설** 의문사가 없는 의문문이므로 「if(whether)+주어+동사」의 어순이 되어야 한다.

해석 그는 나에게 "너는 그녀의 이메일 주소를 아니?" 라고 말했다.

22 **해설** ⑤ 주절의 시제가 과거이므로, 종속절에 현재완료가 올 수 없다. has → had

23 **해설** if로 보아 의문사가 없는 의문문임을 알 수 있다. asked를 said to로 바꾸고, she는 you로 바꾼다.

해석 그는 그녀에게 다쳤는지 물었다.

24 **해설** The rich는 Rich people을 의미하는 복수명사이므로 복수 취급 한다.

해석 부자들은 그들의 돈을 투자할 기회를 찾고 있다.

25 **해설** ④ 현재의 습관은 현재시제로 나타내므로 will go를 goes로 써야 한다.

서술형

26 **해설** 주절이 과거이면 종속절의 시제는 과거 또는 과거완료여야 한다.

해석 그는 시험이 어렵다고(어려웠다고) 생각했다.

27 **해설** 파티에서 그녀를 본 것은 과거의 일이므로, see의 과거형인 saw로 써야 한다.

해석 **A** 너는 그 파티에서 그녀를 보았니?
B 응, 나는 그 파티에서 그녀를 본 게 기억나.

28 **해설** 「the number of+복수명사」는 단수 취급한다.

29 **해설** 불변의 진리는 항상 현재형으로 쓴다.

해석 **선생님** 여러분은 무엇이 사물을 떨어지게 만드는지 아나요?
학생들 물론이죠. 중력이에요.

30 **해설** 동명사구(Looking up new words)는 단수 취급하므로 are를 is로 써야 한다.

해석 새로운 단어들을 찾아보는 것은 언어를 배우는 데 있어서 매우 중요하다.

31 **해설** 의문사가 있으므로 직접화법은 「의문사+동사+주어」의 어순이 된다. could는 현재시제(can)로 쓰고, Sam에게 말한 것이므로 주어는 you가 된다.

해석 나는 Sam에게 그가 어떻게 체스를 그렇게 잘하는지 물었다.
→ 나는 Sam에게 "너는 어떻게 체스를 그렇게 잘 하니?"라고 말했다.

32 **해설** 긍정명령문을 간접화법으로 나타낼 때는 to부정사를 사용한다.

해석 의사는 내게 잠을 충분히 자라고 조언했다.

33 **해설** (1) 「a number of 복수명사」: 복수취급
(2) 「the number of 복수명사」: 단수취급

[34-35]

해석 **Julie** 주말 어땠니, James?
James 좋았어! 나는 서울에 있는 프랑스 마을에 갔어.
Julie 나는 서울에 프랑스 마을이 있는지 몰랐어. 그것에 대해 나에게 더 말해줄 수 있니?

34 **해설** 전달동사가 asked이고, 의문사가 있는 의문문이므로 간접화법은 「의문사+주어+동사」의 형태로 쓴다.

해석 Julie는 첫 번째로, James에게 주말이 어땠는지 물었다.

35 **해설** 전달동사가 asked이고, 의문사가 없는 의문문이므로 간접화법은 「if(whether)+주어+동사」의 형태로 쓴다.

해석 Julie는 두 번째로, James에게 서울에 있는 프랑스 마을에 대해 더 말해줄 수 있는지 물었다.

[36-37]

해석 <보기> 나의 선생님은 내게 도서관에서 공부하라고 말씀하셨다.

36 **해설** 긍정명령문이므로 to부정사를 사용한다.

해석 나의 언니가 나에게 우산을 가져가라고 말했다.

37 **해설** 부정명령문이므로 「not+to부정사」를 사용한다.

해석 Paul은 내게 그것에 대해 더 이상 이야기하지 말라고 말했다.

Chapter 15 특수구문

1 강조 I - 동사를 강조하는 do
▶▶ p.326

A

1 do **2** do
3 does **4** did
5 did

B

1 does have **2** did paint
3 do like watching **4** does play

2 강조 II - It ~ that 강조 구문
▶▶ p.327

A

1 Ernest Hemingway, wrote *the Old Man and the Sea*
2 the film *Harry Potter*, Chris Columbus directed
3 last week, I happened to see Sarah on the street
4 you, helped me get over difficulties

3 도치 I - 장소 부사구
▶▶ p.328

A

1 In the room was a new computer.
2 From around the corner appeared a red car.
3 Next to the museum stand a few tall trees.
4 Next to the bakery is the bank I work for.
5 In warm seas lives the sea horse.
6 Out of the car came an old woman.
7 In the library is a computer lab which students can use.

4 도치 II - so(neither) + 동사 + 주어
▶▶ p.329

A

1 too **2** do
3 am **4** either
5 does **6** has
7 can **8** have

B

1 Neither am I **2** So have we
3 Neither can he

5 도치 III - 부정어
▶▶ p.330

A

1 Never has she been
2 Rarely do I read
3 Seldom does she have
4 Hardly could I understand
5 Never had they heard
6 has he mentioned

6 생략
▶▶ p.331

A

1 I **2** that
3 who was **4** go

B

1 My mother doesn't always buy me everything (that) I want.
2 She received my phone call but (she) didn't talk to me.
3 The girl (who is) waiting at the door is my cousin, Jenny.
4 I asked her to play the violin, but she did not want to (play the violin).
5 She brought me a book (which was) written by one of her favorite writers.
6 The handsome man (who(m)(that)) she spoke to is her English teacher.

Chapter 15 학교 시험 대비 문제

▶▶ p.332~336

01 ③ **02** ③ **03** ② **04** ①, ⑤ **05** ⑤ **06** ② **07** ④ **08** ② **09** ④, ⑤ **10** ④ **11** ② **12** ①, ② **13** ③ **14** ②, ④ **15** ② **16** ① **17** ④ **18** ③ **19** ④ **20** ②

서술형 **21** Neither have I **22** So did I **23** Hardly do I skip my breakfast. **24** Seldom has she missed her music class. **25** Never have they tried Turkish food before. **26** So do I. **27** Neither can she. **28** So has Jane. **29** It was he that helped me find my pen at the library yesterday. **30** It was at the library that he helped me find my pen yesterday. **31** It was yesterday that he helped me find my pen at the library.

01 해설 ③은 일반동사로 쓰였고, 나머지는 동사를 강조하는 do이다.

02 해설 <보기>와 ③은 「It ~ that 강조 구문」으로 쓰였다.
① think의 목적절을 이끄는 접속사
② girl을 꾸며주는 지시형용사
④ 형용사 difficult를 꾸며주는 부사
⑤ 「It ~ that 가주어·진주어 구문」

해석 내가 버스에 두고 내린 것은 바로 나의 스마트폰이다.

03 해설 「장소 부사구 + 동사 + 주어」의 어순이므로 동사 was를 주어 lots of wooden baskets and tables에 맞춰 복수형으로 써야 한다. was → were

해석 그들 주변에 목재 바구니와 탁자들이 많이 있었다.

04 해설 ① 「빈도부사 + 일반동사」
⑤ 「부정어 + do(does, did) + 주어 + 동사원형」

05 해설 ⑤는 「It ~ that 가주어·진주어 구문」으로 쓰였고, 나머지는 「It ~ that 강조 구문」으로 쓰였다.

06 해설 '하다'라는 의미로 쓰인 일반동사 / 동사를 강조하는 do

해석 • 그녀는 저녁 식사 전에 숙제를 했다.
• 나는 일본에서 활화산을 정말 보았다.

07 해설 ④에서 had는 일반동사의 과거형으로 쓰였으므로 did를 써야 한다. had → did

08 해설 「장소 부사구 + 동사 + 주어」 어순의 도치 구문이므로, 동사를 뒤에 이어지는 주어에 수 일치시켜야 한다. 주어 the boys and the girls가 복수이므로 stand가 알맞다.

해석 미술관 뒤에 소년들과 소녀들이 서 있다.

09 해설 ① either → too ② neither → either ③ was → did

10 해설 <보기>와 ④는 「It ~ that 강조 구문」으로 쓰였다.
① bag을 꾸며주는 지시형용사
② believed의 목적절을 이끄는 접속사
③ 주어절을 이끄는 접속사
⑤ 「It ~ that 가주어·진주어 구문」

해석 내가 그녀의 신분증을 찾은 곳은 바로 도서관이었다.

11 해설 ②는 「부정어 + have(조동사) + 주어 + 동사」의 어순으로 쓴다.
Never she has been → Never has she been

12 해설 ① 목적격 관계대명사 생략 → This is the house (which / that) she used to live in.
② 장소 부사구 도치 → A beautiful princess lived in a castle.
③ Hardly he does → Hardly does he
④ neither → either
⑤ which is used에서 which is 생략 using → used

13 해설 ③ 주격 관계대명사는 생략할 수 없다.
①, ④ 「주격 관계대명사 + be동사」는 생략할 수 있다.
② 반복되는 어구는 생략할 수 있다.
⑤ 앞에 나온 동사의 반복을 피하기 위해 to만 쓰고 동사원형을 생략할 수 있다.

14 해설 ② 현재완료에서 빈도부사의 위치는 「have/has + 빈도부사 + p.p.」이며, 도치되지 않은 문장이다.
④ 「부정어 + has(조동사) + 주어 + 동사」의 어순으로 도치된 문장이다.

15 해설 ②는 '하다'라는 뜻으로 쓰인 일반동사이고, 나머지는 동사의 의미를 강조하는 조동사로 쓰였다.

16 해설 ①은 「It ~ that 가주어·진주어 구문」이고, 나머지는 「It ~ that 강조 구문」이다.

17 해설 전치사 뒤에 오는 목적격 관계대명사는 생략할 수 없다. 대신 전치사가 관계사절 끝에 위치할 경우에는 생략할 수 있다.

18 해설 ③ 장소 부사구 Right over our heads가 문장 맨 앞에 위치할 경우 주어 an eagle과 동사 flew가 도치되므로 Right over our heads flew an eagle.의 어순이 되어야 한다.

19 해설 빈칸 뒤에 이어지는 내용으로 보아 B의 빈칸 또한 과학을 잘하지 못한다는 내용이 되어야 한다. 부정문 'I'm not ~'에 대한 동의 표현이 되어야 하므로 Neither am I.가 알맞다.

해석 A 나는 과학을 잘하지 못해.
B 나도 그래. 나는 시험에 합격하지 못했어.

20 해설 ② A의 말이 현재완료시제이므로 B는 have로 대답해야 한다. → So have I.

서술형

21 해설 부정문에 동의하는 표현으로 「neither + 동사 + 주어」가 알맞다, A의 말이 현재완료형이므로 B의 응답에 조동사 have를 사용한다.

해석 A 나는 그렇게 지루한 사람을 만나본 적이 전혀 없어.
B 나도 만난 적이 없어.
= 나도 그래.

22 해설 「So + 동사 + 주어」 : ~도 또한 그렇다
enjoyed가 일반동사의 과거형이므로 B의 응답에 did를 사용한다.

해석 A 훌륭한 저녁 식사였어요. 저는 그 음식을 즐겼어요.
B 나도 즐겼어요.
= 나도 그랬어요.

[23-25]

해석 <보기> 그는 점심을 먹으러 밖에 나가는 일이 거의 없다.

23 해설 동사의 시제가 현재나 과거일 때
→ 「부정어 + do〔does, did〕+ 주어 + 동사원형」

해석 나는 아침 식사를 거의 거르지 않는다.

24 해설 동사의 시제가 완료시제이거나 조동사가 있을 때
→ 「부정어 + have〔조동사〕+ 주어 + 동사」

해석 그녀는 음악 수업을 거의 빠지지 않았다.

25 해설 동사의 시제가 완료시제이거나 조동사가 있을 때
→ 「부정어 + have〔조동사〕+ 주어 + 동사」

해석 그들은 전에 터키 음식을 먹어 본 적이 없다.

[26-28]

해석 <보기> A 그녀는 영어를 잘하지 못해.

26 해설 A의 말이 일반동사이므로 B는 do로 답해야 한다.

해석 A 나는 책 읽는 것을 굉장히 즐겨.
B 나도 그래.

27 해설 A가 부정문이므로 B에는 부정문에 동의하는 표현이 들어가야 한다. 부정문에 동의하는 표현은 「neither + 동사 + 주어」이다.

해석 A 그는 수영을 아주 잘하지 못해.
B 그녀도 그래.

28 해설 A의 말이 현재완료 시제이므로 B의 대답에는 has가 와야 한다.

해석 A 그는 숙제를 끝냈어.
B Jane도 그래.

[29-31]

해설 It ~ that 강조 구문 : 강조어구 자리(It was와 that 사이)에 주로 주어, 장소의 부사구, 시간의 부사구 등을 쓴다.

해석 그는 어제 도서관에서 내 펜을 찾는 것을 도와주었다.

29 어제 도서관에서 내 펜을 찾는 것을 도와준 사람은 바로 그였다.

30 그가 어제 내 펜을 찾도록 도와준 곳은 바로 도서관이었다.

31 그가 도서관에서 내 펜을 찾는 것을 도와준 때는 바로 어제였다.

적중! 중학영문법 3300제

LEVEL 3

워크북

적중! 중학영문법 3300제 Level 3

워크북

단어 암기장

* WORD TEST의 정답은 WORD LIST에서 확인할 수 있습니다.

WORD LIST

□ 01	master [mǽstər]	통 통달하다	
□ 02	impossible [impάsəbəl]	형 불가능한	
□ 03	concern [kənsə́ːrn]	명 관심사 통 염려하다	
□ 04	respect [rispékt]	통 존중하다, 존경하다	
□ 05	waste [weist]	통 낭비하다 명 낭비; 쓰레기	
□ 06	criminal [krímənəl]	명 범인	
□ 07	properly [prάpərli]	부 적당하게	
□ 08	get rid of	~을 없애다	
□ 09	against [əgénst]	전 ~에 반대하여	
□ 10	employee [emplɔ́iiː]	명 종업원, 고용인	
□ 11	pretend [priténd]	통 ~인 척하다	
□ 12	hang out	(~와) 놀다, 어울리다	
□ 13	conference [kάnfərəns]	명 회의	
□ 14	repair [ripέər]	통 고치다, 수선하다	
□ 15	water [wɔ́ːtər]	통 물을 주다 명 물	
□ 16	crawl [krɔːl]	통 기어가다, 기다	
□ 17	apology [əpάlədʒi]	명 사과	
□ 18	complain [kəmpléin]	통 불평하다	
□ 19	complete [kəmplíːt]	통 끝마치다	
□ 20	dine out	외식하다	
□ 21	make money	돈을 벌다	
□ 22	athlete [ǽθliːt]	명 운동 선수	
□ 23	diligent [dílədʒənt]	형 부지런한	
□ 24	foolish [fúːliʃ]	형 어리석은	
□ 25	in secret	몰래, 비밀스럽게	
□ 26	pass [pæs]	통 통과하다	
□ 27	disappoint [dìsəpɔ́int]	통 실망시키다	
□ 28	environment [inváiərənmənt]	명 환경, 주위	
□ 29	repeat [ripíːt]	통 반복하다	
□ 30	policy [pάləsi]	명 정책, 방침	

WORD TEST

A 다음 영어는 우리말로, 우리말은 영어로 쓰시오.

01	master	______	11	~인 척하다	______
02	impossible	______	12	(~와) 놀다, 어울리다	______
03	concern	______	13	회의	______
04	respect	______	14	고치다, 수선하다	______
05	waste	______	15	물을 주다; 물	______
06	criminal	______	16	기어가다, 기다	______
07	properly	______	17	사과	______
08	get rid of	______	18	불평하다	______
09	against	______	19	끝마치다	______
10	employee	______	20	외식하다	______

B 다음 영어를 우리말과 알맞은 것끼리 연결하시오.

21	make money •	•	환경, 주위
22	athlete •	•	통과하다
23	diligent •	•	정책, 방침
24	foolish •	•	돈을 벌다
25	in secret •	•	운동 선수
26	pass •	•	어리석은
27	disappoint •	•	몰래, 비밀스럽게
28	environment •	•	부지런한
29	repeat •	•	실망시키다
30	policy •	•	반복하다

□ 01	lift [lift]	동 들어 올리다
□ 02	humorous [hjúːmərəs]	형 재미있는, 익살스러운
□ 03	driveway [dráivwèi]	명 진입로
□ 04	cheerful [tʃíərfəl]	형 활기찬
□ 05	discussion [diskʌ́ʃən]	명 토론, 토의
□ 06	memorize [méməràiz]	동 암기하다
□ 07	article [áːrtikl]	명 (신문·잡지의) 기사
□ 08	oral [ɔ́ːrəl]	형 구두의, 입의
□ 09	drop by	~에 들르다
□ 10	favor [féivər]	명 호의, 친절
□ 11	trip over	~에 발이 걸려 넘어지다
□ 12	survive [sərváiv]	동 살아남다
□ 13	robber [rɑ́bər]	명 강도, 도둑
□ 14	mechanic [məkǽnik]	명 정비사
□ 15	kneel [niːl]	동 무릎을 꿇다
□ 16	shut [ʃʌt]	동 닫다, 잠그다
□ 17	astronaut [ǽstrənɔ̀ːt]	명 우주 비행사
□ 18	train [trein]	동 훈련시키다
□ 19	gentle [dʒéntl]	형 점잖은
□ 20	messy [mési]	형 어질러진
□ 21	sunrise [sʌ́nràiz]	명 해돋이
□ 22	share [ʃɛər]	동 공유하다
□ 23	disturb [distə́ːrb]	동 방해하다
□ 24	timid [tímid]	형 소심한
□ 25	adviser [ædváizər]	명 충고자, 조언자
□ 26	stand [stænd]	동 견디다
□ 27	regret [rigrét]	명 유감 동 후회하다
□ 28	destination [dèstənéiʃən]	명 목적지
□ 29	head [hed]	동 (어느 지점으로) 나아가다
□ 30	crowded [kráudid]	형 붐비는, 혼잡한

WORD TEST

A 다음 영어는 우리말로, 우리말은 영어로 쓰시오.

01 lift ____________________

02 humorous ____________________

03 driveway ____________________

04 cheerful ____________________

05 discussion ____________________

06 memorize ____________________

07 article ____________________

08 oral ____________________

09 drop by ____________________

10 favor ____________________

11 ~에 발이 걸려 넘어지다 ____________________

12 살아남다 ____________________

13 강도, 도둑 ____________________

14 정비사 ____________________

15 무릎을 꿇다 ____________________

16 닫다, 잠그다 ____________________

17 우주 비행사 ____________________

18 훈련시키다 ____________________

19 점잖은 ____________________

20 어질러진 ____________________

B 다음 영어를 우리말과 알맞은 것끼리 연결하시오.

21 sunrise	•	•	소심한
22 share	•	•	목적지
23 disturb	•	•	붐비는, 혼잡한
24 timid	•	•	유감; 후회하다
25 adviser	•	•	충고자, 조언자
26 stand	•	•	(어느 지점으로) 나아가다
27 regret	•	•	견디다
28 destination	•	•	공유하다
29 head	•	•	방해하다
30 crowded	•	•	해돋이

WORD LIST

□ 01	fond [fand]	형 좋아하는	
□ 02	be poor at	~에 서투르다, ~을 못하다	
□ 03	meal [miːl]	명 식사, 밥	
□ 04	spend [spend]	동 돈(시간)을 소비하다	
□ 05	commerce [kάməːrs]	명 상업, 무역	
□ 06	pleasant [plézənt]	형 기분 좋은	
□ 07	make fun of	~을 놀리다	
□ 08	amaze [əméiz]	동 ~을 놀라게 하다	
□ 09	terrible [térəbəl]	형 끔찍한	
□ 10	yard [jɑːrd]	명 마당, 뜰	
□ 11	satisfy [sǽtisfài]	동 만족시키다	
□ 12	insist [insíst]	동 주장하다	
□ 13	allow for	~을 감안(고려)하다	
□ 14	quickly [kwíkli]	부 빨리, 빠르게	
□ 15	doubt [daut]	명 의심 동 의심하다	
□ 16	be proud of	~을 자랑으로 여기다	
□ 17	entrance [éntrəns]	명 입학, 입구	
□ 18	support [səpɔ́ːrt]	동 지지하다	
□ 19	proposal [prəpóuzəl]	명 제안	
□ 20	congress [kάŋgris]	명 국회; 회의	
□ 21	do a good job	~을 잘 해내다	
□ 22	share the blame for	~에 대해 공동 책임을 지다	
□ 23	let out	입 밖에 내다, 누설하다	
□ 24	idle [áidl]	형 게으른, 할 일이 없는	
□ 25	bite [bait]	동 물다	
□ 26	apologize [əpάlədʒàiz]	동 사과하다	
□ 27	mind [maind]	동 꺼리다, 신경 쓰다	
□ 28	unsatisfied [ʌnsǽtisfàid]	형 불만스러워 하는	
□ 29	delay [diléi]	동 연기하다 명 연기, 지연	
□ 30	postpone [poustpóun]	동 미루다	

WORD TEST

A 다음 영어는 우리말로, 우리말은 영어로 쓰시오.

01 fond ____________________
02 be poor at ____________________
03 meal ____________________
04 spend ____________________
05 commerce ____________________
06 pleasant ____________________
07 make fun of ____________________
08 amaze ____________________
09 terrible ____________________
10 yard ____________________
11 만족시키다 ____________________
12 주장하다 ____________________
13 ~을 감안(고려)하다 ____________________
14 빨리, 빠르게 ____________________
15 의심; 의심하다 ____________________
16 ~을 자랑으로 여기다 ____________________
17 입학, 입구 ____________________
18 지지하다 ____________________
19 제안 ____________________
20 국회; 회의 ____________________

B 다음 영어를 우리말과 알맞은 것끼리 연결하시오.

21 do a good job •	• 연기하다; 연기, 지연
22 share the blame for •	• 사과하다
23 let out •	• 입 밖에 내다, 누설하다
24 idle •	• 불만스러워 하는
25 bite •	• 물다
26 apologize •	• 미루다
27 mind •	• 꺼리다, 신경 쓰다
28 unsatisfied •	• 게으른, 할 일이 없는
29 delay •	• ~을 잘 해내다
30 postpone •	• ~에 대해 공동 책임을 지다

□ 01	quit	[kwit]	동 그만두다
□ 02	imagine	[imǽdʒin]	동 상상하다
□ 03	suggest	[səgdʒést]	동 제안하다
□ 04	consider	[kənsídər]	동 깊이 생각하다
□ 05	novel	[nɑ́vəl]	명 소설
□ 06	offer	[ɔ́:fər]	동 제공하다
□ 07	autumn	[ɔ́:təm]	명 가을
□ 08	tend	[tend]	동 ~하는 경향이 있다
□ 09	choose	[tʃu:z]	동 선택하다
□ 10	agree	[əgrí:]	동 동의하다
□ 11	manage	[mǽnidʒ]	동 해내다, 관리하다
□ 12	afford	[əfɔ́:rd]	동 (~ 할) 형편이 되다
□ 13	have a conversation		대화를 나누다
□ 14	purpose	[pə́:rpəs]	명 목적
□ 15	keep company with		~와 친해지다
□ 16	continue	[kəntínju:]	동 계속하다
□ 17	bath	[bæθ]	명 목욕
□ 18	nap	[næp]	명 낮잠
□ 19	fence	[fens]	명 울타리
□ 20	explain	[ikspléin]	동 설명하다
□ 21	process	[prɑ́ses]	명 과정
□ 22	rule	[ru:l]	명 규칙
□ 23	jump out		뛰쳐나가다
□ 24	spicy	[spáisi]	형 양념 맛이 강한
□ 25	out of habit		습관적으로
□ 26	adapt	[ədǽpt]	동 적응하다
□ 27	surroundings	[səráundiŋz]	명 환경, 주위의 상황
□ 28	floor	[flɔ:r]	명 바닥, 마루
□ 29	celebration	[sèləbréiʃən]	명 축하 행사
□ 30	lazy	[léizi]	형 게으른

WORD TEST

Ⓐ 다음 영어는 우리말로, 우리말은 영어로 쓰시오.

01	quit	________	11	해내다, 관리하다	________
02	imagine	________	12	(~ 할) 형편이 되다	________
03	suggest	________	13	대화를 나누다	________
04	consider	________	14	목적	________
05	novel	________	15	~와 친해지다	________
06	offer	________	16	계속하다	________
07	autumn	________	17	목욕	________
08	tend	________	18	낮잠	________
09	choose	________	19	울타리	________
10	agree	________	20	설명하다	________

Ⓑ 다음 영어를 우리말과 알맞은 것끼리 연결하시오.

21	process	•	• 과정
22	rule	•	• 환경, 주위의 상황
23	jump out	•	• 뛰쳐나가다
24	spicy	•	• 게으른
25	out of habit	•	• 축하 행사
26	adapt	•	• 적응하다
27	surroundings	•	• 규칙
28	floor	•	• 바닥, 마루
29	celebration	•	• 습관적으로
30	lazy	•	• 양념 맛이 강한

WORD LIST

□ 01	firefighter [fáiərfaitər]	명 소방관
□ 02	attend [əténd]	동 참석하다
□ 03	classmate [klǽsmèit]	명 반 친구
□ 04	cheer [tʃiər]	동 응원하다, 환호하다
□ 05	parrot [pǽrət]	명 앵무새
□ 06	chat [tʃæt]	동 이야기하다, 수다 떨다
□ 07	expression [ikspréʃən]	명 표현, 말
□ 08	merrily [mérəli]	부 명랑하게
□ 09	relieved [rilíːvd]	형 안심한, 안도한
□ 10	bark [bɑːrk]	동 짖다
□ 11	surround [səráund]	동 둘러싸다
□ 12	treasure [tréʒər]	명 보물
□ 13	make a speech	연설하다, 발표하다
□ 14	accident [ǽksidənt]	명 사고
□ 15	shout [ʃaut]	동 소리 지르다
□ 16	mend [mend]	동 고치다
□ 17	gladly [glǽdli]	부 즐거이, 기꺼이
□ 18	sight [sait]	명 광경, 시야
□ 19	audience [ɔ́ːdiəns]	명 관객, 청중
□ 20	address [ǽdres]	명 연설; 주소
□ 21	northward [nɔ́ːrθwərd]	부 북쪽으로
□ 22	receive [risíːv]	동 받다
□ 23	in a hurry	서둘러, 황급히
□ 24	biology [baiɑ́lədʒi]	명 생물학
□ 25	beginner [bigínər]	명 초보자
□ 26	turn off	끄다
□ 27	hold out	내밀다, 뻗다
□ 28	sunset [sʌ́nsèt]	명 일몰, 해질녘
□ 29	language [lǽŋgwidʒ]	명 언어
□ 30	vase [veis]	명 꽃병

WORD TEST

Ⓐ 다음 영어는 우리말로, 우리말은 영어로 쓰시오.

01	firefighter	______	11	둘러싸다	______
02	attend	______	12	보물	______
03	classmate	______	13	연설하다, 발표하다	______
04	cheer	______	14	사고	______
05	parrot	______	15	소리 지르다	______
06	chat	______	16	고치다	______
07	expression	______	17	즐거이, 기꺼이	______
08	merrily	______	18	광경, 시야	______
09	relieved	______	19	관객, 청중	______
10	bark	______	20	연설; 주소	______

Ⓑ 다음 영어를 우리말과 알맞은 것끼리 연결하시오.

21	northward	•	•	끄다
22	receive	•	•	내밀다, 뻗다
23	in a hurry	•	•	받다
24	biology	•	•	언어
25	beginner	•	•	북쪽으로
26	turn off	•	•	생물학
27	hold out	•	•	서둘러, 황급히
28	sunset	•	•	일몰, 해질녘
29	language	•	•	초보자
30	vase	•	•	꽃병

□ 01	catch up with		~을 따라잡다
□ 02	scold	[skould]	동 꾸짖다
□ 03	invite	[inváit]	동 초대하다
□ 04	present	[prézənt]	형 참석한
□ 05	situation	[sìtʃuéiʃən]	명 상황
□ 06	confident	[kánfidənt]	형 자신 있는
□ 07	reward	[riwɔ́:rd]	명 보상, 대가
□ 08	behavior	[bihéivjər]	명 행동
□ 09	pace	[peis]	명 속도 동 보조를 맞추다
□ 10	gentleman	[dʒéntlmən]	명 신사
□ 11	asleep	[əslí:p]	형 잠이 든
□ 12	reliable	[riláiəbəl]	형 믿을 만한
□ 13	accent	[ǽksent]	명 억양, 말투
□ 14	correct	[kərékt]	형 옳은
□ 15	accept	[æksépt]	동 받아들이다
□ 16	tightly	[táitli]	부 꽉, 단단히
□ 17	scream	[skri:m]	동 소리치다
□ 18	bill	[bil]	명 지폐
□ 19	life jacket		구명 조끼
□ 20	responsible	[rispánsəbəl]	형 책임이 있는
□ 21	lecture	[léktʃər]	명 강의
□ 22	quality	[kwáləti]	명 질, 특성
□ 23	goods	[gudz]	명 상품
□ 24	modern	[mádərn]	형 현대의
□ 25	cross	[krɔ:s]	동 건너다
□ 26	jewel	[dʒú:əl]	명 보석
□ 27	document	[dákjumənt]	명 서류
□ 28	as usual		언제나처럼
□ 29	reply	[riplái]	동 대답하다
□ 30	wonder	[wʌ́ndər]	동 궁금하다

WORD TEST

A 다음 영어는 우리말로, 우리말은 영어로 쓰시오.

01	catch up with	______	11	잠이 든	______
02	scold	______	12	믿을 만한	______
03	invite	______	13	억양, 말투	______
04	present	______	14	옳은	______
05	situation	______	15	받아들이다	______
06	confident	______	16	꽉, 단단히	______
07	reward	______	17	소리치다	______
08	behavior	______	18	지폐	______
09	pace	______	19	구명 조끼	______
10	gentleman	______	20	책임이 있는	______

B 다음 영어를 우리말과 알맞은 것끼리 연결하시오.

21	lecture	•	• 현대의
22	quality	•	• 질, 특성
23	goods	•	• 언제나처럼
24	modern	•	• 강의
25	cross	•	• 서류
26	jewel	•	• 상품
27	document	•	• 보석
28	as usual	•	• 대답하다
29	reply	•	• 궁금하다
30	wonder	•	• 건너다

□ 01	fly [flai]	동 (비행기를 타고) 가다	
□ 02	outside [àutsáid]	부 밖에서	
□ 03	own [oun]	동 소유하다 형 자기 자신의	
□ 04	resemble [rizémbl]	동 닮다	
□ 05	pet [pet]	명 애완동물	
□ 06	move [muːv]	동 이사하다	
□ 07	restaurant [réstərənt]	명 식당, 레스토랑	
□ 08	elementary [èləméntəri]	형 초급의	
□ 09	president [prézədənt]	명 사장, 회장, 대통령	
□ 10	cough [kɔːf]	명 기침	
□ 11	parcel [pάːrsəl]	명 소포	
□ 12	station [stéiʃən]	명 역, 정거장	
□ 13	take off	이륙하다	
□ 14	airport [έərpɔ̀ːrt]	명 공항	
□ 15	enter [éntər]	동 들어가다	
□ 16	match [mætʃ]	명 경기, 시합	
□ 17	sold out	매진된, 다 팔린	
□ 18	doorbell [dɔ́ːrbèl]	명 초인종	
□ 19	discuss [diskʌ́s]	동 논의하다	
□ 20	stand in line	일렬로 서다	
□ 21	camel [kǽməl]	명 낙타	
□ 22	subway [sʌ́bwèi]	명 지하철	
□ 23	essay [ései]	명 글, 수필	
□ 24	speech [spiːtʃ]	명 연설	
□ 25	series [síəriːz]	명 연속, 시리즈	
□ 26	coast [koust]	명 해안	
□ 27	coat [kout]	명 코트, 외투	
□ 28	purse [pəːrs]	명 지갑, 핸드백	
□ 29	each other	서로	
□ 30	defeat [difíːt]	동 물리치다, 이기다	

WORD TEST

Ⓐ 다음 영어는 우리말로, 우리말은 영어로 쓰시오.

01 fly ________________

02 outside ________________

03 own ________________

04 resemble ________________

05 pet ________________

06 move ________________

07 restaurant ________________

08 elementary ________________

09 president ________________

10 cough ________________

11 소포 ________________

12 역, 정거장 ________________

13 이륙하다 ________________

14 공항 ________________

15 들어가다 ________________

16 경기, 시합 ________________

17 매진된, 다 팔린 ________________

18 초인종 ________________

19 논의하다 ________________

20 일렬로 서다 ________________

Ⓑ 다음 영어를 우리말과 알맞은 것끼리 연결하시오.

21 camel	•	•	연속, 시리즈
22 subway	•	•	서로
23 essay	•	•	해안
24 speech	•	•	연설
25 series	•	•	낙타
26 coast	•	•	지하철
27 coat	•	•	물리치다, 이기다
28 purse	•	•	지갑, 핸드백
29 each other	•	•	글, 수필
30 defeat	•	•	코트, 외투

WORD LIST

□ 01	solve [sɑlv]	통 해결하다
□ 02	pill [pil]	명 알약
□ 03	laptop [lǽptɑ̀p]	명 노트북 컴퓨터
□ 04	follow [fɑ́lou]	통 따르다
□ 05	control [kəntróul]	통 조정하다
□ 06	weep [wiːp]	통 흐느끼다
□ 07	except [iksépt]	전 ~외에는
□ 08	beat [biːt]	통 이기다
□ 09	classify [klǽsəfài]	통 분류하다
□ 10	husband [hʌ́zbənd]	명 남편
□ 11	for free	무료로
□ 12	actress [ǽktris]	명 여배우
□ 13	leave [liːv]	통 떠나다
□ 14	borrow [bɑ́rou]	통 빌리다
□ 15	fresh [freʃ]	형 신선한
□ 16	take care of	~을 돌보다
□ 17	public [pʌ́blik]	형 공공의
□ 18	rent [rent]	통 빌리다, 임대(임차)하다
□ 19	innocent [ínəsənt]	형 결백한
□ 20	witness [wítnis]	통 증언하다 명 목격자
□ 21	party [pɑ́ːrti]	명 정당
□ 22	avoid [əvɔ́id]	통 피하다
□ 23	customer [kʌ́stəmər]	명 손님
□ 24	handle [hǽndl]	통 다루다
□ 25	regain [rigéin]	통 되찾다
□ 26	reject [ridʒékt]	통 거절하다
□ 27	punish [pʌ́niʃ]	통 처벌하다
□ 28	fortress [fɔ́ːrtris]	명 요새
□ 29	temple [témpəl]	명 사원
□ 30	generation [dʒènəréiʃən]	명 세대, 시대

WORD TEST

A 다음 영어는 우리말로, 우리말은 영어로 쓰시오.

01 solve ____________

02 pill ____________

03 laptop ____________

04 follow ____________

05 control ____________

06 weep ____________

07 except ____________

08 beat ____________

09 classify ____________

10 husband ____________

11 무료로 ____________

12 여배우 ____________

13 떠나다 ____________

14 빌리다 ____________

15 신선한 ____________

16 ~을 돌보다 ____________

17 공공의 ____________

18 빌리다, 임대[임차]하다 ____________

19 결백한 ____________

20 증언하다; 목격자 ____________

B 다음 영어를 우리말과 알맞은 것끼리 연결하시오.

21 party	•	•	피하다
22 avoid	•	•	처벌하다
23 customer	•	•	정당
24 handle	•	•	요새
25 regain	•	•	손님
26 reject	•	•	세대, 시대
27 punish	•	•	사원
28 fortress	•	•	되찾다
29 temple	•	•	다루다
30 generation	•	•	거절하다

□ 01	bully [búli]	통 괴롭히다
□ 02	give up	포기하다
□ 03	truth [tru:θ]	명 진실, 사실
□ 04	life span	수명
□ 05	nowadays [náuədèiz]	부 요즈음에는
□ 06	deceive [disí:v]	통 속이다
□ 07	swear [swεər]	통 맹세하다
□ 08	cancer [kǽnsər]	명 암
□ 09	impolite [ìmpəláit]	형 무례한
□ 10	attitude [ǽtitjù:d]	명 태도, 자세
□ 11	convince [kənvíns]	통 납득시키다
□ 12	empty [émpti]	형 빈, 공허한
□ 13	honest [ánist]	형 솔직한
□ 14	educate [édʒukèit]	통 가르치다
□ 15	salesman [séilzmən]	명 영업사원
□ 16	unfortunately [ʌnfɔ́:rtʃənitli]	부 불행하게도
□ 17	luxurious [lʌgʒúəriəs]	형 호화로운
□ 18	earthquake [ə́:rθkwèik]	명 지진
□ 19	spill [spil]	통 엎지르다
□ 20	promote [prəmóut]	통 조장하다; 홍보하다
□ 21	abroad [əbrɔ́:d]	부 해외에
□ 22	vet [vet]	명 수의사
□ 23	nervous [nə́:rvəs]	형 긴장되는
□ 24	pond [pɑnd]	명 연못
□ 25	wander [wɑ́ndər]	통 방랑하다
□ 26	practice [prǽktis]	통 연습하다
□ 27	protect [prətékt]	통 보호하다
□ 28	pale [peil]	형 창백한
□ 29	suburb [sʌ́bə:rb]	명 교외
□ 30	inspiration [ìnspəréiʃən]	명 영감, 자극

WORD TEST

A **다음 영어는 우리말로, 우리말은 영어로 쓰시오.**

01 bully ____________

02 give up ____________

03 truth ____________

04 life span ____________

05 nowadays ____________

06 deceive ____________

07 swear ____________

08 cancer ____________

09 impolite ____________

10 attitude ____________

11 납득시키다 ____________

12 빈, 공허한 ____________

13 솔직한 ____________

14 가르치다 ____________

15 영업사원 ____________

16 불행하게도 ____________

17 호화로운 ____________

18 지진 ____________

19 엎지르다 ____________

20 조장하다; 홍보하다 ____________

B **다음 영어를 우리말과 알맞은 것끼리 연결하시오.**

21 abroad	•	•	교외
22 vet	•	•	긴장되는
23 nervous	•	•	방랑하다
24 pond	•	•	보호하다
25 wander	•	•	수의사
26 practice	•	•	연못
27 protect	•	•	연습하다
28 pale	•	•	영감, 자극
29 suburb	•	•	창백한
30 inspiration	•	•	해외에

WORD LIST

□ 01 thief [θiːf] 명 도둑

□ 02 hand [hænd] 동 건네주다 명 손

□ 03 increase [inkríːs] 동 증가하다

□ 04 traffic [trǽfik] 명 교통

□ 05 launch [lɔːntʃ] 동 쏘아 올리다

□ 06 satellite [sǽtəlàit] 명 위성

□ 07 landscape [lǽndskèip] 명 풍경, 풍경화

□ 08 author [ɔ́ːθər] 명 작가

□ 09 decision [disíʒən] 명 결정

□ 10 career [kəríər] 명 경력

□ 11 sheet [ʃiːt] 명 (종이) 한 장

□ 12 decoration [dèkəréiʃən] 명 장식

□ 13 whale [weil] 명 고래

□ 14 cotton [kɑ́tn] 명 면직물

□ 15 referee [rèfəríː] 명 심판

□ 16 penalty [pénəlti] 명 벌칙, 페널티

□ 17 bunch [bʌntʃ] 명 다발

□ 18 sentence [séntəns] 명 판결; 문장

□ 19 judge [dʒʌdʒ] 명 판사

□ 20 grow [grou] 동 재배하다

□ 21 dynasty [dáinəsti] 명 왕조, 시대

□ 22 prepare [pripέər] 동 준비하다

□ 23 performance [pərfɔ́ːrməns] 명 공연

□ 24 case [keis] 명 사건; 상자

□ 25 colleague [kɑ́liːg] 명 동료

□ 26 governor [gʌ́vərnər] 명 관리자, 우두머리

□ 27 field [fiːld] 명 들판

□ 28 flat [flæt] 형 평평한

□ 29 plot [plɑt] 명 음모

□ 30 at the moment 지금

WORD TEST

A 다음 영어는 우리말로, 우리말은 영어로 쓰시오.

01 thief	______	11 (종이) 한 장	______
02 hand	______	12 장식	______
03 increase	______	13 고래	______
04 traffic	______	14 면직물	______
05 launch	______	15 심판	______
06 satellite	______	16 벌칙, 페널티	______
07 landscape	______	17 다발	______
08 author	______	18 판결; 문장	______
09 decision	______	19 판사	______
10 career	______	20 재배하다	______

B 다음 영어를 우리말과 알맞은 것끼리 연결하시오.

21 dynasty •	• 지금
22 prepare •	• 평평한
23 performance •	• 들판
24 case •	• 준비하다
25 colleague •	• 음모
26 governor •	• 관리자, 우두머리
27 field •	• 공연
28 flat •	• 왕조, 시대
29 plot •	• 동료
30 at the moment •	• 사건; 상자

WORD LIST

Chapter 06 수동태 ❷

□ 01	genius [dʒíːnjəs]	명 천재
□ 02	volunteer [vɑ̀ləntíər]	명 자원 봉사자
□ 03	explore [iksplɔ́ːr]	동 탐험하다
□ 04	tropical [trɑ́pikəl]	형 열대의
□ 05	issue [íʃuː]	명 주제, 쟁점
□ 06	get in touch with	~와 연락(접촉)하다
□ 07	frequently [fríːkwəntli]	부 자주
□ 08	observe [əbzə́ːrv]	동 목격하다
□ 09	presentation [prèzəntéiʃən]	명 발표
□ 10	recipe [résəpi]	명 조리법
□ 11	starve [staːrv]	동 굶주리다
□ 12	orphan [ɔ́ːrfən]	명 고아
□ 13	mistake [mistéik]	명 실수
□ 14	newborn [njúːbɔːrn]	형 갓 태어난
□ 15	gain [gein]	동 얻다
□ 16	weight [weit]	명 무게, 체중
□ 17	extinct [ikstíŋkt]	형 멸종된
□ 18	escape [iskéip]	동 탈출하다
□ 19	passionate [pǽʃənət]	형 열정적인
□ 20	flee [fliː]	동 달아나다
□ 21	million [míljən]	명 100만
□ 22	diligence [dílidʒəns]	명 근면, 성실
□ 23	development [divéləpmənt]	명 발달
□ 24	contain [kəntéin]	동 포함하다
□ 25	extremely [ikstríːmli]	부 극도로, 몹시
□ 26	generous [dʒénərəs]	형 너그러운
□ 27	scenery [síːnəri]	명 경치
□ 28	statue [stǽtʃuː]	명 동상, 조각상
□ 29	temperature [témpərətʃər]	명 기온
□ 30	chairman [tʃɛ́ərmən]	명 의장, 회장

WORD TEST

A 다음 영어는 우리말로, 우리말은 영어로 쓰시오.

01	genius	______	11	굶주리다	______
02	volunteer	______	12	고아	______
03	explore	______	13	실수	______
04	tropical	______	14	갓 태어난	______
05	issue	______	15	얻다	______
06	get in touch with	______	16	무게, 체중	______
07	frequently	______	17	멸종된	______
08	observe	______	18	탈출하다	______
09	presentation	______	19	열정적인	______
10	recipe	______	20	달아나다	______

B 다음 영어를 우리말과 알맞은 것끼리 연결하시오.

21	million •		• 발달
22	diligence •		• 근면, 성실
23	development •		• 기온
24	contain •		• 극도로, 몹시
25	extremely •		• 너그러운
26	generous •		• 경치
27	scenery •		• 동상, 조각상
28	statue •		• 포함하다
29	temperature •		• 의장, 회장
30	chairman •		• 100만

WORD LIST

□ 01	fruit [fruːt]	명 과일
□ 02	laugh at	비웃다
□ 03	paint [peint]	동 그림을 그리다 명 물감
□ 04	alone [əlóun]	부 혼자
□ 05	stupid [stjúːpid]	형 어리석은
□ 06	hurt [həːrt]	동 다치게 하다
□ 07	remote [rimóut]	형 먼, 외딴
□ 08	mirror [mírər]	명 거울
□ 09	introduce [ìntrədjúːs]	동 소개하다
□ 10	effort [éfərt]	명 수고
□ 11	develop [divéləp]	동 발달시키다
□ 12	collect [kəlékt]	동 모으다
□ 13	recycle [riːsáikl]	동 재활용하다
□ 14	marry [mǽri]	동 결혼하다
□ 15	literature [lítərətʃər]	명 문학
□ 16	soldier [sóuldʒər]	명 군인
□ 17	decide [disáid]	동 결정하다
□ 18	stay [stei]	동 머무르다
□ 19	shape [ʃeip]	명 모양
□ 20	triangle [tráiæŋgl]	명 삼각형
□ 21	square [skwεər]	명 정사각형
□ 22	kite [kait]	명 연
□ 23	twin [twin]	명 쌍둥이
□ 24	get along with	어울리다, ~와 잘 지내다
□ 25	economics [èkənámiks]	명 경제학
□ 26	salary [sǽləri]	명 월급
□ 27	challenge [tʃǽlindʒ]	명 도전 동 도전하다
□ 28	material [mətíəriəl]	명 재료, 소재
□ 29	pay [pei]	동 지불하다
□ 30	tradition [trədíʃən]	명 전통

WORD TEST

A 다음 영어는 우리말로, 우리말은 영어로 쓰시오.

01 fruit ______________

02 laugh at ______________

03 paint ______________

04 alone ______________

05 stupid ______________

06 hurt ______________

07 remote ______________

08 mirror ______________

09 introduce ______________

10 effort ______________

11 발달시키다 ______________

12 모으다 ______________

13 재활용하다 ______________

14 결혼하다 ______________

15 문학 ______________

16 군인 ______________

17 결정하다 ______________

18 머무르다 ______________

19 모양 ______________

20 삼각형 ______________

B 다음 영어를 우리말과 알맞은 것끼리 연결하시오.

21 square	•	•	쌍둥이
22 kite	•	•	어울리다, ~와 잘 지내다
23 twin	•	•	경제학
24 get along with	•	•	도전; 도전하다
25 economics	•	•	지불하다
26 salary	•	•	월급
27 challenge	•	•	재료, 소재
28 material	•	•	전통
29 pay	•	•	정사각형
30 tradition	•	•	연

WORD LIST

- □ 01 deserve [dizə́:rv] 통 ~을 받을 만하다
- □ 02 cage [keidʒ] 명 (짐승의) 우리
- □ 03 hard [ha:rd] 부 열심히 형 열심히 하는
- □ 04 worthless [wə́:rθlis] 형 가치 없는
- □ 05 disgust [disgʌ́st] 명 넌더리 통 역겹게 만들다
- □ 06 mountain [máuntən] 명 산
- □ 07 exception [iksépʃən] 명 예외
- □ 08 fit [fit] 통 ~에 맞다
- □ 09 law [lɔ:] 명 법
- □ 10 for a moment 잠시 동안
- □ 11 amusement park 놀이공원
- □ 12 realize [rí:əlàiz] 통 깨닫다
- □ 13 international [ìntərnǽʃənəl] 형 국제적인
- □ 14 mass communication 매스컴, 대중매체
- □ 15 weekend [wí:kend] 명 주말
- □ 16 foreign [fɔ́:rən] 형 외국의
- □ 17 vacation [veikéiʃən] 명 방학, 휴가
- □ 18 quite [kwait] 부 꽤, 상당히, 전적으로
- □ 19 collapse [kəlǽps] 통 붕괴하다
- □ 20 wait in line 줄을 서서 기다리다
- □ 21 seat [si:t] 명 자리, 좌석 통 앉히다
- □ 22 express [iksprés] 통 표현하다
- □ 23 rich [ritʃ] 형 부유한, 돈 많은
- □ 24 rumor [rú:mər] 명 소문
- □ 25 fortunately [fɔ́:rtʃənətli] 부 다행스럽게도
- □ 26 badly [bǽdli] 부 심하게, 몹시
- □ 27 impressive [imprésiv] 형 인상적인
- □ 28 bathtub [bǽθtʌ̀b] 명 욕조
- □ 29 expensive [ikspénsiv] 형 비싼
- □ 30 selfish [sélfiʃ] 형 이기적인

WORD TEST

Ⓐ 다음 영어는 우리말로, 우리말은 영어로 쓰시오.

01 deserve ______________

02 cage ______________

03 hard ______________

04 worthless ______________

05 disgust ______________

06 mountain ______________

07 exception ______________

08 fit ______________

09 law ______________

10 for a moment ______________

11 놀이공원 ______________

12 깨닫다 ______________

13 국제적인 ______________

14 매스컴, 대중매체 ______________

15 주말 ______________

16 외국의 ______________

17 방학, 휴가 ______________

18 꽤, 상당히, 전적으로 ______________

19 붕괴하다 ______________

20 줄을 서서 기다리다 ______________

Ⓑ 다음 영어를 우리말과 알맞은 것끼리 연결하시오.

21 seat	•	• 다행스럽게도
22 express	•	• 표현하다
23 rich	•	• 부유한, 돈 많은
24 rumor	•	• 소문
25 fortunately	•	• 자리, 좌석; 앉히다
26 badly	•	• 심하게, 몹시
27 impressive	•	• 인상적인
28 bathtub	•	• 이기적인
29 expensive	•	• 비싼
30 selfish	•	• 욕조

WORD LIST

□ 01	scene [siːn]	명 경치
□ 02	mere [miər]	형 단순한
□ 03	ashamed [əʃéimd]	형 수치스러운
□ 04	pleased [pliːzd]	형 기쁜
□ 05	improve [imprúːv]	동 개선하다
□ 06	current [kə́ːrənt]	형 최근의
□ 07	pollution [pəlúːʃən]	명 오염, 공해
□ 08	attractive [ətrǽktiv]	형 매력적인
□ 09	take place	발생하다
□ 10	result [rizʌ́lt]	명 결과
□ 11	survey [səːrvéi]	명 조사
□ 12	in person	직접
□ 13	private [práivit]	형 사립의; 사적인
□ 14	local [lóukəl]	형 지역의
□ 15	voluntary [vɑ́ləntèri]	형 자발적인; 자원봉사의
□ 16	announce [ənáuns]	동 발표하다
□ 17	unable [ʌnéibəl]	형 ~할 수 없는
□ 18	physical [fízikəl]	형 신체의
□ 19	devote [divóut]	동 헌신하다
□ 20	park [pɑːrk]	동 주차하다
□ 21	beg [beg]	동 구걸하다
□ 22	social [sóuʃəl]	형 사회의
□ 23	deaf [def]	형 귀가 먼
□ 24	souvenir [sùːvəníər]	명 기념품
□ 25	at any time	언제라도
□ 26	physics [fíziks]	명 물리학
□ 27	refrigerator [rifrìdʒəréitər]	명 냉장고
□ 28	nearly [níərli]	부 거의
□ 29	broke [brouk]	형 파산한
□ 30	perfume [pə́ːrfjuːm]	명 향수

WORD TEST

Ⓐ 다음 영어는 우리말로, 우리말은 영어로 쓰시오.

01	scene	______	11	조사	______
02	mere	______	12	직접	______
03	ashamed	______	13	사립의; 사적인	______
04	pleased	______	14	지역의	______
05	improve	______	15	자발적인; 자원봉사의	______
06	current	______	16	발표하다	______
07	pollution	______	17	~할 수 없는	______
08	attractive	______	18	신체의	______
09	take place	______	19	헌신하다	______
10	result	______	20	주차하다	______

Ⓑ 다음 영어를 우리말과 알맞은 것끼리 연결하시오.

21	beg •		• 향수
22	social •		• 파산한
23	deaf •		• 언제라도
24	souvenir •		• 사회의
25	at any time •		• 물리학
26	physics •		• 냉장고
27	refrigerator •		• 기념품
28	nearly •		• 귀가 먼
29	broke •		• 구걸하다
30	perfume •		• 거의

WORD LIST

□ 01	definitely [défənitli]	부 분명히
□ 02	recently [rí:səntli]	부 최근에
□ 03	arrive [əráiv]	동 도착하다
□ 04	icy [áisi]	형 얼음에 뒤덮인
□ 05	whole [houl]	형 모든, 전체의
□ 06	in silence	조용히
□ 07	heartwarming [há:rtwɔ̀:rmiŋ]	형 마음이 따뜻해지는
□ 08	recognize [rékəgnàiz]	동 알아보다
□ 09	funeral [fjú:nərəl]	명 장례식
□ 10	publish [pʌ́bliʃ]	동 출판하다
□ 11	expect [ikspékt]	동 기대하다
□ 12	price [prais]	명 가격
□ 13	alike [əláik]	형 비슷한
□ 14	treat [tri:t]	동 대접하다
□ 15	raise [reiz]	동 올리다
□ 16	successful [səksésfəl]	형 성공한
□ 17	custom [kʌ́stəm]	명 관습
□ 18	used [ju:zd]	형 사용된
□ 19	provide [prəváid]	동 제공하다
□ 20	government [gʌ́vərnmənt]	명 정부
□ 21	skip [skip]	동 건너뛰다
□ 22	cancel [kǽnsəl]	동 취소하다
□ 23	deny [dinái]	동 거절하다
□ 24	answer [ǽnsər]	동 대답하다 명 대답
□ 25	occur [əkə́:r]	동 발생하다
□ 26	cathedral [kəθí:drəl]	명 대성당
□ 27	overcoat [óuvərkòut]	명 외투
□ 28	character [kǽriktər]	명 등장 인물
□ 29	describe [diskráib]	동 묘사하다
□ 30	creatively [kriéitivli]	부 창의적으로

WORD TEST

A 다음 영어는 우리말로, 우리말은 영어로 쓰시오.

01 definitely ____________

02 recently ____________

03 arrive ____________

04 icy ____________

05 whole ____________

06 in silence ____________

07 heartwarming ____________

08 recognize ____________

09 funeral ____________

10 publish ____________

11 기대하다 ____________

12 가격 ____________

13 비슷한 ____________

14 대접하다 ____________

15 올리다 ____________

16 성공한 ____________

17 관습 ____________

18 사용된 ____________

19 제공하다 ____________

20 정부 ____________

B 다음 영어를 우리말과 알맞은 것끼리 연결하시오.

21 skip	•	•	거절하다
22 cancel	•	•	건너뛰다
23 deny	•	•	창의적으로
24 answer	•	•	대답하다; 대답
25 occur	•	•	대성당
26 cathedral	•	•	등장 인물
27 overcoat	•	•	묘사하다
28 character	•	•	발생하다
29 describe	•	•	외투
30 creatively	•	•	취소하다

WORD LIST

□ 01	plane [plein]	명 비행기
□ 02	half [hæf]	부 반쯤 형 절반의
□ 03	possible [pásəbl]	형 가능한
□ 04	promise [prámis]	동 약속하다
□ 05	save [seiv]	동 저축하다; 구출하다
□ 06	plan [plæn]	동 계획하다 명 계획
□ 07	visit [vízit]	동 방문하다
□ 08	zebra [zí:brə]	명 얼룩말
□ 09	junior [dʒú:njər]	형 나이가 어린
□ 10	senior [sí:njər]	형 손위의, 선배의
□ 11	superior [səpíəriər]	형 상급의, 뛰어난
□ 12	inferior [infíəriər]	형 하위의, 낮은
□ 13	brand new	아주 새로운, 신제품인
□ 14	reasonable [rí:zənəbəl]	형 합리적인
□ 15	question [kwéstʃən]	명 질문
□ 16	taste [teist]	동 맛이 ~하다
□ 17	beautifully [bjú:təfəli]	부 아름답게
□ 18	intelligent [intélədʒənt]	형 총명한
□ 19	usual [jú:ʒuəl]	형 보통의, 평상시의
□ 20	pool [pu:l]	명 수영장, 웅덩이
□ 21	wise [waiz]	형 현명한
□ 22	exercise [éksərsàiz]	동 운동하다
□ 23	fluently [flú:əntli]	부 유창하게
□ 24	weather [wéðər]	명 날씨
□ 25	supply [səplái]	동 공급하다
□ 26	confused [kənfjú:zd]	형 당황한, 혼란한
□ 27	lately [léitli]	부 최근에
□ 28	operation [àpəréiʃən]	명 수술; 작동
□ 29	slowly [slóuli]	부 천천히
□ 30	product [prádʌkt]	명 상품

WORD TEST

A 다음 영어는 우리말로, 우리말은 영어로 쓰시오.

01	plane	______	11	상급의, 뛰어난	______
02	half	______	12	하위의, 낮은	______
03	possible	______	13	아주 새로운, 신제품인	______
04	promise	______	14	합리적인	______
05	save	______	15	질문	______
06	plan	______	16	맛이 ~하다	______
07	visit	______	17	아름답게	______
08	zebra	______	18	총명한	______
09	junior	______	19	보통의, 평상시의	______
10	senior	______	20	수영장, 웅덩이	______

B 다음 영어를 우리말과 알맞은 것끼리 연결하시오.

21	wise •		• 당황한, 혼란한
22	exercise •		• 천천히
23	fluently •		• 유창하게
24	weather •		• 수술; 작동
25	supply •		• 공급하다
26	confused •		• 현명한
27	lately •		• 상품
28	operation •		• 날씨
29	slowly •		• 운동하다
30	product •		• 최근에

□ 01	market [mɑ́ːrkit]	명 시장
□ 02	probably [prɑ́bəbli]	부 아마
□ 03	healthy [hélθi]	형 건강한
□ 04	famous [féiməs]	형 유명한
□ 05	movement [múːvmənt]	명 (정치적 · 사회적) 운동
□ 06	smart [smaːrt]	형 똑똑한
□ 07	transportation [trænspərtéiʃən]	명 교통수단
□ 08	Jupiter [dʒúːpitər]	명 목성
□ 09	solar system	태양계
□ 10	polite [pəláit]	형 예의 바른
□ 11	clearly [klíərli]	부 또렷하게, 알기 쉽게
□ 12	village [vílidʒ]	명 마을
□ 13	a couple of	둘의, 몇 개의
□ 14	mild [maild]	형 온화한
□ 15	climate [kláimit]	명 기후
□ 16	stadium [stéidiəm]	명 경기장
□ 17	activity [æktívəti]	명 활동
□ 18	theater [θíːətər]	명 극장, 영화관
□ 19	clever [klévər]	형 재치 있는, 능숙한
□ 20	friendly [fréndli]	형 친절한
□ 21	warm [wɔːrm]	형 따뜻한
□ 22	influential [ìnfluénʃəl]	형 영향력 있는
□ 23	bridge [bridʒ]	명 다리, 육교
□ 24	subject [sʌ́bdʒikt]	명 과목
□ 25	creative [kriéitiv]	형 창의적인
□ 26	previous [príːviəs]	형 이전의
□ 27	inventor [invéntər]	명 발명가
□ 28	get up	일어나다
□ 29	compact [kəmpǽkt]	형 소형의
□ 30	vehicle [víːikl]	명 차량, 탈것

WORD TEST

A 다음 영어는 우리말로, 우리말은 영어로 쓰시오.

01	market	________	11	또렷하게, 알기 쉽게	________
02	probably	________	12	마을	________
03	healthy	________	13	둘의, 몇 개의	________
04	famous	________	14	온화한	________
05	movement	________	15	기후	________
06	smart	________	16	경기장	________
07	transportation	________	17	활동	________
08	Jupiter	________	18	극장, 영화관	________
09	solar system	________	19	재치 있는, 능숙한	________
10	polite	________	20	친절한	________

B 다음 영어를 우리말과 알맞은 것끼리 연결하시오.

21	warm	•	• 따뜻한
22	influential	•	• 일어나다
23	bridge	•	• 소형의
24	subject	•	• 창의적인
25	creative	•	• 이전의
26	previous	•	• 발명가
27	inventor	•	• 영향력 있는
28	get up	•	• 차량, 탈것
29	compact	•	• 다리, 육교
30	vehicle	•	• 과목

□ 01 dawn [dɔːn] 명 새벽

□ 02 absence [ǽbsəns] 명 결석, 결근

□ 03 bloom [bluːm] 동 꽃이 피다

□ 04 return [ritə́ːrn] 동 돌아오다

□ 05 suffer from ~로 고통 받다

□ 06 graduate [grǽdʒuèit] 동 졸업하다

□ 07 fix [fiks] 동 해결하다

□ 08 surface [sə́ːrfis] 명 표면

□ 09 horizon [həráizən] 명 지평선

□ 10 leap [liːp] 동 뛰어오르다

□ 11 divide [diváid] 동 나누다

□ 12 pigeon [pídʒən] 명 비둘기

□ 13 roof [ruːf] 명 지붕

□ 14 land [lænd] 동 착지하다

□ 15 dive [daiv] 동 잠수하다

□ 16 chopstick [tʃάpstìk] 명 젓가락

□ 17 destroy [distrɔ́i] 동 파괴하다

□ 18 leather [léðər] 명 가죽, 피혁

□ 19 lack [læk] 명 부족

□ 20 disappointment [dìsəpɔ́intmənt] 명 실망

□ 21 refuse [rifjúːz] 동 거절하다

□ 22 national [nǽʃənəl] 형 국가의

□ 23 errand [érənd] 명 심부름

□ 24 translate [trænsléit] 동 해석하다

□ 25 standard [stǽndərd] 형 보통의

□ 26 gather [gǽðər] 동 모이다, 모으다

□ 27 weekday [wíːkdèi] 명 평일

□ 28 hang [hæŋ] 동 걸다

□ 29 bucket [bʌ́kit] 명 양동이

□ 30 celebrate [séləbrèit] 동 축하하다

WORD TEST

A **다음 영어는 우리말로, 우리말은 영어로 쓰시오.**

01 dawn	________	11 나누다	________
02 absence	________	12 비둘기	________
03 bloom	________	13 지붕	________
04 return	________	14 착지하다	________
05 suffer from	________	15 잠수하다	________
06 graduate	________	16 젓가락	________
07 fix	________	17 파괴하다	________
08 surface	________	18 가죽, 피혁	________
09 horizon	________	19 부족	________
10 leap	________	20 실망	________

B **다음 영어를 우리말과 알맞은 것끼리 연결하시오.**

21 refuse	•	• 해석하다
22 national	•	• 평일
23 errand	•	• 축하하다
24 translate	•	• 양동이
25 standard	•	• 심부름
26 gather	•	• 보통의
27 weekday	•	• 모이다, 모으다
28 hang	•	• 국가의
29 bucket	•	• 걸다
30 celebrate	•	• 거절하다

WORD LIST

□ 01	cure [kjuər]	동 치료하다
□ 02	disease [dizí:z]	명 질병
□ 03	shelf [ʃelf]	명 선반
□ 04	neighbor [néibər]	명 이웃
□ 05	nursing home	양로원
□ 06	break down	고장 나다
□ 07	theory [θí:əri]	명 이론, 학설
□ 08	mention [ménʃən]	동 언급하다
□ 09	task [tæsk]	명 일, 과제
□ 10	effect [ifékt]	명 영향
□ 11	found [faund]	동 설립하다
□ 12	check [tʃek]	명 수표 동 확인하다
□ 13	popularity [pɑ̀pjulǽrəti]	명 인기
□ 14	hundreds of	수백의
□ 15	unique [ju:ní:k]	형 특별한
□ 16	worn [wɔ:rn]	형 닳아서 해진, 낡은
□ 17	major [méidʒər]	명 전공 과목
□ 18	ghost [goust]	명 유령, 귀신
□ 19	wheel [wi:l]	명 바퀴
□ 20	capital [kǽpətl]	명 수도, 중심지
□ 21	show up	나타나다
□ 22	millionaire [mìljənɛ́ər]	명 백만장자
□ 23	prove [pru:v]	동 증명하다
□ 24	cradle [kréidl]	명 요람, 유아용 침대
□ 25	grave [greiv]	명 무덤
□ 26	method [méθəd]	명 방법
□ 27	depend on	~에 달려 있다
□ 28	nephew [néfju:]	명 조카
□ 29	drawer [drɔ:r]	명 서랍
□ 30	explanation [èksplənéiʃən]	명 설명

WORD TEST

A 다음 영어는 우리말로, 우리말은 영어로 쓰시오.

01	cure	______	**11**	설립하다	______
02	disease	______	**12**	수표; 확인하다	______
03	shelf	______	**13**	인기	______
04	neighbor	______	**14**	수백의	______
05	nursing home	______	**15**	특별한	______
06	break down	______	**16**	닳아서 해진, 낡은	______
07	theory	______	**17**	전공 과목	______
08	mention	______	**18**	유령, 귀신	______
09	task	______	**19**	바퀴	______
10	effect	______	**20**	수도, 중심지	______

B 다음 영어를 우리말과 알맞은 것끼리 연결하시오.

21	show up	•	• 나타나다
22	millionaire	•	• 무덤
23	prove	•	• 증명하다
24	cradle	•	• 요람, 유아용 침대
25	grave	•	• 백만장자
26	method	•	• 방법
27	depend on	•	• 서랍
28	nephew	•	• 조카
29	drawer	•	• ~에 달려 있다
30	explanation	•	• 설명

- □ 01 passenger [pǽsəndʒər] 명 승객
- □ 02 sculpture [skʌ́lptʃər] 명 조각
- □ 03 injure [índʒər] 동 상처를 입히다
- □ 04 recommend [rèkəménd] 동 추천하다
- □ 05 extra [ékstrə] 형 추가의
- □ 06 tear [tɛər] 동 찢다, 파괴하다
- □ 07 reunification [riːjùːnəfikéiʃən] 명 재통일, 재통합
- □ 08 bankrupt [bǽŋkrʌpt] 형 파산한
- □ 09 heavy [hévi] 형 무거운
- □ 10 arrest [ərést] 동 체포하다
- □ 11 understand [ʌ̀ndərstǽnd] 동 이해하다, 알아듣다
- □ 12 cottage [kɑ́tidʒ] 명 오두막, 시골집
- □ 13 dead [ded] 형 죽은
- □ 14 harbor [hɑ́ːrbər] 명 항구
- □ 15 risk [risk] 명 위험
- □ 16 reconstruction [rìːkənstrʌ́kʃən] 명 복원, 재건
- □ 17 appear [əpíər] 동 나타나다
- □ 18 decline [dikláin] 동 거절하다; 감소하다
- □ 19 talent [tǽlənt] 명 재능
- □ 20 alive [əláiv] 형 살아 있는
- □ 21 exactly [igzǽktli] 부 정확히
- □ 22 hang around 서성거리다, 배회하다
- □ 23 reach [riːtʃ] 동 ~에 도달하다
- □ 24 troop [truːp] 명 군대, 무리
- □ 25 fame [feim] 명 명성
- □ 26 useless [júːslis] 형 헛된, 소용없는
- □ 27 exist [igzíst] 동 존재하다
- □ 28 nickname [níknèim] 명 별명
- □ 29 variety [vəráiəti] 명 여러 가지; 버라이어티 쇼
- □ 30 tourist [túərist] 명 관광객

WORD TEST

A 다음 영어는 우리말로, 우리말은 영어로 쓰시오.

01 passenger ______________

02 sculpture ______________

03 injure ______________

04 recommend ______________

05 extra ______________

06 tear ______________

07 reunification ______________

08 bankrupt ______________

09 heavy ______________

10 arrest ______________

11 이해하다, 알아듣다 ______________

12 오두막, 시골집 ______________

13 죽은 ______________

14 항구 ______________

15 위험 ______________

16 복원, 재건 ______________

17 나타나다 ______________

18 거절하다; 감소하다 ______________

19 재능 ______________

20 살아 있는 ______________

B 다음 영어를 우리말과 알맞은 것끼리 연결하시오.

21 exactly	•	•	~에 도달하다
22 hang around	•	•	서성거리다, 배회하다
23 reach	•	•	관광객
24 troop	•	•	정확히
25 fame	•	•	명성
26 useless	•	•	군대, 무리
27 exist	•	•	존재하다
28 nickname	•	•	헛된, 소용없는
29 variety	•	•	여러 가지; 버라이어티 쇼
30 tourist	•	•	별명

WORD LIST

□ 01	spread [spred]	동	퍼지다
□ 02	prefer [prifə́ːr]	동	선호하다
□ 03	decorate [dékərèit]	동	장식하다
□ 04	password [pǽswə̀ːrd]	명	암호
□ 05	accountant [əkáuntənt]	명	회계사
□ 06	shame [ʃeim]	명	수치심
□ 07	diplomat [dípləmæ̀t]	명	외교관
□ 08	strict [strikt]	형	엄격한
□ 09	comfortable [kʌ́mfərtəbəl]	형	안락한
□ 10	select [silékt]	동	선택하다
□ 11	cold-hearted [kóuldhɑ̀ːrtid]	형	냉정한
□ 12	false [fɔːls]	형	거짓의, 가짜의
□ 13	deal with		처리하다
□ 14	billion [bíljən]	명	10억
□ 15	opinion [əpínjən]	명	의견
□ 16	recover [rikʌ́vər]	동	회복하다
□ 17	pregnant [prégnənt]	형	임신한
□ 18	uncertain [ʌ̀nsə́ːrtən]	형	불확실한
□ 19	achievement [ətʃíːvmənt]	명	업적, 성취
□ 20	exhausted [igzɔ́ːstid]	형	기진맥진한
□ 21	install [instɔ́ːl]	동	설치하다
□ 22	prevent [privént]	동	막다
□ 23	overtime [óuvərtàim]	부	규정 시간 외에
□ 24	throw [θrou]	동	던지다
□ 25	narrow [nǽrou]	형	좁은
□ 26	retire [ritáiər]	동	은퇴하다
□ 27	talented [tǽləntid]	형	재능 있는
□ 28	criticize [krítisàiz]	동	비난하다
□ 29	hire [háiər]	동	고용하다
□ 30	basement [béismənt]	명	지하실

WORD TEST

A 다음 영어는 우리말로, 우리말은 영어로 쓰시오.

01	spread	______	11	냉정한	______
02	prefer	______	12	거짓의, 가짜의	______
03	decorate	______	13	처리하다	______
04	password	______	14	10억	______
05	accountant	______	15	의견	______
06	shame	______	16	회복하다	______
07	diplomat	______	17	임신한	______
08	strict	______	18	불확실한	______
09	comfortable	______	19	업적, 성취	______
10	select	______	20	기진맥진한	______

B 다음 영어를 우리말과 알맞은 것끼리 연결하시오.

21	install	•	• 설치하다
22	prevent	•	• 규정 시간 외에
23	overtime	•	• 막다
24	throw	•	• 던지다
25	narrow	•	• 지하실
26	retire	•	• 은퇴하다
27	talented	•	• 좁은
28	criticize	•	• 비난하다
29	hire	•	• 고용하다
30	basement	•	• 재능 있는

WORD LIST

□ 01	count [kaunt]	통 (수를) 세다
□ 02	hatch [hætʃ]	통 (알이) 부화하다
□ 03	cupboard [kʌ́bərd]	명 찬장
□ 04	cop [kɑp]	명 경찰관
□ 05	rotten [rɑ́tn]	형 썩은
□ 06	spit [spit]	통 뱉다
□ 07	vending machine	자동 판매기
□ 08	further [fə́ːrðər]	형 그 이상의
□ 09	catch a cold	감기에 걸리다
□ 10	forgive [fərgív]	통 용서하다
□ 11	allow [əláu]	통 허락하다
□ 12	patient [péiʃənt]	형 인내심 있는 명 환자
□ 13	flu [fluː]	명 독감
□ 14	in danger	위험에 처한
□ 15	nourish [nə́ːriʃ]	통 ~에게 자양분을 주다
□ 16	agenda [ədʒéndə]	명 안건
□ 17	election [ilékʃən]	명 선거
□ 18	successfully [səksésfəli]	부 성공적으로
□ 19	unusual [ʌnjúːʒuəl]	형 보기 드문
□ 20	recession [riséʃən]	명 불경기
□ 21	safe [seif]	명 금고
□ 22	suspect [səspékt]	명 용의자
□ 23	thankful [θǽŋkfəl]	형 감사하는
□ 24	export [ikspɔ́ːrt]	통 수출하다
□ 25	coal [koul]	명 석탄
□ 26	guilty [gílti]	형 유죄의
□ 27	disappear [dìsəpíər]	통 사라지다
□ 28	approach [əpróutʃ]	통 접근하다
□ 29	naive [nɑːíːv]	형 순진한
□ 30	stranger [stréindʒər]	명 낯선 사람

WORD TEST

A 다음 영어는 우리말로, 우리말은 영어로 쓰시오.

01	count	______	11	허락하다	______
02	hatch	______	12	인내심 있는; 환자	______
03	cupboard	______	13	독감	______
04	cop	______	14	위험에 처한	______
05	rotten	______	15	~에게 자양분을 주다	______
06	spit	______	16	안건	______
07	vending machine	______	17	선거	______
08	further	______	18	성공적으로	______
09	catch a cold	______	19	보기 드문	______
10	forgive	______	20	불경기	______

B 다음 영어를 우리말과 알맞은 것끼리 연결하시오.

21	safe •		• 접근하다
22	suspect •		• 유죄의
23	thankful •		• 용의자
24	export •		• 순진한
25	coal •		• 수출하다
26	guilty •		• 석탄
27	disappear •		• 사라지다
28	approach •		• 낯선 사람
29	naive •		• 금고
30	stranger •		• 감사하는

WORD LIST

□ 01	fatty [fǽti]	형 지방이 많은
□ 02	give a big hand	큰 박수를 보내다
□ 03	swim [swim]	동 수영하다
□ 04	enough [inʌ́f]	형 ~할 만큼 충분한
□ 05	carefully [kέərfəli]	부 주의 깊게
□ 06	position [pəzíʃən]	명 입장, 위치
□ 07	ask for advice	조언을 구하다
□ 08	trouble [trʌ́bl]	명 문제, 골칫거리
□ 09	tired [taiərd]	형 피곤한
□ 10	close [klous]	형 가까운
□ 11	warn [wɔːrn]	동 경고하다
□ 12	hero [híərou]	명 영웅
□ 13	lend [lend]	동 빌려주다
□ 14	speak [spiːk]	동 말하다
□ 15	partner [pɑ́ːrtnər]	명 동반자
□ 16	go fishing	낚시하러 가다
□ 17	health [helθ]	명 건강
□ 18	mall [mɔːl]	명 쇼핑센터
□ 19	chance [tʃæns]	명 기회
□ 20	take part in	참가하다
□ 21	thirsty [θə́ːrsti]	형 목이 마른
□ 22	climb up	~에 오르다
□ 23	surprise [sərpráiz]	동 놀라게 하다
□ 24	horror [hɔ́ːrər]	명 공포
□ 25	keep one's promise	약속을 지키다
□ 26	for a long time	오랫동안
□ 27	travel [trǽvəl]	동 여행하다 명 여행
□ 28	get over	극복하다
□ 29	succeed [səksíːd]	동 성공하다
□ 30	office [ɔ́ːfis]	명 회사, 사무실

WORD TEST

A 다음 영어는 우리말로, 우리말은 영어로 쓰시오.

01	fatty	______	**11**	경고하다	______
02	give a big hand	______	**12**	영웅	______
03	swim	______	**13**	빌려주다	______
04	enough	______	**14**	말하다	______
05	carefully	______	**15**	동반자	______
06	position	______	**16**	낚시하러 가다	______
07	ask for advice	______	**17**	건강	______
08	trouble	______	**18**	쇼핑센터	______
09	tired	______	**19**	기회	______
10	close	______	**20**	참가하다	______

B 다음 영어를 우리말과 알맞은 것끼리 연결하시오.

21	thirsty	•	• 약속을 지키다
22	climb up	•	• 놀라게 하다
23	surprise	•	• 목이 마른
24	horror	•	• ~에 오르다
25	keep one's promise	•	• 공포
26	for a long time	•	• 성공하다
27	travel	•	• 여행하다; 여행
28	get over	•	• 극복하다
29	succeed	•	• 오랫동안
30	office	•	• 회사, 사무실

WORD LIST

□ 01	scholarship [skɑ́lərʃìp]	명 장학금
□ 02	college [kɑ́lidʒ]	명 대학
□ 03	attack [ətǽk]	동 공격하다
□ 04	war [wɔːr]	명 전쟁
□ 05	guide [gaid]	명 안내인, 안내 책자
□ 06	take a good rest	충분히 휴식하다, 편하게 쉬다
□ 07	warning sign	경고판
□ 08	weapon [wépən]	명 무기
□ 09	enemy [énəmi]	명 적, 원수
□ 10	credit card	신용 카드
□ 11	magazine [mæ̀gəzíːn]	명 잡지
□ 12	bored [bɔːrd]	형 지루한
□ 13	well off	잘사는, 부유한
□ 14	company [kʌ́mpəni]	명 회사; 친구
□ 15	have a bad cough	심하게 기침을 하다
□ 16	achieve [ətʃíːv]	동 성취하다
□ 17	goal [goul]	명 목표
□ 18	store [stɔːr]	명 가게
□ 19	read through	통독하다, 다 읽다
□ 20	project [prɑ́dʒekt]	명 기획, 과제, 프로젝트
□ 21	meeting [míːtiŋ]	명 회의
□ 22	map [mæp]	명 지도
□ 23	breathe [briːð]	동 숨을 쉬다
□ 24	in time	제시간에
□ 25	grow up	성장하다
□ 26	gloomy [glúːmi]	형 우울한, 어두운
□ 27	mood [muːd]	명 기분
□ 28	noon [nuːn]	명 정오
□ 29	overcome [òuvərkʌ́m]	동 극복하다
□ 30	grief [griːf]	명 깊은 슬픔, 비통

WORD TEST

A 다음 영어는 우리말로, 우리말은 영어로 쓰시오.

01 scholarship ______________

02 college ______________

03 attack ______________

04 war ______________

05 guide ______________

06 take a good rest ______________

07 warning sign ______________

08 weapon ______________

09 enemy ______________

10 credit card ______________

11 잡지 ______________

12 지루한 ______________

13 잘사는, 부유한 ______________

14 회사; 친구 ______________

15 심하게 기침을 하다 ______________

16 성취하다 ______________

17 목표 ______________

18 가게 ______________

19 통독하다, 다 읽다 ______________

20 기획, 과제, 프로젝트 ______________

B 다음 영어를 우리말과 알맞은 것끼리 연결하시오.

21 meeting	•	•	깊은 슬픔, 비통
22 map	•	•	기분
23 breathe	•	•	숨을 쉬다
24 in time	•	•	회의
25 grow up	•	•	성장하다
26 gloomy	•	•	정오
27 mood	•	•	지도
28 noon	•	•	우울한, 어두운
29 overcome	•	•	극복하다
30 grief	•	•	제시간에

WORD LIST

□ 01	politics [pálitiks]	명 정치학
□ 02	complicated [kámpləkèitid]	형 복잡한
□ 03	locate [loukéit]	동 (~에) 위치를 정하다
□ 04	traveler [trǽvlər]	명 여행자
□ 05	swimsuit [swímsù:t]	명 수영복
□ 06	rapidly [rǽpidli]	부 급속히
□ 07	garbage [gá:rbidʒ]	명 쓰레기
□ 08	regard [rigá:rd]	동 여기다, 간주하다
□ 09	forum [fɔ́:rəm]	명 포럼, 토론회
□ 10	reason [rí:zən]	명 이유
□ 11	absent [ǽbsənt]	형 결석한
□ 12	bright [brait]	형 밝은
□ 13	trousers [tráuzərz]	명 바지
□ 14	unhappy [ʌ̀nhǽpi]	형 불행한
□ 15	advice [ədváis]	명 조언
□ 16	helpful [hélpfəl]	형 도움이 되는
□ 17	encourage [enkə́:ridʒ]	동 격려하다
□ 18	notice [nóutis]	동 알아채다
□ 19	wrong [rɔ:ŋ]	형 틀린
□ 20	worm [wə:rm]	명 벌레
□ 21	break out	(전쟁 등이) 발발하다
□ 22	tight [tait]	형 (옷이) 꽉 조이는
□ 23	invent [invént]	동 발명하다
□ 24	declare [dikléər]	동 선언하다
□ 25	independence [ìndipéndəns]	명 독립
□ 26	professor [prəfésər]	명 교수
□ 27	moss [mɔ:s]	명 이끼
□ 28	timetable [táimtèibl]	명 시간표
□ 29	remind [rimáind]	동 상기시키다
□ 30	scholar [skálər]	명 학자

WORD TEST

A 다음 영어는 우리말로, 우리말은 영어로 쓰시오.

01 politics ______________
02 complicated ______________
03 locate ______________
04 traveler ______________
05 swimsuit ______________
06 rapidly ______________
07 garbage ______________
08 regard ______________
09 forum ______________
10 reason ______________
11 결석한 ______________
12 밝은 ______________
13 바지 ______________
14 불행한 ______________
15 조언 ______________
16 도움이 되는 ______________
17 격려하다 ______________
18 알아채다 ______________
19 틀린 ______________
20 벌레 ______________

B 다음 영어를 우리말과 알맞은 것끼리 연결하시오.

21 break out	•	•	학자
22 tight	•	•	이끼
23 invent	•	•	시간표
24 declare	•	•	선언하다
25 independence	•	•	상기시키다
26 professor	•	•	(옷이) 꽉 조이는
27 moss	•	•	발명하다
28 timetable	•	•	독립
29 remind	•	•	교수
30 scholar	•	•	(전쟁 등이) 발발하다

WORD LIST

□ 01	stewardess [stjúːərdis]	명 여자 승무원
□ 02	honesty [ánisti]	명 정직
□ 03	unify [júːnəfài]	동 통일하다
□ 04	sleepy [slíːpi]	형 졸린
□ 05	be fond of	~을 좋아하다
□ 06	order [ɔ́ːrdər]	동 명령하다
□ 07	fire [faiər]	동 발사하다; 쏘다
□ 08	walk [wɔːk]	동 산책시키다; 걷다
□ 09	make (a) noise	떠들다
□ 10	join [dʒɔin]	동 참가하다
□ 11	careful [kɛ́ərfəl]	형 조심스러운
□ 12	plumber [plʌ́mər]	명 배관공
□ 13	faucet [fɔ́ːsit]	명 수도꼭지
□ 14	garage [gərɑ́ːdʒ]	명 차고
□ 15	immediately [imíːdiətli]	부 즉시
□ 16	plate [pleit]	명 접시
□ 17	dish [diʃ]	명 음식; 요리
□ 18	vote [vout]	동 투표하다 명 투표
□ 19	increasing [inkríːsiŋ]	형 증가하는
□ 20	behave [bihéiv]	동 행동하다
□ 21	cause [kɔːz]	동 야기하다
□ 22	object [ɑ́bdʒikt]	명 물체
□ 23	gravity [grǽvəti]	명 중력
□ 24	clear [kliər]	형 명확한
□ 25	major in	~을 전공하다
□ 26	psychology [saikɑ́lədʒi]	명 심리학
□ 27	look up	(사전 등으로) 찾아보다
□ 28	planet [plǽnət]	명 행성
□ 29	cover [kʌ́vər]	동 뒤덮다
□ 30	invest [invést]	동 투자하다

WORD TEST

A 다음 영어는 우리말로, 우리말은 영어로 쓰시오.

01 stewardess ______________

02 honesty ______________

03 unify ______________

04 sleepy ______________

05 be fond of ______________

06 order ______________

07 fire ______________

08 walk ______________

09 make (a) noise ______________

10 join ______________

11 조심스러운 ______________

12 배관공 ______________

13 수도꼭지 ______________

14 차고 ______________

15 즉시 ______________

16 접시 ______________

17 음식; 요리 ______________

18 투표하다; 투표 ______________

19 증가하는 ______________

20 행동하다 ______________

B 다음 영어를 우리말과 알맞은 것끼리 연결하시오.

21 cause	•	•	행성
22 object	•	•	(사전 등으로) 찾아보다
23 gravity	•	•	~을 전공하다
24 clear	•	•	뒤덮다
25 major in	•	•	명확한
26 psychology	•	•	물체
27 look up	•	•	심리학
28 planet	•	•	야기하다
29 cover	•	•	중력
30 invest	•	•	투자하다

WORD LIST

□ 01	wife [waif]	명 아내
□ 02	of course	물론, 당연히
□ 03	absolutely [æbsəlúːtli]	부 틀림없이, 완전히
□ 04	actually [ǽktʃuəli]	부 정말로
□ 05	math [mæθ]	명 수학(= mathematics)
□ 06	problem [prɑ́bləm]	명 문제
□ 07	direct [dirékt]	동 감독하다, 지휘하다
□ 08	film [film]	명 영화, 필름
□ 09	enjoy [indʒɔ́i]	동 즐기다
□ 10	street [striːt]	명 거리, 도로
□ 11	person [pə́ːrsn]	명 사람
□ 12	along [əlɔ́ːŋ]	전 ~을 따라서
□ 13	road [roud]	명 길
□ 14	castle [kǽsl]	명 성, 성곽
□ 15	hill [hil]	명 언덕
□ 16	corner [kɔ́ːrnər]	명 모퉁이
□ 17	museum [mjuːzíːəm]	명 박물관, 미술관
□ 18	bakery [béikəri]	명 빵집, 제과점
□ 19	lab [læb]	명 실험실(= laboratory)
□ 20	hungry [hʌ́ŋgri]	형 배고픈
□ 21	already [ɔːlrédi]	부 이미, 벌써
□ 22	homework [hóumwə̀ːrk]	명 숙제
□ 23	be good at	~을 잘하다
□ 24	hardly [hɑ́ːrdli]	부 거의 ~아니다
□ 25	bike [baik]	명 자전거
□ 26	library [láibrèri]	명 도서관
□ 27	seldom [séldəm]	부 좀처럼 ~않는
□ 28	strange [streindʒ]	형 이상한
□ 29	idea [aidíːə]	명 생각, 발상
□ 30	single [síŋgl]	형 단 하나의

WORD TEST

A 다음 영어는 우리말로, 우리말은 영어로 쓰시오.

01 wife ____________

02 of course ____________

03 absolutely ____________

04 actually ____________

05 math ____________

06 problem ____________

07 direct ____________

08 film ____________

09 enjoy ____________

10 street ____________

11 사람 ____________

12 ~을 따라서 ____________

13 길 ____________

14 성, 성곽 ____________

15 언덕 ____________

16 모퉁이 ____________

17 박물관, 미술관 ____________

18 빵집, 제과점 ____________

19 실험실 ____________

20 배고픈 ____________

B 다음 영어를 우리말과 알맞은 것끼리 연결하시오.

21 already	•	•	생각, 발상
22 homework	•	•	이미, 벌써
23 be good at	•	•	좀처럼 ~않는
24 hardly	•	•	자전거
25 bike	•	•	거의 ~아니다
26 library	•	•	이상한
27 seldom	•	•	단 하나의
28 strange	•	•	도서관
29 idea	•	•	~을 잘하다
30 single	•	•	숙제

□ 01	evening [íːvniŋ]	명 저녁
□ 02	cousin [kʌ́zn]	명 사촌
□ 03	favorite [féivərit]	형 좋아하는
□ 04	writer [ráitər]	명 작가
□ 05	handsome [hǽnsəm]	형 잘생긴
□ 06	toward [tɔːrd]	전 ~을 향하여
□ 07	period [píːəriəd]	명 기간, 시기
□ 08	wooden [wúdn]	형 나무로 된
□ 09	basket [bǽskit]	명 바구니
□ 10	hear [hiər]	동 듣다, 전해 듣다
□ 11	ID card	신분증(= identity card)
□ 12	important [impɔ́ːrtənt]	형 중요한
□ 13	used to	~하곤 했다, ~이었다
□ 14	active [ǽktiv]	형 활동적인
□ 15	volcano [valkéinou]	명 화산
□ 16	read [riːd]	동 읽다
□ 17	self-confidence [sèlfkɑ́nfidəns]	명 자신감
□ 18	behind [biháind]	전 ~의 뒤에
□ 19	pity [píti]	명 동정, 연민
□ 20	arm [ɑːrm]	명 팔
□ 21	newspaper [njúːzpèipər]	명 신문
□ 22	delicious [dilíʃəs]	형 아주 맛있는
□ 23	doll [dal]	명 인형
□ 24	finally [fáinəli]	부 마침내
□ 25	bench [bentʃ]	명 긴 의자, 벤치
□ 26	eagle [íːgl]	명 독수리
□ 27	ground [graund]	명 땅바닥, 지면
□ 28	pipe [paip]	명 관, 파이프
□ 29	science [sáiəns]	명 과학
□ 30	take a walk	산책하다

WORD TEST

A 다음 영어는 우리말로, 우리말은 영어로 쓰시오.

01 evening ____________
02 cousin ____________
03 favorite ____________
04 writer ____________
05 handsome ____________
06 toward ____________
07 period ____________
08 wooden ____________
09 basket ____________
10 hear ____________
11 신분증 ____________
12 중요한 ____________
13 ~하곤 했다, ~이었다 ____________
14 활동적인 ____________
15 화산 ____________
16 읽다 ____________
17 자신감 ____________
18 ~의 뒤에 ____________
19 동정, 연민 ____________
20 팔 ____________

B 다음 영어를 우리말과 알맞은 것끼리 연결하시오.

21 newspaper •	• 산책하다
22 delicious •	• 독수리
23 doll •	• 인형
24 finally •	• 마침내
25 bench •	• 긴 의자, 벤치
26 eagle •	• 땅바닥, 지면
27 ground •	• 아주 맛있는
28 pipe •	• 관, 파이프
29 science •	• 과학
30 take a walk •	• 신문

적중! 중학영문법 3300제 Level 3

워크북

내신 대비 문제

서술형 대비 문장 연습

+

학교 시험 대비 문제

Chapter 01
부정사

서술형 대비 문장 연습

A 다음 밑줄 친 부분을 어법에 맞게 고쳐 문장을 다시 쓰시오.

1 It is easy for her eat spicy food.

→ ______________________________

2 You are never too old learning.

→ ______________________________

3 She told me what seeing in New York.

→ ______________________________

4 He found that difficult to run a marathon.

→ ______________________________

5 It is dangerous dogs to eat chocolate.

→ ______________________________

6 Please let me to know if you need anything.

→ ______________________________

B 다음 우리말과 일치하도록 괄호 안의 말을 바르게 배열하시오.

1 한 사람도 보이지 않았다. (seen, was, not, to, a man, be)

→ ______________________________

2 그는 그녀를 그리워하는 것 같다. (to, her, seems, he, miss)

→ ______________________________

3 나는 자전거 타는 방법을 배울 것이다. (will, to, a bike, I, ride, how, learn)

→ ______________________________

4 너희들은 도서관에서 조용히 해야 한다. (to, quiet, are, in the library, you, keep)

→ ______________________________

5 내가 거기까지 가는 데 한 시간이 걸린다. (me, to, an hour, it, there, takes, get)

→ ______________________________

6 그는 어디에서 표를 사야 할지 몰랐다. (know, to, a ticket, buy, didn't, he, where)

→ ______________________________

C 다음 우리말과 일치하도록 괄호 안의 말을 이용하여 문장을 완성하시오.

1 다른 사람들을 돕다니 너는 친절하구나. (kind, other people)
→ ______________________________

2 그는 파스타를 만드는 것이 쉽다는 것을 알았다. (find, easy, make)
→ ______________________________

3 우리가 물 없이 사는 것은 불가능하다. (impossible, without)
→ ______________________________

4 나는 쓸 종이가 한 장 필요하다. (piece, write)
→ ______________________________

5 그는 너무 바빠서 그들을 만날 수 없었다. (too, busy)
→ ______________________________

6 나는 내 남동생이 그의 방을 청소하는 것을 도왔다. (clean)
→ ______________________________

D 다음 주어진 문장과 같은 뜻이 되도록 to부정사를 이용하여 문장을 완성하시오.

1 It was so cold that he couldn't sleep.
= It was ______________________________.

2 It seems that he passed the test.
= He seems ______________________________.

3 We are going to arrive at your hotel tomorrow.
= We ______________________________.

4 She is so smart that she can solve the problem.
= She is ______________________________.

5 He didn't tell me when I should call him.
= He didn't tell me ______________________________.

6 We haven't decided where we should go for a picnic.
= We haven't decided ______________________________.

Chapter 02
동명사

서술형 대비 문장 연습

A 다음 밑줄 친 부분을 어법에 맞게 고쳐 문장을 다시 쓰시오.

1 We decided save some money.
→ ______

2 Listening to music make me calm.
→ ______

3 He denied for her being his girlfriend.
→ ______

4 My dad kept me from go out at night.
→ ______

5 On graduated, she worked as a doctor.
→ ______

6 Susan was sorry not for remembering my birthday.
→ ______

B 다음 우리말과 일치하도록 괄호 안의 말을 바르게 배열하시오.

1 그는 조깅하는 데 한 시간을 보낸다. (spends, he, jogging, an hour)
→ ______

2 나는 항상 그녀가 노래하는 것을 좋아한다. (I, singing, like, her, always)
→ ______

3 그 책은 두 번 읽을 가치가 있다. (worth, twice, reading, the, is, book)
→ ______

4 제가 질문을 해도 될까요? (you, a question, me, mind, asking, do)
→ ______

5 그녀는 그의 이름을 기억하려고 노력했다. (tried, name, she, remember, to, his)
→ ______

6 나는 그가 늦을까 봐 걱정된다. (his, late, worried, being, I'm, about)
→ ______

C 다음 우리말과 일치하도록 괄호 안의 말을 이용하여 문장을 완성하시오.

1 나는 일찍 일어나는 것에 익숙하다. (used, get up)
→ ______________________________

2 그는 그녀가 떠나는 것을 막을 수 없었다. (prevent, leave)
→ ______________________________

3 나는 그녀가 자신의 직업에 대해 말한 것을 기억한다. (talk about)
→ ______________________________

4 그녀는 자신의 부모님을 찾아가는 것을 고대했다. (look, visit, parents)
→ ______________________________

5 그는 새로운 사람들을 만나는 것을 두려워하지 않는다. (be afraid of)
→ ______________________________

6 내 여동생은 내가 그녀의 컴퓨터를 사용하는 것을 좋아하지 않았다. (use)
→ ______________________________

D 다음 주어진 문장과 같은 뜻이 되도록 동명사를 이용하여 문장을 완성하시오.

1 I'm worried that I might make her sad.
→ I'm worried about ______________________________.

2 I hate that he tells lies.
→ I hate ______________________________.

3 Jenny doesn't like that I practice dancing.
→ Jenny doesn't like ______________________________.

4 Do you mind if I turn off the TV?
→ Do you mind ______________________________?

5 They didn't know that he quit school.
→ They didn't know about ______________________________.

6 I was angry that they didn't tell me about it.
→ I was angry at ______________________________.

Chapter 03
분사

서술형 대비 문장 연습

A 다음 밑줄 친 부분을 어법에 맞게 고쳐 문장을 다시 쓰시오.

1 Boring, I turned on the TV.

→ ______________________________

2 I saw her waited for a bus.

→ ______________________________

3 Frankly spoken, he is not honest.

→ ______________________________

4 There was nobody at home, we went out again.

→ ______________________________

5 He having no money, he had to walk home.

→ ______________________________

6 Hearding the sad news, I couldn't say anything.

→ ______________________________

B 다음 우리말과 일치하도록 괄호 안의 말을 바르게 배열하시오.

1 비가 와서 경기가 취소되었다. (being, canceled, the game, it, rainy, was)

→ ______________________________

2 그는 불이 켜진 채로 잠이 들었다. (turned, he, on, fell asleep, the light, with)

→ ______________________________

3 저녁을 먹으면서, 우리는 여행 계획을 세웠다. (we, having, planned, dinner, our trip)

→ ______________________________

4 그는 다리를 꼰 채로 앉아 있었다. (his legs, sat, with, he, crossed)

→ ______________________________

5 나는 배가 고프지 않아서 점심을 먹지 않았다. (feeling, not, hungry)

→ ______________________, I didn't eat lunch.

6 그는 무엇을 해야 할지 몰라서 그냥 그곳에 서 있었다. (what, not, to, knowing, do)

→ ______________________, he just stood there.

C 다음 우리말과 일치하도록 괄호 안의 말을 이용하여 문장을 완성하시오.

1 기타를 치고 있는 소녀는 내 사촌이다. (cousin)
→ ____________________

2 그는 그의 차가 수리되기를 원한다. (want, repair)
→ ____________________

3 그 새로운 게임은 흥미로워 보인다. (look, excite)
→ ____________________

4 엄밀히 말해서, 이 답은 정확하지 않다. (answer, correct)
→ ____________________

5 그는 부상당한 사람들을 돌보았다. (look after, injure)
→ ____________________

6 나는 그녀가 나의 이름을 부르는 것을 들었다. (hear, call)
→ ____________________

D 다음 문장을 분사구문으로 바꾸어 쓰시오.

1 As she waited for the bus, she ate some ice cream.
→ ____________________, she ate some ice cream.

2 If you turn to the right, you will find the bank.
→ ____________________, you will find the bank.

3 As it was sunny and warm, we went to the park.
→ ____________________, we went to the park.

4 Because he didn't have anything to do, he was bored.
→ ____________________, he was bored.

5 Because there was no food, she went out to eat.
→ ____________________, she went out to eat.

6 Because she made no effort, now she gets nothing.
→ ____________________, now she gets nothing.

Chapter 04
시제

서술형 대비 문장 연습

A 다음 밑줄 친 부분을 어법에 맞게 고쳐 문장을 다시 쓰시오.

1 I had not seen Amy since she left here.
→ ______________________________

2 The game has just begun when I arrived.
→ ______________________________

3 I will go out when my sister will arrive at home.
→ ______________________________

4 She is preparing for an hour when I entered the kitchen.
→ ______________________________

5 My neighbors have been argued outside since this morning.
→ ______________________________

6 Dave didn't come to school because he has been sick yesterday.
→ ______________________________

B 다음 우리말과 일치하도록 괄호 안의 말을 바르게 배열하시오.

1 나는 방금 점심을 먹었다. (lunch, just, have, I, eaten)
→ ______________________________

2 그녀는 내일 서울로 이사할 것이다. (is, tomorrow, Seoul, she, moving, to)
→ ______________________________

3 나는 2년째 요가 수업을 듣고 있다. (I, taking, have, yoga classes, been)
→ ____________________ for two years.

4 그는 한 시간 동안 신문을 읽고 있다. (has, a newspaper, he, reading, been)
→ ____________________ for an hour.

5 내가 그를 방문했을 때 그는 두 시간째 운동을 하고 있었다. (had, he, exercising, been)
→ ____________________ for two hours when I visited him.

6 John이 도착했을 때, 회의는 이미 끝난 상태였다. (finished, the meeting, already, had)
→ ____________________ when John arrived.

C 다음 우리말과 일치하도록 괄호 안의 말을 이용하여 문장을 완성하시오.

1 너는 유럽에 가 본 적이 있니? (ever, be)
→ ______________________________

2 그녀는 하루 종일 피아노를 치고 있다. (play, all day)
→ ______________________________

3 그는 이미 그 영화를 봤다고 나에게 말했다. (already, see)
→ He told me that ______________________________.

4 그는 2013년부터 한 소설을 써 오고 있다. (write, novel)
→ ______________________________ since 2013.

5 내가 그곳에 갔을 때 그 가게는 이미 문을 닫았다. (store, close)
→ ______________________________ when I got there.

6 내가 도착했을 때 3일째 눈이 내리고 있었다. (snow)
→ ______________________________ for three days when I arrived.

D 다음 주어진 문장과 같은 뜻이 되도록 문장을 완성하시오.

1 I lost the key to my house. I don't have it now.
→ I ______________________________ to my house.

2 She went to Canada last year. She is still there.
→ She ______________________________ Canada.

3 Last Saturday, Helen came to my house. She is still staying here.
→ Helen ______________________________ at my house since last Saturday.

4 The game started at 5 o'clock. I got to the stadium at 5:40.
→ The game ______________________________ when I got to the stadium.

5 He began to make a sandcastle an hour ago. He is still making it.
→ He ______________________________ for an hour.

6 She began to play the violin when she was eight. She is still playing it.
→ She ______________________________ since she was eight.

Chapter 05
조동사

서술형 대비 문장 연습

A 다음 밑줄 친 부분을 어법에 맞게 고쳐 문장을 다시 쓰시오.

1 I will <u>can</u> call you back later.
→ ______________________________

2 You <u>ought to not</u> be here.
→ ______________________________

3 I <u>would rather to stay</u> at home.
→ ______________________________

4 She <u>has not to</u> get up early tomorrow.
→ ______________________________

5 He <u>must</u> wait for her for an hour yesterday.
→ ______________________________

6 There <u>would</u> be a famous restaurant around here.
→ ______________________________

B 다음 우리말과 일치하도록 괄호 안의 말을 바르게 배열하시오.

1 이 케이크는 정말 맛이 달콤하다. (taste, does, this cake, sweet)
→ ______________________________

2 그녀가 실수를 했을지도 모른다. (mistake, she, have, a, made, may)
→ ______________________________

3 그가 네 돈을 훔쳤을 리가 없어. (can't, stolen, money, he, have, your)
→ ______________________________

4 너는 시간을 낭비해서는 안 된다. (ought, waste, your, not, you, to, time)
→ ______________________________

5 우리는 집에 머무는 편이 낫다. (may, well, at home, we, stay, as)
→ ______________________________

6 나는 낚시하러 가느니 등산을 하러 가겠다. (would, go, rather, I, than, hiking)
→ ______________________________ go fishing.

C 다음 우리말과 일치하도록 괄호 안의 말을 이용하여 문장을 완성하시오.

1 그녀가 피곤할 리가 없어. (tired)
→ ______________________________

2 그 수업은 지루했음에 틀림없다. (class, boring)
→ ______________________________

3 당신은 내 이름을 확인했어야 했다. (check)
→ ______________________________

4 그녀는 지금 결정할 필요가 없다. (have, decide)
→ ______________________________

5 그는 어제 그의 여동생을 돌봐야 했다. (take care of)
→ ______________________________

6 그가 그의 아들을 자랑스러워하는 것도 당연하다. (may, be proud of)
→ ______________________________

D 다음 주어진 문장과 같은 뜻이 되도록 문장을 완성하시오.

1 I'm sure that this house is very expensive.
→ This house ______________________________.

2 I am sorry that you didn't tell your mother the truth.
→ You ______________________________ your mother the truth.

3 I'm sure that you left your wallet in the office.
→ You ______________________________ your wallet in the office.

4 This building was a flower shop. Now it is a church.
→ The church ______________________________ a flower shop.

5 I didn't listen to the teacher, but now I regret that.
→ I ______________________________ to the teacher.

6 Amy lived in Seoul when she was young, but now she doesn't.
→ Amy ______________________________ in Seoul.

Chapter 06
수동태

서술형 대비 문장 연습

A 다음 밑줄 친 부분을 어법에 맞게 고쳐 문장을 다시 쓰시오.

1 This pasta was made <u>to</u> her.

→ ______________________________

2 The work <u>will finish</u> in a few weeks.

→ ______________________________

3 They were made <u>wear</u> clean uniforms.

→ ______________________________

4 It <u>said</u> that Superman has special powers.

→ ______________________________

5 Korean history is taught <u>of us</u> by Mr. Lee.

→ ______________________________

6 Many trees <u>have planted</u> in this park since last year.

→ ______________________________

B 다음 우리말과 일치하도록 괄호 안의 말을 바르게 배열하시오.

1 나는 Jake에게 꽃들을 받았다. (was, flowers, by, I, given, Jake)

→ ______________________________

2 이 책은 오늘 반납되어야 한다. (returned, should, this, today, book, be)

→ ______________________________

3 Jenny가 길을 건너는 것이 보였다. (crossing, was, a road, Jenny, seen)

→ ______________________________

4 스트레스는 질병을 유발한다고 한다. (cause, said, stress, is, disease, to)

→ ______________________________

5 그 상자는 지금 막 치워졌다. (has, removed, the, just, box, been)

→ ______________________________

6 교실은 학생들로 가득 차 있다. (filled, the, classroom, with, students, is)

→ ______________________________

C 다음 우리말과 일치하도록 괄호 안의 말을 이용하여 문장을 완성하시오.

1 저녁 식사가 나의 어머니에 의해 준비되고 있다. (dinner, prepare)

→ ______________________________

2 이 스웨터는 그를 위해 그의 아버지에 의해 만들어졌다. (sweater, make)

→ ______________________________

3 나는 어머니에 의해 방을 청소하게 되었다. (make, clean)

→ ______________________________

4 그 산은 눈으로 덮여 있었다. (cover)

→ ______________________________

5 고양이 한 마리가 트럭에 치였다. (run over)

→ ______________________________

6 Tom은 그의 친구들에 의해 천재라고 불린다. (call, a genius)

→ ______________________________

D 다음 문장을 수동태로 바꾸어 쓰시오.

1 Somebody heard the boy screaming.

→ ______________________________

2 My brother was using the computer.

→ ______________________________

3 Her parents bought her a pair of pants.

→ ______________________________

4 They have built a bridge across the river.

→ ______________________________

5 Children under 7 must not take this medicine.

→ ______________________________

6 They say that walking is the best exercise.

→ It ______________________________.

Chapter 07
대명사

서술형 대비 문장 연습

A 다음 밑줄 친 부분을 어법에 맞게 고쳐 문장을 다시 쓰시오.

1 We enjoyed <u>us</u> on our trip to Germany.
→ ______________________________

2 Each of <u>the answer</u> is worth 5 points.
→ ______________________________

3 Every member <u>were</u> present at the meeting.
→ ______________________________

4 Both of my brothers <u>likes</u> outdoor activities.
→ ______________________________

5 Some were angry, and <u>other</u> were confused.
→ ______________________________

6 One of their five children is a girl, and <u>the other</u> are boys.
→ ______________________________

B 다음 우리말과 일치하도록 괄호 안의 말을 바르게 배열하시오.

1 그들 둘 다 수영을 못한다. (them, swim, neither, of, can)
→ ______________________________

2 나의 부모님은 두 분 다 바쁘시다. (of, are, parents, both, busy, my)
→ ______________________________

3 모든 학생들이 코트를 입고 있다. (is, a coat, student, wearing, every)
→ ______________________________

4 내 친구들 중 아무도 커피를 마시지 않는다. (coffee, friends, of, drink, none, my)
→ ______________________________

5 반 친구들에게 네 소개를 해 주겠니? (you, to, yourself, can, the class, introduce)
→ ______________________________

6 그 꽃들 각각은 다른 색을 가지고 있다. (a, has, each, the, different, of, flowers, color)
→ ______________________________

C 다음 우리말과 일치하도록 괄호 안의 말을 이용하여 문장을 완성하시오.

1 그녀는 혼자서 이 집을 지었다. (build, oneself)

→ ______________________________

2 그 가방 둘 다 매우 낡았다. (of, old)

→ ______________________________

3 그는 스스로를 천재라고 생각한다. (think, a genius)

→ ______________________________

4 우리는 우리 자신을 믿어야 한다. (should, believe in)

→ ______________________________

5 이 반에 있는 모든 학생들은 열심히 공부한다. (every, class)

→ ______________________________

6 그는 혼자 힘으로 그 문제들을 해결하려고 노력했다. (solve, oneself)

→ ______________________________

D 다음 <보기>에서 알맞은 대명사를 골라 우리말에 맞게 영작하시오.

<보기>

someone　　something　　somewhere　　anything　　anyone

1 그녀는 아무것도 먹지 않았다. (eat)

→ ______________________________

2 날 위해 무언가를 해 줄 수 있니? (do)

→ ______________________________

3 나는 나를 도와줄 누군가가 필요해요. (need)

→ ______________________________

4 누구 연필 가지고 있니? (have)

→ ______________________________

5 나는 전에 어디선가 그를 본 적이 있다. (see, before)

→ ______________________________

Chapter 08
형용사와 부사

서술형 대비 문장 연습

A 다음 밑줄 친 부분을 어법에 맞게 고쳐 문장을 다시 쓰시오.

1 The restaurant was near empty.
→ ______________________________

2 I bought these pants very cheap.
→ ______________________________

3 Would you have any more chocolate?
→ ______________________________

4 Did you have many fun at the party?
→ ______________________________

5 The young is interested in new trends.
→ ______________________________

6 I had such wonderful a time with my cousins.
→ ______________________________

B 다음 우리말과 일치하도록 괄호 안의 말을 바르게 배열하시오.

1 이것은 정말 훌륭한 영화이다. (is, a, film, such, this, great)
→ ______________________________

2 그녀는 항상 밝게 웃는다. (brightly, she, always, smiles)
→ ______________________________

3 나를 7시에 깨워 줄 수 있니? (at, up, you, wake, can, me, seven)
→ ______________________________

4 나는 네게 말할 중요한 것이 있다. (something, I, important, you, have, to tell)
→ ______________________________

5 그는 점심으로 약간의 빵을 먹었다. (a, had, for lunch, little, he, bread)
→ ______________________________

6 상당수의 학생들이 오늘 결석했다. (students, absent, quite, were, a, today, few)
→ ______________________________

C 다음 우리말과 일치하도록 괄호 안의 말을 이용하여 문장을 완성하시오.

1 그 계획은 흥미롭게 들린다. (sound, interesting)
→ ______________________________

2 그녀는 정말 친절한 선생님이었다. (such, kind)
→ ______________________________

3 이 공원에는 나무가 거의 없다. (there, park)
→ ______________________________

4 그 실수는 나를 긴장하게 했다. (make, nervous)
→ ______________________________

5 Kate는 따뜻한 마실 것이 필요하다. (warm, drink)
→ ______________________________

6 그들은 다음 주 금요일까지 그것을 제출해야 한다. (should, hand in)
→ ______________________________

D 다음 괄호 안의 단어를 알맞은 곳에 넣어서 문장을 다시 쓰시오.

1 I have been to Canada. (never)
→ ______________________________

2 They are ready to go on a trip. (always)
→ ______________________________

3 Is there anything with this computer? (wrong)
→ ______________________________

4 I had such a time with my family in New York. (nice)
→ ______________________________

5 She goes jogging in the morning. (usually)
→ ______________________________

6 I want to do something for my grandmother. (special)
→ ______________________________

Chapter 09
비교

서술형 대비 문장 연습

A 다음 밑줄 친 부분을 어법에 맞게 고쳐 문장을 다시 쓰시오.

1 My bag is heavier than you.
→ ______________________________

2 The train got much and more crowded.
→ ______________________________

3 No player on his team is as fast than Steve.
→ ______________________________

4 She drew the picture as quick as possible.
→ ______________________________

5 He is taller than any other boys in his class.
→ ______________________________

6 The fast you drive, the more dangerous it is.
→ ______________________________

B 다음 우리말과 일치하도록 괄호 안의 말을 바르게 배열하시오.

1 가능한 한 빨리 내게 전화를 줘. (me, as, call, you, soon, can, as)
→ ______________________________

2 요가는 보이는 것만큼 쉽지 않다. (easy, it, as, yoga, not, as, is, looks)
→ ______________________________

3 내 가방은 네 것보다 훨씬 가볍다. (lighter, yours, much, my, than, is, bag)
→ ______________________________

4 당신이 더 행복할수록, 더 잘 일한다. (the, you, work, happier, are, the, you, better)
→ ______________________________

5 그는 나보다 테니스를 더 잘 친다. (plays, better, me, he, than, tennis)
→ ______________________________

6 Tom은 우리 반에서 가장 용감한 소년이다. (in, bravest, is, Tom, class, the, my, boy)
→ ______________________________

C 다음 우리말과 일치하도록 괄호 안의 말을 이용하여 문장을 완성하시오.

1 그의 연필은 내 것보다 두 배 길었다. (long)
→ ____

2 어떤 다른 배우도 Jack만큼 매력적이지 않다. (no, attractive)
→ ____

3 그는 점점 더 인기를 얻고 있다. (become, popular)
→ ____

4 그는 세계에서 가장 훌륭한 축구 선수들 중 한 명이다. (good, soccer)
→ ____

5 그녀는 가능한 한 명확하게 내 질문에 답했다. (clearly, possible)
→ ____

6 네가 운동을 많이 할수록, 너는 더 건강해질 것이다. (exercise, healthy)
→ ____

D 다음 주어진 문장과 같은 뜻이 되도록 문장을 완성하시오.

1 Dan is not as strong as his father.
→ Dan ________ ________ ________ ________ his father.

2 She studied as hard as she could.
→ She studied ________ ________ ________ ________.

3 Kate is not as famous as Grace.
→ Grace ________ ________ ________ ________ Kate.

4 As I sleep more, I feel more tired.
→ ________ ________ ________ ________, the more tired I feel.

5 Her bicycle is worse than my bicycle.
→ My bicycle ________ ________ ________ her bicycle.

6 Russia is the largest country in the world.
→ Russia is ________ ________ ________ ________ ________ countries in the world.

Chapter 10
전치사

서술형 대비 문장 연습

A 다음 밑줄 친 부분을 어법에 맞게 고쳐 문장을 다시 쓰시오.

1 I have no classes <u>at</u> Sunday.
→ ______________________________

2 John stood <u>among</u> two people.
→ ______________________________

3 He lived there <u>since</u> 2000 to 2010.
→ ______________________________

4 My friend was waiting for me <u>on</u> the bus stop.
→ ______________________________

5 She should finish her homework <u>till</u> this Friday.
→ ______________________________

6 I have been working there <u>during</u> almost a year.
→ ______________________________

B 다음 우리말과 일치하도록 괄호 안의 말을 바르게 배열하시오.

1 치즈는 우유로 만들어진다. (is, milk, cheese, made, from)
→ ______________________________

2 그는 그 결과에 놀랐다. (surprised, he, the result, at, was)
→ ______________________________

3 그녀는 창문 쪽으로 걸어갔다. (toward, she, the window, walked)
→ ______________________________

4 그는 주머니에서 지갑을 꺼냈다. (took, out of, he, pocket, a wallet, his)
→ ______________________________

5 그는 보통 오후에 축구를 한다. (usually, soccer, the, he, in, afternoon, plays)
→ ______________________________

6 내가 너에게 내 사진을 이메일로 보내 줄게. (send, my pictures, email, will, you, I, by)
→ ______________________________

C 다음 우리말과 일치하도록 괄호 안의 말을 이용하여 문장을 완성하시오.

1 그는 항상 내 앞에 앉는다. (sit)

→ ____________________

2 그녀는 버스를 타고 그곳에 갈 것이다. (will, go)

→ ____________________

3 그 책들은 한 시간 이내에 배달될 것이다. (will, deliver)

→ ____________________

4 그들은 바닥에 누워 있었다. (lie, floor)

→ ____________________

5 우리는 어제 공항에서 만났다. (meet, airport)

→ ____________________

6 나는 새벽에 누군가가 노래 부르는 것을 들었다. (someone, dawn)

→ ____________________

D 다음 〈보기〉에서 알맞은 전치사를 골라 우리말에 맞게 영작하시오.

〈보기〉

by	for	from	during	until

1 그녀는 한 달째 영어를 배우고 있다. (learn)

→ ____________________

2 나는 월요일부터 금요일까지 일한다. (work)

→ ____________________

3 Kelly는 내일까지 여기에 머물러야 한다. (should, stay)

→ ____________________

4 너는 그 책들을 내일까지 반납해야 한다. (should, return)

→ ____________________

5 너는 이번 방학 동안 무엇을 할 거니? (be going to, vacation)

→ ____________________

Chapter 11
관계사

서술형 대비 문장 연습

A 다음 밑줄 친 부분을 어법에 맞게 고쳐 문장을 다시 쓰시오.

1 This is the book what I've been looking for.

→ ______________________________

2 They are children that parents both work.

→ ______________________________

3 I don't like the way how he looks at me.

→ ______________________________

4 Whatever angry you are, you should have patience.

→ ______________________________

5 I don't remember the store which I bought this shirt.

→ ______________________________

6 I wrote a letter to John, which answered me quickly.

→ ______________________________

B 다음 우리말과 일치하도록 괄호 안의 말을 바르게 배열하시오.

1 그가 내게 준 것은 반지였다. (he, was, me, gave, what, a ring)

→ ______________________________

2 나는 그가 결석한 이유를 알고 있다. (know, absent, I, he, was, why, the reason)

→ ______________________________

3 우리 선생님은 내가 존경하는 분이다. (a person, respect, whom, I, is, my teacher)

→ ______________________________

4 당신이 좋아하는 것은 무엇이든지 살 수 있다. (you, buy, like, you, whatever, can)

→ ______________________________

5 오는 사람은 누구든지 환영받을 것이다. (be, whoever, welcomed, comes, will)

→ ______________________________

6 내가 아무리 열심히 노력해도, 그 일을 끝낼 수가 없다. (I, hard, however, try)

→ ______________________________, I can't finish the work.

C 다음 우리말과 일치하도록 괄호 안의 말을 이용하여 문장을 완성하시오.

1 우리는 그가 말한 것을 믿을 수 없었다. (believe, say)
→ ______________________________

2 나는 어머니가 의사인 친구가 한 명 있다. (have)
→ ______________________________

3 나는 뉴욕에 갔고, 그곳에서 나는 Amy를 만났다. (meet)
→ ______________________________

4 이것이 내가 그 문제를 해결한 방법이다. (solve, problem)
→ ______________________________

5 이곳은 사람들이 자연을 즐길 수 있는 공원이다. (where, nature)
→ ______________________________

6 그 가방이 아무리 좋더라도, 그것은 너무 비싸다. (nice, expensive)
→ ______________________________

D 다음 두 문장을 관계사를 이용하여 한 문장으로 바꾸어 쓰시오.

1 Jenny is a student. She likes playing the piano.
→ Jenny is ______________________________.

2 I know the woman. David fell in love with her.
→ I know ______________________________ David fell in love.

3 I bought a red shirt for a friend. His favorite color is red.
→ I bought a red shirt for a friend ______________________________.

4 That's the way. Babies express their feelings in that way.
→ That's ______________________________.

5 This is the only book. I read it last month.
→ This is ______________________________.

6 We visited the museum. And we saw many paintings there.
→ We visited ______________________________.

Chapter 12
접속사

서술형 대비 문장 연습

A 다음 밑줄 친 부분을 어법에 맞게 고쳐 문장을 다시 쓰시오.

1 Unless you don't study hard, you'll fail.

→ ______________________________

2 Neither Patrick or Dave knows how to skate.

→ ______________________________

3 My brother as well as I like to play soccer.

→ ______________________________

4 I'm not sure that Steve will come or not.

→ ______________________________

5 If he will come tomorrow, I'll prepare dinner.

→ ______________________________

6 Emily is wondering whether does Mom like roses.

→ ______________________________

B 다음 우리말과 일치하도록 괄호 안의 말을 바르게 배열하시오.

1 비가 오지 않는다면, 밖에 나가자. (it, go, unless, let's, rains, outside)

→ ______________________________

2 나는 이 게임이 재미있는지 궁금하다. (this, interesting, wonder, is, I, if, game)

→ ______________________________

3 Tom은 너무 피곤해서 뛸 수 없다. (tired, can't, Tom, run, that, he, so, is)

→ ______________________________

4 나는 서울에 있는 동안 내 친구를 보러 갔다. (I, Seoul, while, was, in)

→ ______________________________, I went to see my friend.

5 겨울이 옴에 따라, 날씨가 점점 추워지고 있다. (getting, it, as, comes, colder, winter, is)

→ ______________________________

6 우리는 제시간에 도착할 수 있도록 일찍 떠났다. (we, on time, so, arrive, that, could)

→ We left early ______________________________.

C 다음 우리말과 일치하도록 괄호 안의 말을 이용하여 문장을 완성하시오.

1 Sue와 Tina 둘 다 안경을 쓰지 않는다. (neither, wear)
→ ______________________________

2 너는 그녀가 왜 울었다고 생각하니? (think, cry)
→ ______________________________

3 너는 그가 언제 여기에 도착할지 알고 있니? (arrive)
→ ______________________________

4 그 소설은 길었을 뿐만 아니라 지루했다. (novel, only, also)
→ ______________________________

5 나는 그 사고가 어디에서 일어났는지 모른다. (accident, happen)
→ ______________________________

6 네가 아니라 John이 그것에 책임이 있다. (be responsible for)
→ ______________________________

D 다음 주어진 문장과 같은 뜻이 되도록 문장을 완성하시오.

1 The movie was moving as well as interesting.
→ The movie was ______________________________.

2 I can visit him tomorrow, or I can visit him this Sunday.
→ I can visit him ______________________________.

3 If you don't leave now, you'll be late.
→ ______________________________, you'll be late.

4 I can't speak Chinese. I can't speak Spanish, either.
→ I can speak ______________________________.

5 Upon getting up, he brushed his teeth.
→ ______________________________, he brushed his teeth.

6 The bag was so big that I couldn't carry it by myself.
→ The bag was ______________________________.

Chapter 13
가정법

서술형 대비 문장 연습

A 다음 밑줄 친 부분을 어법에 맞게 고쳐 문장을 다시 쓰시오.

1 I wish you come to my birthday party yesterday.
→ ______________________________

2 If we took a taxi, we could have arrived earlier.
→ ______________________________

3 He is a student, but he acts as if he is a teacher.
→ ______________________________

4 If Jane drove slowly, she wouldn't have had an accident.
→ ______________________________

5 If John hadn't told a lie, we could have trusted him now.
→ ______________________________

6 If it were not for the homework, I could have played with my friends.
→ ______________________________

B 다음 우리말과 일치하도록 괄호 안의 말을 바르게 배열하시오.

1 내가 더 열심히 일했더라면 좋았을 텐데. (had, harder, I, worked, wish, I)
→ ______________________________

2 내가 너라면 그 셔츠를 사지 않을 텐데. (were, I, buy, if, wouldn't, you, I, the shirt)
→ ______________________________

3 그는 마치 미국에서 살았던 것처럼 말했다. (talked, he, lived, he, as, had, if)
→ ____________________ in America.

4 어젯밤에 잠을 잘 잤더라면, 나는 지금 피곤하지 않을 텐데. (wouldn't, tired, I, be)
→ If I had slept well last night, ____________________ now.

5 인터넷이 없다면, 우리의 삶은 매우 다를 것이다. (it, for, if, were, the Internet, not)
→ ____________________, our lives would be very different.

6 그의 도움이 없었다면, 나는 성공하지 못했을 것이다. (it, been, had, his help, not, for)
→ ____________________, I couldn't have succeeded.

C 다음 우리말과 일치하도록 괄호 안의 말을 이용하여 문장을 완성하시오.

1 내가 더 나은 학생이었다면 좋았을 텐데. (wish, good)
→ ______________________________

2 내가 뛰었더라면, 나는 버스를 놓치지 않았을 텐데. (run, miss)
→ ______________________________

3 그가 없었더라면, 우리는 경기에서 졌을 것이다. (if, lose)
→ ______________________________

4 그는 마치 그가 정직한 것처럼 행동한다. (act, honest)
→ ______________________________

5 내가 시간이 충분하다면 너를 도울 수 있을 텐데. (have, enough)
→ ______________________________

6 내가 어제 지갑을 잃어버리지 않았더라면 좋았을 텐데. (wish, lose, wallet)
→ ______________________________

D 다음 주어진 문장과 같은 뜻이 되도록 문장을 완성하시오.

1 As he doesn't have a car, he can't drive to work.
→ ______________________, he could drive to work.

2 As I wasn't careful, I made a mistake.
→ ______________________, I wouldn't have made a mistake.

3 As I got your advice, I didn't waste my time.
→ ______________________, I would have wasted my time.

4 I'm sorry that you can't join our club.
→ I wish ______________________.

5 I'm sorry that I ate so much chocolate.
→ I wish ______________________.

6 In fact, she doesn't know Dean very well.
→ She talks as if ______________________.

Chapter 14
일치와 화법

서술형 대비 문장 연습

A 다음 밑줄 친 부분을 어법에 맞게 고쳐 문장을 다시 쓰시오.

1 Some of the cheese <u>have</u> gone bad.
→ ______________________________

2 The pants in the store <u>is</u> very expensive.
→ ______________________________

3 Kevin said he <u>will</u> go on a picnic the next day.
→ ______________________________

4 She told me that she <u>have been</u> to England before.
→ ______________________________

5 Jenny asked me <u>where would I</u> travel during winter vacation.
→ ______________________________

6 We learned that the Second World War <u>have ended</u> in 1945.
→ ______________________________

B 다음 우리말과 일치하도록 괄호 안의 말을 바르게 배열하시오.

1 그 돈의 절반은 너의 것이었다. (yours, money, the, half, was, of)
→ ______________________________

2 부자들이 항상 행복한 것은 아니다. (rich, happy, are, always, the, not)
→ ______________________________

3 그는 나에게 그를 기다려 달라고 부탁했다. (asked, him, he, to, for, wait, me)
→ ______________________________

4 Alex는 그가 그 시험을 통과했다고 말했다. (passed, he, Alex, that, had, the exam, said)
→ ______________________________

5 그는 내게 내가 그를 도울 수 있는지 물었다. (asked, I, me, could, he, help, him, if)
→ ______________________________

6 우리는 지구가 둥글다는 것을 배웠다. (learned, Earth, round, we, is, the, that)
→ ______________________________

C 다음 우리말과 일치하도록 괄호 안의 말을 이용하여 문장을 완성하시오.

1 그는 나에게 어디에 사는지 물었다. (ask)
→ ____________________

2 Peter는 매일 운동을 한다고 말했다. (that, exercise)
→ ____________________

3 많은 소년들이 공원에서 놀고 있다. (a number of, play)
→ ____________________

4 그 음식의 대부분은 내 것이다. (most, mine)
→ ____________________

5 그는 나에게 축구를 좋아하는지 물었다. (ask, soccer)
→ ____________________

6 그 학생들 중 3분의 2가 일본어를 배우고 있다. (learn, Japanese)
→ ____________________

D 다음 문장을 간접화법으로 바꾸어 쓰시오.

1 My friends say to me, "You are very kind."
→ My friends ____________________.

2 Steve said to me, "I will go fishing."
→ Steve ____________________.

3 Jane said to me, "Do you like tennis?"
→ Jane ____________________.

4 She said to him, "What did you have for dinner?"
→ She ____________________.

5 The teacher said to us, "Don't be late to class."
→ The teacher told ____________________.

6 The doctor said to me, "Work out regularly."
→ The doctor advised ____________________.

Chapter 15
특수구문

서술형 대비 문장 연습

A 다음 밑줄 친 부분을 어법에 맞게 고쳐 문장을 다시 쓰시오.

1 Amy do like comic books.

→ ______________________________

2 In the room a new desk was.

→ ______________________________

3 Never he has been to Japan before.

→ ______________________________

4 Under the bed were your cat.

→ ______________________________

5 Little I dreamed that I would meet you again.

→ ______________________________

6 It was the guitar what he played on the stage yesterday.

→ ______________________________

B 다음 우리말과 일치하도록 괄호 안의 말을 바르게 배열하시오.

1 올해는 눈이 거의 오지 않았다. (did, snow, rarely, this year, it)

→ ______________________________

2 나는 그에게 이메일을 정말로 보냈다. (send, an email, I, did, him)

→ ______________________________

3 창문을 깬 사람은 바로 John이었다. (John, broke, it, the window, who, was)

→ ______________________________

4 그는 그녀의 말을 거의 이해하지 못했다. (what, hardly, said, did, understand, he, she)

→ ______________________________

5 이것들은 내가 어제 산 신발이다. (I, yesterday, are, the shoes, bought, these)

→ ______________________________

6 그가 여기에 도착한 때는 바로 어제였다. (yesterday, it, he, here, arrived, was, that)

→ ______________________________

C 다음 우리말과 일치하도록 괄호 안의 말을 이용하여 문장을 완성하시오.

1 나는 정말로 열심히 공부한다. (do, hard)
→ ______________________________

2 이 가방은 정말 비싸 보인다. (do, expensive)
→ ______________________________

3 나는 책을 거의 읽지 않는다. (rarely, do)
→ ______________________________

4 내가 어제 잃어버린 것은 바로 빨간 우산이었다. (it, lose)
→ ______________________________

5 그는 그의 부모님을 거의 방문하지 않는다. (seldom, do)
→ ______________________________

6 그 회의가 열린 곳은 바로 서울에서였다. (that, meeting, hold)
→ ______________________________

D 다음 밑줄 친 부분을 강조하는 문장으로 바꾸어 쓰시오.

1 This bread <u>tastes</u> sweet.
→ ______________________________

2 I <u>little</u> imagined that they could win.
→ ______________________________

3 I bought <u>a backpack</u> in the mall last Friday.
→ ______________________________

4 He drew a sunflower <u>on the wall</u>.
→ ______________________________

5 <u>Kate</u> rode a bicycle in the park last week.
→ ______________________________

6 Apollo 11 landed on the Moon <u>in 1969</u>.
→ ______________________________

Chapter 01
부정사

학교 시험 대비 문제

맞힌 개수
_____ / 24

01 다음 문장의 밑줄 친 부분과 쓰임이 같은 것은?

He has no house to live in.

① Father advises me to go there.
② He is the last man to trust you.
③ She was pleased to go with her son.
④ I went to the post office to mail a letter.
⑤ It's easy for me to write a card in English.

02 다음 우리말과 일치하도록 빈칸에 들어갈 말로 알맞은 것은?

네가 원한다면 이 케이크를 먹어도 돼.
➡ You may have this cake if you __________.

① to
② want to
③ want to it
④ want to have
⑤ want have it

03 다음 주어진 문장과 의미가 일치하는 것은?

It seems that no one on earth understands him.

① No one on earth seems to understand him.
② No one on earth seem to understands him.
③ No one on earth seems to be understand him.
④ No one on earth is seeming to understand him.
⑤ No one earth has seemed to understand him.

04 다음 빈칸에 들어갈 말로 알맞지 않은 것은?

I ________ the kids not to worry.

① asked
② wanted
③ ordered
④ had
⑤ advised

05 다음 중 밑줄 친 부분이 의미상 어색한 것은?

① Please tell me how to use this computer.
② I don't know when to say goodbye to her.
③ She doesn't know which to go for her vacation.
④ Did you decide what to buy for her birthday?
⑤ Can you show me how to change the battery for this camera?

06 다음 빈칸에 들어갈 말이 바르게 짝지어진 것은?

• My father allowed me ________ his car.
• She told her son not ________ TV late at night.

① drive — watch
② to drive — watching
③ to drive — watch
④ driving — to watch
⑤ to drive — to watch

07 다음 중 문장 전환이 틀린 것은?

① It seems that she was rich.
➡ She seems to have been rich.
② It seemed that my mother was ill.
➡ My mother seemed to be ill.
③ It seems that John was very surprised.
➡ John seems to be very surprised.
④ It seemed that the robbers were smarter.
➡ The robbers seemed to be smarter.
⑤ It seems that they are satisfied with the results.
➡ They seem to be satisfied with the results.

08 다음 문장의 밑줄 친 부분과 쓰임이 같은 것은?

She woke up to find the whole house on fire.

① My hobby is to play the piano.
② It is not easy to speak in English.
③ He grew up to be a famous actor.
④ Do you have anything cold to drink?
⑤ There are many palaces to visit in Seoul.

09 다음 밑줄 친 부분 중 생략할 수 있는 것은?

I wanted ① to go ② to the concert, but my mom ③ told ④ me not to ⑤ go to the concert.

10 다음 빈칸에 들어갈 말이 나머지 넷과 다른 것은?

① It is strange ________ him to disagree with you.
② It was careless ________ her to forget her keys.
③ It is possible ________ me to exercise every day.
④ It's not easy ________ children to use chopsticks.
⑤ It is dangerous ________ children to play with matches.

11 다음 주어진 문장과 의미가 일치하는 것은?

The shirt is so small that I can't wear it.

① The shirt is too wear to small.
② The shirt is small enough to wear.
③ The shirt is too small for me to wear.
④ The shirt is small enough for me to wear.
⑤ The shirt is too small for me not to wear it.

서술형

12 다음 우리말과 일치하도록 주어진 단어를 바르게 배열하여 문장을 완성하시오.

너는 내가 말했던 것을 생각할 충분한 시간이 있다. (to, time, think, enough) ➡ You have ________________________ over what I've said.

13 다음 빈칸에 들어갈 말로 알맞은 것은?

> She bought some clothes for her children ________.

① putting ② to put ③ put on
④ putting on ⑤ to put on

14 다음 두 문장의 뜻이 같도록 빈칸에 들어갈 말로 알맞은 것은?

> It seems that he was sick for a long time.
> = He seems to ________ sick for a long time.

① be ② was ③ been
④ have been ⑤ had been

15 다음 빈칸에 들어갈 말이 바르게 짝지어진 것은?

> • Sarah saw him ________ off the cap.
> • I want you ________ telling lies to your parents.

① take — stop ② taking — stop
③ take — to stop ④ to take — stop
⑤ to take — to stop

16 다음 우리말을 영어로 바르게 옮긴 것은?

> 나는 그가 피아노를 방으로 옮기게 했다.

① I had him move the piano into the room.
② I had him moving the piano into the room.
③ I had him to move the piano into the room.
④ I got him move the piano into the room.
⑤ I got him moving the piano into the room.

17 다음 중 두 문장의 의미가 서로 <u>다른</u> 것은?

① The boy didn't know where to go.
= The boy didn't know where he should go.
② It seems that there was a car accident here.
= There seems to have been a car accident here.
③ Sora is standing in line to buy a ticket.
= Sora is standing in line in order to buy a ticket.
④ He is wise enough to give me good advice.
= He is so wise that he can't give me good advice.
⑤ If you are to get there on time, you should leave now.
= If you intend to get there on time, you should leave now.

18 다음 밑줄 친 부분이 어법상 <u>틀린</u> 것은?

① It was foolish <u>of you</u> to quit your job.
② It was generous <u>of him</u> to forgive me.
③ It is natural <u>of a child</u> to make a mistake.
④ It is bad <u>of you</u> to shout at your pet dog.
⑤ It is difficult <u>for her</u> to sing in front of people.

19 다음 중 어법상 올바른 문장을 모두 골라 짝지은 것은?

ⓐ Can you tell me which to choose? ⓑ Jerry found it hard giving up bad habits. ⓒ He is too selfish to share his bike with his brother. ⓓ We were very disappointed to not win the match.

① ⓐ, ⓑ ② ⓐ, ⓒ ③ ⓑ, ⓓ
④ ⓐ, ⓒ, ⓓ ⑤ ⓑ, ⓒ, ⓓ

20 다음 중 어법상 <u>틀린</u> 것은?

① I'm really excited to watch the musical.
② Strange to say, I have never eaten kimchi.
③ Turn on the air conditioner if you want to.
④ It took ten minutes her to melt the chocolate.
⑤ I'm looking for a person to carry out the project.

서술형

21 다음 밑줄 친 부분 중 어법상 <u>틀린</u> 것을 골라 바르게 고쳐 쓰시오.

The guard ① <u>didn't</u> let ② <u>me</u> ③ <u>to park</u> ④ <u>my car</u> ⑤ <u>in front of the bank</u>.

__________ ➡ __________

서술형

22 다음 우리말과 일치하도록 괄호 안의 말을 바르게 배열하시오.

우리가 물을 절약하는 것은 중요하다. (us, save, for, water, important, it, to, is) ➡ ______________________

서술형

23 다음 우리말과 일치하도록 괄호 안의 말을 이용하여 문장을 완성하시오.

그녀는 아프지만 그녀를 돌봐줄 사람이 없다. ➡ She's sick but doesn't have ____________ ____________. (look after, anyone)

서술형

24 다음 두 문장의 뜻이 같도록 빈칸에 알맞은 말을 쓰시오.

The girl was so scared that she couldn't open the door. = The girl was ________ ________ ________ ________ the door.

Chapter 02
동명사

학고 시험 대비 문제

맞힌 개수
_____ / 24

01 다음 밑줄 친 부분이 어법상 틀린 것은?

① I enjoy listening to music.
② Would you mind closing the door?
③ She expected him playing the violin.
④ It was very funny. I couldn't stop laughing.
⑤ We usually finish eating at about 8:30 in the evening.

02 다음 우리말과 일치하도록 빈칸에 들어갈 말로 알맞은 것은?

나는 학교 식당에서 그녀를 만난 것이 기억났다.
➡ I remembered ________ her at the cafeteria.

① met ② meet
③ to meet ④ meeting
⑤ have met

03 다음 빈칸에 들어갈 말로 알맞은 것은?

His parents ________ him from coming to the party.

① have ② make
③ keep ④ like
⑤ take

04 다음 중 우리말을 영어로 바르게 옮긴 것은?

① 그녀는 네게 그 이야기를 했던 것을 기억하지 못한다.
➡ She can't remember to tell you the story.
② 상자를 청소해야 하는 것을 잊지 마라.
➡ Don't forget cleaning the box.
③ 나는 음악 듣는 것을 멈추었다.
➡ I stopped to listen to music.
④ 나는 숙제를 해야 하는 것을 기억했다.
➡ I remembered to do my homework.
⑤ 나는 너무 많이 먹은 것을 후회한다.
➡ I regret to eat too much.

05 다음 중 어법상 틀린 것은?

① Tom is busy washing his car.
② Her speech is worth hearing.
③ They're looking forward to seeing him.
④ He cannot help to laugh after looking at her.
⑤ Heavy rain kept them from going on a picnic.

06 다음 우리말과 일치하도록 빈칸에 들어갈 말로 알맞은 것은?

그들은 내가 그들의 음악에 맞춰 춤추는 것을 즐겼다.
➡ They enjoyed ________ dancing to their music.

① I ② my
③ mine ④ they
⑤ their

07 다음 중 어법상 <u>틀린</u> 것은?

① Would you mind to close the door?
② It began to rain this morning.
③ She cannot avoid telling the truth.
④ He finished doing his homework yesterday.
⑤ Don't give up studying English.

08 다음 중 어법상 올바른 문장은?

① There are many places visit in Korea.
② He knows how driving a car.
③ I enjoy to walk in the park.
④ Jenny is good at speaking in public.
⑤ He was exciting to hear the news.

09 다음 영어를 우리말로 <u>잘못</u> 옮긴 것은?

① I remember locking the window.
➡ 나는 창문을 잠근 것을 기억한다.
② They like to go to the movies.
➡ 그들은 영화 보러 가는 것을 좋아한다.
③ I stopped singing.
➡ 나는 노래를 하기 위해 멈추었다.
④ I tried to call you all afternoon.
➡ 나는 오후 내내 너와 통화하려고 애썼다.
⑤ He seems to forget meeting her.
➡ 그는 그녀를 만난 것을 잊은 것 같다.

10 다음 중 어법상 올바른 문장은?

① I need a friend to play.
② His speech was very long and bored.
③ Alice is expecting going out with you.
④ My friends are busy practicing soccer.
⑤ I'm looking forward to visit there soon.

서술형
11 다음 밑줄 친 부분을 어법에 맞게 고쳐 쓰시오.

I had trouble <u>propose</u> to her.

서술형
12 다음 문장에서 어법상 <u>틀린</u> 부분을 찾아 바르게 고쳐 쓰시오.

Minsu regrets studying not English.

__________ ➡ __________

13 다음 빈칸에 들어갈 말이 바르게 짝지어진 것은?

> • You must avoid ________ the same mistakes.
> • Jerry promised ________ hiking with Tom tomorrow.

① make — to go ② making — going
③ to make — going ④ making — to go
⑤ to make — to go

14 다음 빈칸에 공통으로 들어갈 말로 알맞은 것은?

> • I'm not very good at ________ yet.
> • ________ fast at night is dangerous.

① drive[Drive] ② drove[Drove]
③ driving[Driving] ④ driven[Driven]
⑤ to drive[To drive]

15 다음 밑줄 친 부분의 쓰임이 나머지 넷과 다른 것은?

① Taking care of babies is not easy.
② My goal is winning a gold medal.
③ Do you mind joining the book club?
④ Mark is listening to music on a bench.
⑤ The little boy was afraid of riding a horse.

16 다음 빈칸에 들어갈 말로 알맞지 않은 것은?

> Susan ________ painting the walls green.

① denied ② decided ③ stopped
④ finished ⑤ gave up

17 다음 밑줄 친 부분을 바꿔 쓸 때 의미가 달라지는 것은?

① Asking questions is a good habit. (→ To ask)
② Mina likes talking about her problems. (→ to talk)
③ He remembers learning how to skate. (→ to learn)
④ I prefer seeing an older doctor, if possible. (→ to see)
⑤ They continued playing soccer despite the cold weather. (→ to play)

18 (A), (B), (C)의 괄호 안에서 알맞은 것끼리 바르게 짝지어진 것은?

> • What do you feel like (A) [having / to have] for dinner?
> • She was used to (B) [clean / cleaning] her room on weekends.
> • He spends most of his spare time (C) [playing / to play] computer games.

	(A)	(B)	(C)
①	having	— clean	— to play
②	having	— cleaning	— playing
③	having	— clean	— playing
④	to have	— cleaning	— playing
⑤	to have	— clean	— to play

19 다음 우리말을 영어로 바르게 옮긴 것은?

나는 그녀가 Joan을 초대하지 않는 것을 이해할 수 있다.

① I can't understand she inviting Joan.
② I can't understand her inviting Joan.
③ I can understand she not inviting Joan.
④ I can understand her inviting not Joan.
⑤ I can understand her not inviting Joan.

20 다음 대화의 밑줄 친 ①~⑤ 중 어법상 틀린 것은?

A You ①aren't supposed ②to use your cell phone ③during the show.
B Sorry. I ④will stop ⑤to send text messages right now.

21 다음 밑줄 친 부분이 어법상 틀린 것의 개수는?

ⓐ They tried to find their lost dog.
ⓑ Did you finish writing your report?
ⓒ Hiking with friends are very exciting.
ⓓ I'm looking forward to read his new novel.
ⓔ My dad suggested going to the exhibition.

① 1개 ② 2개 ③ 3개
④ 4개 ⑤ 5개

서술형

22 다음 우리말과 일치하도록 괄호 안의 말을 이용하여 문장을 완성하시오.

그녀는 그녀의 계획을 바꾼 것을 후회한다.
(change, her plan)
➡ She regrets ________________.

서술형

23 다음 두 문장을 한 문장으로 나타낼 때 빈칸에 알맞은 말을 쓰시오.

Mary put on sunscreen in the morning. She forgot it.
➡ Mary forgot ____________________ in the morning.

서술형

24 다음 우리말과 일치하도록 괄호 안의 말을 바르게 배열하시오.

소음은 그가 공부에 집중하지 못하게 했다.
(from, on studying, focusing, him)
➡ The noise prevented ________________
____________.

Chapter 03
분사

학고 시험 대비 문제

맞힌 개수
_____ / 23

01 다음 빈칸에 들어갈 말이 바르게 짝지어진 것은?

- I was _________ to see that he was practicing as hard as the others.
- Sarah's birthday party is always _________.

① surprise — excite ② surprised — exciting
③ surprised — excited ④ surprising — excited
⑤ surprising — exciting

02 다음 밑줄 친 부분의 쓰임이 나머지 넷과 다른 것은?

① Science class is boring.
② Do you enjoy listening to music?
③ I've been studying Japanese over 10 years.
④ The soccer game last night was very exciting.
⑤ Be quiet, please. Your sister is sleeping now.

03 다음 문장을 부사절이 있는 문장으로 바르게 바꿔 쓴 것은?

Not having a pen, he couldn't write down her e-mail address.

① As he has a pen, he couldn't write down her e-mail address.
② As he didn't have a pen, he couldn't write down her e-mail address.
③ Because he had not had a pen, he couldn't write down her e-mail address.
④ Because he doesn't have a pen, he couldn't write down her e-mail address.
⑤ Because he has had a pen, he couldn't write down her e-mail address.

04 다음 중 분사구문으로 바꾼 것이 옳지 않은 것은?

① Because I felt tired, I went to bed early.
➡ Feeling tired, I went to bed early.
② Though she was sick, she kept on working.
➡ Though being sick, she kept on working.
③ If you turn to the left, you'll see the library.
➡ Turning to the left, you'll see the library.
④ As it is written in easy English, we can read it.
➡ Written in easy English, we can read it.
⑤ When I was walking along the street, I saw a friend of mine.
➡ Walking along the street, I saw a friend of mine.

05 다음 밑줄 친 부분을 바르게 고친 것은?

Her car broke down, so she had it repair.

① repair ② repairs
③ repairing ④ repaired
⑤ to repair

06 다음 빈칸에 들어갈 말이 바르게 짝지어진 것은?

Before she watched a movie with me, my mom washed the dishes.
= Before _________ a movie with me, my mom _________ the dishes.

① watch — wash ② watching — wash
③ watch — washing ④ watching — washed
⑤ watching — washing

07 다음 중 어법상 틀린 것은?

① The movie was so bored.
② She was interested in plants.
③ I heard an amazing story last night.
④ My friends gave me a surprising gift.
⑤ I'm very excited because my job is very exciting.

08 다음 빈칸에 들어갈 말이 바르게 짝지어진 것은?

- **A** How was the exhibition?
  B It was ________. I want to see it one more time.
- **A** How was the book?
  B It was ________. I quit reading it.
- **A** How was the movie?
  B It was ________. It made me cry.

① interested — bored — sad
② interesting — bored — happy
③ interesting — boring — sad
④ interesting — bored — sad
⑤ interested — boring — happy

09 다음 빈칸에 들어갈 말이 바르게 짝지어진 것은?

The result of the game was very ________, so we were ________.

① disappoint — disappointed
② disappointed — disappoint
③ disappointed — disappointing
④ disappointing — disappointed
⑤ disappointing — disappointing

10 다음 중 분사구문으로 바꾼 것이 옳지 않은 것은?

① As I live in a big city, I can meet a lot of people.
➡ Living in a big city, I can meet a lot of people.
② While I walked along the street, I saw my old friend.
➡ Walking along the street, I saw my old friend.
③ As the book had been written in French, the book was hard to read.
➡ Having been written in French, the book was hard to read.
④ As I finished my exercise, I have nothing else to do.
➡ Finished my exercise, I have nothing else to do.
⑤ Because he had worked hard, he was rich enough to travel abroad.
➡ Having worked hard, he was rich enough to travel abroad.

서술형

11 다음을 <보기>와 같이 분사구문으로 바꿔 쓰시오.

<보기>
As he had found the bead, the poor man went back to his town.
➡ Having found the bead, the poor man went back to his town.

As she was scolded by her teacher, the girl cried for a long time.

➡ ______________________________, the girl cried for a long time.

12 다음 빈칸에 들어갈 말로 알맞은 것은?

> The restaurant's food was nice, but its service was ________.

① disappoint ② to disappoint
③ disappointed ④ disappointing
⑤ to disappointing

13 다음 빈칸에 들어갈 말이 바르게 짝지어진 것은?

> • Mom fell asleep with the TV ________ on.
> • The teacher left the classroom with his students ________ him.

① turned — to follow ② turning — followed
③ turned — following ④ to turn — followed
⑤ turning — following

14 다음 밑줄 친 부분을 분사구문으로 바르게 바꾼 것은?

> <u>Because the game was canceled</u>, I was able to finish my homework on time.

① Canceled
② Being canceled
③ The game canceling
④ Because being canceled
⑤ The game being canceled

15 다음 우리말을 영어로 바르게 옮긴 것은?

> 나는 차가 없기 때문에 버스로 출근한다.

① Having not a car, I go to work by bus.
② Not having a car, I go to work by bus.
③ I not having a car, I go to work by bus.
④ Don't having a car, I go to work by bus.
⑤ Since don't having a car, I go to work by bus.

16 (A), (B), (C)의 괄호 안에서 알맞은 것끼리 바르게 짝지어진 것은?

> • Jerry likes a girl (A) [called / calling] Anne.
> • The man (B) [wore / wearing] a blue shirt is my cousin.
> • There were two children (C) [hurt / hurting] in the accident.

	(A)	(B)	(C)
①	called	— wore	— hurting
②	called	— wearing	— hurt
③	called	— wearing	— hurting
④	calling	— wore	— hurting
⑤	calling	— wearing	— hurt

17 다음 중 밑줄 친 부분을 생략할 수 <u>없는</u> 것은?

① <u>Having</u> much to do, he couldn't go to the movies.
② <u>Being</u> made by my grandma, the soup was delicious.
③ Although <u>having been</u> raised in France, she can't speak French.
④ <u>Being</u> walking along the street, she talked on the phone.
⑤ <u>Being</u> interested in the universe, I want to be an astronomer.

18 다음 중 밑줄 친 부분이 어법상 틀린 것은?

① I felt my shoulder touched by someone.
② The man tried to open the locked car door.
③ As his speech was boring, some audience members yawned.
④ She took a photo of the boys dancing on the stage.
⑤ Jessica wants to watch an excited nature documentary.

19 다음 중 어법상 올바른 문장을 모두 골라 짝지은 것은?

ⓐ Opening the box, I found a drone.
ⓑ Having gotten up early, she wasn't late.
ⓒ Spoken of Mr. Park, he isn't a good leader.
ⓓ The refrigerator been out of order, I called a mechanic.

① ⓐ, ⓑ ② ⓐ, ⓒ ③ ⓑ, ⓓ
④ ⓐ, ⓒ, ⓓ ⑤ ⓑ, ⓒ, ⓓ

서술형

20 다음 우리말과 일치하도록 괄호 안의 말을 바르게 배열하시오. (단, 필요하면 형태를 바꿀 것)

그는 팔짱을 낀 채로 밖에서 기다리고 있었다.
(arms, his, with, fold)
➡ He was waiting outside ________________.

서술형

21 다음 우리말과 일치하도록 괄호 안의 말을 이용하여 문장을 완성하시오.

솔직히 말해서, 나는 네가 돌아올 것이라고 기대하지 않았다. (speak)
➡ _________ _________, I didn't expect you to come back.

서술형

22 다음 괄호 안의 단어를 알맞은 형태로 바꾸어 빈칸에 쓰시오.

His sudden death was _________ news. Many people were _________ by the event. (shock)

서술형

23 다음 밑줄 친 부분을 분사구문으로 바꿔 쓰시오.

Because vegetables are good for health, I like them.
➡ ________________________________

학교 시험 대비 문제

맞힌 개수 ____ / 24

01 다음 두 문장을 한 문장으로 바꿔 쓸 때 빈칸에 알맞은 것은?

- I lost my watch in the park one week ago.
- I found the watch yesterday.

➡ I found the watch I ________ in the park.

① has lost ② have lost
③ had lost ④ was lost
⑤ had been lost

02 다음 밑줄 친 establish의 형태로 알맞은 것은?

He establish the famous Italian restaurant in 1919.

① establish
② establishing
③ established
④ to establish
⑤ has established

03 다음 빈칸에 들어갈 말로 알맞은 것은?

When Sumi came home, she found that somebody ________ the juice.

① spill ② to spill
③ was spilt ④ had spilt
⑤ have spilt

04 다음 두 문장을 한 문장으로 바꿔 쓸 때 빈칸에 알맞은 것은?

- It started to snow yesterday.
- It is snowing now.

➡ It ____________ since yesterday.

① snowed
② is snowing
③ had snowed
④ was snowing
⑤ has been snowing

05 다음 빈칸에 들어갈 말로 알맞은 것은?

He remembered something his mother ________ said.

① is ② was
③ has ④ had
⑤ having

06 다음 빈칸에 공통으로 들어갈 말로 알맞은 것은?

- We have all been hearing music ________ we were born.
- Two years have passed ________ you entered middle school.

① or ② and
③ but ④ since
⑤ that

07 다음 밑줄 친 see의 형태로 알맞은 것은?

> Alex didn't enjoy the movie because he see it before.

① see　② sees
③ had seen　④ have seen
⑤ had been seeing

08 다음 빈칸에 들어갈 말로 알맞은 것은?

> They've been playing a computer game ________ two hours.

① for　② toward
③ during　④ at
⑤ into

09 다음 중 밑줄 친 부분의 쓰임이 <보기>와 같은 것은?

> 〈보기〉
> Have you ever seen *Mission Impossible*?

① He has never been to England.
② She has gone to Africa.
③ I haven't finished my homework.
④ We have lived in Incheon since 2016.
⑤ I have lost my bicycle.

10 다음 두 문장을 한 문장으로 바꿔 쓸 때 빈칸에 알맞은 것은?

> • Cindy started to study English three hours ago.
> • She is still studying it.
> ➡ Cindy ____________ English for three hours.

① studied
② is studying
③ had studied
④ has been studied
⑤ has been studying

11 다음 글의 빈칸에 들어갈 말로 알맞은 것은?

> Last night I started to do my homework at 7. I finished it at 9. Jane came at 9:20. By the time Jane came, I ____________ my homework.

① finish
② finishes
③ was finished
④ had finished
⑤ have finished

서술형

12 다음 우리말과 일치하도록 주어진 단어를 바르게 고쳐 쓰시오.

> 나는 그 전날 산 가방을 잃어버렸다. (buy)
> ➡ I lost the bag that I ____________ the day before.

13 다음 우리말과 일치하도록 빈칸에 들어갈 말로 알맞은 것은?

> 그녀는 몇 달 동안 매일 수영을 해 오고 있다.
> ➡ She ______________ every day for several months.

① had swum ② is swimming
③ was being swum ④ has been swimming
⑤ had been swimming

14 다음 빈칸에 들어갈 말로 알맞지 않은 것은?

> I have read this book ________.

① once ② twice ③ before
④ a week ago ⑤ since yesterday

15 다음 밑줄 친 부분을 바르게 고친 것은?

> When she got on the bus, she found out that she has left her wallet at home.

① leaves ② had left ③ is leaving
④ will leave ⑤ has been leaving

16 다음 빈칸에 들어갈 말이 바르게 짝지어진 것은?

> • The artist has been painting the picture ________ last week.
> • I have used the same smartphone ________ five years.

① for — during ② for — since
③ since — for ④ during — for
⑤ since — since

17 다음 우리말을 영어로 바르게 옮긴 것은?

> 그들은 그때 3년 동안 그 집을 짓고 있는 중이었다.

① They had built the house since 3 years then.
② They have built the house since 3 years then.
③ They are building the house for 3 years then.
④ They have been building the house for 3 years then.
⑤ They had been building the house for 3 years then.

18 다음 밑줄 친 부분의 쓰임이 나머지 넷과 다른 것은?

① He has never seen a celebrity before.
② Have you ever failed an exam at school?
③ They have raised these cats for three years.
④ I have been to the new Chilean restaurant for lunch.
⑤ My sister has forgotten the password for her smartphone before.

19 다음 중 어법상 틀린 것은?

① She has just had a regular checkup.
② James has quit his job four years ago.
③ How long have you been working out?
④ She had never learned to bake before then.
⑤ He spent all the money that I had given him.

20 다음 중 밑줄 친 부분이 어법상 틀린 것은?

① Lucy has seen a shooting star recently.
② We have been looking around here for an hour.
③ Harry told me that he has already solved the problem.
④ It has been 10 years since he opened his store.
⑤ Kate had been feeding her dog when he saw her.

서술형

21 다음 문장에서 어법상 틀린 부분을 찾아 바르게 고쳐 쓰시오.

Daniel has never eaten kimchi before he tried it in Korea.

____________ ➡ ____________

서술형

22 다음 괄호 안의 동사를 이용하여 대화를 완성하시오.

A ______ ______ ______ the palace? (visit)
B Yes, I have. I ______ it with my friend last weekend. (visit)

서술형

23 다음 두 문장을 한 문장으로 나타낼 때 빈칸에 알맞은 말을 쓰시오.

- Mina lost her necklace.
- She doesn't have the necklace now.

➡ Mina ________ her necklace.

서술형

24 다음 우리말과 일치하도록 주어진 〈조건〉에 맞게 영작하시오.

〈조건〉
1. 현재완료진행형으로 쓸 것
2. 괄호 안의 말을 사용하여 총 7단어로 쓸 것

그녀는 지난달부터 요가를 배워 오고 있다.
(learn, yoga, last month)
➡ She ________________.

Chapter 05
조동사

학교 시험 대비 문제

맞힌 개수 ______ / 24

01 다음 주어진 문장과 의미가 일치하는 것은?

> Jane had long hair before, but she doesn't have it anymore.

① Jane liked her long hair.
② Jane used to have long hair.
③ Jane wants to have short hair.
④ Jane wants to have her hair cut.
⑤ Jane changes her hair very often.

02 다음 중 어법상 올바른 것은?

① Do you think that we'll can travel to the moon in 2030?
② Now we won't have to walk to school anymore.
③ She will has to come early tomorrow.
④ Will you are able to go camping on Friday?
⑤ You will must live under the sea.

03 다음 대화의 빈칸에 들어갈 말로 알맞은 것은?

> A What's the matter with you?
> B I have a stomachache. I ______ eaten so much.

① should
② should have
③ should have not
④ not should have
⑤ should not have

04 다음 중 밑줄 친 부분과 바꿔 쓸 수 있는 것은?

> We should eat healthy food, especially much fruit and vegetables.

① can ② might ③ used to
④ ought to ⑤ are able to

05 다음 중 밑줄 친 부분을 have(has) to로 바꿔 쓸 수 없는 것은?

① They must get up early tomorrow.
② You must sit quietly in the library.
③ I must return the book by Tuesday.
④ My room is very dirty. I must clean it.
⑤ She doesn't look well. She must be sick.

06 다음 빈칸에 공통으로 들어갈 말로 알맞은 것은?

> • ______ your homework before dinner.
> • Why ______ you want to be an actor?

① Be(be) ② Do(do)
③ Are(are) ④ Take(take)
⑤ Have(have)

07 다음 중 밑줄 친 May(may)의 쓰임이 나머지와 다른 것은?

① May I see your workbook?
② You may take pictures here.
③ She may know the answer.
④ May I sit here?
⑤ You may not leave the classroom.

08 다음 중 어법상 올바른 문장은?

① He may not know the secret.
② You ought to not give him money.
③ You have not to go on a diet.
④ This job has to be dangerous.
⑤ He looks pale. He should have health problems.

서술형

09 다음 우리말과 일치하도록 주어진 단어를 바르게 배열하여 문장을 완성하시오.

내가 그녀에게 그것을 하도록 하느니 차라리 책임을 지겠다. (rather, than, the responsibility, would, take)
➡ I ______________________________ let her do it.

서술형

[10-12] 다음 빈칸에 알맞은 말을 <보기>에서 골라 쓰시오.

<보기>
must have practiced
should have listened
should have brought

10

We are lost. We ______________________ to the guide.

11

She plays the piano very well. She ________ ____________ a lot.

12

It's raining. We ______________________ umbrellas.

13 다음 빈칸에 들어갈 말로 알맞은 것은?

She has good eyesight. She ________ be wearing glasses.

① may ② can't ③ must
④ should ⑤ used to

14 다음 빈칸에 공통으로 들어갈 말로 알맞은 것은?

• ________ you find the bike for me? • You ________ open the box which I gave you.

① Can[can] ② May[may] ③ Will[will]
④ Must[must] ⑤ Should[should]

15 다음 두 문장의 뜻이 같도록 빈칸에 알맞은 것은?

Robert walked the dog every day, but he doesn't anymore. = Robert ________ walk the dog every day.

① has to ② used to ③ ought to
④ had better ⑤ would rather

16 다음 중 나머지와 의미가 다른 문장은?

① Don't take off your mask indoors.
② You mustn't take off your mask indoors.
③ You shouldn't take off your mask indoors.
④ You ought not to take off your mask indoors.
⑤ You don't have to take off your mask indoors.

17 다음 빈칸에 들어갈 말이 바르게 짝지어진 것은?

• It's snowing outside. I ________ stay at home. • The bank will close soon. We ________ hurry up.

① have to — may not
② may not — ought not to
③ would rather — had better
④ should — would rather not
⑤ had better — don't have to

18 (A), (B), (C)의 괄호 안에서 알맞은 것끼리 바르게 짝지어진 것은?

• He has a stomachache. He (A) [should / must] have eaten too much. • Anna has a cold. She (B) [should / may] have worn a warmer coat. • She (C) [must / can't] have forgotten about the meeting. She sent me a text message about it.

	(A)	(B)	(C)
①	should	— should	— can't
②	should	— may	— can't
③	must	— should	— must
④	must	— should	— can't
⑤	must	— may	— must

19 다음 중 밑줄 친 부분의 쓰임이 나머지 넷과 다른 것은?

① You must keep to the right.
② People must wait in line here.
③ You must be foolish to fight with him.
④ You must remember to say "thank you."
⑤ I must finish the math homework by tomorrow.

20 다음 중 밑줄 친 부분과 바꿔 쓸 수 없는 것은?

① You may choose what you want. (= can)
② There used to be an art gallery here. (= would)
③ Jake can run 100 meters in 13 seconds. (= is able to)
④ We must protect the natural environment. (= have to)
⑤ You should bring a sleeping bag and a flashlight. (= ought to)

21 다음 주어진 문장과 의미가 같은 것은?

I regret that I didn't have an audition for the musical.

① I may have had an audition for the musical.
② I must have had an audition for the musical.
③ I should have had an audition for the musical.
④ I cannot have had an audition for the musical.
⑤ I shouldn't have had an audition for the musical.

22 다음 문장에서 어법상 틀린 부분을 찾아 바르게 고친 것은?

You should study harder. You may can get an excellent grade.

① should → ought to
② study → have studied
③ may → can
④ can → be able to
⑤ get → to get

23 다음 중 밑줄 친 부분이 어법상 틀린 것은?

① You would rather not see this scene.
② You don't have to hide your feelings.
③ You ought not to cook noodles too long.
④ You had not better change your hair color.
⑤ I'm so sleepy that I am not able to focus on the book.

서술형

24 다음 문장을 미래시제로 바꿔 쓰시오.

You can experience different cultures. ➡ ________________

Chapter 06
수동태

학고 시험 대비 문제

맞힌 개수

_____ / 23

01 다음 중 어법상 틀린 것은?

① A tie was bought for my dad by me.
② A shot was given to Tom by the nurse.
③ I was given to a Christmas gift by my aunt.
④ The new toys were given to the boys by me.
⑤ A question was asked of Sora by the foreigner.

02 다음 중 수동태로 잘못 바꿔 쓴 것은?

① He laughed at me.
➡ I was laughed at by him.
② People found the movie boring.
➡ The movie was found boring by people.
③ I saw him enter the room.
➡ He was seen enter the room.
④ I am writing the letter.
➡ The letter is being written by me.
⑤ She gave me a watch.
➡ I was given a watch by her.

03 다음 빈칸에 들어갈 말이 바르게 짝지어진 것은?

• She was satisfied ________ the furniture.
• I was surprised ________ their marriage.

① to — of
② at — of
③ with — at
④ with — for
⑤ for — at

04 다음 중 어법상 틀린 것은?

① He was considered a great scientist.
② I am called a little prince by my sister.
③ Linda's room is always kept clean by her.
④ She was elected chairperson by us.
⑤ He was told give up smoking by them.

05 다음 중 수동태로 바르게 바꿔 쓴 것은?

① People found the story interesting.
➡ The story is found interesting.
② A car ran over the man.
➡ The man was ran over by a car.
③ Tom is painting this house.
➡ This house is painted being by Tom.
④ Did Mr. Kim bring this book?
➡ Was this book brought by Mr. Kim?
⑤ He gave the police the information.
➡ The information was given the police by him.

06 다음 문장을 수동태로 바꿔 쓸 때 빈칸에 알맞은 것은?

He will buy a T-shirt.
➡ A T-shirt ____________ by him.

① was bought
② will buy
③ is bought
④ will be bought
⑤ will be buying

서술형

07 다음 문장을 수동태로 바꿔 쓸 때 빈칸에 알맞은 말을 쓰시오.

(1) My mom is cleaning the room now.

➡ The room ________ ________ ________ by my mom now.

(2) Lisa must clean the room.

➡ The room ________ ________ ________ by Lisa.

서술형

08 다음 문장을 수동태로 바꿔 쓰시오.

(1) The policemen are checking other suspects.

➡ ____________________________

(2) When did you change your phone number?

➡ ____________________________

서술형

09 다음 우리말과 일치하도록 빈칸에 알맞은 말을 쓰시오.

(1) 그는 우리에게 가수로 알려져 있다.

➡ He ________ ________ ________ us as a singer.

(2) 하늘이 구름으로 덮여 있었다.

➡ The sky ________ ________ ________ clouds.

서술형

10 다음 문장을 수동태로 바꿔 쓸 때 빈칸에 알맞은 말을 쓰시오.

(1) People can download it from that site.

➡ It ________ ________ ________ from that site.

(2) Somebody is using this computer.

➡ This computer ________ ________ ________ by somebody.

서술형

11 다음 문장을 수동태로 바꿔 쓰시오.

(1) He made us happy.

➡ ____________________________

(2) They called the boy a soccer star.

➡ ____________________________

(3) We found the book interesting.

➡ ____________________________

(4) They elected Tom captain.

➡ ____________________________

12 다음 빈칸에 들어갈 말로 알맞은 것은?

> He ________ to exercise regularly by the doctor.

① advises ② advised ③ will advise
④ was advised ⑤ has advised

13 다음 빈칸에 들어갈 말이 바르게 짝지어진 것은?

> • My bike ________ several days ago.
> • A thief broke into his house and ________ his computer.

① stole — stole
② stole — was stolen
③ was stolen — stole
④ was stolen — was stolen
⑤ has stolen — was stealing

14 (A), (B), (C)의 괄호 안에서 알맞은 것끼리 바르게 짝지어진 것은?

> • The kite is (A) [being made / been made] by Brad.
> • The sneakers must (B) [been washed / be washed] by hand.
> • The restaurant has (C) [been run / being run] by the family since 2010.

	(A)	(B)	(C)
①	being made	— been washed	— been run
②	being made	— be washed	— been run
③	being made	— been washed	— being run
④	been made	— be washed	— being run
⑤	been made	— been washed	— been run

15 다음 문장을 수동태로 바르게 바꾼 것은?

> Mom made me help my brother.

① I was made help my brother by Mom.
② I was made helping my brother by Mom.
③ I was made to help my brother by Mom.
④ My brother was made help me by Mom.
⑤ My brother was made to help me by Mom.

16 다음 우리말을 영어로 바르게 옮긴 것은?

> 쿠키가 그녀에 의해 구워지고 있었다.

① The cookies were baked by her.
② The cookies were baking by her.
③ The cookies were had baking by her.
④ The cookies were been baking by her.
⑤ The cookies were being baked by her.

17 다음 문장을 수동태로 바꿀 때 빈칸에 알맞은 것은?

> The children laughed at the beggar.
> ➡ The beggar ____________ the children.

① was laughed
② laughed at by
③ was laughed at
④ was laughed by
⑤ was laughed at by

[18-19] 다음 문장을 수동태로 바르게 바꾼 것을 모두 고르시오.

18

The librarian gave me the library book.

① I was given the library book by the librarian.
② The library book was given me by the librarian.
③ I was given to the library book by the librarian.
④ The library book was given to me by the librarian.
⑤ The library book was given for me by the librarian.

19

People think that Seoul is a safe city.

① Seoul is thought being a safe city.
② Seoul is thought to be a safe city.
③ It is thought that Seoul is a safe city.
④ It thinks that Seoul is been a safe city.
⑤ People are thought Seoul to be a safe city.

20 다음 우리말과 일치하도록 빈칸에 들어갈 말로 알맞은 것은?

내 개가 밖에서 짖는 소리가 들렸다. ➡ My dog ________ outside.

① heard barking
② heard to bark
③ was heard bark
④ was heard barked
⑤ was heard to bark

21 다음 빈칸에 들어갈 말이 같은 것끼리 바르게 짝지어진 것은?

ⓐ The bags are filled ________ coffee beans. ⓑ All the furniture was covered ________ dust. ⓒ People are worried ________ food shortages. ⓓ The customer was satisfied ________ the design.

① ⓐ, ⓑ — ⓒ, ⓓ ② ⓐ, ⓒ — ⓑ, ⓓ
③ ⓐ, ⓑ, ⓓ — ⓒ ④ ⓐ, ⓒ, ⓓ — ⓑ
⑤ ⓐ — ⓑ, ⓒ, ⓓ

22 다음 중 수동태로 바꿀 수 없는 문장을 모두 골라 바르게 짝지은 것은?

ⓐ The pink sweater costs over $80. ⓑ Qatar hosted the 2022 World Cup. ⓒ An avocado resembles a pear in shape. ⓓ This book has a lot of information about animals.

① ⓐ, ⓑ ② ⓑ, ⓒ ③ ⓑ, ⓓ
④ ⓐ, ⓒ, ⓓ ⑤ ⓑ, ⓒ, ⓓ

23 다음 중 어법상 틀린 문장의 개수는?

ⓐ I was asked show my driver's license. ⓑ His new book was released last week. ⓒ The car must be returned by next Friday. ⓓ The air conditioner was turned on Jenny. ⓔ We were made to wait in the classroom by the teacher.

① 1개 ② 2개 ③ 3개
④ 4개 ⑤ 5개

Chapter 07
대명사

학교 시험 대비 문제

맞힌 개수 _____ / 24

01 다음 빈칸에 들어갈 말이 바르게 짝지어진 것은?

I have two dogs. ________ is white and ________ is black.

① One — others
② One — another
③ One — the other
④ Some — others
⑤ Some — the other

02 다음 빈칸에 들어갈 말이 바르게 짝지어진 것은?

• The museum ________ was very old.
• He drew the picture for ________.

① it — him
② it — himself
③ itself — him
④ itself — himself
⑤ himself — themselves

03 다음 빈칸에 들어갈 말이 바르게 짝지어진 것은?

I have six dogs. One of them is white, ________ is black, and ________ are brown.

① some — others
② another — the other
③ one — the others
④ one — another
⑤ another — the others

04 다음 밑줄 친 부분과 바꿔 쓸 수 있는 것은?

My sister took a trip to Europe <u>alone</u>.

① for her
② of itself
③ by herself
④ in herself
⑤ from herself

05 다음 밑줄 친 부분이 어법상 틀린 것은?

① All of them <u>are</u> of the same age.
② Every book in the library <u>have</u> been lost.
③ Neither of them <u>is</u> able to play the piano.
④ Neither of my parents <u>likes</u> to grow flowers.
⑤ Both friends <u>are</u> interested in the environment.

06 다음 빈칸에 들어갈 말이 바르게 짝지어진 것은?

• I have two pets. One is an iguana and ________ is a puppy.
• Look at the three boys in the playground. One is running, ________ is riding a bike, and the other is flying a kite.

① one — another
② one — the other
③ another — others
④ the other — another
⑤ the other — others

07 다음 중 어법상 틀린 것은?

① Some people went up the mountain and others stayed at home.
② He has two sisters. One is a cook and the other is a teacher.
③ There are 20 students. Some students like summer and the others don't like it.
④ She has four children. One is a boy and the other are girls.
⑤ Some people are buying tickets and others are waiting for the train.

08 다음 중 어법상 틀린 것은?

① All of the books were so fun.
② Either of you has to wash the car.
③ Every boys in my class likes Sally.
④ Neither of them is good at swimming.
⑤ Each of these books costs 10 dollars.

09 다음 중 어법상 틀린 것을 모두 고르면?

① I got three pencils. One is red, another is blue, and the other is green.
② I don't like this shirt. Show me another one.
③ I have ten apples. One is blue and the other are red.
④ Some people like bananas and other like oranges.
⑤ I invited five friends to the party. But only Judy and Tom came. And the others didn't come.

10 다음 중 어법상 틀린 것은?

① I can't eat anything.
② Somebody used my laptop computer.
③ Maybe somebody thinks that she is very poor.
④ He has something different from other employees.
⑤ If there's something wrong with you, tell me anytime.

11 다음 빈칸에 들어갈 말로 알맞은 것은?

Did Bob and Tony ________ make this doghouse?

① they ② them ③ their
④ theirs ⑤ themselves

서술형

12 다음 문장에서 어법상 틀린 부분을 찾아 바르게 고쳐 쓰시오.

Each of the students in this class are warm-hearted.

____________ ➡ ____________

13 다음 빈칸에 들어갈 말로 알맞은 것은?

> Two children are having lunch. One is having a hamburger, and ________ is having a sandwich.

① some ② other ③ another
④ the other ⑤ the others

14 다음 빈칸에 들어갈 말로 알맞지 않은 것은?

> ________ has been to the amusement park.

① Each of them
② None of the boys
③ Both of my friends
④ Every girl in the room
⑤ Neither of the students

15 다음 우리말을 영어로 바르게 옮긴 것은?

> 모든 정보가 이 지도 안에 있다.

① All informations are in this map.
② All of the information is in this map.
③ All of the informations are in this map.
④ Both of the information is in this map.
⑤ Both of the informations are in this map.

16 다음 문장에서 괄호 안의 단어가 들어갈 위치로 알맞은 곳은?

> She often (①) tells (②) me (③) something (④) about (⑤) my brother. (bad)

17 다음 중 밑줄 친 부분을 생략할 수 없는 것은?

① We set up the tent ourselves.
② Did you make the table itself?
③ My dad took these photos himself.
④ She herself cooked the chicken soup.
⑤ They're ready to fight to protect themselves.

18 (A), (B), (C)의 괄호 안에서 알맞은 것끼리 바르게 짝지어진 것은?

> • Each of the students (A) [has / have] different hobbies.
> • Every animal (B) [need / needs] food and water to survive.
> • All the tables (C) [is / are] already booked this evening.

	(A)	(B)	(C)
①	has	needs	are
②	has	need	is
③	has	need	are
④	have	need	is
⑤	have	needs	are

19 다음 중 밑줄 친 부분의 쓰임이 나머지 넷과 다른 것은?

① To know yourself is not easy.
② Alex seems satisfied with himself.
③ The little girl can ride a bike herself.
④ John gave himself a gift for Christmas.
⑤ Jane introduced herself before starting the job interview.

20 다음 중 밑줄 친 부분이 어법상 틀린 것은?

① Some like dogs, and others like cats.
② There are three shops. On Sunday, one is open, and the others are closed.
③ Some of the sweaters are white, and the others are blue.
④ There are two trees. One is an apple tree, and the other is a pine tree.
⑤ There are three girls. One is playing the piano, other is singing, and the other is dancing.

서술형
21 다음 우리말과 일치하도록 괄호 안의 말을 이용하여 문장을 완성하시오.

그는 혼자서 책을 읽기 시작했다. (by)
➡ He started to read books ____________.

서술형
22 다음 빈칸에 알맞은 대명사를 쓰시오.

They have two children. _________ is 6 years old, and _________ _________ is 3 years old.

서술형
23 다음 우리말과 일치하도록 빈칸에 알맞은 말을 쓰시오.

식당에는 많은 사람들이 있었다. 어떤 사람들은 샌드위치를 먹고 있었고, 다른 사람들은 햄버거를 먹고 있었다.
➡ There were many people in the restaurant. _________ were eating sandwiches and _________ were eating hamburgers.

서술형
24 다음 우리말과 일치하도록 괄호 안의 말을 바르게 배열하시오.

모든 구성원들은 규칙을 따라야 한다.
(the members, follow, of, have to, all)
➡ ________________________________ the rules.

Chapter 08
형용사와 부사

학교 시험 대비 문제

맞힌 개수 ______ / 24

01 다음 중 어법상 틀린 것은?

① It tastes well.
② It sounds simple.
③ It was getting dark.
④ You will grow stronger.
⑤ The poor man was sleeping in the forest.

02 다음 대화의 빈칸에 들어갈 말로 알맞은 것은?

A Did you spend ________ money in L.A.?
B Yes, I did. I spent a million dollars there.

① many　② much
③ lot of　④ a little
⑤ a few

03 다음 중 어법상 올바른 것은?

① I make a few money.
② He bought a little apples.
③ There is few water in the bottle.
④ There are a little students in the classroom.
⑤ He feels lonely because he has few friends.

04 다음 대화의 빈칸에 들어갈 말로 알맞은 것은?

A That music is too loud. Can you ________ please?
B Sure.

① turn on it　② turn it on
③ turn it up　④ turn down it
⑤ turn it down

05 다음 중 밑줄 친 부분의 쓰임이 올바른 것은?

① Henry is only.
② You look happily.
③ It is an alive fish.
④ It sounds really great.
⑤ There was an asleep boy.

06 다음 빈칸에 들어갈 말이 바르게 짝지어진 것은?

• I think you know very little. ________ knowledge is a dangerous thing.
• In the past, ________ women were successful in Korean politics.
• Michael Cane was born in South London, not the East End. ________ people know that.

① A few — few — Little
② A little — few — Few
③ Few — a little — Little
④ Little — little — A few
⑤ A little — a little — Few

07 다음 밑줄 친 부분이 어법상 틀린 것은?

① Do you know someone smart?
② It is a such unique and pretty ring.
③ I felt something cold in the box.
④ How could he live in such a small house?
⑤ She has never bought such an expensive bag.

08 다음 우리말과 일치하도록 빈칸에 들어갈 말로 알맞은 것은?

> 나는 부자들이 세금을 더 부과받아야 한다고 생각한다.
> ➡ I think that ____________ should be taxed more.

① rich ② a rich
③ the rich ④ people rich
⑤ the rich person

09 다음 밑줄 친 부분이 어법상 틀린 것은?

① We got a lot of snow last week.
② You need lots of money to buy it.
③ How much water do you drink a day?
④ He has too many work to finish today.
⑤ Many people want to have an exciting hobby.

10 다음 빈칸에 들어갈 말이 바르게 짝지어진 것은?

> • She has ________ books to read.
> • I cannot breathe well. I think there is ________ air in this elevator.

① few — a lot of ② a few — little
③ little — little ④ a little — a few
⑤ a lot of — a few

11 다음 우리말과 일치하도록 빈칸에 들어갈 말로 알맞은 것은?

> 많은 사람들이 종종 밸런타인데이에 초콜릿을 주고받는다.
> ➡ Many people ______________________ on Valentine's Day.

① give often and receive chocolate
② give and often receive chocolate
③ give and receive often chocolate
④ often give and receive chocolate
⑤ give and receive chocolate often

서술형

12 다음 괄호 안에 주어진 단어를 이용하여 문장을 완성하시오.

> **A** How often does she walk to school?
> **B** She ______________________.
> (always, walk)

[13-14] 다음 빈칸에 알맞지 않은 것을 고르시오.

13

The speaker tried to talk ________.

① loudly ② kindly ③ clearly
④ friendly ⑤ strongly

14

John went to the airport to ____________.

① see her off ② pick up them
③ pick Susan up ④ pick up his uncle
⑤ see his friend off

15 다음 중 밑줄 친 부분과 바꿔 쓸 수 있는 것은?

They ordered lots of food to share.

① much ② many ③ some
④ a few ⑤ a little

16 다음 우리말을 영어로 바르게 옮긴 것은?

몇몇 사람들이 아직 살아 있다.

① Some people are still live.
② A few people are still alive.
③ Some people are still living.
④ A few people are still living.
⑤ A lot of people are still alive.

17 (A), (B), (C)의 괄호 안에서 알맞은 것끼리 바르게 짝지어진 것은?

- (A) [Few / Little] children are playing in the playground.
- I want to drink (B) [a few / a little] tea before I leave.
- There is (C) [many / much] oil in the sea because of the accident.

	(A)	(B)	(C)
①	Few	a few	much
②	Few	a few	many
③	Few	a little	much
④	Little	a few	many
⑤	Little	a little	much

18 다음 빈칸에 들어갈 말이 바르게 짝지어진 것은?

- I find it ________ to express myself in English.
- Linda decided to join the school volunteer club ________.

① hard — late ② hardly — late
③ hard — lately ④ hard — nearly
⑤ hardly — lately

19 다음 밑줄 친 부분을 같은 의미의 어법에 맞는 표현으로 잘못 고친 것은?

① He seems to have many patience. (→ much)

② Don't allow dogs to eat some chocolate. (→ any)

③ My country has much beautiful traditions. (→ a lot of)

④ Henry dropped a little coins on the floor. (→ lots of)

⑤ He had few food, so he feels very hungry. (→ little)

20 다음 중 짝지어진 문장의 밑줄 친 부분의 쓰임이 서로 같은 것은?

① • Jerry is pretty good at dancing.
 • She got up pretty early in the morning.

② • The train often arrives late.
 • I'm afraid you will be late for the party.

③ • He wants to be fast like his friend.
 • The horse is young enough to run fast.

④ • Did the wind blow hard last night?
 • He is having a hard time these days.

⑤ • Katie got a high grade in science.
 • Raise your hand high when you want to speak.

서술형

21 다음 우리말과 일치하도록 괄호 안의 말을 바르게 배열하시오.

나는 긴장할 때 보통 단것을 먹는다. (sweet, have, usually, I, something)

➡ ____________ when I'm nervous.

서술형

22 다음 우리말과 일치하도록 괄호 안의 말을 이용하여 문장을 완성하시오.

그것은 물이 거의 없는 환경에서 산다. (water)

➡ It lives in an environment with ________ ________.

서술형

[23-24] 다음 문장에서 어법상 틀린 부분을 찾아 바르게 고쳐 쓰시오.

23

The homeless is provided a home to live in, food to eat, and clothes to wear.

____________ ➡ ____________

24

This printer is broken. Where can I throw away it?

____________ ➡ ____________

Chapter 09
비교

학교 시험 대비 문제

맞힌 개수
_____ / 24

01 다음 빈칸에 들어갈 말로 알맞은 것은?

Male anacondas are not as ________ as female anacondas.

① big ② bigger
③ biggest ④ less big
⑤ more big

02 다음 우리말을 영어로 바르게 옮긴 것은?

나는 수미가 잡은 것만큼 많은 물고기를 잡았다.

① I caught fish as Sumi did.
② I caught as many as Sumi did.
③ I caught as much fish as Sumi did.
④ I caught as many fish as Sumi did.
⑤ I caught much more fish than Sumi did.

03 다음 빈칸에 들어갈 말로 알맞은 것은?

The article says that Korea gets warm ________ than the world average.

① fast ② faster
③ fastest ④ as fast
⑤ more fast

04 다음 중 문장의 의미가 나머지 넷과 다른 것은?

① Nari is the best middle school in Korea.
② Nari isn't as good as other middle schools in Korea.
③ Nari is better than any other middle school in Korea.
④ No other middle school in Korea is better than Nari.
⑤ No other middle school in Korea is as good as Nari.

05 다음 우리말과 일치하도록 빈칸에 들어갈 말로 알맞은 것은?

기술이 발달하면 할수록, 세계는 점점 더 작아진다.
➡ ________ technology develops, ________ the world becomes.

① The less — the better
② The less — the busier
③ The more — the fewer
④ The more — the smaller
⑤ The lower — the worse

06 다음 중 밑줄 친 부분의 쓰임이 틀린 것은?

① Russia is even larger than China.
② He is very more handsome than his brother.
③ This summer is much hotter than last summer.
④ This experiment is a lot harder than the last one.
⑤ This chair is far more comfortable than that chair.

07 다음 빈칸에 들어갈 말로 알맞지 않은 것은?

> Harry is the ________ boy in his class.

① laziest
② smartest
③ fastest
④ more popular
⑤ most handsome

08 다음 주어진 문장과 의미가 같지 않은 것은?

> Famine is the most serious problem.

① No other problem is as serious as famine.
② All the other problems are as serious as famine.
③ No other problem is more serious than famine.
④ Famine is more serious than any other problem.
⑤ Famine is more serious than all the other problems.

09 다음 중 어법상 틀린 것은?

① Sumi is as tall as Yeonsu.
② He can speak Chinese as better as you.
③ You should get home as early as possible.
④ The bigger animals are, the longer they live.
⑤ Hallasan is the most beautiful mountain I have ever seen.

서술형

10 다음 밑줄 친 부분 중 어법상 틀린 것을 골라 바르게 고쳐 쓰시오.

> This mall is(①) one of(②) the highest(③) building(④) in our city(⑤).

________ ➡ ________

서술형

11 다음 우리말과 일치하도록 주어진 단어를 사용하여 문장을 완성하시오.

> 우리 엄마는 내게 스마트폰을 가능한 한 조금만 사용하라고 하셨어. (little, possible)
> ➡ My mom asked me to use the smartphone ________ ________ ________ ________.

서술형

12 Ann의 가족에 관한 표를 보고, 빈칸에 알맞은 말을 쓰시오.

Member	Dad	Mom	Tim	Ann
Height (cm)	180	165	170	153
Old	42	43	13	15

(1) 비교급 이용
No one in Ann's family is ________ ________ Mom.

(2) 원급 이용
No one in Ann's family is ________ ________ ________ Ann.

(3) 비교급 이용
Tim is ________ ________ ________ ________ member in Ann's family.

13 다음 빈칸에 들어갈 말로 알맞지 않은 것은?

This is the most ________ dress in the shop.

① pretty ② colorful ③ popular
④ beautiful ⑤ expensive

[14-15] 다음 빈칸에 들어갈 말이 바르게 짝지어진 것을 고르시오.

14

• Tiffany is ________ than her sisters. • Fruits are as ________ as fresh vegetables.

① kind — healthy ② kinder — healthy
③ kind — healthier ④ kindest — healthier
⑤ kinder — healthiest

15

The ________ you are, the ________ mistakes you make.

① careful — few
② careful — fewer
③ more careful — fewer
④ more careful — fewest
⑤ most careful — fewest

16 다음 밑줄 친 부분과 바꿔 쓸 수 없는 것은?

These sneakers are much more comfortable than those shoes.

① far ② very ③ still
④ even ⑤ a lot

17 다음 우리말과 일치하도록 할 때 밑줄 친 부분이 어법상 틀린 것은?

그것은 세계에서 가장 인기 있는 스포츠들 중 하나가 되었다. ➡ It has become(①) one(②) of the most popular(③) sport(④) in the world(⑤).

18 다음 우리말과 일치하도록 빈칸에 들어갈 말로 알맞은 것은?

지하철이 점점 더 혼잡해지고 있다. ➡ The subway is getting ____________.

① crowded and crowded
② more and more crowded
③ most and most crowded
④ more crowded and crowded
⑤ most crowded and crowded

19 다음 두 문장을 한 문장으로 나타낼 때 빈칸에 알맞은 것은?

> Billy is 12 years old. His mother is 36 years old.
> ➡ Billy's mother is ______________ Billy.

① three as old as
② three older than
③ three times older as
④ three times as old as
⑤ three times the oldest

20 다음 표의 내용과 일치하지 않는 것은?

	Apple	Orange	Melon
Price	$2	$2	$5
Weight	200g	250g	1500g

① The orange is as cheap as the apple.
② The orange is heavier than the apple.
③ The apple is the lightest of the three.
④ The melon is less heavy than the apple.
⑤ The melon is the most expensive of the three.

21 다음 중 짝지어진 두 문장의 의미가 같지 않은 것은?

① This book is less useful than that one.
= This book isn't as useful as that one.
② My hair is longer than Susan's.
= Susan's hair isn't shorter than mine.
③ I will send it to you as soon as possible.
= I will send it to you as soon as I can.
④ Seoul is the biggest city in Korea.
= No other city in Korea is bigger than Seoul.
⑤ The process is more important than the result.
= The result is less important than the process.

22 다음 중 어법상 틀린 것은?

① She is one of the best figure skaters.
② Sam's farm is twice as large as Andy's.
③ The Earth is much smaller than the Sun.
④ What is the most difficult thing when you study math?
⑤ You had better apologize to her as sooner as possible.

서술형
23 다음 문장들이 같은 뜻이 되도록 빈칸에 알맞은 말을 쓰시오.

> This is the most interesting picture in the museum.
> = No picture in the museum is ________ ________ as this one.
> = This is ________ ________ ________ any other picture in the museum.

서술형
24 다음 우리말과 일치하도록 괄호 안의 말을 이용하여 문장을 완성하시오. (단, 필요하면 형태를 바꿀 것)

> 생선이 신선할수록 맛이 더 좋다. (fresh, good)
> ➡ ________ ________ the fish is, ________ ________ it tastes.

Chapter 10
전치사

학고 시험 대비 문제

맞힌 개수 ____ / 24

01 다음 빈칸에 들어갈 말이 바르게 짝지어진 것은?

- I was surprised ________ Eric's sudden change.
- The inventor of the microwave oven was interested ________ cooking.

① at — to
② in — at
③ of — to
④ at — in
⑤ of — at

02 다음 빈칸에 공통으로 들어갈 말로 알맞은 것은?

- Fast and loud music is full ________ energy.
- She told me to study harder, instead ________ listening to music.

① of
② with
③ at
④ into
⑤ without

03 다음 글의 밑줄 친 부분이 어법상 틀린 것은?

Ella Grasso was born ① on May 10, 1919, ② in America. She graduated ③ from Mount Holyoke College ④ with the highest honors. She married ⑤ to a school teacher, and they spent the next three years in a small town.

04 다음 중 빈칸에 들어갈 전치사가 나머지 넷과 다른 것은?

① We eat soup ________ a spoon.
② Brian helps me ________ the homework a lot.
③ The top of the mountain is covered ________ snow.
④ The streets are full ________ trash and dirty houses.
⑤ My days are very busy ________ work and family.

05 다음 빈칸에 들어갈 말로 알맞은 것은?

My dad gave me a ride ________ the museum.

① over
② to
③ up
④ down
⑤ below

06 다음 두 문장의 뜻이 같도록 빈칸에 알맞은 것은?

He did his homework before eating dinner.
= He ate dinner ________ doing his homework.

① by
② during
③ before
④ after
⑤ within

07 다음 빈칸에 들어갈 말이 바르게 짝지어진 것은?

- She made some friends ________ the summer camp.
- The event was put off ________ a week due to the heavy rain.

① for — during ② for — while
③ while — for ④ during — for
⑤ during — while

08 다음 밑줄 친 부분과 바꿔 쓸 수 있는 것은?

There is a library <u>beside</u> my house, which has a lot of good books.

① near ② around ③ next to
④ between ⑤ far from

09 다음 빈칸에 들어갈 말로 알맞은 것은?

Is it possible for John to finish the work ________ tomorrow?

① to ② by ③ till
④ from ⑤ since

10 다음 우리말과 일치하도록 빈칸에 들어갈 말로 알맞은 것은?

나는 빗속에서 길을 따라 걷고 있었다.
➡ I was walking ________ the road in the rain.

① onto ② along ③ across
④ toward ⑤ through

서술형

[11-12] 다음 우리말과 의미가 같도록 빈칸에 알맞은 전치사를 쓰시오.

11

Tom은 Jane과 준수 사이에 앉아 있다.
➡ Tom is sitting ________ Jane and Junsu.

12

도서관 앞에서 만나자.
➡ Let's meet ________ ________ ________ the library.

13 다음 빈칸에 들어갈 말로 알맞은 것은?

> The festival will last ________ seven days from May 10.

① by ② at ③ for
④ while ⑤ during

[14-15] 다음 빈칸에 들어갈 말이 바르게 짝지어진 것을 고르시오.

14

> • The Earth is suffering ________ climate change.
> • ________ my regret, I have to refuse your offer.

① for — In ② for — To
③ by — For ④ from — To
⑤ from — For

15

> • Chris found his dog sleeping ________ the bed.
> • It takes about 30 minutes ________ car to the airport.

① over — by ② under — by
③ under — on ④ beneath — on
⑤ beneath — with

16 다음 두 문장의 뜻이 같도록 빈칸에 알맞은 것은?

> My school is in front of the bookstore.
> = The bookstore is ________ my school.

① beside ② behind ③ among
④ around ⑤ next to

[17-18] 다음 중 우리말과 일치하도록 빈칸에 알맞은 것을 고르시오.

17

> 두 소년이 운동장을 가로질러 달리고 있었다.
> ➡ Two boys were running ________ the playground.

① from ② past ③ across
④ toward ⑤ between

18

> 그는 주머니 밖으로 구슬 하나를 꺼냈다.
> ➡ He took a marble ________ his pocket.

① up ② into ③ down
④ through ⑤ out of

19 다음 빈칸에 공통으로 들어갈 말로 알맞은 것은?

> • In many countries, the new year begins ________ January 1.
> • Early humans drew pictures ________ the walls of caves.

① on ② at ③ in
④ by ⑤ for

20 다음 중 밑줄 친 부분이 어법상 틀린 것은?

① A robot is walking toward me.
② You must arrive at the terminal till 5:00.
③ She threw my gift in the trash can.
④ He began to dig up the ground with a shovel.
⑤ I think I dropped my wallet around the front door.

21 다음 중 우리말을 영어로 잘못 옮긴 것은?

① 내 남동생은 Brad 뒤에 앉아 있다.
➡ My brother is sitting beside Brad.
② 누군가 그를 계단 아래로 밀었다.
➡ Someone pushed him down the stairs.
③ 청국장은 콩으로 만들어진다.
➡ Cheonggukjang is made from soybean.
④ 그 호텔은 아름다운 전망으로 유명하다.
➡ The hotel is famous for its beautiful view.
⑤ 너희 집 근처에 외식할 좋은 곳이 있니?
➡ Is there a good place to eat out near your house?

서술형

22 다음 우리말과 일치하도록 괄호 안의 말을 바르게 배열하시오.

> 학교는 그녀가 자란 마을에서 멀리 떨어져 있다.
> (far, the town, from, is)
> ➡ The school ______________ where she grew up.

서술형

[23-24] 다음 우리말과 일치하도록 괄호 안의 말을 이용하여 문장을 완성하시오.

23

> 당신은 일주일 이내에 그 물건을 반품해야 한다.
> (a week)
> ➡ You must return the item ________ ________ ________.

24

> 너의 가장 친한 친구가 너의 적으로 변할 수 있다.
> (turn, enemy)
> ➡ Your best friend can ________ ________ ________ ________.

Chapter 11
관계사

학교 시험 대비 문제

맞힌 개수

_____ / 24

01 다음 빈칸에 들어갈 말이 바르게 짝지어진 것은?

- My uncle Tom, ________ lives in L.A., is a doctor.
- We went to Jane's party, ________ we enjoyed very much.

① who — which ② who — that
③ that — that ④ who — what
⑤ which — who

02 다음 빈칸에 공통으로 알맞은 것은?

- He is the first man ________ landed on the Moon.
- This is the only restaurant ________ has never disappointed us.

① who ② whose
③ whom ④ that
⑤ what

03 다음 중 빈칸에 관계부사가 들어갈 수 없는 것은?

① This is the bench ________ they used to sit.
② He looked at the house ________ the bell rang.
③ I went to London, ________ I stayed for two weeks.
④ Tell me the reason ________ you are looking for the magazine.
⑤ Do you know the country ________ the great poet was born in?

04 다음 중 관계대명사가 바르게 쓰인 것을 모두 고르면?

① Ann, which lives next door, is very friendly.
② My uncle has two daughters, who became doctors.
③ This is the restaurant at that I met him.
④ Ms. Kim, which cakes are wonderful, has opened a bakery.
⑤ BART, which is Oakland's subway, connects San Francisco to Oakland.

05 다음 중 밑줄 친 What(what)의 쓰임이 나머지 넷과 다른 것은?

① What she said made me angry.
② That's what I thought.
③ What I want is to buy a new computer.
④ Tell me what you want to drink.
⑤ I wonder what time the concert begins.

06 다음 빈칸에 들어갈 말이 바르게 짝지어진 것은?

- She likes pizza ________ has lots of toppings.
- I know a doctor ________ has lots of experience.

① that — which
② who — that
③ which — which
④ who — which
⑤ which — who

07 다음 중 밑줄 친 부분을 생략할 수 없는 것은?

① I like the boy who dances well.
② There is a girl who is called Mary.
③ The house has a door that is painted green.
④ He is the man that I met yesterday.
⑤ I saw a picture which was painted by Picasso.

08 다음 밑줄 친 부분과 바꿔 쓸 수 있는 것은?

> The dress that she wants to buy is very expensive.

① who ② whom
③ what ④ which
⑤ of which

09 다음 밑줄 친 부분 중 어법상 틀린 것은?

① I can't believe what Justine said.
② This is the notebook whose cover is black.
③ I'm the first man that heard the news.
④ That's the reason how we study English.
⑤ April 5th is the day when we plant trees.

서술형

10 다음 두 문장을 관계대명사를 사용하여 한 문장으로 바꿔 쓰시오.

> • The necklace was beautiful.
> • She was looking at it.
> ➡ ______________________________
> ______________________________

서술형

[11-12] 다음 두 문장을 주어진 지시 사항에 따라 한 문장으로 바꿔 쓰시오.

> • Samuel returned to the village.
> • He was born in the village.

11 관계부사 사용

➡ ______________________________
____

12 관계대명사 사용

➡ ______________________________
____

[13-14] 다음 빈칸에 들어갈 말로 알맞은 것을 고르시오.

13

I saw a program ________ introduces Korea's beautiful tourist attractions.

① who ② what ③ whom
④ which ⑤ whose

14

He approached the tree ________ the bird had landed.

① how ② what ③ why
④ when ⑤ where

15 다음 중 밑줄 친 부분과 바꿔 쓸 수 있는 것은?

She makes a list of <u>the things that</u> she needs before going shopping.

① that ② what ③ which
④ whose ⑤ whichever

16 다음 두 문장의 뜻이 같도록 빈칸에 알맞은 것은?

Call me at any time when you need my help.
= Call me ________ you need my help.

① however ② at which ③ whatever
④ whenever ⑤ whichever

17 다음 중 밑줄 친 부분의 쓰임이 나머지 넷과 <u>다른</u> 것은?

① He helps old people <u>who</u> live alone.
② Do you know <u>who</u> wrote the article?
③ The man <u>who</u> sang at the party is James.
④ I'm proud of my uncle <u>who</u> is a firefighter.
⑤ What is the name of the person <u>who</u> invented the zipper?

18 다음 우리말을 영어로 바르게 옮긴 것은?

나는 Sam의 집을 방문했는데, 그것은 오래되어 보였다.

① I visited Sam's house, that looked old.
② I visited Sam's house, what looked old.
③ I visited Sam's house which looked old.
④ I visited Sam's house where looked old.
⑤ I visited Sam's house, which looked old.

19 다음 우리말과 일치하도록 빈칸에 알맞은 것은?

> 네가 무엇을 요리하든, 나는 그것을 맛있게 먹을 것이다.
> ➡ ____________ you cook, I will enjoy it.

① Which ② However ③ Whatever
④ Whomever ⑤ Anything that

20 다음 빈칸에 들어갈 말로 알맞지 않은 것은?

> The table ______________ is made of wood.

① has three legs
② I bought yesterday
③ whose color is blue
④ which is in the living room
⑤ covered with a table cloth

21 다음 중 밑줄 친 부분을 생략할 수 있는 것을 모두 골라 짝지은 것은?

> ⓐ A ship which is made of steel can float.
> ⓑ I bought a new car last month, which is broken.
> ⓒ Today is the day when we first met.
> ⓓ The girl who is jumping rope in the garden is Sarah.

① ⓐ, ⓑ ② ⓐ, ⓒ ③ ⓑ, ⓓ
④ ⓐ, ⓑ, ⓒ ⑤ ⓑ, ⓒ, ⓓ

22 다음 밑줄 친 부분이 어법상 틀린 것의 개수는?

> ⓐ This is the bench on that I was sitting.
> ⓑ Whoever can play an instrument can join our club.
> ⓒ The doctor told us the way how she takes care of patients.
> ⓓ People like fruits and vegetables which are grown organically.
> ⓔ On her way home, she found a puppy whose life was in danger.

① 1개 ② 2개 ③ 3개
④ 4개 ⑤ 5개

서술형

23 다음 우리말과 일치하도록 괄호 안의 말을 바르게 배열하시오.

> 네가 아무리 바쁘더라도 너는 운동할 시간을 가져야 한다. (busy, are, however, you)
> ➡ ________________, you must take time to exercise.

서술형

24 다음 우리말과 일치하도록 주어진 <조건>에 맞게 영작하시오.

> <조건>
> 1. 관계대명사를 사용할 것
> 2. 괄호 안의 말을 사용하되 필요하면 형태를 바꿀 것
> 3. 과거시제를 사용하여 총 8단어로 쓸 것

> Tony는 그녀에게 거짓말을 했는데, 그것이 그녀를 화나게 만들었다.
> (lie to her, make her angry)
> ➡ ______________________________

Chapter 12
접속사

학교 시험 대비 문제

맞힌 개수

_____ / 24

01 다음 우리말과 일치하도록 빈칸에 알맞은 것은?

> 그 영화는 너무나 감동적이어서 나는 울었다.
> ➡ The movie was ________ touching ________ I cried.

① so — that
② so — to
③ too — to
④ to — that
⑤ enough — to

02 다음 빈칸에 공통으로 들어갈 말로 알맞은 것은?

> • Kelly said ________ she was a pianist.
> • It was my dog ________ came to help me.

① what
② if
③ who
④ that
⑤ which

03 다음 빈칸에 들어갈 말로 알맞은 것은?

> Unless it rains tomorrow, we will go on a picnic.
> = ________________, we will go on a picnic.

① If it will rain tomorrow
② If it don't rain tomorrow
③ If it doesn't rain tomorrow
④ If it will not rain tomorrow
⑤ If it had not rained tomorrow

서술형

04 다음 두 문장을 한 문장으로 바꿔 쓸 때 빈칸에 알맞은 말을 쓰시오.

> • He gave me a present.
> • He also gave me money.
> ➡ He gave me ________ ________ a present ________ ________ money.

05 다음 중 밑줄 친 While(while)의 의미가 나머지 넷과 다른 것은?

① While I eat dinner, I watch TV.
② While John is very tall, his brother is short.
③ He is nice and gentle, while his brother isn't.
④ James is good at math, while he is poor at art.
⑤ Susan likes to go around, while her sister never goes out of the town.

06 다음 두 문장의 뜻이 같도록 빈칸에 알맞은 것은?

> ________ he doesn't come by six, we'll start first.
> = ________ he comes by six, we'll start first.

① As — If
② If — Unless
③ Unless — As
④ Although — As
⑤ Although — While

07 다음 밑줄 친 if의 의미가 나머지 넷과 다른 것은?

① I wonder if John likes Susan.
② I will come with you if I have the time.
③ I will ask mom if he was a brave seaman.
④ I'm not sure if she will come to the party.
⑤ She asked John if he was coming to the meeting.

08 다음 두 문장의 뜻이 같도록 빈칸에 알맞은 것은?

I studied hard, but I didn't pass the test.
= ________ I studied hard, I didn't pass the test.

① If
② As
③ When
④ Although
⑤ Because

09 다음 빈칸에 들어갈 말로 알맞은 것은?

There was a traffic jam. ________, she missed her plane.

① However
② For example
③ In other words
④ In contrast
⑤ As a result

10 다음 밑줄 친 부분의 쓰임이 의미상 어색한 것은?

① She was cooking when he came.
② As soon as he fell asleep, he went to bed.
③ Turn off the light before you leave the office.
④ After you get home, you must wash your hands.
⑤ The baby kept on crying until her mom came back.

11 다음 빈칸에 들어갈 말로 알맞지 않은 것은?

What do you think ____________?

① I should do
② her name is
③ she is looking for
④ the weather looks like
⑤ did James eat for lunch

12 다음 중 밑줄 친 부분과 바꿔 쓸 수 있는 것은?

Kiwis are a good source of vitamin C and minerals. Besides they taste great.

① Therefore
② However
③ In addition
④ For example
⑤ In other words

[13-14] 다음 빈칸에 들어갈 말이 바르게 짝지어진 것을 고르시오.

13

- I canceled the appointment ________ I had a headache.
- The boy was very scared ________ his mom was away.

① after — until
② because — while
③ till — as soon as
④ whether — though
⑤ although — unless

14

- I had to decide ________ I would buy a new sofa.
- Some scientists believe ________ the island will disappear soon.

① if — that
② that — if
③ that — what
④ what — that
⑤ whether — if

15 다음 빈칸에 들어갈 말로 알맞지 않은 것은?

Can you tell me ____________________?

① where my seat is
② what I can do for you
③ why your room is so messy
④ when did the fire break out
⑤ who is responsible for the accident

16 다음 빈칸에 공통으로 들어갈 말로 알맞은 것은?

- Listen carefully and do ________ I tell you.
- Don't forget to bring your smartphone ________ you go out.

① as ② if ③ since
④ while ⑤ when

17 다음 두 문장을 한 문장으로 나타낼 때 빈칸에 알맞은 말이 바르게 짝지어진 것은?

She doesn't throw away old clothes. She doesn't throw away old toys, either.
➡ She throws away ________ old clothes ________ old toys.

① not — but
② either — or
③ both — and
④ neither — nor
⑤ not only — but also

18 다음 중 같은 의미의 문장으로 잘못 바꾼 것은?

① His classes are not only useful but also fun.
= His classes are fun as well as useful.
② The book is too difficult for me to read.
= The book is so difficult that I can't read it.
③ I had enough time, but I was late for the concert.
= Although I had enough time, I was late for the concert.
④ If you don't read him a book, he will be disappointed.
= Unless you don't read him a book, he will be disappointed.
⑤ You should get some rest in order to get well soon.
= You should get some rest so that you can get well soon.

19 다음 우리말과 일치하도록 빈칸에 알맞은 것은?

> 그 결과, 많은 해양 동물들이 미세 플라스틱 때문에 죽어 가고 있다.
> ➡ ________________, many sea animals are dying because of microplastics.

① Therefore
② In addition
③ As a result
④ In other words
⑤ On the other hand

20 다음 중 어법상 <u>틀린</u> 것은?

① Where do you think you lost it?
② I have been your fan since you debuted.
③ Don't speed because animals may appear.
④ Either you or your friend have to pay for it.
⑤ He raised his hand so that she could see him.

서술형

21 다음 두 문장을 한 문장으로 연결하시오.

> • I wonder.
> • Does she know my name?
> ➡ ________________________________

서술형

22 다음 두 문장의 뜻이 같도록 빈칸에 알맞은 말을 쓰시오.

> Unless you follow his advice, you won't pass the interview.
> = If ____________________, you won't pass the interview.

서술형

23 다음 두 문장을 주어진 접속사로 시작하는 한 문장으로 바꾸어 쓰시오.

> • He couldn't stop laughing.
> • The comic book was very funny.
> ➡ Because ________________________________
> ________________________________.

서술형

24 다음 <조건>에 맞게 주어진 문장과 같은 의미의 문장을 완성하시오.

> <조건>
> 1. 접속사를 사용하여 부사절로 쓸 것
> 2. 총 6단어로 쓸 것

> Buy a ticket online, and you will get a 20% discount.
> ➡ ____________________, you will get a 20% discount.

Chapter 13
가정법

학교 시험 대비 문제

맞힌 개수 _____ / 23

01 다음 문장을 가정법으로 바꿔 쓸 때 빈칸에 알맞은 것은?

> As I don't have enough money, I can't buy a new computer.
> ➡ If I ________ enough money, I ________ a new computer.

① have — can buy
② were — would buy
③ had — could buy
④ were not — wouldn't buy
⑤ didn't have — couldn't buy

02 다음 중 두 문장의 뜻이 같은 것은?

① He looks as if he knew my secret.
= In fact, he doesn't know my secret.
② If I were rich, I could buy a car.
= As I am not rich, I can buy a car.
③ I am sorry that I don't have a computer.
= I wish I wouldn't have a computer.
④ If the doctor hadn't come, she would have died.
= As the doctor didn't come, she died.
⑤ He didn't study hard, so he failed.
= If he had studied hard, he would have failed.

03 다음 빈칸에 들어갈 말로 알맞은 것은?

> I failed the test, and I'm upset. I wish I ________ for the test.

① studied ② had studied
③ would study ④ have studied
⑤ would have studied

04 다음 문장을 가정법으로 표현한 것은?

> I am sorry I am not young.

① I wish I am young.
② I wish I were young.
③ I wish I had been young.
④ I wish I have been young.
⑤ I wish I was being young.

05 다음 중 가정법의 쓰임이 옳은 것은?

① I wish I had had no homework now.
② If it didn't rain, I would have played tennis.
③ I would put on a sweater if I am you.
④ Everything would have been OK if I hadn't lost my keys.
⑤ I'm not going to buy a car. If I buy a car, I would spend all my money on it.

06 다음 문장과 의미가 같은 것은?

> As I don't know his phone number, I cannot call him.

① If I know his phone number, I can call him.
② If I know his phone number, I could call him.
③ Had I known his phone number, I could have called him.
④ If I knew his phone number, I could call him.
⑤ If I had known his phone number, I could have called him.

07 **다음 중 문장 전환이 올바른 것은?**

① If Ann were in her office, she would answer the phone.
➡ As Ann is in her office, she doesn't answer the phone.

② If I had the new CD, I would lend it to you.
➡ As I didn't have the new CD, I can't lend it to you.

③ John fell down the stairs, so he hurt his left foot.
➡ If John had fallen down the stairs, he had hurt his left foot.

④ If he were healthy, he would play outside.
➡ Were he healthy, he would play outside.

⑤ If she had taken the medicine, she might have recovered more quickly.
➡ Had taken she the medicine, she might have recovered more quickly.

08 **다음 밑줄 친 부분의 쓰임이 올바른 문장은?**

① I wish I have a yacht.
② I wish I were handsome and rich.
③ If I finish my work, I could go to the movie.
④ If I knew her phone number, I call her right now.
⑤ The dog looked as if it could have understood my words.

서술형

09 **다음 우리말과 일치하도록 빈칸에 알맞은 말을 쓰시오.**

그는 마치 그가 부자인 것처럼 말한다.
➡ He talks ________ ________ ________ ________ rich.

서술형

[10-11] 다음 문장을 가정법으로 바꿔 쓰시오.

10

As I didn't have enough money, I couldn't buy the bike.
➡ ______________________________
____

11

He passed the exam because he studied hard.
➡ ______________________________
____

[12-13] 다음 빈칸에 들어갈 말로 알맞은 것을 고르시오.

12

If he had kept his promise, she ________ him.

① will trust
② has trusted
③ had trusted
④ would trust
⑤ would have trusted

13

If I had a magic wand, I ________ food to the poor.

① gave
② will give
③ had given
④ would give
⑤ would have given

14 다음 문장을 통해 알 수 있는 것은?

If he hadn't called 119, the woman would have died.

① He called 119.
② The woman died.
③ He didn't call 119.
④ The woman will die.
⑤ He has never called 119.

15 다음 문장을 가정법으로 바꿀 때 어법상 틀린 부분을 찾아 바르게 고친 것은?

As I wasn't on that ship then, I am alive now.
➡ If I had been on that ship then, I wouldn't have been alive now.

① had been → were
② had been → hadn't been
③ had been → haven't been
④ wouldn't have been → would be
⑤ wouldn't have been → wouldn't be

16 다음 우리말을 영어로 바르게 옮긴 것은?

그녀가 돈을 절약했더라면 지금 새 차를 살 수 있을 텐데.

① If she saves money, she can buy a new car now.
② If she saved money, she can buy a new car now.
③ If she saved money, she could buy a new car now.
④ If she had saved money, she could buy a new car now.
⑤ If she had saved money, she could have bought a new car now.

17 다음 두 문장의 뜻이 같도록 빈칸에 알맞지 않은 것을 모두 고르면?

Without a wheelchair, I would be very uncomfortable.
= ______________________, I would be very uncomfortable.

① But for a wheelchair
② Were it not for a wheelchair
③ If it were not for a wheelchair
④ Had it not been for a wheelchair
⑤ If it had not been for a wheelchair

18 **다음 두 문장의 뜻이 같도록 빈칸에 알맞은 것은?**

> He talks as if he had lived in Austria.
> = In fact, he ________ in Austria.

① lives ② lived ③ has lived
④ didn't live ⑤ doesn't live

19 **(A), (B), (C)의 괄호 안에서 알맞은 것끼리 바르게 짝지어진 것은?**

> • I'm bad at math. I wish I (A) [were / had been] good at math.
> • He didn't eat lunch. But he acts as if he (B) [ate / had eaten] lunch.
> • If he (C) [were / had been] here, he would have given me some advice.

	(A)	(B)	(C)
①	were	— ate	— had been
②	were	— had eaten	— were
③	were	— had eaten	— had been
④	had been	— ate	— were
⑤	had been	— had eaten	— were

20 **다음 중 어법상 틀린 것은?**

① I felt as if I were floating in the air.
② If it had snowed, I would have a happy Christmas.
③ But for my passion for drawing, I would have given up.
④ If you didn't wear your gloves, you would hurt your hands.
⑤ What kind of movies would you like to make if you were a movie director?

21 **다음 두 문장의 뜻이 서로 다른 것은?**

① I wish I had brothers and sisters.
= I'm sorry I don't have brother and sisters.
② Mike acts as if he didn't know Kelly at all.
= In fact, Mike knows Kelly.
③ I wish she had won the singing contest.
= I'm sorry she doesn't win the singing contest.
④ If he hadn't been tired, he would have watched the match.
= As he was tired, he didn't watch the match.
⑤ If there were apples, she would bake an apple pie.
= As there aren't apples, she doesn't bake an apple pie.

서술형

22 **다음 우리말과 일치하도록 빈칸에 알맞은 말을 쓰시오.**

> 네 도움이 없었다면 나는 운전면허 시험에 합격할 수 없었을 텐데.
> ➡ ________ your help, I couldn't have passed my driving test.
> ➡ If ________ ________ ________ ________ ________ your help, I couldn't have passed my driving test.

서술형

23 **다음 우리말과 일치하도록 〈조건〉에 맞게 문장을 완성하시오.**

> **〈조건〉**
> 1. if로 시작하는 가정법 문장으로 쓸 것
> 2. be, quiet, will, wake up을 시제에 맞게 사용할 것

> 네가 조용히 했더라면 아기가 깨지 않았을 텐데.
> ➡ If you ____________________, the baby ____________________.

Chapter 14
일치와 화법

학교 시험 대비 문제

맞힌 개수 ______ / 24

01 다음 빈칸에 들어갈 말로 알맞은 것은?

The scene with lots of special effects ________ been created by the artist.

① to
② has
③ with
④ have
⑤ having

02 다음 문장을 간접화법으로 바꿔 쓸 때 빈칸에 들어갈 말이 바르게 짝지어진 것은?

She said to us, "Be quiet in the classroom."
➡ She ________ us ________ quiet in the classroom.

① spoke — to be
② asked — being
③ asked — be
④ told — be
⑤ told — to be

03 다음 중 화법 전환이 틀린 것은?

① Ann said to Eric, "Wait a minute."
➡ Ann told Eric to wait a minute.
② I said to him, "Do you like reading books?"
➡ I asked him that he liked reading books.
③ Susan said, "I want to stay here."
➡ Susan said that she wanted to stay there.
④ Julia said, "I'm going away tomorrow."
➡ Julia said that she was going away the next day.
⑤ He said to her, "How do you go to school?"
➡ He asked her how she went to school.

04 다음 밑줄 친 부분이 어법상 틀린 것은?

Part of(①) the hotel(②) have(③) been destroyed(④) by the earthquake(⑤).

05 다음 빈칸에 들어갈 말로 알맞지 않은 것은?

____________ is going to take part in the marathon.

① Each student
② One of the students
③ Nobody in class
④ Some of the students
⑤ Every student in class

06 다음 밑줄 친 부분 중 어법상 틀린 것은?

① It was so hot that I can't sleep.
② I know Matt walks to school every day.
③ She said that three and three makes six.
④ Ron said that he would meet Linda for dinner.
⑤ I warned him that he would fail unless he worked hard.

07 다음 중 화법 전환이 올바른 것은?

① Mike said, "I will go now."
➡ Mike said that I would go then.
② He said to me, "Can you speak English?"
➡ He asked me if he could speak English.
③ The waiter said to me, "What are you drinking?"
➡ The waiter asked what was I drinking.
④ He said to me, "Are you fond of reading?"
➡ He asked me if I was fond of reading.
⑤ I said to students, "Don't make noise in the classroom."
➡ I told students to not make noise in the classroom.

08 다음 빈칸에 들어갈 말로 알맞은 것은?

We often went to Stanley Park when we ________ in Vancouver.

① live ② lived
③ will live ④ have live
⑤ have been lived

09 다음 밑줄 친 부분의 쓰임이 어법상 틀린 것은?

① The poor are not always unhappy.
② A number of potatoes in the garage is rotten.
③ Both skiing and skating are popular winter sports.
④ The sunglasses that she is wearing are made in Italy.
⑤ Ten kilometers is too far to walk.

10 다음 문장을 간접화법으로 쓸 때, 어법상 틀린 것은?

Paul said, "I went to the amusement park yesterday."
➡ Paul said(①) that(②) he(③) had gone(④) to the amusement park yesterday(⑤).

11 다음 밑줄 친 부분이 어법상 틀린 것은?

① He said that the moon is a satellite.
② We learned that water boils at 100℃.
③ People said that no news was good news.
④ We learned that William conquered England in 1066.
⑤ He thought that he was the most popular student in his class.

서술형

12 다음 주어진 문장을 간접화법으로 바꿔 쓰시오.

My homeroom teacher said to me, "Don't be late for school."
➡ My homeroom teacher told ____________
________________________________.

[13-14] 다음 빈칸에 들어갈 말이 바르게 짝지어진 것을 고르시오.

13

• One of my car's tires ________ to be flat.
• A number of people ________ looking forward to watching amazing fireworks.

① seem — is ② seem — are
③ seems — is ④ seems — are
⑤ seemed — was

14

• Chanho said that he ________ to Canada three times.
• Who first said that the Sun ________ the center of the Solar System?

① goes — was ② has been — is
③ had been — is ④ had been — was
⑤ has been — has been

[15-16] 다음 문장을 간접화법으로 바꿀 때, 빈칸에 들어갈 말로 알맞은 것을 고르시오.

15

Matt said to her, "Where are my sunglasses?"
➡ Matt asked her ________________.

① where his sunglasses are
② where were my sunglasses
③ where my sunglasses were
④ where his sunglasses were
⑤ where my sunglasses were

16

Ann said to Paul, "I don't feel well today."
➡ Ann told Paul that ________________.

① I don't feel well today
② I didn't feel well that day
③ she doesn't feel well today
④ he didn't feel well that day
⑤ she didn't feel well that day

17 다음 우리말을 영어로 바르게 옮긴 것은?

그녀는 우리에게 표지판을 보라고 말했다.

① She told us look at the sign.
② She told us to look at the sign.
③ She said us to look at the sign.
④ She said to us look at the sign.
⑤ She told to us to look at the sign.

18 다음 중 밑줄 친 부분을 잘못 고쳐 쓴 것은?

① He said that it will snow the next day. (→ would)
② The teacher said that water froze at 0°C. (→ freezes)
③ She thought that Tom has locked the door. (→ had locked)
④ The doctor said that poor sleep was bad for health. (→ is)
⑤ The teacher said that World War II has ended in 1945. (→ had ended)

19 다음 문장을 간접화법으로 바꿀 때, 어법상 틀린 것은?

She said to me, "Do you have your student ID card?"
➡ She asked(①) me(②) that(③) I had(④) my student ID card(⑤).

20 다음 밑줄 친 부분이 어법상 틀린 것의 개수는?

ⓐ Each shirt costs twelve dollars.
ⓑ Going hiking with friends are exciting.
ⓒ Most of the children like eating candy.
ⓓ He runs so fast that nobody is able to stop him.
ⓔ Three-fourths of the cake were eaten by my brother.

① 1개 ② 2개 ③ 3개
④ 4개 ⑤ 5개

서술형

21 다음 문장에서 어법상 틀린 부분을 찾아 바르게 고쳐 쓰시오.

The number of homeless people are increasing.

__________ ➡ __________

서술형

22 다음 우리말과 일치하도록 괄호 안의 말을 알맞은 형태로 바꾸어 쓰시오.

나는 다이아몬드가 강철보다 강하다고 배웠다. (be)
➡ I learned that diamonds __________ stronger than steel.

서술형

[23-24] 다음 문장을 간접화법으로 바꾸어 쓰시오.

23

Brian said to me, "I'm trying to lose weight now."
➡ Brian told me that __________
__________.

24

Sora said to Tyler, "Are you interested in Korean history?"
➡ Sora asked Tyler __________
__________.

Chapter 15
특수구문

학교 시험 대비 문제

맞힌 개수 ____ / 24

01 다음 중 밑줄 친 부분이 어법상 옳은 것은?

① I do likes cats.
② He does talks a lot.
③ I did had breakfast. But I feel hungry now.
④ He do went to Tom's birthday party. I saw him.
⑤ They do play soccer. In fact, they're very good at it.

02 다음 중 문장 전환이 바르지 않은 것은?

① A book was under the table.
➡ Under the table was a book.
② The woman I love stands near the door.
➡ Near the door stands the woman I love.
③ My grandparents have never tried pizza.
➡ Never have tried my grandparents pizza.
④ An old castle stands on top of the hill.
➡ On top of the hill stands an old castle.
⑤ She never told us about her son.
➡ Never did she tell us about her son.

03 다음 대화의 빈칸에 들어갈 '동의 표현'이 바르게 짝지어진 것은?

• A I found the movie boring.
B ____________________
• A I don't like doing exercise.
B ____________________

① So do I. — Neither I do.
② So I do. — Neither did I.
③ So did I. — Neither do I.
④ So I did. — Neither I did.
⑤ So is she. — Neither does she.

04 다음 중 밑줄 친 It의 쓰임이 나머지 넷과 다른 것은?

① It was you that I loved.
② It is true that he is a good student.
③ It was at the school that I met her.
④ It was last Sunday that we saw the movie.
⑤ It was yesterday that we had the meeting.

05 다음 중 어법상 틀린 것은?

① Never had Dr. Lee driven a car.
② Seldom had I believed rumors.
③ Hardly he looked like a famous dentist.
④ Never does Mina lose her way in the maze.
⑤ Not until the Middle Ages did cheese appear on pizza.

06 다음 밑줄 친 부분 중 생략할 수 있는 것은?

There was(①) a line of(②) wounded people(③) who were(④) waiting(⑤) for treatment.

07 다음 밑줄 친 ①~⑤ 중 어법상 틀린 것은?

> I did played(①) soccer a lot when(②) I was(③) young, but(④) I don't anymore(⑤).

08 다음 빈칸에 공통으로 들어갈 말로 알맞은 것은?

> • It is Jane ________ is wearing a white dress.
> • The students said ________ they had nothing to do.

① who　② which
③ that　④ what
⑤ whether

09 다음 밑줄 친 부분을 강조한 문장이 잘못된 것은?

① She had stolen a diamond ring.
➡ It was a diamond ring that she had stolen.
② Jessica ate my cake.
➡ It was my cake that Jessica ate it.
③ He entered the college in 2019.
➡ It was in 2019 that he entered the college.
④ Judy saw an actor at the bus stop.
➡ It was Judy that saw an actor at the bus stop.
⑤ A big tree used to be over the hill.
➡ It was over the hill that a big tree used to be.

10 다음 우리말을 영어로 바르게 옮긴 것은?

> 수평선 너머에 Tutu라는 섬이 있다.

① Beyond the horizon an island named Tutu is.
② Beyond the horizon is an island named Tutu.
③ Beyond is the horizon an island named Tutu.
④ An island named Tutu beyond the horizon is.
⑤ An island around the horizon has named Tutu.

서술형

[11-12] 다음 문장의 밑줄 친 부분을 <보기>와 같이 강조하는 문장으로 바꿔 쓰시오.

> <보기>
> Tom solved the problem.
> ➡ It was Tom that solved the problem.

11

> Korean War broke out in 1950.
> ➡ ________________________________
> ________________________________

12

> His strong will made John succeed.
> ➡ ________________________________
> ________________________________

13 **다음 빈칸에 공통으로 들어갈 말로 알맞은 것은?**

> • Mom _________ not let me go to the rock concert.
> • She _________ her best to prepare for the exam.
> • He _________ work for the post office when he was young.

① had ② did ③ was
④ took ⑤ made

[14-15] 다음 빈칸에 들어갈 말로 알맞은 것을 고르시오.

14

> Little _______________ about the viruses until recently.

① scientists know ② scientists knew
③ did scientists know ④ did scientists knew
⑤ did scientists have known

15

> Over the amusement park _______________.

① drones flew ② flew drones
③ did drones fly ④ did drones flew
⑤ drones did fly

16 **다음 우리말을 영어로 바르게 옮긴 것을 모두 고르면?**

> 그 여자는 거의 외출하지 않는다.

① Rarely the woman go out.
② The woman rarely goes out.
③ Rarely goes the woman out.
④ The woman does rarely go out.
⑤ Rarely does the woman go out.

17 **다음 대화 중 어법상 <u>틀린</u> 것은?**

① **A** I didn't bring my umbrella.
B Neither did I.
② **A** Sue got a free gift from ABC Mall.
B So did I.
③ **A** I was not satisfied with the movie.
B Neither was I.
④ **A** I haven't seen Kelly since yesterday.
B Neither have I.
⑤ **A** Ted has an important match tomorrow.
B So has Brian.

18 **다음 우리말과 일치하도록 빈칸에 알맞은 것은?**

> 그가 마시고 싶은 것은 바로 따뜻한 물이었다.
> ➡ ____________________ he wanted to drink.

① Warm water was that
② Warm water was which
③ It was warm water that
④ It was warm water who
⑤ It was warm water what

19 다음 문장의 일부를 강조한 문장으로 알맞지 않은 것은?

I borrowed the book last week.

① I did borrow the book last week.
② It was I that borrowed the book last week.
③ It was the book that I borrowed last week.
④ It was borrowed that I the book last week.
⑤ It was last week that I borrowed the book.

20 다음 중 밑줄 친 부분의 쓰임이 나머지 넷과 다른 것은?

① It is true that the Earth is warming.
② It was my sister that turned on the TV.
③ It was in the park that I parked my car.
④ It is Jenny that is cooking in the kitchen.
⑤ It is the alarm clock that wakes me up every morning.

21 다음 중 어법상 올바른 문장은?

① Between Tom and Jerry are a dog.
② On the front door is my parents' names.
③ Never the children have tasted chocolate.
④ She is the woman I helped on the street.
⑤ The man talking to Mira and Somin are a pianist.

서술형

22 다음 밑줄 친 부분을 강조하는 문장으로 바꿔 쓰시오.

She likes to discuss books with others. ➡ ______________________

서술형

[23-24] 다음 문장을 〈보기〉와 같이 바꿔 쓰시오.

〈보기〉

Many books are in his library. ➡ In his library are many books.

23

A parrot sat on her shoulder. ➡ ______________________

24

The terrorists live in an underground shelter. ➡ ______________________

적중! 중학영문법 3300제 Level 3

워크북

정답과 해설

서술형 대비 문장 연습

Chapter 01 부정사

▸▸ p.60~61

A

1 It is easy for her to eat spicy food.
2 You are never too old to learn.
3 She told me what to see in New York.
4 He found it difficult to run a marathon.
5 It is dangerous for dogs to eat chocolate.
6 Please let me know if you need anything.

B

1 Not a man was to be seen.
2 He seems to miss her.
3 I will learn how to ride a bike.
4 You are to keep quiet in the library.
5 It takes me an hour to get there.
6 He didn't know where to buy a ticket.

C

1 It's kind of you to help other people.
2 He found it easy to make pasta.
3 It is impossible for us to live without water.
4 I need a piece of paper to write on.
5 He was too busy to meet them.
6 I helped my brother (to) clean his room.

D

1 too cold for him to sleep
2 to have passed the test
3 are to arrive at your hotel tomorrow
4 smart enough to solve the problem
5 when to call him
6 where to go for a picnic

Chapter 02 동명사

▸▸ p.62~63

A

1 We decided to save some money.
2 Listening to music makes me calm.
3 He denied her being his girlfriend.
4 My dad kept me from going out at night.
5 On graduating, she worked as a doctor.
6 Susan was sorry for not remembering my birthday.

B

1 He spends an hour jogging.
2 I always like her singing.
3 The book is worth reading twice.
4 Do you mind me asking a question?
5 She tried to remember his name.
6 I'm worried about his being late.

C

1 I'm used to getting up early.
2 He couldn't prevent her from leaving.
3 I remember her talking about her job.
4 She looked forward to visiting her parents.
5 He isn't afraid of meeting new people.
6 My sister didn't like me(my) using her computer.

D

1 making her sad
2 his(him) telling lies
3 my(me) practicing dancing
4 my(me) turning off the TV
5 his(him) quitting school
6 their(them) not telling me about it

Chapter 03 분사

▸▸ p.64~65

A

1 Bored, I turned on the TV.
2 I saw her waiting(wait) for a bus.
3 Frankly speaking, he is not honest.
4 There being nobody at home, we went out again.
5 Having no money, he had to walk home.
6 Hearing the sad news, I couldn't say anything.

B

1 It being rainy, the game was canceled.
2 He fell asleep with the light turned on.
3 Having dinner, we planned our trip.
4 He sat with his legs crossed.
5 Not feeling hungry
6 Not knowing what to do

C

1 The girl playing the guitar is my cousin.
2 He wants his car repaired.
3 The new game looks exciting.
4 Strictly speaking, this answer isn't correct.
5 He looked after injured people.
6 I heard her calling[call] my name.

D

1 Waiting for the bus
2 Turning to the right
3 It being sunny and warm
4 Not having anything to do
5 There being no food
6 Having made no effort

Chapter 04 시제

▶▶ p.66~67

A

1 I have not seen Amy since she left here.
2 The game had just begun when I arrived.
3 I will go out when my sister arrives at home.
4 She had been preparing for an hour when I entered the kitchen.
5 My neighbors have been arguing outside since this morning.
6 Dave didn't come to school because he was sick yesterday.

B

1 I have just eaten lunch.
2 She is moving to Seoul tomorrow.
3 I have been taking yoga classes
4 He has been reading a newspaper
5 He had been exercising
6 The meeting had already finished

C

1 Have you ever been to Europe?
2 She has been playing the piano all day.
3 he had already seen the movie
4 He has been writing a novel
5 The store had already closed
6 It had been snowing

D

1 have lost the key
2 has gone to
3 has been staying
4 had started
5 has been making a sandcastle
6 has been playing the violin

Chapter 05 조동사

▶▶ p.68~69

A

1 I will be able to call you back later.
2 You ought not to be here.
3 I would rather stay at home.
4 She doesn't have to get up early tomorrow.
5 He had to wait for her for an hour yesterday.
6 There used to be a famous restaurant around here.

B

1 This cake does taste sweet.
2 She may have made a mistake.
3 He can't have stolen your money.
4 You ought not to waste your time.
5 We may as well stay at home.
6 I would rather go hiking than

C

1 She can't be tired.
2 The class must have been boring.

3 You should have checked my name.
4 She doesn't have to decide now.
5 He had to take care of his sister yesterday.
6 He may well be proud of his son.

D

1 must be very expensive
2 should have told
3 must have left
4 used to be
5 should have listened
6 used to live

Chapter 06 수동태

▸▸ p.70~71

A

1 This pasta was made for her.
2 The work will be finished in a few weeks.
3 They were made to wear clean uniforms.
4 It is said that Superman has special powers.
5 Korean history is taught to us by Mr. Lee.
6 Many trees have been planted in this park since last year.

B

1 I was given flowers by Jake.
2 This book should be returned today.
3 Jenny was seen crossing a road.
4 Stress is said to cause disease.
5 The box has just been removed.
6 The classroom is filled with students.

C

1 Dinner is being prepared by my mother.
2 This sweater was made for him by his father.
3 I was made to clean the room by my mother.
4 The mountain was covered with snow.
5 A cat was run over by a truck.
6 Tom is called a genius by his friends.

D

1 The boy was heard screaming.
2 The computer was being used by my brother.
3 A pair of pants was bought for her by her parents.
4 A bridge has been built across the river (by them).
5 This medicine must not be taken by children under 7.
6 is said that walking is the best exercise

Chapter 07 대명사

▸▸ p.72~73

A

1 We enjoyed ourselves on our trip to Germany.
2 Each of the answers is worth 5 points.
3 Every member was present at the meeting.
4 Both of my brothers like outdoor activities.
5 Some were angry, and others were confused.
6 One of their five children is a girl, and the others are boys.

B

1 Neither of them can swim.
2 Both of my parents are busy.
3 Every student is wearing a coat.
4 None of my friends drink coffee.
5 Can you introduce yourself to the class?
6 Each of the flowers has a different color.

C

1 She built this house by herself.
2 Both of the bags are very old.
3 He thinks himself a genius.
4 We should believe in ourselves.
5 Every student in this class studies hard.
6 He tried to solve the problems for himself.

D

1 She didn't eat anything.
2 Can you do something for me?
3 I need someone to help me.
4 Does anyone have a pencil?

5 I have seen him somewhere before.

Chapter 08 형용사와 부사

▸▸ p.74~75

A

1 The restaurant was nearly empty.
2 I bought these pants very cheaply.
3 Would you have some more chocolate?
4 Did you have much(a lot of/lots of/plenty of) fun at the party?
5 The young are interested in new trends.
6 I had such a wonderful time with my cousins.

B

1 This is such a great film.
2 She always smiles brightly.
3 Can you wake me up at seven?
4 I have something important to tell you.
5 He had a little bread for lunch.
6 Quite a few students were absent today.

C

1 The plan sounds interesting.
2 She was such a kind teacher.
3 There are few trees in this park.
4 The mistake made me nervous.
5 Kate needs something warm to drink.
6 They should hand it in by next Friday.

D

1 I have never been to Canada.
2 They are always ready to go on a trip.
3 Is there anything wrong with this computer?
4 I had such a nice time with my family in New York.
5 She usually goes jogging in the morning.
6 I want to do something special for my grandmother.

Chapter 09 비교

▸▸ p.76~77

A

1 My bag is heavier than yours(your bag).
2 The train got more and more crowded.
3 No player on his team is as fast as Steve.
4 She drew the picture as quickly as possible.
5 He is taller than any other boy in his class.
6 The faster you drive, the more dangerous it is.

B

1 Call me as soon as you can.
2 Yoga is not as easy as it looks.
3 My bag is much lighter than yours.
4 The happier you are, the better you work.
5 He plays tennis better than me.
6 Tom is the bravest boy in my class.

C

1 His pencil was twice as long as mine.
2 No other actor is as attractive as Jack.
3 He is becoming more and more popular.
4 He is one of the best soccer players in the world.
5 She answered my question as clearly as possible.
6 The more you exercise, the healthier you will be.

D

1 is less strong than
2 as hard as possible
3 is more famous than
4 The more I sleep
5 is better than
6 larger than all the other

Chapter 10 전치사

▸▸ p.78~79

A

1 I have no classes on Sunday.
2 John stood between two people.
3 He lived there from 2000 to 2010.
4 My friend was waiting for me at the bus stop.

5 She should finish her homework by this Friday.
6 I have been working there for almost a year.

B

1 Cheese is made from milk.
2 He was surprised at the result.
3 She walked toward the window.
4 He took a wallet out of his pocket.
5 He usually plays soccer in the afternoon.
6 I will send you my pictures by email.

C

1 He always sits in front of me.
2 She will go there by bus.
3 The books will be delivered within an hour.
4 They were lying on the floor.
5 We met at the airport yesterday
6 I heard someone singing(sing) at dawn.

D

1 She has been learning English for a month.
2 I work from Monday to Friday.
3 Kelly should stay here until tomorrow.
4 You should return the books by tomorrow.
5 What are you going to do during this vacation?

Chapter 11 관계사

▶▶ p.80~81

A

1 This is the book which(that) I've been looking for.
2 They are children whose parents both work.
3 I don't like the way(how) he looks at me.
4 However angry you are, you should have patience.
5 I don't remember the store where(in which) I bought this shirt.
6 I wrote a letter to John, who answered me quickly.

B

1 What he gave me was a ring.
2 I know the reason why he was absent.
3 My teacher is a person whom I respect.
4 You can buy whatever you like.
5 Whoever comes will be welcomed.
6 However hard I try

C

1 We couldn't believe what(the thing that/which) he said.
2 I have a friend whose mother is a doctor.
3 I went to New York, where I met Amy.
4 This is the way(how) I solved the problem.
5 This is a park where people can enjoy nature.
6 However(No matter how) nice the bag is, it is too expensive.

D

1 a student who(that) likes playing the piano
2 the woman with whom
3 whose favorite color is red
4 the way(how) babies express their feelings
5 the only book that I read last month
6 the museum, where we saw many paintings

Chapter 12 접속사

▶▶ p.82~83

A

1 Unless you study hard, you'll fail.
2 Neither Patrick nor Dave knows how to skate.
3 My brother as well as I likes to play soccer.
4 I'm not sure whether(if) Steve will come or not.
5 If he comes tomorrow, I'll prepare dinner.
6 Emily is wondering whether Mom likes roses.

B

1 Unless it rains, let's go outside.
2 I wonder if this game is interesting.
3 Tom is so tired that he can't run.
4 While I was in Seoul
5 As winter comes, it is getting colder.
6 so that we could arrive on time

C

1 Neither Sue nor Tina wears glasses.

2 Why do you think she cried?
3 Do you know when he will arrive here?
4 The novel was not only long but also boring.
5 I don't know where the accident happened.
6 Not you but John is responsible for it.

D

1 not only interesting but also moving
2 either tomorrow or this Sunday
3 Unless you leave now
4 neither Chinese nor Spanish
5 As soon as he got up
6 too big to carry by myself

4 He acts as if he were honest.
5 If I had enough time, I could help you.(I could help you if I had enough time.)
6 I wish I hadn't lost my wallet yesterday.

D

1 If he had a car
2 If I had been careful
3 If I hadn't gotten your advice
4 you could join our club
5 I hadn't eaten so much chocolate
6 she knew Dean very well

Chapter 13 가정법

▸▸ p.84~85

A

1 I wish you had come to my birthday party yesterday.
2 If we took a taxi, we could arrive earlier.
3 He is a student, but he acts as if he were a teacher.
4 If Jane had driven slowly, she wouldn't have had an accident.
5 If John hadn't told a lie, we could trust him now.
6 If it had not been for the homework, I could have played with my friends.

B

1 I wish I had worked harder.
2 If I were you, I wouldn't buy the shirt.(I wouldn't buy the shirt if I were you.)
3 He talked as if he had lived
4 I wouldn't be tired
5 If it were not for the Internet
6 Had it not been for his help

C

1 I wish I had been a better student.
2 If I had run, I wouldn't have missed the bus.(I wouldn't have missed the bus if I had run.)
3 If it hadn't been for him, we would have lost the game.

Chapter 14 일치와 화법

▸▸ p.86~87

A

1 Some of the cheese has gone bad.
2 The pants in the store are very expensive.
3 Kevin said he would go on a picnic the next day.
4 She told me that she had been to England before.
5 Jenny asked me where I would travel during winter vacation.
6 We learned that the Second World War ended in 1945.

B

1 Half of the money was yours.
2 The rich are not always happy.
3 He asked me to wait for him.
4 Alex said that he had passed the exam.
5 He asked me if I could help him.
6 We learned that the Earth is round.

C

1 He asked me where I lived.
2 Peter said that he exercises every day.
3 A number of boys are playing in the park.
4 Most of the food is mine.
5 He asked me if(whether) I liked soccer.
6 Two-thirds of the students are learning Japanese.

D

1 tell me that I am very kind
2 told me that he would go fishing
3 asked me if(whether) I liked tennis
4 asked him what he had had for dinner
5 us not to be late to class
6 me to work out regularly

Chapter 15 특수구문

▶▶ p.88~89

A

1 Amy does like comic books.
2 In the room was a new desk.
3 Never has he been to Japan before.
4 Under the bed was your cat.
5 Little did I dream that I would meet you again.
6 It was the guitar that he played on the stage yesterday.

B

1 Rarely did it snow this year.
2 I did send him an email.
3 It was John who broke the window.
4 Hardly did he understand what she said.
5 These are the shoes I bought yesterday.
6 It was yesterday that he arrived here.

C

1 I do study hard.
2 This bag does look expensive.
3 Rarely do I read books.
4 It was a red umbrella that(which) I lost yesterday.
5 Seldom does he visit his parents.
6 It was in Seoul that the meeting was held.

D

1 This bread does taste sweet.
2 Little did I imagine that they could win.
3 It was a backpack that(which) I bought in the mall last Friday.
4 It was on the wall that he drew a sunflower.
5 It was Kate that(who) rode a bicycle in the park last week.
6 It was in 1969 that(when) Apollo 11 landed on the Moon.

학교 시험 대비 문제

Chapter 01 부정사

▸▸ p.90~93

01 ② 02 ② 03 ① 04 ④ 05 ③ 06 ⑤ 07 ③ 08 ③ 09 ⑤ 10 ② 11 ③ 12 enough time to think 13 ⑤ 14 ④ 15 ③ 16 ① 17 ④ 18 ③ 19 ② 20 ④ 21 ③ to park, park 22 It is important for us to save water. 23 anyone to look after her 24 too scared to open

01 ②
주어진 문장과 ② 명사(구)를 수식하는 형용사적 용법, ① ⑤ 명사적 용법, ③ ④ 부사적 용법

02 ②
우리말의 의미상 if절에서 반복되는 부분(have this cake)을 생략한 문장이 되어야 하므로 대부정사를 사용한 want to가 알맞다.

03 ①
주어진 문장의 본동사(seems)와 that절 안의 동사(understands)의 시제가 동일하므로 to부정사(to + 동사원형)로 표현한 ①이 정답이다.

04 ④
사역동사는 목적격보어로 동사원형을 사용한다.

05 ③
문맥상 '어디로 가야 할지'가 알맞으므로 where to go가 오는 것이 알맞다.

06 ⑤
allow와 tell은 목적격보어로 to부정사를 취한다.

07 ③
seems와 that절 안의 동사(was)의 시제가 같지 않다. that절의 동사는 과거시제이므로 완료부정사(to have p.p.)로 나타내야 한다. (to be → to have been)

08 ③
주어진 문장과 ③ 부사적 용법(결과), ① ② 명사적 용법, ④ ⑤ 형용사적 용법

09 ⑤
to부정사구에서 반복되는 동사구(go to the concert)를 생략하고 대부정사 to만 남길 수 있다.

10 ②
careless가 사람의 성격을 나타내는 형용사이므로 of를 써야 한다. 나머지 빈칸에는 모두 for가 들어간다.

11 ③
「so + 형용사[부사] + that + 주어 + can't + 동사원형」은 「too + 형용사[부사] + to부정사」로 나타낼 수 있다. 이때 문장의 주어와 that절의 주어가 다를 경우 to부정사 앞에 의미상 주어(for + 목적격)를 써 주어야 한다.

12 enough time to think
명사를 수식하는 형용사적 용법으로 to부정사를 나타낸다.

13 ⑤
앞의 명사구 some clothes를 수식하는 형용사적 용법의 to부정사로 '입을 옷'이라는 의미가 되어야 하므로, 빈칸에는 to put on이 알맞다.

14 ④
that절 안의 동사(was)가 본동사(seems)보다 앞선 시제이므로, 완료부정사(to have p.p.)로 써야 한다.

15 ③
see는 지각동사이므로 목적격보어로 동사원형이나 현재분사를 취한다. want는 목적격보어로 to부정사를 취한다.

16 ①
사역동사 have는 목적격보어로 동사원형을 취하고, get은 to부정사를 취한다.

17 ④
「형용사 + enough + to부정사」는 「so + 형용사 + that + 주어 + can + 동사원형」으로 바꿔 쓸 수 있으므로, can't give를 can give로 고쳐야 한다.

18 ③
natural은 사람의 성격이나 태도를 나타내는 형용사가 아니므로 to부정사의 의미상 주어는 「for + 목적격」의 형태로 써야 한다.

19 ②
ⓑ it은 가목적어이므로 진목적어로 to부정사가 와야 한다. (giving → to give) ⓓ to부정사의 부정형은 「not + to부정사」의 형태로 쓴다. (to not win → not to win)

20 ④

「It takes + 시간 + for + 사람 + to부정사」 또는 「It takes + 사람 + 시간 + to부정사」의 형태로 써야 한다.

21 ③ to park, park
사역동사 let의 목적격보어로 동사원형을 써야 한다.

22 It is important for us to save water.
「It(가주어) is + 형용사 + 의미상 주어(for + 목적격) + to부정사구(진주어)」의 어순으로 배열한다.

23 anyone to look after her
형용사적 용법의 to부정사구 to look after her가 대명사 anyone을 뒤에서 수식하는 형태로 쓴다.

24 too scared to open
「so + 형용사 + that + 주어 + can't[couldn't]+동사원형」은 「too+형용사 + to부정사」로 바꿔 쓸 수 있다.

Chapter 02 동명사

▸▸ p.94~97

01 ③ **02** ④ **03** ③ **04** ④ **05** ④ **06** ② **07** ① **08** ④ **09** ③ **10** ④ **11** proposing **12** studying not, not studying **13** ④ **14** ③ **15** ④ **16** ② **17** ③ **18** ② **19** ⑤ **20** ⑤ **21** ② **22** changing her plan **23** putting on sunscreen **24** him from focusing on studying

01 ③
expect는 목적격보어로 to부정사를 사용한다.
(playing → to play)

02 ④
「remember + 동명사」: ~한 것을 기억하다(과거)

03 ③
keep *A* from -ing: A가 ~하는 것을 막다

04 ④
「remember + to부정사」: ~할 것을 기억하다(미래)
① → She can't remember telling you the story.
② → Don't forget to clean the box.
③ → I stopped listening to music.
⑤ → I regret eating too much.

05 ④
cannot help -ing: ~할 수밖에 없다
(to laugh → laughing)
① be busy -ing: ~하느라 바쁘다
② be worth -ing: ~할 가치가 있다
③ look forward to -ing: ~하기를 고대하다
⑤ keep *A* from -ing: A가 ~하는 것을 막다

06 ②
동명사의 의미상 주어는 소유격 또는 목적격으로 쓴다.

07 ①
mind는 목적어로 동명사를 사용하는 동사이다.
(to close → closing)

08 ④
be good at -ing: ~을 잘하다
① → places to visit
② → how to drive
③ → enjoy walking
⑤ → He was excited

09 ③
→ 나는 노래하는 것을 멈추었다.
「stop + 동명사」: ~하는 것을 멈추다
「stop + to부정사」: ~하기 위해 멈추다

10 ④
be busy -ing: ~하느라 바쁘다
① → a friend to play with
② → boring
③ → expecting to go out
⑤ → looking forward to visiting

11 proposing
have trouble -ing: ~하는 데 어려움을 겪다

12 studying not, not studying
동명사의 부정형은 동명사 바로 앞에 부정어(not)를 쓴다.

13 ④
avoid는 동명사를 목적어로 취하고, promise는 to부정사를 목적어로 취한다.

14 ③
전치사의 목적어 자리와 주어 자리에 모두 쓰일 수 있는 것은 동명사이다.

15 ④
④는 현재진행형에 사용된 현재분사이고, 나머지는 모두 동명사이다.

16 ②

decide는 목적어로 to부정사를 취한다.

17 ③

「remember + 동명사」는 '(과거에) ~한 것을 기억하다'라는 의미이고, 「remember + to부정사」는 '(미래에) ~할 것을 기억하다'라는 의미이다.

18 ②

(A) feel like -ing: ~하고 싶다

(B) be used to -ing: ~하는 데 익숙하다

(C) spend + 시간 + -ing: ~하는 데 시간을 소비하다

19 ⑤

동명사의 부정형은 동명사 앞에 not을 쓰고, 동명사의 의미상 주어는 동명사 앞에 소유격 또는 목적격으로 나타낸다.

20 ⑤

문맥상 문자 메시지를 보내는 것을 멈추겠다고 하는 것이 자연스러우므로 to send를 sending으로 고쳐야 한다.

stop + 동명사: ~하는 것을 멈추다

stop + to부정사: ~하기 위해 멈추다

21 ②

ⓒ 동명사(구)가 주어로 쓰인 경우 단수 취급하므로 단수동사를 써야 한다. (are → is)

ⓓ look forward to -ing: ~하는 것을 고대하다 (to read → reading)

22 changing her plan

regret+동명사: ~한 것을 후회하다

23 putting on sunscreen

과거에 한 일을 잊어버린 경우이므로 forget 뒤에 동명사를 쓴다.

24 him from focusing on studying

prevent *A* from -ing: A가 ~하지 못하게 하다

Chapter 03 분사

▸▸ p.98~101

01 ② **02** ② **03** ② **04** ④ **05** ④ **06** ④ **07** ① **08** ③ **09** ④ **10** ④ **11** (Being) Scolded by her teacher **12** ④ **13** ③ **14** ⑤ **15** ② **16** ② **17** ① **18** ⑤ **19** ① **20** with his arms folded **21** Frankly speaking **22** shocking, shocked **23** Vegetables being good for health

01 ②

첫 번째 빈칸에는 주어가 놀란 감정을 느끼는 것이므로 과거분사 surprised가 알맞고, 두 번째 빈칸에는 주어가 재미 있는 감정을 일으키는 것이므로 현재분사 exciting이 알맞다.

02 ②

② 동명사, ① ③ ④ ⑤ 현재분사

03 ②

분사구문이 Not으로 시작하고 있으므로 부정의 부사절임을 알 수 있다. 「having + p.p.」가 아니라 「동사원형 + -ing」로 쓰였으므로 부사절과 주절의 시제가 동일해야 한다.

04 ④

부사절의 주어와 주절의 주어가 일치하지 않으므로 분사구문으로 전환할 때 분사구문 앞에 주어를 써 주어야 한다. 따라서 It (being) written in easy English, ~.가 알맞다.

05 ④

'~된, ~해진'을 의미하는 과거분사가 오는 것이 알맞다.

06 ④

부사절과 주절이 과거시제로 동일하므로 분사구문은 「동사원형 + -ing」형태로, 주절은 과거시제로 나타낸다.

07 ①

영화가 '지루한 감정을 느끼게 하는' 것이므로 bored → boring

08 ③

전시회가 '흥미롭게 하는' 것이기 때문에 interesting / 책이 '지루하게 하는' 것이기 때문에 boring / 문맥상 영화가 슬펐다고 해야 하므로 sad

09 ④

주어가 감정을 일으키는 의미일 때 현재분사를 쓰므로

disappointing / 주어가 감정을 느끼는 의미일 때 과거분사를 쓰므로 disappointed

10 ④
부사절의 시제가 주절의 시제보다 앞서므로 분사구문을 「having + p.p.」 형태로 나타내야 한다. (Finished my exercise → Having finished my exercise)

11 (Being) Scolded by her teacher
부사절의 시제와 주절의 시제가 동일할 때 「동사원형 + -ing」 형태로 분사구문을 나타내고, 부사절의 시제가 주절의 시제보다 앞설 때 「having + p.p.」로 나타낸다. 문두에 오는 Being은 생략이 가능하다.

12 ④
주어인 its service가 실망스러운 감정을 일으키는 것이므로 현재분사 disappointing이 알맞다.

13 ③
「with + (대)명사 + 분사」 구문에서는 (대)명사와 분사의 관계가 능동이면 현재분사, 수동이면 과거분사를 쓴다. 첫 번째 빈칸에는 명사인 the TV와 turn on이 수동 관계이므로 과거분사가 알맞고, 두 번째 빈칸에는 명사인 his students와 follow가 능동 관계이므로 현재분사가 알맞다.

14 ⑤
부사절의 주어와 주절의 주어가 일치하지 않으므로 부사절의 주어 the game을 생략하지 않고 분사 being 앞에 그대로 둔다.

15 ②
분사구문의 부정형은 분사 앞에 not을 써서 나타낸다.

16 ②
(A) Anne이라고 '불리는(수동)' 것이므로 과거분사가 와야 한다.
(B) 파란 셔츠를 '입고 있는(능동)'이라는 의미이므로 현재분사가 와야 한다.
(C) 그 사고로 '다친(수동)' 두 명의 아이들이라는 의미이므로 과거분사가 와야 한다.

17 ①
분사구문에 쓰인 being이나 having been은 생략할 수 있다.

18 ⑤
다큐멘터리가 흥미로운 감정을 일으키는 것이므로 현재분사로 고쳐야 한다. (excited → exciting)

19 ①
ⓒ speaking of: ~에 관해 말하면 (Spoken → Speaking)
ⓓ 분사구문의 주어인 냉장고가 고장이 난 주체이므로 been을 being으로 고쳐야 한다.

20 with his arms folded
「with + (대)명사 + 분사」 형태로 배열한다. 이때 명사 his arms와 fold가 수동 관계이므로 fold를 과거분사로 써야 한다.

21 Frankly speaking
frankly speaking: 솔직히 말해서

22 shocking, shocked
첫 번째 빈칸에는 소식이 충격적인 감정을 일으키는 것이므로 현재분사 shocking이 알맞고, 두 번째 빈칸에는 많은 사람들이 충격적인 감정을 느끼는 것이므로 과거분사 shocked가 알맞다.

23 Vegetables being good for health
부사절의 주어(vegetables)가 주절의 주어(I)와 다르므로 부사절의 주어 vegetables를 생략하지 않는 것에 유의한다.

Chapter 04 시제

▸▸ p. 102~105

01 ③ **02** ③ **03** ④ **04** ⑤ **05** ④ **06** ④ **07** ③
08 ① **09** ① **10** ⑤ **11** ④ **12** had bought **13** ④
14 ④ **15** ② **16** ③ **17** ⑤ **18** ③ **19** ② **20** ③
21 has, had **22** Have you visited, visited **23** has lost
24 has been learning yoga since last month

01 ③
시계를 잃어버린 것은 일주일 전이고 찾은 것은 어제이므로, 잃어버린 것이 찾은 것보다 더 먼저 일어난 일이다. 따라서 잃어버린 것을 과거완료(had + p.p.)로 써준다.

02 ③
명확한 과거를 나타내는 표현인 in 1919가 있으므로 과거형인 established가 알맞다.

03 ④
누군가가 주스를 쏟은 것은 수미가 집에 온 것보다 먼저 일어난 일이므로 과거완료(had + p.p.) 형태가 알맞다.

04 ⑤
어제부터 눈이 오기 시작해서 지금도 눈이 오고 있으므로 현재완료진행형인 「have(has) been + -ing」로 표현한다.

05 ④
그의 어머니가 무언가 이야기했던 것이 그가 기억한 것보다 먼저 일어난 일이므로 과거완료(had + p.p.) 형태가 알맞다.

06 ④
문맥상 '~한 이후로, ~한 때로부터'의 의미인 since가 알맞다.

07 ③
Alex가 전에 그 영화를 본 것이 즐기지 않은 것보다 먼저 일어난 일이므로 과거완료(had + p.p.) 형태가 알맞다.

08 ①
문맥상 '두 시간 동안 계속'의 의미를 가진 for가 알맞다.

09 ①
<보기>와 ① 현재완료의 경험 ②⑤ 결과 ③ 완료 ④ 계속

10 ⑤
Cindy가 3시간 전에 영어 공부를 시작해서 지금까지 하고 있다고 했으므로 빈칸에 알맞은 형태는 현재완료진행형이다. 「have(has) been + -ing」: ~해 오고 있다

11 ④
9시에 숙제를 마쳤고, Jane은 9시 20분에 왔으므로, 숙제를 마친 것이 Jane이 온 것보다 먼저 일어난 일이다. 따라서 과거완료(had + p.p.) 형태가 알맞다.

12 had bought
가방을 산 것이 잃어버린 것보다 먼저 일어난 일이므로 과거완료(had + p.p.)로 쓴다.

13 ④
과거부터 현재까지 계속 진행하고 있는 일은 현재완료진행형(have(has) been + -ing)으로 나타낸다.

14 ④
현재완료 시제이므로 명백한 과거를 나타내는 부사구 a week ago(일주일 전)는 빈칸에 들어갈 수 없다.

15 ②
집에 지갑을 두고 온 것이 발견한 시점인 과거시제(found out)보다 이전이므로 has left를 과거완료(had left)로 고쳐야 한다.

16 ③
last week는 과거의 시점을 나타내므로 since를 쓰고, five years는 기간을 나타내므로 for를 쓴다.

17 ⑤
'~ 동안'은 「for + 기간」으로 나타내고, 과거의 특정 시점 이전부터 과거 시점까지 진행되어 온 일은 과거완료진행형(had been + -ing)으로 나타낸다.

18 ③
③은 계속을 나타내는 현재완료이고, 나머지는 모두 경험을 나타내는 현재완료이다.

19 ②
four years ago(4년 전)는 특정 과거 시점을 나타내는 부사구이므로 현재완료와 함께 쓸 수 없다.

20 ③
문제를 푼 것이 말을 한 과거 시점 이전이므로 과거완료(had + p.p.)로 써야 한다.

21 has, had
'한국에서 김치를 먹어 보기 전에'라는 과거의 시점까지의 경험을 나타내므로 과거완료(had + p.p.)를 쓴다.

22 Have you visited, visited
A의 빈칸에는 B의 대답 Yes, I have.로 보아 현재완료 Have you visited가 알맞고, B의 빈칸에는 명백한 과거를 나타내는 부사구 last weekend가 있으므로 과거시제 visited가 알맞다.

23 has lost
목걸이를 잃어버린 과거의 일이 현재까지 영향을 미치므로 현재완료를 사용한다.

24 has been learning yoga since last month
현재완료진행형은 「have(has) been + -ing」의 형태로 쓰고, '~부터'라는 의미로 완료시제와 함께 쓰이는 부사구는 「since + 과거 시점」의 형태로 쓴다.

Chapter 05 조동사

▸▸ p. 106~109

01 ② 02 ② 03 ⑤ 04 ④ 05 ⑤ 06 ② 07 ③
08 ① 09 would rather take the responsibility than
10 should have listened 11 must have practiced
12 should have brought 13 ② 14 ① 15 ② 16 ⑤
17 ③ 18 ④ 19 ③ 20 ② 21 ③ 22 ④ 23 ④
24 You will be able to experience different cultures.

01 ②
예전에는 그랬지만 지금은 아니라는 뜻을 나타내는 used to가 알맞다.

02 ②
①, ⑤ 조동사는 2개가 연달아 쓰일 수 없다.
③, ④ 조동사 뒤에는 동사원형이 온다.

03 ⑤
'~했어야 했다'라는 뜻의 should have p.p.의 부정형은 should not have p.p.이다.

04 ④
의무를 나타내는 should는 ought to로 바꿔 쓸 수 있다.

05 ⑤
have(has) to는 의무를 나타내므로 추측의 의미를 나타내는 ⑤의 must와는 바꿔 쓸 수 없다.

06 ②
첫 번째 문장에는 '하다'라는 뜻의 일반동사 Do
두 번째 문장에는 의문문을 만들어주는 조동사 do

07 ③
③ 추측(~일지도 모른다), ① ② ④ ⑤ 허락(~해도 된다)

08 ①
② ought to not → ought not to
③ have not to → don't have to
④ has to → must(강한 추측)
⑤ should → may(추측)

09 would rather take the responsibility than
would rather *A* than *B*: B하느니 차라리 A하겠다

10 should have listened
should have p.p.: ~했어야 했다

11 must have practiced
must have p.p.: ~했음에 틀림없다

12 should have brought
should have p.p.: ~했어야 했다

13 ②
시력이 좋다고 했으므로 안경을 쓰고 있을 리가 없다는 부정적 추측이 자연스럽다. 따라서 can't가 알맞다.

14 ①
첫 번째 빈칸에는 요청을 나타내는 Can이나 Will이, 두 번째 빈칸에는 허가를 나타내는 can이나 may가 들어갈 수 있다. 따라서 빈칸에 공통으로 알맞은 것은 can이다.

15 ②
과거에 반복적으로 했던 행동을 현재는 더 이상 하지 않는 경우 조동사 used to(~하곤 했다)를 쓴다.

16 ⑤
⑤는 '실내에서 마스크를 벗을 필요가 없다.'는 의미이고, 나머지는 모두 '실내에서 마스크를 벗지 말라.'는 금지의 의미이다.

17 ③
'밖에 눈이 오니까 집에 있겠다'는 의미가 알맞다. (would rather: ~하겠다)
은행이 곧 문을 닫을 것이라고 했으므로 서두르는 게 낫다는 의미가 알맞다. (had better: ~하는 것이 낫다, ~하는 게 좋겠다)

18 ④
(A) must have p.p.: ~했음에 틀림없다
(B) should have p.p.: ~했어야 했다
(C) cannot have p.p.: ~했을 리가 없다

19 ③
③은 '~임에 틀림없다'라는 강한 추측의 의미로 쓰였고, 나머지는 모두 '~해야 한다'라는 의무의 의미로 쓰였다.

20 ②
②의 used to는 과거의 상태를 나타내므로 would로 바꿔 쓸 수 없다. used to가 과거의 습관을 나타낼 경우 would로 바꿔 쓸 수 있다.

21 ③
과거에 하지 않은 일에 대한 후회를 나타낼 때는 「should have p.p.」를 사용한다.

22 ④
조동사는 may can처럼 2개를 나란히 쓸 수 없으므로 can을 be able to로 바꿔 써야 한다.

23 ④

had better의 부정형은 had better not으로 쓴다.

24 You will be able to experience different cultures.

can은 조동사이므로 미래시제 조동사 will과 함께 쓸 수 없다. 따라서 같은 의미의 표현 be able to로 바꿔 will be able to로 쓴다.

Chapter 06 수동태

▸▸ p. 110~113

01 ③ **02** ③ **03** ③ **04** ⑤ **05** ④ **06** ④ **07** (1) is being cleaned (2) must be cleaned **08** (1) Other suspects are being checked by the policemen. (2) When was your phone number changed (by you)? **09** (1) is known to (2) was covered with **10** (1) can be downloaded (2) is being used **11** (1) We were made happy by him. (2) The boy was called a soccer star by them. (3) The book was found interesting by us. (4) Tom was elected captain by them. **12** ④ **13** ③ **14** ② **15** ③ **16** ⑤ **17** ⑤ **18** ①, ④ **19** ②, ③ **20** ⑤ **21** ③ **22** ④ **23** ②

01 ③

4형식의 수동태에서 직접목적어 앞에는 전치사를 쓰지 않는다. (→ I was given a Christmas gift by my aunt.)

02 ③

지각동사의 목적격보어로 쓰인 원형부정사는 수동태 문장에서 to부정사로 바뀐다. (was seen enter → was seen to enter)

03 ③

be satisfied with: ~에 만족하다

be surprised at: ~에 놀라다

04 ⑤

모두 5형식 문장의 수동태이다. ⑤ 능동태(They told him to give up smoking.)의 목적격보어로 쓰인 to부정사는 수동태에서 주격보어가 되며 그대로 to부정사로 써준다. (give up → to give up)

05 ④

① 5형식 문장의 수동태 is found → was found

② 동사구의 수동태 run over: (차가) ~을 치다

was ran over → was run over (run - ran - run)

③ 진행형 수동태 painted being → being painted

⑤ 4형식 문장의 직접목적어를 수동태의 주어로 쓸 때 간접목적어 앞에는 to, for, of와 같은 전치사가 온다. (was given the police → was given to the police)

06 ④

조동사의 수동태: 「조동사 + be + p.p.」

07 (1) is being cleaned

진행형 수동태: 「be동사 + being + p.p.」

(2) must be cleaned

조동사의 수동태: 「조동사 + be + p.p.」

08 (1) Other suspects are being checked by the policemen.

진행형 수동태: 「be동사 + being + p.p.」

(2) When was your phone number changed (by you)?

의문사가 있는 의문문의 수동태: 「의문사 + be동사 + 주어 + p.p. + (by 행위자) ~?」

09 (1) is known to

be known to: ~에게 알려지다(대상)

(2) was covered with

be covered with: ~으로 덮여 있다

10 (1) can be downloaded

조동사의 수동태: 「조동사 + be + p.p.」

(2) is being used

진행형 수동태: 「be동사 + being + p.p.」

11 (1) We were made happy by him.

(2) The boy was called a soccer star by them.

(3) The book was found interesting by us.

(4) Tom was elected captain by them.

(1), (2), (3), (4) 모두 5형식 문장의 수동태이다.

12 ④

그가 의사로부터 '권고를 받은' 것이므로 수동 관계를 나타내는 「be동사 + p.p.」로 쓴다.

13 ③

첫 번째 빈칸은 자전거를 '도난당하는' 것이므로 수동태가 알맞다. 두 번째 빈칸은 도둑이 컴퓨터를 '훔친' 것이므로 능동태가 알맞다.

14 ②

(A) 진행형 수동태: 「be동사 + being + p.p.」

(B) 조동사의 수동태: 「조동사 + be + p.p.」
(C) 완료형 수동태: 「have(has) + been + p.p.」

15 ③
능동태의 목적어를 수동태의 주어로 써야 하므로 주어는 I가 되어야 하고, 사역동사 make의 목적격보어로 쓰인 동사원형은 수동태에서 to부정사로 바뀐다.

16 ⑤
'구워지고 있었다'고 했으므로 과거진행형 수동태(was(were) + being + p.p.)로 써야 한다.

17 ⑤
동사구 laugh at을 하나의 동사로 취급하여 수동태를 만든다.

18 ①, ④
give가 쓰인 4형식 문장의 수동태는 직접목적어와 간접목적어를 각각 주어로 하는 수동태를 만들 수 있는데, 직접목적어를 주어로 할 경우 남아 있는 간접목적어 앞에 전치사 to를 써야 한다.

19 ②, ③
목적어가 that절인 경우 가주어 It을 주어로 하거나, that절의 주어를 문장의 주어로 하는 수동태를 만들 수 있다. that절의 주어를 주어로 하는 경우 that절의 동사를 to부정사로 쓴다.

20 ⑤
지각동사의 목적격보어로 쓰인 동사원형은 수동태에서 to부정사로 바뀐다.

21 ③
ⓐ be filled with: ~으로 가득 차다
ⓑ be covered with: ~으로 덮여 있다
ⓒ be worried about: ~에 대해 걱정하다
ⓓ be satisfied with: ~에 만족하다

22 ④
소유나 상태를 나타내는 타동사 cost, resemble, have는 수동태로 쓸 수 없다.

23 ②
ⓐ 5형식 문장의 목적격보어로 쓰인 to부정사는 수동태에서 과거분사 뒤에 그대로 써야 한다. (show → to show)
ⓓ 동사구 turn on의 수동태에서 행위자 Jenny 앞에 전치사 by를 써야 한다. (Jenny → by Jenny)

Chapter 07 대명사

▸▸ p. 114~117

01 ③ **02** ④ **03** ⑤ **04** ③ **05** ② **06** ④ **07** ④
08 ③ **09** ③, ④ **10** ⑤ **11** ⑤ **12** are, is **13** ④
14 ③ **15** ② **16** ④ **17** ⑤ **18** ① **19** ③ **20** ⑤
21 by himself **22** One, the other **23** Some, others
24 All of the members have to follow

01 ③
「one ~ the other ...」: (둘 중) 하나는 ~, 나머지 하나는 …

02 ④
첫 번째 빈칸에는 주어 The museum을 강조하는 재귀대명사 itself가 알맞다. 두 번째 빈칸에는 '혼자 힘으로'라는 뜻을 나타내는 재귀대명사 관용 표현 for oneself가 알맞다.

03 ⑤
(정해진 범위 안에서) '하나'는 one, '다른 하나'는 another, '나머지 모두'는 the others로 쓴다.

04 ③
by oneself: 혼자서(= alone)

05 ②
「every + 단수명사」는 단수 취급하므로 have → has

06 ④
「one ~, the other ...」: (둘 중) 하나는 ~, 나머지 하나는 … / 「one ~ another ... the other –」: (셋 중) 하나는 ~, 또 다른 하나는 …, 나머지 하나는 –

07 ④
네 명 중 한 명은 남자아이고, 나머지는 모두 여자아이이므로 the others로 써야 한다.

08 ③
every 뒤에는 단수명사가 온다. (boys → boy)

09 ③, ④
③ 「one ~, the others ...」: (정해진 범위 안에서) 하나는 ~, 나머지는 모두 …
④ 「some ~, others ...」: (정해지지 않은 다수 중에서) 몇몇은 ~, 다른 일부는 …

10 ⑤
조건문에서는 anything을 쓴다.
(something → anything)

11 ⑤
Bob and Tony를 강조하는 재귀대명사 themselves가 알맞다.

12 are, is
「each of + 복수명사」는 단수 취급한다.

13 ④
「one ~, the other ...」: (둘 중) 하나는 ~, 나머지 하나는 ···

14 ③
단수동사 has가 왔으므로 빈칸에는 단수 취급하는 표현이 들어가야 한다. both는 복수 취급하므로 빈칸에 들어갈 수 없다.

15 ②
all 뒤에 셀 수 없는 명사가 오면 단수 취급한다. information은 '정보'라는 뜻으로 셀 수 없는 명사이다.

16 ④
-thing으로 끝나는 대명사는 형용사가 뒤에서 수식한다.

17 ⑤
⑤는 재귀 용법으로 쓰인 재귀대명사이므로 생략할 수 없다. 나머지는 모두 강조 용법으로 쓰였으므로 생략할 수 있다.

18 ①
(A) 「each of + 복수명사」는 단수 취급한다.
(B) 「every + 단수명사」는 단수 취급한다.
(C) 「all + (of) + 복수명사」는 복수 취급한다.

19 ③
③은 강조 용법으로 쓰인 재귀대명사이고, 나머지는 모두 재귀 용법으로 쓰인 재귀대명사이다.

20 ⑤
셋 중 하나는 one, 또 다른 하나는 another, 나머지 하나는 the other로 나타내므로 other를 another로 고쳐야 한다.

21 by himself
by oneself: 혼자서

22 One, the other
둘 중 하나는 one, 나머지 하나는 the other로 가리킨다.

23 Some, others
정해지지 않은 다수 중 일부는 some, 다른 일부는 others로 나타낸다.

24 All of the members have to follow
「all of + 복수명사」는 '모든 ~들'의 의미이며, 복수 취급한다.

Chapter 08 형용사와 부사

▸▸ p. 118~121

01 ① **02** ② **03** ⑤ **04** ⑤ **05** ④ **06** ② **07** ②
08 ③ **09** ④ **10** ② **11** ④ **12** always walks to school
13 ④ **14** ② **15** ① **16** ② **17** ③ **18** ③ **19** ④
20 ① **21** I usually have something sweet **22** little water **23** is, are **24** away it, it away

01 ①
taste는 감각동사이므로 보어로 형용사가 와야 한다. 따라서 well → good

02 ②
문맥상 '많은'을 뜻하면서 셀 수 없는 명사인 money를 수식하는 것으로 much가 알맞다.

03 ⑤
(a) little + 셀 수 없는 명사
(a) few + 셀 수 있는 복수명사

04 ⑤
'(소리·온도를) 낮추다'라는 뜻의 동사구는 turn down이다. 타동사와 부사가 동사구를 이룰 때 목적어가 대명사인 경우 항상 타동사와 부사 사이에 위치한다.

05 ④
① only는 한정적 용법으로만 쓰임
② 감각동사 look은 주격보어로 형용사를 취하므로 happily → happy
③ alive, ⑤ asleep은 서술적 용법으로만 쓰임

06 ②
첫 번째 빈칸에는 '조금, 약간의'를 의미하면서 셀 수 없는 명사인 knowledge를 수식하는 것으로 a little이 알맞고, 두 번째와 세 번째 빈칸에는 '거의 없는'을 의미하면서 각각 복수명사인 women과 people을 수식하는 것으로 few(Few)가 알맞다.

07 ②
「such + a(an) + 형용사 + 명사」의 어순으로 써야 하므

로 a such unique and pretty ring → such a unique and pretty ring

08 ③
「the + 형용사」: ~한 사람들(= 형용사 + people)

09 ④
work는 셀 수 없는 명사이므로 many → much[a lot of, lots of, plenty of]

10 ②
books는 셀 수 있는 명사의 복수형이므로 few 또는 a few, a lot of가 알맞다. air는 셀 수 없는 명사이므로 little이나 a little이 올 수 있는데 의미상 '거의 없는'을 뜻하는 little이 알맞다.

11 ④
빈도부사가 일반동사를 수식할 경우 일반동사 앞에 위치한다.

12 always walks to school
always는 빈도부사이므로 일반동사 앞에 위치한다.

13 ④
동사 talk를 수식해야 하므로 부사가 와야 한다. friendly는 '친절한'이라는 뜻의 형용사이므로 빈칸에 들어갈 수 없다.

14 ②
pick up, see off와 같은 「타동사 + 부사」로 이루어진 동사구의 목적어가 대명사일 경우 타동사와 부사 사이에 와야 한다.

15 ①
lots of는 '많은'이라는 뜻이며, 셀 수 없는 명사 food를 수식하고 있으므로 much와 바꿔 쓸 수 있다.

16 ②
'몇몇의'라는 의미로 셀 수 있는 명사를 수식할 수 있는 것은 some과 a few이고, '살아 있는'의 의미로 서술적 용법으로 쓰이는 형용사는 alive이다.

17 ③
(A) children이 셀 수 있는 명사의 복수형이므로 Few가 알맞다.
(B) tea가 셀 수 없는 명사이므로 a little이 알맞다.
(C) oil이 셀 수 없는 명사이므로 much가 알맞다.

18 ③
첫 번째 문장은 영어로 나 자신을 표현하기가 '어렵다'라는 의미가 되어야 하므로 형용사 hard가 알맞다. 두 번째 문장은 '최근에' 학교 자원봉사 동아리에 가입하기로 결정했다는 의미가 되어야 하므로 부사 lately가 알맞다.

19 ④
a little은 '약간의'라는 뜻을 나타내며 뒤에 셀 수 있는 명사의 복수형이 왔으므로 a few로 고쳐야 한다. lots of는 '많은'이라는 뜻이다.

20 ①
① 둘 다 '꽤'라는 뜻의 부사로 쓰였다.
② 늦게(부사) — 늦은(형용사) ③ 빠른(형용사) — 빨리(부사) ④ 세게(부사) — 힘든(형용사) ⑤ 높은(형용사) — 높게(부사)

21 I usually have something sweet
빈도부사는 일반동사 앞에 오고 -thing으로 끝나는 대명사는 형용사가 뒤에서 수식한다.

22 little water
「little + 셀 수 없는 명사」는 '~이 거의 없는'이라는 뜻을 나타낸다.

23 is, are
the homeless는 homeless people의 의미이므로 복수동사를 써야 한다.

24 away it, it away
타동사와 부사 사이에 대명사 목적어가 와야 하므로 it을 부사 away 앞에 써야 한다.

Chapter 09 비교

▶▶ p. 122~125

01 ① **02** ④ **03** ② **04** ② **05** ④ **06** ② **07** ④ **08** ② **09** ② **10** ④ building, buildings **11** as little as possible **12** (1) older than (2) as[so] short as (3) younger than any other **13** ① **14** ② **15** ③ **16** ② **17** ④ **18** ② **19** ④ **20** ④ **21** ② **22** ⑤ **23** as[so] interesting, more interesting than **24** The fresher, the better

01 ①
「not as[so] + 원급 + as」: ~만큼 …하지 않은

02 ④
③ much는 셀 수 없는 명사와 함께 쓴다.
⑤ much more fish than ~보다 훨씬 더 많은 물고기

03 ②
뒤에 than이 있으므로 비교급이 들어가야 하고, fast의 비교급은 faster이다.

04 ②
①, ③, ④, ⑤ Nari는 한국에서 가장 좋은 중학교이다.
② Nari는 한국의 다른 중학교들만큼 좋지 않다.

05 ④
「The + 비교급 ~, the + 비교급 …」: ~하면 할수록, 더 …한

06 ②
very는 원급을 강조하며 비교급을 수식할 수 없다.

07 ④
앞에 정관사 the가 있으므로 비교급 more popular는 빈칸에 알맞지 않다.

08 ②
'다른 모든 문제들이 기아만큼 심각하다.'라는 의미로 기아가 가장 심각한 문제라는 주어진 문장과 의미가 다르다.

09 ②
「as + 원급 + as」이므로 better를 well로 고쳐야 한다.

10 ④ building, buildings
「one of the + 최상급 + 복수명사」: 가장 ~한 것들 중 하나

11 as little as possible
「as + 원급 + as possible」: 가능한 한 ~한(하게)

12 (1) older than
(2) as(so) short as
(3) younger than any other

13 ①
앞에 most가 있으므로 pretty는 빈칸에 들어갈 수 없다. pretty의 최상급은 prettiest이다.

14 ②
첫 번째 빈칸에는 뒤에 than이 있으므로 비교급인 kinder가 알맞다. 두 번째 빈칸에는 빈칸 앞뒤로 as가 있는 원급 비교 구문이므로 형용사의 원급인 healthy가 와야 한다.

15 ③
「the + 비교급 ~, the + 비교급 …」: ~하면 할수록, 더 …한

16 ②
much는 비교급을 강조하는 부사로 far, even, still, a lot으로 바꿔 쓸 수 있다. very는 형용사나 부사의 원급을 강조하며, 비교급은 강조할 수 없다.

17 ④
'가장 ~한 것들 중 하나'라는 의미는 「one of the + 최상급 + 복수명사」로 나타내야 하므로 sport를 sports로 고쳐야 한다.

18 ②
'점점 더 ~한'은 「비교급 + and + 비교급」으로 나타낸다. 비교급이 「more + 원급」의 형태일 경우 「more and more + 원급」으로 쓴다.

19 ④
Billy 엄마의 나이가 Billy 나이의 3배이므로 배수사를 이용한 비교 표현으로 나타낼 수 있다. 배수사 비교 표현은 「배수사 + as + 원급 + as」 또는 「배수사 + 비교급 + than」으로 나타낸다.

20 ④
멜론이 사과보다 더 무거우므로 The melon is heavier than the apple.로 고쳐야 한다.

21 ②
내 머리카락은 Susan의 것보다 길다.
≠ Susan의 머리카락은 나의 것보다 짧지 않다.
두 번째 문장의 isn't를 is로 바꾸거나 shorter를 longer로 바꿔야 한다.

22 ⑤
「as + 원급 + as possible」: 가능한 한 ~한(하게)
(sooner → soon)

23 as(so) interesting, more interesting than
「부정주어 … as(so) + 원급 + as ~」와 「비교급 + than any other + 단수명사」는 최상급의 의미를 나타낸다.

24 The fresher, the better
「the + 비교급 ~, the + 비교급 …」: ~하면 할수록, 더 …한

Chapter 10 전치사

▶▶ p. 126~129

01 ④ 02 ① 03 ⑤ 04 ④ 05 ② 06 ④ 07 ④
08 ③ 09 ② 10 ② 11 between 12 in front of
13 ③ 14 ④ 15 ② 16 ② 17 ③ 18 ⑤ 19 ①
20 ② 21 ① 22 is far from the town 23 within a week 24 turn into your enemy

01 ④
be surprised at: ~에 놀라다
be interested in: ~에 관심이 있다

02 ①
be full of: ~로 가득하다
instead of: ~ 대신에

03 ⑤
marry는 '~와 결혼하다'의 의미를 나타내는 동사이므로 전치사가 필요 없다.

04 ④
④에는 of가 알맞고, ①, ②, ③, ⑤에는 with가 알맞다.

05 ②
방향을 나타내는 to

06 ④
before: ~ 전에 / after: ~ 후에

07 ④
특정한 때를 나타낼 때는 during을, 주로 숫자로 표현되는 일정한 기간을 나타낼 때는 for를 쓴다.

08 ③
beside: ~ 옆에(= next to)

09 ②
'~까지'라는 의미로 동작이나 상태의 완료를 나타낼 때는 전치사 by를 사용한다.

10 ②
along: ~을 따라

11 between
between: (둘) ~ 사이에
among: (셋 이상) ~ 사이에

12 in front of
in front of: ~의 앞에

13 ③
뒤에 숫자를 포함하는 일정 기간이 나오므로 for(~ 동안)가 알맞다.

14 ④
suffer from: ~로 고통받다
to one's + 감정 명사: ~하게도

15 ②
첫 번째 빈칸에는 '~의 바로 아래에 (떨어져서)'라는 의미가 되어야 하므로 under가 알맞다. 두 번째 빈칸에는 뒤에 교통수단이 있으므로 by를 쓴다.

16 ②
in front of: ~의 앞에 / behind: ~ 뒤에

17 ③
across: ~을 가로질러서

18 ⑤
out of: ~ 밖으로

19 ①
날짜 앞에는 on을 쓴다. / 접촉해 있는 표면 위를 나타낼 때는 on을 쓴다.

20 ②
'~까지'라는 뜻으로 동작이나 상태의 완료를 나타낼 때는 by를 써야 한다.

21 ①
'~의 뒤에'는 behind이다. beside는 '~의 옆에'라는 뜻이다.

22 is far from the town
far from: ~에서 멀리 떨어진

23 within a week
within: ~ 이내에

24 turn into your enemy
변화의 결과를 나타낼 때 전치사 into를 쓴다. (turn into: ~로 변하다)

Chapter 11 관계사

▸▸ p.130~133

01 ① 02 ④ 03 ⑤ 04 ②, ⑤ 05 ⑤ 06 ⑤ 07 ① 08 ④ 09 ④ 10 The necklace at which she was looking was beautiful. 또는 The necklace (which / that) she was looking at was beautiful. 11 Samuel returned to the village where he was born. 12 Samuel returned to the village (which / that) he was born in. 또는 Samuel returned to the village in which he was born. 13 ④ 14 ⑤ 15 ② 16 ④ 17 ② 18 ⑤ 19 ③ 20 ① 21 ② 22 ② 23 However busy you are 24 Tony lied to her, which made her angry.

01 ①
관계대명사 that은 계속적 용법으로 쓸 수 없는 것에 주의한다.

02 ④
선행사에 서수나 the only가 포함된 경우 관계대명사 that을 쓴다.

03 ⑤
관계부사 다음에는 완전한 문장이 온다. ⑤의 빈칸에는 관계대명사가 들어가야 한다.

04 ②, ⑤
② 선행사가 사람(two daughters)이므로 계속적 용법의 주격 관계대명사 who가 알맞다. ⑤ 선행사가 사물(BART)이므로 주격 관계대명사 which가 알맞다.
① 사람 선행사 Ann, 주격 관계대명사 자리 which → who ③ 관계대명사 that 앞에는 전치사를 쓸 수 없다. → This is the restaurant that I met him at. ④ 선행사가 사람(Ms. Kim)이고, 뒤에 명사 cakes가 오므로 소유격 관계대명사 whose를 써야 한다.

05 ⑤
⑤의 what은 의문을 나타내는 동사인 wonder와 함께 쓰인 의문사이다. 나머지는 모두 관계대명사 what이다.

06 ⑤
선행사 pizza가 사물이고 관계사절에서 주어 역할을 하므로 주격 관계대명사 which 또는 that이 알맞다. / 선행사 a doctor가 사람이고 관계사절에서 주어 역할을 하므로 주격 관계대명사 who 또는 that이 알맞다.

07 ①
목적격 관계대명사와 「주격 관계대명사 + be동사」는 생략이 가능하나 주격 관계대명사는 생략할 수 없다.

08 ④
선행사 The dress가 사물이고, 관계사절에서 wants의 목적어 역할을 하므로 which로 바꿔 쓸 수 있다.

09 ④
선행사 the reason이므로 how → why

10 The necklace at which she was looking was beautiful. 또는 The necklace (which / that) she was looking at was beautiful.
관계대명사가 전치사의 목적어인 경우 전치사는 관계대명사 앞 또는 관계대명사절 끝에 올 수 있으나 관계대명사 that 앞에는 전치사를 쓸 수 없다.

11 Samuel returned to the village where he was born.
선행사 the village가 장소를 나타내므로 관계부사 where가 알맞다.

12 Samuel returned to the village (which / that) he was born in. 또는 Samuel returned to the village in which he was born.
관계대명사가 전치사의 목적어인 경우 전치사는 관계대명사 앞 또는 관계대명사절 끝에 올 수 있으나 관계대명사 that 앞에는 전치사를 쓸 수 없다.

13 ④
선행사 a program이 사물이고, 관계사절에서 주어 역할을 하므로 주격 관계대명사 which가 알맞다.

14 ⑤
선행사 the tree가 장소를 나타내고, 관계사절에서 부사 역할을 하므로 관계부사 where가 알맞다.

15 ②
the things that은 선행사를 포함하는 관계대명사 what으로 바꿔 쓸 수 있다.

16 ④
at any time when: ~할 때마다(= whenever)

17 ②
②는 간접의문문에 사용된 의문사이고, 나머지는 모두 관계대명사이다.

18 ⑤
집이 오래되어 보인다는 것이 Sam의 집을 부연 설명하는 내용이므로 계속적 용법으로 써야 하고, 선행사 Sam's house가 사물이므로 which가 알맞다. that은 계속적 용법으로 쓸 수 없다.

19 ③

'무엇을 ~하든'은 양보의 부사절이며, 복합관계대명사 whatever나 no matter what으로 나타낸다.

20 ①

본동사 is가 뒤에 있으므로 빈칸에는 주어 The table을 수식하는 말이 와야 한다. 따라서 ①이 들어가려면 which(that) has three legs가 되어야 한다. ②는 앞에 목적격 관계대명사 which 또는 that이 생략된 형태이고 ⑤는 「주격 관계대명사 + be동사(which(that) is)」가 생략된 형태이므로 들어갈 수 있다.

21 ②

ⓐ 「주격 관계대명사 + be동사」는 생략할 수 있다.

ⓒ the day와 같이 일반적인 명사가 선행사로 올 때 관계부사는 생략할 수 있다.

22 ②

ⓐ 관계대명사 that 앞에는 전치사를 쓸 수 없다. (on that → on which 또는 on that I was sitting → that I was sitting on)

ⓒ 관계부사 how는 선행사 the way와 함께 쓸 수 없다. 둘 중 하나를 생략해야 한다. (the way how → the way 또는 how)

23 However busy you are

「however + 형용사/부사 + 주어 + 동사」의 어순으로 써야 한다.

24 Tony lied to her, which made her angry.

앞의 절 전체를 선행사로 하는 계속적 용법의 관계대명사 which를 사용하여 쓴다.

Chapter 12 접속사

▸▸ p. 134~137

01 ① **02** ④ **03** ③ **04** not only, but also **05** ① **06** ② **07** ② **08** ④ **09** ⑤ **10** ② **11** ⑤ **12** ③ **13** ② **14** ① **15** ④ **16** ① **17** ④ **18** ④ **19** ③ **20** ④ **21** I wonder if(whether) she knows my name. **22** you don't follow his advice **23** the comic book was very funny, he couldn't stop laughing **24** If you buy a ticket online

01 ①

「so ~ that ...」: 매우 ~해서 …한

02 ④

첫 번째 빈칸에는 '~라는 것'이라는 의미로 명사절을 이끄는 접속사 that이 알맞고 두 번째 빈칸에는 my dog를 수식하는 관계대명사 that이 알맞다.

03 ③

'~하지 않으면'을 뜻하는 Unless는 If ~ not으로 바꿔 쓸 수 있다. 조건을 나타내는 부사절에서는 현재시제가 미래를 대신한다.

04 not only, but also

not only *A* but also *B*: A 뿐만 아니라 B도

05 ①

①의 while은 '~하는 동안'을 의미하고, ②, ③, ④, ⑤의 while은 '반면에'를 의미한다.

06 ②

If ~ not은 Unless로 바꿔 쓸 수 있다.

07 ②

②의 if는 '~라면'을 의미하고, ①, ③, ④, ⑤의 if는 '~인지 아닌지'를 의미한다.

08 ④

although: (비록) ~이지만

09 ⑤

교통 체증이 원인이 되어 비행기를 놓치게 되는 결과를 낳았으므로 As a result(그 결과)가 알맞다.

10 ②

'그는 잠이 들자마자 잠자리에 들었다.'는 의미상 어색하다.

11 ⑤

빈칸에 절이 들어갈 경우 do you think의 목적어가 되므로 what과 연결되는 간접의문문(의문사 + 주어+ 동사)의 형태가 되어야 한다.

12 ③

Besides(게다가)는 추가의 의미를 나타내므로 In addition으로 바꿔 쓸 수 있다.

13 ②

첫 번째 문장은 두통 '때문에' 약속을 취소했다는 의미가 자연스러우므로 이유를 나타내는 접속사 because가 알맞다. 두 번째 문장은 엄마가 없는 '동안' 무서웠다는 의미가 자연스러우므로 시간을 나타내는 접속사 while이 알맞다.

14 ①

첫 번째 빈칸은 '~인지 아닌지'의 뜻으로 decide의 목적어 역할을 하는 명사절을 이끄는 접속사가 와야 하므로 if나 whether가 알맞다. 두 번째 빈칸은 believe의 목적어 역할을 하는 명사절을 이끄는 접속사가 와야 하므로 that이 알맞다.

15 ④
tell의 직접목적어 자리이므로 의문문이 올 경우 간접의문문(의문사 + 주어 + 동사)의 형태가 되어야 한다. 간접의문문에서 의문사가 주어인 경우는 「의문사 + 동사」의 어순으로 쓴다.

16 ①
'~ 대로'라는 양태의 의미와, '~할 때'라는 시간의 의미로 모두 사용되는 접속사는 as이다.

17 ④
오래된 옷과 오래된 장난감 둘 다 버리지 않는다는 부정의 의미가 되어야 하므로 「neither *A* nor *B*(A와 B 둘 다 아닌)」이 알맞다.

18 ④
unless는 if ~ not의 의미이므로 don't를 삭제해야 한다. (Unless you don't read → Unless you read)

19 ③
as a result: 그 결과

20 ④
「either *A* or *B*」가 주어로 쓰인 경우 동사의 수를 B에 일치시키므로 have를 has로 고쳐야 한다.

21 I wonder if[whether] she knows my name.
의문사가 없는 의문문이 동사 wonder의 목적어 역할을 해야 하므로 간접의문문(if[whether] + 주어 + 동사)의 어순으로 wonder 뒤에 와야 한다.

22 you don't follow his advice
unless는 if ~ not으로 바꿔 쓸 수 있다.

23 the comic book was very funny, he couldn't stop laughing
이유를 나타내는 접속사를 사용해야 하는데, 문맥상 두 번째 문장이 이유에 해당하므로 두 번째 문장을 부사절로 쓴다.

24 If you buy a ticket online
「명령문, and ~」는 접속사 if로 시작하는 부사절을 이용하여 바꿔 쓸 수 있다.

Chapter 13 가정법

▸▸ p. 138~141

01 ③ **02** ① **03** ② **04** ② **05** ④ **06** ④ **07** ④ **08** ② **09** as if he were **10** If I had had enough money, I could have bought the bike. **11** If he had not[hadn't] studied hard, he would not[wouldn't] have passed the exam. **12** ⑤ **13** ④ **14** ① **15** ⑤ **16** ④ **17** ④, ⑤ **18** ④ **19** ③ **20** ② **21** ③ **22** Without, it had not been for **23** had been quiet, wouldn't[would not] have woken up

01 ③
직설법 현재는 가정법 과거로 바꿔 쓸 수 있으므로 「If + 주어 + 동사의 과거형 ~, 주어 + 조동사의 과거형 + 동사원형 …」 형태로 나타낸다.

02 ①
② 가정법 과거는 현재 사실과 반대되는 가정을 나타낸다. (can → can't)
③ 「I wish + 가정법 과거」는 현재와 반대되는 소망을 나타낸다. (wouldn't → would)
④ 가정법 과거완료는 과거 사실과 반대되는 가정을 나타낸다. (didn't come → came, died → didn't die)
⑤ 가정법 과거완료는 과거 사실과 반대되는 가정을 나타낸다. (would → wouldn't)

03 ②
첫 번째 문장이 직설법 과거이므로 「I wish + 가정법 과거완료」가 알맞다. 「I wish + 주어 + had p.p.」: ~했더라면 좋았을 텐데

04 ②
주어진 문장이 직설법 현재이므로 「I wish + 주어 + 동사의 과거형」 형태인 가정법 과거로 나타낸다.

05 ④
④ 가정법 과거완료: 「If + 주어 + had p.p. ~, 주어 + 조동사의 과거형 + have p.p. …」
① had had → had
② would have played → would play
③ am → were
⑤ If I buy → If I bought

06 ④
주어진 문장이 직설법 현재이므로 의미가 같은 것은 가정법 과거인 ④이다.

07 ④

④ 가정법에서 if를 생략하면 주어와 동사가 도치된다.

08 ②
② I wish 가정법 과거(주어 + 동사의 과거형)
① have → had
③ finish → finished
④ call → would〔could〕 call
⑤ could have 삭제 또는 could have → had

09 as if he were
as if + 가정법과거: 「as if + 주어 + 동사의 과거형」

10 If I had had enough money, I could have bought the bike. (직설법 과거 → 가정법 과거완료)

11 If he had not〔hadn't〕 studied hard, he would not〔wouldn't〕 have passed the exam. (직설법 과거 → 가정법 과거완료)

12 ⑤
if절에 「if + 주어 + had p.p.」가 쓰인 가정법 과거완료 문장이므로 주절의 동사를 「조동사의 과거형 + have p.p.」의 형태로 써야 한다.

13 ④
if절에 「if + 주어 + 동사의 과거형」이 쓰인 가정법 과거 문장이므로 주절의 동사를 「조동사의 과거형+동사원형」의 형태로 써야 한다.

14 ①
주어진 문장을 직설법으로 바꾸면 As he called 119, the woman didn't die.이다. 즉, 그는 119에 전화를 했고, 그 여자는 죽지 않았다.

15 ⑤
As가 이끄는 부사절은 과거시제, 주절은 현재시제의 문장이므로 혼합가정법(if절은 가정법 과거완료, 주절은 가정법 과거)으로 써야 한다. 따라서 주절의 wouldn't have been을 wouldn't be로 고쳐야 한다.

16 ④
과거의 사실이 현재까지 영향을 미치고 있는 혼합가정법 문장이므로, if절은 가정법 과거완료, 주절은 가정법 과거를 쓴다.

17 ④, ⑤
주절이 가정법 과거이므로 Without을 '~이 없다면'의 의미인 If it were not for나, If를 생략한 Were it not for로 바꿔 쓸 수 있다. 또한 Without은 But for로 바꿔 쓸 수 있다.

18 ④
「as if + 가정법 과거완료」이므로 주절의 시제인 현재보다 한 시제 앞선 과거의 일을 나타낸다. 과거의 일을 반대로 가정하고 있으므로 ④가 알맞다.

19 ③
(A) 현재 사실과 반대되는 상황을 소망하고 있으므로 「I wish + 가정법 과거(주어 + 동사의 과거형)」의 형태를 취해야 한다.
(B) 과거의 일을 반대로 가정하고 있으므로 「as if + 가정법 과거완료(주어 + had p.p.)」가 알맞다.
(C) 주절에 「주어 + 조동사의 과거형 + have p.p.」가 쓰인 가정법 과거완료 문장이므로 if절은 「if + 주어 + had p.p.」의 형태로 써야 한다.

20 ②
if절은 가정법 과거완료, 주절은 가정법 과거로 된 문장이므로, 주절의 동사를 would have had로 바꾸거나 if절의 동사를 snowed로 고쳐야 한다.

21 ③
「I wish + 가정법 과거완료」는 과거 사실에 대한 유감이나 아쉬움을 나타내는 것이므로 I'm sorry she didn't win the singing contest.로 고쳐야 한다.

22 Without, it had not been for
「without + 명사(구), 주어 + 조동사의 과거형 + have p.p.」 = 「If it had not been for + 명사(구), 주어 + 조동사의 과거형 + have p.p.」: ~가 없었다면

23 had been quiet, wouldn't〔would not〕 have woken up
과거 사실과 반대되는 상황을 가정하고 있으므로 가정법 과거완료(If + 주어 + had p.p. ~, 주어 + 조동사의 과거형 + have p.p. …)로 쓴다.

Chapter 14 일치와 화법

▸▸ p. 142~145

01 ② 02 ⑤ 03 ② 04 ③ 05 ④ 06 ① 07 ④ 08 ② 09 ② 10 ⑤ 11 ③ 12 me not to be late for school 13 ④ 14 ③ 15 ④ 16 ⑤ 17 ② 18 ⑤ 19 ③ 20 ② 21 are, is 22 are 23 he was trying to lose weight then(at that time) 24 if(whether) he was interested in Korean history

01 ②
주어가 단수(The scene)이므로 has가 알맞다.

02 ⑤
긍정명령문을 간접화법으로 바꿀 때에는 to부정사를 사용하여 나타낸다. 전달동사 say to는 tell로 바꾼다.

03 ②
의문사가 없는 의문문을 간접화법으로 바꿀 때는 if(whether)를 사용하여 나타내므로 that → if(whether)

04 ③
part of 뒤에 단수명사 the hotel이 왔으므로 have → has

05 ④
뒤에 이어지는 동사 is가 단수형이므로 주어 자리의 빈칸에는 단수 취급하는 어구가 들어가야 한다. some of 뒤에 셀 수 있는 명사의 복수형이 왔으므로 복수동사가 와야 한다. each, one of ~, nobody, every는 단수동사와 함께 쓰인다.

06 ①
주절과 종속절의 시제를 일치시켜야 하므로, can't를 couldn't로 고친다.

07 ④
의문사가 없는 의문문을 간접화법으로 바꿀 때에는 「if(whether)+주어+동사」의 형태로 나타낸다.
①, ② 간접화법으로 고친 문장에서 인칭의 전환이 되지 않았으므로 정답이 될 수 없다.
③ 의문사가 있는 의문문은 간접화법으로 바뀔 때 어순이 「의문사+주어+동사」이므로 what was I → what I was
⑤ 부정명령문을 간접화법으로 바꿀 때 어순이 「not+to부정사」이므로 to not make → not to make

08 ②
주절이 과거시제이므로 종속절은 과거 또는 과거완료시제로 써야 한다.

09 ②
「a number of+복수명사」는 복수 취급하므로 is → are

10 ⑤
직접화법의 yesterday는 간접화법에서 the day before 또는 the previous day로 바꿔야 한다.

11 ③
No news is good news.(무소식이 희소식이다.)와 같은 격언은 주절의 시제에 상관없이 항상 현재시제로 쓰므로 was → is

12 me not to be late for school
부정명령문을 간접화법으로 바꿀 때에는 「not+to부정사」를 사용하여 나타낸다.

13 ④
「one of+복수명사」는 단수 취급한다.
「a number of+복수명사」는 복수 취급한다.

14 ③
주절이 과거일 때 종속절은 과거나 과거완료로 쓴다. 과학적 사실이나 불변의 진리는 항상 현재시제로 쓴다.

15 ④
의문사가 있는 의문문의 간접화법은 「의문사+주어+동사」의 어순으로 쓰고, 시제는 주절에 맞게 과거시제로 바꾼다. 인칭대명사 my는 주어에 맞춰 his로 바꾼다.

16 ⑤
평서문의 간접화법으로 시제는 주절에 맞게 과거시제로 바꾼다. 인칭대명사 I는 주어에 맞춰 she로 바꾸고, 부사 today는 that day로 바꾼다.

17 ②
긍정명령문 Look at the sign.의 간접화법으로, 명령문을 to부정사 형태로 고치고 전달동사는 told를 쓴다.

18 ⑤
역사적 사실은 항상 과거시제로 쓰므로 has ended는 ended로 고쳐야 한다.

19 ③
의문사가 없는 의문문의 간접화법에서 접속사는 if 또는 whether를 써야 한다.

20 ②
ⓑ 동명사구는 단수 취급한다. (are → is)

ⓔ「분수 of + 단수명사」는 단수 취급한다. (were → was)

21 are, is
「the number of + 복수명사」는 단수 취급한다.

22 are
불변의 진리는 항상 현재시제로 쓴다.

23 he was trying to lose weight then[at that time]
평서문의 간접화법으로 시제는 주절에 맞게 현재진행형을 과거진행형으로 바꾸고, 인칭대명사 I는 주절의 주어 Brian에 맞춰 he로 바꾼다. 또한 부사 now는 then 또는 at that time으로 바꾼다.

24 if[whether] he was interested in Korean history
의문사가 없는 의문문의 간접화법은 「if[whether] + 주어+동사」의 어순으로 쓴다. 시제는 주절에 맞게 과거시제로 바꾸고, 인칭대명사 you는 목적어 Tyler에 맞춰 he로 바꾼다.

Chapter 15 특수구문

▶▶ p. 146~149

01 ⑤ **02** ③ **03** ③ **04** ② **05** ③ **06** ④ **07** ① **08** ③ **09** ② **10** ② **11** It was Korean War that broke out in 1950. **12** It was his strong will that made John succeed. **13** ② **14** ③ **15** ② **16** ②, ⑤ **17** ⑤ **18** ③ **19** ④ **20** ① **21** ④ **22** She does like to discuss books with others. **23** On her shoulder sat a parrot. **24** In an underground shelter live the terrorists.

01 ⑤
do / does / did를 사용해서 일반동사를 강조할 수 있다.
① likes → like ② talks → talk ③ had → have ④ do went → did go

02 ③
③ 부정어의 도치: 「부정어 + have[조동사] + 주어 + 동사」 (동사의 시제가 완료시제이거나 조동사가 있을 때)
Never have tried my grandparents pizza.
→ Never have my grandparents tried pizza.
① 장소 부사구의 도치
② 장소 부사구의 도치
④ 장소 부사구의 도치
⑤ 부정어의 도치

03 ③
「so + 동사 + 주어」: ~도 역시 그렇다
「neither + 동사 + 주어」: ~도 역시 그렇지 않다

04 ②
②는 가주어 · 진주어 구문이고, 나머지는 모두 「It is[was] ~ that ...」 강조 구문이다.

05 ③
부정어 hardly가 강조되어 문장 앞에 위치했으므로 주어와 동사가 도치되어 「부정어 + do[does / did] + 주어 + 동사원형」의 어순이 되어야 한다.(→ Hardly did he look like a famous dentist.)

06 ④
「주격 관계대명사 + be동사」는 생략할 수 있다.

07 ①
일반동사의 의미를 강조할 때는 「do + 동사원형」의 형태로 쓴다. (played → play)

08 ③
첫 번째 문장의 「It is ~ that ...」 강조 구문에서 강조하는 부분이 사람(Jane)이므로 that 또는 who가 알맞다. 두 번째 문장에서는 said의 목적절인 명사절을 이끄는 접속사 that이 필요하다.

09 ②
「It is[was] ~ that ...」 강조 구문에서 목적어 my cake를 강조하여 앞으로 이동했으므로 that절의 목적어 자리에 있는 it을 없애야 한다.(→ It was my cake that Jessica ate.)

10 ②
장소 부사구를 도치하면 「장소 부사구 + 동사 + 주어」의 어순이 된다.

11 It was Korean War that broke out in 1950.
「It is[was] ~ that ...」 강조 구문으로, Korean War를 It was와 that 사이에 쓴다.

12 It was his strong will that made John succeed.
It is[was] ~ that ...」 강조 구문으로, His strong will을 It was와 that 사이에 쓴다.

13 ②
첫 번째 빈칸에는 일반동사의 부정문을 만드는 do동사, 두 번째 빈칸에는 do one's best에 사용되는 일반동사

do, 세 번째 빈칸에는 일반동사 work를 강조해 주는 강조의 do동사가 와야 한다.

14 ③
부정어 little이 문장 맨 앞에 왔으므로 주어와 동사가 도치된다. 이때, 동사가 일반동사일 경우 「부정어 + do〔does / did〕+ 주어 + 동사원형」의 형태가 된다.

15 ②
장소 부사구 over the amusement park가 문장 맨 앞에 왔으므로 주어와 동사가 도치된다.

16 ②, ⑤
rarely는 부정의 의미를 갖는 빈도부사이므로 일반동사 앞에 올 수 있고, 강조를 위해 문장 맨 앞에 올 경우 「부정어 + do〔does / did〕+ 주어 + 동사원형」의 형태로 도치된다.

17 ⑤
has가 일반동사로 쓰였으므로 do동사를 사용하여 So does Brian.으로 써야 한다.

18 ③
drink의 목적어 warm water를 강조하는 문장이므로 「It is〔was〕 ~ that ...」 강조 구문을 사용하여 warm water를 It was와 that 사이에 쓴다.

19 ④
동사는 「It is〔was〕 ~ that ...」 강조 구문으로 강조할 수 없다. 동사는 do동사를 사용하여 강조할 수 있다.

20 ①
①은 진주어 역할을 하는 명사절을 이끄는 접속사 that으로 쓰였고, 나머지는 모두 「It is〔was〕 ~ that ...」 강조 구문의 that으로 쓰였다.

21 ④
I 앞에 목적격 관계대명사 who〔that〕이 생략되어 있다.
① 부사구 도치 문장으로, 주어가 a dog이므로 단수동사를 써야 한다. (are → is)
② 부사구 도치 문장으로, 주어가 my parents' names이므로 복수동사를 써야 한다. (is → are)
③ 부정어 도치 구문이므로 주어와 동사가 도치되어야 한다. (the children have tasted → have the children tasted)
⑤ talking 앞에 who〔that〕 is가 생략된 문장으로, 주어가 The man이므로 단수동사를 써야 한다. (are → is)

22 She does like to discuss books with others.
동사를 강조할 때는 시제와 인칭에 맞는 do동사를 사용하여 「do〔does / did〕+ 동사원형」의 형태로 쓴다.

23 On her shoulder sat a parrot.
장소 부사구 on her shoulder를 문장 맨 앞에 두고 주어와 동사를 도치시킨다.

24 In an underground shelter live the terrorists.
장소 부사구 in an underground shelter를 문장 맨 앞에 두고 주어와 동사를 도치시킨다.